NATIONAL ASSOCIATION OF
STUDENT PERSONNEL ADMINISTRATORS

The National Association of Student Personnel Administrators (NASPA) is the leading national association for college and university student affairs administrators. Since its inception in 1918, student affairs administrators have turned to NASPA for leadership and guidance on a wide range of contemporary issues, including public policies on alcohol and substance abuse, campus dissent, and campus security; campus climate; cultural diversity; student affairs research; student service program evaluations; staff development assistance; and compliance with federal regulations.

NASPA's current mission is to enrich the educational experience of all college and university students. To carry out this mission, NASPA strives to:

Help chief student affairs officers provide knowledgeable and effective leadership to their institutions, staff, and students

Provide a forum for the exchange of ideas, research, information, and opinions about issues in higher education and student affairs

Help colleges and universities provide a campus environment that promotes academic achievement and personal growth and development for all students

Promote the student affairs profession and advance the standing of student affairs professionals in higher education

With 6,000 individual members at 1,100 member campuses, NASPA is one of the largest nonprofit professional associations for student affairs administrators, faculty, and graduate students. Its members provide a variety of student services on campuses nationwide, including residence life, career planning and placement, counseling, athletics programs, minority student support services, student activities, financial aid, and orientation.

For additional information on NASPA or its membership, publications, and professional development programs, contact

NATIONAL ASSOCIATION OF STUDENT
PERSONNEL ADMINISTRATORS
1875 Connecticut Avenue, NW
Suite 418
Washington, D.C. 20009–5728

(202) 265–7500
(202) 797–1157 (FAX)

THE HANDBOOK OF

Student
Affairs
Administration

∽

Margaret J. Barr
and Associates

THE HANDBOOK OF

Student
Affairs
Administration

Jossey-Bass Publishers · San Francisco

Substantial discounts on bulk quantities of Jossey-Bass books
are available to corporations, professional associations, and other
organizations. For details and discount information, contact the
special sales department at Jossey-Bass Inc., Publishers.
(415) 433-1740; Fax (415) 433-0499.

For sales outside the United States, contact Maxwell Macmillan
International Publishing Group, 866 Third Avenue, New York,
New York 10022.

Manufactured in the United States of America

The paper in this book meets the guidelines for permanence and
durability of the Committee on Production Guidelines for Book
Longevity of the Council on Library Resources.

The ink in this book is either soy- or vegetable-based and during the
printing process emits fewer than half the volatile organic compounds
(VOCs) emitted by petroleum-based ink.

Library of Congress Cataloging-in-Publication Data

Barr, Margaret J.
   The handbook of student affairs administration / Margaret J. Barr
and Associates
      p.   cm. — (The Jossey-Bass higher and adult education series)
   Includes bibliographical references and index.
   ISBN 1-55542-506-2
   1. Universities and colleges — United States — Administration.
2. Student activities — United States — Management.   I. Title.
II. Series.
LB2341.B276   1993
378.1'989 — dc20   92-33894
                                                                         CIP

FIRST EDITION
HB Printing   10 9 8 7 6 5 4 3 2   *Code 9310*

The Jossey-Bass
Higher and Adult Education Series

Contents

Preface

The administration and management of student affairs programs, services, and activities have grown increasingly complex. Not only do student affairs professionals work directly with students but they are also required to manage facilities and budgets, participate in policy decisions influencing the life of the institution, plan new construction projects, and deal with emerging campus crises. As student affairs professionals contend with a rapidly evolving agenda for higher education, many are asking for assistance in confronting change and preparing themselves for the future. Student affairs colleagues must grapple with a range of questions: What are the skills, competencies, and knowledge that I need in order to become a more effective administrator in student affairs? What opportunities are available to me to improve my professional effectiveness? How can I assist my staff members in their professional growth and development? What are the issues facing higher education and student affairs?

Purpose

This book has been written to help the student affairs professional begin to answer these questions. It contains broad approaches to problem identification and solution, as well as specific, practical advice from respected practitioners. Although we cannot answer all questions in these pages, we hope that *The Handbook of Student Affairs Administration* will become a basic reference for student affairs professionals at all levels of management and administration.

The handbook is the result of a collaborative effort by many people. The authors contributed both time and expertise and were willing to share their ideas with others. The National Association of Student Personnel Administrators (NASPA) charted a new course by sponsoring the publication, identifying potential authors, and providing editorial guidance through its central staff. The effort was undertaken because all involved felt that there was a need for a practical resource book written *by* practitioners *for* practitioners. We hope that the goal has been met.

Audience

The book is designed to be particularly helpful to individuals assuming middle management or executive positions in student affairs for the first time. It will also be useful to people with background and experience in another area who join student affairs organizations. In addition, the handbook is designed to be of assistance to chief student affairs officers interested in professional renewal and development. It can serve as a reference point for presidents and other administrative officers who wish to improve their understanding of the role of student affairs on the college campus. Finally, the book can be used as a basic text in doctoral preparation programs.

Overview of the Contents

The Handbook of Student Affairs Administration is organized into five parts, which can be read in any order. Within these, the chapters are also designed to be read independently, although references are made to others that expand on particular points and issues.

Part One focuses on the administrative environment for student affairs practitioners. Student affairs does not stand alone; instead it is part of a complex web of structures, missions (Chapter One), cultures, finances (Chapter Four), relationships, constituency groups (Chapter Five), and presidential expectations (Chapter Six). The chapters in Part One describe those issues and their many and varied influences on student affairs professionals and organizations.

In Part Two, the focus shifts to the practical organizational and management issues associated with the field. Administrative relationships, internal management structures for a division of student affairs, and the role of the middle manager in student affairs organizations are discussed in detail in Chapters Seven, Eight, and Nine, respectively. Other chapters emphasize the critical importance of staff selection and training (Chapter Ten), understanding of the political dimensions of our administrative role (Chapter Eleven), facility management (Chapter Twelve), and the influence of the technological revolution on student affairs administration (Chapter Thirteen). Each of these issues influences the ability of student affairs to make the greatest possible contribution to the educational goals of both students and the institution.

The essential skills and competencies necessary to a manager in student affairs are explored in Part Three, whose chapters offer practical ad-

vice to practitioners. Part Three begins with approaches to program planning and implementation, essential competencies in program evaluation and
research, and outcomes assessment issues (Chapters Fourteen through Sixteen). The chapters that follow discuss budgeting and fiscal management
(Chapter Seventeen), translation of theory into practice (Chapter Eighteen),
the legal implications of student affairs practice (Chapter Nineteen), creation of effective campus relationships (Chapter Twenty), conflict management (Chapter Twenty-One), ethical implications of our interactions with
students and others (Chapter Twenty-Two), and the skills needed to manage
campus crises (Chapter Twenty-Three). Each chapter aims to provide guidance to professionals struggling with issues on their own campuses.

Part Four outlines methods and means to acquire and develop administrative skills. The authors of Chapters Twenty-Four through Twenty-Eight
present staff development programs, professional associations, mentoring
and self-directed learning, graduate education possibilities, and administrative
internships as opportunities for professionals who want to increase their
administrative abilities.

The volume concludes with Part Five, which considers the administrative challenges the profession will face in the years ahead: changing student needs and characteristics (Chapter Twenty-Nine), management of fiscal
constraints (Chapter Thirty), achievement of staff diversity (Chapter Thirty-
One), necessary alterations to service delivery systems, student health issues, the shifting governmental role in higher education, and the application of professional standards (Chapters Thirty-Two through Thirty-Five),
to name a few. This part concludes with a summary chapter and suggestions for further reading (Chapter Thirty-Six).

Acknowledgments

I would be remiss if I did not thank those who contributed to this volume. My
colleagues from all across the country deserve special appreciation for their
willingness to contribute to this endeavor. When called, they were more than
willing to help and to share what they have learned during years of successful
professional practice. Particular thanks go to Elizabeth Nuss and Marilyn
Schorr, who helped in getting in touch and working with authors and provided
general support. Jossey-Bass staff members made enormous contributions
to the volume by furnishing critical conceptual feedback as well as editorial
and production expertise. Pamela Gomez, from Texas Christian University
(TCU), deserves special mention for her long hours devoted to the final production of the manuscript. In addition, all of my colleagues at TCU contributed
support and understanding as work on the book progressed. Finally, my thanks
go to NASPA for entrusting me with the leadership of this venture. It has
been a learning experience for me, and for that I am grateful.

Evanston, Illinois   Margaret J. Barr
February 1993

The Authors

Margaret J. Barr currently serves as vice president for student affairs at Northwestern University. She received her B.S. degree (1961) in elementary education from State University College, Buffalo, her M.S. degree (1964) in college student personnel from Southern Illinois University, Carbondale, and her Ph.D. degree (1980) in higher education administration from the University of Texas, Austin.

Author of more than twenty-five books, book chapters, and monographs, Barr received the Outstanding Contribution to Literature or Research Award from the National Association of Student Personnel Administrators (NASPA) in 1986 and the Professional Service Award from the American College Personnel Association (ACPA) in that same year. In 1990, she received the Contribution to Knowledge Award from ACPA.

Long active in professional associations, she served as president of ACPA in 1985, and before that as vice president for commissions and chair of Commission II of that association. She acted as program chair for the ACPA national convention in Cincinnati in 1980. Barr was also a member of the committee that authored *A Perspective on Student Affairs,* a monograph issued by NASPA (1987), and she was director of the Richard F. Stevens Institute in 1989 and 1990.

Among her publications are *New Futures for Student Affairs: Building a Vision for Professional Leadership and Practice* (1990, with M. L. Upcraft and Associates), *Student Affairs and the Law* (ed., 1988), and *Developing Effective Student Services Programs: Systematic Approaches for Practitioners* (1985, with L. A. Keating and Associates). She is currently editor of the New Directions for Student Services series published by Jossey-Bass.

Barr previously served as vice chancellor for student affairs at Texas Christian University, vice president for student affairs at Northern Illinois University, assistant vice president for student affairs at Northern Illinois University, associate dean of students at the University of Texas, Austin, and assistant dean of students at that same institution. She was director of housing and of the college union at Trenton State College and director and assistant director of women's residences at the State University of New York, Binghamton.

David A. Ambler, vice chancellor for student affairs at the University of Kansas, received his B.S. degree (1959) in business administration, his M.P.A. degree (1961) in political science, and his Ed.D. degree (1966) in educational administration, all from Indiana University. He was chair of the ACPA/NASPA Task Force on Professional Preparation and Practice from 1987 to 1989 and has served on both the ACPA and the NASPA journal editorial boards. He is currently a member of the NASPA Task Force on Policy Issues.

Rosalind E. Andreas is vice president for student affairs and assistant professor of organizational, counseling, and foundations studies at the University of Vermont. She earned her B.A. degree (1963) in English from Bethel College in Kansas, her M.A. degree (1973) in speech communication and human relations from the University of Kansas, and her Ph.D. degree (1984) in higher education administration from the University of Michigan. Active in professional associations, she was ACPA's founding chairperson for the commission on commuter programs and is a former member of the *NASPA Journal* editorial board. She also serves on the board of directors of Bethel College. She was a member of the research team and one of the authors for *Involving Colleges.*

John L. Baier is professor and chair of the Department of Higher Education at the University of North Texas. He received his B.S. degree (1966) in industrial engineering from General Motors Management and Engineering Institute and his M.Ed. degree (1968) in counselor education from the State University of New York, Buffalo. His Ph.D. degree (1974) in higher education is from Southern Illinois University, Carbondale, and he has attended the Institute for Educational Management at Harvard University. He is a member of the editorial board of the *Journal of College Student Development* and the *College Student Affairs Journal.* He has served as president of the Texas Association of College and University Student Personnel Administrators. Baier is the author of more than fifteen book chapters and refereed journal articles.

Susan W. Batchelor, director of student activities at Texas Christian University, has a B.S. degree (1968) in education from Ohio University and an M.Ed. degree (1978) from Texas Christian University. She is currently working on an Ed.D. degree at the University of North Texas. Her professional activities include service as the director of the NASPA Region III New Professionals Institute in 1989–90 and membership on the 1993 NASPA conference committee.

Margaret W. Bridwell is director of the University Health Center and adjunct associate professor of health education at the University of Maryland, College Park. She received her B.S. degree (1943) in zoology from Tulane University and her M.D. degree (1946) from the Louisiana State University Medical Center. She is a fellow in the American College of Obstetrics and Gynecology and the American College Health Association (ACHA). Bridwell served as president of ACHA and is treasurer of the BACCHUS board of directors. (BACCHUS is a national undergraduate organization that focuses on substance abuse.) She received the Boyton Award from ACHA in 1988 and was named Outstanding Woman of the Year in 1991 at the University of Maryland, College Park.

Robert D. Brown is the Carl A. Happold Distinguished Professor of Educational Psychology at the University of Nebraska, Lincoln. He received his B.A. degree (1955) in history from Saint John's University in Collegeville, Minnesota, and both his M.A. degree (1956) in psychology and his Ph.D. degree (1966) in educational psychology from the University of Iowa. He is a former president of ACPA and was the recipient of the 1979 Contribution to Knowledge Award from that association. He is the author of numerous publications, including *Student Development in Tomorrow's Higher Education: A Return to the Academy* (1972).

William A. Bryan is vice chancellor for student affairs at the University of North Carolina, Wilmington. He holds a B.S. degree (1960) in social sciences and history from Florida State University, an M.A. degree (1961) in guidance and student personnel from Indiana University, and an Ed.D. degree (1970) in counselor education and student personnel from the University of Wyoming. Bryan served as president of ACPA and as vice president of state divisions for that association. He is the author of more than twenty publications, including *Using Professional Standards in Student Affairs* in the Jossey-Bass New Directions for Student Affairs series (1991, with R. B. Winston and T. K. Miller, eds.).

E. T. "Joe" Buchanan, dean of campus and community relations at Tidewater Community College, received his B.A. degree (1962) in history from Duke University, his J.D. degree (1966) from the University of Florida, and his Ph.D. degree (1972) in higher education from Florida State University. He is former president of NASPA (1981–82) and received the Fred Turner Award from NASPA in 1985. In 1988, he received the First Citizen of Virginia Beach award.

Harry J. Canon is senior associate with Aspen Professional Development Associates. He was formerly vice president for student affairs at Northern Illinois University for nearly a decade and then joined the faculty as professor of counseling. Canon has been a member of the executive council of ACPA and chair of the ACPA Ethics Committee. He also participated on the governing council for the American Association for Counseling and Development.

Don G. Creamer is professor of education at Virginia Polytechnic Institute and State University. He received both his B.A. degree (1960) in American history and his M.Ed. degree (1961) in counseling and guidance from East Texas State University and his Ed.D. degree (1965) in higher education from Indiana University. He is an ACPA senior scholar and former president of ACPA (1978–79). Creamer is the author of more than fifty publications, including monographs, chapters in books, and articles in refereed journals.

Marsha A. Duncan is vice president for student affairs at Lehigh University. She received both her B.S. degree (1969) in government and her M.S. degree (1971) in college student personnel from Southern Illinois University, Carbondale. Active in professional associations, she has served as a member of both the judicial affairs directorate of ACPA and the board of directors for NASPA. She is former president of NASPA.

Ernest H. Ern is completing his nineteenth year as vice president for student affairs at the University of Virginia, where he also serves as professor of environmental sciences. His B.S. degree (1955) was conferred by Bates College and both his M.S. degree (1957) and his Ph.D. degree (1959) by Lehigh University; all three degrees are in geology. He has been a member of the board of trustees of Bates College since 1981 and a member of the board of overseers of Sweet Briar College since 1988. He is also a fellow of the Geological Society of America.

T. Dary Erwin is director of assessment and professor of psychology at James Madison University. He earned both his B.S. degree (1972) in business and his M.S. degree (1975) in educational psychology from the University of Tennessee, and his Ph.D. degree (1978) in student development and measurement from the University of Iowa. He received the Ralph E. Berdie Memorial Research Award from the American Association for Counseling and Development in 1985. Erwin is the author of *Assessing Student Learning and Development: A Guide to the Principles, Goals, and Methods of Determining College Outcomes* (1991).

Michael A. Freeman is a graduate intern and graduate assistant at the NASPA office. He received both his B.G.S. degree (1980) in psychology and sociology and his M.S. degree (1983) in counselor education from the

University of Iowa. He has been involved in both ACPA and NASPA and is currently pursuing doctoral work in counseling and personnel services at the University of Maryland, College Park.

Donald D. Gehring is a professor of higher education at Bowling Green State University. He received his B.S. degree (1960) in industrial management from the Georgia Institute of Technology, his M.Ed. degree (1966) in math education from Emory University, and his Ed.D. degree (1971) in higher education from the University of Georgia. He was the recipient of the NASPA Contribution to Literature or Research Award in 1985, the NASPA Robert Schaffer Award for Excellence as a Graduate Faculty Member in 1990, and the American College and University Housing Officers-International (ACUHO-I) Distinguished Service Award in 1989. He is the author, with D. Parker Young, of the quarterly publication *The College Student and the Courts*.

Barbara Jacoby is director of the office of commuter affairs at the University of Maryland, College Park, as well as director of the National Clearinghouse for Commuter Programs. She received her B.A. degree (1971), her M.A. degree (1972), and her Ph.D. degree (1978), all in French language and literature, from the University of Maryland, College Park. She has long been involved in ACPA, serving on two commission directorate bodies, the national convention committee in 1984, and now the ethics committee. She has been a member of the board of directors of the Council for the Advancement of Standards for Student Services and Development Programs since 1980. Jacoby is the author or coauthor of more than fifteen publications.

Stanley P. Kinder serves as assistant director of the University Health Center at the University of Maryland, College Park. He received his B.A. degree (1974) in psychology from Johns Hopkins University and his M.S. degree (1977) in Business Administration from the Boston University School of Management.

Susan R. Komives is assistant professor of counseling and personnel services at the University of Maryland, College Park, where she is also faculty associate in the division of student affairs. She earned both her B.S. degree (1968) in mathematics and chemistry and her M.S. degree (1969) in higher education and student personnel administration from Florida State University, and her Ed.D. degree (1973) in educational administration and supervision from the University of Tennessee. A former president of ACPA, she has also served as its vice president for commissions and as a member of the ACPA/NASPA Task Force on Professional Preparation and Practice.

George D. Kuh, professor of higher education at Indiana University in the Center for Postsecondary Research and Planning, received his B.A.

degree (1968) in English and history from Luther College, his M.S. degree (1971) in counseling from Saint Cloud State University, and his Ph.D. degree (1975) in counselor education and higher education from the University of Iowa. Kuh was given the Contribution to Knowledge Award by ACPA in 1986 and the Contribution to Literature or Research Award by NASPA in 1987. Named a senior scholar by ACPA in 1989, he was a member of the committee that collaborated on *A Perspective on Student Affairs* (1987). He has authored or coauthored more than 125 publications, including *Involving Colleges: Successful Approaches to Fostering Student Learning and Development Outside the Classroom* (1991, with J. H. Schuh, E. J. Whitt, and Associates).

Peter Likins is president of Lehigh University. He received his B.S. degree (1957) in civil engineering from Stanford University, his M.S. degree (1958), also in civil engineering, from the Massachusetts Institute of Technology, and his Ph.D. degree (1965) in engineering mechanics from Stanford as well. He is a member of the President's Council of Advisors on Science and Technology and the National Academy of Engineers. Likins has published more than fifty works in his field.

James W. Lyons is currently a faculty member at Stanford University, after serving as dean of students there for eighteen years. He received his B.A. degree (1954) in economics from Allegheny College and both his M.S. degree (1956) in counseling and guidance and his Ed.D. degree (1963) in higher education from Indiana University. He received the Scott Goodnight Award for Outstanding Performance as a Dean from NASPA in 1988. Lyons also served as a member of the committee that wrote *A Perspective on Student Affairs* (1987).

Juan E. Mestas is vice provost and dean of students at Portland State University. Before that, he was acting director of educational equity services and director of retention services at California State University, Long Beach. He was awarded his B.A. degree (1966) in Hispanic studies by the University of Puerto Rico and both his M.A. degree (1974) and his Ph.D. degree (1985) in Hispanic languages and literature by the State University of New York, Stony Brook. He served as president of the Western Association of Educational Opportunity Personnel for two terms and also as director of the National Council of Educational Opportunity. He was an American Council on Education fellow in 1989–90.

Donald B. Mills is associate vice chancellor for student affairs at Texas Christian University. He earned his B.A. degree (1968) in government from Harvard University, his M.Div. degree (1972) in Christian ethics from Texas Christian University, and his Ed.D. degree (1985) in higher education administration from the University of North Texas. He received the Distinguished Service Award from the Texas Association of College and University Student Personnel Administrators in 1988. Highly involved in community service, he has served as the president of his local chapter of Planned Parenthood and as a member of the Trinity Valley School Board of Trustees.

Paul L. Moore is vice president for student affairs at California State University, Chico. He received his B.A. degree (1965) from the University of Oregon, his M.A. degree (1966) in counseling from the University of Oregon, and his Ph.D. degree (1977) in social education from the University of Southern California. Active in NASPA, he has served as vice president of Region VI and as a member of the editorial board of the *NASPA Journal*. Moore's most recent publication is *Managing the Political Dimension of Student Affairs* in the Jossey-Bass New Directions for Student Services series.

Richard H. Mullendore is associate vice chancellor for student affairs at the University of North Carolina, Wilmington. He received his B.A. degree (1970) in speech and hearing sciences from Bradley University, his M.S. degree (1975) in higher education from Southern Illinois University, and his Ph.D. degree (1980) in higher education administration from Michigan State University. He was president of the National Orientation Directors Association from 1990 to 1992 and is a member of the directorate of Commission I of ACPA. Mullendore also served as chair of the Interassociation Task Force on the Reaffirmation of the Joint Statement on Rights and Freedoms of Students.

Elizabeth M. Nuss is executive director of NASPA. She received her B.A. degree (1967) in Spanish and secondary education from the State University of New York, Albany; her M.Ed. degree (1969) in higher education and student personnel administration from The Pennsylvania State University; and her Ph.D. degree (1981) in education policy, planning, and administration from the University of Maryland, College Park. She is the author of ten publications and was the recipient of the NASPA Dissertation of the Year Award (1982).

W. John Pembroke is vice chancellor for administration for the Illinois board of regents. He was awarded his B.S. degree (1964) in English by North Central College, his M.P.A. (Master's of Public Administration) degree (1969) in public affairs by Northern Illinois University, and the Certificate for Advanced Study (1971) in public administration and public finance by Northern Illinois University.

Diane L. Podolske is currently graduate assistant for leadership development at the University of Nebraska, Lincoln, where she is pursuing her Ph.D. degree in college student development. She received her B.A. degree (1984) in psychology from Southwest State University in Minnesota and her M.A. degree (1988) in counseling psychology from the University of Nebraska, Lincoln. She has also coauthored two publications.

Frederick R. Preston, vice president for student affairs at the State University of New York, Stony Brook, received his B.S. degree (1967) in business administration from the University of Hartford and his Ed.D. degree (1971) in education from the University of Massachusetts. He has served on NASPA's board of directors and monograph board. In 1987, he received the Outstanding Service Award from the Long Island Student Personnel Association.

Blandina C. Ramirez is director of the office of minority affairs in higher education at the American Council on Education (ACE). She earned her B.J. degree (1967) in journalism and public relations from the University of Texas, Austin, and her Ed.D. degree (1974) in educational leadership and administration from the University of Massachusetts. Ramirez is the recipient of a Ford Foundation fellowship and was a Rockefeller fellow. She also received the National Education Association Human Rights Award in 1983. She is a member of the United States Civil Rights Commission and a board member for many city, state, and national organizations.

Marlene Ross, director of the ACE Fellows Program for the American Council on Education, received her B.A. degree (1959) in psychology from Barnard College, her Ed.M. degree (1960) in education from Harvard University, and her Ph.D. degree (1985) in educational administration from American University. She is the author of numerous publications, her most recent being "The Rules of the Game: The Unwritten Code of Career Mobility" (1990, with M. F. Green) in *Administrative Careers and the Marketplace,* a Jossey-Bass New Directions for Higher Education sourcebook.

Arthur Sandeen is vice president for student affairs at the University of Florida. He received his B.A. degree (1960) in religion and psychology from Miami University (Ohio), his M.A. degree (1962) in college student personnel from Michigan State University, and his Ph.D. degree (1965) in higher education administration from Michigan State University. He served as president of NASPA in 1977–78 and received the NASPA Fred Turner Award in 1983 and the NASPA Scott Goodnight Award in 1990. He chaired the committee that collaborated on *A Perspective on Student Affairs* (1987). A respected author, his most recent work is *The Chief Student Affairs Officer: Leader, Manager, Mediator, Educator* (1991).

John H. Schuh is associate vice president for student affairs at Wichita State University. He received his B.A. degree (1969) in history from the University of Wisconsin, Oshkosh, and both his M.C. degree (1972) in counseling and his Ph.D. degree (1974) in higher education from Arizona State University. He received the Contribution to Knowledge Award from ACPA in 1990 and its Presidential Service Award in 1991. Schuh also received the Contribution to Literature or Research Award from NASPA in 1992 and the ACUHO-I Leadership and Service Award in 1989. He has served as a member of the ACUHO-I executive board, as the ACPA media editor, and as a member-at-large of the NASPA executive board. He is the author, coauthor, or editor of ten books and monographs, eighteen book chapters, and fifty-nine articles, including *Involving Colleges: Successful Approaches to Fostering Student Learning and Development Outside the Classroom* (1991, with G. D. Kuh, E. J. Whitt, and Associates).

Winston G. Shindell is director of the Indiana Memorial Union at Indiana University. He received both his B.S. degree (1961) in education and his M.B.A. degree (1963) in business administration from Oklahoma State University. He is former president of the Association of College Unions-International (ACU-I) and a member of the executive group of that association. He received the Distinguished Service Award from Region IX of ACU-I and has been a keynote speaker and presenter at professional meetings throughout the United States and Canada.

Richard F. Stimpson is assistant vice president for student affairs at the University of Maryland, College Park. He earned his B.S. degree (1965) in secondary education from the State University College, Geneseo, and both his M.A. degree (1968) in guidance and personnel services and his Ph.D. degree (1977) in higher education administration from Michigan State University. He has been actively involved in ACPA and contributed to *Personal Education and Community Education in College Residence Halls* in 1980.

M. Lee Upcraft is assistant vice president for counseling services and program assessment, affiliate associate professor of education, and affiliate at the Center for the Study of Higher Education at The Pennsylvania State University. He received both his B.A. degree (1960) in social studies and his M.A. degree (1961) in guidance and counseling from the State University of New York, Albany, and his Ph.D. degree (1967) in student personnel administration from Michigan State University. He is a member of the advisory board of the National Center for the Study of the Freshman Year and also of the planning group of the U.S. Department of Education Network of Colleges and Universities Committed to the Elimination of Drug and Alcohol Abuse. He currently serves as associate editor of the Jossey-Bass New Directions in Student Services series. He is the author, editor, or coeditor of six books and monographs, nineteen book chapters, and seven articles in refereed journals.

Mark von Destinon, dean of students at Cochise College, has a B.A. degree (1978) in political science, an M.Ed. degree (1985) in higher education, and a Ph.D. degree (1989) in higher education, all from the University of Arizona. He is chair of the NASPA Gay, Lesbian, and Bisexual Concerns Network and member-at-large for the Research and Program Development Division of NASPA. Von Destinon also serves as a member of the ACPA Task Force on Campus Violence.

Dudley B. Woodard, Jr., is professor of higher education at the University of Arizona, where he previously served as vice president for student affairs. Woodard earned his B.A. degree (1962) in psychology from Mac-Murray College; his M.A. degree (1965) in human relations and his Ph.D. degree (1969) in counseling, guidance, and student personnel are both from Ohio University. Currently chair of the NASPA foundation board, he has also served NASPA as chair of the Research and Program Development Division, vice president for Region II, and president.

THE HANDBOOK OF

Student
Affairs
Administration

PART ONE

❧

The Administrative
Environment of
Student Affairs

Institutions of higher education are complex and oftentimes confusing organizations. Whether the institution is large or small, commuter or residential, or four- or two-year, it is essential for the effective student affairs professional to develop a sound understanding of the administrative environment. Part One discusses the framework in which we must practice our profession. Higher education is part of the larger society and is greatly shaped by forces beyond the control of the institution. In addition, campus governance structures and constituent relationships within the institution also influence the role of student affairs. The chapters included in this section discuss the broader issues involved in determining the climate in which we function.

Many factors affect the place of student affairs within institutions of higher education, but none is more important than that of the institutional mission. Each of us must appreciate and use that mission to guide our work with students. In Chapter One, James Lyons discusses the importance of the mission of the institution in developing student affairs programs, activities, and services.

Internal and external governance structures also influence the work of administration in student affairs. Questions of complexity, bureaucracy, unions, councils, and committees plague all of us from time to time. In Chapter Two, W. John Pembroke provides guidance for understanding such organizational structures and the specific parts they play in the effective administration of student affairs.

Campus climate, tradition, community, and other phrases have become part of the lexicon of student affairs. What do they really mean, and how can you

1

as a practitioner begin to assess your campus environment? George Kuh provides helpful assistance in answering these difficult questions in Chapter Three and introduces us to the complexity of that process.

Money — the lack of it, the loss of it, or the prudent use of it — presents a number of challenges for successful practice in student affairs. In recent years, rapid growth of higher education has ended, and fiscal support for the academy has diminished. In Chapter Four, John Schuh provides an overview of the fiscal constraints facing higher education and draws salient conclusions for each of us on our campuses.

Many have called administration an art rather than a science. Good administration is dependent on developing strong working relationships with others both on and off the campus. In Chapter Five, Dudley Woodard and Mark von Destinon provide a framework to assist student affairs professionals in identifying key constituency groups.

In Chapter Six, Peter Likins offers the view of one president on the role of student affairs within colleges and universities and discusses the critical relationship between the functional units of student affairs and the institution's chief executive officer. The chapter provides practical suggestions regarding those relationships and the balance that must be achieved between serving both our students and our institutions.

Part One sets the stage for understanding the complicated administration of student affairs programs and services within institutions of higher education.

1

❧

The Importance of
Institutional Mission

James W. Lyons

Emerson cautions us that "the one thing not to be forgiven to intellectual persons is, not to know their own tasks" (as quoted in Barzun, 1968, p. 207). As student affairs administrators, we must know our tasks, which flow from many sources, including both our students and our institutions. Other chapters in this volume will concentrate on student characteristics, needs, and differences; administrative processes and procedures; and the knowledge and skills essential to the creation of strong student affairs programs. This chapter, however, focuses on one essential element that shapes our work as student affairs professionals: the institutional mission.

There is great diversity in American higher education. "Together, over 3,000 colleges and universities serve about 13 million students" (National Association of Student Personnel Administrators, [1987] 1989, p. 9). Beyond these numbers, however, the astute observer will see a rich landscape filled with differences between institutions of higher education. Each college or university is unique, and that uniqueness derives from a distinctive mission. For student affairs programs to be succesful, a clear understanding of that mission is a necessary first step.

This chapter will first briefly discuss the history of American higher education from its beginnings in the colonial colleges to the present day.

Second, attention will be given to the traditional missions and purposes of higher education. Third, illustrations will be provided of how several factors influence the character and mission of particular institutions and student affairs practice.

A Brief Historical Overview

Knock describes three philosophic orientations to higher education that have influenced its growth and development in the United States: education for the aristocracy, educational opportunities earned through merit, and an open, egalitarian system (1985). "Oxford and Cambridge furnished the original model which the colonial colleges sought to copy" (Brubacher and Rudy, 1976, p. 3). It became evident, however, that transplanting the traditional English model of higher education to the New World would require modification and adjustments. Among the changes were the establishment of collegiate boards of control that were either interdenominational in makeup or in "one case completely secular" (Brubacher and Rudy, 1976, p. 4). In addition, the colonial colleges were influenced by Scottish models and by continental universities and were modified to meet the needs of an expanding colonial population.

The goals of the early colonial colleges were well defined.

> The Christian tradition was the foundation stone of the whole intellectual structure which was brought to the New World. It is equally important, however, to keep in mind that the early colleges were not set up solely to train ministers; their charters make it amply clear that from the very beginning it was intended that they also educate professional men in fields other than the ministry and public officials of various kinds. The civil society would thus get educated orthodox laymen as its leaders; the church would get educated orthodox clergymen as its ministers. This was the ideal that the colonial higher education hoped to attain [Brubacher and Rudy, 1976, p. 6].

Of course, times and purposes changed. In the period intervening between the establishment of the early colonial colleges to the present, a number of forces shaped higher education in the United States. The growing heterogeneity of the colonial population forced some institutions, supported by colonial legislatures, to modify their curricula beyond narrow sectarian ideas. "The nineteenth century witnessed a gradual decline in governmental involvement with sectarian schools. As states began to establish their own institutions, the public-private dichotomy emerged" in American higher education (Kaplin, 1985, pp. 16–17). "The first truly public institution of higher education was founded by Jefferson and became the University of Virginia" (Knock, 1985, p. 19). The Supreme Court case of *Trustees of Dartmouth Col-*

lege v. *Woodward* (1819) ensured the existence of both public and private universities and colleges in the United States, because it ruled that the government could not alter the perpetual charter of a private institution.

During this same period, increased calls for curriculum reform and expanded opportunities could be heard across the country. The first nonmilitary technical school, Rensselaer Polytechnic Institute, was established in 1824. Women's colleges first arose in the South: Wesleyan Female College in Macon, Georgia, in 1836, Judson College in 1838, and Mary Sharp College in 1852 (Brubacher and Rudy, 1976). (It was not until after the Civil War that many of the famous women's colleges (Smith, Vassar, Radcliffe) were established in the North.)

Oberlin established coeducation before 1860, an example that was followed by many institutions in the West. Denominational colleges continued to flourish during the nineteenth century, although there was a distinct separation of church and state. The period of growth for colleges for African Americans occurred in the thirty years after the Civil War (Brubacher and Rudy, 1976, p. 75). Concurrently, other educational models were introduced successfully. The German approach, with its focus on the expansion of knowledge (research), began to be perceived as a legitimate one and still can be found in major research institutions across the country, such as Johns Hopkins, the University of Chicago, and the University of Michigan. Science and mathematics were introduced as respectable subjects in the curriculum, laboratories were developed, and in some institutions a primary emphasis on graduate and professional education became the norm.

The Morrill Land Grant Act of 1862 was a landmark in the expansion of American higher education. Through the Morrill Act, the federal government set aside public lands to finance agricultural and mechanical schools in response to the needs of society. Three models emerged from the Morrill Act: (1) special institutions specifically geared to land-grant objectives in many states; (2) already-established institutions that received money to support new curricular objectives (the University of California, Berkeley, and the University of Minnesota); or (3) a blend of private and public institutions (Cornell) to meet land-grant objectives.

Although the intensive period for establishing colleges occurred from 1790 to 1859, 134 more colleges were founded in the years 1860 to 1890 and another 135 between 1890 and 1929 (Millett, 1952). And all of this growth in number and kind predated the massive community or junior college movement. In 1947, the President's Commission on Higher Education recommended that two more years of study be provided for about the 50 percent of young people who could benefit from formal study beyond high school (President's Commission on Higher Education, 1947). In 1947, there were a total of 650 public and private community or junior colleges, and by 1987 that number grew to 1,224 (Cohen and Brawer, 1989).

Other factors also influenced the history and growth of American higher education. For example, the G.I. Bill (1944 Veterans Readjustment Act) made it possible for veterans to attend institutions of higher education. Desegregation provided a second large wave of new students following the decision of *Brown* v. *Board of Education* (1954). The civil rights movement increased the expectation of minority group members for the right for higher education. The Higher Education Act of 1965 created Basic Educational Opportunity Grants, later renamed Pell Grants, and financial aid increased the opportunity and choice of higher education for financially needy students. The political activism of the 1960s and 1970s caused many institutions to reassess both purpose and governance. Finally, the rise of the adult and part-time learner forever changed the characteristics of American higher education. Consequently, it is a diverse and complicated enterprise.

As described by Balderston (1974), the three traditional missions of higher education are teaching, research, and public service. Others have characterized its traditional purposes as "to preserve, transmit and create knowledge, to encourage personal development and to serve society" (National Association of Student Personnel Administrators, [1987] 1989, p. 9). What creates variation among institutions of higher education is the emphasis placed on each of these three objectives and the type of institution involved. The scope of institutions of higher education in the United States is enormous. Their enrollments range from fewer than five hundred to over fifty thousand. They are located in rural and small towns and in major cities. They may be independent, church-related, church-controlled, or publicly supported. Some are purely undergraduate institutions grounded in the liberal arts tradition. Some, most notably community colleges, are degree-granting institutions with a strong component of public service and public access to nondegree offerings. "Others have multiple purposes and include undergraduate, graduate, professional and technical education and serve students from around the world. Still others are community oriented, and their offerings reflect local or regional needs" (National Association of Student Personnel Administrators, [1987] 1989, p. 9).

Although it would sometimes seem that most institutional mission statements "are remarkable more for their sameness than their distinctiveness and give little symbolic focus for collective action" (Alfred and Weissman, 1987, p. 34), the written and "living mission," statement of any institution can shape the collaborative learning processes within the academic community. Kuh, Schuh, and Whitt (1990) indicate that "the mission provides the rationale for what a college or university is and aspires to be and the yardstick used by students, faculty and others to determine if their institutional policies and practices are educationally purposeful" (p. 4).

The *Involving Colleges* (Kuh, Schuh, Whitt, and Associates, 1991) study concentrated on what made institutions successful in encouraging the achievement of students and a sense of community. Although the missions and philosophies of the institutions studied in *Involving Colleges* are many, all have clarity and coherence.

Discovering the Institutional Mission

Virtually all institutions have a mission statement that sets forth what they do, how they go about it, for whom it is done, and in some cases the larger social, ethical, and educational world view that enlivens them. There is usually more to an institution's mission than a descriptive page or paragraph in the front of a catalogue. The heritage of an institution can be one of the building blocks of its mission. It is *always* worthwhile to ask who founded the institution? When? For whom? And to do what? No two institutions have evolved in the same way, and their history often accounts for their distinctiveness. Yet this history, important as it always is, may be only one of *many* portals that can lead to understanding the full meaning and texture of an institution's mission.

How does one learn what the mission of a college or university really is, especially when it is rarely spelled out? Much of the answer can be found in how those in the institution view what they do, how they live, how they relate to each other and to educational goals, and what they value. As Kuh and Schuh observe, "The 'living mission' of a college is how students, faculty, administrators, graduates, and others describe what the college is and is trying to accomplish" (1991, p. 12). To what extent is the institution residential? Are there educational purposes embedded in its residential programs and arrangements? Is "community" an important concept, and how is it encouraged? Why do students come? What kinds of students attend? What are the key criteria for faculty selection, advancement, and retention? Are there significant organizing principles, such as religious, social, or special educational beliefs? Certainly one way to understand the mission of the institution is to ask what it *does not do*.

Terminology

The meaning of even common terms like *liberal arts* may vary according to the institution. At Allegheny College in Pennsylvania, for example, a liberal arts college, the core of its program is in liberal studies; however, students can major in communication arts, physical education, environmental science, and education and international studies, along with the more classic liberal arts fields (classics, physics, chemistry, history, humanities, and philosophy). Allegheny's idea of the liberal arts has evolved over time in much the same way as has that of many other liberal arts colleges.

Reed College, also a liberal arts institution, embraces a far more traditional and restrictive view of the liberal arts. Any subject matter that appears to be applied may have great difficulty finding its way into Reed's curriculum.

Moreover, the understanding and practice of student affairs are quite different on the two campuses. At Allegheny, the education of the whole person is valued. Attention is paid to students' affective, as well as cognitive, development. Reed, by contrast, focuses almost exclusively on the intellectual development of students. More than other institutions, the college tends to assume that students' social development matters less.

Heritage

Earlham, Haverford, and Guilford colleges are located in widely different parts of the country. They are private, residential, small liberal arts colleges, like many hundreds of others. They are distinctive, however, in that all were founded by Quakers (Society of Friends). Though Quakers constitute a very small proportion of their student bodies, governing boards, and administrations, the Quaker tradition continues to play a significant role in determining how things get done, how members of the campus community relate to each other, and how policy is conceived and implemented. The work of the community (faculty meetings, residence meetings, and student government) is done by consensus, a way of doing business that is characteristically Quaker. Relationships among members of the communities are cemented by a deliberately nourished environment of trust and respect and forthrightness. All of these institutions are influenced by a strong peace testimony. All tend to avoid pretense in its many forms. For example, titles are used infrequently, if at all. These schools' architecture and furnishings are usually elegant in their simplicity. Learning viewed as a means to search for truth in its many forms creates strong bonds to scholarship. To be effective, a professional in student affairs would have to learn, respect, and work within the cultural context of each college's Quaker tradition. Calling for a vote to decide disputed matters, seeking ROTC (or for that matter military) recruiters on campus, and creating prescriptive rules are not part of procedural and programmatic approaches on these campuses, although they are common elsewhere. The mission of these colleges cannot be understood fully without an appreciation of their heritage.

Geography, history, and tradition have thus shaped each of these colleges in a distinctive way.

Distinctive Systems

The University of California is a multicampus system governed by a common board of regents. Its faculty has a governance system that transcends the boundaries of any given campus: a central administration sits at the head of the system. Yet the institutions within the University of California are quite different.

Every institution in the system has its own traditions, culture, distinctive geographical setting, and ways of approaching academics. Although all University of California (UC) institutions emphasize research, two of the older campuses, Berkeley and the University of California, Los Angeles

(UCLA), are preeminent in that regard. UC Santa Cruz, founded in the 1960s, reflects many of the educational ideals that so characterized that decade. It has both academic departments and residential colleges with interdisciplinary themes and tends to emphasize teaching and undergraduate education. UC San Diego also has residential colleges with interdisciplinary themes. In addition, however, it has professional schools and an ambitious research agenda, especially in science and technology. UC Davis is different in other ways. While stressing teaching and research, it is heavily influenced by its agricultural heritage, including a tradition of everyone (as on a farm) pitching in at certain points for the good of the whole, regardless of role and specialty. It is therefore not surprising that UC Davis students take substantial responsibility for governing the institution and, as peer departmental advisers, their home departments.

A student affairs professional should understand these differences, even in a university system characterized by considerable centralized control. Standardization within student affairs might occur in admissions, conduct policies, financial aid processes, certain governance requirements, methods of allocating resources, and other common services. But building an organization to serve the *special* mission of each institution must be done very differently at UC Santa Cruz, UC Berkeley, UCLA, UC Davis, and UC San Diego. Creating and maintaining a high quality of student life will be achieved in distinctive ways on each campus. The skills that work on one campus are not easily transferable to another within the system.

Geography

What effect does geography have on the educational programs of the institution? It can range from subtle to dramatic. For example, it is not surprising that the educational priorities of the University of Alaska in Fairbanks include the education of rural Alaskan natives, fisheries research, and the study of Arctic phenomena. Student affairs staff members know the importance of hockey and cross-country skiing to the well-being of students in the long, dark winters. They also know that orientation activities must include lessons on how to dress for and cope with long periods of intense cold and how to handle the mental health issues that accompany the winters.

At the University of Arizona, Arizona State University, and the University of New Mexico, considerable attention in the curriculum and in campus life is devoted to the education of Native Americans and to the general cultural understanding of Hopi, Navajo, and Pueblo tribal cultures.

Many institutions on the ethnically rich West Coast have long faced the challenge of enriching students' understanding of the ethnic and racial diversity that characterizes their campus and their region. Student affairs professionals are called upon regularly to articulate and help create the ideals of multicultural communities marked by respect, trust, and the comfort needed by students to optimize their academic priorities. This process, of course, happens in many other parts of the country, but it is a regular and obvious feature of many West Coast schools.

An institution's history and location often work together to give it a distinctive mission. Xavier University in New Orleans was founded as a Catholic institution "to serve blacks and persons of color who were denied educational opportunities" (Kuh, Schuh, Whitt, and Associates, 1991, p. 74). The approaches and organization of student affairs are influenced heavily by Xavier's setting in an ethnically rich city and by the guidance of the Catholic faith. These act in concert to produce distinctive ways to recognize, reward, and encourage students to achieve, as well as to foster a special sense of community or family rarely found on campuses.

Geography, then, can have a profound affect on the mission of an institution. Looking at an institution through the lens of its geographical setting is thus another way to understand what it seeks to do and why.

Social Organization of Students

The social organization of students, or the lack of it, may also help one understand an institution's mission and the ways in which it is carried out. An urban institution such as Temple University cannot be evaluated by using criteria appropriate to a residential setting. At such institutions, the social organization and relationships of students may be relatively unimportant when compared with those at residential institutions. If the social organization of students has importance in such urban settings, it will more often than not be realized in the ways schools and departments work to build social structures for their students. The relationship between the institution and the community is also a significant factor in determining the social structures that benefit students. In the case of Wichita State University, one must understand the community in order to comprehend how the community serves as a surprising source of social support and organization for students attending the university.

The social structures of student life at residential institutions may look more alike than they really are and lead to erroneous conclusions about the mission of the institution. Cornell, Miami University (Ohio), and the University of Virginia are schools with fraternities and sororities that affect the social and organizational lives of many students on each campus. Each of the schools depends on residential fraternities and sororities to provide housing for students. Fraternal organizations have a recognizable presence on the campus. Beyond these facts, similarities are less obvious. The relationship between the institution and the Greek organizations—and its support for these groups—varies considerably.

It is fair to observe that Cornell and the University of Virginia tolerate their residential fraternities, though they are often troubled by them. Fraternal organizations have long histories at both schools, are seen by some as anachronisms or antithetical to education or both, and are a frequent source of conduct problems. The relationship between the institution and Greek organizations is sometimes marked by mistrust and suspicion. And the resulting town-and-gown dynamics can be volatile.

Though Miami also has a long history of fraternal organizations, its history is rooted in an early belief in the founding ideals of many fraternities and sororities. Three of the oldest national fraternities were founded there. Hence, Miami's history has been marked by good relationships with its Greek organizations. They are seen as important partners in the creation of a healthy organizational, residential, and university life.

Differences such as these are found throughout higher education and are an area in which student affairs professionals have a special interest and responsibility.

Somewhere in the living mission of each college and university are the expectations, behavioral customs, policies, and ways of relating that will shape the work of students affairs. The success or failure of student affairs may depend, in some measure, on the compatibility of the views of student affairs professionals and the mission of their institution. If they are highly congruent, student affairs work is more likely to be effective.

Institutions with Broad and Far-Reaching Missions

Some institutions, either by design or inadvertently, are many things to many people. It would be difficult to find much overall focus in a sprawling state university with large residential graduate and undergraduate student populations, several branch campuses, several professional schools, and many centers for research and service. The missions of such a mega-university may be little more than to provide an environment in which research, general and professional education and training, and service to the state will flourish. Distinctive purposes *do* exist within the components of such institutions, and it is to them that the student affairs staff should look. The missions of an adult education division are likely to be quite different from those of a school of law or a college of liberal studies. Each of these units will probably have its own student affairs organization and services within the larger whole.

Many student services and programs will be decentralized by necessity and occur within subcommunities such as residences or colleges and schools. Even some central services like unions or intercollegiate sports also have distinctive missions that give definition and substance to the more vague and overarching objectives of the university.

Community Colleges

Community colleges have widely varying missions. They usually exist to respond to the training and educational needs of a specific community or region; the curriculum may therefore be heavily influenced by local social and economic patterns. A community college in a manufacturing town will offer a curriculum that will reflect that industrial focus, whereas a community college in Reno, Nevada, may offer courses to run casino games and operations. A community college will also organize teaching and curriculum to respond to the special requirements and characteristics of the area's residents. Thus, understanding the mission of a community college will be easier to the extent that one understands its location. Nearly all community colleges offer a means to transfer to four-year institutions and provide a place to prove one's scholastic mettle and prepare for the academic specialization that awaits one in the university.

The subtleties of many community colleges' missions can also be understood by identifying what motivates students to attend in the first place. The wise and experienced student affairs vice president of a community college urges that we acknowledge some compelling motivations for attendance that will never be found in the mission statement: "To get out of the house; to feel better or get well; to get out of prison sooner; to please parents; to play basketball; to have status; to escape from _____; to learn English; to get promoted . . . " (Golseth, 1992, p. 20).

Institutions with Focused Missions

American higher education abounds with colleges and universities with specialized goals. Technical institutes like the Massachusetts Institute of Technology, California Polytechnic Institute, Virginia Polytechnic Institute and State University, Harvey Mudd College, and Rochester Institute of Technology are examples of institutions with missions focused on science and technology. Though all have these at their core, they are nevertheless quite different from each other. They are affected variously by geography, size, the relative importance placed on teaching and research and on graduate and undergraduate education, institutional age, sources of funding, admissions standards, the degree to which their students reside on campus, and their public and private status.

Moreover, an institution's religious affiliation may account for some distinctive missions that may have a profound impact on the work and approaches of the student affairs staff. Georgetown University painfully labored in the full glare of the national press in deciding how it would recognize a gay and lesbian organization. Should a Catholic university condone, or seem to condone, an organization that appeared to flout an important tenet of its faith? Our higher educational landscape is full of examples, both visible and subtle, of how an institution's religious affiliation can affect its mission and therefore the work of student affairs.

The Evergreen State College in Olympia, Washington, is a wonderful instance of how influential a focused mission can be. Founded in 1967, its doors opening in 1971, Evergreen was conceived with the objective of providing a sound liberal arts education through nontraditional means. From that founding mission, a most imaginative, successful, and effective educational program has evolved. Traditional (or at least common) approaches to student affairs would thus be out of place and counterproductive at Evergreen.

Berea College is another institution with an unusual purpose. It is a liberal arts college founded to educate able but poor children in Appalachia. Among its several objectives is to demonstrate that labor, mental and manual, has dignity as well as utility. To achieve these aspects of its mission, its student body is limited to those who can pay little or no tuition, and all students must work for the institution for approximately fifteen hours per week. The work of student affairs at Berea will be as distinctive as it is at Evergreen. At both colleges, expectations for student life must be well understood if the professional student affairs staff is to succeed there.

Institutional Missions That Predetermine How Student Services Will Be Organized

The same model of residential colleges found at the University of California campuses at Santa Cruz and San Diego can be found in other institutions as diverse as Yale, the University of Redlands (Johnston College), Western Washington University (Fairhaven College), and Harvard. These universities are organized into residential (except Fairhaven) colleges that have many things in common besides their relatively small size. These include affiliated faculty members who serve as advisers, mentors, and deans to furnish academic advising and help with personal problems. In addition, such faculty members monitor student academic standing, nurture students' self-governance, handle conflicts, and organize rituals such as orientation and graduation. Each residential college will generate its own leisure and extracurricular activities. The colleges usually have distinct personalities — cultures, traditions, rules, norms, and practices that set them apart from each other and from the larger institution and that persist over many generations of students (Jencks and Riesman, 1962). Many institutions have variations of the college or house system. Versions of one sort or another can also be found at Stanford, Bucknell, Cornell, and Princeton.

Professionals in the field working in more traditional settings often wonder just how student affairs activities are organized in such residential colleges. Most of the typical services and responsibilities are found there, but they are often labeled and organized differently. The boundaries between academic and nonacademic are quite permeable because faculty members assume general duties assigned to administrative professionals on other campuses. The line between students and administrators is also vague because students in such settings tend to assume significant responsibility for each other and their community. Highly technical services like financial aid, psychological counseling, career planning, and medical care are provided on a more centralized basis. Even then, these might be supplied in the residential college setting as well. Students routinely take charge of programs like orientation, campus communications, colloquia, admissions recruiting, the community paper or newsletter, or the campus (college) directory. The living mission almost always can be understood more clearly by looking at what students do to maintain their community and how they do it. To illustrate, at Fairhaven College at Western Washington University, a lively and immensely successful 1960s alternative learning community, the campus directory has no separate categories for students, faculty, and staff and is alphabetized by the person's first name.

As illustrated by these examples, the university's goals cannot be well understood without a knowledge of the special missions of its member residential colleges. In addition, the structure of the educational activities and the services of student affairs will be dramatically different in a university organized into colleges.

Summary

We have observed that the role of student affairs will nearly always differ from one institution to another. How the work of student affairs is structured, how its responsibilities are defined, how it is valued, and how it relates to the work and culture of an institution can vary greatly from one university to another and even within an institution.

The most important factor that determines the shape and substance of student affairs is the mission of the institution. There are other factors, of course, but none is as important and compelling. Terminology, heritage, academic focus, geography, the social organization of students, the curriculum, the administrative structure, and faculty involvement all reflect institutional objectives and the place of student affairs. Understanding this mission requires more than merely reading a statement. Homework must be done and understanding achieved. Institutional "fit" between student affairs staff members and their colleges and universities is very important to the success of each. Acceptance of and support for the institutional mission, then, seems a prerequisite to success in the student affairs profession.

References

Alfred, R., and Weissman, J. *Higher Education and the Public Trust.* ASHE-ERIC Higher Education Report, no. 6. Washington, D.C.: Association for the Study of Higher Education, 1987.

Balderston, E. F. *Managing Today's University.* San Francisco: Jossey-Bass, 1974.

Barzun, J. *The American University.* New York: HarperCollins, 1968.

Brubacher, J., and Rudy, W. R. *Higher Education in Transition.* (3rd ed.) New York: HarperCollins, 1976.

Cohen, A. M., and Brawer, F. B. *The American Community College.* (2nd ed.) San Francisco: Jossey-Bass, 1989.

Golseth, A. "Diversity—Beyond Celebration." In J. W. Lyons (ed.), *Student Affairs 1992: How Things Are and Are Becoming: A Collection of Essays.* A collection of essays prepared for the National Association of Student Personnel Administrators Western Regional Conference, 1992.

Jencks, C., and Riesman, D. "Patterns of Residential Education: A Class Study of Harvard." In N. Sanford (ed.), *The American College.* New York: Wiley, 1962.

Kaplin, W. *The Law of Higher Education.* (2nd ed.) San Francisco: Jossey-Bass, 1985.

Knock, G. "Development of Student Services in Higher Education." In M. J. Barr, L. A. Keating, and Associates, *Developing Effective Student Services Programs: Systematic Approaches for Practitioners.* San Francisco: Jossey-Bass, 1985.

Kuh, G., and Schuh, J. *The Role and Contribution of Student Affairs in Involving Colleges.* Washington, D.C.: National Association of Student Personnel Administrators, 1991.

Kuh, G. D., Schuh, J. H., and Whitt, E. J. "Involving Colleges: Characteristics of Colleges and Universities That Promote Involvement in Out-of-Class Learning." Unpublished manuscript, June 1990.

Kuh, G. D., Schuh, J. H., Whitt, E. J., and Associates. *Involving Colleges: Successful Approaches to Fostering Student Learning and Development Outside the Classroom.* San Francisco: Jossey-Bass, 1991.

Millett, J. D. *Financing Higher Education in the United States.* New York: Columbia University Press, 1952.

National Association of Student Personnel Administrators. "A Perspective on Student Affairs." In *Points of View.* Washington, D.C.: National Association of Student Personnel Administrators, 1989. (Originally published 1987.)

President's Commission on Higher Education. *Higher Education for American Democracy.* Washington, D.C.: U.S. Government Printing Office, 1947.

Legal Cases

Brown v. *Board of Education,* 347 U.S. 483 (1954).
Trustees of Dartmouth College v. *Woodward,* 17 U.S. 518 (1819).

2

Institutional Governance and the Role of Student Affairs

W. John Pembroke

Governance structures may be the key element that differentiates colleges and universities from other complex organizations. College and university governance differs markedly from the corporate, hierarchical organizational structures in business and industry (Flawn, 1990). In institutions of higher education, governance more closely resembles a parliamentary form of government where the executive, legislative, and judicial branches are intermingled. Even with the presence of governing boards, state coordinating boards, statutes, and legislative and gubernatorial pressures, the apparatus of state government only marginally impinges on campus-based governance prerogatives in both public and private institutions. Governing boards, statutes, and chartering and licensure requirements do, however, play pivotal roles in establishing the broad parameters within which institutions must operate (Kaplin, 1985). But there is an interactive process of achieving consensus between the governed and those governing in higher education with respect to establishing mission, purpose, agenda, planning, and aspirations. In virtually no other organizational setting are there as many competing ideals, goals, and purposes as on a college or university campus.

One of this country's chief export products, incredibly not even considered in the balance-of-trade calculations, is higher education. Since the expansion of higher education in the mid 1950s, international students have been attracted to American colleges and universities in ever-increasing numbers. The fundamental reason is that the United States has a system of higher education with a multitude of choices between institutions and the broadest array of options anywhere in the world. Such a situation does not either happen overnight or in a vacuum. Underpinning the entire enterprise is a system of governance that in the final analysis works and works quite well.

In this chapter, the key components of college and university governance will be identified. The influence of collective bargaining agreements on governance will be discussed, and the part that student affairs professionals can play in campus governance will be identified.

The Context of Institutional Governance

To the casual observer, colleges and universities are perceived (correctly) as environments where students go to learn, grow, and prepare for their own individual futures and participation in the world at large. The academy is also expected to undertake research regarding everything from the creation of the universe to a cure for cancer, AIDS, and the common cold. In addition, colleges and universities are supposed to provide a focal point for the redress of societal ills ranging from the abuse of the environment to poverty. The academy is assumed to play a contributing or major role in curing virtually every problem or malady. Conflicting agendas and paradoxical situations are the norm for higher education.

The issue of governance is complicated by the harsh fiscal realities now faced by higher education. In fiscal year 1992 alone, nineteen state legislatures and their governors imposed midyear budget reductions upon public higher education. In those states, such as Illinois and New York, that supply substantial public support to private higher education, these reductions also affected private institutions. Thus, fiscal constraints, demands for increased accountability (National Institute of Education, 1984), and a very diffuse agenda require responsiveness, focus, and agreement on the part of campus governance and decision-making bodies.

The Governing Board

Whether public or independent, each institution of higher education is under the control of a governing board. Called the board of trustees, the board of regents, the board of rectors, or the board of overseers, these lay governing boards are the source of the power and authority to operate the institution.

In public institutions, the governing board may be appointed by the governor with the advice and consent of the state senate, or board members may be elected, in the case of constitutionally autonomous institutions (Kaplin, 1985), or chosen by alumni. In any case, the dynamics of the governing board are different from those experienced in private higher education, due to the political nature of the board appointments. Public institutional governing boards are usually of small size and have specific statutory or constitutional powers. They meet frequently and exercise substantial power over component institutions. In addition, governing boards of state-supported institutions are also subject to statutes that influence how the board operates. For example, in both Florida and Illinois, state "sunshine" laws require that board meetings be open and that decisions of the board be discussed in a public setting. This practice creates unusual and often difficult problems for institutional administrators when trying to confront campus issues and resolve conflicts.

Private institutions of higher education are controlled by governing boards that are self-perpetuating, are not subject to sunshine laws, and derive their authority from the charter or license granted by the state to operate the institution. In contrast to public institutional governing boards, private boards are usually larger and include individuals who have made either a substantial service or monetary contribution to the institution. The day-to-day business of the governing board is generally vested in an executive committee of board members who meet often with appropriate campus administrative staff members. Full board meetings, however, are held on a less frequent basis than those of public institutions.

The presence of a broadly based, well-defined, and agreed-upon structure provides a governing board with two important benefits. First, a well-defined governance structure furnishes a legitimate basis for the board to deliberate and make policies and to undertake initiatives compatible with the mission and character of the institution. Second, established governance structures create credibility; divergent points of view can be resolved, and the outcome can gain standing and general acceptance across the campus community.

It is at the board level of formal authority that the character, general reputation, and the mission of the institution are articulated to external constituencies. The governing board also makes key administrative appointments. And although this activity is initially undertaken on a collaborative basis, in the final analysis it is the board's area of exclusive responsibility to render such judgments. Finally, the governing board is where key elements of new institutional initiatives or mission redefinition are sanctioned, rejected, or remanded to the campus for further refinement.

The role of the campus's chief executive officer (CEO) is the most prominent in providing support and direction to the board; however, other administrative officers, as well as advisory mechanisms reflecting the views of faculty, students, and staff, are essential for well-informed board deliberations.

It is at the governing-board level where student affairs divisions lag most notably behind other campus-based constituency groups in the governance process. Perhaps this fact can be attributed to the evolution of student affairs's responsibilities from the concept of in loco parentis to the current understanding of the fundamental role of the division in achieving both student and institutional success. Although its organization may change from one institution to another, the functions of student affairs, irrespective of administrative reporting lines, now span a large spectrum. This changed perspective of student affairs has been accepted on many campuses but is still one that proves illusive to many governing boards. The failure of board members to comprehend the place and function of student affairs results in either a lack of appreciation for its programs, priorities, and services or (in the worst case) in opposition to student affairs plans and priorities. Although boards are at the top of the governance chain, in reality most boards are educated, informed, directed, and otherwise influenced from the bottom up (through committees). Consequently, it is important for student affairs professionals to avail themselves of every chance to engage the board and its individual members in dialogue and to provide direct exposure to the activities, functions, and responsibilities of student affairs. Most members of governing boards are not only open but receptive to opportunities that aid them in better defining the goals of the institution and the discrete roles the various organizational components play in meeting institutional objectives. Many governing boards also either have a committee structure that addresses issues particularly germane to student affairs or provide an annual opportunity to consider relevant issues. Although it might appear simplistic, it is important that student affairs professionals consider relationships with and understanding of the governing board as a priority agenda item.

Campus Governance

At the campus level, most mature institutions have an array of overlapping governance mechanisms. These include institutional governance councils, faculty senates, a variety of committee structures, relationships with other administrative units, and student government organizations.

Institutional Governance Structures

Many campuses have an institutionwide governance body that incorporates a number of campus constituency groups into a single deliberative entity such as a university or college council. Faculty representatives tend to dominate these governance bodies because of their preeminent role in the academic mission of the institution. It is in such forums, however, that representatives from the administrative and professional staff, student government, support personnel, and other segments of the campus community come together to determine institutional priorities and policies. Frequently, these bodies have standing committees or advisory groups that have the twofold purpose of broadening the participation base in institutional governance matters and providing a forum where members of the community with specific expertise can contribute to particular aspects of the governance process.

Again, the most common pattern is that such committees or task groups related to an institutionwide governance body have heavy faculty representation. However, groups that have overarching responsibilities for matters like the budget or planning process usually contain representatives from all campus constituencies.

From a student affairs point of view, there are two basic patterns of involvement in institutionwide governance bodies. First, student affairs staff members are asked to serve on the central body and also on subordinated committees and advisory groups. A second pattern is to involve student affairs professionals in committees that are charged to examine issues immediately related to the responsibilities of the student affairs division. This latter approach, although offering a more focused and in-depth treatment of issues, has the disadvantage of isolating the student affairs perspective instead of integrating it broadly and comprehensively into institutional decision making.

It cannot be stressed too strongly that student affairs personnel who rely almost exclusively upon interaction with student constituency groups and remain divorced from campuswide governance systems often suffer from a "stepchild" syndrome when it comes to institutionwide initiatives, decision making, and policy formulation. The CEO, the faculty, and the students will be better served if all perspectives—including academic, fiscal, budgetary, planning, *and* student affairs—are included in central campus governance.

Of course, shared governance processes can be arduous and extremely time consuming. Decisions that appear to be reasonable and logical from a divisional point of view are often delayed by collective governance scrutiny. Instances arise when the need or rationale is so compelling as to virtually mandate that a judgment be made at the division level and that action be undertaken without more general consultation. More commonly, however, it is the inconvenience of the governance process that deters student affairs professionals from wanting decisions to be subjected to the scrutiny of governance processes. Notwithstanding those observations, the ultimate protection afforded by full and complete participation in campus governance is that a decision or a conclusion, once arrived at, provides a clear and unambiguous sense of direction for the actions that subsequently follow. The other benefit is the opportunity afforded to student affairs professionals to educate other parts of the academy regarding their role and responsibilities. Ultimately, the result is to humanize the environment by demonstrating that a student's higher education experience includes both academic and out-of-class experiences. Such involvement also demonstrates the critical importance of interdependence and mutual respect among all parts of the community. The practical effect is a general recognition that the student affairs division is not only important but essential. And in times of tight fiscal resources, support for student affairs in the budgetary allocation process is strengthened.

Faculty Senate

Most institutions also have some form of faculty senate that influences their governance structure. Mortimer and McConnell (1978) define three categories of faculty senate jurisdiction: legislative, advisory, and forensic. To illustrate the legislative function, through their committee structures faculty senates often have effective control over such matters as curriculum. "The phrase *effective control* means that although legally the decisions of senates or senate committees could be reversed by the administration or the board, they rarely, if ever, are" (Mortimer and McConnell, 1978, p. 27). Advisory functions of faculty senates can be wide ranging and usually revolve around issues of budget, personnel, or planning; the senate is asked for its input, and the decision is made by the appropriate administrative entity. It is extremely important, however, that the differences between the legislative and advisory functions of faculty senates be defined clearly. Finally, the forensic work of a faculty senate consumes a great deal of time and energy as debate occurs on issues. Yet it is frequently this forensic function that brings to light pressing issues or concerns that must be confronted by the institution. Student affairs personnel must develop linkages with such faculty governance groups.

All too often, student affairs professionals abdicate to an articulate minority or faculty "hallway politicians" influence over fundamental institutional decisions. This practice is a grievous error and over time will weaken the viability and standing of the entire institution. The broad array of specializations, genuine disparities in levels of expertise, conflicting perspectives or frames of reference—all serve as a natural, centrifugal force to pull an institution in many simultaneous directions. It is only through governance that these forces can be contained and integrated in a manner that is institutionally beneficial. It is usually easier to ignore faculty governance groups due to the press of day-to-day business and other organizational imperatives; but to succumb to these internal, division-based pressures is to surrender one of the key methods of achieving greater parity and standing for student affairs within the institution.

Committee Structures

The area between formal governance and institutional management is occupied by committees. Committees have been regarded as time-consuming bodies at which little is accomplished; often what *is* accomplished winds up being the proverbial camel that was intended to be the horse. Yet as imperfect as the committee mechanism is for either governance or management, it is a structure most suited to the particular characteristics of the academy. As indicated earlier, the most profound decisions arrived at by an institution actually tend to be rooted in the bottom-up system of committees. A strong committee structure performs the valuable task of communicating to all organizational and governance levels new ideas, refinements of old ideas, reaffirmation of purpose, and suggestions for new initiatives. Committees are inclusionary, often with representation from faculty, staff, and students, where feedback as well as input can be sought and communicated both to the administrative and governance structures. Committees also provide an ideal setting for conflict resolution and rigorous evaluation of competing concepts.

Committees are also effective because of their somewhat more elastic membership and less formalized modes of deliberation. In the absence of a properly defined and mature committee structure, institutions may become mired in situations where there are ongoing clashes between the judgments produced by the governance process and those arrived at by the more hierarchical administrative channels. Although committees come in all shapes and sizes, three broad categories prevail within higher education: standing committees, select or issue-oriented committees, and general-purpose advisory committees.

Standing Committees

The standing committee is a permanent structure that has well-delineated responsibilities and prerogatives related to a specified set of functions within the institution (such as budget or planning). Standing committees not only furnish the opportunity for ideas and suggestions but also provide a critical screening function for proposed alternative courses of action. Because of the overlap between membership on key committees and other governance mechanisms, the real strength and power of campus governance tends to reside in such committees.

Select Committees

Select committees appear to be very much like standing ones and perform similar functions, with one important difference: they are usually impaneled for a specific period of time to accomplish a particular set of objectives. Examples might include a committee to examine and make recommendations about campus diversity or a special investigatory body to examine the role and standards of the athletic program. The select committee is useful in that a range of expertise from across the campus can be brought to bear on a reasonably limited set of issues that require in-depth examination and comprehensive assessment before action can be taken. Not infrequently, select committees become standing ones due to the importance of the issue and the quality of the committee's contribution in understanding it.

Ad Hoc and Advisory Committees

The last type is an ad hoc or advisory committee, which is routinely employed when there is a need to expand the participation of campus constituencies. If either the governance or administrative structure is desirous of broad initial input into policies, ad hoc groups have great utility. When they are effective, they include students, faculty, and staff who have interest in and expertise about the issue under examination.

The student affairs professional is well advised to take advantage of the three-legged committee stool. At their best, all three types of committees develop informal mechanisms to communicate the status of deliberations and pending actions. As many student affairs staff members are well versed in group dynamics, the committee structure provides an ideal forum in which to integrate the student affairs division into the mainstream of institutional life. Committees can also be invaluable in adjusting the administrative structure when it becomes too bureaucratic and cumbersome. Although they are not above byzantine politics, bringing committees back on course is often easier than trying to accomplish an administrative reorganization. Above all, committees constitute the basic building block for the exchange of ideas; they wrestle with difficult institutional challenges and influence the course of governance and the institution. Committee structures may afford the student affairs professional with an opportunity to develop critical relationships on an interdivisional basis. It is an environment within which new ideas, even radical ones, can receive a fair hearing and be refined into proposals or initiatives that are shared both horizontally (with other committees) and vertically (with governance and administrative entities).

Relationships with Other Administrative Units

Student affairs staff members must also develop linkages to each of the other institutional divisions on campus. Failure to do so prevents student affairs professionals from achieving the advancement of their own interests and winning general recognition that their work is a necessary and integral part of the overall operation of the institution.

Whenever occasions occur for the student affairs professional to interact directly with an academic department, a business office, a personnel office, or any other agency where their professional expertise might make a useful contribution, they should be encouraged to do so.

Student Government

The role and influence of student government bodies cannot be ignored when discussing governance. Their pattern of involvement in the affairs of the institution will vary widely from campus to campus, but assistance to these organizations must be high on the agenda for student affairs. During the 1960s, for example, many institutions developed elaborate mechanisms for mandating student involvement in establishing student fees. Although the political climate has changed radically, possibilities for student participation in decision making still exist. Even in institutions that do not mandate involvement, strong and healthy relationships with student government contribute to the overall welfare of the institution. Student affairs professionals usually hold responsibility for advising such groups, but they must also ensure that they are considered by all parts of the university when decisions directly involving students are being made.

Campus Governance: A Summary

The most ideal governance environment for a student affairs division would include a universitywide governance apparatus that would comprehend all constituent groups, augmented by task forces to address either urgent or pervasive institutional concerns. If one were to picture a circle with a core and many spokes, the core would represent a central governance council and the spokes the committees, task forces, and other advisory bodies; ideally, student affairs personnel would be involved in many of the bodies at the ends of those spokes. This approach is, of course, dependent on the willingness of student affairs professionals and colleagues in other divisions to interact as part of the institution's informal organization. At the same time, a bottom-up structure paralleling administrative reporting lines helps to keep internal student affairs issues focused and integrated.

Community colleges have integrated student affairs into the general governance apparatus more effectively than their colleague senior institutions (Cohen and Brawer, 1989). Moreover, within senior institutions, those with an emphasis on undergraduate education tend to incorporate student affairs into campuswide governance structures more often than do research institutions. Each of these institutional cultures, however, is capable of recognizing student affairs and incorporating it into institutional governance. The key for student affairs in each setting is to identify those areas where there is a congruence of interest and ability to contribute to an agenda that will enhance institutional aspirations. Student affairs personnel, and the division as a whole, can frequently provide a very useful "translator" service that enhances communication and understanding across the academy. A contribution to the tone, style, and general atmosphere of a deliberative process will often have just as much effect on the final outcome as attention to the substance of an issue.

In the final analysis, it is the combination of an adequate governance structure and a student affairs professional willing to work closely with other parts of the institution that will yield the most beneficial results, not only for the student affairs division, but also for its counterparts elsewhere in the institution.

The Influence of Collective Bargaining on Governance

Unions and collective bargaining are a reality on many campuses and do influence both governance and decision-making structures.

Unfortunately, collective bargaining is commonly and erroneously perceived to mean faculty collective bargaining. Certainly, the presence of a faculty collective bargaining agent has a profound effect upon institutional governance. Yet what is equally important, though less well recognized, is the influence of other internal collective bargaining on governance. For example, it is not unusual to have personnel in both business affairs and student affairs divisions represented by a collective bargaining agent. Craft employees in many physical-plant departments and administrative and support staff across the country also have collective bargaining agreements. In instances where contracts emphasize wages and general working conditions, the effect upon general institutional governance is usually not very significant. However, as the new fiscal constraints confront colleges and universities, issues of compensation and fringe benefits will consume a much larger proportion of the time of campus-based governance systems. Thus, collective bargaining processes and agreements under these circumstances can have an impact on the governance structure. Often, a natural conflict is created by a governing body's perceptions, fiscal realities, and mandated contract provisions that have fundamental budget implications.

The feature that most strongly determines the influence of collective bargaining on campus governance structures is the character of the relationship between the leadership of the institution and that of the union. In some instances, when matters at the bargaining table and the bargaining agreement do not influence or attempt to replace governance prerogatives, collective bargaining can be fairly unobtrusive. However, when there is an adversarial bargaining situation (referred to as the *industrial model*), the effect on governance is very negative. What appears to be a dual governance structure can develop, with contract negotiations infringing upon many of the deliberative processes built into most campus governance structures. For example, union leadership is often present on key institutional committees, senates, and councils. The result is that the institutional governance structure is weakened because a pervasive union agenda is always present and discussions must be framed with a view to potential or ultimate consequences to contract negotiations. Further exacerbating the situation is the likelihood that many faculty and staff members may not be covered by collective bargaining agreements. When confronted by a governance apparatus that is overly sensitive to a union, these individuals see their ability to be represented diminished, and additional conflict develops.

Fortunately, most collective bargaining environments are not as skewed as the one described above. The academy, due to a historical affinity for collegial decision making and to external changes that have occurred in the nature of these negotiations, has the potential to be a place where institutional governance and collective bargaining can peacefully coexist.

Collegiality and civilized discourse ultimately determine both the caliber and characteristics of governance, whether there is a collective bargaining agreement or not. Faculty and staff unions have been formed many times when there is a sense of frustration with campus governance and the institution. Therefore, it is incumbent upon the institution to recognize problems and make modifications that address concerns and perceptions. It is often merely a matter of opening the process up and broadening the base of participation. Such actions have the benefit of not only allowing genuine issues to be heard but also affording the opportunity for constituent group involvement in governance. If collective bargaining exists, it is important to provide a clear method for union input into campus deliberative processes. Anything short of such actions will result in the need to tackle the issue or problem twice — once in the governance process and again at the bargaining table.

On campuses where as many as a dozen collective bargaining agreements exist, it is useful to have common language in all contracts that delineate the responsibilities and prerogatives of the governance process and those inherent in collective bargaining. This specificity can save all parties from years of confusion and frustration over the appropriate venue for confronting problems. At the same time, administrative attitudes that overemphasize management rights will result in constant challenges from the unions. Institutional governance systems generally recognize the importance of collective bargaining by forming either standing committees or special advisory bodies that link the two systems and keep both the bargaining and governance groups informed.

No substitute exists for effective communication, of course. When campus-based bodies or constituent groups feel that they have been taken advantage of by another group or process, there is instant contention. Such disputes, left to their own devices for a long-enough period, will result in paralysis and undermine the standing of the institution. In the final analysis, the presence of collective bargaining, if properly structured and conducted, need not be a threat to campus governance. Careful delineation of roles, encouragement of collegial relationships, and the incorporation of bargaining unit members, where appropriate, into the governance process can actually serve to strengthen campus governance.

The Role of Student Affairs Staff in Governance

If the committee structure is the basic building block for the governance process, then it is the level and effectiveness of staff support that make it work. Deliberative bodies, by their very nature, must have substantial preparation before action can be taken. Student affairs staff can play a vital role in that process.

Preparing the Governing Board

The need for strong staff preparation is critical at the governing-board level, where far-reaching policies are either adopted or rejected. Quite frequently, staff members are either inadequately prepared or have such singleness of purpose that governing boards are placed in a position of trying to divine what a specific decision means and where it might fit into the institution. Failure to present items to the governing board in a manner that provides a well-defined context and includes a complete explanation of the process used in formulating the recommendation can result in the item's being tabled and remanded or rejected.

Most governing boards are well acquainted with the academic program and budgetary issues. They are less prepared to deal with issues emanating from a student affairs division. Most members of governing boards give freely of their time and serve out of a genuine respect for the institution. That does not mean, however, that they will blindly endorse any initiative that reaches their level. The student affairs professional should regard board members simultaneously as predisposed to be supportive and as relatively uninformed about the breadth and depth of student affairs issues. Therefore, when placing an item before a governing board for action, it is always useful to position the issue within a comparative context of peer institutions, regional profiles, or national standards. Additionally, the matter should have strong grounding as to where it precisely fits into the institution and what its effect will be on other components of the campus.

Serving as a Liaison

Virtually no aspect of governance fails to affect students or alumni, either directly or indirectly. Student affairs personnel, by virtue of training and experience, typically have a greater appreciation of both the intended and unintended consequences of actions and decisions. Although faculty members have a preeminent function in campus governance, there is a strong need for student affairs professionals to represent other campus constituencies. The structure of the academy with its many academic disciplines and specializations, the fact that faculty members identify highly with their disciplines, and the range of issues confronting higher education create conditions where it is essential to focus governance issues on campus-based realities.

Student affairs staff can play a pivotal role in keeping discussions based on institutional imperatives. With the best of intentions, policies are sometimes adopted that are simply inappropriate to the culture of an institution. For example, an institution with a reputation for excellent undergraduate education is probably ill advised to embark on the mission of becoming a major research institution at the urging of a small group of highly qualified, productive research scholars. In such a setting, the appropriate student affairs professional has a responsibility to explain and predict the consequences of such an undertaking—what it may do to the size of the institution, its financial stability, and its reputation.

Serving as a Catalyst

Being a catalytic agent means stimulating open debate and dialogue. Difficult issues are seldom confronted effectively in an environment where governance has become overly compartmentalized. Many institutions have found it useful to designate student affairs professionals as chairs of committees that are grappling with difficult problems. The training and experience of student affairs personnel can assist greatly in assuring that the issue is properly framed and that the deliberative process is civil. In many ways, the student affairs professional can be viewed as an institutional diplomat who not only has the responsibility for advancing and defending a position but has the concomitant charge to make sure that the process is appropriate and balanced.

The ability to operate effectively within the governance structure engenders respect for both the individual involved and the student affairs division. The press of day-to-day business can be a major deterrent to expending the thought and energy required to support campus governance and to do it well. Yet many student affairs divisions that have made that commitment find they are actively supported and helped by the faculty and other segments of the campus community. Governance prerogatives are jealously guarded by faculty, but anyone who can aid the process and make it more open, meaningful, and productive will be supported.

Summary

Governance structures and processes can have far-reaching influence on the student affairs enterprise. The governing board can play a key part in providing support for student affairs, but active efforts must be made to aid governing board members in understanding the role of student affairs.

Attention must also be paid to campus-based governance mechanisms. Active involvement in all levels and types of committees provides the opportunity for student affairs personnel to reinforce their unique contribution to the institution. Care also must be taken to develop strong and effective working relationships with other administrative units, and relationships with student government should be a primary agenda item for student affairs.

Collective bargaining and the presence of unions have the potential to influence both governance and decision making. Astute student affairs professionals understand these realities and strive to establish competent methods for accommodating collective bargaining in their work.

Student affairs has an important function in enhancing the effectiveness of campus governance. Careful staff preparation, combined with the knowledge of how groups work, make student affairs professionals uniquely qualified to assist in the process of communication. Finally, the commitment of student affairs to the principles of conflict resolution and free debate can result in invaluable assistance to the governance process.

References

Cohen, A. M., and Brawer, F. B. *The American Community College.* (2nd ed.) San Francisco: Jossey-Bass, 1989.

Flawn, P. *A Primer for University Presidents.* Austin: University of Texas Press, 1990.

Kaplin, W. A. *The Law of Higher Education: A Comprehensive Guide to Legal Implications of Administrative Decision Making.* (2nd ed.) San Francisco: Jossey-Bass, 1985.

Mortimer, K. P., and McConnell, T. R. *Sharing Authority Effectively: Participation, Interaction, and Discretion.* San Francisco: Jossey-Bass, 1978.

National Institute of Education. *Involvement in Learning: Realizing the Potential of American Higher Education.* Washington, D.C.: U.S. Department of Education, 1984.

3

ॐ

Assessing
Campus Environments

George D. *Kuh*

Colleges and universities have many things in common. Most institutions offer a variety of major fields. Academic years, usually divided into semesters or quarters, run from fall to spring. Classrooms, laboratories, and studios provide structured settings for regular interactions between teachers and students. Out-of-class learning opportunities are available through which students acquire practical competence in, among other things, how to make decisions and how to work with people who are different from themselves.

At the same time, institutions of higher education differ in many respects, such as size, control (public or private), curricular emphasis (for example, liberal arts or science and technology), and the amount and type of external funding. These and other variables frequently are considered by prospective students applying for admission (Nicholson, 1991) and by scholars studying faculty productivity and satisfaction (Bowen and Schuster, 1986). Contrary to popular belief, however, such factors as institutional size, prestige, and affluence are unrelated to student learning and personal development (Braxton, Smart, and Thieke, 1991; Pascarella and Terenzini, 1991).

According to Pascarella and Terenzini (1991), what and how much a student learns is more a function of what the student *does* in college than such institutional characteristics as size and affluence. They also conclude

30

that the contextual conditions of an institution are more important in encouraging involvement than organizational or programmatic variables. The amount of effort students devote to learning is in part a function of the degree to which their institution provides opportunities for, supports, and rewards student learning.

This chapter provides an overview of some of the more important contextual conditions that foster student learning and personal development and the ways that they can be assessed. Also considered are key concepts with which student affairs professionals must be familiar in order to determine how these conditions of their campus influence learning. The relationship between the institutional context and student learning is first briefly summarized. A framework is then presented for identifying and understanding how these conditions work together to affect student learning. Finally, issues that warrant attention when assessing a given campus's contextual conditions are discussed.

The Importance of the Institutional Context for Student Learning and Personal Development

Pascarella and Terenzini (1991) reviewed about 2,600 studies on the impact of college on students. Four of their conclusions point to the importance of contextual conditions on student learning (Kuh, 1992). First, students benefit more from their college experience when their "total level of campus engagement [academic, interpersonal, extracurricular] is mutually supporting and relevant to a particular educational outcome" (Pascarella and Terenzini, 1991, p. 626).

Second, involvement in the academic and social life of the institution enhances student learning (Pascarella and Terenzini, 1991). Students have choices concerning how to allocate their time and effort. Two institutional characteristics are particularly important in engendering student involvement in educationally purposeful activities: (1) a clear, coherent (preferably distinctive) mission that focuses faculty and student behavior and gives direction to student learning and (2) sufficient opportunities for meaningful participation in the life of the institution, such as leadership roles in academic and social organizations, recreation, campus jobs, and off-campus work or internships.

Third, integrated and complementary academic and social programs, policies, and practices increase learning (Pascarella and Terenzini, 1991). No single experience, policy, or program is likely to have a dramatic influence on the attitudes and behaviors of most students. Curricular and cocurricular policies and practices (such as advising and orientation) are more likely to have positive effects on learning when they support students' learning goals and are consistent with the institution's educational purposes and values.

Finally, students who feel that they belong and are valued as individuals are more likely to take advantage of institutional resources, resulting in improved learning (Pascarella and Terenzini, 1991). When ethics of membership and care characterize a college, students perceive that they are not anonymous or marginal, that the institution is concerned about their welfare, and that the psychological "size" of the institution is appropriate, comfortable, and manageable (Kuh, Schuh, Whitt, and Associates, 1991).

Taken together, these four conclusions suggest that an institution's contextual conditions are more important to student learning and personal development than faculty productivity, library holdings, organizational structures, or specific academic or student life programs. Therefore, student affairs professionals must know how the various aspects of their campus environments influence student behavior (National Association of Student Personnel Administrators, 1987). To acquire this knowledge, student affairs staff have to discover how various institutional properties (location and physical, social, and psychological environments) and faculty and student cultures act either to promote or inhibit students' engagement with learning and personal development opportunities.

A Framework for Assessing the Influence of Contextual Conditions on Student Learning

Many institutional properties work together to produce conditions for learning. To identify and analyze these properties, substantive and interpretive frames of reference are required. The substantive frame focuses the student affairs professional on the primary student-institutional points of contact where learning is likely to occur, such as faculty-student interaction outside the classroom. The interpretive frame is used as a filter or lens through which to analyze and understand how students' experiences influence their behavior.

Substantive Frames

In this section, three sets of properties are discussed that illustrate how the institution's contextual conditions affect learning: (1) the institution's mission and philosophy, (2) opportunities for learning, as well as support and rewards for student effort, and (3) faculty and student cultures.

Institutional Mission and Philosophy. As Lyons points out in Chapter One, no institutional factor is more important in directing student and faculty behavior than the institution's mission and philosophy (Kuh, Schuh, Whitt, and Associates, 1991). For this reason, creating conditions that encourage students to take advantage of personal and intellectual opportunities must begin with clarifying institutional aims and translating these into appropriate expectations for student behavior.

Clarifying the mission seems to be a fairly straightforward task. But although every college has a mission, it may or may not be congruent with how the college describes itself in its publications, such as the statement of educational purposes in the catalogue or other documents. For these reasons, student affairs staff members assessing their institution's contextual conditions must verify the institution's mission by talking with students, faculty, administrators, graduates, and others in order to learn what the college is at present and what it aspires to be.

When members of various groups consistently use similar terms to describe what their college is trying to do with its resources, the institution's mission can be said to be clear and coherent. In some instances, particularly at small colleges and universities, the institutional mission may be salient — meaning that even people who are not college "insiders" (people who live and work in close proximity to the institution and call it their own) or who are not members of major constituent groups have a fairly clear understanding of what the institution stands for and is trying to accomplish. For example, the missions of colleges such as Swarthmore and Reed (Clark, 1970) and Berea, Earlham, and Mount Holyoke colleges (Kuh, Schuh, Whitt, and Associates, 1991) set the tone for the campus by attracting students and faculty whose aspirations are consistent with those of the institution and establishing clear expectations for their behavior. Too often, however, institutions are unclear about what they are trying to accomplish or communicate their aims in confused ways. As a result, they send mixed messages about their values. When institutional leaders assert that both research and teaching are important but tenure decisions depend primarily on research contributions, inconsistent signals are sent to the faculty and others about what the institution expects.

A college's philosophy represents the institution's values and beliefs as they are enacted through policies, practices, and standard operating procedures. Just as every college has a mission, each has a philosophy, although it is rare that it is ever stated in written form (Kuh, Schuh, Whitt, and Associates, 1991). However, an institution's philosophy can be discerned in its acts.

One aspect of an institution's philosophy is the degree to which faculty and student affairs staff trust students. For example, at some institutions student codes of conduct include many stipulations. Other institutions rely on academic and social honor codes to foster student responsibility. Student learning can be promoted using either type of philosophy, provided that it is clearly expressed throughout all aspects of institutional life; it must also be compatible with the idea that students can behave in ways that support that philosophy — that is, students have the capacity for responsible, independent judgment and can make good decisions.

As colleges and universities have grown larger, their philosophies have sometimes become incoherent and, worse, inconsistent with their educational aims. When students are told at orientation that the institution has high expectations for their learning, but faculty members rely on multiple-choice tests and provide little or no feedback on written work other than a grade, students understandably may become confused. The same situation will occur if students are told that they are to handle their affairs independently and yet are constantly monitored by the student affairs staff. For this reason, it is difficult for institutional agents to articulate a moral basis for challenging student behavior that is inconsistent with the institution's aspirations.

Opportunities, Support, and Rewards. According to Blocher (1974 and 1978), an optimal learning environment has three subsystems: (1) opportunity, (2) support, and (3) reward. These subsystems warrant the attention of those student affairs professionals assessing how the contextual conditions of their campus promote or discourage learning.

All colleges and universities require that a certain number of students participate in such activities as social-programming bodies, governance structures, theater and the arts, intercollegiate athletic teams, and so on. When the availability, frequency, and the intensity of these opportunities are great, an adequate infrastructure of developmental experiences exists, and "people tend to be busier, more vigorous, more versatile, and more involved" (Walsh, 1978, p. 7). Iowa State University, for example, has more than four hundred formally recognized clubs. Students at the University of North Carolina at Charlotte who need help in developing leadership skills are offered a comprehensive series of training programs. At the University of Louisville, peer tutors assist underprepared students in acquiring academic survival skills; the tutors also benefit by being engaged in educationally purposeful activities (Kuh and Schuh, 1991).

The opportunity subsystem of a college should promote spontaneous interaction—among students and between students and institutional agents—consistent with the institution's educational purposes. Stanford University has four ethnic theme houses and four ethnic community centers to encourage students from historically underrepresented groups to become involved in the life of their university. Grinnell College and Wichita State University make it very easy for student groups to organize themselves and receive funding (Kuh, Schuh, Whitt, and Associates, 1991). When the physical dimensions of a campus are "human scale," students enjoy a sense of being in control; small residences (no more than three hundred students) permit students to identify with and take ownership of their living units more easily.

High expectations for the performance of all students are a characteristic of powerful learning environments. Such settings provide structure and support that enable students successfully to deal with ambiguous, complex, and novel situations that require responses beyond their experience. Support may take the form of an ethic of care, a belief system permeating the institution that encourages faculty, staff, and students to reach out to those in need (Kuh, Schuh, Whitt, and Associates, 1991). Safety nets made up of faculty and staff (paraprofessional as well as professional) must be furnished to students encountering difficulty. The amount of structure that students require may depend on their ability to exercise responsibility, their academic preparation or background, and their religious background. For example, Berea, Xavier University in New Orleans, and Iowa State provide more rules than Earlham, Grinnell, Mount Holyoke, and Stanford.

Students learn best when they receive frequent feedback about their performance relative to institutional expectations (Chickering and Gamson, 1987) and are encouraged to integrate their in-class and out-of-class experiences (Kuh, Schuh, Whitt, and Associates, 1991). Most colleges recognize student achievement through convocations and honors society memberships, athletic banquets, deans' lists, announcements of scholarship and fellowship recipients, and the selection of high-performing students to serve as tutors, laboratory assistants, and peer advisors (Hawley and Kuh, 1986). For instance, at Xavier University in New Orleans, photographs of those admitted to graduate and professional schools are featured on the walls of academic buildings.

When the three subsystems (opportunity, support, and reward) are operating at a satisfactory level, are mutually supporting, and complement the institution's educational purposes, they create excellent conditions for student learning.

Faculty and Student Subcultures. Student learning is also a function of the frequency and quality of interactions between students and important agents of socialization: faculty, student affairs personnel, and peers (Pascarella and Terenzini, 1991). Therefore, it is important to determine whether faculty and student cultures foster or discourage learning.

The amount of time that faculty members devote to students is influenced in large part by the type of institution in which they work and by what institutional leaders and others expect from faculty and student performance. Teachers at many institutions spend less time with undergraduates outside the classroom than their counterparts of several decades ago. Although there are exceptions (institutions that have been successful in encouraging their faculty to engage with students beyond the classroom and laboratory [Kuh, Schuh, Whitt, and Associates, 1991]), the dominant trend is toward expecting faculty to devote more effort to research activities.

Obviously, the more time professors spend doing research, the less they can allot to students and to teaching-related activities. When teaching is a basic institutional commitment, faculty members tend to work more with students and less with their disciplinary community; hence, their research is less specialized, and their identity with the institution is greater. In state-assisted colleges, where the heavy emphasis on undergraduate instruction is often coupled with institutional aspirations to move up in the pecking order, teaching loads remain heavy even as expectations for publications increase. As a result, faculty members often feel torn between research (which was stressed in graduate school) and the daily demands of teaching and student advising. At community colleges, teachers have heavy teaching loads and many students who require compensatory assistance to succeed academically. For these reasons, faculty members rely increasingly on textbooks and teaching assistants, and contact with students is further reduced.

Low faculty expectations for student performance can become pernicious in certain instances. At some institutions, a disengagement compact has been struck; students and faculty enter into a tacit agreement that essentially says, "You leave me alone and I will leave you alone." On such campuses, standards of academic achievement are not rigorous. As a result, students may have considerable discretionary time but do not use it to take advantage of institutional resources for learning and personal development (such as the library and laboratories) because faculty and student affairs professionals do not expect them to do so. At one college, it was discovered that students on average watched about three hours of television per day, with the most popular shows being *Looney-Tunes,* soap operas, and programs on MTV (Wolf, Schmitz, and Ellis, 1991). Allowing students so much free time also may say something about what the faculty members expect of student behavior.

The student culture on that campus is also sending messages about how to use discretionary time. This culture exerts considerable influence on learning because it determines what kinds of people students spend time with and therefore the values and attitudes to which they are exposed (Baird, 1988; Weidman, 1989). No matter what institutional agents say or do, within four to six weeks following the start of an academic term, new students are exposed to the prevailing student culture, which tells them what classes and instructors are to be taken seriously and where and how much to study (Holland and Eisenhart, 1990; Moffatt, 1989; Weidman, 1989).

Most colleges host student groups with values that deviate significantly from those espoused by the institution. The behavioral patterns of these groups, either formally defined or informally developed and supported, often are similar in content and form and typically are sustained over a period of time. Such groups as Greek organizations, honors students, athletes, or members of racial and ethnic groups have their own distinctive interaction patterns and norms that affect how their members behave and relate to others. This situation complicates attempts to describe and understand the influence of the institution's cultures on student behavior.

What the student culture perceives as important may be incompatible with what the faculty esteems. Faculty members are primarily interested in teaching and research, but students are more concerned with other matters: getting good grades, making friends, taking care of themselves, and managing their time. Student groups like fraternities organize around social themes, whereas athletes are focused on competition; both focuses may conflict with those of faculty.

One reason that many colleges and universities condone and support the activities of some student subcultures is that those groups accomplish what no other organization in the institution can achieve. For example, "collegiates" (Clark and Trow, 1966), such as fraternity and sorority members, tend to be satisfied with college life and are loyal to their college. They help their college attract new students and usually support the institution financially after graduation (Nelson, 1984).

Most colleges and universities ignore what student subcultures really teach. Student affairs staffs must become more knowledgeable about the various student cultures on their campuses and experiment with ways to reshape those activities antithetical to the institution's educational aims (Eaton and Manning, forthcoming). Clearly, more must be learned about the influence of these cultures on learning, particularly at colleges and universities with large numbers of students in residence. Of course, institutions must be willing to commit resources to this task.

Interpretive Frames

In this section, three analytical frameworks are presented that can be used to understand an institution's contextual conditions: (1) ecology, (2) climates, and (3) cultures. The terms *ecology, climate,* and *culture* often are used interchangeably; yet they refer to different aspects of a college or university that need to be clarified and understood for student affairs professionals to discover the effect of their campus's contextual conditions. Encompassing both climate and culture, ecology is the broadest of these concepts. The plural form of *climate* and *culture* suggests that the contextual conditions of a college are not monolithic nor do they influence uniformly the behavior of all students. Many subenvironments exist on a campus and can be approximated by examining climates and cultures at various levels of analysis, such as the institution, academic departments, living units, and affinity groups. As a result, campus climates and cultures have multiple, sometimes contradictory, effects on the behavior of students, faculty, and student affairs professionals.

Ecology. Student learning and personal development are products of the reciprocal interactions between individuals or groups of students, faculty and administrators, and the environment of the college. In other words, behavior is a function of students interacting with the college environment broadly defined to include physical space, policies, people, and other physical, biological, chemical, and cultural stimuli. The relationship between students and their college has been described as *transactional* (Aulepp and Delworth, 1976)—that is, students shape their environment and are shaped by it.

Collegiate environments affect the behavior of students; as a result, students behave in similar ways despite their individual differences (Barker, 1968; Huebner, 1989). Some environments are more in harmony with a student's needs than others. For example, "If a student reported a high need for achievement and the campus environment was consensually identified as exerting a press for achievement, a congruent situation would exist, leading to satisfaction and good functioning" (Huebner, 1989, p. 169).

Similarly, if a student is surrounded by people with compatible personality characteristics, the environmental setting can be said to be congruent (Holland, 1973). When the mismatch between environmental demands and student needs is great, dissonance results, and the student becomes dissatisfied, academic performance suffers, and premature departure occurs (Tinto, 1987).

The ecology frame (the institution's size, location, facilities, open spaces, and other permanent attributes) can also be used to interpret the influence of the physical properties on behavior. The amount and arrangement of physical space shape behavior, for instance. The location and dimensions of buildings facilitate or inhibit social interaction and the development of group cohesiveness (Myrick and Marx, 1968). In general, the less crowded and more organized and neat the physical environment (Mehrabian and Russell, 1974), the lower the level of stress (Ahrentzen, Jue, Skorpanish, and Evans, 1982). In densely populated areas, such as high-rise residences, indicators of social pathology (deviant behavior, frustration) tend to be higher (Moos, 1979). Colors are also associated with certain psychological effects, such as arousal (Rapaport, 1982; Schuh, 1980). The physical design of counseling centers (Iwai, Churchill, and Cummings, 1983), the dean of students office (Hurst and Ragle, 1979), college unions (Banning and Cunard, 1986), and commencement programs (Banning, 1983) also have an impact.

Campus policies have an effect on student attitudes and behavior as well. For example, when more stringent alcohol policies are enforced on campus, students shift the locus of drinking to off campus (Hayes-Sugarman, 1989). Providing choice housing assignments for student athletes or fraternity members suggests that some people are more important than others.

As is evident from this brief discussion, the influence of the ecology of a campus can be difficult to determine, though it has multiple, complicated effects on students' behavior. Nevertheless, this interpretive frame has great potential for helping student affairs staff members understand how their institution influences student learning because it emphasizes the interrelatedness of a large number of institutional factors and conditions (Banning, 1989).

Climates. Climate refers to how students, the faculty, the student affairs staff, and other institutional agents *experience* their institution (Baird, 1988; Peterson and Spencer, 1990). For example, institutions differ in the degree to which their students believe faculty and administrators are supportive of their learning and personal development goals (Pace, 1987). If students believe the campus to be inhospitable, this perception can negatively affect their academic performance as well as their feelings toward themselves and others (Lyons, 1990; National Association of Student Personnel Administrators, 1987). Most climate measures focus on (1) perceptions of organizational functioning, such as goal setting, decision making, and resource allocation; and/or (2) affective responses to experiences with the institution, such as feelings of loyalty, commitment, good morale, satisfaction, and a general sense of belonging (Baird, 1988).

Such instruments as the *College and University Environment Scales* (CUES) (Pace, 1969) assess institutional attributes that encourage students to behave in certain ways, such as a high need for achievement or the quality of relations between faculty and students (Astin and Holland, 1961). The *College Student Experience Questionnaire* (CSEQ) (Pace, 1987), although designed primarily to estimate student effort devoted to various learning activities, also includes five scales that depict the degree to which students feel that their college emphasizes scholarship, estheticism, critical thinking, vocational competence, and the practical relevance of courses. In addition, three CSEQ scales refer to the quality of relations among students, faculty, and administrators.

The University Residence Environments Scale (URES) (Moos, 1979) provides information about the climates of residential subenvironments. The URES evelutes whether groups of residents are more interested in social activities or in academic pursuits: it also assesses whether these same students view their living environments as (for example) highly structured and competitive or interpersonally supportive and achievement-oriented. Student affairs professionals can use these data to modify, through indirect or direct means, the climate of residences by grouping students with certain characteristics to create the desired environment (Brown, 1968; Schroeder, 1976 and 1981).

Results from the CUES, CSEQ, URES and similar instruments (*College Student Questionnaire*, Peterson, 1968; *Institutional Functioning Inventory*, Peterson and others, 1970) can be interpreted according to students' sex, year in school, major field, and race and ethnicity to compare the perceptions of different groups of students. (See Baird, 1988, for additional information about these instruments.) As a result, campus climate measures can reflect the many realities that exist among various groups (Kuh, Whitt, and Shedd, 1987). By administering climate measures periodically, student affairs staff can monitor progress toward making living-unit environments, attitudes of subgroups of students (such as fraternities), and the general campus climate more consistent with the institution's educational purposes.

Cultures. Whereas measures of climate reflect individual or group perceptions of certain aspects of the institution, campus culture refers to qualities of an institution's character (Kuh, forthcoming; Peterson and others, 1986). Viewing institutional life through a cultural frame of reference allows the interpretation of the meaning of events and actions on and off campus (Kuh and Whitt, 1988). Institutional culture is the collective pattern shaped by the combination of institutional history, mission, physical setting, norms, traditions, values, practices, beliefs, and assumptions that guide the behavior of individuals and groups in a college or university (Kuh and Whitt, 1988).

Every college's culture is unique and difficult to describe clearly. The reason is that collegiate cultures are composed of holistic, complex webs of artifacts, enduring behavioral patterns, embedded values and beliefs, and ideologies and assumptions that represent learned products of group experience. Cultural values and beliefs are perpetuated through traditions (for instance, graduation ceremonies and induction experiences for new students and faculty), major campus events, heroic individuals, and language (Kuh and Whitt, 1988; Ott, 1989). The meanings that various members of the campus community attach to these cultural elements, however, are not always simple to deduce nor can they be easily grasped by people unfamiliar with the institution.

Institutional cultures tend to be relatively stable, but they are not stagnant. They change over time through a dynamic interplay of forces: the institution's structural and cultural elements, factors in the external environment (shifting demographics), cataclysmic events (destruction of facilities or accidents involving senior administrators or athletic teams [Peterson and others, 1986]), and the presence of people (women and members of underrepresented ethnic and racial groups) whose beliefs and assumptions differ somewhat from those of the majority.

Cultures also change as a result of the mutual influence of cultural properties, such as the physical attributes of a campus, established practices, celebratory events, and symbols and symbolic actions. Moreover, subcultures influence each other while simultaneously affecting the behavior of students, faculty, and staff. Similarly, the presence of newcomers whose backgrounds are different from those of previous cohorts of students and faculty members also has an influence on cultural properties. In this sense, culture is both product and process (Peterson and others, 1986); it influences such behavioral outcomes as student performance and satisfaction and is itself affected by the characteristics, attitudes, and behavior of faculty, staff, and students and of the external environment.

Key Issues in Assessing Campus Climates

To discover how the contextual conditions of a campus have ramifications for student learning and personal development, an institutional audit is recommended. Campus audits can be expensive in both human and fiscal terms, but the outcomes are usually very useful and assist in the planning and policy decisions of the institution. In this section, some major issues associated with conducting such an audit are identified. Detailed discussions of these and related factors are offered by Austin, Rice, and Splete (1991), Crowson (1987), Fetterman (1990), Kuh, Schuh, Whitt, and Associates (1991), Whitt (forthcoming), and Whitt and Kuh (1991). Though audits are labor intensive, they provide high-quality, policy-relevant information that cannot be obtained any other way.

The following suggestions are distilled from Austin (1990), Kuh (forthcoming), Kuh, Schuh, Whitt, and Associates (1991), Schein (1985), and Whitt (forthcoming).

• *Assemble a credible, qualified audit team.* Assuming that campus policy makers have agreed that an audit is needed, the first step is to create a partnership of people familiar with the institution (insiders) and consultants (outsiders) knowledgeable about conditions that foster student learning. Ideally, the audit itself should be commissioned and cosponsored by academic and student affairs as a collaborative endeavor. Outsiders are needed to help insiders "make the familiar strange" (Whitt, forthcoming). Most faculty members, student affairs staffs, and students are too familiar with an institution to assess how its traditions and ritualistic practices positively and negatively influence student learning. The team must be perceived as credible, sensitive, fair, tactful, and truthful by all members of the campus community. Although many student affairs professionals possess these characteristics, it is also important that several faculty members serve on the audit team. Faculty members are more likely to talk freely with others on the teaching staff or with a respected outsider; therefore, an audit team that includes several faculty members will be more likely to obtain higher-quality data.

• *Obtain as much relevant information as possible from different sources.* Some combination of varied sources of information (faculty; current, former, and prospective students; graduates; student affairs staff; and others) and multiple data-collection methods (interviews, observations, survey data, and document analysis) are essential to create a complex, accurate understanding of campus life. To yield the most useful results, audits should incorporate some combination of interviews, observations, and self-report pencil-and-paper instruments (Austin, 1990; Kuh, 1990). One strategy is to use open-ended interviews with students, faculty members, and others to identify critical issues that deserve immediate attention. Based on this information, an appropriate instrument, such as the CSEQ or URES, may be used to collect additional information from a larger number of students. In certain instances, the best approach may be to construct a survey designed to obtain the needed information. Following the collection of survey data, additional interviews with individual and groups of students, faculty members, and student affairs staff will provide more detailed insights into the institutional context.

• *Start anywhere.* It is not important which institutional factor the audit team decides to focus its time on initially, provided that it is committed to conducting a comprehensive audit. An assessment could begin with the campus climate, for example, or with an audit of the influence of certain student subcultures on the learning environment. At some point, however, the team must address the role of the institutional mission in creating an appropriate context for learning.

By examining the written and oral statements of institutional leaders and important institutional documents (the mission statement; past and current catalogues; and statements of student rights, responsibilities, and ethics), the audit team can determine if the values and aspirations of the institution are in harmony with the enacted policies and practices that shape daily interactions. These tacit assumptions and other enacted patterns of behavior and understanding often go unchallenged and unrecognized, and their influence on student learning is thus difficult to evaluate.

• *Seek different points of view.* Obtain as much diverse information as possible by seeking out contradictions and differences of opinion. Avoid simplifying complicated issues and prematurely drawing conclusions. Particular attention should be given to what the institution *espouses* (says about itself in publications and public statements but may or may not actually do) with regard to the philosophy, values, policies, and practices and what seems to be *enacted* (what people put into practice). Espoused values may take the form of institutional aspirations, such as an announced commitment to improving health-enhancing behavior or to increasing the number of students and faculty from historically underrepresented groups. If these goals are not realized, however, the gap between espoused and enacted values can create considerable confusion in students and others.

• *Conduct the audit with integrity, goodwill, and an open mind.* Respect the unique qualities of your institution and the worth of all individuals, groups, and points of view. Keep to a minimum evaluative judgments about the relative merits of the perceptions of individuals and groups, policies, practices, symbols, and other cultural artifacts. Emphasize institutional strengths as well as limitations so that an appropriate tone for campus life can be created. Most importantly, determine what these data mean in the context of your college and how they influence student learning. Whitt's cautions (forthcoming) are worth noting here: (1) obtain the permission of participants; (2) be clear about your purpose and the ways that information obtained from participants will be used; (3) do not report preliminary findings except to check your evolving impressions, explanations, and interpretations; and (4) be explicit about how the results of the campus audit can and cannot be used.

• *Test impressions early and often.* Feedback from insiders about initial interpretations is critical to obtaining high-quality data. As mentioned above, the audit team must have its emerging understandings and impressions validated and corrected by those whose experiences are being described (Lincoln and Guba, 1985). Initial ideas should be treated as speculations to be confirmed and reconfirmed by subsequent data. Feedback should be given to participants throughout the process. The audit experience itself should be educative: that is, through the data collection and reporting processes, the team and various campus constituent groups should learn a good deal about themselves and student learning well before any final report is circulated.

• *Be prepared to spend time.* Certain activities of an audit will take more time than others. For example, examining how the institutional culture and various student subcultures contribute to student learning is much more time consuming than administering campus climate surveys. Moreover, the process of assessing the contextual conditions of a campus is "iterative, involving repeated cycles of data collection and analysis" (Whitt, forthcoming).

• *Treat every participant and every piece of information as important.* Many inextricably intertwined institutional properties influence student learning. Therefore, the audit team must assume that every aspect of institutional life may have an influence, positive or negative, on student learning. Attention must be given to the routine, as well as the more unusual, celebratory aspects of campus life. By focusing on events that are the most obvious or most colorful, such as new student orientation, induction ceremonies, honors programs, scholarship banquets, and commencement, one may overlook the mundane situations in which institutional values are expressed and reinforced for most students and that shape faculty and student aspirations and behavior on an ongoing basis.

• *Recognize that significant improvements in institutional conditions for learning take time.* Creating conditions that improve student learning will not be easy for some colleges and universities. Determine, as early as possible, if the institution is ready to accept feedback about the quality of contextual conditions for learning (Schein, 1985). Audits often shed light on the "shadow side of campus culture," aspects of faculty and student cultures about which just enough is known that people know they are not to discuss such matters (Kuh, forthcoming). Therefore, it probably will be useful to have people from different groups of faculty, students, and administrators participate in some aspects of the investigation. Expect the audit results to challenge one or more assumptions about student life. A recent study at Indiana University, for instance, found that more than 50 percent of undergraduates skip three or more class sessions per course per semester (Wolf, Schmitz, and Ellis, 1991). Although the reasons for missing class varied (some use the time to study for exams in other classes, some to sleep), the fact that so many students missed what amounts to a week or more of instruction surprised and disappointed many faculty and academic administrators.

Certain physical attributes of a campus are not always viewed as welcoming by people who have been historically underrepresented and may belie institutional aspirations to be open to members of these groups. For example, art work and portraits featured in public places often reflect the institution's history and preferences of administrators. As a result, artifacts manifest mostly white, mostly male views. It seems a simple matter to add some artifacts that reflect the experiences of different groups of people, but a college simply cannot exchange one set of paintings for another. Some will also object to what appears to be revisionist history or "politically correct" behavior.

Though it is easy to criticize any current state of affairs, the most important goal of the audit is to help the faculty, student affairs professionals, and students become aware of the rich harvest of learning opportunities inherent in collegiate environments and of the ways that their institution can encourage more students to take greater advantage of these possibilities.

Summary

An institution of higher education is much more than a collection of students and faculty, buildings, and green spaces. Greater than the sum of its many parts, a college or university is at once a setting that regulates the behavior of its members; a theater-in-the-round where the scripts of the past get played out in the process of seeking solutions to contemporary ills; a highly leveraged subsidiary that annually consumes an increasing amount of its parent company's resources; a social club with numerous cliques of faculty, students, and administrators; a cultural and recreational oasis where the number and variety of events and activities outstrip any one individual's capacity to partake of them all; a game of chance in which members of various groups are assigned to physical spaces not always compatible with their personal or academic preferences and aspirations; and an intellectual theme park where the only limits to what one can discover are imposed by the learner.

This maelstrom of activity is more consistent with educational purposes at some colleges than others because the various properties of a college work together in complicated, almost mysterious ways to promote or discourage student learning. Although how these properties work together may *seem* mysterious, the properties themselves are not.

In the final analysis, a college or university is what its faculty, administrators, students, graduates, trustees, and others believe it to be (Wilkins, 1989). Knowledge about graduation rates and library holdings is not enough to create and sustain an educationally purposeful learning community. Students, faculty, and administrators must *believe* in something. In other words, a high-quality learning environment "is a bit like religion. . . . We have to believe in it to make it work" (Murchland, 1991, p. 15).

Student affairs staffs can use the substantive and interpretive frames described in this chapter to identify and better understand the influence of their institution on the learning and personal development of students. Such knowledge, coupled with a firm belief in the importance of their work and what their college stands for, will enable student affairs professionals to make even more valuable contributions to their institutions and students.

References

Ahrentzen, S., Jue, B. M., Skorpanish, M. A., and Evans, G. W. "School Environment and Stress." In G. Evans (ed.), *Environmental Stress*. Cambridge, Mass.: MIT Press, 1982.

Astin, A. W., and Holland, J. L. "The Environmental Assessment Technique: A Way to Measure College Environments." *Journal of Educational Psychology,* 1961, *52,* 308–316.

Aulepp, L., and Delworth, U. *Training Manual for an Ecosystem Model.* Boulder, Colo.: Western Interstate Commission for Higher Education, 1976.

Austin, A. E. "Faculty Cultures, Faculty Values." In W. G. Tierney (ed.), *Assessing Academic Climates and Cultures*. New Directions for Institutional Research, no. 68. San Francisco: Jossey-Bass, 1990.

Austin, A. E., Rice, R. E., and Splete, A. P. *The Academic Workplace Audit.* Washington, D.C.: Council for Independent Colleges, 1991.

Baird, L. L. "The College Environment Revisited: A Review of Research and Theory." In J. C. Smart (ed.), *Higher Education: Handbook of Theory and Research.* Vol. 4. New York: Agathon Press, 1988.

Banning, J. H. "The Built Environment: Do Ivy Walls Have Memories?" *Campus Ecologist,* 1983, *1* (2), 1–3.

Banning, J. H. "Creating a Climate for Successful Student Development: The Campus Ecology Manager Role." In U. Delworth, G. R. Hanson, and Associates (eds.), *Student Services: A Handbook for the Profession.* (2nd ed.) San Francisco: Jossey-Bass, 1989.

Banning, J. H., and Cunard, M. "Environment Supports Student Development." *ACU-I Bulletin,* 1986, *54* (1), 8–10.

Barker, R. G. *Ecological Psychology: Concepts and Methods for Studying the Environment of Human Behavior.* Stanford, Calif.: Stanford University Press, 1968.

Blocher, D. H. "Toward an Ecology of Student Development." *Personnel and Guidance Journal,* 1974, *52,* 360–365.

Blocher, D. H. "Campus Learning Environments and the Ecology of Student Development." In J. Banning (ed.), *Campus Ecology: A Perspective for Student Affairs.* Cincinnati, Ohio: National Association of Student Personnel Administrators, 1978.

Bowen, H. R., and Schuster, J. H. *American Professors: A National Resource Imperiled.* New York: Oxford University Press, 1986.

Braxton, J. M., Smart, J. C., and Thieke, W. S. "Peer Groups of Colleges and Universities Based on Student Outcomes." *Journal of College Student Development,* 1991, *32,* 302–309.

Brown, R. D. "The Manipulation of the Environmental Press in a Residence Hall." *Personnel and Guidance Journal,* 1968, *46,* 555–560.

Chickering, A. W., and Gamson, Z. F. "Seven Principles for Good Practice in Undergraduate Education." *AAHE Bulletin,* 1987, *39* (7), 3–7.

Clark, B. R. *The Distinctive College: Antioch, Reed, and Swarthmore.* Hawthorne, N.Y.: Aldine, 1970.

Clark, B. R., and Trow, M. "The Organizational Context." In T. M. Newcomb and E. K. Wilson (eds.), *College Peer Groups: Problems and Prospects for Research.* Hawthorne, N.Y.: Aldine, 1966.

Crowson, R. L. "Qualitative Research Methods in Higher Education." In J. C. Smart (ed.), *Higher Education: Handbook of Theory and Research.* Vol. 3. New York: Agathon Press, 1987.

Eaton, S., and Manning, K. "Loosening the Ties That Bind: Shaping Student Culture." In G. D. Kuh (ed.), *Using Cultural Perspectives in Student Affairs Work.* Washington, D.C.: American College Personnel Association Media Board, forthcoming.

Fetterman, D. "Ethnographic Auditing: A New Approach to Evaluating Management." In W. G. Tierney (ed.), *Assessing Academic Climates and Cultures.* New Directions for Institutional Research, no. 68. San Francisco: Jossey-Bass, 1990.

Hawley, K. T., and Kuh, G. D. "The Small College as a Developmentally

Powerful Learning Environment." In G. Kuh and A. McAleenan (eds.), *Private Dreams, Shared Visions: Student Affairs Work in Small Colleges.* Washington, D.C.: National Association of Student Personnel Administrators, 1986.

Hayes-Sugarman, K. M. *New York State's 21 Alcohol Purchase Age: Unanticipated Consequences in the College Community.* Unpublished doctoral dissertation, State University of New York, Buffalo, 1989. *Dissertation Abstracts International, 49* (9), 2612-A.

Holland, D. C., and Eisenhart, M. A. *Educated in Romance: Women, Achievement, and College Culture.* Chicago: University of Chicago Press, 1990.

Holland, J. L. *Making Vocational Choices: A Theory of Careers.* Englewood Cliffs, N.J.: Prentice-Hall, 1973.

Huebner, L. A. "Interaction of Student and Campus." In U. Delworth, G. R. Hanson, and Associates, *Student Services: A Handbook for the Profession* (2nd ed.). San Francisco: Jossey-Bass, 1989.

Hurst, J. C., and Ragle, J. D. "Application of the Ecosystem Perspective to a Dean of Students' Office." In L. A. Huebner (ed.), *Redesigning Campus Environments.* New Directions for Student Services, no. 8. San Francisco: Jossey-Bass, 1979.

Iwai, S., Churchill, W., and Cummings, L. "The Physical Characteristics of College and University Counseling Services." *Journal of College Student Personnel,* 1983, *24,* 55–60.

Kuh, G. D. "Assessing Student Culture." In W. G. Tierney (ed.), *Assessing Academic Climates and Cultures.* New Directions for Institutional Research, no. 68. San Francisco: Jossey-Bass, 1990.

Kuh, G. D. "What Do We Do Now? Some Implications of *How College Affects Students.*" *Review of Higher Education,* 1992.

Kuh, G. D. "Appraising the Character of a College." *Journal of Counseling and Development,* forthcoming.

Kuh, G. D., and Schuh, J. H. "The Ecology of Involving Colleges." *Campus Ecologist,* 1991, *9* (4), 1–3.

Kuh, G. D., Schuh, J. H., Whitt, E. J., and Associates. *Involving Colleges: Successful Approaches to Fostering Student Learning and Development Outside the Classroom.* San Francisco: Jossey-Bass, 1991.

Kuh, G. D., and Whitt, E. J. *The Invisible Tapestry: Culture in American Colleges and Universities.* ASHE-ERIC Higher Education Report, no. 1. Washington, D.C.: Association for the Study of Higher Education, 1988.

Kuh, G. D., Whitt, E. J., and Shedd, J. D. *Student Affairs, 2001: A Paradigmatic Odyssey.* ACPA Media Publication, no. 42. Washington, D.C.: American College Personnel Association, 1987.

Lincoln, Y., and Guba, E. G. *Naturalistic Inquiry.* San Francisco: Jossey-Bass, 1985.

Lyons, J. W. "Examining the Validity of Basic Assumptions and Beliefs." In M. J. Barr, M. L. Upcraft, and Associates, *New Futures for Student Affairs: Building a Vision for Professional Leadership and Practice.* San Francisco: Jossey-Bass, 1990.

Mehrabian, A., and Russell, J. A. *An Approach to Environmental Psychology.* Cambridge, Mass.: MIT Press, 1974.

Moffatt, M. *Coming of Age in New Jersey: College and American Culture.* New Brunswick, N.J.: Rutgers University Press, 1989.

Moos, R. H. *Evaluating Educational Environments: Procedures, Measures, Findings, and Policy Implications.* San Francisco: Jossey-Bass, 1979.

Murchland, B. "Knowledge, Action, and Belief." *Public Leadership Education,* 1991, *4,* 13–15.

Myrick, R., and Marx, B. S. *An Exploratory Study of the Relationship Between High School Building Design and Student Learning.* Washington, D.C.: Bureau of Research, Office of Education, U.S. Department of Health, Education and Welfare, 1968.

National Association of Student Personnel Administrators. *A Perspective on Student Affairs.* Washington, D.C.: National Association of Student Personnel Administrators, 1987.

Nelson, T. *A Comparison of Selected Undergraduate Experiences of Alumni Who Financially Support Their Alma Mater.* Unpublished doctoral dissertation, Indiana University, Bloomington, 1984.

Nicholson, J. "A Guide to the Guides." *Change,* 1991, *23* (6), 22–29.

Ott, J. S. *The Organizational Culture Perspective.* Belmont, Calif.: Dorsey Press, 1989.

Pace, C. R. *College and University Environment Scales: Technical Manual.* (2nd ed.) Princeton, N.J.: Educational Testing Service, 1969.

Pace, C. R. *CSEQ Test Manual and Norms: College Student Experiences Questionnaire.* Los Angeles: Center for the Study of Evaluation, Graduate School of Education, University of California, Los Angeles, 1987.

Pascarella, E. T., and Terenzini, P. T. *How College Affects Students: Findings and Insights from Twenty Years of Research.* San Francisco: Jossey-Bass, 1991.

Peterson, M. W., and Spencer, M. G. "Understanding Academic Climate and Culture." In W. G. Tierney (ed.), *Assessing Academic Climates and Cultures.* New Directions for Institutional Research, no. 68. San Francisco: Jossey-Bass, 1990.

Peterson, M. W., and others. *The Organizational Context for Teaching and Learning: A Review of the Research Literature.* Ann Arbor, Mich.: National Center for Research to Improve Postsecondary Teaching and Learning, 1986.

Peterson, R. E. *College Student Questionnaire: Technical Manual.* Princeton, N.J.: Educational Testing Service, 1968.

Peterson, R. E., and others. *Institutional Functioning Inventory: Preliminary Technical Manual.* Princeton, N.J.: Educational Testing Service, 1970.

Rapaport, A. *The Meaning of Built Environments: A Non-verbal Communication Approach.* Newbury Park, Calif.: Sage, 1982.

Schein, E. H. *Organizational Culture and Leadership: A Dynamic View.* San Francisco: Jossey-Bass, 1985.

Schroeder, C. S. "New Strategies for Structuring Residential Environments." *Journal of College Student Personnel,* 1976, *17,* 386–390.

Schroeder, C. S. "Student Development Through Environmental Management." In G. S. Blimling and J. H. Schuh (eds.), *Increasing the Educational Role of Residence Halls*. New Directions for Student Services, no. 13. San Francisco: Jossey-Bass, 1981.

Schuh, J. H. "Housing." In W. Morrill and J. Hurst (eds.), *Dimensions of Intervention for Student Development*. New York: Wiley, 1980.

Tinto, V. *Leaving College*. Chicago: University of Chicago Press, 1987.

Walsh, W. B. "Person-Environment Interaction." In J. Banning (ed.), *Campus Ecology: A Perspective for Student Affairs*. Washington, D.C.: National Association of Student Personnel Administrators, 1978.

Weidman, J. "Undergraduate Socialization: A Conceptual Approach." In J. Smart (ed.), *Higher Education: Handbook of Theory and Research*. Vol. 5. New York: Agathon Press, 1989.

Whitt, E. J. "Making the Familiar Strange: Discovering Culture." In G. D. Kuh (ed.), *Using Cultural Perspectives in Student Affairs Work*. Washington, D.C.: American College Personnel Association Media Board, forthcoming.

Whitt, E. J., and Kuh, G. D. "Qualitative Methods in Higher Investigation." *Review of Higher Education*, 1991, *14*, 317–337.

Wilkins, A. L. *Developing Corporate Character: How to Successfully Change an Organization Without Destroying It*. San Francisco: Jossey-Bass, 1989.

Wolf, B., Schmitz, T., and Ellis, M. "How Students Study: Views from Bloomington Campus Undergraduates." Bloomington: Indiana University Office for Academic Affairs and Dean of Faculties, 1991.

4

ℰ

Fiscal Pressures
on Higher Education
and Student Affairs

John H. Schuh

This is not an easy time to be a budget officer or financial manager in an institution of higher education. As this chapter will describe, states are facing enormous financial problems; students are coming to our institutions inadequately prepared in many cases to do adequate academic work; the federal government is requiring institutions of higher education to comply with new legislation without providing the resources to do so; and the general economic environment is gloomy. In addition, institutions of higher education also face increased costs for services, and deteriorating physical plants place further financial burdens on both public and private institutions.

Fiscal policy, constraints, and conditions all have a profound effect on programs, services, learning opportunities, and activities developed and offered in the student affairs division. This chapter will examine a variety of factors that influence the fiscal environment in which the student affairs division operates. First, the economic implications of demographic trends will be examined. Second, several federal initiatives will be presented in the context of their economic impact on institutions of higher education. Third, a quick look will be taken at states, with a specific emphasis on the budgetary pressures that they are experiencing and the compliance requirements that they are placing on colleges and universities. Finally, a cluster of economic conditions affecting the fiscal environment of higher education will be presented. Brief implications for student affairs will be presented in each section. The environment that we confront as the century concludes will be difficult, as Mills and Barr (1990, p. 21) note: "Student affairs managers and all those associated with higher education are faced with shrinking resources, increased demands, and new expectations for accountability." Let us examine some of the factors that have contributed to that environment.

Demographic Trends

Demographic influences on student affairs will be addressed in detail in Chapter Twenty-Nine. This section will discuss selected demographic trends using a fiscal lens—that is, demographic changes will be viewed in the context of their financial implications for higher education.

Kuh (1990) observes that student affairs officers will have to deal with social issues that will affect the practice of student affairs in the future. In fact, the future is just around the corner. According to a recent study (Evangelauf, 1991), in four states (California, New Mexico, Mississippi, and Hawaii) and in the District of Columbia, students of color will form the majority of the high school graduating class of 1995. By the year 2010, young people of color will constitute 38 percent of all youth under the age of eighteen (Schwartz and Exter, 1989). For reasons that we will examine, many college students of the future may be at risk and may need additional support to be successful. This will take the forms of tutorial help, counseling, financial aid, and other assistance specific to individual campuses. Consider the following information about the students who will be coming to college at the start of the twenty-first century.

The Family

The United States leads a listing of ten developed countries in both marriage and divorce rates. In 1986, for example, there were 21.2 divorces for every one thousand women in the United States, compared with 12.9 in Canada and the United Kingdom, 8.3 in West Germany, 5.4 in Japan, and 1.1 in Italy (U.S. Department of Education, 1991b). Thus, disruption of the family affects children in the United States more frequently than in other developed countries against which it is in fierce economic competition.

Traditional-age college students will continue to come from homes where divorce has occurred. As a result, these students will have been forced to adjust to the trauma of divorce and may need help from their institution of higher education in such forms as support groups, individual counseling, or other assistance. As they tend to be labor intensive, these kinds of services will result in additional pressures on student affairs divisions.

In addition to the effect of divorce rates, the increasing proportion of single-parent families also influences young people. The U.S. Department of Education (1991b) reports that the percentage of children living in single-parent families nearly doubled from 11 percent in 1970 to 21.9 percent in 1989. More than half (54.8 percent) of all African-American children lived in single-parent households in 1990, compared with 19 percent of white children and 30 percent of Hispanic children, according to O'Hare, Pollard, Mann, and Kent (1991). These statistics point to the second demographic trend that will affect students of the future: economic deprivation.

Poverty

Absence of the father often means limited financial support, lack of nurturing, and negative psychological and social effects on children (Bianchi, 1990). The economic consequences of growing up in single-parent households are particularly dramatic and disturbing. The U.S. Department of Education (1991b) indicates that 54 percent of children under eighteen in female-headed households were part of families with an income under $10,000. Yet nearly 26 percent of children in married-couple families had parents with an income of $50,000 or more (p. 36). In addition, O'Hare, Pollard, Mann, and Kent (1991) estimate that the median family income for two-parent families was $31,757, compared with $9,590 for families with only the female parent present.

Another interesting fact is that the average number of children in households with children bears an inverse relationship to family income. Families with an average income under $10,000 in 1987 had nearly two children per household, whereas those with incomes over $75,000 per year had 1.65 children per household (U.S. Department of Education, 1991b, p. 36). Perhaps the most telling statistic is offered by Hodgkinson (1985), who writes that every day in America forty teenage girls give birth to their third child. One wonders what opportunities will be available to the children who grow up in these families.

In fact, the U.S. Department of Education (1991b, p. 38) determined that 51 percent of all children in female-headed households lived in poverty. About 43 percent of all African-American children and 36 percent of Hispanic children lived in poverty in 1989. Moreover, the rate of increase of poor children coming from female-headed households has grown dramatically since 1960, from 24 percent to 57 percent for all children. Children of the unmarried are also more likely to live in poverty as adults (Griffith, Frase, and Ralph, 1989).

Perhaps the only glimmer of hope in these discouraging statistics is that the number of affluent African-American households has grown by 360 percent during the time period of 1967 to 1987. Unfortunately, affluence among African-American families still trails white families substantially (O'Hare, 1989).

The difficult financial situation in which single-parent families find themselves is not due to a lack of effort to find work. On the contrary, in 1988 the mother was part of the workforce in 67.2 percent of families headed by a female only, up from 59.9 percent in 1975 (U.S. Department of Education, 1991b).

Many of the traditional-age students of the future will come from one-parent families where the only provider was the mother. As we have seen, the data show that the income of these families is below the poverty line. Students from these families will need substantial amounts of financial aid to be able to afford to come to college. Additionally, the students may very well require special efforts on the part of the colleges and universities to attract them to college in the first place, as many of them may come from families where the remaining parent has not graduated from college or even thought about attending an institution of higher education. This situation in turn will make it more costly to recruit these students. It may be incumbent on institutions to provide more programming for parents that describes the benefits of college attendance. An individual unfamiliar with institutions of higher education may find the language, traditions, and culture of colleges complex and difficult to understand (Kuh and Whitt, 1988).

School Enrollment

The percentage of whites in the school-age population is projected to drop from 73 percent in 1985 to 66 percent by the year 2000 (Griffith, Frase, and Ralph, 1989). The percentage of young people of color enrolled in elementary and secondary schools has grown dramatically over the past two decades and should be an indication of the next century's college population. Unfortunately, young people of color are not even now represented in university student bodies to the extent that they are in elementary and secondary schools, according to the U.S. Department of Education (1991b). For example, in 1989 whites composed 79.7 percent of the enrollment in elementary schools and 79.6 percent of that in high schools; however, they accounted for 84.7 percent of the students enrolled in institutions of higher education. African Americans have increased their numbers from 14.2 percent of children attending elementary schools in 1960 to 16 percent of those enrolled in 1989; they have also become a greater proportion of students enrolled in high schools — up from 11 percent in 1960 to 16.2 percent of all high school students in 1989. But they constitute only 10.3 percent of all students attending college in 1989 (although that percentage was up from 6.4 percent in 1960 [U.S. Department of Education, 1991b]).

Similarly, the representation of Hispanic young people has increased in elementary and secondary schools, but they are not enrolled proportionately in institutions of postsecondary education. The number of Hispanic children in elementary school grew from 6.8 percent of all those enrolled in 1975 to 11 percent in 1989. Six percent of all high school students were

Hispanic in 1975, as opposed to 9.9 percent in 1989. But Hispanics made up only 5.8 percent of college students in 1989, a modest increase from 4.2 percent in 1975 (U.S. Department of Education, 1991b).

Perhaps the most promising news in this brief review of the country's demographics is that Asian Americans, the most affluent group in the country, are also the fastest-growing one of people of color, mostly due to immigration (O'Hare, 1990). O'Hare estimates that 21 percent of all Asian Americans have completed college, and another 14 percent have attended universities, figures that far exceed comparable statistics for any racial group in the United States, including whites (O'Hare, 1990).

It is clear that student bodies of the future will contain more students of color. Campuses are already struggling with providing appropriate support to historically underrepresented students. As the number of students of color increases on college campuses, additional staff time, perhaps staff members, and additional program support may be required.

Aging Faculty and Staff

One other demographic trend is worthy of note: attracting and retaining qualified faculty and staff will become increasingly difficult in the coming years. The U.S. Department of Education (1991a) describes the situation this way: "Many of today's faculty began their careers during the 1950s and 1960s when higher education was expanding very rapidly. These faculty will be approaching retirement age during the late 1990s and early 21st century. . . . When these faculty do begin to retire, there may be an increased demand for new faculty" (p. 95). The same is true for senior student affairs officers, and institutions will have to search for new leaders for their student affairs units. We in student affairs will be challenged to find and develop new senior leaders. This process should begin with attracting bright young people to our profession, retaining them (through advanced graduate preparation), and then providing work experiences that will keep them committed to a career in student affairs. For a more complete discussion of this issue, see Barr (1990).

Federal Higher Education Initiatives

At the time of this writing, the Bush administration's primary educational thrust was captured in the document *America 2000: An Education Strategy* (1991). This document is the nation's blueprint for improving education by the year 2000. Depending on one's political point of view, *America 2000* has the potential to produce success or failure. The document is concerned primarily with elementary and secondary education; postsecondary education is mentioned only in passing, mostly in the context of graduating more students with majors in the sciences, mathematics, and engineering. The document also briefly considers issues of accountability and financial aid, but much of that discussion focuses on how well current resources are used by colleges and universities. Using existing resources more effectively may well be the key to understanding how the federal government will approach higher education from a fiscal perspective for the next several years. This section is dedicated to reviewing several selected federal legislative and regulatory developments of recent years in detail.

Access for Those with Disabilities

One category of federal regulation of higher education stems from legislation adopted in 1973. This mandates that programs offered by campuses be accessible to persons with disabilities. Certainly, no one could argue with the premise that everyone ought to be able to pursue a college education; indeed, there are tremendous benefits to making higher education available so that disabled people can more easily become independent, productive citizens. However, this legislation (like other, more recent, laws) makes requirements without providing funding for their implementation.

In the years immediately following the passage of this legislation, attention was directed toward removing physical barriers to the physically challenged. With the passage of the Americans with Disabilities Act (1990) and an increasing emphasis on including individuals who heretofore had been shut out of campus life, additional costs will be incurred by colleges and universities. Students with learning disabilities who previously may not have been welcomed by institutions of higher education are now enrolling and requiring costly special services. For example, students with hearing impairments are provided interpreter services at substantial expense to their universities. There is no question that governmental spending on programs and services for persons with disabilities is growing. For example, spending on programs and services for persons with disabilities rose from $19.3 billion in 1970 to $164.9 billion in 1986 (Smith, 1990). But the cost of providing services and renovating facilities is exceeding even this substantial increase.

Among the implications of this legislation for student affairs officers are that housing reserves must be tapped for residence hall modifications; that staff must be identified and programs developed to assist those with disabilities; that documents, brochures, and other printed material may have to be provided in braille; and that those with disabilities will expect student affairs officers to serve as their advocates, even though the potential costs associated with the changes they desire may be substantial.

Regulatory Compliance

Another category of federal initiatives deals with regulatory compliance as exemplified by draft registration and illegal immigration. The burdens of these regulations are relatively light in that all that is required is a certain degree of documentation. Nevertheless, the regulations themselves point to the philosophical direction in which the federal government appears to be heading: institutions will have to keep more records and assist the federal government in achieving its objectives. In the case of draft registration, the goal is that all eighteen-year-olds eligible for draft registration will comply with the law. In the case of immigration legislation, the objective is that all persons hired by institutions of higher education will conform with federal law concerning eligibility for employment.

Other regulatory initiatives affect the daily conduct of business in the various departments in the student affairs division. For example, the Occupational Safety and Health Administration (OSHA) regulations require actions protecting safety in the workplace. Obviously, no one would take the position that an unsafe workplace is desirable. However, the costs of bringing it into compliance with OSHA regulations can be expensive, and the costs must be borne by the employer. In another case, if the student affairs division includes a student health service, additional regulations related to the handling of hazardous materials and medical waste have an impact on daily business. Improper handling of these materials can result in fines or other forms of sanctions.

Institutions should not look to their states for relief from regulation. State governmental regulation has also placed additional burdens on colleges and universities. State involvement has taken on many forms (budgeting, program assessment, and political intrusion) and exists for many purposes (improving academic quality, economic competitiveness, and access and degree attainment [Fenske and Johnson, 1990]). "Public colleges and universities, and to a lesser but still significant extent, private institutions, are just beginning to sense the dimensions and long term impact of state governors, legislatures, and statewide higher education agencies" (Fenske and Johnson, 1990, p. 124).

Consumer Protection

A third category of the federal agenda, which might be termed consumer protection legislation, has placed more substantial financial burdens on colleges and universities for the foreseeable future. Recent laws have stipulated that institutions of higher education notify faculty and students on a regular basis about the institution's substance-abuse policy, laws related to the use of alcohol and other drugs, and programs available to provide assistance to those who seek help (Drug-Free Schools and Communities Act Amendments of 1989, Public Law 101-226). Starting in the 1992–93 academic year, institutions will be required to provide a variety of individuals (including current and prospective students) with information related to graduation rates, campus safety, and criminal activity (Student Right-to-Know and Campus Security Act, Public Law 101-542). In each case (substance abuse and criminal activity), failure to comply with Department of Education regulations will result in the forfeiture of financial aid dollars. As Fenske and Johnson (1990, p. 120) assert, "The federal government is now willing to use the threat of withdrawal of student aid as a club to enforce desired student behaviors unrelated to and beyond the direct control of the colleges and universities."

Although one can only speculate about what may be next on the agenda of the federal government, it is clear that recent activities will have an impact on the financial resources of colleges and universities for several reasons. The first is obvious. As we have seen, failure to comply with the regulations may result in the loss of financial aid (see U.S. Department of Education, 1990). Of course, these directives are taken seriously on college campuses, and virtually all would be able to pass a federal audit if one were to be conducted.

Less apparent is the aggregate cost of compliance. One higher education professional estimated that the annual cost to all postsecondary institutions of compliance with the Drug-Free Schools and Communities Act exceeds $500 million in expenses related to the duplication and distribution of materials (D. Roberts, personal communication, June 4, 1991). It is highly likely that the cost of implementing the crime-awareness legislation will approximate the cost of the substance-abuse legislation. As a whole, the expense of compliance with these two recent initiatives could easily approach $1 billion — or, stated another way, more money than the federal government spent on the entire college work-study program during the 1990–91 academic year ("Almanac," 1991).

Financial Aid

During the past decade, the pattern of financial aid has changed to the point where the majority of federal dollars are now devoted to loans rather than grants. For example, of the approximately $19.5 billion allocated to financial aid programs by the federal government in 1990–1991, over half of the aid was earmarked for loan programs ("Almanac," 1991). Margolin (1989) summarizes the mix of grants and loans in the following way: "The loan share of student aid from Washington has increased from 26% to 52% since 1978, while the grant share has dropped from 70% to 45%" (p. 31). As a result, students are forced to take on debt to pay their college bills in ever-increasing amounts. For example, the typical financial aid package in the late 1970s consisted of approximately 80 percent grants, 17 percent loans and 3 percent student employment; in the late 1980s, the mix was 50 percent loans, 46 percent grants, and 4 percent student employment (Margolin, 1989). Only 16 percent of freshmen received Pell Grants in 1988, fewer than half the number of students who received Pells in 1980 (Cutler, 1989).

Not only has there been a shift from grants to loans (which moves some of the financial aid responsibility from the federal government to the student), there has also been a change in the funding composition of the college work-study program. In 1964, this program consisted of 80 percent federal and 20 percent institutional funding (Organization for Economic Co-operation and Development, 1990), whereas in 1991, federal funding accounted for 70 percent, with the balance coming from institutions.

Recall that students of the twenty-first century will increasingly come from single-parent families or families with modest financial resources. To pay for the costs of attending college, these students will be forced to assume larger debts than those of preceding generations. As a result, when they graduate from college and enter the work force, they will have to defer any additional debts because of their student loan obligations. Moreover, those interested in attending private institutions must contemplate even more substantial debt if their resources are insufficient to finance their education. For private institutions, the potential burden of student debt is a real problem if they would like to attract a diverse student body as some economic classes will simply be excluded from attendance. In addition, private institutions must balance increased tuition rates against the dollars required for financial aid.

As an economic policy issue, this matter of students' increasingly turning to loans to finance their college education does not augur well for the future financial health of the United States, where consumer spending represents approximately two-thirds of all economic activity. Students who are strapped with heavy college loan debts will be less able to buy appliances, cars, homes, or other items that require long-term financing.

Issues Related to State Finance

Before reviewing specific factors and trends influencing the financing of higher education, it is useful to take a moment to describe some of the financial issues faced by the states. Although public institutions rely on state support to a much greater degree than private institutions, virtually every college or university in the country is affected to some degree by the amount of financing that the states can provide, whether through direct aid to institutions or aid programs to students. State governments have had to contend with fundamental shifts in their relationship with the federal government that have dramatic implications for their budgets. Consider several issues, listed here in cursory form, that have both short- and long-term implications for higher education.

Transfer of Fiscal Responsibility to the States

During the 1980s, the federal government transferred partial or full responsibility for many domestic programs to the states (McGuire, 1991). General revenue sharing (GRS) ended in 1987 (Steel, Lorrich, and Soden, 1989). As GRS accounted for 5 percent of cities' general funds and 3 percent of all operating revenues (Marando, 1990), cities and counties have turned to their state government for increased aid (Gold and Erickson, 1989). Local governments have become competitors with higher education for state funds.

Hazardous Waste. High-level radioactive waste from the nation's 111 active nuclear plants will increase from 20,000 metric tons currently to 38,000 tons by 1999 (Winegrad, 1991). The authority to deal with hazardous waste has been shifted to the states (Fitzgerald, McCabe, and Folz, 1988), so they will now have to develop mechanisms to dispose of this waste safely.

Transportation. In the early 1980s, it appeared that the states and federal government had developed a partnership to deal with highway and mass transportation issues. But more recently, Congress has decreased its financial commitment to transportation programs—roads and mass transit (Gosling, 1988).

Health Care. It was estimated that by 1995, Americans will spend $660 billion on health care, up from $550 billion spent in 1988. Approximately $60 billion of this cost will be financed by state and local governments (Califano, 1990). Indeed, the financial burden for health care will be increasingly borne by the states. This is also true for the prison system.

Prisons. In 1990, 3.5 million adults were under some sort of correctional care. In Illinois, which has the fastest growing prison population in the country, the prison inmate population grew by 21 percent in one year. It would cost the state of Illinois $1.4 billion to build the twenty-six prisons necessary to keep up with the inmate flow (Reeves, 1991).

Welfare. The states' share of spending on welfare programs has increased, while the federal share has declined. From 1980 to 1987, state spending on welfare programs as a percentage of the gross national product increased from 1.73 percent to 1.87 percent; the federal share decreased from .7 percent to .58 percent (McGuire, 1991).

Housing. The burden of funding housing programs is shifting from the federal government to state and local governments. Each year, states and localities dig more deeply into general revenues to fund these programs (Stegman and Holden, 1987).

These six trends demonstrate the increased financial obligation of the states for programs for which the federal government formerly had greater responsibility. Higher education finds itself in a position of competing for revenues with prison reform or health care for the elderly, for example. As a result of increased burdens and declining revenues, the states have been challenged to remain solvent. During 1990, twenty states cut their budgets by $2.6 billion because of revenue shortfalls (Miller, 1990). According to Miller (1990), the states are barely solvent, with end-of-year fund balances falling dangerously close to zero. For example, end-of-year balances for all states dropped from $12.6 billion at the end of fiscal 1989 to $8.3 billion at the close of fiscal 1990. It is estimated that the balance will drop further at the close of fiscal 1991. Funding trends vary dramatically from state to state. Nonetheless, the current picture is quite bleak, according to recent reports (Cage, 1991). For example, during the 1990–91 fiscal year, thirty states cut their higher education budgets in the middle of the fiscal year (Cage, 1991); for the 1991–92 fiscal year, state governments allotted less money to higher education than for the previous year for the first time in thirty-three years (Jaschik, 1991).

This brief discussion of some of the pressures on state budgets, which appear to be getting worse rather than better, makes clear that most institutions of higher education will not be able to turn to their legislatures for substantial increases in funding. In the best scenario, public institutions may be able to receive adjustments in their budgets that correspond to the cost of inflation. But it is highly unlikely that a majority of public colleges and universities will be successful in their attempts to receive much more support from their state governments. Private institutions face similar pressures due to the current and projected economic climate in the country. Private support cannot meet *all* the perceived needs of the institution.

As institutions of higher education are affected adversely by state budget problems, student affairs units will be fortunate to maintain the status quo. Those units funded by general revenues (state support and tuition) will be in fierce competition with academic units for resources. Those funded by user fees and fees for service (such as student housing or student unions) can expect to put more money back into their institutions through overhead charges for such items as utilities, accounting and purchasing services, security, and the like. Regardless of the funding source, student affairs units will be forced to struggle to maintain an adequate funding base for the foreseeable future.

The Public-Private Dilemma

An especially difficult issue confronting state financing of higher education is the extent to which government ought to support private institutions. Though private colleges and universities constitute over half of the country's institutions of higher education ("Almanac," 1991), their total enrollment is only approximately 20 percent of all individuals attending institutions of higher education ("Almanac," 1991). The average cost of attending a residential public institution in 1990–91 was just under $7,000, whereas similar costs at a residential private institution were just over $15,000 ("Almanac," 1991). As a result of a variety of factors, there is a spirited debate over just how much state support should go to private institutions. Among the questions in this debate, according to Floyd (1982), are the following:

1.   What is the desirability of government aid to private institutions?
2.   What is the appropriate differential between tuition for public and private institutions?
3.   If the private sector in a particular state is especially large, should the government choose between having to subsidize it or absorb increased public sector enrollments?
4.   If states provide money to private institutions, most commonly through financial aid programs to students, should these institutions participate in statewide planning efforts?
5.   If states provide support to private institutions, how will the institutions maintain their traditional role of independence?

The answers to these questions and others do not come easily. In those states where 40 percent or more of high school graduates attend private or out-of-state institutions, the debate will be more vigorous than in the fifteen states where fewer than 20 percent of high school graduates attend such schools (Halstead, 1987) because the financial implications are far greater. Nonetheless, there is no doubt that the competition between public and private institutions for state dollars—often revolving around whether states ought to provide direct support to students (through financial aid programs, thereby favoring private colleges) or direct support to institutions (thereby favoring public colleges)—has the potential to become more heated.

Factors Affecting State Finance of Higher Education

When one examines the relationship of higher education to the states, it is important to remember that the United States does not have a national system of higher education. As Levy (1986, p. 255) points out, "Discussions about U.S. higher education finance should really be pursued on a state-by-state basis. The fifty state systems, not to mention more local networks, put intra-nation comparative analysis at a premium. Variation is enormous." There are, however, some factors influencing state financing of higher education.
       Munitz and Lawless (1986) identify several issues related to resource allocation that are germane to the current fiscal environment.

Scrutinization of Expenditures

Increasingly, expenditures of higher education institutions are being scrutinized by governing boards, legislatures, coordinating councils, students, parents, and virtually anyone else who has a perceived interest in this area. As mentioned earlier, state funding is being squeezed, and the result is that careful attention is being paid to how financial resources are being spent.
       Munitz and Lawless (1986) posit that a fundamental shift has occurred in the framework being used to determine if higher education institutions are expending their funding wisely. Their position is that through the 1970s,

higher education was viewed in a broader context, and such ideas as encouraging lifelong learning and viewing vocational achievements over a lifetime were considered important. Munitz and Lawless assert that a philosophical change occurred in the 1980s: higher education has come to be regarded as an experience that provides immediate socioeconomic mobility and strengthened earning potential. The result of this shift is that resources have had to be reallocated and curricula and other learning experiences have had to be revised. Moreover, a new aspect of this approach may be in the process of emerging. Higher education may be seen as having direct economic benefit to individuals, rather than to society as a whole. Those holding this position believe that the recipients of higher education ought to pay more since they gain directly from the experience (Kassebaum, 1991).

Student affairs officers can expect that their expenditures will receive careful scrutiny for the balance of this century and perhaps beyond. This is not to suggest that care has not been exercised in the past. It has. But as resources become increasingly tighter, institutions will examine their funding for student affairs with an increasing degree of care and possibly with an eye to finding resources that could be diverted to other institutional purposes.

Disenchanted Taxpayers

As witnessed by the tax revolt in California (Proposition 13), taxpayers across the country are demanding and winning cuts in property taxes (Yinger, 1990). From the late 1970s through the late 1980s, states increasingly have limited the growth of municipal spending (Preston and Ichniowski, 1991). The relative priority of higher education compared to other governmentally funded activities has been questioned. As noted previously, higher education has become a *competitor* with other activities for state funds: "Citizen movements like California's Proposition 13 can have an impact on higher education, as a decline in local tax revenues places greater burdens on the state to provide services previously assumed by the localities" (Hauptman, 1990, p. 16).

Academic Productivity

As part of the call for increased accountability, institutions have been asked to develop measures of productivity. Munitz and Lawless (1986, p. 69) argue, "In higher education there are no indices as quantifiably specific as widgets produced per hour of labor." Though they feel that demonstrating productivity will result in greater taxpayer and legislative confidence in institutions of higher education, conducting such studies is not an easy task, especially in an environment embracing the new philosophy described above. Kuh and Nuss (1990), citing Scott, Wards, and Yeomen (1978), point out that student affairs expenditures usually receive even greater scrutiny than those of academic units because the former have been justified more on the basis of idealistic or humanistic grounds than on tangible evidence or results.

Increased productivity will be sought across institutions of higher education. Student affairs will be no exception. Its staff can expect to work more efficiently, harder, and perhaps longer, and it cannot count on technology to make jobs easier or to help it be more productive. "Introduction of new technology rarely, for example, reduces personnel requirements or saves money" (Mills, 1990, p. 139). New programs can be added only by eliminating others or by stretching existing personnel and operating expenses.

Factors Influencing the Financial Health of Institutions

Brinkman (1990) has identified four factors that determine the financial circumstances of institutions of higher education.

Revenues

Revenues have a dramatic and important effect on the financial status of colleges and universities. Among the revenue sources for institutions of higher education are students, government, private donors, corporations, and financial markets. Students pay tuition, fees, and room-and-board expenses and buy books and supplies. State governments, as mentioned earlier, provide direct aid to public institutions and financial aid to students who attend private institutions. The federal government sponsors financial aid programs and supports research and creative activities. Individuals, foundations, and corporations furnish gifts and grants to colleges and universities; and financial markets provide income for these institutions through revenue generated from investments. Brinkman (1990) reports that student revenue is a key source for all institutions of higher education, although it is more critical to private institutions, where tuition can account for more than two-thirds of their income.

As stated previously, the federal government has changed its emphasis in financial aid programs from grants to loans. Federal revenues are badly lagging behind expenditures, so it is unlikely that substantial amounts of new dollars will be available for program support. Additionally, with the exception of projects introduced as part of specific legislation (as opposed to competitive review), the federal government is not providing support for the construction and renovation of facilities as it did several decades ago.

Private colleges depend more on private and corporate contributions than public institutions, but the latter have also begun to rely more on donations — a situation that puts them squarely in competition for these funds with the private sector. During the 1989–90 fiscal year, twelve of the twenty institutions receiving the most in voluntary (gift-donor) support were private ("Almanac," 1991).

Revenues from investments reflect the fruits of gifts and donations. In recent years, the return on investments has been substantially greater than the rate of inflation. For example, the consumer price index has increased at an annual rate of 4.4 percent from June 30, 1980, through June 30, 1990; however, the return on all investment pools for institutions of higher education has been 13.4 percent ("Almanac," 1991). Thus, the real return on these funds (the rate of return minus the rate of inflation) has been substantial, though it may not be sustainable in the future. In fact, some institutions suffered a decline in investment income in the last year due to the sluggish economy.

Prices

Institutions of higher education purchase goods and services and are affected by general economic conditions. The inflationary years of the late 1970s and early 1980s, for instance, resulted in increases in faculty salaries far less than general rises in the cost of living. Lower inflation rates in recent years have provided institutions with an opportunity to gain ground in this area. Data provided by Research Associates of Washington (1989) indicate that faculty salaries exceeded the Consumer Price Index (CPI) from 1962 through the late 1960s, trailed the CPI until 1984, and then exceeded the CPI through 1988.

Research Associates of Washington (1989) makes the case that the normal components of CPI are inappropriate for measuring the inflationary costs associated with institutions of higher education. Instead, they suggest four factors affecting fiscal operations of institutions of higher education: current operations, sponsored research, building construction, and capital equipment. Current operations, in their terms, consists of the following items: personnel compensation, including professional and nonprofessional salaries, wages, and fringe benefits; contracted services, including data processing, communications, transportation, and printing; supplies and materials; equipment; books and periodicals; and utilities. These items are aggregated to form a Higher Education Price Index (HEPI). Using the HEPI as a guide, the general cost of operating institutions from 1977–78 through 1988–89 has accelerated at a rate faster than the CPI: 6.8 percent for the HEPI compared with 6.2 percent for the CPI.

Other indices make it difficult to come to definite conclusions about inflationary costs to colleges and universities. Although the HEPI grew at a higher annual rate than the CPI for every year from 1985 through 1989, the Boeck Building Construction Index (cited by Research Associates of Washington, 1989) lagged behind the CPI for the same reporting period. Similarly, the Capital Equipment Price Index (consisting of commercial and classroom furniture, office machines and equipment, general-purpose machinery and equipment, and electrical machinery and equipment) also trailed the CPI for each of the same reporting years. By contrast, the Research and Development Price Index exceeded the CPI for each of the same reporting years. It is important to note that the HEPI and the Research and Development Price Index, which exceeded the CPI, are heavily weighted with personnel costs.

If these trends continue (and no one can state with absolute assurance what direction inflation will take), the cost of operating student affairs units, with the possible exception of student housing and other similar facility-intensive units, will exceed the CPI because student affairs budgets tend to be very labor intensive. Most student affairs divisions spend relatively little on capital equipment and construction; most costs, with some exceptions, reflect personnel compensation.

With luck, student affairs may be able to receive minor adjustments, but a windfall of new revenues is highly unlikely. Although there will be little change in revenues, student affairs should expect costs (as measured by the HEPI) to increase at a rate slightly higher than the CPI. Competition for staff will occur both within institutions and with business and industry, where higher initial compensation packages and a more predictable career path make employment very attractive (Barr, 1990).

Technological Change

According to Brinkman (1990), technology is a mixed blessing. On the one hand, improvements in technology—including improved energy conservation, data processing, and the like—will result in lower costs for most enterprises. On the other hand, technological changes often result in increased costs for higher education because the changes rarely result in improved productivity (Brinkman, 1990). The teaching and learning process is labor intensive and although technology can enhance that process it cannot replace interaction. Furthermore, statutory requirements and calls for accountability have forced institutions to respond to new demands for data. Productivity has certainly not increased as a result. Chapter Thirteen provides a wealth of information on technology issues that need to be resolved by student affairs administrators.

Social Change

The final environmental factor affecting higher education is social change. According to Green (1986), the federal government has been attempting to expand educational opportunity to a number of historically underrepresented groups of people, including African Americans, American Indians, Hispanics, the poor, women, and the physically challenged. This expansion has not come without cost. In some instances, students come underprepared to do college-level academic work; in others, the students do not have the funds to enroll in college. In the former case, programs providing academic assistance are in order, whereas in the latter case, financial aid is indicated. Regardless, however, the cost of enrolling these students is greater than it would be for those from a traditional background, who (as we have established elsewhere in this chapter) will be in shorter supply as we move into a new century.

Summary

This chapter has examined four wide-ranging issues that influence the fiscal environment of higher education and student affairs. Demographic trends promise that our future students will more commonly be people of color, less likely be affluent, and more often be from single-parent families. All of these trends have specific implications for student affairs. Federal initiatives of this last decade have resulted in a shift of the mix of financial aid from grants to loans. Legislation has been passed that requires institutions to initiate what could be classified broadly as consumer information activities, but funding has not been forthcoming to help institutions comply. The shift of the responsibility for many programs from the federal government to the states has created substantially increased obligations for state governments that have often had to contend simultaneously with a dismal economic climate. Higher education has therefore to compete vigorously for state support. Finally, we find that economic conditions, as measured by a variety of indices and trends, are rather unfavorable toward higher education in general and toward student affairs in particular.

Yet there is some reason to hope—for example, the call for community articulated by Boyer (Carnegie Foundation, 1990), which could result in greater prominence for student affairs at those institutions that take this work seriously. Not all states are in dire financial straits. Some institutions have completed highly successful fund-raising campaigns, and still others have a steady growing enrollment of bright, able students. But in the main the fiscal waters upon which our student affairs efforts of the future must sail appear choppy at best and hazardous at worst.

References

"Almanac." *Chronicle of Higher Education.* Aug. 28, 1991, pp. 3–38.

America 2000: An Education Strategy. Washington, D.C.: U.S. Department of Education, 1991.

Barr, M. J. "Growing Staff Diversity and Changing Career Paths." In M. J. Barr, M. L. Upcraft, and Associates (eds.), *New Futures for Student Affairs: Building a Vision for Professional Leadership and Practice.* San Francisco: Jossey-Bass, 1990.

Bianchi, S. M. "America's Children: Mixed Results." *Population Bulletin,* 1990, *45* (4), 3–41.

Brinkman, P. T. "College and University Adjustments to a Changing Financial Environment." In S. A. Hoenack and E. L. Collins (eds.), *The Economics of American Universities.* Albany: State University of New York Press, 1990.

Cage, M. C. "30 States Cut Higher-Education Budgets by an Average of 3.9% in Fiscal 1990–91." *Chronicle of Higher Education,* June 26, 1991, pp. A1, A17.

Califano, J. A., Jr. "Ways to Cut America's Health Bill." *State Government News,* 1990, *33* (5), 12-14.

Carnegie Foundation for the Advancement of Teaching. *Campus Life: In Search of Community.* Princeton, N.J.: Carnegie Foundation for the Advancement of Teaching, 1990.

Cutler, B. "Up the Down Staircase." *American Demographics,* 1989, *11* (4), 32-26, 41.

Evangelauf, J. "Study Predicts Dramatic Shifts in Enrollments." *Chronicle of Higher Education,* Sept. 18, 1991, p. A40.

Fenske, R. H., and Johnson, E. A. "Changing Regulatory and Legal Environments." In M. J. Barr, M. L. Upcraft, and Associates, *New Futures for Student Affairs: Building a Vision for Professional Leadership and Practice.* San Francisco: Jossey-Bass, 1990.

Fitzgerald, M. R., McCabe, A. S., and Folz, D. H. "Federalism and the Environment: The View from the States." *State and Local Government Review,* 1988, *20* (3), 98-104.

Floyd, C. E. *State Planning, Budgeting, and Accountability: Approaches for Higher Education.* AAHE-ERIC Higher Education Research Report, no. 6. Washington, D.C.: American Association for Higher Education, 1982.

Gold, S. D., and Erickson, B. M. "State Aid to Local Governments in the 1980s." *State and Local Government Review,* 1989, *21* (1), 11-22.

Gosling, J. J. "Changing U.S. Transportation Policy and the States." *State and Local Government Review,* 1988, *20* (2), 84-93.

Green, K. C. "Government Responsibility for Quality and Equality in Higher Education." In S. K. Gove and T. M. Stauffer (eds.), *Policy Controversies in Higher Education.* Westport, Conn.: Greenwood Press, 1986.

Griffith, J. E., Frase, M. J., and Ralph, J. H. "American Education: The Challenge of Change." *Population Bulletin,* 1989, *44* (4), 3-37.

Halstead, H. *State Profiles: Financing Public Higher Education 1978 to 1987.* Washington, D.C.: Research Associates of Washington, 1987.

Hauptman, A. M. "Helping Colleges Survive Bad Times." *State Government News,* 1990, *33* (9), 16-17.

Hodgkinson, H. L. *All One System: Demographics of Education, Kindergarten Through Graduate School.* Washington, D.C.: Institute for Educational Leadership, 1985.

Jaschik, S. "State Funds for Higher Education Drop in Year; First Decline Since Survey Began 33 Years Ago." *Chronicle of Higher Education,* Nov. 6, 1991, pp. A1, A38.

Kassebaum, N. L. "Perspectives from Washington." Speech presented at the Kansas Conference on Postsecondary Education, Topeka, Oct. 1991.

Kuh, G. D. "The Demographic Juggernaut." In M. J. Barr, M. L. Upcraft, and Associates, *New Futures for Student Affairs: Building a Vision for Professional Leadership and Practice.* San Francisco: Jossey-Bass, 1990.

Kuh, G. D., and Nuss, E. M. "Evaluating Financial Management in Student Affairs." In J. H. Schuh (ed.), *Financial Management for Student Affairs*

Administrators. Washington, D.C.: American College Personnel Association, 1990.

Kuh, G. D., and Whitt, E. J. *The Invisible Tapestry: Culture in American Colleges and Universities,* ASHE-ERIC Higher Education Report, no. 1. Washington, D.C.: Association for the Study of Higher Education, 1988.

Levy, D. C. "Policy Controversies in Higher Education Finance: Comparative Perspectives on the U.S. Private-Public Debate." In S. K. Gove and T. M. Stauffer (eds.), *Policy Controversies in Higher Education.* Westport, Conn.: Greenwood Press, 1986.

McGuire, T. J. "State and Local Tax Reform for the 1990s: Implications from Arizona. *Journal of Policy Analysis and Management,* 1991, *10* (1), 64–77.

Marando, V. L. "General Revenue Sharing: Termination and City Response." *State and Local Government Review,* 1990, *22* (3), 98–107.

Margolin, J. B. *Financing a College Education.* New York: Plenum Press, 1989.

Miller, G. H. "Goodbye to Good Economic Times." *State Government News,* 1990, *33* (7), 9–10.

Mills, D. B. "The Technological Transformation of Student Affairs." In M. J. Barr, M. L. Upcraft, and Associates, *New Futures for Student Affairs: Building a Vision for Professional Leadership and Practice.* San Francisco: Jossey-Bass, 1990.

Mills, D. B., and Barr, M. J. "Private Versus Public Institutions: How Do Financial Issues Compare?" In J. H. Schuh (ed.), *Financial Management for Student Affairs Administrators.* Washington, D.C.: American College Personnel Association, 1990.

Munitz, B., and Lawless, R. "Resource Allocation Policies for the Eighties." In S. K. Gove and T. M. Stauffer (eds.), *Policy Controversies in Higher Education.* Westport, Conn.: Greenwood Press, 1986.

O'Hare, W. "In the Black." *American Demographics,* 1989, *11* (11), 24–29.

O'Hare, W. "A New Look at Asian Americans." *American Demographics,* 1990, *12* (10), 26–31.

O'Hare, W. P., Pollard, K. M., Mann, T. L., and Kent, M. M. "African Americans in the 1990s." *Population Bulletin,* 1991, *46* (1), 1–40.

Organization for Economic Co-operation and Development. *Financing Higher Education: Current Patterns.* Paris: Organization for Economic Co-operation and Development, 1990.

Preston, A. E., and Ichniowski, C. A. "A National Perspective on the Nature and Effects of the Local Property Tax Revolt, 1976–1986." *National Tax Journal,* 1991, *44* (2), 123–145.

Reeves, R. "Corrections: Elderly Criminals and Computer Crimes Will Be Among the Challenges Facing States." *State Government News,* 1991, *34* (10), 27.

Research Associates of Washington. *Higher Education Price Indexes: 1989 Update.* Washington, D.C.: Research Associates of Washington, 1989.

Schwartz, J., and Exter, T. "All Our Children." *American Demographics,* 1989, *11* (5), 34–37.

Scott, R. A., Wards, S., and Yeomen, D. *Collegiate Middle Managers and Their Organizations.* AAHE-ERIC Research Report, no. 7. Washington, D.C.: American Association of Higher Education, 1978.

Smith, V. P. "An Answer to the Labor Shortage." *State Government News,* 1990, *33* (2), 14.

Steel, B. S., Lorrich, N. P., and Soden, D. L. "A Comparison of Municipal Responses to the Elimination of Federal General Revenue Sharing in Florida, Michigan, and Washington." *State and Local Government Review,* 1989, *21* (3), 106–115.

Stegman, M. A., and Holden, J. D. "States, Localities, Respond to Federal Housing Cutbacks." *Journal of State Government,* 1987, *60* (3), 110–116.

U.S. Department of Education. "Drug-Free Schools and Campuses: Final Regulations." *Federal Register,* Aug. 16, 1990, 34 CFR Part 86, pp. 33,580–33,601.

U.S. Department of Education. *The Condition of Education, 1991. Vol. 2: Postsecondary Education.* Washington, D.C.: National Center for Education Statistics, U.S. Department of Education, 1991a.

U.S. Department of Education. *Youth Indicators, 1991: Trends in the Well-Being of American Youth.* Washington, D.C.: Office of Educational Research and Improvement, U.S. Department of Education, 1991b.

Winegrad, G. W. "Environment: Too Many People, Too Few Resources Spell Trouble for States." *State Government News,* 1991, *34* (10), 7.

Yinger, J. "States to the Rescue? Aid to Central Cities Under the New Federalism." *Public Budgeting & Finance,* 1990, *10* (2), 27–44.

5

⁊

Identifying and Working with Key Constituent Groups

Dudley B. Woodard, Jr.
Mark von Destinon

We hear from and read about them all the time. The news media identify them as interest groups, political scientists study them as pressure groups, sociologists refer to power groups, and elected officials speak of constituents. Even in a nonpolitical context, their influence is recognized when service providers speak of clientele and economists talk of consumers. Regardless of the label, "they" are individuals organized to promote a cause, represent an issue, monitor an activity, or express an interest. This broad definition helps us focus on the differing roles of the many constituencies in higher education.

This chapter concentrates on identifying student affairs constituency groups (student organizations, parents, alumni, governing entities, community leaders, business, industry, and others). Theoretical constructs are presented to help in understanding the dynamics of constituent relations. Methods to establish effective relationships, to make positive use of the talents and energy of constituent groups to effect change, and to maintain integrity and accountability are also detailed.

In the late 1960s, the American Association of University Professors stated that the business of institutions produced an "inescapable interdependence among governing boards, administrators, faculty, and students" (American Association of University Professors, American Council on Education, and Association of Governing Boards of Universities and Colleges, 1966, p. 376). Baldridge (1971) notes that "the university has several nations of students, of faculty, of alumni, of trustees, or public groups. Each has its own territory, its jurisdiction, its form of government. . . . Governance [decision making] often becomes negotiation, strategy becomes a process of jockeying between pressure groups, [and] administration even more becomes 'politics'" (p. 122) (see also Chapter Eleven). Finally, Henderson and Henderson (1974) explain that today's faculty members want to be consulted, students demand to be involved, and interest groups of various types wish to organize in order to influence the outcome of administrative decisions (Penn and Cornthwaite, 1977).

Whatever the makeup, influence, or interests of constituent groups, they are usually classified as internal or external. Students, faculty, and staff form the primary internal constituent groups, and the student affairs professional works closely with the associations formed to serve the interests of these groups. The role of the practitioner would be uncomplicated if all the players' attitudes toward and interests in any given issue were known. Instead, the infinite possible divisions and coalitions among these three groups, based on their interests, values, and perceptions, add complexity to the challenge of identifying and working with key campus constituencies.

External constituent groups for purposes of this chapter are defined as parents, alumni, donors, retired faculty and staff, community leaders, business leaders, civic groups, governing boards, and legislators. Each has a stake in the institution, and each has different beliefs and values. Additionally, there are other constituency groups or coalitions that are not visible or heard from until something occurs. Success in some cases hinges on appreciating the role and influence of both known and unknown external constituents.

Theoretical Constructs

The theoretical models discussed in this section attempt to describe and explain the energies fueling the power components of constituent relations. A theoretical construct helps to illuminate the behavior, motivation, and actions of constituent groups. Acquiring an understanding of these characteristics increases the practitioner's effectiveness because the relationship is based on objectivity and a knowledge of the group's etiology rather than on suspicion and misinformation. The three models that we explore are symbolic interaction, social power, and political decision making.

Symbolic Interaction Theory

Symbolic interaction theory is rooted in social psychology and describes the relationship between individuals and society. People not only create society but are influenced by it. Symbolic interaction focuses on how people interpret events, objects, and situations and how different interpretations result in varied behaviors (Blumer, 1969). The meaning that people attach to their experiences is expressed in thoughts and actions and can be understood only to the extent that their frame of reference is clear (Bogdan and Biklen, 1982). Therefore, symbolic interaction is helpful in interpreting how constituents perceive a decision, and it can shed some light on their subsequent actions.

Take, for example, the case of the University of Arizona, which is attempting to construct an observatory on a mountaintop in a southern Arizona wilderness area. The university has been besieged by interest groups who have formed a coalition to prevent construction. The coalition includes members of the San Carlos Apache nation, several environmental groups, and animal-rights activists. On the basis of their beliefs, each of these groups has an interest in stopping the observatory project. For the Apache nation, the mountain has been a site of religious significance. Even though it is not on their reservation, the Apaches are concerned about permitting further erosion of their religious traditions. The environmental groups wish to prevent what they consider wanton development of a wilderness area, and the animal-rights groups are worried about the loss of habitat and possible extinction of a species of red squirrel that inhabits the mountain. At the same time, others have actively promoted the project. The scientific community, especially astronomers, favor construction. Many community leaders and business people in the surrounding communities support the project because of the impact that they hope it will have on the local economy. All of these are valid interests, and the groups' differing frames of reference provide clues to the meanings that each attaches to decisions made by the university. Even within the coalitions they have formed, there are different belief structures and values that influence not only their interpretations of events but also their behavior.

Social Power

The second theoretical foundation for understanding constituent relations also draws on social psychology. The concept of social power was developed by French and Raven (1959). Social power can be defined as the force capable of being exerted by a constituent group in an attempt to influence another person, organization, or institution. French and Raven identified five bases of social power: reward, coercive, legitimate, referent, and expert. An understanding of those five bases provides an answer to, "What's going on here?" That question is often the first to be asked when attempting an analysis of social interactions (Freeman, 1980).

The five bases are most easily understood when the concept of power is applied. The basic question being asked is, "Why should *I* do *this* for *you*?" Reward power responds, "Because *you* may want *me* to do *something* for *you*." This kind of power is the institution's ability to offer rewards to a constituency. Examples of reward power include recognition, release time, or a salary bonus to faculty members who have consistently been "good citizens" in working through controversial policies.

A coercive power response would be, "Because *I* am *bigger* than *you.*" This concept is rooted in the idea that an institution may be publicly punished for not conforming to the interests of a constituent group. For example, alcohol-beverage companies may threaten to withdraw financial support from campus scholarship events if they are not permitted to promote their products on campus.

A legitimate power answer might be, "Because *I* am your *boss.*" It is best defined as the perception that a constituency has a legitimate right to behave or act in a certain way. The state legislature may flex its muscle by adjusting funding based on a revised workload for faculty and staff.

Use of referent power might involve saying, "Because *others* do it." This source of power is similar to peer pressure. The concept is that other groups of stature are supporting a certain position on an issue; therefore, it is acceptable for our group to lend support. Most national professional associations, for example, have publicly called for an end to ROTC discrimination based on sexual orientation.

An expert power response could be, "Because *I* know something *you* do not." This reply refers to a constituency that has some special knowledge. For example, an institution should seriously consider the results of an environmental-impact study sponsored by a local environmental group before finalizing construction of a facility on disputed land.

These five definitions of social power are useful in analyzing interaction and provide an understanding of the nature of that interaction. They can explain the "why" of a behavior based on the meaning, or interpretation, of a decision as identified through symbolic interaction. These two theoretical foundations have great utility for providing insights into constituent behaviors and the reasons behind them.

Political Decision Making

Symbolic interaction and social power help practitioners understand group behavior, whereas political decision-making theory helps us to grasp how decisions are influenced or made. The model developed by Baldridge (1971) describes decision making in academic institutions as a political process. The model is based on six assumptions about policy making within that (decision-making) process. Even if the decision is believed to be final and has been in force for several years, a twist of fate may result in its review. Indeed, decision-making processes have no end, and constituent interests can raise an issue again and again. Baldridge's six assumptions, which we now describe, indicate the transient nature of decisions.

1. *Prevalent inactivity* addresses the issue that not everyone is included in policy making within a political process. When given the opportunity, people choose not to participate, and decisions are made by small groups.

2. *Interest group pressures* refer to the actions of specific stakeholders within the political process.
3. *Fluid participation* recognizes that participants will move in and out of the decision-making process; their movements both affect it and allow decisions to be made by those who persist.
4. *Conflict* is viewed as natural to the process and an asset in promoting healthy organizational change.
5. *Limitations on formal authority* assume that decisions come about through conflict compromises and will be the direct result of interests or conditions affecting the issue.
6. *External interest groups* are those external agencies attempting to influence the policy-making process (Baldridge, 1971).

Each of the six assumptions in the decision-making theory is influenced by the varying interpretations of actions within the symbolic interaction paradigm, as well as by the type of social power the constituent group is attempting to exercise.

Environmental Scanning Theory

An understanding of the theoretical concepts of symbolic interaction, social power, and political decision making will not ensure successful constituent relations. More practical advice is needed. What can a student affairs professional do, what concrete action can be taken to anticipate constituent concerns?

The technique known as environmental scanning surveys the campus and community for groups that may have an impact on the institution. Environmental scanning refers to an early-warning system that collects information on external forces and their impact on the organization (Michman, 1983). Alvin Toffler (1970) indicated that students must learn to anticipate the direction and rate of change. Environmental scanning looks for any trend or event that may have an impact on the institution; it must include sensitivity to all environmental influences and identify both the issues as well as the stakeholders.

Cope (1981) offers one model of environmental scanning that has four dimensions reflecting the arenas of greatest impact on the institution: social, economic, political, and technological.

1. *Economic changes* relevant to decision making in student affairs will be in the areas of personal income, interest rates, availability of loans, and financial aid. What is the economic profile of the student body? How will changes in the state or national economy affect enrollment? What is the effect of a tuition increase on enrollment?

2. *Social and cultural changes* reflect changing societal values, the shifting roles of women and minorities, and changes in life-styles and families. All have implications for the issues that we face in our institutions. The "new" student typology identified by Cross in her book (1971) has become the college student of the 1990s. The impending "demographic juggernaut" (Kuh, 1990) of older students, women, and people of color seeking higher education

is transforming our campuses. As professionals, we must be prepared to deal with those changes.

3. *The political and legal landscape* takes into account the federal and state agencies and legislatures that affect institutions through their regulatory policies and appropriations. Rather than as faits accomplis, their policies and legislation should be looked upon as negotiable items that can be influenced by constituent group pressure. Of course, it is harder to have an impact on national legislation than it is to affect state or local policies.

4. *Technological advances* play a major role in the way that we conduct business. The advent of integrated data bases that can provide information within seconds has strong implications for student- and family-privacy rights. The technological-ecological interface presents concerns that must be considered. The waste of paper and other limited resources, as well as questions about laboratory experiments and animal rights, has also become an issue on most campuses.

Outcomes of Environmental Scanning

In working with constituent groups, environmental scanning identifies issues, stakeholders, sources of influence, possible options, and formal and informal leadership.

Identify Issues

Issues that may influence the institution need to be monitored in order to keep abreast of developments (Michman, 1983). Issues management asks questions about the probability that problems will emerge, their consequences to the institution, and the time frame in which they are apt to develop (Heydinger, 1983). Advance awareness of issues permits the institution to determine a constructive response.

Identify Constituents and Sources of Influence

The monitoring system involves the identification of the players (groups, individuals, or organizations), recognition of boundaries that limit change, identification of conflicts in the system among constituents and between them and the process, and recognition of possible future forces (Michman, 1983). Feedback is necessary to ensure flexibility of issues management, which permits the system to adjust strategies to accord with objectives. The major constituency, students, has already been identified, and the proper place to begin is by enlisting their interest and support. The major vehicle to generate support will be student government, but the practitioner should not stop there; other constituents who may have a stake in the outcome of the issue need to be identified and actively involved.

Identify Options

As the future is uncertain, administrators may next choose to develop possible responses to the issues and constituencies that they face. These responses create an awareness of the issues and of the constituent groups surrounding them. This technique is termed multiple-scenario analysis (Heydinger, 1983). In response to the changing conditions of the institutional environment, a wide range of strategic alternatives must be determined to address them (Michman, 1983). Scenarios for institutional planning require more focus on internal environmental variables and in most cases a regional or local emphasis. Scenarios integrate environmental trends and events into possible strategies. By considering multiple scenarios, administrators are able to examine the various response strategies and plot an informed course of action.

Identify Leadership

A harmonious working relationship with constituency groups is often based on locating the leaders of each group. This process is often as difficult as identifying the constituent group itself, as many constituencies do not have strong organizational structures. Leadership is especially important in a confrontational situation. Those in student affairs must attempt to attach some form of legitimacy to both the constituency and its leadership. Were the leaders appointed, elected, or self-anointed? Do they represent a coalition of groups or individuals, or are they acting for themselves as "free agents"? Both the membership and leadership requirements of each group must be examined so that the institution knows whom it is dealing with at all times.

Classification of Constituent Groups

Sandeen (1991) identifies seven constituencies: faculty, community, parents, governing board, legislature and federal government, alumni, and the student affairs staff. Constituent groups are usually organized around a constitutional function, common interest, or a social or service function. There are countless possible permutations of constituencies and their interests; the student affairs professional should therefore identify those groups that have a legitimate interest in student affairs or that are likely to claim a role in the activities and functions of the division of student affairs. Environmental scanning, networking, and probing questioning will help the practitioner discover groups that may be helpful, influential, or combative. Double-check your road map to make certain you have not missed any hidden constituencies! Another way to classify key constituencies is as follows: faculty, staff, student government, formal and informal student organizations, the local and state community, and nationally based groups.

Faculty

There are several faculty governance groups, such as the faculty senate, undergraduate and graduate councils, and college and departmental councils or advisory groups; there are also groups like the American Association of University Professors (AAUP) or self-appointed "watchdog" groups. Learn which have campuswide support and have been effective in institutional governance. Identify the splinter groups and learn more about their issues and power base. Do not underestimate the influence and role of different factions and even temporary organizations. Gain an understanding of the issues that drive a group: for example, institutional governance, personnel, budget, curriculum, or quality of the educational experience. Make use of different governance and advisory groups, according to function, through information sharing, consultation, and (where appropriate) presentation of agenda items for debate and resolution. Be seen as someone who understands and respects the role of faculty governance.

Staff

There are usually one or two staff advisory groups: (1) classified staff (clerical, secretarial, physical-plant employees, and so on) and (2) professional and administrative staff. The classified staff council or advisory group is generally organized for the purpose of representing employees on the conditions of employment (salary raises, merit distribution, paid holidays, child care, or tuition reimbursement for family members). The professional-administrative council's work is usually to handle concerns related to the functions and operations of the institution. Some councils, however, consider employment conditions either as a recognized responsibility or on a case-by-case basis when requested by the administration.

Staff and professional advisory councils serve useful purposes but are often ignored or paid little attention. Not recognizing the actions and presence of these groups leads to alienation and cynicism. Understand their functions and their decision-making powers. As with the faculty groups, know their leaders, ask to meet with them occasionally, and request mailings, newsletters, or other materials. Support the groups by sponsoring some of their programs and advocating some of their causes. Make certain, however, that you do not go beyond the groups' institutional roles and power or unintentionally grant authority that they do not or should not have.

Student Government

Most institutions recognize some form of student governance. The most common form is an elected executive branch, senate or assembly, and judicial branch. Depending on the size and complexity of the institution, there may be separate governance functions for undergraduates, graduates, and those attending professional schools. The interests, characteristics, temperament, and composition of these groups are changeable; therefore, the student affairs professional must always guard against stereotypical judgments and insensitivity to the varying interests and characteristics of student government. Remember that student government is a learning experience, and an accepting attitude helps to shape students' experiences, actions, and futures. And above all, stay out of student politics. Be an advocate, adviser, information giver, and challenger and arrange opportunities for a fair hearing of student issues regardless of your position or the perceived position of the institution.

Other Student Organizations

As noted, many constituent groups exist, but the most important ones to the student affairs professional are formal or informal student organizations. Working with student organizations is the core of the practitioner's work. Like student governance associations, student organizations reflect the size, type, and complexity of an institution and are dynamic and changing in nature.

Formal Groups. Formal groups are usually (1) recognized by some student government or institutional process; (2) organized for a social, service, educational, or honorary purpose; and (3) function according to an approved constitution or statement of purpose. Formal organization and recognition by the institution provide certain privileges to the group, such as funding assistance, a meeting place, and use of facilities and services.

Informal Groups. Informal groups tend to be temporary and created because of some issue or interest. For example, during the Persian Gulf war, many student protests were held on campuses, though those participating were often not registered or chartered organizations. These groups varied and vanished as the war changed and ended. Informal groups also tend to be campus barometers—thus, the interest that they represent should be taken seriously (though it is important to take other soundings to validate their claims). It is equally essential not to invalidate the legitimate concerns of other recognized campus groups.

Local and State Community

Groups representing another major constituency—the local and state community—are just as varied as those on campus and represent a wide range of governance, professional or business, and special-interest groups, as well as friends and graduates. Governance groups include trustees, regents, city or town councils, and state legislatures. Professional and business organizations include school boards, other higher education institutions, and businesses that rely on graduates. Special-interest groups include those organized to lobby for a specific cause, minority groups, neighborhood associations, donors, sports fans, or parents. Constituents in this category are not directly connected to the institution through employment or enrollment. Their interest is based on an experience, concern, conflict, or program related to the institution. And their expressions of interest are not always supportive of institutional actions.

National Groups

Nationally organized bodies are less likely to have a physical presence on the campus. Their interests in it may be equally as strong, but they are less apt to be directly involved in a debate over campus issues. Instead, their presence and pressure are more exerted in subtle ways. National constituencies include Congress, educational associations (like the American Council on Education and the American Association of Community and Junior Colleges), and professional organizations (like the American Association for Counseling and Development or the National Association of Student Personnel Administrators).

Working Guidelines

After issues, leaders, and options have been identified through environmental scanning, some practical guidelines should be followed in working with constituent groups. These expect to be treated with respect and taken seriously. Action by the institution that suggests otherwise will antagonize them, create unnecessary barriers, and perhaps doom discussions before they begin. Taking the time to understand the characteristics and power sources of constituent groups will facilitate discussions and secure relationships. Although some of these suggestions appear elementary, attention to all of them is essential.

• *Schedule meetings carefully.* Make sure certain people have agreed on time, place, and agenda for meetings. A letter of confirmation should be sent to participants, and when possible, the meeting place should alternate between the institution's choice and the preferred site of the constituent group.

• *Know constituents.* Both formal and informal leaders should be identified. It is also important to become acquainted with some of the group members. Learn something in advance about the members, their jobs, families, community service, children. Actively work on establishing personal relationships, and make certain to attend some functions sponsored by the group. This should be an ongoing commitment by the professional.

• *Recognize legitimate groups.* Groups often believe that the institution does not recognize their legitimacy. Established groups can be recognized by the institution in many ways: sending representatives to group-sponsored functions or honoring the group or its leaders during a campus ceremony.

Less well known or temporary groups may be recognized through acknowledgment of their mission or through public statements supporting or describing their efforts or action.

• *Seek advice.* If you have an upcoming decision that you know will interest or affect one or more constituencies, then seek their advice. You may have to mediate disputes, but the situation can sometimes be defused by allowing the groups to have input, or feel that they have input, before the decision is made. After the fact, it is impossible to include the opinions and interests of the differing constituencies.

• *Hold briefings.* Once an issue arises, constituents should be kept informed and involved in its development. Serve constituents by presenting a positive attitude toward the issue and not permitting it to become a point of controversy. Provide constituents with the data that they need to assist them in their decision making and to educate them on the scope of the issues involved. Do not withhold information unless it is confidential or cannot be released due to legal concerns or personnel policies. Trust is built on openness, and a group will quickly distrust the institution if it believes it is withholding information. Remember your symbolic interaction theory — any action on your part will be interpreted by the group — so try to give a clear message.

• *Secure feedback.* This strategy helps to keep a high level of interest in the issue and gives all groups an opportunity to take part in the decision-making process. Securing feedback involves both quantitative and qualitative data collection. Not only will important information be collected, but the constituents will have been provided a documented opportunity to participate.

• *Recognize differences.* Constituent groups may come from diverse cultural backgrounds or may have value that are different from the community norm. Through words and actions, the institution can influence how the issues are addressed and how divergent values are viewed. Demonstrating acceptance behaviors may have as strong an effect on the outcome as any other factor in the negotiations. In addition, a little sensitive foresight may facilitate the decision process. During the Vietnam War, for example, the Paris peace talks were held up for months over arguments about the shape of the table and who should sit where.

• *Accept responsibility.* At times, you may also have to accept the responsibility for enforcing unpopular decisions made by others. In such a case, do not express your disagreement with the decision; rather, indicate that you are upholding the decision and that you believe that particular constituency group also has the obligation to recognize the decision.

• *Do not procrastinate.* Answer each constituency's questions as soon as possible. Delays will be inevitable, but dragging your heels over an issue that you know will provoke dissent may only increase the magnitude of that dissent.

• *Keep no secrets.* Be open about the decision-making process — clear on whose responsibility it is to make it, how and when the decision will be made, and where the meeting will be held. Being secretive about the process will only serve to increase curiosity and foster distrust.

• *Approve releases and agreements.* Most accords reached by an institution and a constituent group run the risk of disintegration if there is not a written document signed by both parties and approved press releases. It is also appropriate to designate spokespeople for both groups. Letting others speak usually runs the risk of unintentionally giving misinformation or false impressions.

Summary

Working with constituent groups is based on (1) sound working knowledge of the beliefs, behavior, and power source of the group; (2) understanding of how decisions are influenced and made; (3) identification of the leadership, issues, and options through environmental scanning; and (4) adherence to some simple suggestions for success regarding working with constituent groups. Each institution should set into motion an ongoing program of educating constituents about the critical issues that it faces and the choices to be made in order to gain their support and prepare them for change (Haenicke, 1991). And the more an institution knows about the attitudes, life-styles, tastes, and opinions of constituent groups, the more easily it can cultivate a meaningful relationship with them.

Perhaps the best way to describe and assess the conditions characterizing successful constituent relationships is to reframe the Carnegie principles based on the report *Campus Life: In Search of Community* (Carnegie Foundation, 1990). These principles are a necessary condition to establishing strong constituent relationships. Constituent relations should be based on

• *A clear and agreed-upon purpose and direction:* An institution is an educational community where faculty, staff, and students share academic goals and work together for teaching and learning. This is the foundation in building strong constituent relationships.

• *Openness, freedom of expression, and civility:* The Carnegie Foundation affirms that freedom of expression and civility on campus should be recognized and protected. This important principle should be remembered, especially in light of the vigorous campus debates on fighting words, hate speech, and First Amendment rights.

• *A sense of fair play and respect for each individual:* A campus should be a just community where individual rights, differences, and diversity are valued and balanced.

• *Sensitivity to and caring for others:* A campus should be a caring place that offers not just compassion, but empathy and outreach. The well-being of each member of the community is of concern, and service to others is respected.

• *Concern for the common good:* Members of the campus community must recognize and accept their obligation to the group and agree to procedures intended to guide behavior for the common good.

• *Respect for the heritage, traditions, and rituals of other groups:* Members of different groups must recognize, celebrate, and learn from the many historical and cultural traditions present on campus. Whether these are the customs and traditions of the campus, of an ethnic or religious group, or of the locality, appreciating that heritage is an important learning experience.

Each of the Carnegie principles is essential to establishing strong and functional constituent relationships. The university, as a microcosm of society, has a duty to educate students about the fundamental values of human rights. If we as practitioners and educators can transmit that idea to students and instill in them an awareness of and respect for the beliefs and actions of others, then we help to fulfill our responsibility for shaping society. One important step in that direction is the way that we demonstrate appropriate behaviors in our challenging work with constituent groups.

References

American Association of University Professors, American Council on Education, and Association of Governing Boards of Universities and Colleges. "Statement on Government of Colleges and Universities." *AAUP Bulletin,* Winter 1966, pp. 375–379.

Baldridge, J. V. *Academic Governance: Research on Institutional Politics and Decision Making.* Berkeley, Calif.: McCutchan, 1971.

Blumer, H. *Symbolic Interactionism: Perspective and Method.* Englewood Cliffs, N.J.: Prentice-Hall, 1969.

Bogdan, R. C., and Biklen, S. K. *Qualitative Research for Education: An Introduction to Theory and Methods.* Needham Heights, Mass.: Allyn & Bacon, 1982.

Carnegie Foundation for the Advancement of Teaching. *Campus Life: In Search of Community.* Princeton, N.J.: Carnegie Foundation for the Advancement of Teaching, 1990.

Cope, R. G. "Environmental Assessments for Strategic Planning." In N. L. Poulton (ed.), *Evaluation of Management and Planning Systems.* New Directions for Institutional Research, no. 31. San Francisco: Jossey-Bass, 1981.

Cross, K. P. *Beyond the Open Door: New Students to Higher Education.* San Francisco: Jossey-Bass, 1971.

Freeman, C. R. "Phenomenological Sociology and Ethnomethodology." In J. D. Douglas (ed.), *Introduction to the Sociologies of Everyday Life.* Needham Heights, Mass.: Allyn & Bacon, 1980.

French, J.R.P., Jr., and Raven, B. "The Bases of Social Power." In D. Cartwright (ed.), *Studies in Social Power.* Ann Arbor: University of Michigan Press, Institute of Social Research, 1959.

Haenicke, D. "Presidential Perspective." *Currents,* 1991, *17* (1), 18–21.

Henderson, A. D., and Henderson, J. G. *Higher Education in America: Problems, Priorities, and Prospects.* San Francisco: Jossey-Bass, 1974.

Heydinger, R. B. "Using External Information in Planning: Some Tools for Expanding Vision and Enhancing Strategic Thinking." In M. Waggoner and others (eds.), *Academic Renewal: Advancing Higher Education Toward the Nineties.* 1983. (ED 267 680)

Kuh, G. D. "The Demographic Juggernaut." In M. J. Barr, M. L. Up-craft, and Associates, *New Futures for Student Affairs: Building a Vision for Professional Leadership and Practice.* San Francisco: Jossey-Bass, 1990.

Michman, R. D. *Marketing to Changing Consumer Markets: Environmental Scanning.* New York: Praeger, 1983.

Penn, J. R., and Cornthwaite, D. "Administration by Consensus: A Look at Committee Decision Making." *Journal of College Student Personnel,* 1977, *17* (2), 105–108.

Sandeen, A. *The Chief Student Affairs Officer: Leader, Manager, Mediator, Educator.* San Francisco: Jossey-Bass, 1991.

Toffler, A. *Future Shock.* New York: Random House, 1970.

6

ℰ

The President:
Your Master
or Your Servant?

Peter Likins

Understanding the president's view of the world of student affairs can be helpful to success in meeting the many challenges and resolving the endless conflicts that are encountered by the student affairs professional. Sometimes presidents can care very much about students and at the same time have little knowledge of the specialized domain that we have come to know as student affairs, with all its diversity and complexity. In other instances, the president may be very aware of student affairs's problems and issues. In either case, a positive and productive working relationship with the chief executive officer is essential for effective management of the division. This chapter explores strategies to engage the institutional president in the out-of-class lives of students without requiring that he or she be expert in the work of student affairs. The field's professionals must provide the expertise. The president's talents can be used to meet shared responsibilities to students.

The chapter will focus on the various perspectives that shape the president's view of students and of the student affairs enterprise. Attention will be given to a number of its functional areas, and ways to involve the president in each will be provided.

Students: The View from the President's House

Although a president's attitude toward students is often filtered through an intermediary, such as a professor or a dean of students, the personal experiences of the president with individual students can also create unique and significant impressions. If student affairs staff members hope to understand a president's position with regard to their domain, it is essential to determine the president's personal contacts and consider their implications.

Why do these experiences matter? Whether the president frequently finds time for students or not, there will come a moment of crisis when his or her attention is focused in the direction of student affairs. Staff members will at that moment become either part of the problem or a valued partner in the solution. If staff members know enough about the president's basic attitudes, values, and experiences, a stronger partnership can be formed to solve the problem.

For example, does the president continue to interact with students in the classroom? Does the president meet with students in their residences? What athletic or cultural events on campus does the chief executive officer attend? Are students ever in the president's house? Can they see the president easily in his or her office? Do they? Does the president see only student leaders or only students in crisis? What is the view from the president's house at 2 A.M., when faculty members are tucked into their beds at home and undergraduate social life is at its peak?

What is the nature of the relationship of the president with the parents of your students? Does he or she ever meet them directly or respond personally to their letters and phone calls? Does that person understand (and thus share) the natural concerns of parents?

It may be helpful to know the president's personal experiences as a student, even if that was a long time ago. Was the president involved in student government, athletics, theater, or the student newspaper? Was she in a sorority, or he in a fraternity? Was the CEO once a scholarship student? Where was the president educated, and in what fields? None of us can entirely escape the biases created by personal experience, and anticipating your president's prejudices can be very important.

Review the president's job history. Was he or she once a professor, a dean, and then a provost? Where? In large institutions or small? Public or private? All of these experiences shape attitudes permanently.

With rare exceptions, presidents come to their jobs with no formal preparation in student affairs. Still, it is very likely that they are quite concerned about students. A college or university presidency is a very demanding assignment, and few among us will take on such responsibilities without powerful motivations to help students. The combination of the specialized expertise of student affairs staff leaders with the president's personal talents and professional power can result in an outcome that serves students better than either could individually. If that partnership is characterized by mutual respect and communication, there will be no question about the equality of the relationship.

Student Affairs as the President's Lens

As a practical necessity, presidents must rely substantially on the view of students provided by student affairs and by the faculty, deans, and provosts. Even presidents who devote many hours of time to students every week must understand the limitations of their perspective. Presidents need student affairs's point of view, and it must be presented squarely and honestly.

Protecting the president from student problems is dangerous for both. If your president sees students through "rose-colored glasses" and reflects that distorted perception in dealings with the trustees and the public, no one will be prepared to make sound decisions when the next crisis hits the campus.

Yet presidents should be spared chronically negative interpretations of student behavior. Otherwise they will wonder what joy can be found in work with students. There is no inspiration without joy, and a president wants inspirational leadership in student affairs.

The province of student affairs on a modern campus is enormous and exceedingly diverse. Each of the many departments in a typical division has a relationship to the president, and each influences his or her perspective by offering a different lens. The president's impressions come from the admissions and financial aid offices, the dean of students, the chaplain, the campus police, health services, counseling services, the registrar, the athletics department, and the career services department. In the next section, each point of view is treated separately.

The President's View: Through the Office of Admissions

In times past, many college and university presidents often regarded the admissions office as a valve (with filter) used to control the number and quality of incoming undergraduates (relying upon the academic departments for such controls at the graduate student level). The pressure was from the outside, in the form of students trying to get in. The president's major admissions problem was coping with valued alumni and benefactors whose favorite candidates got rejected. The challenge was deciding which of the applicants to admit, not whom to recruit, and the president's obligation was to respect the admissions process without unwarranted intervention. The critical factors consisted of the many dimensions of student quality, not tuition revenues. Presidents were able to take a great deal for granted from the admissions office.

Times have changed. Caught in the vise between demographics and economics, most presidents are making critical decisions based on their perspective of students as shaped by the admissions office. Can enrollments be sustained without sacrifice of quality? What improvements in quality can be achieved by increasing recruiting efforts or reducing class size? These crucial questions will be considered by every institution in the future, and the president cannot answer them alone. The director of admissions has become truly an essential officer of every college and university in America, both public and private.

Stimulated by competition, American institutions of higher education are reacting as American industry has responded to the pressures of the global economy by learning the lessons of the "quality" movement. By reexamining their missions, institutions are rediscovering their primary obligations to students and recognizing the need to present themselves most favorably to prospects. Because admissions officers are often the institution's first contact with future freshmen, their performance is critical to the success of the institutional mission. Every president has learned to place a special value on the good work of the office of admissions. And to assure its success, the president is now eager to help.

Given current priorities, any president must listen carefully to any proposal that might help attract the finest students. Is there a presidential role at that spring reception for top-quality prospects for the next freshman class or even at the barbecue for recruited women athletes? Would a speech to parents or to minority students be useful? Even an individual student and family may be worth the president's time. Certainly, it will make sense for him or her to address a group of high school guidance counselors when they visit the campus.

It seems unlikely that a president will volunteer for any of these roles. There are many claims on limited time, and the choice must be made among options presented. The job of admissions is to develop a reasonable strategy for using the president to advance its mission and then to submit a proposal. In these days, such proposals will not be ignored.

The President's View: Through the Financial Aid Office

The financing of higher education has become an extremely complex business of consuming importance to every college and university CEO. Such preoccupations often take presidents away from students and from student affairs, but these concerns come together in the office of financial aid.

In most private colleges and universities, financial aid is no longer a marginal institutional activity for a few impoverished students. Financial aid policies and strategies are now major elements of college or university management and therefore of keen interest to the president.

Financial aid issues are equally important in the public sector. In either kind of institution, lack of appropriate financial aid can create massive problems for the president and students. In the coming decade, rapid increases are expected in public university tuition, with corollary increases in need-limited financial aid. Thus, the lessons for the private sector will have increasing importance in the public sector.

Presidents get involved with financial aid decisions, not only at the policy level, but also in individual cases—particularly for continuing students whose future enrollment is threatened by financial problems. These are difficult decisions, and the president must be confident of the wisdom and compassion of the staff in the financial aid office and respectful of budgetary constraints. The only way to earn this confidence is by treating students fairly and kindly; it is hard to predict which case might find its way to the president's desk. Financial aid officers should welcome the president's questions, because each case is so different and illustrates the complexity of the rules, regulations, and constraints influencing financial aid decisions. The lessons learned by the president while attempting to solve an individual student's financial aid problem can create an atmosphere of strong support in matters of budget and staffing for financial aid.

If they appreciate the political and economic complexities of these issues, presidents also can help to influence state and federal policies relating to financial aid. Government financial aid policies can be essential to the preservation of the pluralistic system of higher education, so it is important for the president to develop some expertise in this area. Moreover, in a congressional hearing, a president will not be able to refer questions to the financial aid staff, so he or she must be truly conversant with this subject. If necessary, financial aid officers must provide materials to educate the president.

The President's View: Through the Dean of Students

Deans of students were not often very prominent on the college campuses of the 1950s and 1960s. Yet as president of Lehigh University, I see the dean of students and his dedicated team as absolutely critical to the institution's success in the 1990s (and perhaps to that of UCLA and Stanford too). That is a big difference, and it requires some adjustments, particularly in the thinking of the faculty. It is important for people in student affairs to recognize that attitudinal changes of this magnitude require time and patience.

Why is it, I wonder, that students (even graduate students) seem to need and expect so much more personal attention today, outside of the academic sphere? Are they receiving less personal support from their faculties and from their families? Or is society generally less accepting of the idea that there will be casualties on campus: young people devastated by such personal problems as failed relationships, alcohol abuse, and poor physical and mental health? Maybe we accept a greater responsibility for the personal success of students when they are paying $100,000 for their undergraduate education. Yet even in the public sector of higher education, with its large state universities, parental and student expectations for higher education have increased. Responsiveness to the individual needs of students is expected, and the "sink or swim" mentality is no longer acceptable when dealing with student consumers of education. In any event, we have assigned an enormous set of responsibilities to the dean of students office.

A president will feel a special kinship with deans, assistant deans, and residence hall counselors if he or she shares with them the stress of life "after hours" on campus. Together, they may deal with suicide, murder, rape, dangerous illnesses, and violent accidents of all kinds, not to mention distraught parents and disoriented young people. These experiences are painful, and shared pain can create strong bonds.

The president must not be isolated from the dark and dangerous side of life on campus; ultimately, he or she must understand and explain events and problems to others. No campus is an island, removed from the realities of modern society, and the president must be prepared to handle every contingency. Assistance can be provided to the president, if trust and respect are developed *before* the crisis. It may be too late for partnership if relationships are attempted only when the press tells the story.

There is a sunnier side to life for the dean of students, in which the president should also share (if only for the preservation of mental health). College life is a great adventure in learning, and we all have an opportunity to guide that learning experience along healthy and productive paths. Student affairs professionals who work in the dean of students office should actively seek ways to involve the president in positive interactions with students. These efforts should occur with the full knowledge and involvement of the immediate supervisor in the area. Again, the president may not volunteer, because crises seem more compelling and other demands compete for his or her time. But the president must engage young people in the normal, healthy experiences of their college lives, or the burdens of the job will soon become unbearable.

The President's View: Through the Chaplain

On some college and university campuses today, the preachings of the president sound like secularized versions of the chaplain's sermons. These people are natural allies, even when experience suggests otherwise.

Even in public and secular private colleges and universities, there is a growing recognition of the contribution of religious faith to the personal sense of well-being that permits the productive pursuit of advanced education. Campus chaplains have learned to foster many religious faiths simultaneously, and to advance the moral and ethical positions common to all (or virtually all). At the same time, presidents are abandoning the posture of ethical neutrality that paralyzed many of them as institutions became more secular in recent decades and as the demise of the doctrine of in loco parentis redefined obligations. Presidents and chaplains are moving closer together, and they should unite in common cause while respecting their differing roles in the service of students.

The President's View: Through the Campus Police

A campus police department has a delicate task, combining citizenship education with the enforcement of the laws and regulations that preserve order in the campus community. Probably few people appreciate the difficulty of these responsibilities, including institutional presidents. Expectations for a safe environment have increased for all types of institutions, and recent federal legislation (see Chapter Thirty-four in this volume) requiring that crime data be reported has heightened the awareness of the campus police's role for all institutional officers. Today, many college and university presidents do not live directly on the campus and therefore do not see the campus police function at all times of the day and the night. For those presidents, the chief student affairs officer and campus police chief must provide accurate and timely information regarding the important role of the campus police. But those of us who actually live on our campuses quickly learn to respect and value the people who serve the community as peace officers.

Because I do live on campus, I see the university police in a special light. We call for their help with bats in the president's bedroom, and they cheer me on as I run the campus hills at dawn, when we alone are awake on campus. Our police have coached my children's teams after school and tried to keep them on the straight and narrow path. These people really do serve as the friendly neighborhood cops where I live.

Any president who occasionally reads incident reports prepared by campus police must wonder if the residence halls are all populated by Jekyll and Hyde characters, who are transformed hideously from their familiar forms. The puzzle is of course easily solved; students are almost always on their best behavior when they meet the president.

Our police must deal with students who can be in their ugliest state: either drunk or angry at some imposed constraint. They also must act perfectly in times of genuine, life-threatening crisis. And because they represent the authority of the institution, and indeed the president, they must be unfailingly kind, helpful, cheerful, and positive in their attitudes. That is a great deal to ask, particularly of men and women who may sometimes resent the presumptions of students preparing to take their place as leaders of society. Yet we do ask for all of these qualities and more, because we must. The least we can do is demonstrate our respect and appreciation for the work of the campus police.

The president can play a key part in guiding campus police policy by a simple announcement that justice is to be served, even if the institution is consequently embarrassed or otherwise diminished. Campus police must understand that they are to do the right thing, without fear of institutional retribution.

The President's View: Through Health Services

People in campus communities also get sick, and sometimes they die. Even students occasionally (if rarely) die. Unfortunately, most do not really understand their own mortality, so they press the limits of life and good health very hard. The responsibility of the campus health services is to keep them alive and well, and what could be more important?

Every college or university president must give some thought to three terrors of the campus: AIDS and other sexually transmitted diseases, alcohol, and accidents. The health services unit is properly engaged in both prevention and treatment of afflictions in all three areas, and it therefore has the potential to perform a constructive role on campus or to contribute to a major disaster. The president must care about health services, and ultimately he or she must trust the specialists to perform under pressure every time. That kind of trust is built when the president follows the activities of health services rather closely, but the initiative for that active interest will probably have to come from someone other than the president.

On one issue, the president's voice must be heard. He or she must make it clear to those in the health service (and everyone else) that the students' well-being is more important than short-term concerns for the institution. For example, the threat of an epidemic must be faced immediately, even if alarm bells might empty the campus.

The President's View: Through Counseling Services

All it takes is one letter from a grateful parent to enlighten a president regarding the role of counseling services on campus today: one suicide averted or one addiction recognized in time for recovery. The opposite outcomes can also bring the work of counseling services into the president's field of view.

The confidential nature of most of the work in counseling services conceals from the public (and from the president) much that is worthy of attention. Statistical reports may help, but only marginally. Counseling is thus another area in which the president must have confidence in the professionals, and that is best developed through personal contact. An occasional meeting with the counseling staff can help to develop the necessary relationships and to educate the president at the same time.

The President's View: Through the Registrar

The responsibilities of the registrar look very different from different perspectives. For students and faculty, the registrar is a facilitator of course enrollment and associated matters, such as scheduling and grade reporting. Alumni and trustees rely upon the registrar as the guardian of the scared records. And the president looks to this person for up-to-date and accurate information.

Any president must shudder to imagine the damage that can be done by a registrar who is unresponsive to the concerns of students, faculty, and alumni and slow to provide information of high quality. It seems that everyone depends upon the registrar.

Through this office, the president sees the student body in statistical terms. How well the president understands critical characteristics of and salient trends in the student population depends largely on the registrar. High-quality information is critical for successful management in this uncertain age, and a good registrar is the president's valued ally.

The President's View: Through the Athletics Department

For better or for worse, an American college or university is usually most visible to the public on the sports pages of the local newspaper and through the reports of sportscasters in the electronic media. No president can afford to ignore the behavior of the school's intercollegiate athletes, in competition or elsewhere. The emerging role of the President's Commission in the National Collegiate Athletic Association (NCAA) is evidence of the importance of this responsibility.

At universities like Lehigh, where varsity athletes are also serious students, the general quality of student life seems to depend strongly on the richness of opportunity to compete in superior and varied athletic programs at all levels: intercollegiate, intramural, and recreational. Every president knows that recognized high quality of student life is a keen competitive advantage in these days, when excellence in teaching and research is not enough for the success of a college or university.

For smaller colleges or universities with more than twenty intercollegiate teams, a significant fraction of each freshman class is recruited primarily by the coaching staff. The extensive involvement of students in sports is something that every president must take seriously.

Finally, coaches touch students in a way that few teachers ever can; they reach students emotionally and can influence their lives significantly. Coaches can teach most effectively the virtues of perseverance and hard work; they can develop the capacity to recover from defeat and the will to succeed in the presence of adversity. They can communicate standards of decency and fair play and cultivate respect for a healthy life-style. The wrong kind of coach can, however, invalidate all of these lessons and damage students permanently. Coaching involves great moral obligation, and no president can dismiss the importance of the coaching staff in defining the character of the college experience.

If a president is willing to invest the time, he or she can shape the environment of sports competition beyond the campus by active participation in the formation and operation of athletic leagues and the agencies of the NCAA. As a charter member of the NCAA President's Commission and a founder of the Patriot League, I have tried to improve the environment in which Lehigh athletic teams compete. This is a challenge for all institutional presidents and one that student affairs professionals can help meet. Whether an institution is private or public, large or small, residential or nonresidential, Division I or Division III of the NCAA, the intercollegiate athletic program does a great deal to set the tone of the campus community.

The President's View: Through the Career Services Office

Just as students enter institutions through the admissions office, they usually leave for another phase of life in a job or graduate school, often with the assistance of the career services office. The first encounter is most critical to enrollment, but the final service may be the one best remembered. Good career services make good alumni, and every president knows how important it is to have loyal and supportive graduates working successfully all over the world.

Presidents usually take note of the career services function in times of recession, when jobs are scarce and letters to the president from disheartened students and disappointed parents begin to arrive. A better indication of career services performance is corporate support, which often depends primarily on satisfaction with employee recruiting programs. Another factor of natural concern to presidents is the availability of career services counseling for students majoring in the liberal arts, which have less obvious connection to specific employment than engineering or accounting.

In recent years, the focus of career services agencies on campus has expanded to include services to graduates, powerful sources of institutional support. In addition, career planning and placement agencies can provide essential data to the president regarding student and alumni placement and relationships with business and industry that can serve purposes far beyond the immediacy of the career function.

Summary

It should be obvious by now that a successful relationship between student affairs and the presidency must be based on a kind of partnership in a common cause: the healthy development of students. There can be no effective master-servant relationship, because the president lacks the expertise to be the master and both the humility and the time required for servitude.

With this relationship understood, it remains the responsibility of the chief student affairs officer to conceive and advance the role of the president in relation to students. Moreover, the chief student affairs officer must coordinate the work of the agencies in the division and provide strong leadership and support to those efforts. A prime responsibility of such an institutional leader is to take the initiative to make a difference on the campus. Only if proposals are presented and options defined can the president make sensible plans for a role in student affairs. If responsibility for these initiatives remains with the president, they will be random and sporadic, as permitted by demands on the president's time from other sectors of the college or university.

Working together with the president, student affairs professionals can best serve the interests of their students. To strive to represent these interests is a president's first duty, as it is that of student affairs. If this obligation is not met, both parties can abandon hopes and dreams for the institution. If it is, student affairs officers can relax and let the president deal with all the other necessary conditions for the success of their college or university.

PART TWO

❧

Organizational and Management Issues

No one correct model exists for organizing the services and functions related to student affairs. Higher education is much too diverse for that. A number of organizational and management issues exist, however, that influence the direction and character of the student affairs enterprise on the college and university campus. Part Two is designed to concentrate on those issues relating directly to the organizational structure and the role of student affairs administrators within higher education.

Chapter Seven focuses on basic models for administrative oversight of student affairs. An assessment is made of the strengths and weaknesses of alternate reporting structures for a division of student affairs, and suggestions are provided for analyzing the optimum reporting relationship on a specific campus.

David Ambler evaluates various methods of organizing the internal functions of student affairs in Chapter Eight. Through assessing the strengths and weaknesses of each method, Ambler provides valuable insight for the student affairs administrator.

Most student affairs professionals serve in middle management positions within their divisions. Department heads, deans, and others in the field will profit from the analysis that Donald Mills provides in Chapter Nine of the function of the middle manager within student affairs.

Staff members are our greatest resource to meet our professional and institutional objectives of furnishing high-quality services to students. In Chapter Ten, Richard Stimpson discusses the issues, procedures, and problems associated with selecting and training competent staff. Specific attention is given to the need for affirmative action programs in student affairs.

Although many would like to believe otherwise, higher education is an extremely political environment. In Chapter Eleven, Paul Moore reviews the political dimensions of administration in student affairs and gives suggestions to aid the professional in negotiating this difficult area of administration.

Planning for and managing facilities such as student centers, residence halls, and recreational sports complexes has become a major part of the portfolio of student affairs administrators. Winston Shindell in Chapter Twelve provides a sound approach to facility management that will assist practitioners in confronting these concerns.

Technological advances present both problems and opportunities for our field. In Chapter Thirteen, John Baier provides an overview of the issues associated with the introduction of technology into a division of student affairs. The chapter both identifies problems and suggests solutions to technological questions.

Understanding of these management issues is essential to the success of a student affairs administrator. Part Two thus provides options to consider when organizing a student affairs division to provide effective services and programs within our institutional environments.

7

ᔪ

Organizational and
Administrative Models

Margaret J. Barr

To whom do you report? That question is often the first asked of chief student affairs officers when they meet with colleagues from other institutions. To some student affairs professionals, there appears to be only one correct and appropriate answer: the president. The reality of higher education is, however, that the chief student affairs officer may have any one of a number of reporting relationships. Institutions can and do differ, and those differences are reflected in the organizational structures supporting the work of the campus.

In this chapter, a brief introduction to general organizational models in higher education will be provided. The variables that influence the organizational structures in place on a specific campus will then be identified. Four major designs for administrative oversight of the student affairs function will be discussed and their strengths and weaknesses analyzed. Finally, the necessary conditions for success of the student affairs enterprise, no matter what the model of administrative oversight, will be presented.

Throughout this chapter, the terms *chief student affairs officer, vice president for student affairs,* and *dean of students* will be used interchangeably. As with organizational structures, no one title describes the individual who holds primary responsibility for the student affairs function on campus.

One caveat is also necessary in any discussion of organizational models and their effectiveness. No universal reporting structure exists that will assure the effectiveness of the student affairs organization. These structures only acquire meaning by demonstrating their worth within the context of a specific institution. The informed practitioner must analyze each institutional context prior to making the decision about whether a particular reporting relationship is appropriate.

Organizational Models in Higher Education

Most colleges and universities are organized according to functions and have hierarchical relationships within them. It is not uncommon to have a number of divisions within an institution, each holding prime responsibility for matters within a specific functional domain: for example, academic affairs, student affairs, finance, and development. A student affairs division is usually headed by a chief student affairs officer who directs the work of the units in the functional area and whose title clearly reflects the authority and job responsibility that the individual holds within the larger organization (Kuh, 1989). The simplistic notion of neat organizational charts and clearly defined responsibilities for those with titles and authority ignores the reality of the organization of most college and universities.

Rarely, for instance, are functional areas defined in the same way from one institution to another. Indeed, within the context of a particular institution, an argument can be made that the admissions and financial aid functions should report to either student affairs or academic affairs. To illustrate further, maintenance functions in residence halls may either be the responsibility of student affairs or of business affairs. The anomalies within functional areas can be many and complex and are often dependent on the unique circumstances and history of a specific institution.

Kuh (1989) indicates, however, that there are four conventional approaches to organizing the work of most colleges and universities. These include the rational model, the bureaucratic model, the collegial model, and the political model.

The Rational Model

The rational model asumes that the institutional organization is bound by rules of logic and order, purposeful direction, and nonrandom behavior. As Kuh, Whitt, and Shedd (1987) indicate, this approach is very appealing to colleges and universities because it emphasizes the primacy of reason and intellect over intuition and emotion. But although the rational model "helps us to see certain patterns of action as legitimate, credible and normal" (Morgan, 1986, p. 135), it does not aid us in dealing with the complicated agendas and legitimate stakeholders within the higher education enterprise (Kanter and Stein, 1979).

The Bureaucratic Model

The bureaucratic model is based on the work of Max Weber (1947) and stresses hierarchical authority, limits on authority, division of labor, technical competence, standard operating procedures, rules for work, and differential rewards (Hage, 1980). Although examples of this design can be found within most colleges and universities, including in student affairs (Strange, 1983), it is not entirely effective in an academic enterprise. To illustrate, standard operating procedures are useful and provide a structure regarding how to respond to a given set of events; most institutional organizations have such procedural guidelines. However, members of the organization are often expected to respond to the unusual set of circumstances, the unanticipated problem or a behavioral crisis among members of the community. Under such conditions, adherence to a pure bureaucratic approach to decision making may limit the ability of individuals within the organization to respond to changing conditions.

The Collegial Model

The collegial model holds as an ideal the participation of members of the academic community in the decision-making processes influencing institutional goals and direction. Kuh (1989) cites four major advantages of the collegial model: consistency with academic traditions, responsiveness to persuasive arguments, roots in democratic traditions, and guarantee of representation in the decision-making structure. Yet Kuh also indicates that the collegial model is inefficient and insensitive to power differentials, resource availability, and the practical issues of policy implementation.

The collegial model for higher education is also discussed by Millett (1978), who argues that "colleges and universities [have produced] organizations different from other familiar types of organizational entities. . . . A unique characteristic of this organized entity [is] its bringing together of several different types of groups with quite different roles to fill" (1978, p. 14). Yet Millett notes flaws in the collegial model: it consumes a great deal of time and is inefficient; it involves inappropriate persons in issues that should be the domain of the faculty; and it entails faculty involvement in conflicts that they would prefer to avoid, such as student conduct or budgets.

The Political Model

The political model of higher education is not new; in fact, Baldridge (1971), Baldridge and Tierney (1979), Hines and Hartmark (1980), Lipsky (1980), Richman and Farmer (1974), and Saunders (1983) have all conducted extensive studies of the political environment of the academy. "College and universities are political bodies and in that sense provide a reflection of the broader society" (Barr, 1985, p. 64).

Kuh (1989) indicates that the political model acknowledges the importance of power and conflict resolution, encourages the involvement of disparate groups in the decision-making process, and emphasizes policy as the means for managing complex issues. Millett (1978), however, identifies a disadvantage to this design for higher education organizations: "The political model of campus governance further assumed a political product to be derived on a campus wide basis. Experience on various campuses called this assumption into serious question. For the most part it was evident that faculty and student actors on the campus scene were too individualistic, too little inclined to a common group viewpoint and to a common group action, too self centered and inner directed to be able to join together to advance more than a very simple common interest. In this kind of environment, the art of political compromise could not and did not flourish" (p. 229).

Each model has strengths and weaknesses, and probably the most effective organizational structures are composed of a blend of them. Further, organizational structures and the decisions that result from them are not necessarily rational (Kuh, Whitt, and Shedd, 1987) — a situation that makes colleges and universities both fascinating and frustrating environments in which to work. Answering the question of what is the proper administrative oversight for student affairs requires understanding of these basic organizational designs and the ability to analyze the variables that will influence the specific mix of decision-making structures on a given campus. Thus, these structures reflect both the people involved and the context of the institution.

Institutional Variables

What institutional variables are most likely to influence the organizational reporting relationship of student affairs?

The President

The organizational philosophy of the chief executive officer of the institution will certainly play a major role, and if he or she adopts one of the models outlined in the previous section, there may be predictable results for student affairs. More importantly, the tasks and functions that must be performed by the president or chancellor will influence internal organizational structures and demands. For example, if the chief executive officer must spend a great deal of time off campus raising funds, then it is likely that an executive vice president or provost will be designated as the chief internal operating officer of the institution. If the president remains on campus most of the time, a different organizational structure will probably evolve. Nevertheless, most chief executive officers are pragmatic souls who adapt to the realities of the institution; those realities become the most important factors in determining to whom and under what conditions does student affairs report.

Institutional Size

Peter Flawn asserts, "The organized efforts to care for students are usually called student support services or just student services. . . . They are administered by a vice president for student affairs or a dean of students" (pp. 91–92). However, this statement may not be true on many campuses. Institutional size is a definite variable in determining whether there is even a division of student affairs. In small, traditional campuses, the functions of a division of student affairs may be absorbed by a variety of individuals: staff in the office of the president, the chaplain, or faculty members. In larger or midsized institutions, student affairs may emerge as a distinct organizational entity. Although the functions generally associated with student affairs are present on almost all campuses, a centralized or decentralized approach to fulfilling them may be in direct relationship to the size of the institution.

Institutional Mission

As James Lyons points out in Chapter One, the mission of the institution has the greatest impact in determining the ethos of the campus. The campus climate or ethos is also reflected in organizational structures within the institution. A large institution with a major commitment to research is likely, for example, to have a vice president for research. Smaller institutions without a research emphasis are unlikely to have any type of separate research organizational unit. In addition, if the institution is a commuting campus with a student population of older adults attending on a part-time basis, the internal organizational structure must differ markedly from that of a traditional residential campus. Different missions obviously require distinctive forms of organizational support.

The most significant aspect of the mission influencing the organizational structure of student affairs relates to how the institution views students. Examination of admissions brochures and public statements of institutional officers can assist in identifying the institution's philosophy in relation to its students. If emphasis is placed on caring, support, and individual attention, student affairs will be viewed as central to the purposes of the college or university. If the importance of individual scholarship and the research role of the institution are stressd, student affairs may be accorded less importance.

History and Tradition

Perhaps more than any other factor, the history and tradition of the institution form the framework for organizational structures. (See Chapter One in this volume.) If something has always been done a certain way and if tradition is venerated in the campus community, changing or modifying organizational relationships is difficult at best. Many organizational structures have evolved over time, and an overriding attitude in higher education is resistance to change.

Other Players

More often than not, the organizational reporting pattern for student affairs and other administrative entities has been based on people. Personal friendships, work styles, and compatibility of values often determine who works directly with whom. Though most members of the academy would like to believe otherwise, people's personalities, their needs, and their wants all make a difference in the organization and administration of the enterprise.

Major Models for Administrative Oversight for Student Affairs

Four major models exist for administrative oversight in student affairs: direct reporting to the chief executive officer of the institution, reporting through another institutional officer to the president, a dual reporting relationship, and a decentralized model.

Reporting to the Chief Executive Officer

A direct reporting relationship to the institution's chief executive officer is often seen as optimal. Its proponents believe that it sends an important and clear message to the entire academic community regarding the centrality of the role of student affairs within the institution. When all executive officers of the institution report directly to the president, disputes are more likely to be resolved on the basis of the collegial relationship rather than on that of perceived power. The agenda of student affairs can be presented to the president in person, issues can be discussed candidly, and information can be more readily shared. The chief student affairs officer can take responsibility to assure that the president is informed about pressing campus issues and is seldom surprised by unfolding events or problems. Under such conditions, the chief student affairs officer has an opportunity, as a member of the institutional executive staff, to contribute to major decisions that will influence the future of the institution. William Monat, former president of Northern Illinois University, explains his preference for this reporting relationship:

> As the chief executive officer at a large state-assisted university and one who takes seriously his campus management responsibilities, I much prefer an administrative structure that places the chief student affairs administrator in a direct reporting relationship to the president. My experience has led me to the conclusion that there simply are too many potential and occasional actual problems about which the chief executive officer "has a

need to know" and that the direct reporting relationship provides the greatest likelihood that that need will be served. For essentially the same reason, I also believe the chief student affairs administrator should be part of the central management team for the campus and a major actor in the decision and information processes involving the chief administrators of other university divisions [1985, p. 52].

What then are the disadvantages of a direct reporting relationship? If the chief executive officer is often unavailable or is off campus to meet other obligations, time may be lost responding to crisis situations. In addition, if the president is presiding over a very complex enterprise, student affairs may not get the time and attention needed to make sound decisions and to engage in planning. The span of direct control exercised by the president will make a great difference in the effectiveness of such a reporting relationship. Often, if the president has a large and complicated agenda, personal communication is difficult, and other communication such as electronic mail and interoffice memorandums must substitute. Finally, if an analysis of the organization reveals that operational decisions regarding routine fiscal and management matters are vested in another institutional official, then direct reporting to the president may not be an asset. The critical question to ask is whether the student affairs organization will receive sufficient consideration under such an organizational structure. If not, one of the other alternatives may better meet the needs of the institution and student affairs.

Reporting Through Another Institutional Officer

On many campuses, student affairs and other institutional entities report to the president through another executive officer of the institution. When the president's time, attention, and ability to focus on issues of concern are limited, this may be a most viable and useful approach to administrative oversight. Whether it is the provost, the chief academic officer, or the chief financial officer, reporting to an intermediate supervisor may have advantages. Some of these are similar to those outlined as positive reasons for a direct reporting relationship to the president. Access may be easier, communication more fluid, and decisions made in a shorter time frame. As noted previously, if day-by-day operational control over budgetary matters rests with an institutional officer other than the president, increased access to that individual has the potential to assure that a complete hearing on matters of concern to student affairs administrators will occur. Finally, reporting to another executive officer increases the possibility that collegial bonds can be formed with unit heads in the other administrative areas. In one instance, a new vice president for student affairs was assured that within a year a direct reporting relationship to the president would be established. During the interim, this vice president reported to the institution's provost. Rather than reacting negatively, this new vice president viewed this as a unique opportunity to forge collegial ties with the academic deans and other members of the provost staff. That experience of shared meetings and discussions resulted in the development of strong and cooperative relationships between the academic affairs and student affairs areas. And even though the vice president for student affairs now reports to the president, he is invited to and attends meetings with the academic deans and the provost on a regular basis and keeps channels of communication open.

The disadvantages of reporting through another executive officer often have to do with campus perceptions. If student affairs seems a secondary function organizationally, it may not be seen as an equal partner in the educational enterprise. The division's concerns, even when communicated to the president, are filtered through an intermediary, and some agenda items may not even reach the CEO's desk. There are a number of potential and actual problems that the president must be aware of in order to do a good job. Unless the intermediary officer is comfortable with the chief student affairs officer, the president may not receive the necessary information. Finally, a reporting relationship through another administrative officer must be characterized by conditions of trust and respect, or student affairs will not receive the attention it merits.

The Dual Reporting Relationship

To combat the inherent weaknesses in either reporting directly to the president or through an intermediary officer, some institutions have developed a dual reporting relationship. In this situation, the vice president for student affairs sits as a full member of the president's cabinet, participates in policy development and decision making, and regularly meets with the president on issues of policies, priorities, or problems. Day-to-day operational issues are resolved with an executive vice president and usually involve financial issues or policy interpretation. Particularly if the chief executive officer is frequently required to be off campus, this reporting structure can ease the daily flow of business for the chief student affairs officer. Usually, decisions can be made quickly, and valuable time is not lost.

In reality, many institutions operate on this model, although it may not be reflected in the formal organizational chart. The nuts and bolts of financial matters, for example, are usually resolved with the appropriate administrative official, and it is only when disputes arise that the chief executive officer is called in. In order to make such a dual reporting relationship viable, however, a high level of mutual trust must be established. Finally, all the persons involved must demonstrate patience, have a high tolerance for ambiguity, and err on the side of communicating too much rather than too little.

Obviously, this type of organizational structure requires clear guidelines regarding communication and supervision. If these are not established and if the conditions of confidence and respect are not present, a dual reporting relationship can be an invitation to disaster.

A Decentralized Organizational Structure

Many institutions have chosen a decentralized approach to providing student services, programs, and activities. Under such a plan, functions that might normally be a part of a student affairs organization are subsumed into a variety of other administrative structures on campus. Academic units take responsibility for the lives of students enrolled in their school or college; career planning and placement, discipline, advising, support for major related student activities, and other functions are coordinated by the office of the academic dean. Residence halls, food services, and student centers may fall under the oversight of the unit that has administrative responsibility for other physical facilities on campus. Recreational programs may be placed under the guidance of either the intercollegiate athletics program or a department of health and physical education. Psychological services may become part of a department of psychology and provide a clinical experience for enrolled graduate students. Health services, if a medical school is present, may become part of that unit or may be contracted to an outside agency. Services for international students often become part of the admissions function, which then usually reports to the chief academic officer. Student activities are supervised by students and are usually under the control of a faculty oversight committee. Some institutions may also offer entering students a "university college" experience with the full array of services and then decentralize them after a major has been elected. The list of possible placements for student affairs functions could go on and on and is highly dependent on the ethos and culture of the campus.

Proponents of a decentralized approach to student services see it as a method that more fully integrates the need for high-quality student services into the life of the institution. The individual student is more apt to be seen as a whole person, for example, if both academic and nonacademic components of his or her experience are coordinated through one unit. Administrative overhead can be reduced, and another layer of bureaucracy is removed for the student or parent negotiating a complex administrative system. Finally, many believe this is a more cost-efficient approach to providing services.

Decentralization is not, however, without problems. In many institutions that have abandoned a traditional line-and-function approach to student affairs, cost savings have not been realized. In fact, when services are provided concurrently in the many schools and colleges of an institution, wasteful duplication may result. Students who wish to change majors or college affiliation may have no easy access to support. Coordination between and among units can be difficult, and efforts must be made to assure consistency regarding application of both policies and procedures. Supervision of some functions may not be optimal, and confusion may exist regarding the purpose of providing some student services. For instance, should the clinical training of potential psychologists be more important to the institution (and the counseling center be part of the department of psychology), or is the provision of direct services to students the primary goal? Obviously, a number of questions must be answered. Decentralization appears to work only when common values are shared and concerted efforts are made to communicate and handle problems.

The Reality

No "pure" approach to the administrative oversight for student affairs exists. As stated earlier, most institutions have developed a blend of approaches that seems to meet their unique needs. Institutional size is one of the biggest factors in determining what approaches or blends might be taken. To illustrate, a large multiuniversity may have a vice president for student affairs who reports directly to the president and carries administrative responsibility for a wide array of student services; yet career planning and placement functions are decentralized in the various schools and colleges.

Personal style of the president or chief executive officer is also another key variable. The vice president for student affairs or dean of students may report through another administrative officer; however, the expectation of the president is for full and complete communication on matters of student concern.

It is true that any time a group of vice presidents for student affairs is together, it will illustrate greatly varied administrative reporting relationships. The astute practitioner must therefore not be quick to judge that a reporting relationship is inappropriate but must assess instead whether the conditions for success are present within the environment.

Conditions for Success

As Barr and Albright said, "For student affairs to be successful, both institutional and internal organizational conditions must be met" (1990, p. 195). In this volume, six factors are identified that contribute to the success of student affairs: a distinctive institutional mission (see Chapter One), open communication (see Chapters Five and Twenty), encouragement of innovation (see Chapter Fourteen), access to the "real" decision makers on campus (see Chapter Eleven), partnership in the resource allocation process (see Chapters Seventeen and Thirty), and a clear institutional philosophy. Each condition is difficult to achieve and can be either enhanced or complicated by the nature of administrative oversight for student affairs.

The responsibility for an effective student affairs enterprise lies equally with its professional leadership. Barr and Albright (1990) also list seven conditions for a strong practice that are internal to the student affairs organization: clear articulation of goals and purposes (see Chapters One and Three);

participation in research and in evaluation and sharing of those results (see Chapters Fifteen and Sixteen); a strong base of knowledge about students and their cultures (see Chapters Three, Eighteen, and Twenty-Nine); strong management skills (see Chapters Nine, Ten, Fifteen, Eighteen, Twenty, and Twenty-Two); the ability to anticipate and resolve problems (see Chapters Five, Nine, Twelve, Fifteen, Seventeen, Nineteen, Twenty-One, and Twenty-Two); and the enthusiastic involvement of student affairs staffs in their work. As indicated, the authors of other chapters in this book will expand on these issues in greater detail, and the reader is referred to those sources. But perhaps the most important condition for success is for the chief student affairs officer and practitioners to assess the organizational structure of the institution, its antecedents, and the current conditions that support a specific administrative oversight model. After that assessment is complete, careful questions must be asked to determine student affairs professionals' personal degree of "fit" with the organizational climate of the institution. Once that harmony is achieved, then student affairs professionals must engage in the practice of the profession with good humor, ideals, and a commitment to serve both the students and the institution.

Summary

Organizational models and organizational structures for student affairs are highly dependent on the unique characteristics of the institution. Factors such as the organizational philosophy and style of the president, institutional size, mission, history, tradition, and individuals will dictate the appropriate organizational structure for student affairs. Across the country, there are many models for administrative oversight of these units. Each has strengths and weaknesses, and the astute student affairs practitioner must analyze the institution carefully to determine what structure is appropriate in that specific context.

References

Baldridge, J. V. *Power and Conflict in the University.* New York: Wiley, 1971.

Baldridge, J. V., and Tierney, M. L. *New Approaches to Management: Creating Practical Systems of Management Information and Management by Objectives.* San Francisco: Jossey-Bass, 1979.

Barr, M. J. "Internal and External Forces Influencing Programming." In M. J. Barr, L. A. Keating, and Associates, *Developing Effective Student Services Programs: Systematic Approaches for Practitioners.* San Francisco: Jossey-Bass, 1985.

Barr, M. J., and Albright, R. L. "Rethinking the Organizational Role of Student Affairs." In M. J. Barr, M. L. Upcraft, and Associates, *New Futures for Student Affairs: Building a Vision of Professional Leadership and Practice.* San Francisco: Jossey-Bass, 1990.

Flawn, P. T. *A Primer for University Presidents: Managing the Modern University.* Austin: University of Texas Press, 1990.

Hage, J. *Theories of Organization: Form, Process, and Transformation.* New York: Wiley, 1980.

Hines, E. R., and Hartmark, L. S. *Politics of Higher Education.* Washington, D.C.: American Association of Higher Education, 1980.

Kanter, R. M., and Stein, B. A. *Life in Organizations.* New York: Basic Books, 1979.

Kuh, G. D. "Organizational Concepts and Influences." In U. Delworth, G. R. Hanson, and Associates, *Student Services: A Handbook for the Profession.* (2nd ed.) San Francisco: Jossey-Bass, 1989.

Kuh, G. D., Whitt, E. J., and Shedd, J. D. *Student Affairs Work 2001: A Paradigmatic Odyssey.* Washington, D.C.: American College Personnel Association, 1987.

Lipsky, M. *Street Level Bureaucracy: Dilemmas of the Individual in Public Service.* New York: Sage Foundation, 1980.

Millett, J. D. *New Structures of Campus Power: Success and Failures of Emerging Forms of Institutional Governance.* San Francisco: Jossey-Bass, 1978.

Monat, W. R. "Role of Student Services: A President's Perspective." In M. J. Barr, L. A. Keating, and Associates, *Developing Effective Student Services Programs: Systematic Approaches for Practitioners.* San Francisco: Jossey-Bass, 1985.

Morgan, G. *Images of Organizations.* Newbury Park, Calif.: Sage, 1986.

Richman, B. M., and Farmer, R. N. *Leadership, Goals, and Power in Higher Education: A Contingency and Open-Systems Approach to Effective Management.* San Francisco: Jossey-Bass, 1974.

Saunders, L. E. "Politics Within the Institution." In J. W. Firnberg and W. F. Lasher (eds.), *The Politics and Pragmatics of Institutional Research.* New Directions for Institutional Research, no. 38. San Francisco: Jossey-Bass, 1983.

Strange, C. C. "Traditional Perspectives on Student Affairs Organizations." In G. D. Kuh (ed.), *Understanding Student Affairs Organizations.* New Directions for Student Services, no. 23. San Francisco: Jossey-Bass, 1983.

Weber, M. *The Theory of Social and Economic Organization.* London: Oxford University Press, 1947.

8

Developing Internal Management Structures

David A. Ambler

Writing about the early days of student affairs, James Rhatigan suggests that the profession "was predicated upon being out of the mainstream; how to become (or whether to become) a part of the mainstream is our continuing dilemma" (Appleton, Briggs, and Rhatigan, 1978, p. 12). Yet Knock observes, "While the student personnel point of view calls for an institutional response to the education of the whole student, the most visible organizational development at most colleges and universities during the 1950's, 1960's, and 1970's was the creation of a separate student personnel services structure [student affairs division]" (1985, p. 36). Whether intentionally or accidentally, the student personnel movement did in fact become a legitimate part of the higher education bureaucracy in the boom days following World War II and has flourished as a result of being in the mainstream of the administrative structure of American colleges and universities.

The wisdom of adopting the corporate or bureaucratic model for student affairs is now widely debated. Kuh (1983) and others have challenged the assumptions on which this model rests and have provoked a useful debate on this issue that should serve the profession well as we approach the economic, social, and educational uncertainties of the next century. Yet it is the premise of this chapter that the corporate model has by and large served higher education and the student affairs profession very well in the past and is not likely to be greatly altered in the near future. Although the corporate model will be in place, if this profession is to remain a viable element of the American higher education establishment, the student affairs profession must become more sophisticated in its ability to deliver services and programs that contribute directly to the achievement of institutional goals. The general literature on management systems should be studied by any student affairs administrator developing internal organizational structures. *Designing Complex Organizations* (Galbraith, 1973), *High-Involvement Management* (Lawler, 1986), *Integrating the Individual and the Organization* (Argyris, 1964), and *Organizational Culture and Leadership* (Schein, 1985) are representative of the range of management literature that can be of assistance to student affairs professionals. Effective management in student affairs, including the development of an internal organization structure, can be enhanced through transfer of knowledge gained in other settings to the domain of higher education.

The intent of this chapter, however, is to identify and analyze the unique management structures that have evolved within student affairs organizations. It will examine the current status and the principles that undergird the administrative organization of student affairs and present an analysis of the various models of internal management.

The Development of the Student Affairs Bureaucracy

The development of student affairs as a highly organized unit in American higher education did not emerge until the postwar period of the late 1940s brought large numbers of diverse and first-generation college students to a rapidly expanding number of college campuses. The need to accommodate the various needs of these students forced an expansion of curricular and social services and some fundamental changes in the manner in which personnel workers performed their responsibilities.

The student affairs profession has seen an evolution in its organizational structure and management style in the several decades since the "personnel deans" were the principal, if not the only, administrators of the program:

> The deans of men and deans of women had relied heavily on the force of their personalities, and their reputation as effective teachers, in their work as deans. They held no special corner on administrative skills. . . . The dean of students position was established to bring some order out of the substantial overlapping which resulted on some campuses. Persons with administrative skill were hired to direct the various staff and offices involved in working with students outside the classroom. . . . The leader was no longer (necessarily) an inspirational figure, but

was more likely selected for his/her ability to develop or manage a variety of programs and services in behalf of students [Appleton, Briggs, and Rhatigan, 1978, p. 20].

Though the period of years immediately following World War II greatly altered the form and content of student personnel services, it was not until the 1960s that student affairs programs grew into large, complex, and independent administrative units headed by a chief student affairs officer (CSAO) at the vice-presidential level. Several social and political movements contributed to this change in the organization of student affairs. The civil rights movement of African Americans spilled onto the nation's campuses, creating tension and confrontation over long-ignored societal ills. The tactics of civil rights activists were quickly adopted by the antiwar groups and those who sought reform on campus in the so-called student rights movement. Disruption of the academic routine, court rulings redefining the relationship between the student and the university, and the politicization of the campus contributed to an expansion of the role of the CSAO and, consequently, to the complexity of the student affairs mission.

Thus, it has been only in the profession's recent history that much attention has been devoted to understanding and developing effective management styles and structures to address these new organizational assignments and political realities. In many ways, student affairs professionals have found it difficult and uncomfortable to adapt to these new roles and assignments. The recent history of student affairs is replete with an unfortunate debate over whether those in the profession are educators or administrators. Chief student affairs officers frequently express guilt or remorse at their inability to attend equally to the needs of the students and of the organization. The many functions that student affairs officials undertake as officers of the institution on the one hand and advocates for student concerns on the other are often presented as unreconcilable. It is this author's contention that the failure to resolve this dilemma has delayed our development of internal management systems appropriate to our various campuses. The student affairs profession has been slow to provide the would-be chief student affairs officer with the necessary administrative mental outlook, the organizational skills, and the management techniques to be successful in our increasingly complex and technical institutions.

The Current Status of Student Affairs Organizational Development

To understand the concepts involved in developing adequate internal management structures, it is necessary to review the current status of organizational development of student affairs programs at many types of higher educational institutions across the country. In preparing this chapter, the author surveyed over one hundred student affairs organizational structures at various public, community, and private colleges. One hundred and thirteen institutions from forty-seven states responded to a request for their student affairs organizational charts. Various aspects of the organizational plans were studied, including services, organizational model, location in the university structure, nomenclature and titles, and span of control.

Seventy-eight of the universities were public, of which forty-three were identified as "flagship," comprehensive, or land-grant institutions. The other thirty-five public institutions were of the state-university classification, and twenty-nine of these had enrollments of at least ten thousand students. The twenty-five private institutions that responded represented the diversity of private colleges and universities and ranged in enrollment from fewer than four hundred students to twenty thousand or more. The typical private college, however, had in the range of twelve hundred students. Most of the ten community colleges were of the single-campus variety with enrollments of several thousand students. Several were more complex, however; one had a multicampus program with over twenty thousand students.

It is difficult to ascertain all of the complexities of administrative design and reporting relationships from a simple review of these organizational charts, but there are a number of useful observations that can be made. These charts reveal some of the progress that has been made in the assignment of various service programs to the chief student affairs officer and the degree to which student affairs has achieved a role in executive management and policy making within the college or university structure. Although not scientific, the following empirical observations on the status of student affairs organizational development are offered.

Responsibilities

The scope of responsibilities assigned to the student affairs organization has continued to expand during the past several decades. This expansion is particularly noticeable at the large, comprehensive, public universities, but it is true in all four of the institutional categories studied. Many of the chief student affairs officers in the public institutions have been assigned all of the activities identified as student services in the program classification structure of the National Center for Higher Education Management Systems of the Western Interstate Commission for Higher Education (Myers and Topping, 1974). Admissions, records, advising, and remedial and tutorial services that were formerly the responsibility of the chief academic officer are now frequently found in the student affairs division. Some anomalous responsibilities, such as police and campus security, athletics, alumni affairs, and public relations, are also vested in some student affairs units, particularly in the smaller private and the community colleges. In short, the student affairs programs at institutions of all classifications and sizes have often become large, comprehensive, and very diverse.

Auxiliaries

Many student affairs programs have now been assigned full responsibility for both the programmatic and financial operations of the traditional student services auxiliaries. For some services (such as housing, health services, and student unions), the previous separation of the financial and program management functions between student affairs and business affairs is disappearing at institutions of all types. Chief student affairs officers and their respective subordinates are now responsible for multimillion dollar operations, including construction, personnel, plant maintenance, purchasing, budgeting, and policy determination. The elimination of this dichotomy has allowed for more "holistic" programming and consistent management philosophy in these important student services.

Reporting Relationships

The elevation of the chief student affairs officer to the vice-presidential or executive-management level of institutional administration is virtually universal in all classifications of higher educational institutions. Although this phenomenon is more evident in the comprehensive public universities, it is even true at smaller or private institutions (even though the vice-presidential title has not always been awarded to the student affairs officer). In a growing number of institutions, the student affairs officer, along with the other vice presidents, reports to a campus chief administrative officer, such as an executive vice president or a provost. (See Chapter Seven in this volume.) In any event, it is apparent that the student affairs officer participates in many aspects of institutional management as an equal with the other executive officers in academic affairs, business management, plant management, general administration, and university relations.

Organizational Structures

The structures of student affairs divisions have become highly complex and specialized in all types of colleges and universities. As a result of the changing role of the chief student affairs officer, an organization has been necessary that would allow the CSAO to perform a variety of different and sometimes conflicting roles. The results include delegating of supervisory functions, clustering of like services, increasing of subunit autonomy, and surrendering to vicarious relationships (through deans, directors, and other managers) with staff.

Span of Control

The span of control exercised by the CSAO varies greatly among institutions in all four classifications. In spite of the similarities in organizational structures just mentioned, the number of staff members supervised directly by the chief student affairs officer ranges from as few as two to as many as sixteen in the institutions studied. Interestingly, those having the largest number of subordinates reporting to the chief student affairs officer are not the large, comprehensive, public institutions. Whereas many of the public institutions average between six and seven reporting units, community colleges tend to have many more units reporting to the chief student affairs officer. Community colleges often have more diverse student services functions reporting to the chief with fewer assistants or subordinates to assume middle-management functions. The typical midsized private institutions are very consistent; five or six units report to the student affairs officer. Larger private institutions mirror the organizational plans of their counterparts in the public sector.

Titles

The titles given to both student affairs offices and staff positions differ widely in all categories of institutions. This situation is particularly true for offices and staff positions below the chief student affairs officer: "The terms director, dean, assistant dean, assistant director, coordinator, specialist, university staff, and professional staff are used freely to describe the roles and functions of the student affairs staff. Further, there is no agreement about what these terms mean from one campus to another. Academic rank conveys a certain sense of meaning from campus to campus, but this is not true for student affairs" (Barr and Albright, 1990, pp. 186–187). Many offices carry traditional and recognizable titles, but most parents or faculty members would have difficulty understanding the nature of some of the new and specialized services offered by the student affairs division from their names.

As noted, the titles used by the CSAO have become more consistent in recent years. Clearly, the preferred one in the public universities is vice president or vice chancellor for student affairs. Vice provost for student affairs is the most common title in those institutions using the provost model. Some private institutions use similar vice-presidential titles, but they more frequently use *dean* to designate the chief student affairs officer. In most of these cases, the position is called dean of student services or of student affairs. The title dean of students seems to be fading as a designation for the chief student affairs officer, but it is still often used to describe the major officer who is responsible for student life and who reports to a vice president or vice chancellor. Finally, there are a declining number of institutions in both the private and public sectors that use the combination title dean and vice president to mean the chief student affairs officer.

As student affairs programs mature and expand their influence over the direction and development of the college or university, it is important that professional staff members, especially the chief student affairs officer, increase their knowledge and skill in developing effective administrative systems and internal organizational structures. Sandeen observes:

Effective student affairs managers will want organizations that encourage open communications among departments, enable students and faculty to participate in them, and keep the CSAO well informed about issues and problems. . . . The organization of the division should be clear and understandable to those outside student affairs as well as to the staff itself. Reporting lines should be unambiguous and should reflect real responsibility and authority . . . . The organizational chart is not just an inert piece of paper used once per year in an annual report. It should be an accurate description of how the CSAO wants the division to operate, a dynamic instrument that changes as the needs of the campus dictate [Sandeen, 1991, pp. 92–93].

Guiding Principles of Student Affairs Organization and Management

Earlier, a rationale was suggested for using the administrative or corporate model for student affairs' internal management systems. The rationale is based on five assumptions that reflect the history of the profession and the political realities in which it operates:

First, the effective development and delivery of services and programs are the historical and legitimate basis of the profession and its only viable means of accomplishing its educational goals. . . . Second, there is no inherent conflict or dichotomy between the profession's administrative orientation and its educational and developmental goals. . . . Third, in order to effect desired educational outcomes, student services must be effectively managed and coordinated with academic programs and services. . . . Fourth, identification with the administrative structure permits student services to influence policy formulation and resource allocation to effect its educational goals. . . . Fifth, the administrative model provides the student services profession with the greatest flexibility for responding to student and institutional needs and with the ability to reach large segments of the student population [Ambler, 1989, pp. 250–251].

Once the student affairs professional appreciates the basis of the administrative model in higher education, some guiding principles can be established that will be useful in the development of effective internal management systems. These principles have evolved as much from the observation and practice of the profession as they have from any systematic study of administrative theory and practice.

Origins of Organizational Structures

Organizational structures are more the result of history and personality than any particular administrative or management theory (see Chapter Seven). As Sandeen (1989) suggests, few if any executives are given a clean slate when developing their organization. The history of the institution, its mission, the personalities and competencies of its people, its environment, and other such nonobjective factors have all played an important part in developing the unique character of the structure of an institution. A wise administrator takes cognizance of such factors in planning any organizational change.

Role

The desired or ascribed role of the CSAO is the single most important factor in shaping the design of the division of student affairs. If the institution desires that the chief student affairs officer function as a member of the executive management team, then the internal administrative structure of the division must be developed to permit that role. (Of course, chief student affairs officers are sometimes given the vice-presidential title without the expectation that they will be more than a chief counselor of students or a cocurricular policeman.) Regardless of the title used, such executive images will necessarily dictate their own supporting organizational structure.

Symmetry

Organizational symmetry is important internally and externally to the efficient operation of a student affairs division. Organizational symmetry suggests that officers of an organization holding positions of similar importance or value should be located in the same administrative stratum. Traditionally, great importance is attached to good communication up and down the organizational structure. However, equally important is the horizontal interaction and integration of the various units within the division and the ability of student affairs officers to relate on an even footing to their counterparts in other sectors of the university. The group of middle managers reporting to the chief student affairs officer must perceive themselves as equals, even if their titles suggest otherwise, if voluntary integration of services and cooperative programming is to occur. (See Chapter Nine in this volume.) Individuals holding the title personnel dean must feel some kinship with their academic counterparts if genuine coordination of student services with academic instruction is to be realized. However, student affairs officers should be cautious in assigning titles that may not reflect the true status of the position or that undermine organizational symmetry.

Stability

Organizational stability and permanence have virtue. Although organizations must be dynamic and capable of change in responding to new challenges and opportunities, important advantages accrue in maintaining some stability over time regarding the structure, titles, and administrative responsibilities of the various student affairs programs. With the advent of coeducation and the women's equality movement, the student affairs profession was quick to retire the time-honored titles of dean of men and dean of women. In retrospect, it has taken the profession some time to recover some of the institutional identity and perceived prestige that it lost in the process. Today's deans of student services and student development probably do not have the same kind of identity and respect as their predecessors. When a unit has developed a history and reputation for good service, a student affairs officer should be cautious about initiating precipitate or superficial organizational changes.

Autonomy

Organizational autonomy must be balanced with program integration. The value of permitting individual administrative units to achieve a high degree of organizational independence is constantly debated. Clearly, this practice usually promotes responsibility and creativity; yet the danger of isolation from the needs of students and other services and insensitivity to the larger picture are always possible. An effective chief administrator devises systems and strategies to prevent one unit from becoming oblivious to other units and needs. Functional interdependence of units within the division must be balanced with concern for the integrity of individual units.

Staff Involvement

Individual staff members must have a part in designing the organizational structures in which they will be expected to operate. The corporate model is frequently described as a "top-down" model with little latitude for individual participation. However, a good administrator clearly understands the need to make allowances for individual differences and participation. Such involvement in the design and development of the organizational structure is possible without fear of administrative anarchy. In conceptualizing organizational structures, a wise chief administrator will draw broad parameters and allow subordinates to fill in most of the missing details. Encouraging participation in organization design releases creativity and ensures a sense of responsibility for the outcome.

Importance of Titles

Titles are important both to people and to institutions. The student affairs profession has not been fortunate enough to instate consistent and recognizable titles similar to those used by faculty and academic administrators. As we have seen, moreover, the field has a historical proclivity for bestowing esoteric names on its functions and officers. This situation, coupled with many organizational changes, has created considerable confusion for the profession. Assigning titles that are descriptive and simple but that reflect the value of the position and the function should be a goal of every chief student affairs officer. Developing some consensus regarding student affairs nomenclature should become an objective of national student affairs professional organizations.

Organizational Structures

Student affairs organizational structures should be viewed as efficient communications systems with a primary goal of minimizing violations of the organization's integrity. As stated previously, effective communication across the division, as well as up and down the structure, should be a major factor in organizational design. A clear sign of a defective organization is when the classic "end run" becomes a necessary or accepted behavior. The chief student affairs officer must have a system and a style that permit communications to flow in various directions without risking offense to individuals or to the organization. It should be possible for the chief executive to listen to the person on the lowest rung of the organizational ladder.

Models of Internal Management Structures for Student Affairs

On first examination of more than one hundred student affairs divisions at public and private colleges and universities across the country, there seem to be numerous unique and varied organizational structures. This research appears to confirm the principle that organizational structures are indeed a product of institutional history and personality. Upon analysis, however, four basic models emerge as common organizational formats in all kinds of institutions. Many of the more complex and comprehensive student affairs programs, however, represent a hybrid of several of these basic models. The four basic formats can be characterized as those based on (1) revenue sources, (2) the affinity of programs and services, (3) an infrastructure of staff associates, and (4) direct CSAO supervision of all student affairs offices.

The Revenue Source Model

This model is more common in public universities, where a more complete separation of revenue sources is frequently mandated by state statute. Auxiliary units in public universites are often required to pay all costs associated with a program from its unit revenue stream. Examples include bond debt, utilities, maintenance, and staff salaries in other agencies that provide services to the auxiliary program. Educational and general funds and tuition revenue cannot be used to support auxiliary activities. Similarly, excess revenue and reserve funds generated by auxiliary units may not be used for other functions of the institution. Though many private colleges and universities maintain similar separated funds, these institutions appear to be less concerned about the differentiation of revenue sources as "comingling" of funds is sometimes permissible and desirable.

How services are organized using this model will depend on the number of auxiliary units involved, the financial restrictions and requirements of each service, the amount of funds involved, and the extent of other student affairs functions that are funded by the general or state-appropriated budget of the institution. If there are a number of large, separate, and complex auxiliary units involved, the director of each unit may report directly to the chief student affairs officer. Agency heads, holding responsibility for general or state-funded operations, usually also are in a direct reporting relationship. A more simplified version would be two associates responsible for the two different revenue strands reporting to the chief student affairs officer.

This model is relatively new because only in recent years have many chief student affairs officers been given responsibility for the financial management of auxiliary services. These often include housing, student unions, health services, food services, and book stores. It is not uncommon for the management of these auxiliary or restricted-use funds to represent 80 percent or more of the chief student affairs officer's fiscal responsibility. Put in that context, the viability and popularity of this model are easily understood. It has the primary advantage of direct accountability for these important financial functions. Because programmatic responsibility is also included, the chief student affairs officer can ensure that the program or service operates on a unified philosophy, balancing student needs and financial requirements. The format's basic disadvantage is the disproportionate amount of time that the CSAO must spend on financial matters, sometimes at the neglect of other student life concerns.

The Affinity of Services Model

In those student affairs divisions where the services and programs offered are quite numerous and diverse, the affinity model is perhaps the most common. Services are clustered by the nature or similarity of their purpose, usually along the lines of some standard taxonomy or classification of services. A popular set of classifications for this model would include (1) enrollment services (admissions, records, financial aid, registration, orientation), (2) student life (student activities, discipline, residential programs, Greek organizational advising), (3) student services (counseling, placement, foreign-student services, remedial services), and (4) auxiliary services (student housing, student unions, health service, bookstore).

In this organizational model, specialists responsible for each cluster of services will generally report to the CSAO. They may go by the title of personnel deans, associate or assistant vice presidents, or some other descriptive, executive-level title. Each supervisor becomes an expert on the services in that area or cluster and maintains a certain degree of autonomy in fulfilling the responsibilities of the position. The chief student affairs officer will often rely on these subordinates to provide information and advice on the status or needs of the various services or to ensure that they are well coordinated with the other units in the division. The model permits the CSAO to exercise executive control over all the functions assigned to the division of student affairs while being free to participate in central university management functions. Specialization remains the fundamental feature and chief virtue of this model. Advocates argue that the high-tech nature of our society will require even greater degrees of specialization, and this model thus reflects those realities. The executive nature of the chief student affairs officer position works to assure that the efforts of the unit specialists are integrated and consistent with the student development goals of the organization.

Several potential problems are associated with the affinity of services model. Most obvious is a highly elongated and bureaucratic structure. The chief student affairs officer is at some distance from the various services in the division and runs the danger of becoming isolated from staff and student concerns. Communication becomes a constant concern, and decisions affecting a variety of activities are delayed because of the difficulty in cross-unit consultation. Specialization frequently creates problems of territorial boundaries. In spite of these inherent problems, however, it remains the most common model at large public and private universities.

The Staff Associates Model

As a compromise between the elongated, bureaucratic model and the "flat" organizational plan associated with direct supervision, this approach permits the chief student affairs officer to provide general leadership to the various units within the division, while controlling technical and administrative tasks through a cadre of staff assistants. Such associates operate in staff capacities and exercise little or no line authority. They may function with such titles as assistant, associate, coordinator, or staff specialist. They usually specialize in such areas as budgeting, personnel, program development, research, or systems development and create an infrastructure of services that support the division as well as the chief student affairs officer.

These staff associates or specialists are readily available to assist the various line officers as necessary. The staff associates will frequently meet with several unit heads to resolve a mutual problem, plan a common program, or mediate a conflict. Likewise, they meet with the chief student affairs officer to provide data and advice about their area of competence, particularly as it affects the whole division. They may also assist the CSAO in performing central university administrative functions.

This model has the primary advantage of permitting the CSAO to maintain close contact with each unit and furnish leadership for program development and integration. It makes possible the technical and specialized assistance that unit leaders need without encumbering the chief student affairs officer. Specialization is possible without creating artificial territorial boundaries between units. Finally, the chief student affairs officer can function with ease as part of the executive management of the institution.

Disadvantages must also be noted. Staff associates can frequently become power brokers within the organization. When this occurs, the staff function appears to assume line authority, and this is frustrating and confusing to line officers. Units tend to be treated in fragments as no one staff associate can deal with a problem comprehensively or conclusively. Because of the high degree of specialization and the loyalty of the staff associates to the CSAO, it is difficult for a unit head to appeal an action successfully to that level.

The Direct Supervision Model

Usually found in units with a limited number of programs and services or where the chief student affairs officer plays only a minor role in institutional management, the "flat" or direct supervision model is a fast-disappearing operational plan. The expanding scope of responsibilities in student affairs, the complexity of student needs, and the multiple roles of the chief student affairs officer have spelled the doom of the traditional relationships that this model represents. Yet it has its virtues; some long for its return.

Under this approach, all student services units report directly to the chief. Assistant vice presidents or assistant deans fulfill staff functions only, and regular contact between the chief and the unit directors is possible. The chief becomes both a generalist and a specialist in the areas that compose the division of student affairs. Communications are complete, and decision-making channels are clearly identified and understood. The chief student affairs officer is well known to staff, other colleagues, and students.

As suggested above, the primary disadvantage of this model is that there are few institutional settings today where it can be effectively implemented. Few chief student affairs officers are afforded the luxury of operating in such an uncomplicated fashion. Add one or two institutional management functions to the responsibilities of the chief, and the need for a different organizational model is triggered.

Summary

As the survey of the student affairs organizational structures at major American colleges and universities reveals, the profession has recently been developing effective delivery systems for services and programs to meet the contemporary needs of students. No one organizational model can be imposed on all the unique institutions that make up American higher education. Four major internal organizational structures have emerged in student affairs units: the revenue source model, the affinity of services model, the staff associates model, and the direct supervision model. Each has strengths and weaknesses, and careful analysis of the institutional context is required before choosing any one approach. The profession must continue to enhance its understanding of administrative science if it is to remain viable in the high-tech, fast-paced world of the next century. Projecting that future, Barr and Albright suggest, "All student affairs organizations must define clear roles and purposes consistent with the missions of their institutions, and they must resolve issues of organizational uncertainty and professional identity if student affairs is to prosper (1990, p. 197). And Kuh reminds us, "As professionals, we owe it both to ourselves and to our student clients that we make nothing less than our best effort to understand and use the organization to pursue the institution's purpose while maintaining a clear focus on the raison d'être of student affairs, encouraging students' development" (1983, p. 77).

References

Ambler, D. "The Administrator Role." In U. Delworth, G. R. Hanson, and Associates, *Student Services: A Handbook for the Profession.* (2nd ed.) San Francisco: Jossey-Bass, 1989.

Appleton, J. R., Briggs, C. M., and Rhatigan, J. J. *Pieces of Eight.* Portland, Oreg.: National Association of Student Personnel Administrators Institute of Research and Development, 1978.

Argyris, C. *Integrating the Individual and the Organization.* New York: Wiley, 1964.

Barr, M. J., and Albright, R. L. "Rethinking the Organizational Role of Student Affairs." In M. J. Barr, M. L. Upcraft, and Associates, *New Futures for Student Affairs: Building a Vision for Professional Leadership and Practice.* San Francisco: Jossey-Bass, 1990.

Galbraith, J. *Designing Complex Organizations.* Reading, Mass.: Addison-Wesley, 1973.

Knock, G. H. "Development of Student Services in Higher Education." In M. J. Barr, L. A. Keating, and Associates, *Developing Effective Student Services Programs: Systematic Approaches for Practitioners.* San Francisco: Jossey-Bass, 1985.

Kuh, G. D. "Tactics for Understanding and Improving Student Affairs Organizations." In G. D. Kuh (ed.), *Understanding Student Affairs Organizations.* New Directions for Student Services, no. 23. San Francisco: Jossey-Bass, 1983.

Lawler, E. E., III. *High-Involvement Management: Participative Strategies for Improving Organizational Structures.* San Francisco: Jossey-Bass, 1986.

Myers, E. M., and Topping, J. R. "Information Exchange Procedures Activity Structure." Technical Report, no. 63. Boulder, Colo.: National Center for Higher Education Management Systems, Western Interstate Commission for Higher Education, 1974.

Sandeen, A. "Issues Influencing Organization." In U. Delworth, G. R. Hanson, and Associates, *Student Services: A Handbook for the Profession.* (2nd ed.) San Francisco: Jossey-Bass, 1989.

Sandeen, A. *The Chief Student Affairs Officer: Leader, Manager, Mediator, Educator.* San Francisco: Jossey-Bass, 1991.

Schein, E. H. *Organizational Culture and Leadership: A Dynamic View.* San Francisco: Jossey-Bass, 1985.

9

✌

The Role of
the Middle Manager

Donald B. Mills

To paraphrase Charles Dickens, middle management is the best of jobs, it is the worst of jobs. Middle managers frequently have significant responsibility but may not have final authority. They implement policy but may not always feel an integral part of the decision-making process. They often supervise other staff, but final decisions about staffing levels and compensation may be made by others. But even with these limitations, the middle manager plays a vital role in the student affairs function on the campuses of institutions of higher education.

This chapter will discuss the parameters of the middle management role in student affairs and the responsibilities and issues associated with it. The importance of developing positive relationships with subordinates and supervisors will be examined. Career and mobility questions will be presented, and the chapter concludes with recommendations for effective practice as a middle manager.

Defining Middle Management in Student Affairs

A precise definition of what constitutes a middle manager proves to be as elusive as developing an exact definition of middle age. Clearly, there are differences between entry-level staff members and executive-level administrators. But where do the middle managers fit, and what do they do?

One place to start is to examine an organizational chart. Young indicates that middle managers provide support services and other administrative duties linking vertical and horizontal levels of an organizational hierarchy (1990). Allison and Allison declare that a middle management position is the first rung on a career, rather than just a job (1984). A middle manager always provides supervision of programs (Young, 1990). Depending on institutional size, middle managers may also supervise staff. The work is fundamentally different from that of a junior staff member.

Because of their position in the organizational hierarchy, middle managers implement and interpret policy but do not create it. Policy decisions are generally the prerogative of executive-level administrators. Middle managers most often have influence, however, in those decisions directly influencing their area of expertise and responsibility. In contrast to lower-level management staff, the middle manager may not be in direct contact with students but may have a primary relationship with staff.

Positions in student affairs that would be classified as middle management include directors and associate directors of functional departments, facilities, and programs such as admissions, residence life, counseling center, student center, alcohol education, and recreation.

Managing Information

Drucker has indicated that industry's definition of a middle manager as responsible for the production of goods and services is no longer a complete one. Whereas the traditional middle manager was in charge of carrying out production routines, management responsibilities have evolved so that now the middle manager has the added role of knowledge professional (Drucker, 1974). This concept is transferred easily to student affairs and higher education.

Like organizations everywhere, the importance of information in student affairs can not be underestimated. As institutions of higher education have grown increasingly complex, the need for gathering and interpreting information has become more important. Successful institutions adapt to changing environmental conditions. Such conditions can be determined only by accurate information. Therefore, the middle manager can assure the success of programs and services only by receiving information and making decisions based on an appropriate interpretation of it. The implication is that managing information is as integral to the middle manager's job as supervising and as providing programs for students, faculty, and staff.

Types of essential information include demographic data for admissions, retention, housing, and financial aid. In addition, changes in student life-styles affect virtually all student affairs departments, and economic conditions of the society influence programs like food and health services and the student employment or placement center. Successful managing of data and data collection will maximize the ability of the middle manager to serve students well.

Managing Funds

Perhaps the most obvious use of information is involved in managing funds. As these either become more scarce or have more stringent accountability requirements, the middle manager must not only understand changing conditions but must also develop alternative means of supporting programs.

The budget is the basic planning document for the middle manager. The process of creating an annual budget requires setting programmatic priorities, evaluating staffing needs, and determining levels of material support necessary to accomplish objectives. After budgets have been approved, it is the middle manager's responsibility to execute departmental objectives within them. Funds must be spent for the purpose for which they were budgeted. Changing priorities within a fiscal year should occur only in unusual circumstances and with approval of executive-level officers. Failure to maintain budget integrity has a significant impact on the entire division of student affairs and the institution.

Regardless of the most careful budgeting, situations arise when funds available differ from estimates used in budgeting. The effective middle manager will have contingency plans ready. If priorities have been established clearly during the budget process, then the programs and services to be deferred during a shortage of funds should easily be determined. In the instance of surplus funds (admittedly more rare), the middle manager should have programs and services identified that could usefully be added to those already existing.

Managing funds, however, also means maintaining an accurate record of expenditures (and income, if appropriate) throughout the fiscal year. Financial reviews should occur on a regular and relatively frequent basis. Midyear corrections due to unexpected expenditures should be initiated by the middle manager. If the middle manager does not make a regular, careful review of financial status, then corrections will be imposed by higher management.

Influencing the Culture

The middle manager in student affairs has a unique opportunity to understand and change the culture of an institution. By their nature, academic programs are composed of particular knowledge and fields; by contrast, administrative functions are more specific to the institution. Additionally, frequent interaction with students places the profession's middle managers in a unique position to hear institutional myths and traditions and to gain access to institutional information. All these are items that play a part in defining the institutional culture. A skilled middle manager in student affairs processes and shares such information in order to assist in solving problems.

Kuh and Whitt (1988) provide valuable insight in understanding the complexity of the culture of institutions of higher education, and middle managers will profit from reading their work.

At the center of the culture of higher education, however, is the academic enterprise. Faculties sometimes maintain that the functions performed by middle managers in student affairs take funds from necessary academic programs. Yet the astute middle manager can develop positive and fruitful relationships with the faculty. Even though the institutional culture may have an academic core, middle managers can still be in the best position to understand that culture.

Managing a Career

Executive-level positions will usually be filled from the ranks of the middle manager. Because of this potential for advancement, middle managers must be conscious of the career aspects of a position, not just the job requirements (Allison and Allison, 1984). Of course, not all of these managers want to be promoted to an executive level. Whatever their ultimate career decision—movement up the organization or the equally important role of increasing skills and competency at the current job level—a path and goals must be established.

Benke and Disque (1990) describe the difficulty of promotion for the middle manager in higher education. Typically, the higher education hierarchy is organized as a pyramid with many jobs at the base and fewer positions as one moves up the organization. Although this situation is true of other organizations as well, in higher education the concept of a career ladder is not well defined and the number of midrange positions compared to entry-level positions is limited. Further, the means of promotion in institutions is often ill defined (Young, 1990). It is therefore incumbent upon a middle manager to make deliberate decisions about career aspirations. Individuals should establish career and personal objectives, determine the additional training or information necessary to advance, and develop an individual career plan (Allison and Allison, 1984).

Advancement to executive levels in student affairs also requires another important decision on the part of the middle manager. The chief student affairs officer has a general control over a broad range of functional areas. The typical middle manager has specific responsibilities. In preparing for advancement, the middle manager must determine whether a career path should include experience in several areas or a concentration in just one (Allison and Allison, 1984).

Several issues must be considered when planning a career. Factors include individual choice (individual desires, goals, and life-styles), institutional promotion practices and criteria, and economic conditions (supply and demand). Recognition that promotions can be won both by staying within an organization and by moving to another institution is important in determining career path (Young, 1990).

Role Issues for Middle Management

The middle manager must resolve many issues to function effectively within the organization, including: scope of authority, supervision responsibilities, and the importance of staff development.

Authority

Questions of power and authority arise. What can the middle manager decide, and what must receive approval from a higher authority? Should decisions be approved before implementation, or is notification of them appropriate? These questions are especially difficult to resolve when the middle manager has recently been appointed to the position.

Role ambiguity occurs when there is a conflict between expectations and the actual issues that confront the middle manager. Drucker indicates that an efficient organization demands clear decision-making authority. The participants in the process must agree on what determinations can be made and at what level. Unless authority for them is precisely articulated, confusion will result (1974). The responsibility for clarifying any questions rests with both the middle manager and the supervisor. However, experience indicates that the clarification should be initiated by the middle manager as the results are more critical to his or her performance.

The question of power is fraught with ambiguity. Although power has its roots in authority, it has many other dimensions of importance to the middle manager. The organizational chart and clarification of authority will create guidelines, but the middle manager must also recognize the power that comes from a variety of sources. In addition to those that are structural elements of a student affairs division (position, budget, size of staff), other sources of power include knowledge, skills, longevity at the institution, and strength of personality. Additionally, some individuals are able to stop projects (passive power) even though their position in the institution is outside student affairs. Recognition of those who have influence greater than their position would indicate will assist the middle manager in determining how to make decisions within the power structure (Allison and Allison, 1984; see also Chapter Five).

Supervision of Staff

Managing staff is a critical element of the middle manager's responsibility. Although it is never an easy task, it is frequently the most rewarding. As stated previously, entry-level staff members work primarily with students, but the middle manager probably works most closely with staff. The ability to manage staff successfully is generally the determinant of success for the middle manager.

In acting as a supervisor, the middle manager must be more than a manipulator; he or she must be a leader. The middle manager must develop the skills of motivation, delegation, performance appraisal, and staff selection.

In essence, any manager accomplishes goals by working through others. Therefore, inspiring staff to accomplish goals is the essential task of management. Carr (1989) suggests that managers cannot do their other jobs and be constantly "motivating." Only staff members can motivate themselves, so the manager's job is to create an environment in which excellent work will prove beneficial to staff. Congruence must exist between what the student affairs division needs and how staff members are rewarded. Staff should be commended for good work and highly rewarded for great work. Mediocre work does not deserve special acknowledgment. Further, the manager has the responsibility to assure that a person's skills and interests are appropriate for the task to be accomplished.

Salary is one form of reward, but not the only one. Other forms include praise, more challenging work assignments, autonomy, and a pleasant work environment. The good manager understands what is important to each staff person. A necessary and effective reward is to involve staff in setting objectives and priorities. Failure to take critical motivating factors into account can lead to diminished work quality (Carr, 1989).

Careful delegation frees the manager to do the job of managing and allows staff the role of accomplishing specific tasks. Three principles are central. First, both responsibility and authority for work should be delegated, and certain boundaries must be clearly understood. Second, middle managers must delegate only what a staff person is ready to handle. Third, they must keep abreast of the items that have been delegated (Carr, 1989).

Performance appraisals are one of the middle manager's most useful tools. Brown (1988) recommends that performance appraisal be approached the way a coach views working with a player or a mentor with a student. It is designed to improve performance and to enhance an individual's skills. Appraisal should be conducted consistently as part of the developmental process for staff. Lack of a formal approach to performance appraisal leads to a system that does not improve morale, appears biased, and may be considered ineffective. A successful program provides the manager with information that can be used to improve performance, determine goals, and evaluate progress (Brown, 1988).

The process of staff selection is obviously key to good staff performance. A well-developed position description is the first condition for hiring competent staff. (See Chapter Ten for a complete discussion of these issues.)

Staff Development

Staff development is a necessary aspect of the middle manager's work. Programs should be designed that not only improve skills but also challenge individuals intellectually and philosophically. Staff members must be made to feel that they are not stagnating but are continuing to grow. Staff development can occur through formal programs, individual mentoring, performance appraisals, and self-directed learning (Bryan and Mullendore, 1990). (Part Four of this volume discusses in detail the full range of staff development options.)

The middle manager should consider encouraging staff to continue formal education. The development of communication and critical-thinking skills is always an addition to the group. Further, involvement in research and exposure to a breadth of knowledge will provide valuable support to the middle manager (Young, 1990). The value placed on scholarship within the academy will translate into an improved image of the division of student affairs as the educational levels of staff members increase.

Finally, a commitment to a comprehensive staff development plan for staff members in a unit is in the manager's best interest. Drucker indicates that one criterion for promotion of a middle manager is whether or not staff members in the unit are prepared to fill the midmanagement role, at least on a temporary basis (1974).

Relationships with the Supervisor

Just as the relationship with those being supervised is crucial to the success of the middle manager, so too is the relationship with the supervisor—most generally the chief or associate chief student affairs officer. The quality of that connection is dependent on a number of factors. As stated previously, a clear authority structure is critical to the middle manager and the whole functional unit. In addition, the person who will make decisions in an emergency situation when the chief student affairs officer may not be present must be clearly designated. Although emergencies cannot be predicted in advance, the responsibility to respond to them can be preassigned (Drucker, 1974; see also Chapter Twenty).

Responsibility

Although there is a close link between authority and responsibility, there are distinct differences as well. Middle managers may have both responsibility and authority in some areas, but they are also charged with implementing decisions from a higher level. The unpopular message as well as the popular one is often delivered by the middle manager. The middle manager may have to bear the brunt of such a decision, but it is inappropriate to transfer the responsibility for management decisions to the supervisory level. Developing an ability to handle unpopular decisions assists the manager in confronting the inevitable difficulties that are part of management.

Communication

It is especially useful for the middle manager to provide information about issues not related to student affairs. An effective student affairs division will interact with units across campus, and keeping the chief student affairs officer informed about these relationships is most important. There must be constant communication between the middle manager and the chief student affairs officer. The supervisor should never be surprised by events on campus. Even though unforeseen problems will develop, middle managers must try to keep the supervisor up to date. It is equally true that the chief student affairs officer should work to keep middle managers well informed about issues being discussed at the executive level.

The communication system should encompass both formal and informal routes. Regularly scheduled, frequent meetings are important, but informal communication is important as well. The middle manager should use all forms of communication, including the phone, written reports, and memorandums. Communication should cover both the status of present conditions and also future issues, goals, and plans. These will form a basis for new programs and activities with ongoing guidance from and approval of the supervisor. Any concerns will be resolved before extensive work has been completed. Work will progress in a more orderly and efficient fashion when communication is open and frequent.

Accountability

The middle manager must be accountable to a variety of constituencies — a difficult balancing act as there are competing needs associated with each. Among these constituencies are students, supervised staff, the chief student affairs officer, colleagues, and the institution itself. These competing groups and individuals require a different level of accountability and especially that the midmanager set priorities. It may not be possible to please all constituencies, but acting responsibly toward the institution and chief student affairs officer will almost always assure that other constituencies are taken care of.

A relationship also exists between accountability and authority. To be accountable for performance, middle managers must have the authority to control the functions for which they are answerable. This requirement does not diminish the function of the chief student affairs officer; rather, it is a positive statement of the necessity to clarify lines of control and authority (Drucker, 1974). The need for control reinforces the importance of regular communication with the chief student affairs officer.

Middle Manager as Politician

The middle manager by definition serves between other institutional managers. The nature of the position thus requires that political skills be honed and employed as part of the work routine. It should be noted that the word *politician,* as used in this context, carries neither positive nor negative connotations. It is merely a statement of a specific type of necessary skill. (See Chapter Eleven for a discussion of political issues.)

Decision Making

Every middle manager must develop a style for making decisions. Obviously, all these are made within an environmental context. Hersey and Blanchard (1972) indicate that the style of decision making is dependent on the qualities present in those who make up the organization. The middle manager must make judgments about what style best suits the situation. The goal is to choose the style that produces the most effective results. It becomes an important task to assess staff members accurately to determine their readiness to participate in decisions.

Some would maintain that a democratic approach is the most fair way to make decisions, but that is impossible in a bureaucratic organization. The majority does not rule. However, the more a middle manager can share responsibility for decision making, the more staff members are willing to support decisions and are motivated to achieve common objectives. Involvement is dependent on factors such as experience, staff attitudes, executive staff attitudes, the guidelines for the decision, the amount of time available, and preferred style (Allison and Allison, 1984). Of course, one should not confuse involvement with authority; decisions must still rest with appropriate levels of the organization. Still, effective middle managers will seek ways to share responsibility with both their staffs and their chief student affairs officers.

Competition

The middle manager may choose to seek advancement within the student affairs division or within the institution. Although it is generally true that decisions for advancement are based on ability, political aspects are also present. Most student affairs organizations are not blatantly political, but they too have their grapevines.

Advancement within the existing structure can occur in three ways. First, a vacancy occurs at a position above the present level, and the middle manager is promoted. Second, the middle manager has assumed more responsibility and has demonstrated worth to the organization beyond what was expected. A position may then be created to promote the middle manager. Third, the middle manager may move to other responsibilities that bring new opportunities and challenges within the organization. In any case, the middle manager must have a career track in mind, a plan to achieve career goals (including additional education, if necessary), and a commitment to the performance levels necessary for advancement (Allison and Allison, 1984).

For advancement to occur, one must also become known to the administrative decision makers. The best means of increasing visibility is to perform at a high level. Volunteering for institutionwide responsibilities provides that opportunity. Institutional culture and traditions will also determine to a great extent how middle managers interact with those at the top.

Middle managers may find themselves in competition with colleagues for advancement to senior-level positions. This competition should not be allowed to degenerate into an open political fight for the appointment. Neither the individuals nor the institution would benefit. White, Webb, and Young (1990) state that a significant amount of intrinsic support in a student affairs middle management position comes from colleagues. Support from within the institution is much more important to job satisfaction than that from colleagues outside the institution. Therefore, competition for a position can be a source of organizational and personal disruption. The professional attitude of all interested parties should deter the negative aspects of competition for advancement.

The middle manager must also serve as a mediator at times to control competition that may occur between members of the departmental staff. The successful middle manager must recognize and assist those seeking to elevate themselves, but their desire for advancement can never be allowed to come at the expense of another staff member.

Mobility

For many middle managers, respect from their superiors is a highly significant aspect of their positions. However, almost equally significant is a career commitment and a desire to move to more responsible positions. White, Webb, and Young (1990) state that most middle managers expect to relocate to achieve advancement. Movement to another institution seems to be required for many student affairs middle managers with fewer than ten years of experience who wish to advance. For those with more than sixteen years' experience, institutional loyalty has increased significantly, and advancement is often achieved by accruing more and varied responsibilities within the organization.

Benke and Disque (1990) report that the tenure of chief student affairs officers in their positions is increasing. Moreover, some institutions appoint faculty members to executive-level positions, a situation creating limited opportunities for advancement from midmanagement positions. Mobility then must be considered both within the institution and externally.

Though lateral moves may be seen as negative, there is evidence that the path to the chief student affairs office is smoothed by obtaining experience beyond a specific functional unit (Young, 1990). The middle manager interested in mobility would do well to investigate lateral moves as providing necessary experience for later opportunities.

Professional Development

The middle manager must seek means to develop new skills and competencies. Although these are key to advancement, Drucker argues that they are important for performance as well. He maintains, "We need . . . manager development precisely because tomorrow's jobs and tomorrow's organization can be assumed, with high probability, to be different from today's job and today's organization" (1974, p. 424). The effective middle manager will make new skills a priority.

This kind of development can come from a variety of sources. But a crucial aspect of the undertaking is the evaluation of which skills are to be developed. Both the National Association of Student Personnel Administrators and the American College Personnel Association have provided survey results indicating those skills and competencies that college presidents and chief student affairs officers consider important (Young, 1990). These include the ability to communicate with a variety of constituencies, analyze needs and create programs, establish policies, understand students, and select and train staff. Obviously, there are others unique to particular institutions, but those listed demonstrate the chief student affairs officer operates from a much more general point of view than the functional unit manager.

Professional associations can be critical for the mobility of middle managers. Not only do they provide opportunities to increase knowledge, develop new abilities, and learn of professional developments, but they can also be used to build networks with colleagues across the country or within a region. A network proves exceedingly useful to a person interested in moving to another institution as well as to someone attempting to understand the opportunities available for advancement. The placement centers operated by professional associations are of limited value; however, the informal network can be most helpful. Middle managers should be active in professional associations for several professional reasons, but forging links with colleagues is a major one. (See Chapter Twenty-Four for more information.)

Opportunities for formal education should not be dismissed by the middle manager. The doctorate is essential for advancement in many institutions. Further, it fosters improved communication and critical thinking skills, improves the ability to conduct research, and exposes the middle manager to a breadth of knowledge necessary for advancement (Young, 1990). (See Chapter Twenty-Seven for a more complete discussion.) For those who have completed their formal education, many associations and institutions of higher education offer seminars and training sessions designed to respond to critical issues in the field. These have both immediate and long-term benefits for the middle manager.

Some Career Issues

The midlife crisis has become a point of discussion in much of the popular literature of recent years. The scientific literature has also examined the transitions that coincide with middle age. During this time, adults examine careers and career aspirations, take a closer look at family and those relationships, and search for a sense of meaning to life (Schlossburg, Lynch, and Chickering, 1989). These issues are particularly relevant to the middle manager, especially one who has been in a position for several years. The middle manager is "likely to find himself in a spiritual crisis in his early or mid-forties. By that time the great majority will have reached, inevitably, their terminal positions. . . . .Suddenly their work will not satisfy them anymore" (Drucker, 1974, p. 420). The successful middle manager will seek ways to ensure a meaningful career.

Middle managers examine their relationship to employing institutions as they might ties to family. The motivation to continue in student affairs and to excel is frequently based on this relationship. The meaning of a position, and ultimately a career, has its roots in the fundamental relationship between the manager and the institution. Failure to find a satisfactory answer to the quest for meaning in the relationship often causes persons to seek career opportunities outside student affairs (White, Webb, and Young, 1990).

Those elements that create the most satisfaction throughout a career have been investigated by White, Webb, and Young (1990). They report that extrinsic sources are support from a supervisor, ability to develop or influence policy, the degree of authority in the position, salary, staff development opportunities, and support from colleagues outside the institution. Intrinsic sources of satisfaction are opportunities to influence students' development, flexibility and freedom to establish daily routine, variety of job responsibilities, freedom to control or change job responsibilities, respect from superiors, and respect from colleagues. An environment that makes possible these elements enhances job satisfaction for the middle manager and minimizes the likelihood of a career midlife crisis.

Summary

The role of middle managers in student affairs, as of those in other organizations, is difficult to define. The nature of the position almost assures ambiguity about the exact nature of responsibilities. However, middle managers can adopt several approaches to aid in achieving success.

First, they should define clearly for themselves the position, its authority, and its accountability. The middle manager and the supervisor should agree on this definition.

Second, middle managers should commit themselves to provide the best supervision of staff possible and to meet institutional goals and objectives.

Third, they must adopt a management style that helps staff members while enabling the managers to meet performance expectations.

Fourth, the relationship with the chief student affairs officer or other supervisor should be open and designed to enhance the middle manager's role in the institution.

Fifth, middle managers must take responsibility for personal development of new skills and competencies.

Sixth, they should be involved in professional associations to create a network of colleagues for assistance and support.

Seventh, they should establish a personal career path, with contingencies, to keep professional decisions in focus.

Eighth, middle managers should analyze those factors that provide job satisfaction and create situations where those can be exploited to the maximum extent.

The middle manager has a unique function in a student affairs program. Midlevel managers must select, train, and develop staff. They must implement policy and programs. They must furnish communication both up and down the organizational ladder. They may provide direction to a specific functional program and yet are expected to have an institutional view on issues. Finally, middle managers may have designs on a chief student affairs position, but a direct path to that position in one organization is unlikely.

Even with the ambiguities and seeming contradictions inherent in their positions, middle managers provide the leadership of functional areas that form the basis of student affairs programs. They are the knowledge professionals of student affairs programs and have an important influence on each student's development and that of staff members who will be the professional leaders of the next generation.

References

Allison, M. A., and Allison, E. *Managing Up, Managing Down.* New York: Simon & Schuster, 1984.

Benke, M., and Disque, C. S. "Moving In, Out, Up, or Nowhere? The Mobility of Mid-Managers." In R. B. Young (ed.), *The Invisible Leaders: Student Affairs Mid-Managers.* Washington, D.C.: National Association of Student Personnel Administrators, 1990.

Brown, R. D. "The Need for and Purpose of a Performance Appraisal System." In R. D. Brown (ed.), *Performance Appraisal as a Tool for Staff Development.* New Directions for Student Services, no. 43. San Francisco: Jossey-Bass, 1988.

Bryan, W. A., and Mullendore, R. H. "Professional Development Strategies." In R. B. Young (ed.), *The Invisible Leaders: Student Affairs Mid-Managers.* Washington, D.C.: National Association of Student Personnel Administrators, 1990.

Carr, C. *The New Manager's Survival Manual.* New York: Wiley, 1989.

Drucker, P. F. *Management: Tasks, Responsibilities, Practices.* New York: HarperCollins, 1974.

Hersey, P., and Blanchard, K. H. *Management of Organizational Behavior: Utilizing Human Resources.* Englewood Cliffs, N.J.: Prentice-Hall, 1972.

Kuh, G. D., and Whitt, E. J. *The Invisible Tapestry: Culture in American Colleges and Universities.* ASHE-ERIC Higher Education Report, no. 1. Washington, D.C.: Association for the Study of Higher Education, 1988.

Schlossberg, N.K., Lynch, A. Q., and Chickering, A. W. *Improving Higher*

Education Environments for Adults: Responsive Programs and Services from Entry to Departure. San Francisco: Jossey-Bass, 1989.

White, J., Webb, L., and Young, R. B. "Press and Stress: A Comparative Study of Institutional Factors Affecting the Work of Mid-Managers." In R. B. Young (ed.), *The Invisible Leaders: Student Affairs Mid-Managers.* Washington, D.C.: National Association of Student Personnel Administrators, 1990.

Young, R. B. "Defining Student Affairs Mid-Management." In R. B. Young (ed.), *The Invisible Leaders: Student Affairs Mid-Managers.* Washington, D.C.: National Association of Student Personnel Administrators, 1990.

10

∽

Selecting and Training
Competent Staff

Richard F. Stimpson

"Effective student affairs programs are built on competent staff. Student affairs is a very people-intensive enterprise, and our greatest strength, as well as our greatest potential liability, lies with staff members who work with students and design programs and services for them" (Barr, 1990, p. 160). Staff members are the critical variable in the success of the student affairs program. Thus, it is essential that student affairs administrators devote time and attention to the processes of staff selection and subsequent training of selected individuals.

In this chapter, the essential elements in designing sound staff selection processes will be discussed. These are complicated and colored by a variety of legal and ethical issues. It is hoped that the suggestions contained in this chapter will assist student affairs administrators in managing this responsibility. Attention is also given to the important process of integrating new staff members into the student affairs organization and the campus community as well as that of aiding new staff members in meeting their job responsibilities. Information will be presented throughout the chapter regarding the factors that those responsible for selection and training should consider as they meet these important obligations.

Selection and training are interdependent components of a human resources management program that also includes the maintenance of complete and up-to-date job descriptions and periodic performance evaluations. Each component contributes its part to successful employee performance.

Selection and training must be integrated properly within the overall management plan for each student affairs division. Fiscal resources need to be incorporated into budget submissions; dates must be reserved on management calendars so that time requirements for staff participation are recognized; planning for space reservations may be necessary; committee assignments must be made and a variety of administrative tasks completed if selection and training programs are to produce positive results. In addition, if management plans require staff members to possess additional or different skills, knowledge, and experience to implement new initiatives, modifications in both selection and training programs must be made to assure that individuals possess the characteristics needed to meet changed expectations. Effective implementation begins with the formulation of a well-written job description.

The Job Description as a Guide

The job description for a position should reflect a clear understanding of (1) the mission of the institution and the student affairs division, (2) the contribution of the staff position in question to the accomplishment of that mission, (3) the responsibilities assigned to the position, and (4) the activities a person holding the position will be expected to complete in meeting those responsibilities. To ensure effective performance, the employee and the supervisor should have the same understanding of the requirements. If necessary, changes in the job description should be initiated to make certain that agreement about performance expectations exists within the organization.

The job description should describe the position, clarify specific performance requirements, and state the amount of time to be devoted to the accomplishment of assigned responsibilities. Once developed, it should be used as the guide for the clarification of skills, knowledge, and experience that a staff member should possess in order to satisfy expectations. Without a clear grasp of these, it will be difficult if not impossible to design good selection and training programs.

To be most effective, an understanding of the attributes needed for successful job performance should be developed with the intended work setting (the location where performance is actually going to occur) clearly in mind. Accomplishing the responsibilities identified within a job description may require employee attributes that vary depending upon the particular work setting. For example, student affairs administrators are familiar with the differences in employee characteristics needed for successful performance in one residence hall versus another one or in a counseling center as opposed to a campus activities office. Appreciating such differences and reflecting them accurately in job descriptions are an essential endeavor.

It is important to keep in mind that a job description and the attributes necessary to complete a set of assigned responsibilities must be reevaluated and altered as trends influence institutional characteristics and performance expectations: for example, as the number of older students increase, as student populations become more diverse, or as changes in enrollment place added emphasis upon student retention. The skills, knowledge, and experience that student affairs professionals must possess may also change. As organizations respond to their evolving student populations and as job descriptions are modified accordingly, it will be necessary to adjust selection and training programs to assure that student affairs staff members continue to possess the characteristics needed for effective performance.

With an accurate job description in place and necessary employee attributes identified, responsible administrators are in a position to determine which abilities an employee can be expected to bring to a position and which should be developed through training. Selection programs must be developed to locate and hire individuals who possess the skills, competencies, and attitudes that are expected. Training programs must be designed to teach individuals to develop and apply their skills within the work setting. The rest of this chapter examines the course that should be taken to ensure that selection and training are implemented to achieve intended outcomes.

The Selection Committee

The steps leading to a final selection begin with the identification of the individual who will directly supervise the process and chair the team (committee) of individuals who will actually implement related activities. The chair should be appointed by the administrator who will be making the final hiring decision, if the position of chair is not filled by that administrator. Clearly, the chair should be familiar with the organization and have an appreciation for the importance of the responsibilities assigned to the committee. The individual should be a respected community member who will lend credibility to the selection process; he or she should also possess the skills necessary to motivate selection team members, organize selection activities, and impress prospective candidates.

Once a chair has been appointed, the involved administrator should make sure that the person is aware of the following information.

First, the chair must understand the organization's mission and responsibilities. A review of mission statements, organizational charts, budgets, annual reports, and the like will facilitate this process.

Second, the chair must have a clear sense of the position to be filled. He or she should undertake a complete review of the job description, the placement of the position within the organizational structure, and the skills, knowledge, and experience necessary to meet assigned responsibilities.

Third, the chair must be familiar with the principles and procedures that should be followed to assure fairness throughout the process. The affirmative action goals for the division and institution, the importance of consistent treatment of all candidates, and a review of why stated candidate qualifications (knowledge, education levels, experience, skills, personal characteristics) are relevant to successful job performance should be reviewed and thoroughly discussed. Specific attention should be given to the institution's affirmative action–equal employment guidelines. As a general principle, the courts are more concerned with the procedures involved in personnel searches than with their substance (Kaplin, 1985). The College and University Personnel Association has a variety of excellent resources that can help student affairs administrators conduct searches in a manner consistent with legal guidelines.

Fourth, the chair must fully understand the role the committee will play in the selection process. Limits on responsibility for identifying a certain number of finalists and the degree of participation in final hiring decisions should be considered and agreed upon.

Fifth, the chair must be aware of the desired schedule for completion of the selection process. There must be accord on dates and time lines. The budget and support staff available to assist in the management of the process and the support available for candidate (and spouse, if appropriate) travel, food, and lodging should be evaluated.

Finally, the chair should know the degree to which the administrator appointing the committee and making the final hiring decision expects to be kept informed and involved in the selection process.

Discussions that include topics such as these will assure that the chair has a well-developed understanding of the position and the expectations placed upon the committee and the selection process. In addition, they will provide an opportunity for the administrator and chair to establish an effective working relationship. These individuals should meet periodically throughout the process to exchange information, pursue answers to questions, and deal with issues that may arise.

Once the chair has established a working familiarity with the organization, the position, and the selection process, the administrator and chair are in a position to discuss committee composition. Although the committee needs to be of reasonable size, the number of its members will vary depending upon the breadth of responsibility assigned to the position or the range of interactions that the person holding the position is likely to have with other staff members or agencies. At a minimum, colleagues (peers) who will be working with the individual hired, students, and subordinates should be included. Committees should incorporate minorities, women, and others who represent the diversity of the student affairs staff and campus community. Further, if the position requires interaction with units elsewhere in the institution or direct interaction with faculty, individuals from these populations should also be included. In some instances — again depending upon the responsibilities assigned to the position — parent, alumni, or student government representatives should be included. In short, a general rule to follow in committee appointments is to include individuals to serve on behalf of all those with whom the selected individual must work.

Having finalized committee composition, the administrator should invite individuals to participate on the committee and call the initial committee meeting. At that session, he or she should take charge of introductions, present the committee's charge (its assigned responsibilities), discuss the job description and the position's place within the organization, and answer questions. The administrator should also carefully review the role of the committee, the importance of affirmative action, and the necessity for confidentiality.

The Role of the Committee

The administrator should explain the degree to which the committee is expected to be involved in the final selection decision. Will it advise, provide a list of finalists, give a ranking to its recommendations, or directly participate in the final decision? "Search committee members must be clear about their role in selecting finalists and making the job offer. As a rule it is usually best for the supervisor to reserve final authority for the hiring decision and to make sure at the outset that the committee members know that the supervisor has this authority, so that there is no misunderstanding" (Dalton, 1988, p. 336).

Regardless of its role, the committee should be provided with a rationale and given an opportunity to ask questions in order to clarify its assigned function and to minimize the chance of a misunderstanding as the process draws to a close. The issues associated with role clarification should be resolved by the administrator; they should not be left to the chair. Individuals who are uncomfortable with the function as defined should feel free to withdraw from the committee before the selection process gets under way.

Affirmative Action

Expectations for affirmative action should be handled in an open and frank discussion. Goals for affirmation action continue to be a topic of debate within society and on campuses throughout the country. Even when institutions have carefully formulated affirmative action plans and the rationale supporting them, individuals will retain differing views regarding certain aspects of the plan. Further, in some instances, some of those serving may wonder just how committed to affirmative action the administrator or other committee members are. Examination of the institution's expectations regarding openness, consistency of treatment, selection criteria (which should accurately reflect the skills, knowledge, and experience needed to meet job performance expectations), and recruitment efforts to locate qualified candidates from populations underrepresented within the division will help resolve differences and assist committee members in understanding and supporting the plan.

A common perspective regarding steps that can be taken to meet affirmative action objectives should be developed. A clear demonstration of support for the affirmative action plan by the administrator appointing the committee and that person's participation in the discussion of relevant issues should help to achieve this goal. Understanding and support may also be improved through the distribution of appropriate reading material. Good advice on the legal issues associated with the hiring process can be found in Seaquist (1988).

Confidentiality

Within the confines of committee sessions, it will obviously be necessary to share information about individuals, including assessments of their strengths and weaknesses as well as their previous successes and failures. The content of these discussions, names of candidates, and reactions to committee decisions should not be revealed outside the committee. When candidates are dropped from active consideration, committee members should refrain from "announcing" such decisions to colleagues or friends. This restraint is particularly important when in-house candidates who may not yet have been informed of committee actions are involved. The content of letters of recommendation or reference checks should not be discussed outside the committee. In short, the committee's business is forever confidential.

With an understanding of the position to be filled, of the performance expectations that the individual hired will need to meet, and of its own responsibilities, the committee is in a position to formulate and implement the selection process. It should be noted that although the discussion presented in this chapter assumes that a committee will be convened, the process that is described is applicable to other ways of selecting personnel.

Development of Position Announcement

Using the job description and information gathered from the administrator as points of reference, committee members should carefully craft a position announcement; this should state job responsibilities, salary range, application deadline, required application materials (résumé, completed application form, work sample, and so forth), the starting date for employment, and necessary qualifications. It is of particular importance that these qualifications be carefully defined and clearly stated. A review of the announcement should enable a candidate to decide if the position in question is of interest and whether he or she has the skills and experience to be a competitive candidate.

To make certain that the candidate pool is as broadly based as possible (that it includes women and underrepresented populations), the committee should be careful that the qualifications stated in the position announcement accurately reflect the characteristics necessary to perform successfully in the position. Qualifications (years of experience, degrees earned, and the like) should not be overstated. Yet it is equally inappropriate to understate qualifications in the position announcement and then pursue more rigorous qualifications later on. Either extreme can be avoided by being sure that the position announcement accurately reflects the performance requirements represented in the job description.

Posting the Position and Other Recruitment Initiatives

The extent of recruitment efforts should be defined by the nature of the position, the availability of a qualified pool of candidates within a particular geographic area, and the fiscal resources to support specific initiatives. For example, recruitment for undergraduate resident assistants would most likely be limited to the campus undergraduate population, whereas that for a budget officer or a student union assistant director might extend to a certain geographic region. If the pool of qualified candidates within an area is likely to be limited or if defined affirmative action goals require efforts to include underrepresented populations within the candidate pool, recruitment might be expanded to a nationwide basis; if funds are available, the search might include an extensive mailing and telephone initiative to encourage applications from designated populations.

Once the committee has clarified its recruitment goals, the most effective use should be made of media, mailings to professional associations, mailings to other institutions or colleagues, and listings at placement services offered by professional conventions. Committee members and other staff interested in the outcome of the process should pursue recruitment through personal contact with colleagues. Postings in journals or newsletters serving individuals who belong to targeted affirmative action populations should be initiated. Finally, current staff members within the institution where the opening exists should be fully informed of the position and encouraged to participate as candidates.

Review of Applications to Determine Qualified Candidate Pool

As interested candidates turn in their application materials, the committee needs to review each submission to determine those individuals who meet the posted qualifications. A screening form listing the stated qualifications (required and preferred) necessary to receive consideration should be developed and used by those reviewing applications. This form will help assure uniform consideration of each candidate's submission. The candidates who meet these criteria will often exceed the number of individuals who can be brought to campus for a complete interview. In such cases, the pool should be narrowed by placing those candidates who meet required and preferred qualifications in one group; those who only meet required qualifications should be held for possible consideration if the first group does not yield an adequate candidate pool.

As the process unfolds, it is important to keep candidates fully informed of their status. Those eliminated after an initial screening and those with an "on-hold" status should be kept informed. Professional etiquette requires regular updates to each candidate. Further, institutional reputation and the willingness of colleagues to be candidates in the future dictate such action as well. Those continuing as active candidates should be provided a contact person to call if they have questions about the process.

If the list of active candidates needs to be further narrowed, a telephone interview should be pursued as a reasonably cost-effective screening technique. This interview should occur at a time prearranged with the candidate. At least two committee members should complete each interview so that more than one perspective is considered.

At the point that telephone interviews or subsequent on-campus visits are planned, questions for use during these interviews should be designed and their appropriateness discussed. In order to assure that information exists that can be used to compare candidates, each person should be asked the same questions. Those that are discriminatory in nature must be avoided. For example, candidates should not be asked about race, religion, sexual orientation, age, marital status, and political views. Questions related to such issues as physical condition, military experience, other commitments, and organizational memberships may only be asked if they are directly related to some aspect of job performance and should clearly be avoided if they suggest a discriminatory bias.

In addition to formulating standard questions, the committee should take the time to develop unique questions to be asked during each interview. They should be designed to elaborate on points that a candidate makes in his or her written application or résumé, to gather information that the candidate failed to provide, or to explore a particularly interesting or confusing point.

Formal Interview Processes

With completed applications (and the information available from any telephone interviews) in hand, the committee is in a position to determine who should be invited for on campus interviews. These interviews are the most visible and important part of the selection process for both the candidate and the committee. It is at this point that the candidate has an opportunity to learn about the position and the institution firsthand, and the committee is able to evaluate the candidate's credentials and characteristics face to face.

Prior to the campus visit, candidates should be provided with written material to help orient them to the position, organization, and campus. Organizational charts, student handbooks, and sections of annual reports would be helpful. Further, interviews should be scheduled to include sufficient time for both the candidate and the committee to learn from and about each other. In fact, the very best candidates will reconsider their interest in a particular position if they do not have a chance to pursue questions and gather information.

Good decisions result when a well-developed and mutual understanding exists between candidates and their prospective employer. In a very direct way, each should be in the process of assessing (and potentially selecting) the other. Accordingly, the committee and the candidates should have an opportunity for extensive interaction; the candidates and others (potential colleagues, students, subordinates) with a vested interest in the selection outcome should have the chance to exchange views; the candidates and their prospective supervisor (and if at all possible the supervisor's supervisor) should be allotted a period for extended discussion; and the candidates should have an opportunity to tour the institution and learn about its resources, problems, and goals.

Although there is a temptation to "run the candidate around" to meet everyone who might have an interest in the selection process, it is much wiser to plan well-organized contacts where sufficient time is provided for the candidate and interviewers to reach thoughtful conclusions about each other. Each candidate should be treated the same; those interviewing should understand the position being filled and the qualifications being sought; and measures should be taken to make sure that everyone treats each candidate with professional courtesy and avoids inappropriate questions. In addition, the interview schedule should be well organized. Candidates should be provided with a written schedule that identifies whom they will be meeting and how they will get from place to place. Appropriate moments for relaxation should be provided.

To assure that information gathering throughout the interview process is presented to the committee in a reasonably uniform manner, feedback about the candidates should be provided on an evaluation form developed and distributed before interviews are initiated. This form should reflect the position requirements established at the outset and should therefore enable comparisons between candidates.

With interviews complete, the committee should be able to narrow further the list of candidates. Once again, individuals who are no longer under active consideration should be notified at the earliest possible date, and if at all possible, should receive feedback regarding their involvement in the process.

Reference Checks

The order of procedures presented here suggests that reference checks be completed as the last step before making a selection. However, it is also reasonable to complete them before on-campus interviews are scheduled. Placing them earlier would be especially useful if the committee is unable to narrow the candidate pool sufficiently after the completion of the telephone interviews and the screening of applications. Regardless of when it takes place, the committee needs to guard against treating this step too casually, especially when it is the final one before candidates are recommended. When the candidates have been on campus for an interview, committee members may conclude that they know each individual sufficiently to feel that not much else can be learned from a reference check. Such a conclusion should be rejected.

Written references are often not very complete or candid, and telephone conversations about references can consist of vague or superficial inquiries. Good reference checks should include specific questions regarding prior performance, current responsibilities, and ability to meet the performance requirements of the position applied for. The person checking references should also be prepared to ask for elaboration on some points. Though not wishing to be dishonest, individuals being asked questions may be reluctant to examine areas of concern unless specifically asked to do so. Therefore, the questioner will need to pursue points raised indirectly.

The number may vary depending upon the scope of responsibility assigned to the position, but two or three references are advisable for most professional-level positions within student affairs. At least one of the reference checks should be with the individual's current supervisor. If the checks need to include contacting individuals in addition to those listed on the original application or résumé, the candidate should be consulted. Contacts should not be made without the candidate's permission.

Committee Recommendation and Decision

With interviews and reference checks complete, the committee is in a position to meet and formulate its recommendation(s) to the administrator responsible for making the final hiring decision. As candidate information is reviewed, the committee should focus on posted qualifications and carefully consider previously identified affirmative action goals.

Once the committee's list of qualified candidates has been forwarded to the administrator, he or she may wish to complete additional reference checks, review the candidate selection file that has been developed throughout the process, meet with the committee, and discuss the final decision with his or her supervisor. When a broad range of responsibilities are assigned to the position, consideration should be given to inviting the candidate back for additional discussions with the administrator or other senior administrators. At the point that a decision is reached, the administrator should contact the final candidate directly to make an offer and finalize salary, starting date, and other details.

If the process has not identified qualified candidates or if affirmative action goals have not been met, consideration should be given to a reexamination of applicants in the on-hold group. Interviews with additional candidates might be scheduled. In the worst case, if qualified candidates have not been identified, the committee might be faced with the reality of a "failed" search. In such instances, the chair should meet with the administrator who initiated the process to discuss the reexamination of qualifications, the reposting of the position to a wider geographic area, and so forth. The committee should be kept informed, and discussion of the revised process should occur before the search is reopened.

Postselection Activities

Once an offer of employment is accepted, committee members should be notified that the process has reached a successful conclusion and thanked for their contribution. In addition, any candidates still involved should be notified. Individuals should be thanked for their interest, encouraged to consider other campus positions for which they may be qualified, and reminded that they may call the contact person if they have questions about the process or their involvement in it. Each candidate should also be offered the possibility to evaluate the selection process and provide feedback that could be helpful in the design and implementation of future processes.

The successful candidate should be supplied the name, address, and telephone number of the person assisting with transition activities. The new employee should also be given a description of the assistance that will be provided to facilitate transition and orientation to the institution and position. Orientation activities should include reading materials, an overview of benefits and other campus employee programs or services, and an opportunity to meet key people with whom the new employee will work. Such initiatives should form a bridge between the selection process and preservice training activities.

Training

Individuals selected as staff members bring with them abilities, knowledge, and experience that have been specifically identified as necessary for or helpful to the accomplishment of assigned job responsibilities. However, these new employees cannot be expected to arrive with a complete understanding of performance expectations or with mastery of every skill needed for success. Therefore, staff training programs must be an important part of each division's human resource management program in order to foster understanding of organizational goals, procedures, programs, and resources and to furnish guidance about how to meet job expectations in the most productive manner.

Training programs should be deliberately incorporated within each division's management activities, and the organization should demonstrate clear support for such programs. Participation in them should be expected and rewarded, budget and time allocations should reflect their importance, and commitment to them should be strongly expressed by organizational leaders. Such tangible evidence of organizational support will encourage motivation to participate in and benefit from training opportunities.

Training should be divided into two categories. First, preservice training should be designed to help new employees become familiar with organizational expectations and structure, the resources available to meet performance requirements, and the existence of programs to develop the skills or perspectives necessary to respond to a given situation. Second, in-service training should be designed to enable current employees to remain informed about new developments within the organization, learn how to satisfy new expectations, and refresh or improve specific skill areas. A well-developed staff training program incorporates both types of training activity.

Preservice Training

Preservice activities include new-employee orientation but should be recognized as starting when information is provided to candidates during the selection process. Clear job descriptions; information about the institutional and divisional mission, goals, and programs; and opportunities for prospective employees to pursue items of interest, tour facilities, and meet key personnel begin the preservice training program. As previously stated, these initiatives should be continued prior to a new employee's arrival on campus with the mailing of documents describing key programs, policies, and procedures and through interaction with a colleague designated as a contact person or mentor. Preservice training usually ends with some form of well-structured class, retreat, or set of sessions on campus designed to furnish new employees with information about organizational expectations and the chance to develop the skills and perspectives needed to assume assigned responsibilities effectively.

In-Service Training

In-service training should be a priority for new and continuing staff members and should include regularly scheduled opportunities set aside during staff meetings or at other times designated for staff to meet; opportunities to attend workshops, professional conventions, and teleconferences; interaction with consultants with expertise in particular areas of interest; enrollment in classes; and regular reading of selected books, journals, and newsletters. However, quite possibly *the* most important in-service training opportunity is the maintenance of a well-developed relationship with the supervisor.

Because the supervisor understands job requirements and the areas of knowledge and skill development that would be most beneficial to an employee, he or she is also in an especially good position to provide training directly or suggest relevant learning experiences for the employee to pursue. Further, the supervisor can identify and best take advantage of the moment when employee motivation is the highest and educational intervention will be most beneficial. Any good teacher knows that people learn best when they are ready to do so.

Regardless of whether necessary learning experiences occur during preservice or in-service training, whether they happen in a structured group setting or during a specific occasion tailored to an individual's needs, or whether they are designed to serve as a refresher or to provide entirely new information or perspectives, there are certain steps that should be taken to assure the achievement of desired outcomes. In addition to those reviewed in this chapter, the reader is encouraged to draw upon the discussion in Chapter Twenty-Four.

Focused Purpose and Clear Objectives

Training activities are designed and implemented because a requirement for information or skill development has been identified — one that if fulfilled will assist employees in the accomplishment of particular responsibilities. To be effective, the need both for training and for specific instructional activities that will help staff members satisfy performance expectations for their actual work must be determined. The individual responsible for a training activity should begin program design by understanding the setting (work environment) where employee performance will take place and the exact training that is required.

With the performance setting and job expectations in mind, the trainer is in a position to formulate objectives. Robert Mager suggests that the development of clear goals is an especially important part of the design of sound instructional programs because they give the trainer a basis to assess "how well the student can demonstrate his acquisition of desired information" (1962, p. 4). He further notes, "An additional advantage of clearly defined objectives is that the student is provided the means to evaluate *his/her own* progress at any place along the route of instruction" (1962, p. 4). Mager believes that an objective is well conceived if the trainer is able to answer each of the following questions in the affirmative. First, does the statement describe what the learner will be doing when he or she is demonstrating that he or she has reached the objective? Second, does the statement describe the important conditions under which the learner will be expected to demonstrate his or her competence? And finally, does the statement indicate how the learner will be evaluated? Does it describe at least the lower limit of acceptable performance? (Mager, 1962, p. 52)

As formulating well-written objectives requires time and diligence on the part of the trainer, it may be tempting to bypass the process or complete it superficially. However, such objectives assure that training programs remain focused and achieve their intended outcome. In addition, they should help participants understand the purpose of the training experience. Individuals learn best when the desired outcome (objective) of the educational experience is clear. In addition, if employees are taking time from their work schedule to attend a training session, their motivation will be enhanced if they appreciate how participation will assist them in their work.

Relevant Educational Materials

Closely related to the development of clear objectives for the training program is the selection of instructional materials or experiences that facilitate the achievement of the stated educational outcome. It is all too easy for trainers to become too wrapped up in the use of a particular type of instructional activity that they are comfortable with or that has worked previously; insufficient thought may be given to whether or not a technique or activity is relevant to the training objectives.

The phrase "form should follow substance" is certainly applicable when selecting instructional materials for use in a training program. There are endless resources and techniques available (films, courses, books, speakers, manuals, and the like). The educational resources and techniques selected should reflect as much as possible the actual work setting where the skill or knowledge learned is going to be applied. For example, a video produced in a similar environment or a role-playing situation involving individuals (for example, students) from the work setting are the types of activities that should be used. It is also wise to consider whether the training should occur in a group setting or if a program tailored to a single person is called for. Frequently, it is one person who needs to improve performance. Carelessly sending that individual to a group session could prove unproductive if the content is not relevant.

Training Program Evaluation

In order to assess the effectiveness of training programs, structured evaluations should be created. Program participants should be provided with an opportunity to critique the training sessions. In addition, participants and supervisors should assess performance in the work setting to determine if the instruction has had the desired result. Finally, individuals (students, parents) who make use of or are affected by services or programs should periodically be given the chance to complete surveys as a further assessment of whether instruction is having the desired impact.

When evaluation data suggest that employee performance does not meet expectations and that the quality of the training has been inadequate, steps should be taken to modify the design of the instructional program so that it works better in the future. Previous participants can furnish valuable input as efforts to assess evaluation data and plan program modifications are implemented. They should be asked to be members of future planning teams so that their expertise can be taken into consideration.

Trainer Support and Supervision

Those responsible for training activities or who serve as trainers within a particular division must receive the support and guidance necessary to meet organizational expectations. As with any assigned responsibility, efforts must be made to ensure that these individuals are competent and receive regular supervision, especially when staff members are periodically called upon to serve as trainers. For example, at the University of Maryland, individuals who serve as full-time hall staff members are occasionally selected to teach sections of a resident assistant training course offered each spring. To provide the necessary support and supervision, these individuals meet weekly with a training professional to discuss upcoming class sessions and to review instructional objectives and materials. Trainers are supplied with a manual that contains materials designed to help them be competent instructors. Finally, they are provided feedback gathered from class evaluations so that appropriate improvements in class sessions can take place.

Relationship with Performance Evaluation

Both the supervisor and employee should recognize that a strong relationship exists between training and performance evaluation. Each employee should be allowed to participate in periodic sessions to review performance and clarify expectations. Both the supervisor and the employee should recognize these sessions as constructive occasions for two-way communication. Sessions should be scheduled ahead of time in a comfortable setting and should include opportunities for self-assessment as well as supervisor feedback. These sessions will be particularly important for new employees who will benefit from early identification of performance problems.

Once these observations have been shared, the supervisor and employee should develop a mutual understanding about areas for improvement, problems that need to be corrected, and additional responsibilities that might be undertaken. When these goals are identified, a plan for their achievement should be developed. This plan may call for resources or support from other staff in order to meet desired outcomes, but in some cases the plan will entail additional training. In these instances, the supervisor should work with the employee to determine how additional skills or knowledge can be gained. The supervisor should keep in touch with the employee to assure that training experiences are having the desired impact.

Although the emphasis throughout this discussion on training has been upon the development of the skills, knowledge, or experiences, the supervisor needs also to recognize that a portion of the process should be devoted to an examination of potential opportunities to pursue advancement or acceptance of more complex responsibilities. These employee development goals should be recognized as legitimate, and plans should be made to reach them through developmental experiences or education. (See Part Four of this volume on acquiring and developing administrative skills.)

Encouraging development is not only a supervisor's professional responsibility, but it also helps motivate an employee to pursue additional commitments. Further, the pursuit of these objectives will improve the prospect that current employees will be qualified candidates when positions become available. In a very direct way, staff development initiatives are the logical extension of a human resource management program that seeks to hire and train individuals who will meet the organization's needs. Encouraging employees also demonstrates that the organization is interested in preparing current staff for additional responsibilities. This approach not only motivates current performance but also assists the recruitment of current employees as qualified candidates for future positions. Such investment supports the continued ability of the organization to meet its goals and fulfill its mission.

Summary

Those responsible for the administration of student affairs programs must effectively utilize many resources to achieve institutional objectives, assure the delivery of student services, and implement established educational programs. These resources include facilities, supplies and services, and staff members. Although each is essential to the achievement of established responsibilities, within institutions of higher education in general and student affairs agencies in particular, staff members are the most important resource. They represent the largest area of investment; moreover, as each institution's responsibility involves a significant degree of direct interaction between staff members and students, ensuring the proper skill level and performance of individual employees is one of the most important management issues for student affairs administrators. The thoughtful consideration of those steps that will enable staff members to have their desired impact on service or program delivery will return large dividends to students and to the institution.

To help staff members to fulfill organizational goals and performance expectations, selection and training programs must be carefully planned and implemented. Their design must incorporate a clearly focused understanding of the organization. This understanding should be reflected in the position's job description and should clarify the skills, knowledge, and experience to be identified during selection or improved during training.

This chapter has noted the importance of job descriptions, suggested a number of steps to follow in the development and implementation of selection and training, and presented perspectives for consideration by those responsible for the management of such programs. Literature devoted to organization development, affirmative action, and classroom instruction will expand upon the points presented. Student affairs professionals should examine these resources to enrich their understanding of these important management functions. The commitment made to improving staff selection and training will be well worth the investment and must be conscientiously pursued.

References

Barr, M. J. "Growing Staff Diversity and Changing Career Paths." In M. J. Barr, M. L. Upcraft, and Associates, *New Futures for Student Affairs: Building a Vision for Professional Leadership and Practice.* San Francisco: Jossey-Bass, 1990.

Dalton, J. "Employment and Supervision of Student Affairs Personnel." In M. J. Barr and Associates, *Student Services and the Law: A Handbook for Practitioners.* San Francisco: Jossey-Bass, 1988.

Kaplin, W. A. *The Law of Higher Education: A Comprehensive Guide to Legal Implications of Administrative Decision Making.* (2nd ed.) San Francisco: Jossey-Bass, 1985.

Mager, R. F. *Preparing Instructional Objectives.* Palo Alto, Calif.: Fearon, 1962.

Seaquist, G. "Civil Rights and Equal Access: When Laws Apply—And When They Do Not." In M. J. Barr and Associates, *Student Services and the Law: A Handbook for Practitioners.* San Francisco: Jossey-Bass, 1988.

11

✌

The Political Dimension of Decision Making

Paul L. Moore

In organizational life, the term *politics* may be the most employed and least understood concept among those we use to describe important aspects of our work. For many faculty members and administrators, it has negative connotations, suggesting trickery, manipulation, and self-interest; as a result, it causes some discomfort when used (Block, 1987; Pfeffer, 1981). It is a topic we would prefer to talk about privately or euphemistically. The training of student affairs professionals with its anchors in the helping professions and our focus on the personal development of students may create greater ambivalence for us than others when confronted with "politics." At the same time, however, we understand it to be a necessary and ubiquitous process through which important decisions are made in society and in our institutions. As Appleton (1991, p. 5) notes, "Political behavior is inevitable in every organizational setting, is found at every level in the hierarchy, and intensifies as the decision making possibilities are greater and more important."

Clearly, an understanding of institutional decision making must be a priority for all those who hope to make and influence policies affecting their work and institutions. Whether an institution is large or small, secular or nonsecular, whether it is a research university or community college, an important part of its management involves decision making about direction, strategy, and resource allocation. How these decisions are made is the essence of organizational politics.

One important caveat is that the political approach is not the only useful one in understanding organizations in general and higher education in particular. Bolman and Deal (1984) have identified four major theoretical frameworks for organizations: rational, human resource, political, and symbolic. Each has an interesting perspective that adds to our understanding of organizations. Rational theorists deal with the goals, roles, and technology of organizations. The human resource writers are concerned with the interaction of the needs and capabilities of people with the roles and relationships within organizations. Meaning within organizations is the interest of symbolic theorists. Power, conflict, and resource allocation are the concerns of political theorists. Each approach has its strengths and weaknesses; and although we have emphasized in this chapter the political perspective as being useful to student affairs professionals, it is helpful to acknowledge Pfeffer's (1981, p. 2) caution when speaking of politics and its essential ingredient, power: "While power is something, it is not everything."

The purposes of this chapter are to identify and define key concepts necessary to an understanding of organizational politics, highlight elements of institutions of higher education that distinguish them from other societal institutions and affect their political processes, and suggest political perspectives strategies and tactics for student affairs practitioners.

Basic Concepts

As used in this chapter, *politics* refers to the processes that influence the direction of and allocate resources for an organization. Political behaviors are those designed to shape or determine institutional direction and policy and are as rational or irrational, altruistic or self-serving as the people involved. As we are concerned here with the political processes and activities that occur within colleges and universities, Pfeffer's (1981, p. 7) definition of organizational politics is instructive: "Organizational politics involves those activities taken within organizations to acquire, develop, and use power and other resources to obtain one's preferred outcomes in a situation in which there is uncertainty or dissensus about choices."

Key aspects of this definition are power, preferences, and uncertainty. *Power* may be defined as "the ability to produce intended change in others, to influence them so that they will be more likely to act in accordance with one's own preferences" (Birnbaum, 1988, p. 13). *Preferences* suggest what an individual or group would like to see happen within the organization. And *uncertainty* implies that a decision is yet to be made or a direction chosen.

In his study of New York University as a political system, Baldridge (1971, p. 24) describes its major elements: "The broad outline of the political system looks like this: a complex social structure generates multiple pressures, many forms of power and pressure impinge on the decision makers, a legislative stage translates these pressures into policy, and a policy execution phase finally generates feedback in the form of new conflict." Important ideas in this description are differing interests, intergroup disagreement or conflict, use of power in pursuit of interests, efforts to influence decision makers, and decision making itself.

Important Conceptual Considerations

The purpose of this section is to introduce major elements that will help with the discussion of power and politics and perhaps encourage the reader to pursue an independent review of the literature. The intent is not to review in depth all the theoretical concepts that underpin a discussion of organizational politics; excellent discussions of these already exist (Baldridge, 1971; Pfeffer, 1981; Bacharach and Lawler, 1980; and Birnbaum, 1988).

The Political Model

This view of organizations assumes that they are not completely rational and harmonious entities but are composed of constantly shifting coalitions that bargain for desired outcomes and use strategies and tactics designed to influence results. Organizational life is seen as a series of political transactions involving the use of power to obtain resources or achieve other ends (Bacharach and Lawler, 1980). Organizations are not typically homogeneous but rather pluralistic, being composed of all sorts of subgroups and subcultures. Conflicts arising from these differences are natural and are to be expected in political organizations (Baldridge, 1971). Power, differing preferences, conflict, influence, coalitions, negotiation, and compromise are key ingredients in a political system.

To suggest that a college or university is a political system that experiences the use of power, conflict, and mutual influence is not to argue that rational processes, bureaucratic incrementalism, and strong organizational cultural tendencies are not at work or nonexistent. Other methods of making decisions and controlling activity exist that assist with the ongoing activity of an organization. Careful accumulation of information and examination of alternatives frequently inform academic, student welfare, and fund-raising decisions. Organizations will make some decisions based on closely held values, such as those that might be made in an institution with religious roots. And certainly incrementalism will determine many budget allocations.

Political activities tend to be accentuated when normal patterns or processes do not produce coherent direction, strategies, or accepted resource allocations. Active disagreement may be stimulated by external sources, such as an important institutional constituency, or by internal sources, such as a proposal of a new program having perceived negative financial implications for others in the organization. Pfeffer (1981) has identified several elements that produce political activity in organizations: interdependence of the interest groups or actors, goals that are inconsistent, resource scarcity, issues of importance, and decentralized decision making.

The political model assumes that the power of the various participants will determine the outcome. Thus, understanding "who participates in decision making, what determines each player's stand on the issues, what determines each actor's relative power, and how the decision process arrives at a decision" is an important managerial and political consideration (Pfeffer, 1981, p. 28). All groups and individuals are not concerned with all issues. Even when interested, they will exhibit differing levels of intensity and ability to influence a particular decision. And as the results are primarily the consequence of negotiation and compromise, they are rarely the perfect expression of any specific individual or group preferences (Pfeffer, 1981).

Power

Earlier, power was defined as the ability to influence others in such a way that they will more likely do what we prefer. Compared to influence, "power is the potential for influence, and influence is the result of actualized power" (King, 1975, p. 7). Power describes relationships among people that are given particular meaning by the organizational context. Further, the person to be influenced assigns meaning to the behavior or communications that are designed to influence (King, 1975). All relations need not require or manifest the ingredient of power. The organizational setting and the roles of individuals significantly affect the nature and extent of power in the relationship.

French and Raven (1959) identify five bases of power relating to organizational context that describe what groups or individuals use to affect the behavior of others: coercive, reward, expertise, referent, and legitimate power. Some writers have added a sixth: information (Bacharach and Lawler, 1980).

Coercive power suggests the ability to punish, such as dismissal or demotion or, in a group situation, job action by a labor union.

Reward power involves giving something of value (a promotion or raise) if certain behavior is exhibited; in a group situation, it might mean representation on an important board of directors.

Expert power is specialized knowledge about issues or activities of interest to the organization. Examples are the special knowledge of lawyers, medical doctors, and accountants.

Referent power is based on identification with another person, such as the deference shown to charismatic leaders. An example is the credibility often accorded the assistant to a college president.

Legitimate power, sometimes called bureaucratic power, is "power based on rights of control and concomitant obligations to obey" (Bacharach and Lawler, 1980, p. 33). Legitimate power is essentially authority as ascribed to senior university officers, such as presidents, vice presidents, and deans. By virtue of their positions, they are empowered to make certain decisions and are expected to do so by others.

Legitimate power or authority is not the same as influence. Authority is the ability and right to make and enforce decisions; either one has the right to make decisions or not. Influence, by contrast, is the opportunity for almost anyone in an organization to seek to affect decisions arising from any of the bases of power rather than from organizational right (Bacharach and Lawler, 1980).

Information refers to the opportunity that social actors have to gain information about internal matters or the organization's relations to the environment.

Influence does not occur in a vacuum; it requires both that someone wishes to influence and that someone is willing to be influenced. Writing about social influence and communication, King (1975, p. 12) states: "For communication and social influence to occur, the receiver must be affected. The receiver assigns meaning to behavior." The bases of power noted above are conceived similarly; someone employs one or a combination of these sources to induce someone else to do something. These processes therefore cannot exist independently of context.

Needs, Motivation, and Expectations

How people behave in an organization reflects in part their motivations for being there, such as pay, prestige, or fellowship, and expectations about how the organization will treat them or respond to certain behaviors on their part (Appleton, 1991). What motivates them and what they expect from an organization are strongly related to their perceived needs. Personal needs may include safety and security, love and affiliation, social esteem and prestige, power and autonomy, self-esteem and competence, and achievement and creativity (Webber, 1979). Needs, motivations, and expectations are as varied as the people who work in an organization and will be influenced by personal values, beliefs, age, experience, gender, and ethnicity.

Political behavior, designed to influence organizational direction and policy through the use of power and other resources, is directly connected to individual motivations and personal or group expectations of the organization. How people respond to efforts to influence them requires that they give meaning to the actions taken, and that meaning is affected and filtered by needs, motivations, and expectations. The exercise of power does not guarantee that the person or group that is to be influenced will respond as hoped. It all depends on the context—individual perceptions, immediate or long-term needs, personal values and beliefs, and the stakes to be won or lost.

Self-Serving Versus Productive Behavior

If behavior depends in part on the motivations and expectations of the individual, how can an organization elicit behavior that supports its goals? Is self-serving behavior necessarily negative, as some have contended (Block, 1987)? If a person is behaving politically, is that necessarily at odds with institutional goals and culture? How can one distinguish between political activities that support institutional goals and those that do not?

The answer lies in part in the extent to which the political actor's expectations and the results of specific actions are congruent with the goals of the organization. Figure 11.1 illustrates the notion of congruence.

We know, of course, that the motives of the involved actors and purposes behind particular actions are not always apparent. Organizational politics are consequently complex and ambiguous; things may not be as they appear. Although long-term results may provide definitive answers to questions of motivation and purpose, decisions will be made in the short run based on perceptions of those purposes, whether clearly articulated or not.

Figure 11.1. Goal: Functional Behavior.

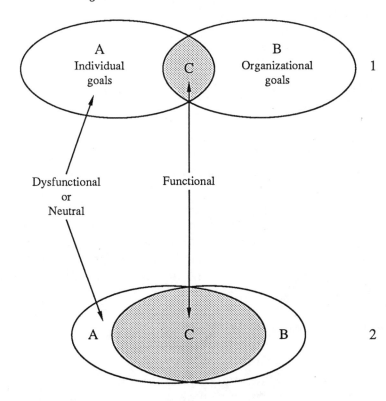

Source: Appleton, 1991, p. 12. Reprinted by permission.

Into those judgments are brought all the contextual elements of organizational life — the individual and organizational values, purposes, technologies, histories, and perspectives. Whether or not political behavior is fundamentally self-serving or in the interest of both the individual and organization is frequently a matter of opinion.

Leadership

Influence, and by implication the use of power, is basic to managerial leadership (Webber, 1979). What then is the role of leadership in a political organization? Appleton (1991, p. 13) argues, "The leader must be prepared to use power in an effective manner and to understand the extent to which individual differences and expectations and self-serving political interests will affect the functioning of an organization." Managing the political process and political conflict is at the heart of leadership (Yates, 1985).

Important Elements of Institutions of Higher Education

If power, influence, and politics exist, are based upon relationships and organizational structures, and are central to administrative life (Pfeffer, 1981; Yates, 1985), then it follows that the practitioner ought to understand the unique aspects of institutions of higher education that shape their political environments.

Goal Diffusion

Colleges and universities typically exhibit a lack of clarity and agreement on institutional goals (Birnbaum, 1988; Baldridge, 1973). Teaching, research, and service are the three most frequently stated goals, but they exist in differing combinations and degrees of emphasis on each campus; moreover, goals may even be assigned a different importance on a single campus. However, other goals may be widely embraced, such as intercollegiate athletics or a particular religion. The result is often a lack of agreed-upon, mutually consistent goals — that is, a number of conflicting or inconsistent goals are accepted. Almost inevitably, such an environment sets the stage for disagreement and competition over institutional direction and the allocation of resources.

Uncertainty of Means or Technologies

Not only are the goals of higher education diffuse, but the means that should be used to educate students are not always clear. Which classroom strategies (lectures, small-discussion seminars, laboratory activity, or independent study) are most productive and when? Many techniques seem to work, but how they create change in students and which ones are best are not known (Birnbaum, 1988). Because our technologies are not clear, major choices about how to allocate resources are often not easily and decisively made. Again, the stage is set for disagreement and political activity.

Dual Control

Another feature of higher education that contributes to political activity is the dual nature of institutional control (Birnbaum, 1988). Responsibility for decision making is vested in an administration, including a board of trustees, a president, and a generally elaborate structure. Simultaneously, responsibility is endowed upon faculty structures, schools, departments, senates, and committes, which make a number of important curricular and personnel decisions. The authority in the former tends to be hierarchical and in the latter professional. Moreover, the two structures are not necessarily clearly defined and integrated; thus, opportunity for dissent and conflict abounds.

Structural Uniqueness

Not only do colleges and universities have dual decision-making systems, they are filled with other distinctive features adding ambiguity and complexity to their functioning. As noted above, there is both a management structure and an employee governance structure. In each, labor unions may organize employees in a context structured by complex state government regulations. Outside groups, particularly the federal government, alumni associations, supporters (such as athletic or arts fund-raising groups), and accrediting associations, have their say. And staff and students may be effectively organized and represented in official governance bodies. Clearly, the variety of interests, institutional complexity, and the nature of the decision-making apparatus, whether direct or advisory, suggest the conditions necessary for a political organization.

Organizational Culture

Culture, according to Schein (1985, p. 9), is "a pattern of basic assumptions—invented, discovered, or developed by a given group as it learns to cope with its problems of external adaptation and internal integration—that has worked well enough to be considered valid and, therefore, to be taught to new members as the correct way to perceive, think, and feel in relation to those problems." Colleges and universities have cultures, as do the structures within them: schools, departments, senates, and groups. In addition, those affiliated with the institution, such as accrediting associations, alumni and support groups, and professional associations, exhibit cultural characteristics. The cultures of universities differ from those of other societal institutions as well as from each other. Culture, then, affects how a particular organization reacts to issues of organizational strategy, technology, conflict, communications, socialization, and productivity. Culture helps deal with issues of organizational survival and internal functioning (Schein, 1985).

Limits on Leadership

Birnbaum (1988) has analyzed the limitations on leadership in higher education brought about by the organizational, governance, and cultural uniqueness of colleges and universities. Dual decision-making systems, decentralization of academic decision making, the influence of external authorities and interests, and the lack of agreement on institutional goals — all impose constraints on leadership. It is no wonder that although transformational leadership is almost always desired, it is much less frequently achieved.

Nonetheless, the importance of leadership remains. An understanding of the political dimension of universities is a critical element in providing effective leadership. Strategies and tactics are available to the student affairs leader that can be helpful in managing the political environment for the benefit of students and the institution.

Perspectives and Strategies

The assumption of this chapter is that most of us experience sufficient organizational politics in our daily administrative lives to warrant thinking about ways to improve our effectiveness in dealing with it. The following suggestions may provide some guidance.

The President and Senior Colleagues

Depending on professional level, the term *boss* may be substituted for *president;* the ideas are the same. Although we might wish it were not so, the most important relationship is with the boss. Without a strong or at least respectful relationship, a student affairs leader will struggle with many aspects of his or her responsibility. It is important to take whatever time and do whatever is necessary to secure this relationship, including informing, training, protecting, and supporting senior colleagues. There are, of course, personal and ethical limits that must be understood and acted on, even if it means resignation (Brown, 1991).

Senior colleagues, particularly at the vice-presidential level, require attention. Without good, constructive relationships, a sense of teamwork cannot be cultivated, and the normal turf, budget, and policy battles may take on a more partisan tone. Student affairs professionals must recognize their colleagues' biases, strengths, and weaknesses in order to strengthen their relationships, shape their approaches, and protect their interests.

Roles, Issues, and the Institution

To perform well in the political arena, it is critical for those in student affairs to understand thoroughly their role, whether as the chief student affairs officer (Sandeen, 1991) or as a middle manager (Young, 1990; Ellis and Moon,

1991). Being clear about the expectations of one's boss and key constituencies will translate into personal confidence when dealing with the managerial as well as the political dimensions of a position. For example, Brown (1991) sees key aspects of the chief student affairs officer role as being surrogate and shield and defender for the president. Without an appreciation of these expectations, the student affairs vice president may be paralyzed by the conflicting expectations of the president, faculty, and students.

It is equally important to know the issues. Although it is not possible to be aware of all that goes on in a division or large department, it is nonetheless critical to have a good sense of the substance of everything within a job's area of responsibility, especially where criticism or territorial battles are likely.

Following and understanding institutional issues is necessary, whether or not they impinge directly on responsibilities. This practice will be helpful in establishing a reputation as an officer or professional with institutionwide interests and role. Such a perception by others may lead to greater involvement in and influence on the full range of institutional concerns. On the formal side, student affairs officers must keep abreast of relevant current issues through perusal of their professional journals and general publications such as the *Chronicle of Higher Education* and the *Journal of Higher Education*. It may be useful to have a working knowledge of the informational sources followed by other important administrators, such as the publications of the National Association of College and University Business Officers typically reviewed by business and administrative vice presidents.

The Importance of Competence

The power of personal competence cannot be overly emphasized. We normally think of competence in relation to student affairs "business" or management, but as a source of power it goes well beyond professional expertise. Professionals in the field must strive to be highly skilled in their work, but that is not sufficient if they are to play a broader institutional role. Political competence, the subject of this chapter, suggests an understanding of power and its uses, of the personal motivations of others in the organization, of the opportunities provided to influence decisions about institutional direction and resource allocation, and of the potential of staff work to shape alternatives.

Proper Positioning

One cannot influence decisions unless one is organizationally, professionally, and personally in a position to do so. Opportunities for influencing unit or institutional decisions do not necessarily occur because an individual knows a lot or is recognized as a strong professional by colleagues on other campuses; such opportunities usually occur because that person has taken steps to be known as competent, interested, and involved in the fortunes of his or her unit, division, or institution.

Visibility on the campus, and perhaps in the larger community in which the institution resides, is an important and not-always-understood notion. Being visible simply means attending meetings, socials, and programs of importance to various important constituencies within and without the college or university. Participation may be seen by others as much more beneficial to a program or idea than might be obvious. The positive aspects of visibility can, however, be squandered through overexposure or participation in unimportant activities. One must therefore monitor the importance and frequency of involvement.

Officers in student affairs must keep track of what they and their units accomplish. Acknowledgment of accomplishments serves both as a reinforcement of strong and innovative performance and a method of ensuring that organizational efforts are directed toward unit goals.

Accomplishments should also be shared with senior administration officials, colleagues, and faculty members. A performance will be judged with or without information; thus, it is important that others are informed of activities and achievements. Informing others also has the benefit of establishing competence, interest, and involvement in institutional issues and strengthening the ability to participate effectively in the institution's political environment.

Being informed about campus issues and individual responsibilities is, of course, required of those who would influence the course of institutional development. This requirement extends to a clear understanding of institutional history and culture.

Those in the field should also be thoughtful about their public presence — that is, their personal style, which relates to how they do things and how they are perceived by others: "Personal style is the professional demeanor by which each of us is known. It denotes how we behave in our work, as distinguished from what we do" (Appleton, Briggs, and Rhatigan, 1978, p. 139). Style, though rooted in personal characteristics and experiences, can be understood and shaped to enhance effectiveness in the educational and political environment. Do student affairs officers use jargon or language readily understood and accepted by their audiences? Do they and those on their staffs show a level of professionalism appropriate for students, their parents, or trustees? Do they dress in a way that meets the expectations of important constituencies? Are they willing and accomplished public speakers readily available to campus and community groups? The point of these and other similar questions is to argue that one needs to act, look, and see oneself as a major player in institutional decision making and leadership.

Relationships, or Getting to Know Others

Like close ties to the president, relationships with others are essential to effective participation in the political processes of colleges and universities. With the possible exception of legislative activities such as faculty senates, relationships are the best vehicle for building coalitions, resolving conflict, and creating consensus. With such a pivotal function, building and maintaining relationships must be an active concern for student affairs officers (see Chapter Twenty).

Brown (1991) refers to the "positive value of gossip," information that gives some hint of situations, motives, or fast-moving events. By working at knowing others, those in student affairs position themselves in key places in the informal communication network of their campus. The information gained can be enormously helpful in countering resistance or informing others of interests or proposals.

Moore (1991) describes a strategy for getting to know and routinely working with academic deans through regular visits or lunches. These periodic contacts need not require agendas other than simply checking in to see how faculty members and students are doing, what issues are developing, and what else might be done. The contact will be appreciated and may build a relationship that will prove mutually beneficial during extraordinary situations.

Time Requirements

It must be clear by now that managing the political dimension of a job can be and frequently is enormously time consuming. The time requirement seems to increase as the organizational level of a position rises: the higher and more central the responsibilities, the greater the opportunities for political activity and the higher the demand on time. In an unpublished study of the political involvement of chief student affairs officers (Moore and Moore, 1991), 74 percent of the 243 responding chief student affairs officers reported that political activities consumed a significant amount of their work time.

Politics is not a function to be managed like budget or planning; it is a backdrop. It is not our work, but it affects our work. Its effect on our time must be accommodated and managed so that it does not overwhelm the requirements of our institutions and our students.

Perhaps politics should be thought of as a consideration — one that must be factored into our efforts at conflict resolution, pursuit of goals, and decision making. In some sense, it is like the notion of student development, which guides and influences much of our work. As such, the time that it takes can be managed so as not to squeeze out other productive activities.

The importance of spending sufficient time on the political process is illustrated by Birnbaum (1988), who writes, "People who spend time on a decision will be disproportionately successful."

Accepting Conflict

Conflict will be more or less present, more or less visible, and more or less a factor in student affairs depending on institutional culture and history and the personalities and motivations of current players. Whatever its degree, however, university administrators must anticipate that conflict over priorities, turf, and resources will occur. It is not unusual or extraordinary.

Differences, and indeed conflict, are necessary ingredients to a political system. This observation implies that student affairs officers must be able to deal with conflict, understand the political system, and know how to operate in it. The marriage of the two, conflict and institutional politics, is a fact that must be considered in confronting problems both between individuals in student affairs and between student affairs personnel and representatives of other areas within the institution.

On a personal level, student affairs officers may not wish to deal with conflict but must have a willingness and strategies to manage it. Individual styles will obviously reflect personal and contextual characteristics.

Fighting, or the Rules of Battle

Inevitably, all administrators will encounter disagreements over territory or resources that will require a struggle. Personal values and style will, of course, determine much of what they do. Nevertheless, there are some points to keep in mind.

Battles should not be fought if they cannot be won. There will be some matters of principle that require a fight even though winning is very unlikely; however, fighting hopeless battles will only dissipate energy and resources. Fighting uses resources, may damage relationships and future interactions, and thus should be engaged in only for important reasons. Personal ego is not such a reason.

It is essential to be well informed. Until preparation is complete, the battle should be postponed. A neutral ground for the conversation should be chosen and privacy ensured. Above all, student affairs officers must maintain their dignity. Fights have consequences, and nothing is worth the loss of one's self-respect and the regard of others.

Integrity

In the final analysis, consistent ethical behavior is the most important strategy. When the battles are over and the dust settles, people will follow leaders of high integrity even when the won-lost record is less than they would hope. To lose integrity is to lose claim to leadership and the support of the boss, staff, and students.

Other Tactics

There are a great number of tactics that might be identified as potentially useful in addition to those formally explored above. Several of these deserve brief mention.

1. The participation of the opposition should be encouraged (Birnbaum, 1988). Participation may help opponents appreciate the real constraints

faced by the institution and the consequences inherent in any particular political situation. It may have a tempering effect.

2. Birnbaum (1988) describes another method for dealing with politically sensitive issues. The "garbage can" strategy is based on the notion that new proposals often attract all sorts of unrelated solutions and problems. By increasing the possible solutions, one may reduce the probability that a specific idea or strategy will survive the process. Committees often serve the function of developing so many ideas and solutions that none can get support or be implemented. In addition, sometimes it is strategically important to overload the decision-making system with proposals on various matters. When that occurs and time is limited, chances increase that some proposals will not get through the process of evaluation and decision making by committees and other governance groups.

3. Efforts should be focused on the relevant persons and situations related to an objective. "[The] persons who are there have the power" (Baldridge, 1971, p. 26).

4. Service on committees is crucial; they are where the work gets done (Baldridge, 1971). By being present, doing the work of the committee, and staying until the job is done, student affairs officers will influence what happens.

5. Persistence is vital (Birnbaum, 1988; Baldridge, 1971). Even though a policy is written, the issue may not be settled. Evolving interpretations should be constantly monitored.

6. Management should be unobtrusive (Birnbaum, 1988). Managing small changes without much fanfare may elicit less attention and resistance.

Staff Education

Although many will be reluctant to involve their staffs in the normal political skirmishes, it is important that they understand institutional history and culture. For example, many business schools have faculty consultants in the area of organizational culture who can be quite helpful to student affairs staffs. An informed staff will be more sensitive to issues and interactions that may have political overtones; the result is that the leadership's network is expanded and more consistent organizational responses to political situations can be made. It is also helpful to inform senior staff members of the details of situations either that may cause political disagreement or that invite collaboration with others.

Clear Purposes and Values

A clearly and consistently stated set of purposes and supporting values can help provide a context within which actions and initiatives related to responsibilities can be understood and interpreted. Explicitness is a virtue in itself in that it informs the opinions of others and helps reduce uninformed speculations and the suspicion of secret motivations and agendas. Speculation will always be present in organizations and should therefore be anticipated and countered by information. Actions rooted in core values are more understandable and less subject to misunderstanding.

Explicit and consistently stated values and purposes are important not only to external but also to internal audiences, such as the staff or division. Staff members, fully cognizant of organizational values and direction, will act more reliably in pursuit of them and will likely make fewer mistakes that can be seized upon by other interest groups within the organization.

At the same time, it is important that student affairs leaders and staffs work to attain and respond to an institutional perspective. Partisan politics is frequently rooted or finds its voice in narrow matters. Budget requests and program proposals that respond to general institutional goals will more likely gain supporters and ultimate approval and less likely attract opposition because of petty issues. Further, embracing institutional purposes and values signals membership on a team committed to institutional advancement.

Performance

Extremely competent people performing at high levels are more likely to be successful in pursuit of objectives and able to counter opposition to organizational activities and initiatives. A uniformly able staff is an invaluable political asset. Political competence can be encouraged through consistent investment in staff development activities.

Faculty

A widely understood and broadly applicable approach to faculty is an important institutional strategy. Faculty members will be supporters or opponents depending on what they know or how they are involved and supported in a given process by student affairs personnel. Importantly, such a strategy must reflect the typical commitments of the faculty, as well as the values and mission of the institution (Bloland, 1991). Managers should think often of faculty in their program planning and evaluation and follow through when faculty participation is secured or interest expressed. (See Chapter Twenty in this volume.)

Staffs should also be encouraged to develop strong relations with academic units through teaching, writing, or consultation. Teaching is the most traditional approach, but consultation on such issues as the handling of difficult students or training on student diversity is increasingly possible. Staff members should be encouraged to respond to faculty concerns quickly and positively, regardless of how insignificant or uninformed the request or question might seem.

Faculties will influence institutional decisions through their senates, institutional standing committees, and school and department governance structures. Although many faculty members may be uninformed about student affairs issues and commitments, they will influence, perhaps negatively, decisions affecting student affairs.

Communication

The student affairs organization must actively communicate with those it would seek to influence. Communication must be consistent, frequent, and of high quality and should originate in all parts of the organization, not just from the top. Each office or function has a constituency with which communication is vital. Its form may be a newsletter, a computer bulletin board, or a personal visit, depending on institutional size and purposes. It may involve the sharing of ideas about common interests through the circulation of articles. Internal articles on student trends or interests can furnish useful information about reentry student characteristics or employment trends. Communication strategies must also contain active opportunities for listening and feedback through an open-door policy, letters to the editor, or a constituent survey.

Ethical Considerations

A number of good resources on ethics are available for the student affairs practitioner (Canon and Brown, 1985; Upcraft and Poole, 1991). It seems, however, that the issue of ethical behavior is more important when examining our political roles within the organizations in which we work — perhaps especially because institutions of higher education are committed to the pursuit of truth. The perceived importance of this behavior also stems from our understanding that when we confront institutional politics, we are not necessarily dealing with an idealized good but with a world in which people do not always act nobly.

Yet groups and individuals disagree on institutional direction and resource allocation decisions, attempt to influence decisions that have an impact on themselves or their interests, and exercise power when they do so. Organizational politics are real and ubiquitous and are thus an important aspect of administrative decision making and life. As such, organizational politics must be considered from an ethical perspective. After all, as Appleton (1991) states, it is "the acquisition and right use of power" (p. 6) that ought to be of great interest to the professional operating in the political dimension of administrative life.

Special Considerations

Although institutions and personal situations will provide an array of administrative and political challenges, some deserve special mention to encourage practitioners to think differently or more broadly about them; these include issues of gender, ethnicity, institutional size, and institutional affiliation or sponsorship.

Gender and Ethnicity

There are expected differences in administrative experiences related to gender and ethnicity, but these factors may present special challenges. In a study of female and African-American chief student affairs officers (Mamarchev and Williamson, 1991), respondents reported a number of common issues that affected their ability to manage their political environments. There were perceived differences in the ways that they had been socialized, in the availability of mentors during the formative years of their careers, in familiarity with the territory of senior administration, in their inclusion in some informal social and information-sharing situations, and in others' understanding of their role and competence because of their gender or ethnic background. These situations caused the respondents to find ways to augment their training and experience and to develop strategies to help them cope with a political environment perhaps different from that normally associated with the position held.

Institutional Size

Institutional size clearly affects how one operates, administratively and politically. Size may limit access to decision making, create administrative decentralization and specialization, lessen social interaction, and diminish the accuracy of communication (Smith, 1991). Each of these dimensions will require the tailoring of strategies and tactics designed to influence institutional decision making. Birnbaum (1988) provides an excellent discussion of institutional function based partly on organizational size.

Mission

Institutional sponsorship and therefore mission can have an enormous impact on institutional goals. A Jesuit college, for example, may well have a different social agenda because of a commitment to service than a public, technical university. Private institutions may more vigorously defend their independent status than some other values that public institutions may deem more important, such as broad student access (see Chapter One). These differences, as well as those in institutional culture, will also influence the approaches to political systems and situations that student affairs officers will adopt.

Summary

This chapter has argued that the political dimension of institutional life exists and is important, and manageable. The student affairs practitioner will be affected by political struggles about institutional direction, plans for pursuing these purposes, and allocation of resources to implement the plans. It is therefore critical for student affairs administrators to know the history, culture, and people in their institutions and to take into account their colleagues who also wish to influence events. They should know their business, actively participate in institutional life, and be students of the inevitable political processes of their institutions, including the tactics, strategies, and possibilities that are available to them. Institutional politics should be understood, appreciated for its potential and limitations, and practiced as competently as possible.

Certainly, the practice of politics without values is bleak. Lacking a clear sense of fairness, high level of integrity, and commitment to the students, faculty, and institutions we serve, organizational politics can disintegrate to the distasteful, self-serving spectacle too often seen in our political institutions. There is another way—one that understands the processes necessary to create consensus about where we are going and how we will get there but that demonstrates the best values of higher education.

References

Appleton, J. R. "The Context." In P. L. Moore (ed.), *Managing the Political Dimension of Student Affairs*. New Directions for Student Services, no. 55. San Francisco: Jossey-Bass, 1991.

Appleton, J. R., Briggs, C. M., and Rhatigan, J. J. *Pieces of Eight*. Portland, Oreg.: National Association of Student Personnel Administrators Institute of Research and Development, 1978.

Bacharach, S. B., and Lawler, E. J. *Power and Politics in Organizations: The Social Psychology of Conflict, Coalitions, and Bargaining*. San Francisco: Jossey-Bass, 1980.

Baldridge, J. V. *Power and Conflict in the University*. New York: Wiley, 1971.

Baldridge, J. V. "Organizational Change Processes: A Political Systems Approach." In J. R. Appleton (ed.), *Selected Major Speeches and Excerpts from NASPA's 55th Annual Conference*, Monograph no. 4. Washington, D.C.: National Association of Student Personnel Administrators, Oct. 1973.

Birnbaum, R. *How Colleges Work: The Cybernetics of Academic Organization and Leadership*. San Francisco: Jossey-Bass, 1988.

Block, P. *The Empowered Manager: Positive Political Skills at Work*. San Francisco: Jossey-Bass, 1987.

Bloland, P. A. "Key Academic Values and Issues." In P. L. Moore (ed.), *Managing the Political Dimension of Student Affairs*. New Directions for Student Services, no. 55. San Francisco: Jossey-Bass, 1991.

Bolman, L. G., and Deal, T. E. *Modern Approaches to Understanding and Managing Organizations*. San Francisco: Jossey-Bass, 1984.

Brown, R. M. "Working with the President and Senior Administrators." In P. L. Moore (ed.), *Managing the Political Dimension of Student Affairs*. New Directions for Student Services, no. 55. San Francisco: Jossey-Bass, 1991.

Canon, H. J., and Brown, R. D. (eds.), *Applied Ethics in Student Services*. New Directions for Student Services, no. 30. San Francisco: Jossey-Bass, 1985.

Ellis, H., and Moon, J. "The Middle Manager: Truly in the Middle." In P. L. Moore (ed.), *Managing the Political Dimension of Student Affairs.* New Directions for Student Services, no. 55. San Francisco: Jossey-Bass, 1991.

French, J.R.P., and Raven, B. H. "The Bases of Social Power." In D. Cartwright (ed.), *Studies in Social Power.* Ann Arbor: University of Michigan Press, 1959.

King, S. W. *Communication and Social Influence.* Reading, Mass.: Addison-Wesley, 1975.

Mamarchev, H. L., and Williamson, M. L. "Women and African Americans: Stories Told and Lessons Learned — A Case Study." In P. L. Moore (ed.), *Managing the Political Dimension of Student Affairs.* New Directions for Student Services, no. 55. San Francisco: Jossey-Bass, 1991.

Moore, P. L. "Ideas for the Chief." In P. L. Moore (ed.), *Managing the Political Dimension of Student Affairs.* New Directions for Student Services, no. 55. San Francisco: Jossey-Bass, 1991.

Moore, P. L., and Moore, S. C. "Survey of Political Involvement of Chief Student Affairs Officers." Unpublished data, 1991.

Pfeffer, J. *Power in Organizations.* Marshfield, Mass.: Pitman, 1981.

Sandeen, A. *The Chief Student Affairs Officer: Leader, Manager, Mediator, Educator.* San Francisco: Jossey-Bass, 1991.

Schein, E. H. *Organizational Culture and Leadership: A Dynamic View.* San Francisco: Jossey-Bass, 1985.

Smith, D. G. "Small Colleges and Religious Institutions: Special Issues." In P. L. Moore (ed.), *Managing the Political Dimension of Student Affairs.* New Directions for Student Services, no. 55. San Francisco: Jossey-Bass, 1991.

Upcraft, M. L., and Poole, T. G. "Ethical Issues and Administrative Politics." In P. L. Moore (ed.), *Managing the Political Dimension of Student Affairs.* New Directions for Student Services, no. 55. San Francisco: Jossey-Bass, 1991.

Webber, R. A. *Management: Basic Elements of Managing Organizations.* Homewood, Ill.: Irwin, 1979.

Yates, D., Jr. *The Politics of Management: Exploring the Inner Workings of Public and Private Organizations.* San Francisco: Jossey-Bass, 1985.

Young, R. B. (ed.) *The Invisible Leaders: Student Affairs Mid-Managers.* Washington, D.C.: National Association of Student Personnel Administrators, 1990.

12

Ꙅ

Facilities
Management Issues

Winston G. Shindell

It has been said that funding of higher education in this decade will make the 1980s look like a picnic. As we move through the 1990s, that statement is proving to be true. For auxiliary enterprise administrators within student affairs divisions, this changing economic climate has brought new challenges and frustrations. College unions, residence halls, food service operations, and recreational sports facilities are all influenced by the current economic and political climate. From campus to campus, all facility managers are being bombarded with mixed messages. Managers are expected to expand and improve services and programs and to maximize revenues and reduce costs. They are being asked to increase existing market shares and to penetrate new markets in politically fragile environments while the private sector is claiming unfair competition. Finally, facility managers are expected to be competitive with the private sector and to produce products and provide services of the highest quality.

To survive in this climate, institutions need professional staffs that can manage complex facilities, understand and appreciate student development theory, and know how to combine the two in supporting the overall mission of the institution. For the purpose of this chapter, a *complex facility* is defined as one that serves all populations of the institution (students, staff, faculty, alumni, and guests), generates the majority of its revenue (at least 85 percent) through the sale of goods and services, has no more than 10 to 15 percent of its operating costs underwritten by student fees and private funds, and offers a variety of programs through student boards and services (meeting rooms, lounges, art galleries, theaters, food and other retail outlets, offices, guest rooms, parking, conference support facilities, and so forth). Although the chapter's reference point is college unions, the information is equally applicable to managers of residence hall systems, recreational sports complexes, and other facilities.

Properly managed facilities have the potential to create revenue to underwrite additional programs and services, fund scholarships, and reduce dependence by auxiliary units on other fund sources such as general funds and student fees. Such facilities support and promote feelings of community while serving as connectors to the institution. Most importantly, well-managed and attractive unions, residence halls, dining halls, and recreational sports facilities can provide a competitive edge in the recruitment and retention of students and faculty. Such enterprises must be connected to and supportive of the mission of the institution and the division of student affairs.

This chapter will highlight some of the issues and problems associated with facility management and offer the practitioner suggestions and resources to improve professional practice. The discussion will focus on the internal and external factors in the current environment that influence facility management, the need to develop a mission statement for the facility, examination of management style and organizational structures, strategic planning, planning for construction and renovation, and the future of campus facilities.

The Current Environment

Change is the one thing that is certain in today's management environment. The rapidity of change and the volume of information available to the facility manager must be constantly evaluated as decisions are made. The successful facility manager will recognize factors internal and external to the institution, will understand their potential impact, and will develop strategies to respond effectively to the most important ones. These factors will influence the quality of facility management in the years to come.

A More Diverse Student Population

Changing demographics will continue to produce a more diverse student population. Older students, single parents, students of color, international students, and physically and economically disadvantaged students are increasing in numbers and influence (see Chapter Twenty-Nine). Facilities and the programs using them must adjust to these changes in positive ways.

Fiscal Pressure

Public and private funding of higher education continues to erode. All facility managers face increased pressure to generate more revenue to cover costs of operation. Traditional programs, services, and spaces within facilities are under threat of elimination in favor of a more cost-effective utilization of spaces and resources. On many campuses, facilities are being judged more as revenue centers than as places to promote community and provide a unifying force for campus life. Balance must be achieved, however, in order to meet the primary goal of serving both the students and the institution.

Technological Change

A technological revolution has hit the college campus and student affairs (see Chapter Thirteen). There are many and specific applications of technology to facility management. Use of computers to aid in scheduling facilities and to conduct space utilization studies, for example, can increase the efficiency of staff response to inquiries. Videotaped programs, connections to satellite programs, and interactive computer programs for information requests can add a dimension to service. The rapidity of such changes, however, requires constant reevaluation of management and information systems. Advances in technology, however, also create a constant cycle of training and retraining of employees.

Career Orientation

Students continue to be focused on careers and interested in those activities that will improve their competitiveness and marketability. Such a focus results in less time spent on traditional programming and activities and also has implications for space use in all facilities.

Volunteerism

Student volunteerism is growing. Formal programs are available on many campuses that recruit and place student volunteers in campus and community service areas. Interest in the social sciences is also increasing. With diminished government support of the arts and social services, private funding and volunteer labor have become even more critical. In response, students are seeking opportunities to improve their understanding of philanthropy and their skills in volunteerism.

Breakdown of Community

Pressures continue that splinter and divide campus communities. These pressures come primarily from growing competition for limited resources (human and financial), a more diverse student and faculty population, societal conditions beyond the campus, and technology that lessens the need for education with human interaction (see Chapter Three).

Increased Need for Financial Aid

Students continue to absorb more costs for higher education through increased tuition, student fees, user fees, and the like. This trend creates a greater demand for student employment; a rise in student consumerism focused on cost, value, and quality; a need for more scholarships and grants; and greater dependence on loans to finance educational pursuits.

Greater Stress

Decreased funding, fragmentation of community, rapid change, increased competition, and environmental and social issues create more stress for employees at all levels of the organization.

Competition with the Private Sector

While institutions are calling for more revenue, the private sector claims unfair competition and looks for relief through state legislation that would limit and in some cases prohibit the sale of certain products and services by institutions. Unrelated business income and the taxing of that income are increased concerns for facility managers.

Privatization

The movement of the private sector into services and programs that institutions have historically operated themselves is gaining momentum. Facility managers are held accountable for financial performance and consistent production of a level of product and service matching or in some cases exceeding the private sector.

Government Regulations

Federal, state, and local governments are increasingly regulating items that directly affect facility planning; construction; ongoing maintenance; the environment; and employee recruitment, hiring, training, performance evaluation, and termination (see Chapters Nineteen and Thirty-Four).

Targeting and Specialization

Targeting specific segments of the campus market with specialized programs and services is becoming more important as campus populations continue to diversify. Although all-campus programs continue to be important in promoting a sense of community, the movement toward specialization and targeting will continue.

Litigation

The trend toward increasing litigation throughout American society has not escaped college campuses. Managers must be informed on changing codes, regulations, and conditions within their facilities that could put their institutions at risk. Safety training for all employees and frequent safety audits are mandatory. In addition, student affairs facility managers must assure that all employees understand and implement fairly all institutional regulations and policies when scheduling and supervising facilities.

Customer Service

Customer satisfaction has never been more important. Knowing customers, their needs, and their levels of satisfaction is extremely critical. Of more importance is flexibility and the ability to respond quickly in order to create acceptable levels of customer satisfaction.

The successful facility manager is constantly monitoring the environment looking for trends that will affect or have the potential to affect the operation. Good managers think strategically on how to utilize positive change as an advantage for the organization and how to eliminate or minimize the negative aspects of other changes. The ability to anticipate produces a competitive edge. The process is greatly enhanced and the chance for success increased immeasurably when an understanding exists as to the facility's purpose on the campus.

Mission Statement

One of the most important yet often ignored and misunderstood items for any organization is a clearly defined statement of mission. This statement for a facility explains its purpose and why the organization exists. To be effective, the unit's mission statement must relate to and support the overall one of the institution. Successful facility managers understand the critical importance of the mission statement, they review it often, and they communicate it frequently both inside and outside the organization.

Too often, no agreement exists among the various customers being served as to the purpose of the facility. Lacking that agreement, every constituent group measures satisfaction of programs, products, and services from a different perspective. Each has its own set of expectations. As a result, planning becomes a haphazard process, resources are wasted, and general support for programs and services is practically nonexistent. Good mission statements for facilities in institutions of higher education should be developed by those being served but also must reflect the values of the institution. Consensus among user groups on the mission of the facility is preferred but is not always possible or necessary. It is critical, however, for all user groups to understand the mission of the facility, for it provides a focus for the expenditure of energy and resources.

A mission statement provides a foundation for decision making and a standard for evaluating success. Mission statements help employees at all levels of the organization to have a better understanding of who they are, where they fit in the larger institution, and, most importantly, why they do what they do. It gives an employee a sense of worth that results in better service to the customer (students, faculty and staff members, and visitors).

The mission statement should be reconsidered regularly using a constant monitoring of environmental factors to ensure that it continues to be understood by and relevant to the campus community. The constant review and communication of mission becomes more critical as shifts in leadership occur among individuals in positions of power and influence over the organization.

Management Style and Organizational Structure

You can throw away your management book! Almost everything has changed. For facility managers to achieve success, careful attention must be paid to the way that staff members are supervised and to the organizational structure that supports the goals of the student affairs unit. This is a particularly critical requirement in service- and program-oriented units in student affairs, such as college unions and residence halls. An organizational structure and management style that works in the 1990s bears little resemblance to the traditional pyramid with the manager sitting at the top, the line employees at the bottom, and several layers separating the two. The traditional model placed value on position, title, control, order, and compliance. Communication was primarily vertical, and information was selectively shared because it was a source of power and influence.

Today's marketplace, both on and off the campus, is creating demands for new organizational models that are leaner, more flexible, flatter, and more responsive to changing conditions. Management skills required by this new environment have also radically changed. No longer is the management culture based on control over others. It is now directed toward empowerment of employees, delegation of responsibility, and creation of a sense of ownership. Managers of facilities associated with student affairs should take note of these changes in the corporate world and learn from them.

Evered and Selman discuss "shifting from coaching as a possible tool or technique within the prevailing paradigm of management, to a new paradigm in which the process of creating an organizational culture for coaching becomes the core managerial activity" (1989, p. 16). They note five attributes of good managers:

1. Observing a truly effective manager in action is much like watching an artist at work.

2. Managers who attend to what is actually going on outperform those who try to apply remembered techniques, canned prescriptions, and rational models.
3. Work results spring from the quality of the communication (speaking and listening) between managers and staff members.
4. The effectiveness of management flows from the level of partnership that is created between managers and the people with whom, through whom, and by whom the job gets done and the results are generated.
5. Effective managers are skillful in generating an empowering organizational climate [1989, p. 16].

Evered and Selman also state, "Reduced to its barest essentials, management may be viewed as a people-based art that focuses on creating and maintaining a climate, environment, and context which enable/empower a group of people to generate desired results, achievements, and accomplishments. Coaching, as we use the term, refers to the managerial activity of creating, by communication only, the climate, environment, and context that empowers individuals and teams to generate results" (1989, pp. 17–18).

Rosabeth Moss Kanter describes the new postentrepreneurial corporation and the type of managers who will be needed (1989). Kanter indicates that the corporation of today is not only leaner and flatter but also has more channels for action. She sees cross-functional projects, business-unit joint ventures, innovation funds for activities outside mainstream budgets and reporting lines, and strategic partnerships with suppliers or customers combining in ways that ignore the traditional chain of command. Today's managers must be competent negotiators, networkers, delegators, communicators, and collaborators; they must be trustworthy and empathetic. She also notes, "Today's executive must bargain, negotiate, and sell ideas like any other politician" (1989, p. 90).

What implications do the new corporate management philosophies have for facility managers in student affairs? As most facilities are created to serve students and others associated with the college or university, at first glance these issues may not appear to be relevant. Yet that is an incorrect perception. The internal and external forces influencing programming require that facility managers create environments that are both responsive to changing user needs and consistent with the philosophy, goals, and limitations of the institution.

Even in those institutions operating from a traditional pyramid, facility managers can still develop and promote a more responsive structure within their units that emphasizes employee empowerment, networking, collaboration, and strategic partnerships. For these individuals, to do otherwise is to hasten their own demise. In a future filled with consumerism and higher expectations for value, service, and quality of product, the manager will be judged more often against the private sector. When performance is found to be inferior, the manager will be replaced, the service will be discontinued or privatized, or some combination of these remedies will occur.

Strategic Planning

To be successful, the student services facility manager must be adept at planning and thinking strategically. With the rapidity of change in the marketplace and in technology, a process must be in place that is constantly assessing the external and internal environment, quickly identifying and responding to issues, anticipating problems, and focusing on action. A strategic planning process can meet the previous criteria while becoming the basis of establishing priorities and conducting financial planning with limited resources. Strategic planning is therefore essential.

At the 1990 Association of College Unions–International Annual Professional Conference, Manuel R. Cunard argued that strategic planning can encourage the move from a static perspective of management to a dynamic and active approach to decision making (1990). Cunard also noted that strategic thinking and acting are always more important than the planning exercise. In fact, if the approach or process used in the planning gets in the way of strategic thinking and action, the planning approach should be modified or abandoned.

Many reasons can be given for institutional facility managers becoming involved in strategic planning. Cunard (1990) states that most contemporary literature on the subject acknowledges that this planning can benefit organizations and hence facilities in eight critical areas. First, it provides a clarification process for the future direction of the organization. Second, it creates a focused opportunity to assess, modify, or reconfirm the mission of the organization. Third, it assists the manager in assigning priorities to responsibilities. Fourth, strategic planning promotes improvement of organizational effectiveness and performance. Fifth, it assists members of the organization and consumers to develop a sense of collaborating and being part of a team. Sixth, it offers a good method for responding to rapidly changing environments and constituencies. Seventh, strategic planning helps increase managers' appreciation of and responsiveness to economic market conditions and competition. Finally, it promotes the creation of an internal environment supportive of preferred behavior in the organization.

Cunard (1990) also indicates that there are a number of identified planning models that could be useful for facility managers in a student affairs environment.

Bryson (1988) proposes a strategic planning process for nonprofit organizations. He emphasizes participation of all concerned parties and suggests the following eight steps. First, agreement must be achieved on the specific process to be used. Second, all institutional mandates (policies) must be identified. Third, the mission and values of the organization (facility) must be clarified. Fourth, the external environment should be assessed and both opportunities and threats identified. Fifth, the strengths and weaknesses of the internal environment should be considered. Sixth, the strategic issues facing the organization must be determined. Seventh, strategies must be developed to manage those issues. Finally, the organization must establish a vision for the future.

Strategic planning allows the organization to take an inventory of resources and apply these to areas of highest priority. Strategic thinking promotes responsiveness and action. Finally, this kind of planning and thinking focuses attention on those issues that truly influence the positioning of the organization in the institution. It helps the manager prepare for the future, whether that future focuses on programs, services, or facilities.

Construction and Renovation

A study by the Association of College/University Physical Plant Administrators ("Higher Education Faces a $20 Billion Backlog," 1988) notes that the nation's 3,400 colleges and universities are facing a $20 billion backlog of urgent facility repairs plus an additional $60 to $70 billion required for renovation and renewal projects. The Data Bank of the Association of College Unions–International (1989) supports the necessity of construction and renovation dollars as 50 percent of the present college unions are twenty-five to thirty years old.

Funding for major repairs, renovation, and new construction is difficult at best. Although many auxiliary units (particularly in the public sector) have reserve accounts, available funds are often inadequate to meet identified needs. Therefore, the facility manager is faced with a very difficult dilemma: facilities are deteriorating, losing customer support, failing to meet mandated health and safety codes, and incapable of taking advantage of new technology. With inadequate funding to address these problems, what is the facility manager to do?

This chapter's earlier emphasis on the importance of thinking strategically is critical to the process of securing adequate funding. Those who are in a position to provide that funding must perceive the programs, services, and products of the facility as having value for them and for the greater institution. As funding usually comes from a variety of sources (student fees, generated income, general fund support, and private donations), it is critical for the facility manager to establish understanding and, if possible, agreement among all parties regarding the mission of the facility.

Once the mission statement has been accepted and the facility is perceived to have value from those being served, the manager is now in a position to put a planning committee together to develop a program statement and a funding plan for new construction or renovation. The mission statement is an essential checkpoint for all planning. Space assignment and functional locations must constantly be compared with the mission statement. If revenue production is an important element of the funding plan, for example, retail outlets should be located in heavy traffic areas of the facility.

If development of community is an important mission, spaces such as lounges, common seating areas, and office environments must be included. The planning group must constantly be aware of functional relationships as spaces are being assigned.

Successful facility managers know that the most important phase of any construction or renovation project is the planning. That is the time when support for the project is generated, funding is finalized, and excitement can start to build for the completed project.

The *Task Force 2000 Final Report* of the Association of College Unions–International notes an extensive list of items generated by Christopher (1989), Brubaker (1989), and Kratzer, Todd, Brattain, and Cherrey (1984) that should be considered in the future design of educational facilities with specific emphasis on college unions. The reader is referred to the chapter in the report by Yates and Canavit (1990) that provides useful guidance for all facility planners whether they are looking at unions, residence halls, dining services, or recreational space. Important concepts in the report include adapting to future innovations, establishing networks with campus and community computer and communication systems, and identifying the needs of the community being served.

The latter is essential if the project is to receive support and funding. The educational, recreational, social, and cultural needs of the entire college or university community must be specifically reviewed. The planning document must recognize the unique characteristics of the institution and the best way for the facility to respond to these. For example, a college union on an urban commuter campus may need amenities such as locker space that would be inappropriate for a residential campus. Finally, the specific requirements of the persons who will teach at, clean, live in, and administer the facilities must be identified.

Practical issues such as availability of funds, energy consumption, accessibility for the disabled, safety, architectural style, location, and an inventory of other existing facilities can not be ignored. Yates and Canavit also focus on intangibles such as the desired aesthetic quality, the attitude of the institution toward competition, the importance of correlation between design and development, and the functionalism of the facility (1990).

The effective manager of today must be a negotiator, a salesman, and a collaborator with an action-oriented style that is constantly in touch with the customer. All of those skills will be needed in facing and solving the challenges of getting funding for new construction and renovation and of meeting the financial goals for a new or renovated facility.

Summary

Given the definition of a complex facility as one generating at least 85 percent of its operating budget through the sale of goods and services, the facility manager knows that the customer's perception of value is critical. If one trend for the future is increasing competition for fewer resources, every manager must ensure that the right combination of services, product quality, and pricing is being offered. The successful manager will understand that quality is defined by the customer and will ensure an organizational climate that is free of barriers to teamwork and employee pride and that actively promotes efforts for improvement.

The facility manager of tomorrow will lead an organization that is more efficient, less hierarchical, and more responsive to the changing marketplace. This manager must be a skilled communicator, motivator, facilitator, negotiator, and strategic thinker. The manager will recognize that the future of any facility or program in a university environment will be greatly enhanced by developing a closer relationship with the faculty.

Managers of complex facilities lead operations that create a significant amount of revenue, control space, and work closely with student leaders. Facility managers must understand and recognize that these functions are perceived as sources of power within the academic community, and they must search for ways to share that power within the institution to improve the customer's perception of value in the quality of its products, programs, and services.

A special report called *Campus Life: In Search of Community,* released by the Carnegie Foundation for the Advancement of Teaching, notes, "What is needed . . . is a larger, more integrative vision of community in higher education, one that focuses not on the length of time students spend on campus, but on the quality of the encounter" (1990, p. 7).

The facility manager must always keep the mission of the facility in mind; as defined by that statement, maintain a proper balance in operations, programs, and services; and make day-to-day decisions on principles that support and strengthen the mission.

With a community framework in place, a genuine commitment to quality throughout the organization, an understanding of who the customer is and what the customer wants, and an openness to new paradigms for operation, the facility manager of the future can and will be successful. In the end, as it always has been, that success will be measured by those who are served — students, faculty, staff, alumni, and guests of the institution. They are the final judges of value, and they always have the final word.

References

Association of College Unions–International. Data Base. Bloomington, Ind.: Association of College Unions–International, 1989.

Brubaker, B. "College and University Planning and Design: The State of the Art." *CEFPI's Educational Facility Planner,* 1989, *27* (1), 21–22.

Bryson, J. M. *Strategic Planning for Public and Nonprofit Organizations: A Guide to Strengthening and Sustaining Organizational Achievement.* San Francisco: Jossey-Bass, 1988.

Carnegie Foundation for the Advancement of Teaching. *Campus Life: In Search of Community*. Princeton, N.J.: Carnegie Foundation for the Advancement of Teaching, 1990.

Christopher, G. "Ten Trends for Education Design." *CEFPI's Educational Facility Planner*, 1989, *27* (1), 15.

Cunard, M. R. "The Process of Strategic Planning." *1990 ACU-I Proceedings*. Bloomington, Ind.: Association of College Unions–International, 1990, 58–62.

Evered, R. D., and Selman, J. C. "Coaching and the Art of Management." *Organizational Dynamics*, Autumn 1989, *18* (2), 16–32.

"Higher Education Faces a \$20 Billion Backlog in Urgent Facility Repair Needs, NACUBO Survey Finds." *Business Officer*, Oct. 1988, *22* (4), 7–8.

Kanter, R. M. "The New Managerial Work." *Harvard Business Review*, Nov.–Dec. 1989, pp. 28–32.

Kratzer, D., Todd, R., Brattain, W. E., and Cherrey, C. "Creative Remodeling and Construction." *Proceedings of the 63rd Meeting of the Association of College Unions–International*. Bloomington, Ind.: Association of College Unions–International, 1984.

Yates, M., and Canavit, F. "The College Union Facility of the Future." In J. W. Johnston (ed.), *Task Force 2000 Final Report*. Bloomington, Ind.: Association of College Unions–International, 1990.

13

∽

Technological Changes
in Student Affairs
Administration

John L. Baier

Student affairs organizations in America's 3,400 colleges and universities are usually an administrative cluster of interrelated services, programs, activities, and facilities that primarily provide vital cocurricular advising and personal support to the institution's student body. For that reason, as Mills (1990) indicates, "Student affairs is typically viewed as a professional area that focuses on the person. . . . There is little mention of technology in the student affairs literature. . . . Indeed, student affairs is considered by many to be the 'high-touch' counterpart to the 'high-tech' aspects of campus life" (p. 138).

By using modern computer and information technology, however, student affairs organizations can enhance the delivery of student services, activities, and programs and increase the overall effectiveness and efficiency of administrative functions. The benefits of using technology include but are not limited to reduced administrative overhead costs related to maintaining files; assistance in generating reports and keeping statistics; a reduced number of human errors resulting in improved record accuracy; improved intra- and interdepartmental communications; better collection and use of administrative data (fiscal, usage, personnel, and facility) needed for planning and decision making; reduced publication costs and improved appearance of handbooks, brochures, course schedules, directories, calendars, forms, letters, and flyers; increased speed and simplification of data collection, analysis, and report production; and possible reductions in clerical staff.

All student affairs professionals should therefore learn how to use modern technology and apply it in their daily activities. In *New Futures for Student Affairs,* Barr, Upcraft, and Associates (1990) include among their twelve recommendations for the future of the profession, "We must join the computer and information system revolution" (p. 299). More specifically, they suggest that student affairs organizations should continue to develop computer-assisted ways of managing information about students, services, programs, and facilities; make better use of computer technology for planning, facilities management, resource allocation, record keeping, and other management functions; ensure that student affairs staff are "computer literate"; and serve as guardians against the dehumanization of students and staff that can occur with the increased use of technology.

Although computer and information technology has been widely integrated into the general administrative and instructional functions of most colleges and universities for over two decades, it is only recently that very many student affairs divisions have attempted a comprehensive approach in applying modern computer and information technology to the administration of their departments and programs. The slowness of many student affairs divisions in the 1980s to embrace the use of technology was probably due to a number of factors: the lack of the funding needed to procure and maintain computer hardware, the lack of suitable software, the technological illiteracy of many student affairs staff members, and the general discomfort and apprehension of professionals for a "people-oriented" profession in using an impersonal technology (machines, cables, and discs) in their daily work.

For the most part, those practitioners who pioneered the computerization of student affairs programs and services in the 1980s had to rely on the materials supplied by computer hardware and software vendors, information obtained by word of mouth from professional colleagues at other campuses, or recommendations extracted from a small number of presentations at professional conferences. Most computerization was therefore accomplished through trial and error or with the assistance of campus computer center personnel who had very limited knowledge of the nuances and priorities of student affairs practice. This situation resulted in costly errors, both in time and dollars, and adversely influenced staff member attitudes about and confidence in the potential benefits of modern computer and information technology.

But during the past decade, there has been a significant increase in the use of new technologies in student affairs all over the nation and in all types of institutions. This change has been brought about by a number of factors. First, there has been an explosion in the availability of new, affordable, and "user-friendly" computer equipment and software programs that can be readily utilized in the management and delivery of student affairs programs and services. Second, more student affairs professionals have become technologically literate, own their own microcomputers or have them available at work, and are willing to experiment with application of computer technology to their day-by-day activities. Third, most of today's college students have been exposed to computers and technology during their primary and secondary education. Students thus not only appreciate and use technology on a daily basis but also expect administrators and faculty to be able to utilize current technology in the administrative and instructional programs of the institution. A college or university that does not take advantage of modern technology for teaching, research, and administration will not be able to compete successfully for the best students, faculty, and staff.

As more student affairs professionals become familiar with computers and discover that most traditional high-touch student affairs functions and activities can be enhanced rather than diminished through the use of modern technology, the computerization of student affairs functions should continue. Organizations that have already begun the process of computerization will need to upgrade hardware and software in order to integrate new technologies into administrative operations. To accomplish this, most student affairs professionals will need to acquire or increase their technological literacy and comfort level with using technology in daily activities. Professionals must learn how to use high tech rather than to fear it, but they must do it in a way that "ensure[s] that [the] student affairs administrator is managing the system—rather than the system managing the administrator" (Mills, 1990, p. 151).

The purpose of this chapter is to describe how the advances in computer and information technology can be positively applied to student affairs and to discuss their implications for the future. The chapter is organized into three sections. The first describes how technology is currently being applied to the day-by-day work of student affairs. The second section offers a brief discussion of the administrative considerations and issues that must be considered in order to ensure the effective and efficient use of technology. The final section provides a list of recommendations for meeting the technology challenges of tomorrow.

Current Applications of Technology in Student Affairs

There are many different ways to apply modern technology to traditional student affairs functions, programs, and student services. In a recent American College Personnel Association publication (Baier, Strong, and Associates, forthcoming) over a hundred current applications are described in considerable detail and evaluated for their utility and effectiveness. A brief summary of some described in that book follow. They are presented by functional area for the convenience of the reader.

Admissions, Registration, and Records

Admissions offices across the nation were among the first areas in student affairs to adopt modern information and computer technology. The earliest applications dealing with admissions, records, and registration used the mainframe computer to manage course scheduling, academic records, grade production, centralized registration functions, generation of student bills, and student address files. In more recent years, the mainframe has been utilized to manage on-line and telephone registration systems, degree audits, report production, class schedule printing, catalog production, and student data analysis and correspondence. On large campuses, all of these functions require continuous entry, updating, storage, inter- and intradepartmental communication, and manipulation of large data bases — all functions ideally suited to the mainframe computer. However, they also usually necessitated the purchase of expensive hardware and software systems and extensive customized program revisions to meet the specific needs of a campus. The services of a full-time computer programmer and data analyst–coordinator to maintain and update the systems were also required.

Until recently, many smaller campuses found the computer hardware and software acquisition and maintenance costs prohibitive. But during the past five years, with the increased power of microcomputers and the availability of inexpensive software (for example, Dialog) for them, even small colleges can now utilize computer technology to perform most of the common tasks of an admissions and records office.

The computerization of admissions office data bases has also improved the accuracy and speed with which student data and records can be gathered, maintained, manipulated, and retrieved. It has also allowed for the development of improved enrollment management programs; it is now a quick and inexpensive matter to run computer simulations of the influence of class and course sizes on the institution's overall enrollment strategies. For example, instead of designing recruitment and retention strategies just for the freshmen class, it is now possible to develop ones for increasing enrollments in selected academic departments and majors without having to increase faculty size or class size. Without the use of computer technology, this type of enrollment management would be very difficult and costly to do.

Academic Advising

Surveys of the perceptions of students on many campuses reveal that one of their greatest concerns is the availability of good academic advising. There is usually little time or incentive for faculty members on campuses to serve effectively as academic advisers, especially when confronted with heavy teaching loads and pressures to engage in research and scholarly publication. In addition, at many institutions, the complexity of the curriculum and the multitude of degree options, course prerequisites, and requirements have made effective and accurate academic advising a monumental task. But through the use of modern technology, it is now possible to audit students' progress toward the completion of their degree programs and to provide faculty members with the timely and comprehensive data they need to advise students on academic programs and future registrations. For large campuses, several excellent, relatively inexpensive (less than $100,000) degree audit–academic advising software programs that run on a mainframe are now commercially available (for example, On Course). And for smaller campuses with a more restricted curriculum, fewer degree options, and fewer students (under two thousand), there are several excellent software programs (for example, Action Trac) that can run on a minicomputer and can then be networked to microcomputers in individual faculty member offices throughout the campus.

Financial Aid

Another major user of information and computer technology during the past decade has been offices of financial aid. Most financial aid programs generally take advantage of the mainframe to manipulate large amounts of data, make awards, keep records, and gain access to student data files to mail award notifications and credit financial aid to student tuition and fee bills. Financial aid offices historically have been the second-largest student affairs user of the mainframe computer on large campuses. But until recently, on small campuses, most financial aid processing, packaging, awarding, and record keeping have been done manually because of the lack of affordable and suitable computer hardware and software. There are now excellent inexpensive financial aid software programs enabling microcomputers to perform these functions as well as manage student part-time employment services, job location and development programs, college work-study programs, scholarship records, and veterans benefits programs.

Financial aid offices also find it is cost effective and advantageous to participate in the federal government's Pell Grant electronic data exchange program and similar state electronic data exchanges and computer networks. These electronic networks and tape-exchange programs save weeks of application-processing time, lessen human errors, and significantly reduce the number of fee deferments that otherwise would have to be given to a large number of Pell Grant and state grant applicants waiting to receive official notification of their awards at the beginning of each new semester, quarter, or term.

Housing and Residential Life

The use of the computer as an administrative tool is not new in the administration of a housing office. Housing offices have used the strengths of the mainframe or minicomputer for accounting, application processing, room assignments, and the collection of housing data for over a decade. With the development of the powerful microcomputer and a wider variety of excellent software, however, all housing offices, whether they be large or small, are now able to improve many additional functions through computerization. These include roommate matching; in-house purchasing systems; student development programming; production of housing brochures, forms, and publications; inventory control; personnel record systems; rate studies; project management; occupancy-income forecasting; conference scheduling; and space utilization modeling. Also, because many residence hall systems now provide microcomputer labs and have wired individual student rooms for cable TV and computer networking, it is possible to use electronic communications (for example, E-Mail) throughout the halls and to provide information and educational video programs twenty-four hours per day.

Counseling and Testing

An area of student affairs that has quite recently adopted new technology in the delivery and management of student services and programs has been the counseling and testing center. Recent software developments for the microcomputer now enable these centers to expand and improve a variety of programming and administrative functions without adding additional clerical or professional staff. Examples of software available for use in counseling include programs for test-anxiety diagnosis, psychoactive drug information, alcohol consumption counseling, alcohol assessment and treatment profiles, intake and apppointment scheduling, and counseling session summary note filing. Examples of software for testing services include vocational-interest inventories, personality tests, graduate and professional school entrance exam preparation and practice tests, and faculty test-scoring services. The use of this new technology has reduced the cost and time required to obtain the results of diagnostic tests and allowed professional staff members to spend more hours counseling and attending to the needs and emotional health of their student clientele.

Teaching and Learning Resource Centers

A teaching-learning skills program is one of the most recent services in the evolution of student affairs organizations. Most of these programs depend on high-tech labs for teaching, tutoring, and course enrichment. These functions are readily being served by the rapid advances in video, microcomputer, CD-ROM (a high-density data storage device read by laser), and interactive multimedia technology, and the hundreds of computer software and CD-ROM programs now available in virtually all academic disciplines (Brady, 1989). Inexpensive microcomputer software is also available for program evaluation, resource utilization, individual diagnostic programs, tutorial scheduling, and preprofessional exam preparation.

Many campuses now also have the capability to produce high-quality instructional and tutorial videotapes of their own faculty that can be used to enrich and supplement their own course instruction. Institutions that have established teaching-learning resource centers have found that they can provide academic support programs to thousands of students for a fraction of the operating and personnel costs common to many other student services. For example, with approximately $100,000 for start-up video and computer hardware and software, two professional staff members, one secretary, a couple of graduate students, several student assistants, and a small operating budget, it is possible to offer excellent and comprehensive teaching-learning assistance programs to five to six thousand students each semester. This type of service not only improves learning and retention rates but also symbolically demonstrates to the faculty and the campus community at large that student affairs is committed to the centrality of learning and the academic mission at the institution.

Career Planning and Placement

There is also an array of video, computer, and interactive microcomputer hardware and software that can be used to support career counseling and placement functions. For years, software programs such as SIGI + and Discover have proven to be excellent tools for career counseling, and videotapes and computer software on topics such as interviewing techniques and résumé writing have been shown to be excellent teaching aids for career-planning programs. There are also first-rate inexpensive software programs to support placement functions in such areas as recruiter scheduling; student interview scheduling; maintenance of credential files; generation of reports; and production of routine publications, job listings, and brochures. Additionally, through the use of facsimile machines and computer linkages with government agencies, corporate offices, employment agencies, and school systems (such as Job Link and KINEXUS), career centers are now able to obtain information on job vacancies throughout the country instantly and supply employers with résumés of qualified applicants.

Career centers that have embraced these technologies have discovered that they are able to serve more effectively larger numbers of students, alumni, and recruiters with the same size staff as before; at the same time, they can also better utilize the time of their professional staff members to meet the counseling needs of the growing numbers of less prepared, self-directed, or self-motivated students who are now attending college.

Student Life, Student Activities, and Student Centers

There is also an abundance of microcomputer software for the student activities professional. Software is available for tracking fraternity and sorority statistics, maintaining membership rosters, managing student activity accounts, scoring student elections, evaluating programs, managing student government budgets, overseeing rush programs, and maintaining student organization data bases.

Microcomputer software that is inexpensive and easy to learn and use also exists to assist student center activities. These include managing building reservations and scheduling, coordinating events, printing and auditing tickets, controlling inventory, managing utility usage, monitoring security systems, managing food service operations, running maintenance schedules, and supervising building budgets. Standard desktop-publishing and word-processing software can also be used by student activities professionals to produce high-quality (but inexpensive) brochures, newsletters, and flyers quickly and to generate routine correspondence, policy documents, and statistical management reports in a fraction of the time previously required.

Recreation Programs

Many elements of traditional recreation and personal fitness programs have also been computerized during the past five years. For example, fitness software has been designed that tailors fitness programs for individuals, tracks their progress, and updates exercise prescriptions on a periodic basis. Like the student activities and housing areas, customized software programs developed specifically for recreation professionals are now available. They allow them to schedule intramurals quickly and accurately, compile and graphically present usage data, maintain equipment inventories, coordinate maintenance schedules, manage locker rental and equipment checkout, reserve facilities, control entry systems, and manage leisure class programs. Recreation centers can now also employ modern technology and media equipment to provide both group and self-paced instruction in sports activities and fitness areas.

It is also possible to purchase interactive multimedia equipment to simulate and teach individual sports such as golf and archery. Although this equipment is currently very expensive to purchase and maintain, recreation-fitness professionals anticipate that it will soon come down in price much as basic computer systems did. When prices are reduced, this technology should find many new applications in the recreation area.

Health Service and Wellness Programs

Although some health services adopted high-tech solutions for their operations during the late 1980s, most still remain only partially computerized today. The reason is that until recently, most health care management computer software was developed for large-hospital use or for small doctors' offices and clinics and was geared for processing insurance applications and generating patient bills. As most health services operate on a prepaid basis, they do very little of either function. Thus, the commercially available software was not well suited for their operations. However, with the emergence of health maintenance organizations (HMOs), a commercial need developed for software that could be used to monitor the use of supplies, laboratory tests, X rays, and pharmaceuticals and to assist nurses and physicians with scheduling appointments, charting, and maintaining patient records. As HMOs operate much like student health centers, the new computer software created for HMOs can easily be adapted to meet student health needs. Software is thus obtainable that will enable student health centers to do all of the above, plus maintain pharmacy records, order drugs and supplies, and keep track of student immunizations.

Software for wellness programs has also become available. Computer programs and videos can be acquired on substance abuse, AIDS, sexually transmitted disease, eating disorders, smoking cessation, exercise, dietary guidance, stress education, and sickle cell anemia. Touch-screen and other interactive computer systems that allow patients to test their health knowledge can be installed in patient waiting rooms. The use of all of this technology allows health services to serve students better while saving both staff members' time and fiscal resources.

The Office of the Chief Student Affairs Officer

Most of the functions performed in the office of the chief student affairs officer (CSAO) lend themselves to modern microcomputer applications. By using standard word-processing, data-base, spreadsheet, and desktop-publishing software, it is possible to be more efficient in responding to routine correspondence and in producing and updating organizational charts, personnel records, student fee schedules, budgetary data, and policy documents. Through both Local Area Networks (LANs) and Wide Area Networks (WANs), it is possible to be on line with the campus's student data base, fiscal information system, personnel system, alumni office files, security department, and all of the other student affairs offices. This situation allows for instant retrieval and updating of essential management information. Communicating through electronic mail with all departments and critical personnel on the campus can also be useful. The wise use of technology in the chief student affairs officer's office not only allows CSAOs to keep their offices small and efficient but also to set a positive example to the rest of the division on the benefits of modern technology.

Administrative Considerations and Issues

Because the advantages of computer and information technology in the delivery and administration of student services are so great, continued application of such tools and preparation for the future are both required. To take proper advantage of these opportunities, a number of management, legal, and ethical issues must first be considered and resolved.

Keeping the Profession's Focus

Mills (1990) cautions, "While technology advances have great potential to provide increased communication, data analysis, and speed, they do not solve all of our problems. . . . Reliance on technology has the potential to decrease human contact and define relationships more rigidly. . . . Dependence on technology may aggravate a lack of attention to the individual characteristics of students and staff" (p. 139).

Student affairs professionals must remember that student affairs is a helping profession. A century-old tradition of providing understanding and support services to a constantly changing student body made up of unique individuals with their own special needs, goals, gifts, and personalities undergirds student affairs practice. Therefore, before we apply a new technology to the delivery of a student service or program, three questions should be answered: (1) Will it help our students? (2) Will it save us time or money? (3) Will it assist our institution? If the answers to all three questions are yes, then we should probably proceed with all deliberate speed. However, if the answer is no to any one of the questions, we should probably defer proceeding until conditions or further advances warrant further consideration of that technology.

Planning

It is also very important that student affairs organizations develop sound plans for both applying and maintaining the use of technology in all areas of responsibility. To date, most planning for the use of microcomputers and other information technology in higher education has not been very good. As Ferrante, Hayman, Carlson, and Phillips (1988) put it, "Most institutions seem to have been muddling through or merely reacting to technology. . . . A more proactive stance is probably more appropriate" (p. 79). To develop, implement, and update plans for using modern technology, they recommend that universities should use strategic planning methodology, establish a strong central authority to coordinate the planning process, provide networking and access to computers and data bases, involve as many staff members in the planning and decision-making process as possible, and develop an infrastructure that supports the use of technology (staff training programs, equipment repair, replacement accounts, and the like). Because student affairs organizations usually have limited budgets, it is critical that they give very careful consideration to proper planning, implementation, and use policies in order to avoid wasting their very limited resources.

Staff Training and Development

Access to modern computer and information technology is of little value if staff members do not know how to use it properly. Because so many current student affairs practitioners entered the profession before much of today's computer and information technology was even invented and because most people attracted to the profession are not technically oriented, it is vital that all student affairs organizations embark upon a major technological literacy training effort within existing staff development programs. Methods include short courses, workshops, technology-related newsletters, tutoring programs, self-paced video-learning modules, contests, and incentive grants (Baier, forthcoming). Professional preparation programs must also embrace technological competency as an essential part of the curriculum.

Each student affairs graduate training program should follow the Council for the Advancement of Standards (CAS) master's-level graduate preparation program guidelines (1988). These guidelines call for the inclusion of a computer literacy and applications component in all student affairs graduate preparation programs, regardless of their emphasis. Although this standard was adopted by the profession nearly a decade ago, it has yet to be followed by most of the eighty-seven graduate programs that collectively graduate approximately five hundred new professionals each year (Keim and Graham, 1990). If graduate programs follow the CAS guidelines and a better job is done of training existing staff members (and those who enter the profession from other routes) via staff development programs, it would only take a few years to raise significantly the technological competence of the entire student affairs profession.

Networking

The full benefits of using computer technology cannot be obtained if microcomputers are not fully connected to each other and to the central campus mainframe computer. Networks allow for on-line interactive communication with any other connected computer. The proper development of LANs that link computers within a single building or portion of a building and WANs that connect computers between buildings and between campuses is very important to the efficient use of computer data bases, software programs, and electronic communications. Therefore, student affairs organizations must carefully design appropriate networking systems to meet the particular needs of their campus. BITNET, a national electronic mail service, is also useful.

Legal and Ethical Issues

In our litigious society, student affairs administrators must be concerned with the legal liabilities that occur as a result of specific acts, omissions, and decisions. Over the past decade, a considerable amount of case law specific to the use of computers has accrued. Patricia A. Hollander, the general counsel of the American Association of University Administrators, has written extensively on this topic (Hollander, 1983, 1984, 1986, and forthcoming); all student affairs professionals who utilize computer technology in their work should carefully read her publications. Then, in conjunction with institutional legal counsel, written policies should be developed that address the legal and ethical issues related to computer use. Programs designed to develop an awareness and working knowledge of computer law and the institution's specific computer-related policies should also be offered as a part of ongoing staff development programs.

Hollander (1986, and forthcoming) points out that the law of computers is for the most part the law of copyrights. Today's courts are applying copyright laws to computer-related matters with increasing frequency. She further indicates that the acquisition and use of computers generally fall into one of three legal-ethical categories. First, there are intellectual-property issues, including who owns the software copyright. Can software programs be copied, and can computer software created by employees and students be exploited? The second category involves contract and tort concerns (such as computer warranties or negligent and wrongful use of programs) and liabilities related to employment (such as radiation dangers and physical injuries). The third category consists of educationally related issues, including abuse of computers by students. For example, should a student who "breaks" an access code be prosecuted criminally or within the campus discipline system? Care in protecting the confidentiality of data, records, and research stored in computers is also critical. Basic knowledge about each area of the law is essential to minimizing legal liabilities and risks.

Summary

The computer will continue to play an important role in the instructional programs and management of our colleges and universities. Other technologies, such as video, CD-ROM, interactive multimedia, and other systems not yet invented or perfected, will also be crucial. All technology will likely become both more sophisticated and easier to use. Exactly how these advances will influence our lives, education, and student affairs functions is unknown. Forecasting is difficult, but the successful student affairs administrator must be ready for change and prepared to take advantage of every opportunity. The following recommendations may provide some guidance for the profession:

1. Continue to keep the focus of the student affairs profession on students, their learning, and their development. Do not let technology dominate the work of the profession. Instead, use technology to enhance the efficiency, effectiveness, and quality of our work with students.

2. Remembering *The Student Personnel Point of View* (American Council on Education, [1937] 1949), develop and constantly update a strategic plan for adapting modern technology to the day-by-day administration and delivery of high-quality and responsible student affairs programs and services to our campus communities.

3. Continue developing the technological literacy, comfort, and competency levels of all student affairs staff members.

4. Expect basic computer skills and minimal technological literacy from all new employees. In addition, assist staff members in staying up-to-date

on new technological applications in student affairs in order to be eligible for merit increases and promotions.

5. Continue development of computer-assisted approaches to collect, maintain, manage, and use pertinent data about students, programs, facility use, program effects on learning and student development, retention, and financing and operations.

6. Persist in using technology to improve communications with students, faculty and staff members, and other administrators whenever possible.

7. Attempt to utilize technology in all new program development and administration, but be certain that its use will benefit both students and the institution before proceeding.

8. Continue serving as custodians of student records and data bases to guard against their misuse.

9. Ensure that student codes of conduct contain prohibitions (and appropriate sanctions) against the misuse and theft of computer equipment, systems, files, software, and others' work.

10. Routinely have legal counsel review all current and planned technological applications and policies to reduce exposure to legal liability and to make certain that they are in full compliance with existing laws.

If these suggestions are followed, student affairs should be able to derive enormous benefits from technological advances without sacrificing its traditional roots as a helping profession interested in meeting the ever-changing educational and developmental needs of college students. Student affairs professionals need not fear technology; instead, whenever practical and appropriate, they should use it to enhance high-touch programs and services. All of higher education, and especially students, will expect no less.

References

American Council on Education. *The Student Personnel Point of View*. Washington, D.C.: American Council on Education, 1949. (Originally published 1937.)

Baier, J. L. "Assessing and Enhancing the Technological Literacy and Competencies of Student Affairs Staff." In J. L. Baier, T. S. Strong, and Associates, *Technology in Student Affairs: Using High-Tech to Enhance High-Touch*. Washington, D.C.: American College Personnel Association, forthcoming.

Baier, J. L., Strong, T. S., and Associates. *Technology in Student Affairs: Using High-Tech to Enhance High-Touch*. Washington, D.C.: American College Personnel Association, forthcoming.

Barr, M. J., Upcraft, M. L., and Associates. *New Futures for Student Affairs: Building a Vision for Professional Leadership and Practice*. San Francisco: Jossey-Bass, 1990.

Brady, H. "Interactive Multimedia: The Next Wave." *Classroom Computer Learning*, Sept. 1989, pp. 56–61.

Council for the Advancement of Standards for Student Services/Development Programs. "Master's-Level Graduate Preparation Program Guidelines." In *Council for the Advancement of Standards: Standards and Guidelines for Student Services/Development Programs*. Washington, D.C.: Council for the Advancement of Standards for Student Services/Development Programs, 1988.

Ferrante, R., Hayman, J., Carlson, M. S., and Phillips, H. *Planning for Microcomputers in Higher Education: Strategies for the Next Generation*. ASHE-ERIC Higher Education Report, no. 7. Washington, D.C.: Association for the Study of Higher Education, 1988.

Hollander, P. A. "University Computing Facilities: Some Ethical Dilemmas." In M. C. Baca and R. H. Stein (eds.), *Ethical Principles, Problems, and Practices in Higher Education*. Springfield, Ill.: Thomas, 1983.

Hollander, P. A. "An Introduction to Legal and Ethical Issues Relating to Computers in Higher Education." *Journal of College and University Law*, Fall 1984, *11* (2), 215–232.

Hollander, P. A. *Computers in Education: Legal Liabilities and Ethical Issues Concerning Their Use and Misuse*. Higher Education Administration Series. Asheville, N.C.: College Administration Publications, 1986.

Hollander, P. A. "Legal Liabilities and Ethical Issues." In J. L. Baier, T. S. Strong, and Associates, *Technology in Student Affairs: Using High-Tech to Enhance High-Touch*. Washington, D.C.: American College Personnel Association, forthcoming.

Keim, M., and Graham, J. W. (eds.). *Directory of Graduate Preparation Programs in College Student Personnel, 1990*. Washington, D.C.: American College Personnel Association (Commission XII Publications), 1990.

Mills, D. B. "The Technological Transformation of Student Services." In M. J. Barr, M. L. Upcraft, and Associates, *New Futures for Student Affairs: Building a Vision for Professional Leadership and Practice*. San Francisco: Jossey-Bass, 1990.

PART THREE

❦

Essential Skills
and Competencies
for Student Affairs
Managers

In Part Three, the skills and competencies necessary for a successful student affairs administrator are defined. Although all may not agre with this list, the wide range of issues and skills discussed here bears witness to the complexity of the management function in student affairs.

Effective program planning and implementation are expected of most student affairs managers. Rosalind Andreas provides a model for program planning and uses extensive case examples to show the applicability of that model in Chapter Fourteen.

In an era of tight fiscal resources, student affairs administrators are called on more frequently to defend program expenditures and show that funding is being allocated in such a way as to make a positive impact on the lives of students. In Chapter Fifteen, Robert Brown and Diane Podolske provide a model to implement sound evaluation procedures for student affairs programs.

We are expected to be experts on students, but many of us do not engage in research about them on a routine basis. Further, outcomes assessment is becoming critical as institutions try to demonstrate that the collegiate experience does make a difference. Dary Erwin offers a primer on research and outcomes assessment in Chapter Sixteen to assist professionals in beginning to deal with these complex questions.

How does one go about making a budget? What models work? These questions and others are addressed by Dudley Woodard in Chapter Seventeen. The budget preparation and management suggestions furnished in this chapter will be equally helpful to the vice president and the unit manager.

Theory application remains an elusive goal for many of us. How can understanding of theory in all its forms assist the student affairs administrator in developing high-quality programs and services? In Chapter Eighteen, M. Lee Upcraft gives a quick overview of theories that provide guidance to student affairs professionals and presents a model of translating theory into practice that can serve as a useful tool.

Ignorance is not bliss for administrators when it comes to the legal dimensions of our work. A fundamental understanding of the legal ramifications of student affairs policies and practices must be mastered and continually updated. Chapter Nineteen, by Donald Gehring, introduces the critical legal questions for student affairs administrators and includes suggestions for practice and continual renewal in this important arena.

The most time-consuming task for the student affairs administrator is working with people. In Chapter Twenty, Arthur Sandeen draws on his years of experience as a chief student affairs officer and offers excellent advice on the art of developing effective campus relations.

Conflict is no stranger to higher education or to student affairs. It is an inherent part of the academy. In Chapter Twenty-One, Don Creamer identifies strategies to resolve conflicts and offers suggestions for the practitioner who must deal with such issues on a daily basis.

Ethics issues are not abstract; they are a real part of the life of any student affairs administrator. In Chapter Twenty-Two, Harry Canon supplies an overview of the ethical implications of our work with specific concentration on the inherent conflicts involved in resolving ethical dilemmas.

Some have said that the nineties will cause us to look with longing to the sixties. Even those who do not agree with that statement would recognize that media concern with higher education, the threat of litigation, and the calls for accountability have all grown dramatically in recent years and that it is a trend likely to continue in the future. Dealing with large- and small-campus crises has become the norm for student affairs administrators. In Chapter Twenty-Three, Marsha Duncan thoughtfully considers how student affairs professionals might master this most difficult area of responsibility.

Each of the issues discussed in Part Three is complex, but all relate to the daily work of administration and management in student affairs. If we are to be effective, we must be able to master this complicated agenda in our daily work.

14

ﾟ

Program Planning

Rosalind E. Andreas

Any scrutiny of position openings in student affairs reveals a high number that call for skills in program conceptualization, implementation, and evaluation. Positions frequently require experience in applying student development theory to program design. Whether the position is in residence life, student activities, Greek affairs, specialized student services, recreation, judicial affairs, multicultural affairs, retention services, or other units, the duties will most likely include some phase of program offering.

This chapter focuses on program design and implementation and presents a model for conceptualizing program planning. Three case examples are presented to demonstrate how the model can be applied. Finally, a series of recommendations for program planners is provided. The chapter is designed to aid practitioners in moving from an idea for a program to its realization. The chapter will focus on issues and considerations in determining the need for a program, setting goals, and establishing and implementing the plan in a specific context.

For purposes of this discussion, the term *program* refers to a major administrative unit, a series of activities, or a single event (Barr, Keating, and Associates, 1985). Thus, an office for alcohol education, a series of events (such as a six-week leadership training seminar in intervention skills), or a drug awareness media campaign would each be characterized as a program. This chapter uses the definition of a program as "a theory based plan, under which action is taken toward a goal within the context of institutions of higher education" (Barr, Keating, and Associates, 1985, p. 3).

Program Components

Barr, Keating, and Associates (1985) have isolated three components of theory-based program development — context, goal, and plan. They further assert that the three must be congruent in order to achieve program success.

Context

Context refers to an array of conditions in the setting into which a program idea will be introduced. Institution type and mission will influence program initiatives and structure. As an example, it would probably not be easy to attempt a pro-choice student organization or program at a private, liberal arts, Catholic institution. Institutional mission and church policy would dictate otherwise.

Public policy context also needs to be considered in program design. In states in the American Southwest, for example, public policy makers are keenly aware of the changing demographics in elementary schools and realize that higher education must be prepared to encourage, attract, and retain rapidly growing student populations now and into the future if they are to develop an educated citizenry. Policy makers offer incentives to help influence program direction at colleges and universities. Successful programs in both public and private sectors will consider demography, state needs, and state aspirations.

Within the institution, governance structure also becomes a critical factor. For example, does a new program need to be approved by the student life committee of the faculty senate, or can it simply be added with the approval of the vice president? What role do trustees play in new program additions? What are the funding sources involved? What other offices and agencies must be engaged in the development of the project?

Closely related to context is the political influence structure within the institution. Baldridge and Riley (1977), who have analyzed interest-group pressures and conflict over resources in academic settings, provide useful background on the political perspective of decision making. Knowledge of pressure groups and decision structures within an institution can help determine the appropriate steps to take. Although the student life committee of the faculty senate may not have authority over a program addition, it is important to assess if that committee is of sufficient political strength that its involvement is needed in the proposed program's rationale and plans.

In almost any college or university, it seems unwise ever to consider a program addition without full participation of students and student government. From a practical standpoint, such participation can help shape successful plans. Some occasions will also require looking beyond the walls of the college or university to the community when planning a program change or addition: student housing, facility expansion, parking modifications, or off campus programming.

Thus, it is important to analyze institutional context and apply findings during the conceptualization of the program. Planners should consider public policy direction, institutional mission, institutional governance procedures, the political influence structure, and external community influence.

Goal

A key assumption underlying student affairs work is that the academic mission of the institution is preeminent (National Association of Student Personnel Administrators, 1989). Thus, the goal of successful student affairs programs should be to support learning in out-of-class settings.

In addition, the goal should be framed in terms of a particular theoretical or conceptual framework. As an applied field, student affairs has borrowed theoretical frameworks from many disciplines and used them to enhance student learning and personal development. In specifying the goal, it is thus important to articulate the theoretical base as well.

Plan

Barr, Keating, and Associates (1985) label both the techniques used in the design of the program and the end product itself as the plan or method. Examples of techniques will be given in the planning process section of the chapter's case studies.

The Barr, Keating, and Associates components of theory-based program development provide a useful model for a discussion of three cases in program planning. The first is about the development of a student recreation center; the second concerns the combination of two administrative units into one; and the third involves an attempt to link two international program units.

Case One: A Student Recreation Center

As stated previously, close analysis of the many facets of the context into which a program idea will be introduced can help determine program success. For the recreation center, great care was taken to analyze not only its appropriateness vis-à-vis mission and goals but also the history of the idea, the leadership role required by the division, institutional influence patterns, resource capabilities and constraints, and—above all—student need.

Institutional Context

A new vice president arrived at a major research land-grant university. In assessing areas of student life, he quickly learned from students that the campus needed recreation space. In fact, the thirty-four thousand students relied on one playing field, an old gym (when it was not being used for classes or athletic practice), and racquetball courts in the field house. Those three areas attempted to accommodate open recreation, intramural, and sports club activities and were inadequate. For example, when playing softball on the field, limits were placed on hits, or the balls would sail through the library windows.

History of the Idea

Seven years earlier, the student association had expressed the need for recreation space and had placed before the students a referendum to determine if they would pay a fee for a recreation center. The referendum was supported. Students took the results forward, as they needed administrative and trustee approval to proceed. Fearing that the referendum — which came one year after a failed parking garage referendum — was not representative of student thinking, university administrative leaders decided not to go ahead.

Role of Division

Although there was turnover among student leaders, the student government did not lose commitment to the idea; instead, it began to build an agenda for improvement of undergraduate education and life. The recreation center idea remained on that agenda. Two years after the vice president of student affairs arrived, the newly elected student body president approached the newly hired dean of students and informed her that a very high priority for his year was to gain recreation space and, most specifically, to win approval for a student recreation center. In fact, he asked the assistance of the dean's staff to conduct a survey that would assess both student interest in and the need for recreation space and facilities at the same time that the student government conducted a second referendum. The referendum questions would be brief; the survey, conducted in classes, would contain the same questions.

   Concurrently, the vice president began to meet with finance and facilities planning colleagues to research costs and payment mechanisms. Facilities planners and institutional research colleagues gathered materials from other universities that had just completed recreation centers or were at more advanced planning stages. Land options were examined on the landlocked campus.

Institutional Influence Patterns

Work began immediately with the appropriate institutional research staff and with faculty leadership to gain support for a classroom survey about recreation to be conducted in mid-October. In the meantime, the dean of students staff and the student government leaders began to plan fall activities leading up to the referendum. The student body president felt strongly that he should not take a position on the referendum but would make sure that students were well informed about the choice before them. He agreed to assemble a small information committee of student government senators and a program director. One committee member identified the critical need for information and requested assistance in identifying representatives from campus constituent groups to come to a series of information sessions about the proposed center. Representatives from the residence halls, fraternities and sororities, multicultural student organizations, disabled students association, off-campus student association, family housing, nontraditional student association, international students, intramurals, athletes, graduate students, and others began to meet. Von Destinon (1987) would call this strategy identifying and organizing the clientele.

Who would pay? When would they pay? How much? Who could have access to the center? What would a center include? Who would decide what was to be included? Why should students pay for such a center if they would graduate before it opened? Who could guarantee that the athletic department would not take over the space in the same way that it had in the past? How could the university be kept from giving it up to other uses? Students had never paid directly for a building before, so why should they be asked to do so now? Should not such a center be considered an important part of a student's educational experience and thus be paid for by tuition? How accessible would all aspects of the proposed center be to persons with disabilities, to children of students, to guests? Could it be like a community center? Could faculty members also use the facilities? If so, what would they pay? Would wellness activities occur there? Why should current students vote to raise the fees of future students?

The questions and discussion gave direction not only for the survey but also for the design of the planning stages and composition of the planning bodies. In addition, the dialogue generated important messages to campus and community media. Student peers were very interested in why students should agree to fund a building. The dean of students office helped by briefing reporters and framing questions and answers at this critical stage of ascertaining campus support for the concept.

Resource Capabilities and Constraints

From financial analysis, it was clear that the only reasonable means to finance construction was to sell bonds and fund the debt through a student fee. Costs estimates had to consider the size and contents of such a center, land costs, and the size of the fee that students could afford or agree to pay. As a matter of public policy, the state had kept tuition and education costs to students and their families low. Thus, in order to gain trustee and legislative approval required to sell bonds, arguments needed to be framed to meet objections related to increased costs.

Land costs were of grave financial and political concern. If land needed to be purchased from neighbors in a newly expanded area, the dollar and political costs could be enormous. High dollar costs would shrink the facility size; high political costs could create endless delays and major public relations problems.

In anticipation that costs might exceed the amount of a fee that students would agree to pay, the president and his cabinet also agreed to add the recreation center to the capital campaign as a gift opportunity for donors. As such, it would need to compete with other very attractive projects.

Relationship to Institutional Mission

Leaders at this major research university believed strongly in the importance of a solid foundation of undergraduate education and life as a basis for excellence in graduate and research efforts. They recognized the importance of good facilities and programs for the campus to attract and retain high-quality students and faculty members. In addition, campus leaders felt that the campus had a role in educating people about responsible life-style choices as a means to advance the health of the citizenry. Adding a student recreation center to the campus would be consistent with institutional mission and aspirations.

Student Need

Upon the vice president's arrival, he had established task forces to ascertain student needs and to help frame his agenda. The requirement for a recreational facility had emerged from both student leader discussions and divisional studies. In addition, the vice president had asked facilities planners to review studies from other institutions on relative amounts of space devoted to recreation. The university ranked very low on these measures. Comparative data became useful as decisions were made along the way. In addition, divisional studies had gathered useful information about the various populations within the student body. The classroom survey also sought information about recreational needs and interests according to student subgroup.

The referendum was held, and students voted to assess themselves a fee of $25 per semester after the doors of the recreation center had opened. The referendum was approved by a margin of 54 percent. The survey yielded similar results with a margin actually higher than the referendum—56.2 percent. The survey also yielded important information about students' interests and needs by subgroup, information that would be used in the planning stage.

Program Goals

Formulating program goals can be an elusive process. However, as this case illustrates, students had articulated a need, which staff homework had verified. The need could then be translated into theory-based goals consistent with the academic mission, educational purposes, and divisional objectives.

Needs into Goals

By late October, the campus's intention to build a student recreation center was clear. It was not certain at that time what the recreation center would include. The referendum also created awareness of other campus recreation needs — field space, sand volleyball courts, improved tennis courts, satellite spaces. The referendum and early discussion expanded recreation goals to include these program components. The program objctive was further refined in the committees and task forces conceptualizing the recreation center program and was expanded to include other recreation goals for the campus.

Theoretical Bases

Colleges and universities have a responsibility to create environments that encourage the development of the whole person. They do so by providing occasions both inside and outside the classroom for students to develop their intellects and also their social, physical, esthetic, occupational, and other abilities (American Council of Education, [1937] 1949). All aspects of campus life must contribute to a sense of wholeness (Boyer, 1987). A university needs spaces where an academic community can assemble, and a recreation center creates the opportunity for students, faculty, and staff to come together to answer health and physical needs in a spirit of cooperative community (DeArmond, 1987). Recreation also provides an important means of education: "Learning to use leisure time in a healthy, constructive, and creative manner; learning to achieve quality of life through physical fitness, increased skills and improved social relations" (Miller, 1987, p. 1). Others refer to this educational function as teaching students about wellness and life-style choices (Hettler, 1986).

The pressures created by academic life also require safe outlets. Recreation activities act as "a safety valve for 'blowing off steam,' a catharsis to relieve aggression, a way to reduce stress and slow pace" (Miller, 1987, p. 1). Thus, recreation teaches ways to manage emotions and deal with the tensions and complexities of contemporary society.

Recreation also assists healthy living by satisfying "the basic human urge and need to play, the human adult version of kittens pawing at string, colts romping in the pasture, children digging in the sandbox, without which the years would be dull and wearisome" (Miller, 1987, p. 2). In this sense, recreation can become re-creation and renewal of perspective.

Recreation activities further contribute to academic achievement in that "they help replace energy which has been used in work and studies; they restore, refresh, revitalize, and create anew — thus giving renewed vigor for academic endeavors" (Miller, 1987, p. 1).

The recreation center was viewed as a facility that would contribute to the development of the whole person, provide a place where the community could come together, teach about constructive use of leisure time and healthy life-style choices, provide a constructive outlet for tensions of academic life, encourage play and recreation, and enhance academic achievement.

Compatibility with Institutional Mission, Educational Purposes, and Student Affairs Goals

Because of its profile as a major research and land-grant university, excellence in instruction, research, and service were at the core of the institution's mission. The university prided itself on the creation of knowledge to advance society. The goals of the recreation program included a wellness component and envisioned research opportunities for interested faculty. Most importantly, however, the mission included enriching student life experiences. The divisional efforts were directed at improving those experiences. The recreation center would greatly improve the quality of student out-of-class life, a goal of the division of student affairs. The program concept fit well with the institution mission, educational purposes, and divisional goals.

Planning Process

The complexity of planning a facility requires a clear objective and the adaptability of planning structures and formats to respond to client pressures and conflict over power and authority. Von Destinon (1987) cites the importance of organizing the clientele, expanding it, serving it, gaining feedback, and working within the structure. The student clientele was therefore enlarged at this stage to gain support for the plan, identify obstacles, and resolve conflicts. Nurturing of clientele interests and identification of different decision structures helped to solve conflicts as they emerged.

Players

It was critical to choose with great care the recreation committee members who would determine the center's program plan. Membership included an assistant vice president in administrative affairs who had responsibility for facilities and who had been a long-term director of the student union, the athletic director, students from four different subgroups, a physical education faculty member, the chair of the faculty senate, the vice president for university relations, the associate vice president for undergraduate affairs, and the dean of students. The vice president for student affairs chaired the committee. The recreation committee analyzed the survey data, interviewed information sources, met with an external consultant, reviewed materials on other recreation centers, and specified the elements to be included.

Formats and Structures for Decision Making

Two special problems emerged. Students greatly feared that given past institutional history, recreation budgets and space would be usurped by a vigorous intercollegiate athletics program. Recreation activities at that time were supervised by the department of athletics.

As a result, an ad hoc committee was established to identify an appropriate administrative location of the recreation function in order to improve it and to integrate it into the fabric of student life. Again, the clientele base was expanded; because students, alumni, the faculty, the staff, the health sciences center, and the athletic department had high stakes in the outcome, all were represented on the task force. The task force was chaired by the director of the student health service. He was an advocate for the community center and wellness components of the recreation center and was highly respected by campus groups. This ad hoc group alleviated the students' concern and came to a consensus that recreation ought to be removed from athletics and made a part of student life. The group also established principles for inclusion of faculty, staff, and alumni once the center opened.

The second problem was where to locate the center. Recreation centers are of such a size and magnitude that they may require the equivalent of a city block or more. High competition existed for campus space, and no good options for location had been identified. Because expanded residential housing space was also being considered for the campus, the vice presidents for student affairs, finance and administration, and university relations agreed to bring in a consultant to see if the two projects could be linked in any way. The consultant confirmed that space was at a premium and found that linkage did not seem feasible. However, he helped university leaders creatively examine alternate use of space. The athletic director was brought into the discussion. As a result, agreement was forged to tear down a somewhat marginal building housing research functions and tennis courts in need of repair, to relocate the research units to temporary space in the sports arena, to move and expand the tennis courts in an open area near the physical education building, to move the football practice field to the vacated space where the office building and the tennis courts had been, and to situate the recreation center on the old practice field. The moves, though charged to the recreation center project, eliminated the need to purchase new land and made more dollars available for the center itself. Every unit emerged with improvements.

The design committee, a successor to the recreation committee, was constituted. It included a highly respected campus architect from the planning office, as well as students and faculty and recreation staff members. The campus architect taught the committee about critical architectural concepts. In addition, he influenced the recreation center architect and his firm in creating a unique design. Further, his presence on design committee visits to recreation centers on other campuses helped the committee decision-making process. The faculty member added valuable insight into space design suitable for teaching. Recreation staff members communicated their program needs. Each member of the committee also kept his or her constituents informed of progress so that the campus was ready for the announcement of the plans.

Almost concurrently, planning for the integration of recreation into campus student life occurred, including a plan to hire a director of recreation. The director of student health chaired that search committee, which again was composed of faculty and staff representatives and students, some of whom had also served in other phases.

The Effect of Planning on Implementation: Some Considerations

This phase clearly established the wisdom of expanding clientele groups by including influential persons, affected constituent groups, specialists from on campus, and consultants from off campus. In this manner, problems, objections, and conflicts could be faced at the planning stage. The process mobilized different interests and assisted students in gaining the power and resources in the system necessary to move the recreation center forward. This political approach to planned change (Crowfoot and Chester, 1976) also demonstrated that by keeping the student clientele's concerns central, the campus could come to healthy resolution of difficult problems while moving toward a goal. Further, it proved that multiple decision structures and formats were needed to resolve complex political and planning issues.

Continuity of personnel was maintained on the committees and task forces so that prior decisions and resolutions could serve as the basis for future decisions. In total, after the referendum, five key decision groups moved the idea forward: the recreation planning committee, an ad hoc committee on recreation, the recreation director search committee, the architect-selection committee, and the design committee. Student leader presence and continuity were maintained on all the committees. The dean of students and the director of student health also remained on all the committees so that subsequent plans could take advantage of previous learning.

Program Implementation

The administrative reorganization and hiring of the director of campus recreation were timed so that the new director could serve on the architect-selection and design committees. In addition, that person was required in order to project staffing needs and help build the budget and financing plan. Staff members in the recreation department were actively involved in expanding the vision of campus recreation; they also attended training sessions to prepare them for new facilities and grounds.

The director also worked with those who conceptualized the recreation center program to shape a development brochure and prepare for contact with donors. University relations representatives, finance and administration officials, facilities planners, faculty members—all worked together with students to meet a major need.

The recreation center ground-breaking ceremony occurred in August, four years after the second referendum. The doors opened a year later. The center has become a campus community center where students meet friends, learn new leisure activities, gain new knowledge at the wellness center, shoot hoops with faculty, maintain an active exercise program, and participate in the latest sports club competition or intramural tournament. It exists today as a lively reminder of student initiatives and leadership, the will to form a student agenda, and careful planning to ensure that context, goal, and plan converged to ensure program success.

Case Two: Reorganizing a Unit
to Serve Commuter Students Better

In this case, planners reexamined divisional goals in light of student characteristics through a careful analysis of institutional context. The program that emerged accomplished the institutional mission in a more effective manner.

Institutional Context

A comprehensive university founded to bring high-quality liberal education to first-generation college students, many of them commuters, was nearing its twentieth year. The university had begun without the traditional departmental and college organization and had sought to teach the liberal arts to students who would major in education, management, or engineering. As the campus grew, the faculty organized along more traditional lines but continued to offer strong undergraduate education to a largely commuter student population.

Located in a suburban area, the institution attracted approximately 85 percent of its students from the larger metropolitan area. In the early 1970s, the university had established an office for commuters designed to define and act as advocate for these students' particular needs as well as to provide services to them (car pools, off-campus housing assistance, locker rentals, volunteer service coordination, noontime programming, and legal aid service). The office staff, comprising a director, a secretary, an undergraduate intern, and five student employees, had worked closely with the director of institutional research to describe the requirements of commuters for the campus. The student staff had served active roles on committees all across campus.

Yet a dilemma always confronted the office. The director and the staff would be asked by other staff and faculty members to address problems facing commuter students in their own functional areas—in as well as out of class. The director and the student staff would always try to help analyze the problem and would propose potential solutions. However, the commuter services staff felt that more units on campus needed to assume responsibilities for *all* of their students. Staff members were also aware that the office's services did not reach all students who commuted.

When the director of student activities resigned to take a position at another campus, the director of commuter services began to discuss a possible merger of student activities and commuter services. Residential life staff, faculty colleagues, student activities staff, student union staff, students, and the dean of student life discussed the idea. Would not the mission of the institution be better served if the commuter services office were eliminated and the students could go to one office that could provide accurate and timely information? Students could acquire information, borrow jumper cables, file a parking ticket appeal, form a carpool, buy a ticket to a campus event, become acquainted with student organizations, rent a locker, get the week's program listings, sign up for leadership training, and more. Could not a reorganization combine the functions in such a way that they could form a hierarchy of services and programs corresponding to that of student needs? If moved from a high-traffic site on the first floor to the lower level across from the campus radio station, pool tables, Ping-Pong tables, and a snack bar, might not the location of the office itself invite students to engage themselves with other students, office staff, and faculty conducting business in the area?

At that time, Chickering (1974) and Astin (1975) were contrasting the development and involvement of residential and commuting students. Chickering found that the residential environment contributed to better student development. Astin found higher satisfaction and persistence among residential students than among commuter students.

History of the Idea

In this case, the idea had emerged from a problem in the commuter services office. Few students identified themselves as commuters. Rather, their contacts with the university were determined by their needs. Their most frequent interactions on campus were with faculty in the classroom, persons in the parking lot, food service and bookstore workers, and staff in the business office as problems occurred. Commuter services and student activities responded to many needs but in a less integrated way than the educational mission of the institution dictated.

Role of the Division

A significant number of faculty members were engaged with students as advisers to student organizations and clubs on the campus. Academic departments also worked well with student life staff in coprogramming events and lectures. For their part, student affairs staff members participated on faculty senate committees and worked collaboratively with faculty to serve evening students and nontraditional students. The division had enjoyed a history of strong leaders and was generally respected for its ability to improve the quality of students' lives and humanize their experiences on the campus.

Institutional Influence Patterns

To make such a change was within the purview of the division of student affairs. Those affected by the decision were the students, the student center office, the commuter services and student activities offices, the student life office, and related student life units. Students felt the idea was a good one, and the divisional staff felt the idea had merit. The critical relationships that could influence the outcome were between the staffs in the two offices.

Resource Capability or Constraints

As the reorganization involved the elimination of one director position, it was possible to redefine roles of existing personnel within the salary dollars available. A merger did require change in office structure and roles. As such, the planning stages needed to involve each staff member carefully in defining and shaping the overall office structure and team relationships as well as the individual roles. The physical combination of the two offices required a move and renovation of an underutilized space outside the existing student activities office into an open-landscape reception and office area. The costs were manageable within the divisional and physical plant budgets.

Relationship to Institutional Mission and Goals

As noted previously, the proposed change appeared to carry out the university mission more effectively than the retention of separate offices. Further, the proposal improved the location of the student center office. Vacating the commuter services office left space for a more visible and accessible student center office.

Student Need

Institutional research data on student interests, curricular patterns, credit-load patterns, age, gender, ethnicity, commuting distance and time, work patterns, and other variables provided the kind of background information for staff to make informed decisions about program response to student needs. The office also had utilized the National Clearinghouse for Commuter Programs needs analysis instrument to gather information from commuter students. A great deal was known about the population, a situation that made it possible to shape student requirements into a hierarchy.

Program Goals

The staff constructed office functions based on Maslow's (1970) hierarchy of needs. This theory asserts that survival needs must be met before moving on to address higher-level ones. In particular, physiological requirements and then safety needs must be satisfied before a sense of belonging can be created. At that point, self-esteem, which precedes self-actualization, can also develop (Maslow, 1970). The reorganized office—Campus Information, Programs, and Organizations—helped students find the basic information and assistance they desired. While students were there, they could also become informed about student organizations, leadership training, and other out-of-class opportunities, all of which contributed to a sense of belonging. The thinking was that if these busy students could become introduced in a comfortable environment to those aspects of campus life that required more time and involvement, they could then make connections with others and address higher-level psychological and educational needs. Once involved in clubs or training, students could be challenged and encouraged by peers to participate at their highest level.

Planning Process

Critical steps in planning the program engaged each affected staff member in the conceptualization of the office organization, roles, and relationships. Separate meetings were held with each staff person and then with the entire group to establish direction. By consensus, the staff was organized into four groups: the information and services team, the program group, the organization and budget team, and the reception group. Each staff member drafted team goals and team-leader role responsibilities. Much good will was generated as each staff member played a major part in defining his or her place in the new unit, relationships to the other teams, and design of the reorganized space. Student employees also helped review the plans.

The principle of extensive staff involvement in program planning was followed in implementation. Regular meetings of team leaders permitted balancing of work load and shifting of people to best advantage. The reorganization also cemented relationships with public information, fine arts, athletics, and other units, making it possible to resolve problems more easily as they arose. The reception staff was trained rigorously in referral and information skills. It also helped to coordinate events calendars for the campus, resulting in better public relations as well. The one-stop concept not only assisted students but made it easier for faculty investing out-of-class time with students. Because staff members also worked with faculty, they could make connections between students and faculty with similar interests. The staff could see immediate results of its efforts. The involvement of students in campus events and in student organizations increased, and they demonstrated a better sense of belonging as they became involved in new ways on campus.

The Effect of Planning on Implementation: Some Considerations

In this case, careful involvement of professional and student staff members in planning the office organization and team structure contributed to a sound plan. Their knowledge of the student experience on the campus, as well as their individual strengths, brought the best information to bear on the office program and physical design. Further, the availability of excellent planning data from the institutional research director had made complete data about subgroups of the student population available to the campus and to the office staff.

Case Three: An International Center

It is always useful to analyze an idea that never came to fruition. Two unit heads at a major land-grant research university thought that it would be advisable to coordinate units with an international focus and bring them under the same administrative leadership. One of these, an international programs office, was closely linked to one of the large colleges on the campus but had a few ties to other colleges. An entrepreneurial unit, it assisted faculty engaged in research around the world. Another, the international students office, served students as well as faculty and visiting scholars on visas throughout the university. One unit reported to the dean of a college and the other to a supervisor within the division of student affairs.

Discussions began at the level of the director and dean of students. The thinking was that if the two units could be combined (they were located in the same building), they could share conference space and possibly even some receptionist functions. Further, the programs office, with its contacts abroad, could introduce new students and faculty who needed the services of the international students office. Thus, it was believed that communication with persons coming into the university would be improved.

Although the need for space proved to be a common point, the concerns that were shared ended at that point. The programs office focused the bulk of its efforts on one college, whereas the student office sought to serve the entire university. The programs office was interested in rewarding faculty entrepreneurial activity, the student office in providing direct service to students and visiting scholars. The culture of one office reflected more clearly the faculty culture; in the other, the administrative culture dominated. In addition, the larger university had not articulated a coordinated international mission. With no overriding mission and goals, the different emphases of the offices could not be reframed. Thus, the idea was dropped and appropriately so.

Summary

In program planning, student affairs people do best when they use strategies that will move ideas to a workable reality. The recommendations that follow are practical reminders derived from the cases. It is our hope that they can assist planners to create successful programs.

- *Understand the mission.* Begin with clear working knowledge of the campus mission and goals and the division's complementary role and objectives. Read mission statements, the president's speeches, planning documents, and annual reports to gain this understanding.

- *Learn about students.* As programs serve students, glean all information possible about them — their mix, needs, and characteristics by subgroups. Read institutional research studies and discover who else on campus has studied your students.

- *Do research.* Be prepared to conduct those surveys or studies that will help the campus understand a problem or need. Utilize strengths and interests of faculty members and student affairs colleagues, both on your campus and from other campuses facing similar problems.

- *Involve students.* You will find that student self-knowledge and creativity help frame alternative solutions. Foster early involvement in defining student problems and needs.

- *Attend to politics.* Do your homework to determine who should be involved at each phase in the process. Know the political influence structure on your campus and identify the key players. Anticipate opposition and plan how to meet it through expanding the clientele, consultants, or other means. Know the governance structure of your campus and follow the appropriate process to gain the necessary approvals. In order to improve chances of success, involve affected persons in planning in order to incorporate the thinking of those doing the work or those served.

- *Use the media.* Apply what has been learned in needs analysis to media presentations. Plan these to tell the story of what the program is trying to accomplish. Determine *what* you want to convey in the story and *when* those messages need to be communicated.

- *Seek help.* Utilize consultants to provide necessary special skills. Consultants are available both within and without the institution. Look for untapped resources and make use of them. Be sure that the program goal is in harmony with mission and that plan methods fit the institutional context. Failure to do so will result in failure.

The importance of careful analysis of institutional context and planning cannot be overemphasized. Program goals that relate to an institution's mission and culture and that involve users, interest groups, and the people who will carry out the program will most likely succeed when implemented.

References

American Council on Education. *The Student Personnel Point of View.* Washington, D.C.: American Council on Education, 1949. (Originally published 1937.)

Astin, A. W. *Preventing Students from Dropping Out.* San Francisco: Jossey-Bass, 1975.

Baldridge, J. V., and Riley, G. *Governing Academic Organizations.* Berkeley, Calif.: McCutchan, 1977.

Barr, M. J., Keating, L. A., and Associates. *Developing Effective Student Services Programs: Systematic Approaches for Practitioners.* San Francisco: Jossey-Bass, 1985.

Boyer, E. L. *Colleges: The Undergraduate Experience in America.* New York: HarperCollins, 1987.

Chickering, A. W., and Associates. *Commuting Versus Resident Students: Overcoming Educational Inequities of Living Off Campus.* San Francisco: Jossey-Bass, 1974.

Crowfoot, J. E., and Chester, M. A. "Contemporary Perspectives on Planned Social Change: A Comparison." In W. G. Bennis and others (eds.), *The Planning of Change.* Troy, Mo.: Holt, Rinehart & Winston, 1976.

DeArmond, M. "Student Recreation Center Case Statement." Tucson: University of Arizona, 1987.

Hettler, B. "Strategies for Wellness and Recreation Program Development." In F. Leafgren (ed.), *Developing Campus Recreation and Wellness Programs.* New Directions for Student Services, no. 34. San Francisco: Jossey-Bass, 1986.

Maslow, A. H. *Toward a Psychology of Being.* New York: Van Nostrand Reinhold, 1970.

Miller, D. M. "Recreation Position Paper." Tucson: University of Arizona, 1987.

National Association of Student Personnel Administrators. "A Perspective on Student Affairs: A Statement Issued on the 50th Anniversary of the *Student Personnel Point of View.*" In *Points of View.* Washington, D.C.: National Association of Student Personnel Administrators, 1989. (Originally published 1987.)

von Destinon, M. "Student Fees: The Politics of Funding Recreation Facilities." 1987. (ED 286433)

15

༄

A Political Model
for Program Evaluation

Robert D. Brown
Diane L. Podolske

The director of new student enrollment, Oliver "Ollie" Orientation, slumped wearily in his chair. He held in his hands the vice chancellor for student affairs's memorandum on the latest round of budget cuts. She reported that she believed that the summer orientation program for new students was redundant in view of the "welcome week" program held a week before classes began. The vice chancellor stated that she could not fund duplicate programs during tight budget times, so one would have to be cut. The vice chancellor's deadline for the final budget cut was the beginning of the next fiscal year. Ollie had one year to conduct evaluation activities and give a recommendation on which orientation program should be eliminated.

Evaluation is a natural activity; people make judgments almost every moment of their lives. Ollie Orientation is also going to be making evaluative judgments and decisions. Program evaluation, by definition, is the act of making value judgments about the worth of a program. Because that worth is its social utility, it is determined in a social context using a social and political process. Usually this kind of judgment leads to decisions such as to revise, retain, expand, or drop a program (Brown, 1979; Guba and Lincoln, 1989).

This chapter presents a political decision-making strategy. This strategy recognizes that evaluations in student affairs are conducted for the purpose of making decisions about programs and that the evaluation and decision-making processes are political (Guba and Lincoln, 1989; Weiss, 1991). Deciding which student affairs programs to sponsor, how to implement and manage them, which outcomes are important and successful is a political process. The values of the entire campus community play a role in these decisions, though the power to make the final ones may reside in a small group of administrators. Program success is affected by investments of time and energy of many persons beyond the program administrators. The definition of program success will vary according to the planners, participants, and other stakeholders and thus is political.

Skills that an individual needs to conduct an evaluation range from being a good observer, thinker, and politician to possessing high-level consultation, negotiation, research design, and measurement abilities. This chapter offers a context in which these skills will be most effective and suggests resources for further information as required. The first part of this chapter describes the political decision-making evaluation strategy; the second part provides a case study of how the strategy can be used to design an evaluation for specific student affairs programs.

Political Decision-Making Evaluation Strategy

The political decision-making evaluation strategy is composed of five steps: (1) identify who the decision makers and stakeholders are, (2) establish the purpose of the evaluation, (3) decide what information is needed, (4) determine when, how, and from whom to collect information, and (5) decide when and how the evaluation information will be reported.

Decision Makers

Determining who ultimately makes decisions about the program being evaluated and who is affected by the decision is critically important when planning and conducting a program evaluation. It is not much help if a student affairs director collects evaluative information for the vice chancellor of student affairs only to discover that the university's chancellor is going to make the final decision. The unit director may gather information regarding the number of students served during a semester when the chancellor is interested in the number of minority students served. Knowing who the ultimate decision makers are makes it possible to conduct the evaluation using appropriate questions and relevant information.

Stakeholders

Potential stakeholders in student affairs programs include professional staff, office staff, involved students, faculty, administrators, parents, taxpayers, and funders (Brown, 1979). Realistically, the scope of stakeholder involvement is restricted by what is feasible, fiscally responsible, politically prudent, and socially relevant. At a minimum, those directly affected by the program should be involved in planning and conducting the evaluation.

Professional staff members have a clear stake in the evaluation of programs for which they are responsible. Decisions about programs could easily affect their job status. Evaluations that focus on day-to-day program operations need staff input. Discovering that posters for an admissions recruitment program are not reaching the high schools in time for the college day program or that the health-aide training program did not include a unit on flu symptoms is going to demand some significant changes. The participation of staff during the planning phases of evaluation, as well as throughout the program, can prevent snags and make adjustments easier.

Students are the primary target of student affairs programs, and they will often be surveyed, tested, and observed to determine the amount of learning and development that has occurred. Students are asked at the end of a program what they liked, would they return again, what suggestions they have for improving the program, and would they recommend the program to another student. Outcome data regarding achievement of learning and developmental goals are also collected. But these efforts are insufficient. Students should be involved early in the process through consultation with student government representatives, through focus groups, or through participation on the evaluation planning team. Students can generate ideas about effective program components, important outcomes, and alternative approaches to achieving the program's goals. (Excellent sources on the use of focus groups in the evaluation process include Jacobi, 1991, and Morgan, 1988.)

Similarly, other stakeholders such as faculty or parents should take part in planning the evaluation for programs in which they participate or that directly affect them. A new student orientation program involving parents should have their input; a program designed to assist faculty members in assuming mentoring roles should benefit from their advice. The suggestions and reactions of stakeholders can be obtained by conducting interviews and surveys, or having those concerned formally represented on the evaluation team.

One final helpful criterion for determining which stakeholders to involve in planning an evaluation is to consider which groups will receive information about the results of the evaluation. If they are important enough to receive reports of the results, even for public relations purposes, they should also play a role in designing the evaluation.

The Purpose of the Evaluation

Decisions made about programs usually fall into two categories — formative or summative (Scriven, 1967 and 1991). Formative evaluations and decisions are those made to improve the program. Summative decisions are made at the end of a program or when its continuance, expansion, or reduction is being debated. This categorization is important because it influences the conduct of the evaluation and particularly the kind of information needed to make a decision.

Formative Evaluations. Formative decisions focus primarily on the process of a program rather than its products or final outcomes. If a residence hall staff is providing a series of workshops on human sexuality, formative decisions must be made as they progress. Is the room large enough? Do the overhead projector and screen work well in the setting? Are the workshop presenters sufficiently knowledgeable and clear? The purpose of conducting a formative evaluation is to collect information that permits the workshop director and staff to make changes during the semester to improve the environment, the materials, or the presentation. Formative evaluations are usually conducted by the staff involved through observations, surveys at the end of sessions, and interviews. Formative, ongoing evaluations should be part of every student affairs program. Student service units must have systematic ways to obtain feedback from students and other stakeholders. A formative evaluation can be informal and does not have to include information from every program participant, but it should systematically provide timely information. The focus of a formative evaluation is to improve the program and provide better services to students, not to assign blame. A collaborative problem-solving approach permitting honest responses is the best strategy.

Summative Evaluations. All summative evaluations should be considered as the act of judging the relative worth of two programs rather than one alone. There are several reasons. First, rarely is a formal decision made to drop a major student affairs program. More likely, programs merge or fade away when directors retire or relocate. Second, most student affairs programs will have at least some impact, so they must be assessed in relation to another program or to a standard. Most importantly, we believe student affairs administrators need to think of program planning and evaluation from the perspective of student needs; the ultimate evaluation question concerns how well the program addresses student needs. The campus might close the student counseling center and the career planning and placement office. Eliminating these programs, however, does not eliminate the necessity for them. Students still have personal and academic problems, and seniors still have to make career decisions. How is one program beneficial as compared to another, or how does one program meet these needs as compared to having no program at all?

Along with establishing the purpose of the evaluation, it is important to identify the political issues involved. The persons requesting an evaluation may be sincerely interested in how a program can be improved or how well it accomplishes its objectives. But there are often other motives and concerns. Perhaps it is a concern about how parents or the regents will react to the program. Or maybe a personality clash inspires the call for an evaluation. Decisions in many matters, including those about programs, are influenced by the amount of risk that people are willing to take (Janis and Mann, 1977), and this risk will also affect how we process evaluation information (Brown, Newman, and Rivers, 1984). Evaluative judgments are often influenced by factors other than so-called objective information. It is essential to ferret out why an evaluation is being conducted as well as what decisions will be made as a result of it.

Necessary Evaluative Information

Three kinds of information are helpful in making judgments and arriving at decisions: (1) formative, (2) summative, and (3) political. The relative emphasis depends on the purpose of the evaluation and the issues involved. If the evaluation is formative and its purpose is to find ways to improve an ongoing program, then the evaluation is going to focus on information about the process. A description of what should occur should be developed and then information collected to ascertain what is actually happening. Are the right students participating in the program and in the appropriate numbers? Is the counseling center offering a career planning workshop intended for first-year students, but the participants are all seniors? Are the materials available and the program activities taking place as intended? Gathering information through observation or short surveys will permit program staff to make changes on short notice.

Besides determining whether or not the intended activities and events are occurring, be alert to unintended events, some of which may have positive as well as negative effects. Perhaps the program is working exceptionally well, but program coordination and the logistics are taking considerably more staff time than anticipated. This situation may necessitate realigning job assignments. Or you may find students in a career planning workshop exploring other developmental issues, such as autonomy, so the staff decides to build these issues into the program. Being watchful can help program staff make immediate adjustments to respond to weaknesses or to fulfill needs. The objectives of the program may even need changing as a result.

If the reason for evaluating a program is to decide whether or not to terminate it or to assess which program among several to continue, a summative evaluation will be necessary, and decision makers are likely to be interested in the outcome. Outcome information often includes data about student knowledge and attitudes, but it can also encompass program variables such as efficiency as indicated by cost and time involved. Student perceptions about the program (for example, would they recommend the program to friends?) and changes in students as a result of the program (are they more self-confident about their career choice?) are important outcome data and are generally easy to document.

Knowledge gained from a program or its impact on behavior should be among the basic outcome indicators for program decisions, but unfortunately this information is gathered infrequently. A knowledge outcome question might ask whether students know how to use career library information. Determining the achievement of developmental goals is not so easily accomplished as assessment of academic objectives; however, more measures of student development outcomes are now available (Erwin, 1991), and behavioral indicators like retention rates and job placements are highly meaningful outcome measures. Interest in outcome assessment is increasing in higher education (Astin, 1991; Erwin, 1991), and student affairs staffs are becoming involved in the planning (Woodard, Hyman, von Destinon, and Jamison, 1991). Evaluators and administrators must be creative and persistent in finding useful behavioral outcome measures. Unobtrusive measures are particularly helpful. For example, damage reports in the residence halls, the number of students waiting in registration lines, the amount of trash in community areas of the college union are all points of evaluation. The time and energy expended on designing good outcome indicators should pay off when making evaluative decisions and especially when seeking continued funding support.

Cost-analysis data such as cost effectiveness or benefit-cost ratios are also influential factors for decision making in the 1990s. These indices tell us much more than "can you do it for less money?" Cost effectiveness indicates the cost of an outcome in terms of the dollars per unit of that outcome. If two alternatives to meet the same student needs are being considered, cost-effectiveness indices can be compared. If a retention program using an individual tutoring service costs $50 per student and a program using group tutoring services costs $20 per student, the group tutoring service is more cost effective. To arrive at a cost-effectiveness index, an indicator of the outcome (in this case the number of students retained) and the total dollars used to achieve the outcome must be evaluated. Comparisons of cost effectiveness can be made only when the programs have identical goals and outcome measures. These indices can be useful for examining student services, where information like the number of students served is a valuable and acceptable indicator of success.

A benefit-cost analysis is a useful cost-outcome measure when programs have different goals and outcome indicators. For example, in deciding whether to continue or expand a speaker program or a student leadership training program, a dollar value must be placed on the outcomes (the dollar value of the impact of a speaker program on a large number of students and the dollar value of a leadership training program on relatively few students). This is not an easy task, but the programs' relative worth will be compared whether they are assigned a dollar value or not. The next step is determining the cost of the program and the ratio of benefits to costs.

Relatively little work has been done in student affairs using formal benefit-cost analysis. Placing dollar values on educational objectives is difficult and an objectionable process for many. However, the process is intended to create a fair measure to use in making tough choices and decisions. Working through the process more formally might provide helpful insights; several resources could be helpful (Levin, 1983 and 1991; Thompson, 1980).

The entire thrust of the proposed evaluation strategy centers around the political nature of the evaluation enterprise, but the importance of considering the information needed should be stressed once again. What are the political issues surrounding the program evaluation? This information needs to be gathered throughout the process from the time the decision is made to conduct an evaluation to when the results are reported. New programs are often innovative, and their developers and implementers have a heavy personal and professional investment in their success. Sometimes staff members can become so involved in the program that they react to criticism as if it were personal. They may become defensive and resistant. New programs may also mean that some people have to change the way that they are doing their jobs. The result may be tension and even hostility. These staff members may not want the program to fail; but their enthusiasm may be limited, or they may want to see the program implemented in a different fashion. These are just a few examples of the political issues that might surround the installation and evaluation of a new program.

Established programs also involve similar political issues. The initiation of such an evaluation suggests a concern on the part of someone and will often be viewed as a potential threat. Camps may already be established among staff members and participants; some may feel that the program is doing fine, and others believe changes are required. Staff members may have already taken sides about which particular changes are needed.

This brief discussion should make apparent the importance of asking three questions before beginning the evaluation process: (1) what process information is necessary? (2) what outcome information is required? and (3) what are the political issues involved in this program?

When, How, and from Whom to Collect Information

Collect information with two fundamental concerns in mind: (1) it should relate specifically to the evaluation questions and issues, and (2) it should describe what it is like to be a participant in the program being evaluated. Satisfying the first concern should flow from efforts in the first three steps of the political decision-making strategy. If the decision makers indicate that retention information will be helpful, collect it. If they decide cost information is necessary, provide it. Do not forget the information needs of significant stakeholders as well. It is quite likely that their concerns may change or broaden the evaluation questions. This situation will require negotiation among the decision makers and the stakeholders to determine what are the primary information needs and what is reasonable within the scope of the evaluation.

Descriptive information about the program makes it possible for the decision makers to understand what it is like to be a participant in the program being evaluated. This second category should go beyond the customary demographic description of the participants, such as their age, class, gender, academic major, and other information. A significant component should be a portrayal of what happens to participants in the program. What is it like when a student goes through the course registration process? What is it like to seek help from the student health center? What happens to a student who participates in a workshop on cultural diversity? If a student becomes an officer in a campus organization, what are his or her responsibilities and duties? Descriptions provide answers to these questions and also furnish details about unintended side effects that may not be the focus of the evaluation questions.

It is useful to make a chart listing the information needs and sources. In column one are listed the decision makers and stakeholders. In column two are the questions and issues of concern to these people. In column three are the information needs that relate to each of the questions and issues. Column four indicates from whom the information is going to be obtained, and column five describes how the information is going to be collected (surveys, observations, or interviews). Additional columns can be used to indicate time lines, costs, and who is responsible for the data collection and analysis.

How to Report Evaluation Information

Boring and highly statistical evaluation reports gather dust on shelves after a cursory reading. Late and long reports suffer a similar fate. If these reports are going to be helpful, they must be timely, brief, and focused. If a formative evaluation of an ongoing health-aide training program is being conducted, the program staff must be supplied with information they can use immediately, not information that would have been useful to them a month ago. Frequent, informal reports will be useful. If information is being provided to the regents regarding the relative effectiveness of two student retention programs, the information should be in a brief and understandable format.

Writing good evaluation reports is a journalistic task and calls for creativity, as reports do not have to fit the traditional mold of the research journal article. The purpose of the report is to communicate useful information to an audience unfamiliar with the issues. One strategy is to furnish the report audience with a vicarious experience about the program being evaluated. This can be done with photographs, video presentations, quotations, and case studies (Brown, Petersen, and Sanstead, 1980; Merriam, 1988; Yin, 1989). Often evaluation information will be offered with the intent of persuading the audience (decision makers) to support a program or select the preferred option. Nothing is wrong with this approach, if it is presented candidly. In this case, a picture of long lines for course registration, for example, is probably going to have more punch than a recitation of numbers. Quotations from several students will have more meaning than mean scores on an attitude scale. And a case presentation of how a student with a physical handicap is helped by an entrance ramp will have more impact than a report describing the number of ramps built. Even if the intent is not to persuade but to remain neutral, every effort must be made to make the reports timely and interesting.

The Political Decision-Making Evaluation Strategy in Action

In this section, an in-depth illustration is provided of how the political decision-making evaluation strategy worked for Ollie Orientation, who had to evaluate two programs.

"It is going to be difficult to decide which orientation program to cut," Ollie thought. Ollie leaned back in his chair and pondered the two orientation programs. The summer program consisted of a one-day blitz of information for the new students, including sessions on campus life, university offices, and student conduct. The program included a tour of campus, lunch in the union dining room, and preregistration for fall classes. Parents and spouses were encouraged to attend the summer program, and a special orientation program was provided to answer their questions and give information. Ollie estimated that approximately three-fourths of the new students attended the summer program.

Ollie knew his staff provided a high-quality one-day orientation for new students; yet he also knew that it was becoming more difficult to cram all of the information the new students needed into one six-hour program. Every day he received a call about another component that should be added to the summer orientation. The university's health center requested time for a presentation on AIDS information, the women's center wanted to add date-rape hot-line phone numbers, and the affirmative action office wanted to include a lecture on the university's sexual harassment policies. Ollie agreed that these topics would be valuable additions to the information sessions, but there was not enough time to cover everything.

Ollie shifted in his chair as he thought about the welcome week festivities that his office sponsored every fall. These activities had been planned as mostly social events to promote friendships among the new students and to provide an opportunity to answer any last-minute questions. Registration for classes was conducted for those students who were not admitted in time for the summer orientation program. Attendance at the events was voluntary, with an average of about one-third of the new students attending each of the week's events.

Ollie noticed the new-student enrollment office was filled with students wanting campus tours and orientation information during welcome week. Many students had attended the summer program but had forgotten the information presented on that day. On the first day of welcome week, one staff member reviewed the entire summer orientation program information with a group of students, and the response was overwhelmingly positive.

The students with questions tripled on the second day, and the staff began to reiterate the summer program information for larger and larger groups. The planned social events began to be more like large information sessions and impromptu tours of campus. An informal poll of the students showed that they remembered hearing some of the information during the summer program, but the day had been so overwhelming that the details were lost. It was no wonder the vice chancellor thought the two orientation programs were duplicates, as the welcome week was quickly becoming a second summer program.

Ollie had strong positive feelings about both of the orientation programs. He felt that the summer program was extremely valuable in framing the students' attitude toward the upcoming academic year. The orientation leaders provided a large volume of important information throughout the course of the day. The program provided the students' families or spouses an opportunity to visit the campus and have their own orientation to campus life. The welcome week program also served new students' needs to make new friends and have questions answered. Ollie was going to need detailed information on the benefits that students received from each program to arrive at his recommendation.

Ollie decided to use a political decision-making evaluation strategy to help him formulate his recommendation. He decided to start by determining the decision-makers and stakeholders. The final decision makers were the vice chancellor and the board of regents. The stakeholders were the new students and their families, Ollie and the rest of those involved in new-student enrollment, the vice chancellor, the university community, and ultimately the state's taxpayers. Ollie decided to add a committee of student affairs staff to the decision makers. He wanted to be sure that any recommendation made about funding for orientation programs would be made by people personally familiar with and invested in both programs. He also felt a committee's recommendations about the programs would be more representative of the student affairs division and have more political weight than his personal recommendations. Ollie quickly selected key student affairs staff members, on the basis of each person's political power on campus and past involvement with the orientation programs, and formed his committee.

The committee's first meeting consisted of clarifying the purpose of the evaluation. The vice chancellor's memo about cutting programs indicated a summative evaluation would be appropriate. The memo stated that she wanted to cut one program, but the committee discussed the possibility of keeping both programs by reducing costs within each. The memo also stated that one of the university's major concerns was to retain more students, so the committee reviewed strategies to link that goal with the evaluation results to present a convincing argument. The committee also considered other ramifications of cutting an orientation program, including loss of revenue for the food service, loss of parental involvement, and increased registration confusion. Ollie volunteered to propose the idea of reducing the budget of both programs to the vice chancellor. The committee members agreed that it was appropriate to keep the vice chancellor informed on their ideas and progress throughout the process. The committee members also voted to add student leaders and faculty advisers to the evaluation committee to get their feedback about and support of the final recommendation.

Ollie added the requested members to the committee and scheduled a second meeting to determine the necessary evaluation information and when and how to collect information. He reported that the vice chancellor was willing to consider retaining both programs if the total budget was reduced. The committee decided that an outcome-based evaluation of three areas of orientation—student knowledge about campus living, student satisfaction with the orientation program, and student retention rates—would supply information needed to make a recommendation to the vice chancellor. The committee planned to measure a student's knowledge about campus living with a paper-and-pencil test at the conclusion of the summer and fall orientation programs. A random sample of students using student services during the first semester would reveal where and how they heard about the service. Student satisfaction with each component of the orientation programs, along with demographic information, would also be assessed at the end of the orientation day with a simple evaluation form. Student retention rates would be measured at the end of the fall semester and would be compared with past years and also with the retention rates of peer institutions that only had one orientation day.

After the meeting, Ollie began the process of developing the paper-and-pencil test to assess knowledge about campus life. He shuffled through his files and located the list of students who had participated in the summer orientation program a year ago. Ollie randomly called eight of the students from the list and invited them to participate in a focus group to develop a campus knowledge questionnaire. The students met with Ollie a week later, and they identified information that they felt was vital for any new students. Ollie was pleased to discover that all the topics identified were covered during the summer orientation program. From the topic areas, the focus group developed questions and answers to measure the new students' knowledge of the campus. The topic areas were arranged in columns in a format similar to the *Jeopardy* game show, with the answers underneath each topic area. The new student could test his or her knowledge of campus life by guessing the right question for each answer provided. The focus group hoped this format would encourage the new students to complete all of the items.

Ollie also reported the evaluation committee's progress to the vice chancellor and asked her what information would assist her decision making about the future of the orientation programs and their budgets. The vice chancellor suggested including a detailed budget report for both orientation programs, the food service's revenue figures for the summer orientation day, and parent-family attendance figures for each orientation session as appendix items.

The topics for the evaluation committee's third meeting included information reporting and dividing responsibilities for implementing the evaluation plan. The committee members discussed several methods for presenting their evaluation findings and recommendations to the vice chancellor. Ollie and his staff would administer the evaluation questionnaires on student knowledge and student satisfaction, and they would compile the data from the measures. The committee would review the data and come to a consensus.

The committee would then divide the responsibility of interpreting the data and writing the report. Ollie reported the information requested by the vice chancellor, and two committee members volunteered to develop graphs and tables to present that information. One of the regents and her son were active participants in the summer orientation program, and they agreed to provide a description of what the experience was like for them in a format that would capture the interest of other board members.

The committee also discussed strategies for presenting its recommendations in a way that would garner the support of the campus community, including new publicity pieces to promote the orientation services offered for new students. One of the student leaders volunteered to write an article for the student newspaper about new-student enrollment services. The members decided to plan a meeting to discuss the evaluation results and recommendations with the vice chancellor and also to include narrative comments from the new students' evaluation forms in the written report. The committee would ask the vice chancellor's permission to present the results to the board of regents.

The political decision-making strategy was a successful one for Ollie's evaluation. The vice chancellor, after reading the evaluation report and listening to the committee members' comments, decided to retain both orientation programs. She followed the guidelines outlined in the evaluation report and reduced the budgets without a substantial loss of quality for the programs. She was also quite impressed with the evaluation effort and wondered if this process should be a part of every student affairs program. Specifically, she wondered about doing a similar evaluation with the new-student mentoring program and the university's 101 course. She asked Ollie to consult with the staff members of the campus activities and programs office who would be conducting these evaluations.

Summary

The political decision-making evaluation strategy recognizes the political realities of the decision-making process for student affairs programs. The evaluation process is subjective and highly dynamic. Much as we would like to think that our decision-making and evaluation judgments are rational, objective, and free of values, they are not. This is not to say that the processes are irrational or not based on information. In fact, decision makers consider a broader array of data than is traditionally characterized as objective. However, in order to conduct useful evaluations, a determination must be made about what data are needed, how to collect them, which methods for reporting the data should be used, and who the audience is for the evaluation. Many people mistakenly get the impression from their research training that research and evaluation are highly objective processes and that subjectivity, politics, and conflicts over values are kept to a minimum, if not eliminated completely. Yet whatever the readers' administrative experience, they should recognize by now that politics is an important part of the reality of administrative life. It is essential not only to understand that politics and value judgments are a part of the evaluation process, but that this awareness be incorporated into evaluation planning.

References

Astin, A. W. *Assessment for Excellence: The Philosophy and Practice of Assessment and Evaluation in Higher Education.* New York: Macmillan, 1991.

Brown, R. D. "Key Issues in Evaluating Student Affairs Programs." In G. Kuh (ed.), *Evaluation in Student Affairs.* Washington, D.C.: American College Personnel Association, 1979.

Brown, R. D., Newman, D. L., and Rivers, L. S. "A Decision Making Context Model for Enhancing Evaluation Utilization." *Educational Evaluation and Policy Analysis,* 1984, *6* (4), 393–400.

Brown, R. D., Petersen, C., and Sanstead, M. "Photographic Evaluation: Use of the Camera as an Evaluation Tool for Student Affairs." *Journal of College Student Personnel,* 1980, *21* (6), 558–563.

Erwin, T. D. *Assessing Student Learning and Development: A Guide to the Principles, Goals, and Methods of Determining College Outcomes.* San Francisco: Jossey-Bass, 1991.

Guba, E., and Lincoln, Y. *Fourth Generation Evaluation.* Newbury Park, Calif.: Sage, 1989.

Jacobi, M. "Focus Group Research: A Tool for the Student Affairs Professional." *NASPA Journal,* 1991, *28* (3), 195–201.

Janis, I. J., and Mann, L. *Decision-Making.* New York: Free Press, 1977.

Levin, H. M. *Cost-Effectiveness: A Primer.* Newbury Park, Calif.: Sage, 1983.

Levin, H. M. "Cost-Effectiveness at Quarter Century." In M. W. McLaughlin and D. C. Phillips (eds.), *Evaluation and Education: At Quarter Century.* Chicago: University of Chicago Press, 1991.

Merriam, S. B. *Case Study Research in Education: A Qualitative Approach.* San Francisco: Jossey-Bass, 1988.

Morgan, D. L. *Focus Groups as Qualitative Research.* Newbury Park, Calif.: Sage, 1988.

Scriven, M. "The Methodology of Evaluation." *Perspectives of Curriculum Evaluation.* In R. F. Stake (ed.), AERA Monograph Series on Curriculum Evaluation, no. 1. Skokie, Ill.: Rand McNally, 1967.

Scriven, M. "Beyond Formative and Summative Evaluation." In M. W. McLaughlin and D. C. Phillips (eds.), *Evaluation and Education: At Quarter Century*. Chicago: University of Chicago Press, 1991.

Thompson, M. S. *Benefit-Cost Analysis for Program Evaluation*. Newbury Park, Calif.: Sage, 1980.

Weiss, C. H. "Evaluation Research in the Political Context: Sixteen Years and Four Administrations Later." In M. W. McLaughlin and D. C. Phillips (eds.), *Evaluation and Education: At Quarter Century*. Chicago: University of Chicago Press, 1991.

Woodard, D. B., Jr., Hyman, R., von Destinon, M., and Jamison, A. "Student Affairs and Outcomes Assessment: A National Survey." *NASPA Journal,* 1991, *29* (1), 17–23.

Yin, R. *Case Study Research: Design and Methods*. Newbury Park, Calif.: Sage, 1989.

16

⸾

Outcomes Assessment

T. Dary Erwin

What do students gain from college? And how could one demonstrate that benefit at any institution? To what extent are programs and services of proven worth, worth based on information and not just logic or intuition? These questions are the essence of assessment in higher education. Although similar ones have been studied for decades as college impact research (Bowen, 1977; Feldman and Newcomb, 1969; Jacob, 1957; and Pascarella and Terenzini, 1991), these questions were posed in the 1980s by the public and government officials from outside the academy. Research about college impact predates assessment by several years; yet the current focus on evaluation suggests new practices and directions for the student affairs profession. Assessment on our individual campuses is a pervasive strategy that touches our mission, governance, campus relationships, program planning, technology, and professional standards, all of which are addressed in other chapters in this volume. What will be presented here is an update for the student affairs professional about several current trends and issues in evaluation that will be useful in future practice.

First, an analysis of the differences between research and assessment

Note: The author wishes to thank Cynthia Olney for reviewing an earlier version of this manuscript.

will be provided. Next, the pressures involved with calls for increased accountability for colleges and universities will be discussed. The specific issues surrounding the purposes and objectives of assessment, appropriate assessment methods, and the use of assessment information will then be discussed in detail.

Comparing Research and Assessment

Studies of student affairs impact or effectiveness may be viewed from a research or an assessment perspective. Research and assessment share most processes in common; however, they differ at least in two basic aspects. First, although assessment and research are both concerned with program impact, the findings of assessment have some policy implications (Ewell, 1988). In other words, assessment is oriented toward practice and usually toward some action. Action in this context means program reinforcement, modification, or removal. Research may contribute new knowledge, but it may not suggest that programs need improvements or are functioning well. Assessment guides practice: research guides our theory and conceptual foundation. Second, assessment has implications for a single institutional setting; research should have broader implications for student affairs and higher education. Of course, assessment findings replicated across several institutional settings can have more general ramifications for theory and research.

Assessment and educational research share the goal of an educational emphasis that differs from traditional program evaluation. That kind of evaluation is concerned with the effectiveness of institutional operations that may be only tangentially related to the educational mission of the institution. For example, an evaluation of a college's purchasing system may well be in order, but its findings are at best indirectly related to the education of students. Assessment and research are concerned with the learning and development of students. This focus in assessment also requires that the profession of student affairs have a clearer purpose about itself within higher education (Erwin, 1989).

Calls for Accountability

The major driving forces behind assessment have been and still are the external needs for evidence of effectiveness. The story of assessment is a familiar one to readers of the higher education literature. Calls for accountability in higher education have led to state mandates and accreditation standards (U.S. Department of Education, 1988) requiring that the value of programs and services be demonstrated. The National Governors' Association (Alexander, Clinton, and Kean, 1986) and state legislators around the country have issued proclamations and legislation focusing on institutional effectiveness.

Existing measures of quality about the higher education experience were deficient in several ways. First, most were simple counts of resources, such as number of full-time students or number of library books. Accreditation associations (Bennett, 1985) that heavily stressed such measures of quantity or resources also came under criticism for their lack of credibility and rigor. In fact, these questions remain today. There are calls for a national test and a single federal accreditation agency replacing the current groups (Ewell, 1991).

Within higher education, the weaknesses of assessment were also recognized and admitted. A Southern Regional Education Board (1985) report warned that "the quality and meaning of undergraduate education [have] fallen to a point at which mere access has lost much of its value" (p. 9). Another report by the Association of American Colleges (1985) claimed that the absence of institutional accountability was "one of the most remarkable and scandalous aspects of higher education" (p. 33). Although most critics concentrated on the lack of learning or direct measures of student quality, it was the *Involvement in Learning* Task Force (Study Group on the Conditions of Excellence in American Higher Education, 1984) that drew attention to the fact that the scope of assessment had been broadened to include development: "Adequate measures of educational excellence must thus be couched in terms of *student outcomes,* principally such academic outcomes as knowledge, intellectual capacities, and skills. Outcomes also may include other dimensions of student growth such as self-confidence, persistence, leadership, empathy, social responsibility, and understanding of cultural and intellectual differences" (p. 16).

Initially, higher education was slow to respond to assessment partially because of concern about government meddling in internal governance. Such concerns have been proven ill founded for institutions that have made the effort to assess outcomes. Recently, institutions that resisted assessment had structures such as specific tests imposed from the outside (Ewell, 1989). In fact, higher education now has new impetus for conducting assessment. First, if higher education does not assume a greater and more credible role in its evaluation, other groups outside of education will. It is better for regulation to occur from inside. Second, documenting effectiveness is to higher education's benefit, not its detriment. Pressures for increased state funding to entitlements (such as Medicare), to human services (such as mental health), to children (such as K–12 education and aid to dependent children), and to judicial edicts for new prison construction leave higher education in a vulnerable budgetary position. The average percentage of state appropriations for higher education fell from 8.3 percent in 1981–82 to 6.9 percent in 1990–91 (Research Associates, 1991). Under such conditions, it is in the best interest of institutions to conduct assessment studies and share the results with key constituencies.

Issues of public policy and assessment mandates relate to student affairs programs in two ways. First, assessment will help student affairs defend its continued existence. With cuts in higher education funding during the early 1990s, college presidents are looking for ways to redirect funds. Tuition and fee increases in double-digit percentages (Evangelauf, 1991) cause students, parents, and others to question more closely how money is being spent on campus (Boulard, 1988). There is rhetoric that challenges student affairs, like academic affairs, to prove its worth. Recently, Mayhew, Ford, and Hubbard (1990) have called for a reduction in student services. Assessment results or lack of them may be used to assist in these decisions. Second, the evaluation process will clarify the role of student affairs within the institution. The nature of how student affairs contributes to students' education is still unclear. Whether mandated or not by external groups, assessment can provide a better understanding of the purposes and effectiveness of services.

What Is to Be Assessed?

High-stakes assessment was introduced to higher education initially in the area of basic skills. Assessment, of course, has been present in higher education for years; however, its use in decisions of accountability or high stakes has been very limited. Statewide testing programs for the basic areas of reading, writing, and mathematics arose in many states, including New Jersey, Florida, Georgia, and Texas. Evaluation in students' majors and general education followed. Tennessee passed a performance funding model (Bogue and Brown, 1982) that linked assessment results to 2 percent and later 5 percent of the total instructional budget.

Nationally, many institutions responded to evaluation of major programs but are still struggling with measuring the worth of general education. General education remains an elusive area for most institutions that have no core curriculum. Skills such as writing can usually be determined early, but general knowledge in natural science or social science is more difficult to define and assess.

Student development is a logical component of general education, and it is one where student affairs can have an impact. Areas of moral and intellectual reasoning and psychosocial tasks are nurtured on many campuses, both through student affairs and in general education course work. These developmental abilities are not unique to any particular discipline but can be fostered across the curriculum and in student affairs.

Assessment of student affairs is following that of basic skills, major programs, and general education. New Jersey and South Carolina, for instance, now specifically mandate assessment in student development. More institutions are placing student affairs in the mainstream of the educational mission and are anxious to demonstrate positive impact (Mable, 1988). Although budget constraints may be the reason prompting some divisions of student affairs to defend their mission on campus, the opportunity is also created to learn more about our value in higher education.

For student affairs divisions participating in these efforts, the following sections will outline briefly some strategies for beginning outcome assessment.

Defining Purposes and Objectives

Student affairs divisions on some campuses are being forced to describe their educational mission. The first step in doing that involves identifying the skills, knowledge, and developmental objectives that student affairs seeks to foster and accomplish. Of course, some student affairs divisions may claim no ties to education; such offices would presumably not need to fund activities to enhance students' personal and social development and therefore would not participate in assessment. For example, if an institution viewed housing as an operational necessity rather than as a developmental experience, residence life programming there would be nonexistent. Similarly, a career services office might provide only scheduling and physical facilities but have no personnel devoted to career development.

The next step for most student affairs units is the specification of developmental or other educational objectives by each student affairs office or group. It is necessary to describe carefully how students' lives will be changed, not just how the program is to be conducted. For instance, stating the objective that students become more decisive in their choices about careers and career decision making is preferable to proposing a career development workshop. In student activities, professionals might define what is meant by developing leadership in more specific terms. Is leadership demonstrated through public speaking skills, assertiveness, ability to achieve a consensus in a group, or something else? Does multicultural awareness mean the student can speak the language of another country, can tolerate other people, has knowledge of another culture, or something else? What is meant by growth in counseling or awareness of health at the health center?

Although most goals in student affairs will be developmental, others may involve acquisition of knowledge or skills. A student activities workshop objective may be to design a LOTUS spreadsheet file for maintaining a student organization budget. A health center goal may be that students are able to describe safe sex practices. See Erwin, Scott, and Menard (1991) for examples of other kinds of objectives in student affairs.

Invariably, when an institution is in the process of defining general education objectives, shared responsibilities between student and academic affairs will emerge (Kuh, Shedd, and Whitt, 1987). For instance, most institutions have some course work requirements in the fine arts, such as art or music appreciation. Esthetic development is obviously accomplished in part by the classroom experience. However, participation in or attendance at plays, concerts, art shows, or other artistic activities may enhance esthetic development. Although art, music, or theater departments would claim some responsibility for their classroom instruction, it is logical for them to recognize the potential contribution of other events that an office of student activities might sponsor. Other common ground between academic and student services offerings might include physical education–wellness course requirements and recreation-intramural activities, social science classes and leadership development, and philosophy-humanities course work and service-experimental learning. The recognition of shared responsibility for general education between academic and student affairs usually brings the two areas closer together and is a very positive benefit of the assessment process.

The specification of objectives in student affairs will generate much discussion about purposes and practices. If done seriously, natural disagreements will occur. For example, does intellectual development have a place in student affairs (Barr, 1986)? Are our current developmental theories and approaches relevant to our students? If this objective-setting step is done well, student affairs staff members should be able to articulate clearly what each program or service is trying to accomplish.

Assessment Methods

Assessment methods should be selected according to their availability, quality of information, and purpose. Availability implies that an instrument exists for measuring the given objective. Some sources for developmental instruments include the ACPA Commission IX Clearinghouse for Tests (Bowling Green State University, Bowling Green, Ohio 43403); *The Iowa Student Development Inventories* (HiTech Press, Box 2341, Iowa City, Iowa 52244); Educational Testing Service Test Review, D-420 (Educational Testing Service, Princeton, New Jersey 08541); Student Development Associates, *Student Development Task and Lifestyle Inventory Manual* (110 Crestwood Drive, Athens, Georgia 30605); Dr. James Rest, *Defining Issues Test* (University of Minnesota, Center for Study of Ethical Development, Minneapolis St. Paul, Minnesota 55455); Developmental Analytics, *Scale of Intellectual Development* and *Erwin Identity Scale,* (Box 855, Harrisonburg, Virginia 22801); Hanson (1989); Baxter Magolda (1987); Mines (1982); Pace (1984); and Robinson and Shaver (1973). Guidelines for selecting assessment instruments may be found in Erwin (1991). For a specific objective, however, it is likely that no instrument exists. Probably one of the greatest needs in student affairs is for easily scored instruments that measure new developmental approaches. See Gable (1986) and Erwin (1991) for information about method design strategies.

Quality of information involves issues of reliability and validity for a given assessment instrument. Because these issues are covered in detail in other sources (Erwin, 1991), only definitional information about these concepts will be presented here.

Reliability means the consistency and precision of the information gathered by the instrument. Are students understanding the words and phrases in the same way? Are the test items measuring the same constructs? In observational or performance situations, would another rater produce the same result? Many problems with reliability can be prevented with clearly worded test statements derived from precisely conceived constructs.

Validity has to do with the worth, credibility, and demonstrated use of the assessment method. Does the method follow some developmental theory or conceptual approach? Is it correlated to other methods measuring a similar construct? Does it differentiate between different groups of students, such as students who have participated in an intervention and those who have not? Does the method *not* make inappropriate discriminations between groups, such as between minority and Caucasian students? A more complete discussion of validity may be found in Messick (1989).

In choosing an instrument, the quality of the information is particularly important because much of that used by higher education in the past to direct programs is currently under criticism. The quality of information used in high-stakes decisions should be proven through evidence of the instrument's reliability and validity.

The purpose or application of the information also influences the formality of the assessment method. If the information is to be used with other measures for program improvement, more informal methods may be appropriate. Informal methods in this context may be existing archival data such as student government minutes or user service surveys. More formal methods would include tests and structured, behaviorally anchored rating scales for which good reliability has been demonstrated. Formal methods are more defensible for external audiences concerned with funding considerations.

Collecting Assessment Information

Typically, assessment information is gathered just after the program intervention or impact — after a workshop is delivered or a service is rendered, such as the end of the residence life experience. Weiss (1972) refers to this analytical approach as the "after-only" study.

A problem with after-only studies is that one cannot evaluate the development or knowledge students bring with them. Some students may be performing well at the end of a program or service because they entered at a high level of functioning, not because of the intervention. The before-and-after approach, also known as the pretest-posttest design, allows some control for different levels of preexisting development or knowledge.

Another approach involves the comparison of participants in a program or service to a group of students who have not participated — a control group. The control group should be as similar as possible to the participating group. Instead of a control group, it may be more convenient to compare subgroups of students participating in various program options (Oetting and Cole, 1978). For example, Martin and Erwin (1991) compared average identity scores among students categorized as either major campus leader, committee chairperson, student organization participant, student nonparticipant, or nonstudents of similar ages. Another example of alternative program comparison may be found in Erwin and Love (1989), in which students' average autonomy scores were compared among students who had loans, scholarships, work-study aid, part-time jobs, or no financial aid. Mostly, these groups were intact, meaning students were not

randomly assigned to them. Very few studies based on random information are possible in higher education, so it is important to compare intact-
group scores or ratings with similar students who have not experienced
the intervention. One study where random data were used concerned roommate assignment in residential life (Erwin, 1983). Instead of analyzing a
program or service, institutions may generalize about students as they
progress through the undergraduate years. For instance, how have students changed during their first two years of college? More sophisticated,
analytical strategies are discussed elsewhere in Pascarelli and Terenzini (1991)
and Erwin (1991).

The following example illustrates a practical application of assessment
and the way that it was used to improve program effectiveness.

An Example

An example of an assessment plan that utilized a before-and-after control
group design is reported in Kilgannon and Erwin (forthcoming). They studied
the impact of sororities and fraternities during students' first two years in
college. Stated succinctly, the objectives of the Greek programs were to increase students' assurance and confidence and to enhance students' moral
reasoning abilities. Developmental information about students was collected
at two points: the beginning of the freshman year and the end of the sophomore year. Both times, the same random samples of Greek and non-Greek
students were assessed using the Erwin Identity Scale and Defining Issues
Test. Statistically, the entering freshmen score levels were controlled to equalize preexisting differences as much as possible. The Greeks' sophomore scores
were then compared to non-Greek sophomore scores to explore the two
groups' development. Of course, Greek sophomore scores could have been
compared to some expected standard or level of development, instead of to
those of a non-Greek control group. Moreover, this study could have tapped
seniors instead of sophomores, but the first two years were of institutional
interest.

The institution in this example regularly assesses development at the
beginning, middle, and end of the undergraduate years. Information is collected at the beginning during students' orientation, which is a very convenient time. Having an institutional data base of assessment information
facilitates other group comparisons, such as student leaders versus participants versus nonparticipants. Other comparisons might include trends or
differences over time.

Using Assessment Information

In the past, assessment in student affairs was largely practiced through diagnostic testing at the counseling center or through student perception surveys. In the future, institutions may likely expand individual student feed-

back with evaluation information collected primarily to gauge program effectiveness. Student affairs professionals are very adept at counseling or consulting with individual students, and feedback from individual assessment represents a powerful, informed way to promote student growth.

For instance, let us consider the use of developmental information for student affairs programs or service-learning placement. Analogous to academic affairs's testing of mathematical abilities, the development of entering freshmen might be assessed during orientation. The collected information could be used to target students with similar needs for support and challenge. For instance, one institution informed freshmen who had low scores on identity measures about a program sponsored by counseling center staff designed to help freshmen adjust to college life and to being on their own. Another institution advertised a career decision-making workshop for students scoring low on the establishing-and-clarifying-purpose subscale of the Student Development Task and Lifestyle Inventory (Winston and Miller, 1987). Another institution divided freshmen who had enrolled in its student organization leadership workshops into two groups. Based on students' scores on the dualism subscale of the Scale of Intellectual Development, students who were more rigid in their thinking were placed in one group and students who were more accepting of new ideas and diversity in the other group. The first workshop group particularly challenged students' rigidity of thinking from a multicultural point of view. Most of these student affairs programs were already in place, but they became more of a focus group when students were organized according to developmental needs.

In the future, it is likely that more student affairs staff members will be regularly conducting assessment studies. Existing student affairs programs should be periodically studied, and new ones should demonstrate their effectiveness in helping students. In the past, our profession assumed that the existence of programs produced positive results. As has been discussed, this assumption is being contested. Like any other profession, student affairs should be able to offer proof of effectiveness for any ongoing program. It may not mean that every program has to be assessed all the time but that positive evidence has been collected recently.

The responsibility for conducting assessment studies lies with each of us and should not be totally relegated to an assessment or institutional research office. Many institutions do not have these applied research units, or if they do exist, these specialists often do not have knowledge of developmental outcomes and instrumentation. Moreover, the field of evaluation has taught us that stakeholders involved in the evaluation effort are more likely to use the results (Patton, 1986). Fortunately, many student affairs staff members have had training in introductory statistics and testing. As a profession, student affairs also has the impetus for program standards through the Council for the Advancement of Standards for Student Services Development Programs (1986).

Summary

The student affairs profession is proud of its heritage of fairness toward and support for students. Assessment represents another mechanism for advancing beyond old models of decision making based on logic, politics, or intuition. According to Ewell (1991), external pressures that higher education furnish evidence of effectiveness are stronger than ever. Most recently, the U.S. Department of Education (1991), through the National Center for Education Statistics, has assembled persons for discussion about a national test for college students. Certainly, intuition and politics will continue to influence decision making, but evaluation for improvement purposes presumes that information will at least be part of the decision-making process.

A number of questions must be answered if student affairs programs are going to respond effectively to the demands of accountability. How clear are the stated objectives of student affairs programs and services? Is information available about their strengths and weaknesses? Has this assessment information been used to improve the institution's programs and services? If not, why not? The advantage exists for those of us who will have answers to these questions for our external constituents, for our students, and also for ourselves. This opportunity to provide proof of our developmental role may not be available for long.

References

Alexander, L., Clinton, B., and Kean, T. H. *Time for Results: The Governors' 1991 Report on Education.* Washington, D.C.: National Governors' Association, 1986.

Association of American Colleges. *Integrity in the College Curriculum: A Report to the Academic Community.* Washington, D.C.: Association of American Colleges, 1985.

Barr, M. J. "Should We Be Surprised?" *Journal of College Student Personnel,* 1986, *27,* 304–305.

Baxter Magolda, M. "A Rater-Training Program for Assessing Intellectual Development on the Perry Scheme." *Journal of College Student Personnel,* 1987, *28,* 356–364.

Bennett, W. J. Foreword. In C. P. Adelman (ed.), *Assessment in American Higher Education.* Washington, D.C.: U.S. Government Printing Office, 1985.

Bogue, E. G., and Brown, W. "Performance Incentives for State Colleges." *Harvard Business Review,* 1982, *60,* 123–128.

Boulard, G. A. "Higher-Education Commissioners Urge State Systems to Limit Tuition Raises and to Explain Costs to Public." *Chronicle of Higher Education,* 1988, *35,* 1.

Bowen, H. R. *Investment in Learning: The Individual and Social Value of American Higher Education.* San Francisco: Jossey-Bass, 1977.

Council for the Advancement of Standards for Student Services/Development Programs. *Council for the Advancement of Standards: Standards and Guidelines for Student Services/Development Programs.* College Park: University of Maryland, College Park, 1986.

Erwin, T. D. "The Influence of Roommate Assignments upon Students' Maturity." *Research in Higher Education,* 1983, *19,* 451–459.

Erwin, T. D. "New Opportunities: How Student Affairs Can Contribute to Student Assessment." In U. Delworth, G. R. Hanson, and Associates (eds.), *Student Services: A Handbook for the Profession.* (2nd ed.) San Francisco: Jossey-Bass, 1989.

Erwin, T. D. *Assessing Student Learning and Development: A Guide to the Principles, Goals, and Methods of Determining College Outcomes.* San Francisco: Jossey-Bass, 1991.

Erwin, T. D., and Love, W. B. "Selected Environmental Factors Associated with Change in Students' Development." *NASPA Journal,* 1989, *26,* 256–264.

Erwin, T. D., Scott, R. L., and Menard, A. J. "Student Outcome Assessment in Student Affairs." In T. K. Miller and R. B. Winston, Jr. (eds.), *Administration and Leadership in Student Affairs.* Muncie, Ind.: Accelerated Development, 1991.

Evangelauf, J. "Sharp Rise Reported in Public-College Tuition; Rate of Increase Drops at Private Institutions." *Chronicle of Higher Education,* 1991, *38,* 1, A30.

Ewell, P. T. "Outcomes, Assessment, and Academic Improvement: In Search of Usable Knowledge." In J. C. Smart (ed.), *Higher Education: Handbook of Theory and Research.* New York: Agathon Press, 1988.

Ewell, P. T. "Hearts and Minds: Some Reflections on the Ideologies on Assessment." Speech for the American Association for Higher Education Fourth National Conference on Assessment in Higher Education, Atlanta, Ga., June 1989.

Ewell, P. T. "Assessment and Public Policy: Shifting Sands, Uncertain Future." *Assessment Update: Progress, Trends, and Practices in Higher Education,* 1991, *3,* 1–7.

Feldman, K., and Newcomb, T. *The Impact of College on Students.* San Francisco: Jossey-Bass, 1969.

Gable, R. K. *Instrument Development in the Affective Domain.* Boston: Kluwer-Nijhoff, 1986.

Hanson, G. R. *The Assessment of Student Development Outcomes: A Review and Critique of Assessment Instruments.* Trenton: College Outcomes Evaluation Program, New Jersey Department of Higher Education, 1989.

Hood, A. B. (ed.). *The Iowa Student Development Inventories.* Iowa City, Iowa: HiTech Press, 1986.

Jacob, P. I. *Changing Values in College: An Exploratory Study of the Impact of College Teaching.* New York: HarperCollins, 1957.

Kilgannon, S. M., and Erwin, T. D. "A Longitudinal Study About the Identity and Moral Development of Greek Students." *Journal of College Student Development,* forthcoming.

Kuh, G. D., Shedd, J. D., and Whitt, E. J. "Student Affairs and Liberal Education: Unrecognized (and Unappreciated) Common Law Partners." *Journal of College Student Personnel,* 1987, *28,* 252–260.

Mable, P. "Student Performance Assessment: The Student Affairs Obligation." *NASPA Region III Review,* Fall 1988, p. 143.

Martin, S., and Erwin, T. D. "Degree of Involvement in Student Activities as Related to Identity and Moral Development." Unpublished manuscript, 1991.

Mayhew, L. B., Ford, P. J., and Hubbard, D. L. *The Quest for Quality: The Challenge for Undergraduate Education in the 1990s.* San Francisco: Jossey-Bass, 1990.

Messick, S. "Meaning and Values in Test Validation: The Science and Ethics of Assessment." *Educational Researcher,* 1989, *18,* 5–11.

Mines, R. A. "Student Development Assessment Techniques." In G. R. Hanson (ed.), *Measuring Student Development.* New Directions for Student Services, no. 20. San Francisco: Jossey-Bass, 1982.

Oetting, E. R., and Cole, C. W. "Method, Design, and Implementation in Evaluation." In G. R. Hanson (ed.), *Evaluating Program Effectiveness.* New Directions for Student Services, no. 1. San Francisco: Jossey-Bass, 1978.

Pace, C. R. *Measuring the Quality of College Student Experiences.* Los Angeles: Higher Education Research Institute, University of California, 1984.

Pascarella, E. T., and Terenzini, P. T. *How College Affects Students: Findings and Insights from Twenty Years of Research.* San Francisco: Jossey-Bass, 1991.

Patton, M. W. *Utilization-Focused Evaluation.* Newbury Park, Calif.: Sage, 1986.

Research Associates of Washington. *State Profiles: Financing Higher Education 1978–91.* Washington, D.C.: Research Associates of Washington, 1991.

Rest, J. *Guide for the Defining Issues Test.* Minneapolis, Minn.: Center for the Study of Ethical Development, 1987.

Robinson, J. P., and Shaver, P. R. *Measures of Social Psychological Attitudes.* Ann Arbor: University of Michigan, 1973.

Southern Regional Education Board Commission for Educational Quality. *Access to Quality Undergraduate Education.* Reprinted in *Chronicle for Higher Education,* 1985, *33,* 9–12.

Study Group on the Conditions of Excellence in American Higher Education. *Involvement in Learning: Realizing the Potential of American Higher Education.* Washington, D.C.: U.S. Government Printing Office, 1984.

U.S. Department of Education. "Secretary's Procedures and Criteria for Recognition of Accrediting Agencies." *Federal Register,* 1988, *53* (127), 25,088–25,099.

U.S. Department of Education. "Assessment of Student Learning in Postsecondary Education." Higher-Order Thinking and Communication Skills Study Design Workshop, Arlington, Va., Nov. 1991.

Weiss, C. H. *Evaluation Research: Methods for Assessing Program Effectiveness.* Englewood Cliffs, N.J.: Prentice-Hall, 1972.

Winston, R. B., Jr., and Miller, T. K. *Student Development Task and Lifestyle Inventory Manual.* Athens, Ga.: Student Development Associates, 1987.

17

❦

Budgeting and
Fiscal Management

Dudley B. Woodard, Jr.

The electronic and printed media have reported at great length on the financial and confidence crisis facing higher education. Is the budgetary crisis of the early 1990s any different from previous ones? Is it fueled more by enrollment declines and shortfalls in revenue, or are these real factors symptomatic of something more systemic? Zemsky and Massy (1990) state that higher education institutions are increasingly "less in control of their own destinies—lumbering along, awkward in their steerage, weighted down by decision-making processes that all but preclude the possibility of funding new investments through savings from current programs. . . . We're over-reaching, we're losing our sense of discipline and control, we're heading for trouble" (p. 16). The economic reality for the twenty-first century will be very different from the unprecedented economic and enrollment growth of the past fifty years. Franklyn Jenifer, president of Howard University, captured the essence of this new reality when he said, "Higher education has to develop a strategy that will be good in the good times and sustain us in the bad times" (Cage, 1991, p. A-1).

Note: The author acknowledges and appreciates the assistance of Mark von Destinon in the writing of this chapter.

The winds of change are not simply driven by economic and enrollment changes; the currents of a new reality have been stirred by the very public debate over the soundness and cost effectiveness of higher education. The public has lost confidence in higher education because of increases in tuition and fees considerably in excess of inflation, and "the perception that research and scholarship—not teaching—are the primary interests of university faculties" (Langfitt, 1990, p. 8).

Many colleges and universities have utilized a cost-plus pricing strategy rather than one of growth by substitution. The cost-plus pricing strategy relies on new revenues to support both increases in base operations and the financing of any new programs. The result is a bloated administration and misplaced priorities by faculty. Zemsky and Massy (1990) describe this as the administrative lattice and the academic ratchet. The administrative lattice is the "proliferation and entrenchment of administrative staff at American colleges and universities over the past two decades" (p. 22). The academic ratchet is "the steady, irreversible shift away from the goals of a given institution, toward those of an academic specialty. . . . the advancement of an independent, entrepreneurial spirit among faculty nationwide, leading to increased emphasis on research and publication and on teaching one's specialty in favor of general introduction courses, often at the expense of coherence in an academic curriculum" (p. 22). The growth-by-substitution philosophy, also known as cost containment, is based on the principle "that sheer expansion beyond a certain point weakens an institution by skewing its focus, diluting its sense of mission, and compromising its ability to provide a quality service in an efficient way" (Zemsky and Massy, 1990, p. 22). The substitution principle requires the elimination or consolidation of programs in order to finance new program growth.

The loss of public confidence amidst some scandals of misused funds has led many presidents and governing boards to review their strategic plans based on a financial plan of cost containment through retrenchment and reallocation. To restore public confidence, institutions must establish new administrative structures, values, and principles based on cost containment, or growth by substitution. They must establish a philosophy that emphasizes accountability and a reshaped mission tied to future budget realities. The public must be convinced that institutions understand that cost containment does not mean less quality and that getting "meaner and leaner" can lead to a more focused and reinvigorated institution (Zemsky and Massy, 1990).

This chapter reviews higher education finance and budgeting trends. It discusses budget definitions and process, including types of budget and revenue sources. Strategies and models for the student affairs practitioner are offered along with a presentation of five theoretical approaches to budgeting. The budgeting cycle in student affairs and analytical guidelines are reviewed and some practical advice offered.

Trends

During recent decades, costs for higher education have risen faster than inflation, and state support and endowment earnings have fallen off. Charges of misuse and inefficiency are also plaguing institutions. A study on institutional costs noted that with two exceptions, "In each decade since 1930 tuition in both public and private sectors has gone up more than general inflation as measured by the Consumer Price Index" (Halstead, 1991a, p. 16). Overall, tuition and fees increased at a rate between two and three times the rate of inflation from 1980 to 1990 (Higher Education Surveys, 1990). A college education is more expensive today than in the past compared to increases in other consumer goods and services because higher education is more susceptible to inflationary influences. Industry can achieve cost savings from increased productivity and new technology, but unfortunately these benefits do not affect higher education in the same way (Halstead, 1991a).

States have shifted priorities by allocating less to public education during the last decade. Halstead (1991b) reports, "State and local governments are allocating a seriously declining share of their tax revenues to public higher education — 7.8 percent in 1989–90 compared to the recent peak of 9.2 percent in 1980–81" (p. 8). And according to a College Board report (1990) on financial aid trends, the cost of attendance for both public and private institutions has risen dramatically since 1980, pricing many students out of their first collegiate choice. Adjusted for constant dollars, cost of attendance (tuition, fees, and room and board) has risen by 40 percent for public universities and 60 percent for private universities since 1980. However, per capita personal income increased only 18 percent in constant dollars during this same period, and during the 1980s the federal share of financial aid decreased from 83 to 73 percent. Loans grew faster than grant aid for students, resulting in an increase in debt at graduation; the maximum Pell Grant award decreased by $54 (constant dollars) during this period. Based on these trends, the conclusion was that "neither student aid nor family incomes kept pace with rising college costs in the 1980s" (College Board, 1990, p. 3).

When describing the higher education economic outlook for the 1980s, Frances (1980) concludes "Enrollments will grow, but the financial squeeze of fiscal 1980 will be worse than those we have weathered in recent years" (p. 36). Frances goes on to say that the higher inflation rate of past years and experience gained in budget reductions should thus result in increased sophistication in financial management and creative approaches to the wise use of human, physical, and financial resources of the institution (1980). Unfortunately, this advice was not taken by those institutions whose fortunes grew for a short time during the economic recovery of the mid 1980s. Rather than using new resources to strengthen basic programs and fund new efforts through reallocation of existing funds, these institutions participated in a bogus game of adding new programs and services based on a cost-plus pricing mentality, driven by their belief that these actions were necessary in order to remain competitive.

Despite the countertrends of the late 1980s, financial officials remain optimistic about their institutions' ability to raise revenues (Higher Education Surveys, 1990) through traditional strategies such as reducing the dropout rate, increasing voluntary contributions, recruiting more nontraditional students, and attracting more federal and state aid.

When asked to identify actions that they could take to control costs, the officials mentioned implementing institutionwide budget cuts, delaying new construction, and increasing the use of part-time faculty. They were also asked about management initiatives that could have a positive effect on either revenues or expenditures. Their most frequent suggestions were to improve the budgeting process, develop a strategic plan, and implement or modify a management information system (Higher Education Surveys, 1990). Clearly, the financial officers responding to the survey intended to rely on traditional budgeting approaches to solve problems.

Budget Definitions

The budget process can be viewed either as a creative process or a routine task. The latter view frequently results in activity designed to satisfy an institutional or governing board requirement. However, budgeting can also be a creative process designed to help those involved make choices, sort out priorities, and agree on a plan for the future.

Budget Process

Meisinger and Dubeck (1984) describe budgeting as a process, a plan of action, a control mechanism, a way of communicating, a contract, and a political tool. As a process, a budget allows for the participation of constituents and consensus building with regard to levels of funding by program, revenue source, and standards of accountability. As a plan, it is a mechanism for setting priorities for activities consistent with the institution's strategic plan and forecasted resources. The budget is a contract based on commitments reflected in the strategic plan and on receipt of restricted funds from donors, federal agencies, and state appropriations. As a control mechanism, the budget regulates the flow of resources to support each activity in accordance with approved institutional policies and procedures. As a communication network, the budget allows each department or unit to communicate its objectives, needs, and the resources required to fund them. And finally, a budget is a political tool because it reflects the outcomes of negotiations with different constituents about funding sources and about which activities will be supported and at what level (Meisinger and Dubeck, 1984). Budgeting should be viewed as a dynamic, creative, consensus-building process that involves key decision makers in an effort to set priorities that best serve students and societal needs.

Budget Types

An institution, depending on size, complexity, and type of control, will generally have two major budgets, the operating budget and the capital budget. There may also be other separate budgets for local funds, auxiliaries, and special function units, like hospital operations. The operating budget is the main budget and includes "all of the regular unrestricted income available to the institution plus those restricted funds (for example, endowed professorships and sponsored programs) that are earmarked for instructional activities and department support" (Meisinger and Dubeck, 1984, pp. 7–8).

As the core budget, the operating budget includes funds allocated for instructional activities and support, student services, libraries, administration and finance, public service and development, and the unrestricted portion of endowment income, gifts, and student aid. The capital budget usually includes the cost of approved new construction and renovation. Local-fund or restricted budgets usually encompass federally sponsored research, grants and contracts, nongovernmental grants, some endowment and gift income, and student aid from federal and other external sources. Auxiliary budgets support those activities that are self-supporting, such as residence halls, intercollegiate athletics, student unions, and copy centers (Meisinger and Dubeck, 1984).

Sources of Revenue

Colleges and universities have many sources of revenue, including tuition and fees, auxiliary income, state appropriations, endowment, federal grants and contracts, federal and state financial aid programs, and fund balances. Based on the character of the institution, the mix of these funds will vary considerably. For example, public colleges generally rely more on state appropriations than tuition, whereas private institutions depend more on tuition and earned interest from endowments. Understanding the sources, the mix of funds, and likely changes in contribution to the overall budget is a prerequisite to sound budget planning. A miscalculation on revenue projection of 2 percent could translate into a 4 or 6 percent cut on the operating side (Meisinger and Dubeck, 1984).

Budget Models

During the last decade, most institutions of higher learning have developed a strategic plan based on the outcomes of environmental scanning and designed to capture the future requirements and needs of the institution. The strategic plan serves as the basis on which the academic, support services, facilities, and financial plans are built. It represents the funding required to implement all the other plans. And once the financial plan for a given year is developed, an operating budget is generated that supports the strategic goals and objectives for that fiscal year. Monthly operating statements then allow for comparison to the budget and evaluation of how well the objectives are being met (Morrell, 1989).

Many different budget models exist. And the shifts in public confidence, declining enrollments, and reductions in financial resources have rendered some approaches less useful than others. The following models represent the array of budget approaches, and any one, or a combination, will fulfill the requirement of establishing an annual budget. However, as Morrell (1989) points out, the operating budget must take into account the assumptions and decisions on which the financial plan is based by providing the tools and information necessary to implement and evaluate the institution's long-range strategic plan successfully.

Incremental Budgeting

Incremental budgeting is one of the most frequently used approaches. It is based on the previous year's allocation, and the budget is adjusted based on guidelines provided by the budget office. The underlying assumptions are (1) that financial resources from one budget cycle to another change only modestly, (2) that expenditure patterns for the department represent continuing commitments that are difficult to alter, and (3) that institutional needs and priorities remain relatively unchanged from one budget cycle to the next (Meisinger and Dubeck, 1984). For example, the next year's budget adjustment factors might represent a salary projection of a 5 percent increase, a 2 percent increase in operations, and no increase in travel and capital. General practice is to adjust all unit budgets by these projected changes rather than making adjustments based on priorities.

Incremental budgeting does not force the institution to examine priorities in a way that encourages annual reallocation, reductions, and elimination of programs. Meisinger and Dubeck (1984) argue that its strengths are also its weaknesses: "It is simpler, easier to apply, more controllable, more adaptable, and more flexible than modern alternatives . . . [but] incrementalism does not encourage rational examination of the full spectrum of policy choices and selection of the best one; the object of incremental decision making is to minimize conflict rather than to make the best policy choice; incremental budgeting does not examine the budget base or the array of existing fiscal commitments, but focuses on changes to those commitments; incrementalism is driven more by political demands than by analytical assessments of requirements" (Meisinger and Dubeck, 1984, p. 183).

Zero-Based Budgeting

Zero-based budgeting is one of the more appealing approaches but also one of the most cumbersome. It is appealing because "administrators must justify from base zero all of their departmental or agency budgeted expenditures. . . .

Nothing is taken for granted or simply continued at some previous level. Everything must be justified or discontinued through the use of cost-benefit analysis" (Boyd, 1982, p. 429). Zero-based budgeting requires an annual review of each department's performance, cost benefit, and relationship to the institution's strategic plan. It is easier to consolidate, reduce, or eliminate programs under a zero-based model, but it also can be very disruptive or anxiety producing since commitments may only last one year. Also, the process is time consuming, makes it difficult to reach consensus on priorities, and generates a lot of paperwork. Many institutions using such an approach fix the budget base at some percentage, such as 90 percent, and then use the principles of zero-based budgeting to allocate the remaining 10 percent. However, this variation undercuts the basic principle of complete program reviews based on performance, cost, and relationship to the strategic plan (Meisinger and Dubeck, 1984).

Planning, Programming, and Budget Systems

Planning, Programming, and Budget Systems (PPBS) is a way of linking strategic planning elements to resource allocation. PPBS focuses on a clear and detailed description of program activities and the cost effectiveness of these in terms of attaining desired objectives. Meisinger and Dubeck (1984) define PPBS as organizing and presenting "information about the cost and benefits of an organization's activities and programs. A program plan establishes goals and objectives for the organization and relates them to the organization's activities. The costs and benefits of alternative ways of reaching the goals and objectives are established through an examination of resources required for and estimated benefits to be gained from alternative programs. An important aspect of the program budget is projection of the costs and outputs of programs over a number of years to provide a long-term view of the fiscal implications of those programs" (p. 183).

According to Schuh (1990), some of the difficulties of PPBS are defining outputs of higher education, quantifying program activities, determining cost-benefit ratios, and calculating cost benefits of alternative programs. Finally, the costs of information gathering and analysis of program alternatives can be overwhelming. Because of these time-consuming activities and their costs, PPBS has not been successfully implemented in governmental and educational settings (Meisinger and Dubeck, 1984).

Formula Budgeting

Formula budgeting is a way of allocating or appropriating dollars to an activity based on quantifiable work-load measures. The most common measure is the conversion of enrollment into a mathematical ratio—for example, every student enrolled for fifteen instructional hours is equivalent to one full-time student, and each full-time student is worth x dollars. According to Brinkman (1984), formula budgeting is both a political and technical process; in other words, policy is forged out of political agreements and mathematical equations that express those agreements. Several criteria ensure the validity of formula budgeting: formula budgeting should recognize the varying costs of different activities, should only use factors that can be quantified, should make comparisons only to comparable peer institutions, should use a factor or methodology appropriate to the activity to be funded, and should take into account differing needs of the institution (Brinkman, 1984). "Taken together, then, the evaluative criteria indicate that a good formula is technically correct, representative of certain basic values, and helpful in making the budgeting process work smoothly" (Brinkman, 1984, p. 25).

The advantages of formula budgeting are (1) an appearance of objectivity as the activity is quantified, (2) the reduction of conflict because individuals understand the basis of funding, (3) built-in equity, (4) diminished uncertainty of the budgeting process, and (5) guarantee of more autonomy for public institutions as state appropriations are formula driven (hence less politically driven) (Meisinger and Dubeck, 1984). The weaknesses of formula budgeting are (1) that it does not anticipate change, as it is usually based on past behavior, such as the previous year's enrollment; (2) that the calculations tend to be simplistic and economies of scale, variable costs, and enrollment shifts are therefore not easily accommodated; (3) that if system based, there is a tendency to treat all institutions alike, resulting in a "leveling effect"; (4) that it discourages new-program development to meet emerging needs because dollars are tied to existing activity (for example, the number of electrical engineering majors); (5) that the reward structure, such as enrolling more students, encourages institutions to behave in ways that favor the reward but penalize the teaching environment; and (6) that reaction to price changes in the marketplace (for instance, faculty and staff salaries) may not be adjusted at the same rate of change for service and production employees (Brinkman, 1984). Formula budgeting is widely used, but its utility should be questioned since it does not encourage program assessment or respond in a timely way to emerging needs or recognize differences between institutions.

Metropolitan institutions and community colleges are often negatively affected by formula budgeting. These institutions often enroll many part-time students; however, the cost for enrollment services such as admission, registration, and advising is the same as for full-time students. Credit-hour production formulas do not account for these constant administrative costs, and resource allocation is not sufficient.

Cost-Centered Budgeting

Cost-centered budgeting is based on the principle that every unit or department pays its own way. Each unit is viewed as self-supporting and is expected to raise sufficient revenues to cover its costs. This type of budgeting works more successfully with "units that are relatively independent in the sense that the instructional and research programs are self-contained" (Meisinger and Dubeck, 1984, p. 188). This is a useful approach for auxiliaries but not for instructional and support functions such as student and academic support services or such items as the physical plant. These units frequently provide assistance to other areas, and a full-cost approach for some units will discourage student use. Several prime examples of services that are much needed but may not be used because of the costs are tutoring, counseling, and health care.

Student Affairs Budget Cycle

It is not uncommon for a department head to be simultaneously involved in three budget cycles. The first involves closing out the previous fiscal year. This is an important activity from the standpoint of determining whether or not budgetary program and expenditure goals were met. This information is critical to the allocation process for the next fiscal year and preparation of the budget request for the subsequent fiscal year. Institutional rules are also important and must be considered when closing out a fiscal year. For example, at many institutions, any unit budget that finishes a fiscal year in a deficit situation may have funds deducted from the allocation for the next fiscal year—a circumstance that should be avoided.

The second cycle is the next fiscal year. Most institutions use a July 1st through June 30th year. This cycle represents the allocation of resources based on the final budget request. It is essential to establish an ongoing monitoring process to make certain that expenditures are in line with actual resources and, equally important, that progress is being made toward meeting program goals. The most frequent mistake made by department heads is to wait until near the end of the fiscal year to check on progress. A monthly review process should be implemented and adjustments made based on the rate of expenditures and any approved variations from the approved budget (for instance, unanticipated expenses or changes in direction based on new information or needs).

The third cycle is the preparation of the budget request for the succeeding year. This request usually begins fourteen to sixteen months in advance of the actual fiscal year, such as March of 1992 for July of 1993. Preparing for the succeeding year's budget cycle is the main focus of this section.

There are seven distinct steps in preparing a budget request for the next fiscal year. These steps do not include the institutional stages of governing-board review and action, legislative submission and action if appropriate, and final institutional process of allocation based on actual and projected resources for the coming fiscal year. The practitioner should be well acquainted with the following steps in order to anticipate likely resources, timing of budget decisions, and especially points of intervention. It is important to know when to take action to clarify a budget issue, to provide additional information, or simply to argue to protect the integrity of the request or offer an alternative based on current and projected conditions.

Establish Assumptions and Constraints

The first step in developing the succeeding budget request is to gather information about next year's likely fiscal environment (Meisinger and Dubeck, 1984). Will enrollments change and how? Has the stock market negatively or positively affected projected earned interest from the endowment? What are the prospects for new gifts? Are there changes in program offerings? What is happening with federal financial aid? What is the prospect for grants and contracts? What are the costs of any new mandated changes? What is the outlook for the state economy? These are some of the many questions that must be addressed by senior management in establishing the framework for preparing the budget. Executive officers must make a realistic assessment of all sources of income, including investment income, as budget parameters are set. Assumptions about sources of revenue, enrollment, and program offerings and constraints like mandated requirements and fixed costs must be understood and shared with all individuals responsible for developing the budget.

Establish Guidelines and Timetable

Once the assumptions and constraints have been established, the division head should send out written guidelines to be used in preparing the budget. These should reflect the general guidelines outlined above as well as the institutional assumptions and constraints agreed to. Expectations should be clear and an opportunity provided to discuss the instructions. A time line for hearings and final submission of the budget request should also be included.

Encourage Involvement

Divisional or unit instructions should encourage the involvement of departmental staff, students, and, where appropriate, faculty. This is also an opportunity for the division or unit head to review financial conditions, institutional priorities, and likely financial scenarios. This is the time to share information and excite individuals to think creatively about achieving goals with the same or fewer resources.

Hold Hearings

Hearings for each unit in student affairs should be scheduled and students, staff, and faculty invited (if appropriate in the institutional setting). A department can then demonstrate whether or not it has been a good steward of its resources and how well it has met its objectives. It is a time to ask tough questions of the department head—including what alternatives were considered in preparing the budget request. A unit hearing will help individuals be more sensitive to the needs of the community, to perceptions on how well those are being met, and to highest priorities.

Allow for Central Staff Debate

After the hearings, each department should finalize its budget and submit it to the central staff or the management team of the division. These are the senior officers of the division of student affairs who have the responsibility of finalizing the division's budget request for approval and action by the chief student affairs officer (CSAO). These individuals will need to take into account assumptions, constraints, unit requests, and results of public hearings, as well as short- and long-term divisional priorities. The CSAO is a member of this group and should participate fully.

Develop Alternatives

Each department and the senior management team should develop alternatives based on likely financial scenarios. This process requires a great deal of goodwill and trust. In some cases, alternatives will describe a reorganized division of student affairs, elimination of programs or units, or transfer of functions to academic departments or other college units. Maintaining flexibility will help the division effectively respond to new opportunities as well as to tough financial challenges.

Stay Informed and Keep Others Informed

In today's environment, the status of a budget is like the daily newspaper. There are new headlines, and yesterday's information is out-of-date. People must be kept informed of changing events, and occasional briefing sessions must be held. This practice will help to control rumors and keep people involved in the process and committed to working through the eventual budgetary circumstances.

Budget Guidelines

This section is intended as assistance to student affairs practitioners in successfully navigating the shifting tides of the budget-setting process. The guidelines will help in the preparation of a budget regardless of the fiscal climate. They should be used to evaluate the contributions of each student affairs unit, both to the mission of the student affairs division and to that of the institution. Careful application of the guidelines will determine whether or not the student affairs unit should remain as is, grow, be reduced, be eliminated, or be consolidated with another. These suggestions are directed at developing a strategy for the good times and the bad times.

Does the Unit Contribute to the Divisional and Institutional Mission?

The connections between the unit and institutional mission should be clear and documentable. Lyons indicates that all "programs and activities are important, but not all are equally important" (1991, p. 3). Although this statement sounds much like Orwell's admonition to society that "all animals are equal, but some animals are more equal than others," (1954), it is true that the mission, purpose, and nature of programs do make some programs more valuable than others. The tighter its connection to the mission, the stronger is the rationale for keeping the program.

Has Each Unit Developed Credible Work-Load Factors?

The scope and magnitude of a service or program and who is served and benefited by it are important to document (Lyons, 1991). Each unit should develop work-load measures and analyze the characteristics of its clientele. These data will help solicit support, for example, from the mathematics department if it can be proved that a number of its students are served, that they value the service, and that student performance is enhanced.

Are There Measurable Outcomes?

Beyond developing work-load factors, each unit should attempt to quantify the desired outcomes for its service or program in relation to the institution's stated outcomes for the educational experience. Does the collegiate experience improve one's ability to think reflectively, analytically, and critically? Does it facilitate personal growth and identity (Pascarella and Terenzini, 1991)? Developing outcome measures and demonstrating the role of the unit or division in increasing student growth in these areas will greatly enhance the unit's worth and future role.

Do Most Activities Help Students Do Things for Themselves?

The authors of *Involving Colleges* observe, "Involving colleges encourage student responsibility and freedom of choice. . . . Students are trusted and expected to be responsible for their own learning and development, as well as for handling violations of community norms. For the most part, students are given the freedom to learn from their own decisions, experiences, and, in some cases, mistakes" (Kuh, Schuh, Whitt, and Associates, 1991, p. 137). It is clear that activities promoting individual responsibility and helping students to do things for themselves should be valued and protected in the budget-setting process (Lyons, 1991).

Are Services Designed to Maintain Ethical, Health, and Safety Standards Protected?

The difficult decisions made during tight fiscal times must be made in such a way as to protect essential services. This does not mean that essential services are exempt from cuts but rather that responsible action should be taken to maintain campus standards for those services. Responsible actions may include using competitive bidding for the services, utilizing students for safety and health tasks, or seeking volunteers for low-risk functions in order to protect high-risk activities (Lyons, 1991).

Is Progress in Building Community and Diversity Protected?

Frequently, programs that were created to meet affirmative action goals and diversity are the first to see the ax blade of budget cuts. These programs are a necessary condition for today's institution to meet the highly publicized statements of commitment to diversity and community. Actions that undercut these obligations will seriously jeopardize the academy's long-stated goal of a community that values and celebrates diversity.

Are Operating Practices Changed to Effect Cost Savings?

The task of changing operating practices is both difficult and essential, and the practitioner should examine alternative ways of providing services. Some possibilities are (1) to contract out services so as to generate cost savings or new revenues without sustaining loss of quality, (2) to develop appropriate, improved work-load standards, (3) to take advantage of staff openings to consolidate and reorganize functions, (4) to target high-cost goods and services such as computing, printing, and reproduction for cost containment, (5) to utilize creative personnel policies and practices to reduce costs — for example, early retirement, flextime, and ten-month contracts, (6) to reduce administrative services inefficiencies, such as duplicate accounting practices, and (7) to streamline reporting and recording activities (University of Arizona, 1991).

Are Weaker Programs Eliminated?

In times of budget cuts, across-the-board or vertical cuts simply reduce everything to a lower level of functioning and effectiveness. Instead, it is possible to protect the efficiency and effectiveness of some programs by eliminating weak, low-demand, or inappropriately duplicative programs (University of Arizona, 1991).

Are Savings Real?

A reduction in one unit will not generate a savings or funding for reallocation if another unit will be pressed to compensate (Lyons, 1991). Cuts should not be made in isolation. Each unit has the obligation to discuss the probable impact of certain actions with those affected in order to avoid later recriminations and confusion among students. The community should be well advised in advance of the curtailment in services and elimination of programs.

Is the Partnership with Faculty Genuine?

Boyer (1991) and others say that we need to reengage faculty. There are functions that faculty should be encouraged to assume as a trade-off for reducing support services. If these kinds of negotiations do not take place and battles rage over turf, then students will continue to be the losers. Student services will not be eliminated, but we must look at new arrangements and at ways that some student service functions could be assumed by faculty in exchange for protecting the integrity of the instructional mission through a reallocation of student service dollars to the instructional budget.

Suggestions for Practice

This section provides practical advice for thinking about and participating in the budget-setting process. These tips cover most problems and should be occasionally reviewed to maintain perspective and a sense of humility.

Be Flexible

The practitioner must be open to new ways of doing things even if the current method is successful. Change occurs either by force or cooperation. Maintaining an open stance will help facilitate a thorough discussion of options and the eventual discarding of dysfunctional ideas and the adoption of new strategies.

Do Not Dawdle

As Lyons so aptly states, "There is more pain and institutional trauma when the decision and implementing processes are stretched out over a long period of time" (1991, p. 2). Determine a reasonable time frame for completing the task and stay on schedule. Be decisive and do not fret about consulting with everyone. If you have designed a solid process with input from staff, students, and faculty, then you should pay attention to agreed-upon procedures and get the job done!

Play It Straight

Nobody likes to find out after the fact that information has been withheld or even edited. Take care to provide all relevant information, such as cost, work-load measures, outcome data, and peer comparison data. Respond to requests on a timely basis and ask for feedback about whether the information was understood and useful. "A lie, an attempt to blatantly cover up some misdeed, a tricky move of any kind, can lead to an irreparable loss of confidence" (Wildavsky, 1988, p. 106).

Accept Responsibility

Make certain the staff understands the decision-making tree and line-staff functions (Halfond, 1991; Lyons, 1991). Accept responsibility for your actions and do not look for scapegoats. Reallocation and reduction are not pleasant businesses, but remember you are paid to make decisions!

Involve People

You must build a sense of community and shared responsibility by involving people in the information-gathering and decision-making process. In order for decisions to have validity and be accepted by the larger community, campus leaders must be valued for their input and be seen by others as involved members of the budgetary process. This approach will reduce friction and help mute the dissidents.

Seek Advice

The many knowledgeable students, staff members, and faculty members on campus can provide valuable advice. Create an advisory committee and test out ideas and possible alternatives with them. "Advisory groups are rarely 'professional student affairs folks.' That's their strength. They can, among other things, ask some brilliant dumb questions—the very kind that often result in some very imaginative thinking" (Lyons, 1991, p. 2).

Avoid Extreme Claims

In an effort to describe the worth of a program, sometimes claims are made that cannot be supported with any evidence. Do not make sweeping assertions or lead with your heart when candor would have scored more points! The faculty has the same problem of documenting the outcomes of the educational experience. Indicate what the research does demonstrate but do not go beyond a reasonable interpretation of the evidence (Wildavsky, 1988).

Decentralized Decisions

Seek the involvement of unit heads and allow for decision making at that level. "Central leaders are best at setting the parameters and the goals. Leaders (and their followers) in the units are in the best position to bring good judgment to bear and, hence, to find the most sensible and creative alternatives to choose from" (Lyons, 1991, p. 2).

Secure Feedback

Everyone claims that his or her service or program is popular and serves its clientele well. Before making such a claim, make certain you have secured feedback from the individuals served and from secondary sources likely to be affected, such as the student's department, residence hall, or place of employment. Direct feedback from those served can be helpful, but if possible, be aware of its content in advance of any presentation. You will then be able to check on the accuracy of the information and be prepared to answer questions. Do not try to avoid bad news. Objective listeners will sort through the information and determine what is helpful based on client feedback and your responses to questions (Wildavsky, 1988).

Be a Good Politician

Wildavsky states that being a good politician requires three things: "Cultivation of an active clientele, the development of confidence among other governmental officials, and skill in following strategies that exploit one's opportunities to the maximum. Doing good work is viewed as part of being a good politician" (1988, p. 101). The student affairs practitioner should lobby for key programs and services as long as the process is open and does not run counter to the priorities established by the division. Spending time explaining the nature of a valued program and its virtues to a faculty colleague, an academic department head, or a dean is a practice that should be ongoing and not prompted solely because of a budgetary crisis.

Summary

Budgeting, once viewed as someone else's job and a tiresome task, has become an important management tool for today's practitioner. Everyone should develop an understanding of the financial and budgetary practices of the institution. This understanding is essential for successful participation in budget-setting practices. The process should be viewed as a creative, adventurous one. Honesty and openness, coupled with adequate data, are the foundation for the development of sound budget approaches for student affairs. To meet the challenge of a cost-containment environment, practitioners must develop the sophistication to assess the costs of different program options that are linked to the priorities of the institution's strategic plan. Anything less will disadvantage the division of student affairs in the preparation of the budget and the allocation of resources for the coming year.

References

Boyd, W. L. "Zero-Based Budgeting: The Texas Experience." *Journal of Higher Education*, 1982, *53*, 429–438.

Boyer, E. L. *Scholarship Reconsidered.* Princeton, N.J.: Carnegie Foundation, 1991.

Brinkman, P. T. "Formula Budgeting: The Fourth Decade." In L. L. Leslie (ed.), *Responding to New Realities in Funding.* New Directions for Institutional Research, no. 43. San Francisco: Jossey-Bass, 1984.

Cage, M. C. "Recession Expected to Bring Long-Term Changes in State Colleges' Relations with Governments." *Chronicle of Higher Education*, 1991, *37* (44), A1.

College Board. *Trends in Student Aid: 1980 to 1990.* New York: College Entrance Examination Board, 1990.

Frances, C. *The Short-Run Economic Outlook for Higher Education.* Washington, D.C.: American Council on Education, 1980.

Halfond, J. A. "Too Many Administrators: How It Happened and How to Respond." *AAHE Bulletin*, Mar. 1991, pp. 7–8.

Halstead, K. *Higher Education Revenues and Expenditures: A Study of Institutional Costs.* Washington, D.C.: Research Associates of Washington, 1991a.

Halstead, K. *State Profiles: Financing Public Higher Education, 1978–1990.* Washington, D.C.: Research Associates of Washington, 1991b.

Higher Education Surveys. *The Finances of Higher Education Institutions.* Higher Education Survey Report, no. 8. National Science Foundation, National Endowment for the Humanities, and U.S. Department of Education, 1990.

Kuh, G. D., Schuh, J. H., Whitt, E. J., and Associates. *Involving Colleges: Successful Approaches to Fostering Student Learning and Development Outside the Classroom.* San Francisco: Jossey-Bass, 1991.

Langfitt, T. W. "The Cost of Higher Education: Lessons to Learn from the Health Care Industry." *Change*, 1990, *22* (6), 8–15.

Lyons, J. W. *A Perspective on Cutting Student Affairs Budgets or How to Run a Blood Bank When Your Only Volunteers Are Turnips.* Unpublished paper presented at the NASPA Richard F. Stevens Institute, July 1991.

Meisinger, R. J., and Dubeck, L. W. *College and University Budgeting: An Introduction for Faculty and Academic Administrators.* Washington, D.C.: National Association of College and University Business Officers, 1984.

Morrell, L. R. "Financial Strategy in Higher Education." *Business Officer*, 1989, *22* (10), 34–38.

Orwell, G. *Animal Farm.* Orlando, Fla.: Harcourt Brace Jovanovich, 1954.

Pascarella, E. T., and Terenzini, P. T. *How College Affects Students: Findings and Insights from Twenty Years of Research.* San Francisco: Jossey-Bass, 1991.

Schuh, J. H. (ed.). *Financial Management for Student Affairs Administrators.* Washington, D.C.: American College Personnel Association, 1990.

University of Arizona. *Advisory Budget Priorities Planning Task Force.* Tucson, Ariz.: Unpublished report, 1991.

Wildavsky, A. *The Politics of the Budgetary Process.* (3rd ed.) Boston: Little, Brown, 1988.

Zemsky, R., and Massy, W. E. "Cost Containment: Committing to a New Economic Reality." *Change,* 1990, *22* (6), 16–22.

18

∽

Translating Theory
into Practice

M. Lee Upcraft

We have made remarkable progress in the last quarter-century in developing a theoretical grounding for the practice of student affairs. We have borrowed and adapted our theories from a variety of academic disciplines, including anthropology, psychology, sociology, management and organizational development, human development, philosophy, ethics, and health education. In some cases, we have developed our own. This progress is even more remarkable when we consider that the first comprehensive scholarly attempt to theorize about college students, *The American College,* was published only thirty years ago (Sanford, 1962). Prior to that time, with the exception of theory borrowed from psychology and sociology, we devoted very little time and attention to the theoretical grounding of student affairs practice.

In spite of this substantial progress, there is a suspicion, usually felt by the researchers in our field, that our theories are not used enough by practitioners as they develop policy, make decisions, solve problems, deliver services and programs, manage budgets, and in general do their jobs. This suspicion was recently confirmed by an administrative colleague of mine; when I asked if he had read a recent and very influential book on student affairs, he replied, "I don't have time to read anything. How about an hour when you tell me all about it?"

In defense of my beleaguered colleague, he is not a mindless practitioner with no interest in the theoretical. But he was telling the truth about his day-to-day existence. Most of us in student affairs do not have the time to read, analyze, and contemplate if we want to get our jobs done. And when we do read, we want to cut out the extraneous. We want the answers, not the questions, and we need them now. This attitude is understandably an affront to researchers and theoreticians in student affairs, who believe that their very fine scholarly efforts may contribute to knowledge but not to practice.

This chapter will review the theories that I believe are most important and relevant to student affairs. These will not be discussed in any detail, and readers who wish to know more about them should consult the citations contained in the bibliography at the end of this chapter. Next, I will analyze the problems in translating theory to practice and present a model originally developed by Wells and Knefelkamp; this describes a process by which practitioners can implement programs based on student development theories. The chapter concludes by offering some advice to both theoreticians and practitioners on how we might better translate theory to practice.

Early Theoretical Foundations of Student Affairs

For about the first three hundred years of American higher education, relationships with students were essentially guided by the principle of in loco parentis. Early colonial colleges believed that they had a responsibility to act on behalf of parents for the good of their students in a way that reflected good Christian moral values. This theory was translated into practice through a highly controlled and contained environment governed by extensive rules, strictly enforced by the president and the faculty. They were in the business of developing Christian moral character, and theology was their guide.

About the turn of the twentieth century, more secular influences were being felt, with the emergence of psychology and sociology as academic disciplines. For example, as the field of psychology developed, theorists such as B. F. Skinner (1938, 1953), Erik Erikson (1950, 1968), Jean Piaget (1964), and especially Carl Rogers (1951, 1961) influenced the student affairs profession. The vocational guidance movement, initiated by Frank Parsons (1909), also contributed to the theoretical underpinnings of our profession, with later help from Donald Super (1957), John Holland (1966), and others.

Another major influence on theory was the publication in 1937 by the American Council on Education of *Student Personnel Point of View*. Although this publication did not contain any theory per se, it did offer some basic assumptions about how students grow and develop in the collegiate environment. Later, writers such as Gilbert Wrenn (1951), Esther Lloyd-Jones and M. R. Smith (1954), Kate Hevner Mueller (1961), and E. G. Williamson (1961) began to focus on college students and higher education as a legitimate field of study.

Theories About College Students and Campus Environments

In the early 1960s, social scientists began to theorize more specifically about college students for the first time. Nevitt Sanford's *American College* (1962) was a landmark publication because it contained many postulates about students (integration-differentiation, support-challenge) that are still relevant today. Chickering (1969) expanded Sanford's (1962) and Erikson's (1950) concepts to include what he called seven vectors of development, which he considered vital to student growth and development in the collegiate setting. Other social scientists began to apply their ideas to college students, including Roy Heath (1964), Clark and Trow (1966), Douglas Heath (1968), Florence Brawer (1973), and Jane Loevinger (1976).

About the same time, theories of reasoning and cognitive development were emerging. William Perry (1970) devised a theory of intellectual and ethical development in which persons moved from a simplistic, categorical view of the world to a more relativistic, committed view. Similarly, Lawrence Kohlberg (1971) formulated a cognitive stage theory of the development of moral judgment. Later on, the cognitive development of students was explored more fully by David Kolb (1984).

Also in the 1960s and 1970s, several sociologists argued that to have a complete understanding of college students, one had to look also at the environments in which they lived. Newcomb and Wilson (1966) were among the first to introduce the idea of the peer group's powerful influence on students. In the mid 1970s, the study of student environments expanded beyond the peer group to a more generalized concept of campus ecology, including the work of Barker (1968), Stern (1970), and Pervin (1968). In 1973, the Western Interstate Commission for Higher Education offered some basic assumptions about the ecological perspective, which defined the environmental conditions under which students could best grow and develop. The work of Banning (1978), Banning and McKinley (1980), and Schroeder (1982) was also helpful in understanding campus environments. A more specific theory about residential environments was offered by Moos (1979), in which he assessed three ways of looking at the climate of a residence hall using relationships, personal growth, and system maintenance.

Theories of Gender and Diversity

In the 1980s, we recognized that the theories of the last two decades failed to explain fully the development of women; racial and ethnic groups; older students; international students; gay, lesbian, and bisexual students; student athletes; honors students; and commuters, to name a few. Theories developed specifically for these students proliferated in the 1980s and drew on the theoretical and methodological resources of other fields of study, such as medicine, women's studies, various racial and ethnic studies, theology, wellness, and anthropology.

Recently, a great deal of theory has evolved from attempts to explain the unique development of persons of color. Wright (1987) argues that theories specific to students from underrepresented racial and ethnic groups are based on the assumption that being raised in a minority culture in the middle of a majority society creates different outcomes for the youth of that culture. Several theories and models are emerging for underrepresented racial and ethnic groups, including African Americans (Fleming, 1984; Cross, 1978; Asante, 1988), Hispanics (Martinez, 1988; Grossman, 1984), Asian Americans (Chew and Ogi, 1987; Sue and Sue, 1971, 1985; Atkinson, Morten, and Sue, 1983), and American Indians (LaCounte, 1987; Scott, 1986).

Similarly, the inadequacy of traditional approaches to explaining the development of women has led to important newer theories, including those of Gilligan (1982); Gilligan, Ward, and Taylor (1988); Belenky, Clinchy, Goldberger, and Tarule (1986); and O'Neil and Carroll (1988). Traditional theories have also been criticized for assuming that all students are young and for neglecting adult student development. Important works in this area include the writings of Cross (1981), Schlossberg, Lynch, and Chickering (1989); and Knowles (1980). Theories about gay, lesbian, and bisexual students are also emerging—for example, Cass (1979, 1984) and Henderson (1984). Minority-majority relations have also been explored in Helms (1990), Farley (1988), and Herek (1985).

More Recent Theories Relating to
the Development of All Students

Also during the 1980s, newer theories emerged that attempted to explain the development of all students. For example, Chickering made some adjustments to his original seven vectors, making them more responsive to today's national and international conditions and to the changing demographics of students (Thomas and Chickering, 1984). By far the most influential student development concept of the 1980s was student *involvement*. Astin (1985) proposed five basic postulates about that involvement and its relationship to personal and academic success. Schlossberg, Lynch, and Chickering (1989) formulated a theory of mattering and marginality that they believed helped to explain student success.

First-year student development is explored by Tinto (1987), who conceptualizes freshman development as occurring in three distinct stages: separation, transition, and incorporation. Upcraft, Gardner, and Associates (1989) identify a model that includes six developmental dimensions of the first-year student's experience. Theories about the spiritual development of students, often neglected by development theorists, have been offered by Fowler (1981 and 1987), Westerhoff (1976), and Parks (1986). A wellness model conceived by Dunn (1961) has been extended to higher education by Hettler (1980), who defined six aspects of wellness.

More Recent Counseling and Career Development Theories

More recent theories of psychological counseling and psychotherapy are in many instances extensions or reinterpretations of earlier theorists. Most counseling practitioners use an eclectic approach, drawing from behavioral, psychoanalytic, psychoeducational, person-centered or humanistic, neuropsychological, moral developmental, cognitive behavioral, and ecological theories (D'Amato and Rothlisberg, 1992).

For career development practitioners, theory development has centered around personality approaches to careers (Roe, 1956; Bordin, Nachmann, and Segal, 1963), trait-oriented approaches to career development (Holland, 1985; Loftquist and Davis, 1969; Krumboltz, 1976), and developmental theories (Super, 1957; Ginzberg, Ginzberg, Axelrad, and Herma, 1951). Osipow (1983) not only reviews these theoretical approaches but also includes career development concepts in which gender, race, ethnicity, and other demographic factors are taken into account.

Organizational Theories

But the theoretical underpinnings of our profession extend beyond student development, campus culture, psychological counseling, and career development. Many of us are student affairs administrators, and theories underlying our organizational, leadership, and management responsibilities are also important. Up until the middle of the twentieth century, our organizations were essentially based on a hierarchical, authoritarian, bureaucratic chain of command model, invented originally by the Roman Catholic Church but first described by sociologist Max Weber (1947). More recently, organizational theories have become more humanistic and participative and less bureaucratic and hierarchial, including McGregor's theory X and theory Y (1960), Blake and Mouton's (1964) managerial grid, Hersey and Blanchard's (1977) situational leadership, Davis and Lawrence's (1977) matrix management, and Keller's (1983) strategic planning. By far the "hottest" organizational theory today is total quality management, based upon Japanese models of organization but originally proposed by American W. Edwards Deming (1982).

The Problem of Translating Theory into Practice

Seventy-five references have been cited that in one way or another contribute to the theoretical basis for the student affairs profession, and there are hundreds more. The most optimistic guess is that most student affairs professionals have a passing acquaintance with many of these theorists, and a few have actually read them. A more cynical assessment is that many would recognize only a few, and too few would have firsthand knowledge of them.

As stated earlier, the fundamental problem is that in spite of very good scholarly efforts by our academicians, theory is rarely known; and even then, it is seldom integrated into practice. As my previously quoted colleague also said to me, "With so much to read, how do you sift the good out from the goofy?" His solution, you may remember, was for me to spend an hour with him and tell him all about a recent influential publication. Later in this chapter, I will offer some practical suggestions to administrators for integrating theory into practice and for sifting the good out from the goofy.

Theory into Practice Issues

The gap between theory and practice does not arise entirely from the fact that busy practitioners have no time for reading. Researchers, academicians, and theoreticians are frequently guilty of writing in ways that though contributing to the scholarly literature, do little to help the practitioner. It appears to some that real scholarship disdains the practical and that it is in part defined by how specialized, esoteric, complex, and irrelevant to practice it is. Scholars developing theory are often so isolated from campus realities that their ideas have little to do with campus problems and issues.

The current means by which we transmit theory to practitioners are by using books on theory, articles in professional journals, and presentations at national or regional workshops. Other efforts include the Jossey-Bass New Directions for Student Services quarterly sourcebooks, whose basic purpose is to deliver timely and relevant information on issues of importance to practitioners, based on emerging theory, research, and literature. But in spite of these efforts, the gap continues to exist. So what is to be done?

The Wells and Knefelkamp Model

Elizabeth Wells and Lee Knefelkamp (1982) were among the first researchers to tackle this issue by suggesting a "practice to theory to practice" model. They developed an eleven-step process in which suggested educational goals are examined in the light of appropriate theory *before* interventions are designed and implemented.

Step 1: Identify pragmatic concerns. Define student, faculty, and staff concerns about something that is a problem or issue or that needs to be enhanced or initiated.

Step 2: Determine educational goals and outcomes. Specify the educational goals and outcomes that would be desirable for students to acquire, including information, concepts, and intellectual and auxiliary skills.

Step 3: Examine which theories may be helpful. Evaluate clusters of theories and specific ones to determine those related to goals and outcomes. From each theory or cluster chosen, identify those concepts that illuminate their developmental content and process, including psycho-social, cognitive development, maturity, and typology models.

Step 4: Analyze student characteristics from the perspective of each theoretical Cluster. Select those theories that are most helpful in understanding the students involved. Use each of the clusters selected as a filter for viewing students, and assess their characteristics both informally and formally.

Step 5: Analyze environmental characteristics from the perspective of each theoretical cluster. Choose those characteristics that are most useful in understanding the students involved. Use each of the characteristics selected to assess environmental characteristics both informally and formally.

Step 6: Analyze the source of developmental challenge and support in the context of both student and environmental characteristics. Translate descriptive characteristics into prescriptive educational designs. Review the theoretical descriptions of both student and environmental characteristics. Identify specific sources of supports and challenges, and ensure a proper balance between the two.

Step 7: Reanalyze educational goals and outcomes. Determine whether students are ready for the learning goals intended. Determine if these objectives should be modified as a result of applying the first six steps. Design the learning process in such a way as to facilitate learning.

Step 8: Design the learning process using methods that will facilitate mastery of educational goals. Develop sequence and structure for teaching, content, process, and evaluation consistent with learning goals.

Step 9: Implement the educational experience.

Step 10: Evaluate the educational experience. Assess learning outcomes, student satisfaction, and educator satisfaction. Develop suggestions for the future.

Step 11: Redesign the educational experience if necessary.

Wells and Knefelkamp provide an excellent model for integrating developmental theory with practice, but it is not without some problems. First, their model was intended to translate *developmental* theory to practice. Although it is possible that other theories forming the basis of the student affairs profession, such as counseling or organizational theory, could be applied to the model, to my knowledge this work has never been done.

But more important, this model neglects the essential step of reconsidering theory in the light of practice. After several interventions based on a particular approach, it may become obvious that the theory needs to be revised in the light of practice, not the other way around. Perhaps a "practice to theory to practice to theory" model is more appropriate, where the final step is to revise or confirm a theory on the basis of its practical application. What is needed, then, is a process by which theoreticians can develop and revise their ideas on the basis of practice and by which practitioners can integrate theory into their practice.

Advice to Researchers and Theoreticians

In my opinion, researchers and theoreticians have a responsibility to communicate theory to practitioners, to help practitioners translate theory to practice, and to revise theory based on its application. What is my advice to the researchers and theoreticians?

Develop at least part of your research agenda on the basis of the concerns and needs of practitioners. It is always tempting to pursue one's own esoteric interests or, more importantly, to follow a research agenda that will result in tenure and promotion. But if theory is to have an impact, it must be relevant to the issues faced on a day-to-day basis by the practitioner.

Accept the responsibility for not only developing theory but translating it to practice as well. There are many instances of available theories that have been translated into practice. For example, much work has been done applying Lawrence Kohlberg's (1971) theory of moral and intellectual development to college students. Arthur Chickering's work has been put into operation in part through the creation and use of the Student Development Task and Lifestyle Inventory by Winston, Miller, and Prince (1987). Programs and services based on William Hettler's (1980) wellness model have been developed and marketed. Many other examples exist, so it can be done.

Collaborate with practitioners in the development of theory. Such collaboration improves both theory and practice. But if theory and practice are to be brought closer, theoreticians must be more in tune with feedback from practitioners.

Conduct research that tests the efficacy of theory. The most skeptical practitioner, when confronted with a theory, will ask, "Does it work?" It is the responsibility of the theoretician to conduct research that confirms, revises, or refutes theory. For example, researchers are attempting to determine if Lawrence Kohlberg's theory of moral development applies equally to men and women (Walker, 1984; Gibbs, Arnold, and Burkhart, 1984), with mixed results.

Theoreticians must observe what is really going on within student affairs practice today. They must resist the temptation to think of practitioners as bureaucrats who never think about or apply ideas. Theoreticians must examine all sources of data, including the characteristics of students and the interventions that have been tried and worked. In other words, theoretical thinking must be translated into observation and self-test theory into practice.

Advice to Practitioners

For their part, practitioners have the responsibility to know and use the scholarly work of researchers and theoreticians. At a minimum, practitioners should possess knowledge of and should use theory in developing policy, making decisions, managing budgets, creating programs, offering services, and advocating for students. What is my advice to practitioners?

Take the time to stay current with the theory that guides our profession, even if that time is away from the job. As an administrator with almost thirty years' experience in student affairs, I can understand the pressures that practitioners feel when confronted with the choice between reading and digesting theory on the one hand and providing direct service to students and responding to bureaucratic demands on the other. At many institutions, we are paid to deliver service, and professional development, particularly reading and studying, is expected to be done on our own time. But even without an organizational climate that is supportive of reading and studying, it is incumbent on professionals to use their own time in pursuit of theory if they are to be truly effective.

Take the time to keep researchers and theoreticians informed about the issues confronted on a day-to-day basis. One of the best ways for practitioners to do this is to use theory in their work, so they know what to say to theoreticians about the efficacy of their proposals. Then a dialogue with them can be created through direct contact, publications, or professional conferences.

Collaborate with researchers and theoreticians in the development of theory. One of my most exciting and rewarding experiences in the last two years was collaborating with a colleague on the development of an approach to administrative ethics. I was confronted with several ethical issues that I was having trouble resolving. My colleague, an ethicist by training, was interested in developing a model in this area. He lacked the administrative experience; I lacked the knowledge of ethics. After several long discussions (and a few arguments), we devised a model that we presented at a national conference, revised, and later published (Upcraft and Poole, 1991).

Direct resources toward the promotion of professional development in general and theory in particular. Convincing the people who control the purse strings in our profession to devote resources to the translation of theory to practice is difficult, but not impossible. Administrators can be convinced if a demonstrable connection between theory to practice translation and quality of services or programs can be established.

Practitioners should not dismiss theory as irrelevant or impractical because it does not fit into some idea of reality or because of an aversion to any theoretician who has never practiced. A conscious effort must be made to develop theory-based programs and to assess them in ways that confirm, revise, or refute the theory.

Summary

When I entered this profession in the early sixties, most of the theory that I studied and applied was drawn from psychology. Most student affairs professionals trained in this era were disciples of Carl Rogers or other psychological theorists—not so much because they had so much to say to us, but because they were among the very few theorists who were relevant to what we did. I remember the excitement that we felt over the publication of Sanford's *American College* because it was the first comprehensive text focusing on theory and research about college students. A whole new world opened up to us, and to our credit theories that are the foundation of our profession were developed and are still being formulated today.

But the separate traditions of the theoretician and the practitioner die hard, and there is still a significant time lapse between the development of theory and its integration into practice. It is ironic that the practitioners who pride themselves on being up-to-date on what is happening on today's campuses are the same ones who lag significantly behind in their knowledge and application of theory. It is also ironic that the theoreticians who push themselves to produce timely and relevant scholarly works are the same ones who sometimes seem hopelessly out of touch with the current generation of students.

What is the solution to this problem? To start with, the dialogue between those who develop theory and those who practice should be expanded. Better yet, each of them should be more directly involved in the work of the other. Perhaps the real goal should be the development of more scholar-practitioners and practitioner-scholars whose identities are rooted in both theory and practice. Individuals in our field who earn their living by teaching and conducting research should enter or reenter the world of the practitioner by regularly providing direct service to students or presenting programs. Concurrently, those in our field who earn their living by providing services and programs to students should be encouraged to hold faculty rank, teach graduate or undergraduate courses, and conduct research. Perhaps only then will theory and practice become truly integrated.

References

American Council on Education. *The Student Personnel Point of View.* Washington, D.C.: American Council on Education, 1937.

Asante, M. K. *Afrocentricity.* Trenton, N.J.: Africa World Press, 1988.

Astin, A. W. *Achieving Educational Excellence: A Critical Assessment of Priorities and Practices in Higher Education.* San Francisco: Jossey-Bass, 1985.

Atkinson, D. R., Morten, G., and Sue, D. W. *Counseling American Minorities: A Cross Cultural Perspective.* (2nd ed.) Dubuque, Iowa: Brown, 1983.

Banning, J. (ed.). *Campus Ecology: A Perspective for Student Affairs.* Portland, Oreg.: National Association of Student Personnel Administrators, 1978.

Banning, J. H., and McKinley, D. L. "Conceptions of the Campus Environment." In W. Morrill, J. Hurst, and E. Oetting (eds.), *Dimensions of Interventions for Student Development.* New York: Wiley, 1980.

Barker, R. G. *Ecological Psychology: Concepts and Methods for Studying the Environment.* Stanford, Calif.: Stanford University Press, 1968.

Belenky, M. F., Clinchy, B. M., Goldberger, N. R., and Tarule, J. M. *Women's Ways of Knowing: The Development of Self, Voice, and Mind.* New York: Basic Books, 1986.

Blake, R. R., and Mouton, J. S. *The Managerial Grid.* Houston, Tex.: Gulf, 1964.

Bordin, E. S., Nachmann, B., and Segal, S. J. "An Articulated Framework for Vocational Development." *Journal of Counseling Psychology,* 1963, *10,* 107–116.

Brawer, F. *New Perspectives on Personality Development in College Students.* San Francisco: Jossey-Bass, 1973.

Cass, V. C. "Homosexual Identity Formation: A Theoretical Model." *Journal of Homosexuality,* 1979, *4,* 219–235.

Cass, V. C. "Homosexual Identity Formation: Testing a Theoretical Model." *Journal of Sex Research*, 1984, *20*, 143–167.

Chew, C. A., and Ogi, A. Y. "Asian American College Student Perspectives." In D. Wright (ed.), *Responding to the Needs of Today's Minority Students*. New Directions for Student Services, no. 38. San Francisco: Jossey-Bass, 1987.

Chickering, A. W. *Education and Identity*. San Francisco: Jossey-Bass, 1969.

Clark, B. R., and Trow, M. "The Organizational Context." In T. M. Newcomb and E. K. Wilson (eds.), *College Peer Groups: Problems and Prospects for Research*. Hawthorne, N.Y.: Aldine, 1966.

Cross, K. P. *Adults as Learners: Increasing Participation and Facilitating Learning*. San Francisco: Jossey-Bass, 1981.

Cross, W. E., Jr. "The Thomas and Cross Models of Psychological Negrescence: A Review." *Journal of Black Psychology*, 1978, *5*, 13–31.

D'Amato, R. K., and Rothlisberg, B. A. (eds.). *Psychological Perspectives on Intervention*. White Plains, N.Y.: Longman, 1992.

Davis, S., and Lawrence, P. *Matrix*. Reading, Mass.: Addison-Wesley, 1977.

Deming, W. E. *Out of the Crisis*. Cambridge, Mass.: Productivity Press, 1982.

Dunn, H. A. *High-Level Wellness*. Arlington, Va.: Betty, 1961.

Erikson, E. *Childhood and Society*. New York: Norton, 1950.

Erikson, E. *Identity: Youth and Crisis*. New York: Norton, 1968.

Farley, J. E. *Majority-Minority Relations* (2nd ed.) Englewood Cliffs, N.J.: Prentice-Hall, 1988.

Fleming, J. *Blacks in College: A Comparative Study of Students' Success in Black and in White Institutions*. San Francisco: Jossey-Bass, 1984.

Fowler, J. W. *Stages in Faith: The Psychology of Human Development and the Quest for Meaning*. New York: HarperCollins, 1981.

Fowler, J. W. *Faith Development and Pastoral Care*. Philadelphia: Fortress Press, 1987.

Gibbs, J. C., Arnold, K. D., and Burkhart, J. E. "Sex Differences in the Expression of Moral Judgment." *Child Development*, 1984, *55*, 1,040–1,043.

Gilligan, C. *In a Different Voice: Psychological Theory and Women's Development*. Cambridge, Mass.: Harvard University Press, 1982.

Gilligan, C., Ward, J. V., and Taylor, J. M. (eds.). *Mapping the Moral Domain*. Cambridge, Mass.: Harvard University Press, 1988.

Ginzberg, E., Ginzberg, S. W., Axelrad, S., and Herma, J. L. *Occupational Choice: An Approach to General Theory*. New York: Columbia University Press, 1951.

Grossman, H. *Educating Hispanic Students*. Springfield, Ill.: Thomas, 1984.

Heath, D. *Growing Up in College*. San Francisco: Jossey-Bass, 1968.

Heath, R. *The Reasonable Adventurer*. Pittsburgh, Penn.: University of Pittsburgh Press, 1964.

Helms, J. E. (ed.). *Black and White Racial Identity: Theory, Research, and Practice*. New York: Glenwood Press, 1990.

Henderson, A. F. "Homosexuality During the College Years: Development Differences Between Men and Women." *Journal of American College Health,* 1984, *32,* 216–219.

Herek, G. M. "Beyond Homophobia: A Social Psychological Perspective on Attitudes Toward Lesbians and Gay Men." In J. P. De Cecco (ed.), *Bashers, Baiters, and Bigots: Homophobia in American Society.* New York: Harrington Park, 1985.

Hersey, P., and Blanchard, K. *Management of Organizational Behavior: Utilizing Human Resources.* Englewood Cliffs, N.J.: Prentice-Hall, 1977.

Hettler, W. "Wellness Promotion on a University Campus." *Family and Community Health Promotion and Maintenance,* May 1980, *3* (1), 77–95.

Holland, J. L. *The Psychology of Vocational Choice.* Waltham, Mass.: Blaisdell, 1966.

Holland, J. L. *Making Vocational Choices: A Theory of Vocational Personalities and Work Environments.* Englewood Cliffs, N.J.: Prentice-Hall, 1985.

Keller, G. *Academic Strategy: The Management Revolution in American Higher Education.* Baltimore, Md.: Johns Hopkins University Press, 1983.

Knowles, M. S. *The Modern Practice of Adult Education: From Pedagogy and Andragogy.* (2nd ed.) New York: Cambridge Books, 1980.

Kohlberg, L. "Stages of Moral Development." In C. M. Beck, B. S. Crittenden, and E. V. Sullivan (eds.), *Moral Education.* Toronto, Canada: University of Toronto Press, 1971.

Kolb, D. *Experiential Learning: Experience as a Source of Learning and Development.* Englewood Cliffs, N.J.: Prentice-Hall, 1984.

Krumboltz, J. D. "A Social Learning Theory of Career Selection." *Counseling Psychologist,* 1976, *6,* 71–81.

LaCounte, D. W. "American Indian Students in College." In D. Wright (ed.), *Responding to the Needs of Today's Minority Students.* New Directions for Student Services, no. 38. San Francisco: Jossey-Bass, 1987.

Lloyd-Jones, E. L., and Smith, M. R. *Student Personnel Work as Deeper Teaching.* New York: HarperCollins, 1954.

Loevinger, J. *Ego Development: Conceptions and Theories.* San Francisco: Jossey-Bass, 1976.

Loftquist, L. H., and Davis, R. V. *Adjustment to Work.* Englewood Cliffs, N.J.: Prentice-Hall, 1969.

McGregor, D. *The Human Side of Enterprise.* New York: McGraw-Hill, 1960.

Martinez, C. "Mexican Americans." In L. Comas-Diaz and E.E.H. Griffith (eds.), *Cross Cultural Mental Health.* New York: Wiley, 1988.

Moos, R. H. *Evaluating Educational Environments: Procedures, Measures, Findings, and Policy Implications.* San Francisco: Jossey-Bass, 1979.

Mueller, K. H. *Student Personnel Work in Higher Education.* Boston: Houghton Mifflin, 1961.

Newcomb, T. M., and Wilson, E. K. (eds.). *College Peer Groups: Problems and Prospects for Research.* Hawthorne, N.Y.: Aldine, 1966.

O'Neil, J. M., and Carroll, M. R. "A Gender Role Workshop Focused on

Sexism, Gender Role Conflict, and the Gender Role Journey." *Journal of Counseling and Development,* 1988, *67,* 193–197.

Osipow, S. H. *Theories of Career Development.* Englewood Cliffs, N.J.: Prentice-Hall, 1983.

Parks, S. *The Critical Years: Young Adult Search for Faith to Live By.* San Francisco: HarperCollins, 1986.

Parsons, F. *Choosing a Vocation.* Boston: Houghton Mifflin, 1909.

Perry, W. G. *Forms of Intellectual and Ethical Development.* Troy, Mo.: Holt, Rinehart & Winston, 1970.

Pervin, L. A. "Performance and Satisfaction as a Function of Individual-Environment Fit." *Psychological Bulletin,* 1968, *69,* 56–68.

Piaget, J. *Judgment and Reasoning in the Child.* Patterson, N.J.: Littlefield Adams, 1964.

Roe, A. *The Psychology of Occupations.* New York: Wiley, 1956.

Rogers, C. *Client-Centered Therapy: Its Current Practice, Implications, and Theory.* Boston: Houghton Mifflin, 1951.

Rogers, C. *On Becoming a Person.* Boston: Houghton Mifflin, 1961.

Sanford, N. (ed.). *The American College.* New York: Wiley, 1962.

Schlossberg, N. K., Lynch, A. Q., and Chickering, A. W. *Improving Higher Education Environments for Adults: Responsive Programs and Services from Entry to Departure.* San Francisco: Jossey-Bass, 1989.

Schroeder, C. C. "Human Development and the Campus Environment." *Council of Independent Colleges,* May 1982, pp. 5–10.

Scott, W. J. "Attachment to Indian Culture and the 'Difficult Situation': A Study of American Indian College Students." *Youth and Society,* 1986, *17* (4), 381–395.

Skinner, B. F. *Behavior of Organisms.* New York: Appleton-Century-Crofts, 1938.

Skinner, B. F. *Science and Human Behavior.* New York: Macmillan, 1953.

Stern, G. G. *People in Context.* New York: Wiley, 1970.

Sue, W. S., and Sue, D. W. "Chinese-American Personality and Mental Health." *Amerasia Journal,* 1971, *1,* 36–39.

Sue, W. S., and Sue, D. W. "Asian-Americans and Pacific Islanders." In P. L. Pedersen (ed.), *Handbook of Cross Cultural Counseling and Therapy.* Westport, Conn.: Greenwood Press, 1985.

Super, D. E. *The Psychology of Careers.* New York: HarperCollins, 1957.

Thomas, R., and Chickering, A. W. "Education and Identity Revisited." *Journal of College Student Personnel,* 1984, *25,* 392–399.

Tinto, V. *Leaving College: Rethinking the Causes and Cures of Student Attrition.* Chicago: University of Chicago Press, 1987.

Upcraft, M. L., Gardner, J. N., and Associates. *The Freshman Year Experience: Helping Students Survive and Succeed in College.* San Francisco: Jossey-Bass, 1989.

Upcraft, M. L., and Poole, T. G. "Ethical Issues and Administrative Politics." In P. L. Moore (ed.), *Managing the Political Dimension of Student Affairs.* New Directions for Student Services, no. 55. San Francisco: Jossey-Bass, 1991.

Walker, L. J. "Sex Differences in the Development of Moral Reasoning: A Critical Review." *Child Development,* 1984, *55,* 677–691.

Weber, M. *The Theory of Economic and Social Organization.* New York: Oxford University Press, 1947.

Wells, E. A., and Knefelkamp, L. L. "A Process Model of Practice to Theory to Practice." Unpublished manuscript, 1982.

Westerhoff, J. *Will Our Children Have Faith?* New York: Seabury Press, 1976.

Western Interstate Commission for Higher Education. *The Ecosystem Model: Designing Campus Environments.* Boulder, Colo.: Western Interstate Commission for Higher Education, 1973.

Williamson, E. G. *Student Personnel Services in Colleges and Universities.* New York: McGraw-Hill, 1961.

Winston, R. B., Jr., Miller, T. K., and Prince, J. S. *Student Development Task and Lifestyle Inventory.* Athens, Ga.: Student Development Associates, 1987.

Wrenn, G. *Student Personnel Work in Colleges and Universities.* New York: Ronald Press, 1951.

Wright, D. (ed.) *Responding to the Needs of Today's Minority Students.* New Directions for Student Services, no. 38. San Francisco: Jossey-Bass, 1987.

19

∽

Understanding
Legal Constraints
on Practice

Donald D. Gehring

Kaplin (1985) notes that the law "has spoken forcefully and meaningfully to the higher education community and will continue to do so" (p. ix). Since the *Dixon* v. *Alabama State Board of Education* (1961) case, colleges and universities have witnessed a steady stream of state and federal laws and judicial opinions having implications for everything from changing light bulbs to awarding degrees. Student affairs practitioners, often at the center of the interaction between students and the institution, can ill afford not to listen to what the law has to say. Though administrators need not be lawyers, their failure to understand and stay abreast of legal implications in developing and administering programs, policies, and practices can have devastating consequences for themselves, the institution, and the students.

Yet a morass of laws, interpretations, rules, rights, and regulations exists. How does one approach bringing order out of this seeming chaos? Every discipline has a classification system, and the law is no exception. By examining the legal relationships that students have with institutions of higher education and asking what their implications are for practice, student affairs administrators can begin to understand the legal implications of their work. The purpose of the chapter is thus to familiarize the reader with these relationships. Case law interpreting those relationships is also provided. Although this chapter focuses on students, employees have similar relationships to the institution.

Students, as residents of the United States, have certain guarantees set forth in the first amendments of the federal Constitution (the Bill of Rights) and other amendments. They are also residents of a particular state and thereby enjoy certain rights provided for in state constitutions. It is necessary to understand the rights that students have under both the federal and state constitutions and to apply those to student affairs programs, policies, and practices. Careful analysis must be made, for constitutional protections are not necessarily guaranteed in private institutions.

Another legal relationship stems from the rights and responsibilities defined in specific state and federal laws pertaining to students. These laws are often very general in nature, and therefore rules and regulations are written to enforce the law. Such rules and regulations carry the full force of the law.

Students also contract for goods and services with their college or university. These contracts are both explicit and implicit and define yet another relationship with the college or university. Finally, students, and all others, have a right to be free from intrusion upon their person, their property, and their reputation. In almost all states, certain minimum rights and duties are defined by judicial precedent developed from English common law and thereby define our relationships with others. A violation of the minimum standards constitutes a tort. Thus, the four primary relationships between students and their institutions can be classified as (1) constitutional, (2) statutory, (3) contractual, and (4) torts.

The Judicial System

The function of the judicial system is to settle controversies, decide the constitutionality of laws, and interpret them. Thus, the courts have a significant influence on student and institutional relationships. Both state and federal courts exist. State courts generally decide disputes between state residents, decide on the constitutionality of state laws, or interpret them. They are limited in their jurisdiction to the laws of that state and its geographic area. Federal courts, in terms of this discussion, decide questions pertaining to federal laws and settle disputes between citizens of different states. These courts also have jurisdiction over a specific geographic area. The decision of a court of geographic jurisdiction is only binding on that particular area. A decision by a California court, therefore, does not bind administrators in New Jersey. However, the reasoning of the California court may be persuasive and adopted by New Jersey courts (see, for example, *Tarasoff* v. *Regents of the University of California,* 1976). Similarly, a decision by the U.S. Fifth Circuit Court of Appeals is not binding on and may even be the opposite of a similar case decided by the Second Circuit Court of Appeals. Only cases decided by the U.S. Supreme Court are binding on everyone.

Finally, administrators must understand that the laws of the various states, as well as the interpretation of their courts, may differ with respect to the same legal relationship. To illustrate, in a tort situation in Pennsylvania, a student organization may be held liable in the case of someone injured by an intoxicated guest who was served alcoholic beverages at one of the organization's parties. The same situation in Virginia may not attach any liability to the organization.

Torts

The word *tort* comes from the Latin word *torquere,* meaning to twist. Thus, a tort would constitute a "twisted relationship." Torts present the greatest potential for financial damages; for that reason, administrators should be most familiar with the minimum standards established for the student-institutional relationship. Specifically, a tort is a civil wrong, other than a breach of a contract, for which the courts will provide a remedy. The remedy is generally in the form of money damages of which there are two types: compensatory and punitive. Compensatory damages seek to make injured persons "whole" again, or as well as possible to put them back into the position that they were in before the injury was suffered. It is therefore easy to understand why damages are sometimes assessed at such high levels. Punitive damages, by contrast, are assessed where the injury is caused by willful acts without regard for another's person, property, or reputation and serve as punishment.

Negligence

The tort of negligence involves the breach of a duty owed. To be found liable for negligence, four elements must exist. First, a duty must be present. Second, the duty must have been breached. Third, an injury must occur as a result of the breach of duty. Fourth, the breach of duty must be the proximate cause of the injury.

If there is no duty, there can be no breach and thus no negligence. It is therefore imperative to understand what duties exist. Prosser (1971) cautions, "'Duty' is not sacrosanct in itself, but only an expression of the sum total of those considerations of policy which lead the law to say that the particular plaintiff is entitled to protection" (p. 326).

The courts have recognized three general duties: (1) to provide proper supervision, (2) to furnish proper instruction, and (3) to maintain equipment in a reasonable state of repair. College students are generally legal adults and therefore require less supervision (*Mintz* v. *State,* 1975); however, as those under eighteen years are considered "children of tender years" by the courts, the concept of in loco parentis may still be applicable. In one case, a high school student attended a special summer program party at Montana State University (MSU) where alcoholic beverages were served. The

Montana Supreme Court noted, "When MSU undertook to have Kimberly live on its campus and supervise her during the MAP program, it assumed a custodial role similar to that imposed on a high school because Kimberly is a juvenile" (*Graham* v. *Montana State University*, 1988, at 304). Once a university permits the enrollment of a student, reasonable care in supervision must occur. With minors, an entirely separate and more restrictive set of regulations may be imposed to meet the obligation of closer supervision (*Stone* v. *Cornell University*, 1987).

In several jurisdictions, it has been held that unless a "special relationship" exists, there is no custodial duty or duty to control the conduct of students (*Bradshaw* v. *Rawlings*, 1979; *University of Denver* v. *Whitlock*, 1987; *Smith* v. *Day*, 1987). However, in Delaware the supreme court has recognized a unique relationship between students and their institutions in which the university does exercise some control over the lives of students and may be held liable for failing to exercise supervision over fraternity hazing activities (*Furek* v. *University of Delaware*, 1991).

Student affairs practitioners engage in a variety of instructional activities and in doing so are held to a standard of providing proper instruction. They must provide careful information on the operation of equipment such as stage equipment in productions (*Potter* v. *North Carolina School of the Arts*, 1978) or the correct adjustment of ski bindings on spring-break outings (*Meese* v. *Brigham Young University*, 1981), for example.

The institution is also required to make inspections of the premises for defects and then to make the necessary repairs. An Ohio court of appeals held that a university had not met a standard of reasonable care, regardless of the fact that it had made periodic inspections of every window in the residence halls (*Shetina* v. *Ohio University*, 1983). Intramural directors should also regularly inspect playing surfaces (*Drew* v. *State*, 1989; *Henig* v. *Hofstra University*, 1990).

Violence

Violence is a significant problem on campuses. Although colleges and universities are generally under no duty to protect students from the violent acts of third persons (Prosser, 1971), there are certain special relationships that involve a duty to protect. The landlord-tenant relationship is a well-defined special relationship; although "the landlord is no insurer of his tenants' safety, . . . he certainly is no bystander" (*Kline* v. *Massachusetts Avenue Apartment Corp.*, 1970, at 481). Not being a bystander includes taking preventative action to minimize predictable risks (*Miller* v. *State*, 1984). A university is also a common carrier when it operates elevators, and as such a special relationship exists with those who ride, requiring that the university protect them from unreasonable risk of harm (*Houck* v. *University of Washington*, 1991). In addition, a landowner (institution) has a duty to protect invitees (students) from unreasonable risks (*Bearman* v. *University of Notre Dame*, 1983;

Schultz v. *Gould Academy,* 1975). Where the risk is not foreseeable, however, liability will not attach (*Relyea* v. *State,* 1980; *Hall* v. *Board of Supervisors, Southern University,* 1981). As a general guide, what must be remembered is that "the risk reasonably to be perceived defines the duty to be obeyed" (*Palsgraf* v. *Long Island R.R. Co.,* 1928, at 100).

Universities do not normally take custody of students, and the courts generally agree that institutions do not exercise control over adult students. Nevertheless, in at least one jurisdiction, it has been held that when students elect to live in campus housing they yield control over their own protection (in other words, no weapons, no dogs, and prohibitions against changing or modifying door hardware). Thus, they surrender control to the institution (*Duarte* v. *State,* 1978). In this case, the university has a special relationship to resident students and thus a duty to protect them from foreseeable violence.

The courts have also defined the relationship between a therapist and a client to be a special one. If in the exercise of professional judgment the therapist determines that the client's conduct needs to be controlled and that there is a foreseeable victim, the therapist has a legal duty to warn or protect the intended victim (*Tarasoff* v. *Regents of the University of California,* 1976; *McIntosh* v. *Milano,* 1979). The circumstances will determine whether therapists need only warn the intended victim or whether they have a duty to protect. This duty is applicable to *professional* therapists, and an attempt to apply the standard to a paraprofessional who failed to report a suicidal youth was rejected in the same jurisdiction that heard *Tarasoff* (*Nally* v. *Grace Community Church of the Valley,* 1987). In at least one case, it has been held that the intended victim need not be a person but could also be a property (*Peck* v. *Counseling Service of Addison County, Inc.,* 1985). At least a dozen states now have specific legislation defining the duties of mental health professionals who deal with violent clients. As significant differences exist between the states in this area of the law, administrators should consult with counsel concerning the applicable law in their specific jurisdiction. It would also be advantageous to develop a policy of consulting with other mental health professionals when dealing with dangerous clients because the law will hold therapists to a standard of care exercised by members of the profession (Gehring, 1991).

Providing security or police services on campus creates yet another duty related to care. The law recognizes that if an institution voluntarily renders a service for the protection of another and the other person relies on that service, then reasonable care must be exercised in providing it (Prosser, 1971). This duty was the basis for finding Pine Manor College liable for the rape of one of its students (*Mullins* v. *Pine Manor College,* 1983). The Massachusetts Supreme Judicial Court stated, "Colleges generally undertake voluntarily to provide their students with protection from the criminal acts of third parties . . . . Adequate security is an indispensable part of the bundle of services which colleges, and Pine Manor, afford their students" (*Mullins* v. *Pine Manor College,* 1983, at 336).

Alcoholic Beverages

Violent acts and alcoholic beverages often seem to be connected (Gadaleto and Anderson, 1986). Administrators should be familiar with the laws of their particular state pertaining to liability associated with violation of alcoholic beverage statutes. In some states, violating alcoholic beverage laws constitutes negligence per se. Two of the more significant areas of alcohol-related liability are dramshop and social-host liability. The two are similar except that dramshop liability usually applies to licensed vendors, whereas social-host liability applies to those who are not licensed. The potential for liability arises when one sells or provides alcoholic beverages to a minor or an intoxicated person and that individual causes injury to another as a result of their intoxication. In addition to suing the person who caused the injury, the dramshop and social-host liability theories hold that the injured person may also sue the provider of the alcoholic beverages for negligence. Not all states recognize dramshop liability, and even fewer recognize social-host liability. The trend, however, seems to be favoring the imposition of liability on the provider (Gehring and Geraci, 1989).

At least two states—Louisiana and Wisconsin—have also passed laws that hold the provider of alcoholic beverages liable for injuries suffered by individuals who have been forced to consume or who have been falsely told a beverage contains no alcohol. In Illinois, the courts have held that fraternities have a duty to refrain from requiring pledges to consume excessive amounts of alcohol; in South Carolina, the court has held that fraternities have a duty not to harm pledges (*Quinn* v. *Sigma Rho Chapter Beta Theta Pi Fraternity,* 1987; *Ballou* v. *Sigma Nu General Fraternity,* 1986).

Because of differences in state laws and judicial interpretations, student affairs administrators must stay current regarding statutes involving alcoholic beverages. To do less would represent both the failure to protect themselves and their institutions against the tremendous cost of liability and the loss of essential opportunities to educate students. Added incentives are the Drug-Free Schools and Communities Act Amendments of 1989, which require that institutions annually notify *each* student of the local, state, and federal laws for unlawful possession, use, or distribution of alcohol.

Defamation

False statements about students or others that hold them up to ridicule or disgrace may constitute the tort of defamation. Both libel (written) and slander (spoken) are included in defamation. Student affairs practitioners who engage in "shop talk" about students risk slander whenever the conversation varies from the truth. In order to be defamatory, a statement must be a false statement made by one person to another about a third person that ridicules or disgraces the third person. Generally, the false statement must injure the third person's reputation; however, it is often not necessary for that person to show injury if he or she is falsely accused of having a loathsome social disease, being unchaste (*Wardlow* v. *Peck,* 1984), or having committed a crime.

Administrators acting without malice and within the scope of their responsibility enjoy a qualified privilege if the statements that they make are to another who has an interest in the matter (*Olsson* v. *Indiana University Board of Trustees,* 1991). The best advice is to speak and write the truth. If the statements being made are professional opinions, the recipient of that communication should be so informed and the basis for the opinion should be stated.

Student editors are accountable for what they publish and therefore risk liability when they print false information (*Ithaca College v. Yale Daily News Publishing Co., Inc.,* 1980). When a student editor responded to a critical letter with a rebuttal that contained sexual innuendo, the court held that the statement presented a libel question for the jury (*Brooks* v. *Stone,* 1984). In New York, student editors were held liable for defamation when they published a letter purportedly sent by two students who said they were gay. The two complained that they had never written the letter and were not gay, and the newspaper printed a retraction and an apology. The court held that the failure of the editors to check the authorship of the letter was irresponsible, negating any qualified privilege that they might have had (*Mazart* v. *State,* 1981).

Tort Liability Defenses

The best defense is to meet all responsibilities. The courts will not generally attach liability when students engage in activity known to be dangerous. When a twenty-five-old student, overweight with high blood pressure and an enlarged left ventricle, died after completing a two-and-a-half-mile race in the tropics, the college sponsoring the race was not held to be liable. The student assumed the risk of injury by participating in the activity with knowledge of his condition and the environment (*Gehling* v. *St. George University School of Medicine,* 1989). In addition, students who contribute to their own negligence may be barred from recovering damages. Some states, however, have comparative liability where damages are assessed on the basis of the degree of fault (*Zavala* v. *Regents of the University of California,* 1981). Sovereign immunity, which insulates public officials from suit when carrying out duties requiring exercise of judgment, should generally not be relied upon for several reasons. Sovereign or governmental immunity only applies to public institutions, and many states have now abrogated the concept; a check with institutional counsel would be prudent. The best defense against tort liability is to know legal duties and fulfill them. If the act is reasonable and treatment to others is proper, then liability will probably not attach.

Contracts

Contract law, a civil matter that can lead to damages, differs from state to state. Although there is no way to cover all the differences and nuances of contract law in this chapter, several general principles will be provided. Understanding some of these will aid in avoiding liability.

A *contract* is defined generally as "a promise or set of promises for the breach of which the law gives a remedy or the performance of which the law in some way recognizes as a duty" (American Law Institute, 1981, p. 5). The elements that must be present in a contract are (1) a promise or set of promises, (2) an offer and an acceptance, (3) an agreement of what is to be gained and what is to be given up to gain it, and (4) an agreement between the parties so that both have the same understanding.

Contracts may be either explicit or implicit, written or oral. The implicit understanding exists that if students pay tuition and meet the established academic requirements, they will receive a degree:

> The elements of a traditional contract are present in the implied contract between a college and a student attending that college, and are readily discernable. The student's tender of an application constitutes an offer to apply to a college. By "accepting" an applicant to be a student at the college, the college accepts the applicant's offer. Thereafter, the student pays tuition (which obviously constitutes sufficient consideration), attends classes, completes course work and takes test. The school provides the student with facilities and instruction and upon satisfactory completion of the school's academic requirements (which constitute performance), the school becomes obligated to issue the student a diploma [*Johnson* v. *Lincoln Christian College,* 1986, at 1348].

One court has held that this implied contract intends that the degree awarded will be an accredited one, if that is required for the licensure examination (*Behrend* v. *State,* 1977). Where students are not required to be graduates of accredited programs to take such licensure examinations, failing to inform them that the degree was not accredited does not constitute a breach of contract (*Lidecker* v. *Kendall College,* 1990).

Explicit contracts are created with students for housing and other services and for admission to the institution. When a medical school stated in a brochure that applicants would be judged on the basis of criteria listed in the brochure and then assessed them on an additional criterion (of being able to contribute financially to the school), this action was held to be a breach of contract with the applicant (*Steinberg* v. *Chicago Medical School,* 1977).

The terms and conditions of the contract found in brochures, handbooks, and other documents published by the institution that set forth promises are usually interpreted by the courts by applying the normal meaning of the words (*Warren* v. *Drake University,* 1989; *Delta School of Business, Etc.,* v. *Shropshire,* 1981).

As stated previously, not all contracts are written, and even oral statements can constitute promises offered. The U.S. Merchant Marine Academy officials promised several midshipmen immunity if they spoke freely about marijuana use at the academy. After admitting their own use, the midshipmen were dismissed from the academy. The court reversed the dismissals, saying, "As agents, the questioners were authorized to make promises. . . . Plaintiffs, by speaking freely, accepted this offer, and a contract was made. The academy is bound by this agreement" (*Krawez* v. *Stans,* 1969, at 1235).

In some cases, the terms and conditions of the contract may be changed without breaching the contract. When Vassar changed the rules to allow male visitation in the residence halls, the mother of one of the students unsuccessfully sued for breach of contract (*Jones* v. *Vassar,* 1969). When a graduate student was obliged to take a comprehensive exam that was not part of the requirements for a degree listed in the catalogue, the change was not held to breach the contract. The court stated that "implicit in the student's contract with the university upon matriculation is the student's agreement to comply with the university's rules and regulations, which the university is definitely entitled to modify so as to properly exercise its educational responsibilities" (*Mahavongsana* v. *Hall,* 1976, at 450).

In the current environment, where students are at a premium and so are dollars, it may be tempting to entice students with promises of extraordinary services. Yet that practice is also risky. The best advice is to provide everything that is promised and do not promise anything that cannot be provided. Catalogues, brochures, and handbooks should be reviewed with counsel. As a final word of caution, to protect themselves against individual liability for goods and services that administrators may contract for as agents of the institution, they should always sign both their names and their official titles. This practice will indicate that the officials were acting for the institution and were not contracting in an individual capacity.

Statutes

Many state and federal laws provide students with specific rights in their relationship with institutions. Violating these can lead to criminal action as well as to civil liability. Administrators must be aware of these laws and their proscriptions. Although it is not possible to cover the laws of each state in this chapter, the campus library will maintain a set of statutes. These volumes are indexed and can be retrieved by looking under headings for "colleges and universities" or "schools and colleges".

This section will focus on the federal laws that affect student affairs programs, policies, and practices. Such statutes are authorized by the power of the Congress to regulate interstate commerce and to provide for the general welfare. The law, once enacted, must be implemented by the appropriate agency of the executive branch, and sometimes statutes are interpreted by the judicial branch. It is not enough to know the law; those in student affairs must also understand what the regulations say and the judicial interpretations of those laws and regulations.

Although the federal government has been making laws affecting higher education since before the 1862 Morrill Act, the most recent, direct impact has been the Civil Rights Act of 1964. Title VI of that act states, "No person in the United States shall, on the ground of race, color or national origin, be excluded from participation in, be denied the benefits of, or be subjected to discrimination under any program or activity receiving federal financial assistance" (42 USC 2000-d).

Title IX of the Higher Education Amendments of 1972 (prohibition against sex discrimination) and Section 504 of the Rehabilitation Act of 1973 (prohibition against discrimination on the basis of handicap) were modeled after Title VI. Therefore, cases interpreting the general application of Title VI would be the same for Title IX and Section 504. Although Title VI has been interpreted to mean that a recipient of federal financial assistance was any institution where even one student attended under any type of federal aid (*Bob Jones University* v. *Johnson*, 1974; *Grove City College* v. *Bell*, 1984), the question of how to define a program or activity remained. The Civil Rights Restoration Act of 1987 defined a program or activity under all three statutes to constitute all operations of the college or university. Thus, whether a specific program receives any federal funding is immaterial. If there is one student attending the institution who receives federal financial aid, everything that school does must conform to Title VI, Title IX, and Section 504, including noncredit and nondegree courses (*Radcliff* v. *Landau*, 1989; *United States* v. *Board of Trustees for University of Alabama*, 1990).

The most famous Title VI case involved the denial of admission to medical school of a white applicant because the institution had specifically reserved a number of spaces for minority candidates (*Regents* v. *Bakke*, 1978). The Supreme Court held that an admissions quota violated Title VI, but institutions could *consider* race as one of several factors in their admissions decisions. Two subsequent cases in which race was considered but was not the sole factor in the admission decision were *McDonald* v. *Hogness* (1979) and *DeRonde* v. *Regents of University of California* (1981). The state supreme court in both cases upheld the process. Thus, when race is the sole factor in making an admissions or other decision, it probably violates Title VI (*Uzzell* v. *Friday*, 1979).

Regulations implementing Title VI (34 CFR 100), Title IX (34 CFR 106), and Section 504 (34 CFR 104) each provide a mechanism for administrative procedures against those who violate the law. If those attempts are not successful, the Department of Education must seek approval from Congress to revoke the institution's federal financial assistance — the penalty for violations. Students, however, may initiate their own legal action and need not wait for the government to act (*Cannon* v. *University of Chicago,* 1979).

Title IX also prohibits sexual harassment by institutional officials, including faculty and staff (*Alexander* v. *Yale University,* 1980; *Bougher* v. *University of Pittsburgh,* 1989). Regulations implementing Title IX (34 CFR 106) have specific sections dealing with campus rules, athletics, student organizations, and the provision of housing, counseling, and placement services.

Section 504 prohibits discrimination against "otherwise qualified handicapped" persons. A handicapped person is one who is physically or mentally impaired to the point that one or more major life activities is substantially limited, has a record of having such an impairment, or is considered to have the impairment. An otherwise qualified handicapped individual is one who can perform the essential functions in spite of the handicap (*Southeastern Community College* v. *Davis,* 1979); *Doe* v. *New York University,* 1981). However, reasonable accommodations such as having a guide dog, taping lectures, or having a sign-language interpreter, may be required to permit the handicapped individual to perform essential functions. Recent judicial decisions have indicated that auxiliary aids are to be paid by state rehabilitation agencies and not colleges and universities (*Jones* v. *Illinois Department of Rehabilitation Services,* 1981; *Schornstein* v. *New Jersey Division of Vocational Rehabilitational Services,* 1981). The Washington Supreme Court, however, upheld the denial of state rehabilitation funds to a blind student who wanted to pursue a ministerial degree because the state constitution prohibited providing public monies for religious instruction (*Witters* v. *State Commission for the Blind,* 1989). Although drug addicts and alcoholics are considered handicapped, they like all handicapped students must conform to the institution's reasonable rules and regulations (*Anderson* v. *University of Wisconsin,* 1988).

In *School Board of Nassau County, Florida,* v. *Arline,* 1987), the U.S. Supreme Court ruled that a contagious disease constituted a handicap under Section 504. The disease in *Arline* was tuberculosis, and the Court held that fear of contagion alone was not sufficient for dismissal of a handicapped person. In determining whether a handicapped person is otherwise qualified, administrators should seek medical advice including (1) how the disease is transmitted, (2) how long the carrier will be capable of transmitting the disease, (3) what the potential risk is to third parties, and (4) what the probability is that the disease will be transmitted and cause harm. Obviously, symptomatic AIDS is a contagious disease but even more difficult to transmit than tuberculosis. For purposes of Section 504 as it relates to employment, the Civil Rights Restoration Act of 1987 states that a handicapped person "does not include an individual who has a currently contagious disease or infection and who, by reason of such disease or infection, would constitute a direct threat to the health and safety of other individuals, or who by reason of currently contagious disease or infection, is unable to perform the duties of the job" (PL 100-259, Sec. 9).

Other federal laws directly affecting colleges and universities include the Family Educational Rights and Privacy Act (FERPA) (or the Buckley Amendment, as it is commonly known). FERPA states, "No funds shall be made available . . . to . . . any institution of higher education . . . which has a policy of permitting the release of personally identifiable records . . . of students without the written consent of their parents" (PL 93-380, Sec. 438-a1). The rights of the parent revert to the student once he or she attains eighteen years of age or enters a postsecondary institution.

Administrators should read the law (20 USC 1232g) and the implementing regulations (34 CFR 99) in their entirety to understand their requirements and exceptions. For example, it is permissible to send copies of grades or disciplinary actions to the parents of college students who are financially dependent on their parents (claimed as deductions on the parents' federal tax return). However, the law is permissive and also allows institutions to withhold such information under institutional policy. Any policy, however, must be written and available to everyone in the college community. Students may not sue to enforce their FERPA rights but must rely on the government to effectuate compliance (*Smith* v. *Duquesne,* 1985).

One court has held that campus police incident reports were not protected from disclosure under FERPA (*Bauer* v. *Kincaid,* 1991). The court noted that FERPA is a law that imposes the *penalty* of withdrawal of funds from institutions that have policies favoring disclosure of personally identifiable information rather than prohibiting such disclosure. This is an interesting and as yet unsettled interpretation of the law.

Two newer federal laws influencing student affairs programs are the Drug-Free Schools and Communities Act of 1989 Amendments and the Student Right-to-Know and Campus Security Act (PL 101-542, 104 Stat. 2381). As mentioned earlier, the Drug-Free Schools and Communities Act mandates that institutions annually distribute to each student and employee specific information regarding (1) standards of conduct that prohibit unlawful possession, use, and distribution of drugs and alcohol; (2) a description of applicable local, state, and federal laws concerning the unlawful possession, use, or distribution of illicit drugs and alcohol; (3) a description of the health risks associated with illegal drugs and alcohol; (4) a description of rehabilitation and treatment programs available; and (6) a statement that the institution will impose sanctions for violations of its standards. It is not enough simply to make the information available. Institutions must also conduct a biennial review of drug and alcohol policies to determine if they are effective and whether disciplinary sanctions are consistently enforced.

The Student Right-to-Know and Campus Security Act requires institutions to report graduation rates for athletes and others and statistics for major crimes. The regulations for this statute will be published during 1992. There are aspects of the law that are somewhat troubling (Gehring, 1991), and administrators must stay abreast of developments.

The Civil Rights Act of 1871 (42 USC 1983) creates civil liability for those public officials who violate the constitutional or statutory rights of others.

The law has been interpreted to apply to public officials carrying out their duties when doing so violates the "basic unquestionable" rights of students (*Wood* v. *Strickland,* 1975). Damages assessed under Section 1983 are limited to $1.00 unless specific injury beyond the violation of one's rights can be shown (*Carey* v. *Piphus,* 1978). The U.S. Supreme Court has also held that Section 1983 can be used as the basis for liability "where the failure to train amounts to deliberate indifference to the rights of persons with whom the police come into contact" (*City of Canton, Ohio,* v. *Harris,* 1989, at 426). The same reasoning was applied in a case where police received no training about AIDS and told a woman that she needed to wash after touching the truck of a neighbor who had AIDS (*Doe* v. *Borough of Barrington,* 1990). Thus, resident assistants, campus police, or any other state employee who works directly with students must be properly trained, as actual damages are likely where there is a deliberate-indifference judgment; and actual damages will be considerably higher than the $1.00 nominal charge that can be assessed under Section 1983.

Many other federal laws have a more indirect impact on student affairs programs and policies. These include the Copyright Revision Act (Title 17 USC with regulations at 37 CFR 201-204), Human Subjects Research Act (45 CFR 46), and Americans with Disabilities Act (42 USC 12101 *et seq.*). In addition, personnel laws affect hiring and employment: for example, Title VII of the Civil Rights Act (42 USC 2000-e2) with regulations at 29 CFR 1601 and sexual harassment guidelines at 24 CFR 1604), the Equal Pay Act of 1963 (29 USC 206-d) with regulations at 29 CFR 806), the Age Discrimination in Employment Act of 1967 (29 USC 621), the Fair Labor Standards Act of 1938 (29 USC 201), Executive Order 11246 as amended (32 FR 14303 with regulations at 41 CFR 60, 41 CFR 60-2, and employee selection guidelines at 42 FR 29016), and the Age Discrimination Act of 1975 (42 USC 6101). Institutional personnel offices can assist in understanding both rights and obligations under these laws.

Constitutional Issues

The U.S. Constitution is the highest law of the land and describes the relationship between the three branches of government. The Bill of Rights, as noted in a previous section, sets forth the minimum rights of persons residing in the country. No state constitution or federal or state law may conflict with the federal Constitution. Although no state constitution may grant fewer rights than the federal Constitution, many states grant more rights than are found in the federal Constitution (*State* v. *Schmid,* 1980; *Witters* v. *State Commission for the Blind,* 1989; *Washington* v. *Chrisman,* 1982). The guarantees set forth in the federal Constitution, however, only protect persons against actions by the government or its agencies. The Constitution "erects no shield against purely private conduct" (*Shelley* v. *Kraemer,* 1947, at 1180). Only if private institutions are shown to be engaged in "state action" are they required to conform to the guarantees in the federal Constitution.

The courts determine state action by "sifting facts and weighing circumstances" (*Burton* v. *Wilmington Parking Authority,* 1961). The mere receipt of federal or state funding is certainly not enough (*Grossner* v. *Trustees of Columbia University,* 1968; *Torres* v. *Puerto Rican Junior College,* 1969), nor is the fact that the state approves the curriculum, accredits the institution, grants a tax exemption, or grants powers of eminent domain (*Rowe* v. *Chandler,* 1971; *Berrios* v. *Inter American University,* 1976; *Browns* v. *Mitchell,* 1969, and *Blackburn* v. *Fisk University,* 1971, respectively). The courts are generally reluctant to find state action and attempt to preserve the public-private distinction. However, racial discrimination is a circumstance that weighs heavily; where it has been present, a private college has been held to have engaged in state action (*Hammond* v. *Tampa,* 1965).

The First Amendment

The First Amendment, which permeates almost every aspect of student affairs administration, states: "Congress shall make no law respecting an establishment of religion or prohibiting the free exercise thereof; or abridging the freedom of speech, or of the press; or the right of people peaceably to assemble; and to petition the Government for a redress of grievances."

Establishment and Free Exercise of Religion

This prohibition is primarily involved in situations in which federal or state assistance of some type is provided to religiously affiliated institutions. The assistance need not be financial; it can be any type of aid that puts the government's "stamp of approval" on a sectarian activity. Determination if there is a violation of the establishment clause rests on a three-pronged test established by the U.S. Supreme Court. If any one of the three criteria is offended, the establishment clause is violated. The test asks whether the aid (1) reflects a clearly secular purpose, (2) has a primary effect that neither advances nor inhibits religion, and (3) avoids excessive entanglement between the church and the government (*Lemon* v. *Kurtzman,* 1971).

State and federal financial assistance may be provided either to students or institutions without offending the establishment clause as long as the aid meets the *Lemon* test (*Tilton* v. *Richardson,* 1970; *Roemer* v. *Board of Public Works,* 1976; and *Americans United* v. *Rogers,* 1976). If public institutions permit student religious groups to use facilities for services, there is also no violation of the establishment clause (*University of Delaware* v. *Keegan,* 1975; *Widmar* v. *Vincent,* 1981). However, when a public institution placed a student teacher at a parochial school, a federal court found that although the placement served a valid secular purpose, it advanced religion by creating a perception that the state endorsed the religious mission of the school (*Stark* v. *St. Cloud State University,* 1986).

Freedom of Speech and the Press

The freedom of speech and the press guaranteed in the First Amendment is not absolute. One cannot yell "fire" in a crowded theater (*Schenck* v. *United States,* 1919) and "utterances in a context of violence, involving a definite and present danger, can lose significance as an appeal to reason and become part of an instrument of force . . . unprotected by the Constitution" (*Siegel* v. *Regents of the University of California,* 1970, at 838). In *Tinker* v. *Des Moines Independent School Dist.* (1969), the Supreme Court held that institutions may regulate speech and expression that would "materially and substantially disrupt the work and discipline of the school" (at 742). The institution, however, must bear the burden of showing clear and convincing evidence that the speech or expression would be disruptive (*Molpus* v. *Fortune,* 1970). The mere belief that speech will become disruptive is not enough (*Brooks* v. *Auburn University,* 1969). Colleges and universities may impose reasonable time, place, and manner restrictions on the exercise of free speech and expression (*Bayless* v. *Martine,* 1970; *Sword* v. *Fox,* 1971), but those restrictions are valid only when there is no reference to content and when they are narrowly tailored to serve a significant governmental interest and leave open ample alternatives for communication of information (*Students Against Apartheid Coalition* v. *O'Neil I,* 1987).

Whenever decisions are made on the basis of the content of oral, symbolic, or printed expression, a violation of the First Amendment will probably be found. Thus, institutional officials have been found to be in violation when they have eliminated editorials critical of the state governor (*Dickey* v. *Alabama State Board of Education,* 1967), removed editorial advertisements (*Lee* v. *Board of Regents of State Colleges,* 1969; *Lueth* v. *St. Clair County Community College,* 1990), restricted speakers (*Pickings* v. *Bruce,* 1970), prohibited the wearing of black arm bands to protest a war (*Tinker* v. *Des Moines Independent School Dist.,* 1969), or prohibited students from erecting shanties to protest South Africa's policy of apartheid (*University of Utah Students Against Apartheid* v. *Peterson,* 1986; *Students Against Apartheid Coalition* v. *O'Neill II,* 1988).

The landmark decision of the Supreme Court in *Papish* v. *Board of Curators of the University of Missouri* (1973) involved a student distributing newspapers that showed a police officer raping the Goddess of Justice and another raping the Statue of Liberty and an article including the headline "M_____F_____ Acquitted." The university suspended the student for violating regulations prohibiting indecent conduct or speech. The Court, reaffirming that college and universities "are not enclaves immune from the sweep of the First Amendment" (*Healy* v. *James,* 1972, at 279), said, "The mere dissemination of ideas — no matter how offensive to good taste — on a state university campus may not be shut off in the name alone of 'conventions of decency'" (*Papish* v. *Board of Curators of the University of Missouri,* 1973, at 662).

Recent incidents of racially motivated behavior have caused institutions to promulgate regulations. This is not a new phenomenon. A student editor at a historically black, state-supported institution published an editorial espousing segregationist views, and the president of the university withheld funds that supported the newspaper on the grounds that funding the editorial violated the Civil Rights Act and the equal protection clause of the Fourteenth Amendment (*Joyner* v. *Whiting,* 1973). The court ordered the funding reinstated since the Civil Rights Act or the Fourteenth Amendment prohibited the state from discriminatory action but did not prohibit advocacy.

The policy of the University of Michigan prohibiting "any behavior, verbal or physical, that stigmatizes or victimizes an individual on the basis of race, ethnicity, religion, sex, sexual orientation, creed, national origin, ancestry, age, marital status, handicap, or Vietnam-era veteran status" was struck down as overly broad and vague as its prohibitions could include speech protected by the First Amendment (*Doe* v. *University of Michigan,* 1989, at 853). Institutional policies brought about unwelcome legislative reaction. Congressman Hyde introduced legislation that would provide students a right to bring civil suits against institutions violating their First Amendment rights (HR 1380). Obviously, more creative and lawful ways must be found to deal with hurtful speech and behavior, which have no place in a collegiate setting.

Right to Peaceable Assembly

Institutions are not required to provide any sort of official recognition or endorsement of student organizations; however, once they open the door to recognition, they must treat all who request it equally and may not differentiate in granting recognition on the basis of goals or philosophy as long as they are lawful. In *Healy* v. *James* (1972), the Supreme Court said that merely disagreeing with the philosophy of the organization, no matter how repugnant it seemed, was not sufficient to deny recognition. However, the Court also stated that recognition could be denied if the organization should advocate views directed to inciting or producing imminent lawless action, fail to show willingness to comply with reasonable institutional rules, or engage in unlawful or disruptive action.

Organizations recognized by an institution gain no new rights, nor is the institution required to assist them to exercise their rights (*National Strike Information Center* v. *Brandeis,* 1970; *Maryland Public Interest Research Group* v. *Elkins,* 1977). Once recognized, however, organizations must be afforded all the rights and privileges generally accorded to other recognized groups. The law does not require equal support for each group, but it does not permit the denial of privileges based on a disagreement with the group's lawful goals (*Gay and Lesbian Student Association* v. *Gohn,* 1988).

Administrators must recognize that the right of association also guarantees the reciprocal right not to associate. Institutions sometimes impose an activity fee on students that is used in part to support the student government association and other campus activities. In some instances, once students pay the fee, they automatically become members of the student government association. The Washington Supreme Court was asked if this practice was constitutionally permissible and had "no hesitancy in holding that the state, through the university, may not compel membership in an association, such as Associated Students of the University of Washington (ASUW) which purports to represent all the students at the university" (*Good* v. *Associated Students,* 1975, at 768). Courts have, however, permitted institutions to collect and distribute activity fees from all students to provide a forum for the expression of ideas (*Veed* v. *Schwartzkoph,* 1973).

The clear language of the First Amendment guarantees students the right to assemble on campus and to demonstrate for particular causes so long as these demonstrations are not disruptive (*Esteban* v. *Central Missouri State College,* 1969). Prior registration may be required to ensure that the demonstration does not interfere with other scheduled activities and to prepare for the demonstration. The right to assemble cannot be denied on the basis of the content of the message (*Shamloo* v. *Mississippi State Board of Trustees, Etc.,* 1980).

The Fourth Amendment

The Fourth Amendment states, "The right of the people to be secure in their persons, houses, papers, and effects, against unreasonable searches and seizures, shall not be violated, and no warrants shall issue, but upon probable cause, supported by oath or affirmation, and particularly describing the place to be searched, and the persons or things to be seized."

The Supreme Court in *New Jersey* v. *T.L.O.* (1985) allowed a warrantless search of a fourteen-year-old schoolgirl's purse, stating that such a search is permissible "when there are reasonable grounds for suspecting that the search will turn up evidence that the student has violated the law or the rules of the school" (at 735). In striking a balance between a student's Fourth Amendment rights and the legitimate interests of school officials, the Court said that "reasonableness" would be determined by the age of the student, that which was sought, past history, and the degree of individualized suspicion. The Supreme Court has yet to address the issue as it relates to adult college students, but prior to *New Jersey* many state and federal jurisdictions have upheld warrantless searches of student rooms where administrators had reasonable cause to believe that the student had contraband in the room (*Moore* v. *Student Affairs Committee of Troy State University,* 1968). Warrantless searches of students' suitcases (*United States* v. *Cole,* 1969), automobiles (*Keene* v. *Rodgers,* 1970), and rooms (*Ekelund* v. *Secretary of Commerce,* 1976) have even been upheld on federal property.

Although it appears that the greater weight of precedent supports warrantless searches under the conditions outlined above, college officials may not delegate the lower standard of reasonable cause to police who seek criminal evidence. Where criminal evidence is sought, police must meet the higher standard of "probable cause" and obtain a warrant as called for in the amendment (*Piazzola* v. *Watkins,* 1971).

There are, in addition to the reasonable-cause standard, other reasonable searches and seizures that do not require a warrant. Contraband observed in "plain view" may be seized and used for disciplinary purposes (*State* v. *Kappes,* 1976). During a monthly health and safety inspection conducted after twenty-four hours' notice, two resident assistants observed drugs in plain view on a student's desk. The seized drugs were then turned over to law enforcement agents. The state court of appeals applied the plain-view doctrine and upheld the seizure.

An emergency situation also provides an exception to the necessity for a warrant. The California Supreme Court upheld the conviction of a student for possession of marijuana where the drug had been treated with a chemical substance and caused a foul odor to emanate from his library carrel, where it was stored. The librarian, acting on the basis of complaints, sent the custodian to find the source of the odor. The discovery of the student's briefcase with small bags of greenish-colored weeds surprised the custodian, and neither he nor the librarian recognized the substance. They called the police, who recognized it as marijuana and seized it. The court held that it was reasonable to assume control of the briefcase under the emergency doctrine (*People* v. *Lanthier,* 1971). The court also held that it was reasonable to call the police for identification and that the police had obtained the evidence under the plain-view doctrine. Good-faith inventories of furniture and equipment, fire safety devices, and the like are also seen as reasonable, and contraband observed in the inventory may be seized (*State* v. *Johnson,* 1975).

The Fourteenth Amendment

The Fourteenth Amendment was passed shortly after the Civil War to protect the former slaves. The amendment provides in part, "Nor shall any State deprive any person of life, liberty, or property, without due process of law; nor deny to any person within its jurisdiction the equal protection of the laws." The amendment refers to any *person* rather than any *citizen.* Thus, the protections of due process and equal protection are guaranteed to everyone in the United States, including international students.

The *Dixon* case was the landmark decision applying the due-process guarantees of the Fourteenth Amendment to student discipline (*Dixon* v. *Alabama State Board of Education,* 1961). M. M. Chambers (1972), however, uncovered a decision by a county court seventy-four years before *Dixon* that also required that due-process rights be afforded to students facing disciplinary charges (*Commonwealth ex rel. Hill* v. *McCauley,* 1887). Time and circumstances, however, have made *Dixon* the landmark that it is today.

The process that is due depends upon the nature of the right that is deprived. Thus, a minor noise violation in a residence hall would not demand the same amount of process as if the student faced expulsion. Due process is not a fixed standard; rather, it is defined "by the gradual process of judicial inclusion and exclusion" (*Davidson* v. *New Orleans,* 1877, at 104).

The Fifth Circuit Court of Appeals in *Dixon* set standards for due process in student discipline. First, the court indicated that students should receive a specific notice of charges and the grounds that, if proven, would justify expulsion. Second, the notice should include the nature of the evidence; furnish the time, date, and place of the hearing; and provide reasonable time for the student to prepare a defense. Third, the court indicated that the circumstances of a specific case would influence the type of hearing to be held. Serious cases required the institution to have a more formal hearing with an opportunity to hear both sides of the case in considerable detail. Fourth, students should be given the names of witnesses and an oral or written report of their testimony. Fifth, students should be provided an opportunity to present a defense, including written or oral testimony of witnesses. Sixth, the hearing must be held before an impartial individual or board. Finally, the findings of the hearing should be furnished in written form for the students' inspection. "If these rudimentary elements of fair play are followed in a case of misconduct of this particular type, we feel that the requirements of due process of law will have been fulfilled" (*Dixon* v. *Alabama State Board of Education,* 1961, at 159).

In their consideration of due process, administrators should also read the *General Order on Judicial Standards of Procedure and Substance in Review of Student Discipline in Tax-Supported Institutions of Higher Education* (1968) issued by a federal district court in Missouri. The *General Order* differentiates between college discipline and criminal jurisprudence and concludes that any analogy between them is not sound. It also points out the lawful missions of higher education and provides an excellent set of procedural standards for campus discipline.

The procedural requirements outlined in *Dixon* and the *General Order* have been refined over the years as they have been applied to specific factual situations. Students should be given written notice of the charges in enough detail to allow them to prepare a defense (*Esteban* v. *Central Missouri State College,* 1969). Violated regulations must be specific enough to provide a reasonable person with notice of what is prohibited (*Soglin* v. *Kauffman,* 1969). Students may not frustrate the notice process by moving or failing to keep the university apprised of their current address (*Wright* v. *Texas Southern University,* 1968). There is no general requirement that witnesses be confronted or crossexamined (*General Order,* 1968), but where questions exist about the credibility of witnesses, crossexamination may be essential (*Blanton* v. *State University of New York,* 1973). A hearing may be conducted when after proper notice the student charged decides not to attend (*Merrow* v. *Goldberg,* 1968; *Swanson* v. *Wesley College,* 1979). Special circumstances, such as when the university uses an attorney to present its case (*French* v. *Bashful,* 1969), require that the student be allowed to be represented by counsel. Where the student faces criminal charges, the advice of counsel at the hearing may also be required (*Gabrilowitz* v. *Newman,* 1978). Students have no absolute rights to record hearings (*Gorman* v. *University of Rhode Island,* 1988). Nor is it necessary for the university to make a full transcript of the hearing (*Sohmer* v. *Kinnard,* 1982; *Due* v. *Florida Agricultural and Mechanical University,* 1963). Hearings on campus need not wait until criminal charges are settled (*Nzuve* v. *Castleton State College,* 1975). Hearings must be closed unless those students defending against the charges agree in writing to have them open; then the choice is the university's (*Marston* v. *Gainesville Sun,* 1976). Finally, decisions should be based on substantial evidence (*Dixon* v. *Alabama State Board of Education,* 1961; *McDonald* v. *Board of Trustees of University of Illinois,* 1974; *Jackson* v. *Hayakawa,* 1985).

Certain circumstances may require more or less due process than that outlined above. The Supreme Court has held that where students are suspended or expelled for academic reasons, the decision rests on the academic judgment of college officials, and a hearing is not required (*Board of Curators* v. *Horowitz,* 1978; *Regents of the University of Michigan* v. *Ewing,* 1985). Questions of acts of academic dishonesty, however, are disciplinary in nature and would require some form of due process (Gehring, Nuss, and Pavela, 1986).

Finally, administrators need not wait for the time-consuming due-process requirements to run their course before protecting the community from those who present a real and serious threat to the health, safety, or welfare of persons or property. A student who poses such a threat may be suspended immediately on an interim basis pending a subsequent hearing (*Gardenhire* v. *Chalmers,* 1971; *Swanson* v. *Wesley College,* 1979). This is a very serious step and should be carefully considered before being taken.

The Fourteenth Amendment also guarantees that the government may not deny anyone equal protection of the law. Obviously, this does not mean that everyone is treated the same. The equal-protection clause means that if an institution is engaged in state action, *similarly situated individuals* must be treated equally. Unless a fundamental right (such as voting or interstate travel) is denied to a class of people or a "suspect class" (based on, for example, race, alienage, or national origin) is created, only a rational relationship between the classes of people created by the different treatment and the legitimate interests of the state must be demonstrated. For example, requiring all students under twenty-three years of age to live on campus for educational reasons has been upheld (*Pratz* v. *Louisiana Polytechnic Institute,* 1971), whereas requiring all women but only freshman men to live on campus has been held to serve no legitimate state interest and thus violates the equal-protection clause (*Mollere* v. *Southeastern Louisiana College,* 1969).

Although admission to an institution of higher education is not a fundamental right, classifying students on the basis of their alienage creates a suspect class, and thus the state must be able to show a "compelling interest" in creating the classification. During the hostage crises in Iran, the state of New Mexico passed legislation denying enrollment to any student whose home country held American citizens hostage. The law was held to be a violation of the equal-protection clause because a suspect class was created and the rationale for creating the class did not serve a compelling state interest (*Tayyari* v. *New Mexico State University,* 1980).

Classifications based on gender are not suspect and therefore do not require a compelling interest, but they have been held to require more than a simple rational relationship to justify them. In a case involving the admissions policy of Mississippi University for Women (which excluded men), the Supreme Court held that gender classification must serve "important governmental objectives" and that the classification must be substantially related to accomplishing those objectives. Furthermore, the classification must be free of stereotypes concerning the roles and abilities of men and women (*Mississippi University for Women* v. *Hogan,* 1982). Applying these same tests to the males-only admission policy of the Virginia Military Institute had an entirely different result. There the court found that the institute provided a unique instructional program in meeting the state's objective of providing a diverse educational system and that the program would need to be altered substantially if women were admitted (*United States* v. *Commonwealth of Virginia,* 1991).

Summary

The law has definitely arrived on campus. It permeates every program, policy, and practice of the institution. Because student affairs programs and practices are often where the student and the institution come together, student affairs administrators must understand the legal guidelines that define the basic relationships between students and their institutions. The law is not static but ever-evolving, and thus administrators must not only understand the basic guidelines but must also stay current with new developments. The specific facts, the current state of the law, and the private or public nature of the institution of higher education will all influence the legal aspects of the work of student affairs. Competent legal advice is necessary and should be sought. This chapter has attempted to provide the basic information for understanding student and institutional relationships. It becomes the responsibility of the astute student affairs administrator to stay current.

References

American Law Institute. *Restatement of Contracts, 2d.* St. Paul, Minn.: American Law Institute, 1981.

Chambers, M. M. *The Colleges and the Courts: The Developing Law of the Student and the College.* Danville, Ill.: Interstate, 1972.

Gadaleto, A., and Anderson, D. "Continued Progress: The 1979, 1982, and 1985 College Alcohol Surveys." *Journal of College Student Personnel,* 1986, *27,* 499–509.

Gehring, D. "Abreast of the Law." In *NASPA Forum*. Washington, D.C.: National Association of Student Personnel Administrators, Nov. 1991.

Gehring, D., and Geraci, C. *Alcohol on Campus: A Compendium of the Law and a Guide to Campus Policy*. Asheville, N.C.: College Administration Publications, 1989.

Gehring, D., Nuss, E., and Pavela, G. *Issues and Perspectives on Academic Integrity*. Washington, D.C.: National Association of Student Personnel Administrators, 1986.

General Order on Judicial Standards of Procedure and Substance in Review of Student Discipline in Tax-Supported Institutions of Higher Education. 45 FRD 133 (W.D. Mo. 1968).

Kaplin, W. A. *The Law of Higher Education: A Comprehensive Guide to Legal Implications of Administrative Decision Making* (2nd ed.) San Francisco: Jossey-Bass, 1985.

Prosser, W. *Law of Torts* (4th ed.). St. Paul, Minn.: West, 1971.

Cases Cited

Alexander v. *Yale University*, 631 F.2d 178 (2nd Cir. 1980).

Americans United v. *Rogers*, 45 L.W. 3429 (1976).

Anderson v. *University of Wisconsin*, 841 F.2d 737 (7th Cir. 1988).

Ballou v. *Sigma Nu General Fraternity*, 352 S.E.2d 488 (S.C. App. 1986).

Bauer v. *Kincaid*, 759 F.Supp. 575 (W.D. Mo. S.D. 1991).

Bayless v. *Martine*, 430 F.2d 873 (5th Cir. 1970).

Bearman v. *University of Notre Dame*, 453 N.E.2d 1196 (App. Ind., 3rd Dist. 1983).

Behrend v. *State*, 379 N.E.2d 617 (Ct. App. Ohio, Franklin, Cty. 1977).

Berrios v. *Inter American University*, 535 F.2d 1330 (1st Cir. 1976).

Blackburn v. *Fisk University*, 443 F.2d 121 (6th Cir. 1971).

Blanton v. *State University of New York*, 489 F.2d 377 (2nd Cir. 1973).

Board of Curators v. *Horowitz*, 46 L.W. 4179 (1978).

Bob Jones University v. *Johnson*, 396 F.Supp. 597 (D. S.C. Greenville Div. 1974).

Bougher v. *University of Pittsburgh*, 882 F.2d 74 (3rd Cir. 1989).

Bradshaw v. *Rawlings*, 612 F.2d 135 (3rd Cir. 1979).

Brooks v. *Auburn University*, 296 F.Supp. 188 (M.D. Ala. E.D. 1969).

Brooks v. *Stone*, 317 S.E.2d 277 (Ga. App. 1984).

Browns v. *Mitchell*, 409 F.2d 593 (10th Cir. 1969).

Burton v. *Wilmington Parking Authority*, 365 U.S. 715 (1961).

Cannon v. *University of Chicago*, 99 S.Ct. 1946 (1979).

Carey v. *Piphus*, 98 S.Ct. 1024 (1978).

City of Canton, Ohio, v. *Harris*, 103 L.E.D.2d 412 (1989).

Commonwealth ex rel. Hill v. *McCauley*, 3 Pa. Co.Ct. 77 (1887).

Davidson v. *New Orleans*, 96 U.S. 97 (1877).

Delta School of Business, Etc., v. *Shropshire*, 399 So.2d 1212 (La. App. 1st Cir. 1981).

DeRonde v. *Regents of University of California,* 172 Calif. Rptr. 677 (1981).

Dickey v. *Alabama Board of Education,* 273 F. Supp. 613 (M.D. Ala. E.D. 1967).

Dixon v. *Alabama State Board of Education,* 294 F.2d 150 (5th Cir. 1961); cert. den. 386 U.S. 930 (1961).

Doe v. *Borough of Barrington,* 729 F.Supp. 376 (D. N.J. 1990).

Doe v. *New York University,* 666 F.2d 761 (2nd Cir. 1981).

Doe v. *University of Michigan,* 721 F.Supp. 852 (E.D. Mich. So. Div. 1989).

Drew v. *State,* 536 N.Y.S.2d 252 (A.D. 3rd Dept. 1989).

Duarte v. *State,* 148 Calif. Rptr. 804 (Calif. App. 4th Dist. 1978).

Due v. *Florida Agricultural and Mechanical University,* 233 F.Supp. 396 (N.D. Fla. 1963).

Ekelund v. *Secretary of Commerce,* 418 F.Supp. 102 (E.D. N.Y. 1976).

Esteban v. *Central Missouri State College,* 415 F.2d 1077 (8th Cir. 1969).

French v. *Bashful,* 303 F.Supp. 1333 (E.D. La. N.O. Div. 1969).

Furek v. *University of Delaware,* 594 A.2d 506 (Del. 1991).

Gabrilowitz v. *Newman,* 582 F.2d 100 (1st Cir. 1978).

Gardenhire v. *Chalmers,* 326 F.Supp. 1200 (D. Kans. 1971).

Gay and Lesbian Student Association v. *Gohn,* 850 F.2d 361 (8th Cir. 1988).

Gehling v. *St. George University School of Medicine,* 705 F.Supp. 761 (D.E.D. N.Y. 1989).

Good v. *Associated Students,* 542 P.2d 762 (Wash. 1975).

Gorman v. *University of Rhode Island,* 837 F.2d 7 (1st Cir. 1988).

Graham v. *Montana State University,* 767 P.2d 301 (Mont. 1988).

Grossner v. *Trustees of Columbia University,* 287 F.Supp. 535 (S.D. N.Y. 1968).

Grove City College v. *Bell,* 104 S.Ct. 1211 (1984).

Hall v. *Board of Supervisors, Southern University,* 405 So.2d 1125 (App. La. 1st Cir. 1981).

Hammond v. *Tampa,* 344 F.2d 951 (5th Cir. 1965).

Healy v. *James,* 33 L.E.D.2d 266 (1972).

Henig v. *Hofstra University,* 533 N.Y.S.2d 479 (A.D. 2nd Dept. 1990).

Houck v. *University of Washington,* 803 P.2d 47 (App. Wash. 1991).

Ithaca College v. *Yale Daily News Publishing Co., Inc.,* 433 N.Y.S.2d 530 (S.Ct. 1980).

Jackson v. *Hayakawa,* 761 F.2d 525 (9th Cir. 1985).

Johnson v. *Lincoln Christian College,* 501 N.E.2d 1380 (Ill. App. 4th Dist. 1986).

Jones v. *Illinois Department of Rehabilitation Services,* 504 F.Supp. 1244 (N.D. Ill. E.D. 1981).

Jones v. *Vassar,* 299 N.Y.S.2d 283 (S.Ct. Duchess Cty. 1969).

Joyner v. *Whiting,* 477 F.2d 456 (4th Cir. 1973).

Keene v. *Rodgers,* 316 F.Supp. 217 (D. Maine N.D. 1970).

Kline v. *Massachusetts Avenue Apartment Corp.,* 439 F.2d 477 (D.C. Cir. 1970).

Krawez v. *Stans,* 306 F.Supp. 1230 (D.E.D. N.Y. 1969).

Lee v. *Board of Regents of State Colleges,* 306 F.Supp. 1097 (W.D. Wis. 1969).

Lemon v. *Kurtzman,* 403 U.S. 602 (1971).

Lidecker v. *Kendall College,* 550 N.E.2d 1211 (Ill. App. 1st Dist. 1990).

Lueth v. *St. Clair County Community College,* 732 F.Supp. 1410 (E.D. Mich. S.D. 1990).

McDonald v. *Board of Trustees of University of Illinois,* 375 F.Supp. 95 (D.N.D. Ill. E.D. 1974).

McDonald v. *Hogness,* 598 P.2d 707 (Wash. 1979).

McIntosh v. *Milano,* 403 A.2d 500 (N.Y. Super., Law 1979).

Mahavongsana v. *Hall,* 529 F.2d 488 (5th Cir. 1976).

Marston v. *Gainesville Sun,* 341 So.2d 783 (Dist.Ct. App. Fla. 1st Dist. 1976).

Maryland Public Interest Research Group v. *Elkins,* 565 F.2d 864 (4th Cir. 1977).

Mazart v. *State,* 441 N.Y.S.2d 600 (Ct. Clms. 1981).

Meese v. *Brigham Young University,* 639 P.2d 720 (Utah 1981).

Merrow v. *Goldberg,* 674 F.Supp. 1130 (D. Vt. 1986).

Miller v. *State,* 478 N.Y.S.2d 829 (1984).

Mintz v. *State,* 362 N.Y.S.2d 619 (App. 3rd 1975).

Mississippi University for Women v. *Hogan,* 73 L.E.D. 1090 (1982).

Mollere v. *Southeastern Louisiana College,* 304 F.Supp. 826 (W.D. Ark. Fayetteville Div. 1969).

Molpus v. *Fortune,* 311 F.Supp. 240 (N.D. Miss. 1970).

Moore v. *Student Affairs Committee of Troy State University,* 284 F.Supp. 725 (M.D. Ala. N.Div. 1968).

Mullins v. *Pine Manor College,* 449 N.E.2d 331 (Mass. 1983).

Nally v. *Grace Community Church of the Valley,* 240 Calif. Rptr. 215 (App. Calif. 2nd Dist. 1987).

National Strike Information Center v. *Brandeis,* 315 F.Supp. 928 (D. Mass. 1970).

New Jersey v. *T.L.O.,* 83 L.E.D.2d 720 (1985).

Nzuve v. *Castleton State College,* 335 A.2d 321 (Vt. 1975).

Olsson v. *Indiana University Board of Trustees,* 571 N.E.2d 585 (Ct. App. Ind. 4th Dist. 1991).

Palsgraf v. *Long Island R.R. Co.,* 162 N.E. 99 (N.Y. 1928).

Papish v. *Board of Curators of the University of Missouri,* 35 L.E.D.618 (1973).

Peck v. *Counseling Service of Addison County, Inc.,* 499 A.2d 423 (Vt. 1985).

People v. *Lanthier,* 97 Calif. Rptr. 297 (1971).

Piazzola v. *Watkins,* 442 F.2d 284 (5th Cir. 1971).

Pickings v. *Bruce,* 430 F.2d 595 (8th Cir. 1970).

Potter v. *North Carolina School of the Arts,* 245 S.E.2d 188 (N.C. App. 1978).

Pratz v. *Louisiana Polytechnic Institute,* 316 F.Supp. 872 (W.D. La. 1970); cert.den. 401 U.S. 1004 (1971).

Quinn v. *Sigma Rho Chapter Beta Theta Pi Fraternity,* 507 N.E.2d 1193 (Ill. App.4th Dist. 1987).

Radcliff v. *Landau,* 883 F.2d 1481 (9th Cir. 1989).

Regents v. *Bakke,* 98 S.Ct. 2733 (1978).

Regents of the University of Michigan v. *Ewing,* 106 S.Ct. 507 (1985).

Relyea v. *State,* 385 So.2d 1378 (Dist.Ct. App. Fla. 4th Dist. 1980).

Roemer v. *Board of Public Works,* 96 S.Ct. 2337 (1976).

Rowe v. *Chandler,* 332 F.Supp. 336 (D. Kans. 1971).

Schenck v. *United States,* 249 U.S. 47 (1919).

School Board of Nassau County, Florida v. *Arline,* 55 L.W. 4245 (1987).

Schornstein v. *New Jersey Division of Vocational Rehabilitational Services,* 519 F.Supp. 773 (D. N.J. 1981).

Schultz v. *Gould Academy,* 332 A.2d 368 (Maine 1975).

Shamloo v. *Mississippi State Board of Trustees, Etc.,* 620 F.2d 5168 (5th Cir. 1980).

Shelley v. *Kraemer,* 92 L.E.D.1161 (1947).

Shetina v. *Ohio University,* 459 N.E.2d 587 (Ohio App. 1983).

Siegel v. *Regents of the University of California,* 308 F.Supp. 832 (N.D. Calif. 1970).

Smith v. *Day,* 538 A.2d 157 (Vt. 1987).

Smith v. *Duquesne,* 612 F.Supp. 72 (W.D. Pa. Civ. Div. 1985).

Soglin v. *Kauffman,* 418 F.2d 163 (7th Cir. 1969).

Sohmer v. *Kinnard,* 535 F. Supp. 50 (D. Md. 1982).

Southeastern Community College v. *Davis,* 442 U.S. 397 (1979).

Stark v. *St. Cloud State University,* 802 F.2d 1046 (8th Cir. 1986).

State v. *Johnson,* 530 P.2d 910 (Ariz. App. Div. 2 1975).

State v. *Kappes,* 550 P.2d 121 (Ct. App. Ariz. Div. 1 Dept.A. 1976).

State v. *Schmid,* 423 A.2d 615 (N.J. 1980).

Steinberg v. *Chicago Medical School,* 371 N.E. 634 (Ill. 1977).

Stone v. *Cornell University,* 510 N.Y.S.2d 313 (A.D. 1987).

Students Against Apartheid Coalition v. *O'Neill I,* 660 F.Supp. 333 (W.D. Va. 1987).

Students Against Apartheid Coalition v. *O'Neill II,* 838 F.2d 735 (4th Cir. 1988).

Swanson v. *Wesley College,* 402 A.2d 401 (Del. Sup. Ct. Kent Co. 1979).

Sword v. *Fox,* 446 F.2d 1091 (4th Cir. 1971).

Tarasoff v. *Regents of the University of California,* 551 P.2d 334 (Calif. 1976).

Tayyari v. *New Mexico State University,* 495 F.Supp. 1365 (D. N.M. 1980).

Tilton v. *Richardson,* 403 U.S. 627 (1970).

Tinker v. *Des Moines Independent School Dist.,* 21 L.E.D.2d 731 (1969).

Torres v. *Puerto Rican Junior College,* 298 F.Supp. 458 (D. P.R. 1969).

United States v. *Board of Trustees for University of Alabama,* 908 F.2d 740 (11th Cir. 1990).

United States v. *Cole,* 302 F.Supp. 99 (D. Maine N.D. 1969).

United States v. *Commonwealth of Virginia,* 766 F.Supp. 1407 (D.W.D. Va. Roanoke Div. 1991).

University of Delaware v. *Keegan,* 349 A.2d 14 (Del. 1975); cert.den. 424 U.S. 934 (1975).

University of Denver v. *Whitlock,* 744 P.2d 54 (Colo. 1987).

University of Utah Students Against Apartheid v. *Peterson,* 649 F.Supp. 1200 (D. Utah C.D. 1986).

Uzzell v. *Friday,* 591 F.2d 997 (4th Cir. 1979).

Veed v. *Schwartzkoph,* 353 F.Supp. 149 (D. Nebr. 1973); aff'd 478 F.2d 1407 (8th Cir. 1973); cert.den. 414 U.S. 1135 (1973).

Wardlow v. *Peck,* 318 S.E.2d 270 (SC App. 1984).

Warren v. *Drake University,* 886 F.2d 200 (8th Cir. 1989).

Washington v. *Chrisman,* 102 S.Ct 812 (1982).

Widmar v. *Vincent,* 102 S.Ct. 269 (1981).

Witters v. *State Commission for the Blind,* 771 P.2d 1119 (Wash. 1989).

Wood v. *Strickland,* 95 S.Ct. 992 (1975).

Wright v. *Texas Southern University,* 392 F.2d 728 (5th Cir. 1968).

Zavala v. *Regents of the University of California,* 178 Calif. Rptr. 185 (App. 2nd Dist. Div. 4 1981).

20

~

Developing Effective
Campus and Community
Relationships

Arthur Sandeen

Student affairs, perhaps more than any other area of an institution, depends on cooperation and collaboration with others. The most serious error student affairs professionals can make is to isolate themselves, thinking they are an independent entity. If programs and policies are to achieve success, the student affairs staff will need to develop effective campus relationships. This process is an ongoing one for student affairs staff, one that requires thoughtful planning and considerable skills. The groups that are most important to student affairs staff are students, faculty, administrators, and the community. However, none of these groups is homogeneous; and to establish good relationships with them, student affairs staff must recognize and understand the many special cultures that are represented in each group.

In this chapter, the essential elements of good campus relations as well as key campus and community relationships, are identified. The benefits and outcomes of establishing positive working relationships are discussed, and the chapter closes with a practical set of issues that must be resolved on any campus.

Essential Elements of Good Campus Relations

Good campus relationships do not happen by accident. The development requires attention to detail and to the persons and constituency groups in-

300

volved in the situation or issue and is founded on certain essential elements: the administrator's personal and ethical characteristics; staff competence; willingness to listen and involve others; commitment to confidentiality; effective planning; and follow-up, where needed and appropriate.

Being Trustworthy and Honest

The most important quality in establishing good campus relations is honesty. Programs and policies must be represented in an open manner. When problems are encountered, they should be acknowledged and confronted. Trust is not granted automatically in an academic community; it has to be earned, and student affairs staff members must be worthy of it every day in their actions and words. Most members of the staff are quite visible in the campus community and are thus subjected to frequent scrutiny. Misrepresenting or exaggerating a program, problem, or issue will easily be noticed and will quickly result in a lack of credibility and support for student affairs staff. This situation is especially true of relationships with students, who may be testing their "elders" to see if they are honest and consistent in their actions. Chief student affairs officers should be sensitive to the integrity of their staff in its dealings with the campus community. They should set an example with their own actions and help their staffs understand that the credibility of all programs and policies in student affairs is a shared responsibility. Programs and policies, no matter how brilliant they may be, do not succeed on their own simply because they are good ideas. They succeed because student affairs staff make honest and persuasive proposals regarding them and implement them with skill and sensitivity. The most important factor in achieving such success is the trust that student affairs staff members have established in the campus community.

Being Competent

In order to establish good relationships with the various constituencies in the campus community, the student affairs staff must be able to demonstrate a high level of competence. The best way to "sell" a program or policy is to do a very good job with it! If a student, faculty, or community group benefits, it is very likely to continue support for a program. A poor performance by an individual can damage the reputation of the entire student affairs division; thus, a strong emphasis on high-quality work should characterize all the staff members' efforts. This is not to suggest that high risk or controversial initiatives should not be undertaken, for fear of failure. However, the staff should recognize its limitations and not assume the lead role in areas for which it is not prepared. Some student affairs staff members are so anxious to serve others and to be helpful that they may become involved in areas beyond their training. This practice can be damaging to students and will certainly erode the confidence of others. Establishing good relationships in the campus community requires the student affairs staff to show its ability to handle difficult problems and issues. It is important that the staff use its skills and training effectively in areas where it can make a positive contribution.

Listening and Involving

Earning the support and confidence of students, faculty, and community groups takes place primarily as a result of listening to their concerns and involving them in programs and policies. The student affairs staff rarely establishes good relationships in the campus community as a result of speech making and authoritative pronouncements. In their eagerness to establish themselves as powerful administrators, some in student affairs have erred by equating strength with the title of their position or with bold-sounding statements. Such actions inevitably antagonize others and damage, rather than develop, campus relationships. The most successful student affairs staff takes the time to learn about the special talents of faculty, students, and community members and then finds useful ways to involve these people in programs and policies. This approach requires sensitivity to the various campus and community cultures and a recognition that the campus is not one community, but several. A student affairs staff must have an open mind and be able to understand these several communities and their needs.

A common error that student affairs staff members who are new to a campus may make is to put programs and policies in place before listening to and understanding the special nature of the group being targeted. There are many similarities from one campus to another, but staff members should not assume that what they have done before will automatically work again on their new campus.

Maintaining Confidentiality

A student affairs staff in the course of its work learns about personal problems and other difficulties being experienced by students, faculty, and staff. If staff members are to establish and maintain good relations with these various groups, they must demonstrate that they can be trusted with confidential information. Engaging in campus gossip might be tempting at times, but it will surely diminish respect for the student affairs staff. Moreover, to share confidential information without adequate justification is a violation of professional obligations. If students and faculty and staff members perceive that some people in student affairs do not protect confidential information, then it will be impossible to create positive relationships with them.

Ensuring Effective Planning

The worst time to try to establish good relationships with various campus groups is during a crisis. Thus, it is important to build trust and to get to know student, faculty, and community groups before there are difficult problems to face. Student affairs staff members should know key elected officials, the police, community mental health staff, hospital personnel, and the city manager. They also should know the most influential faculty in the various academic organizations, as well as the formally elected leaders in the academic senate. Student affairs staff members should be visible participants and contributing members in campus and community organizations. This activity is very supportive of building effective relationships and is essential to the successful resolution of problems when they occur. All of this requires student affairs staff members to get out of their offices and into the campus's many communities. Planning ahead by creating strong support with these groups is often the basis of solving difficult problems.

Following Up

In delivering effective programs and policies, student affairs staff members must follow up with various campus groups; regular contacts are essential. If the student affairs staff is only seen with student, faculty, and community groups when there are problems, then its real commitment may be questioned. The best relationships are built as a result of genuine, regular contacts over a period of time. Following up often means simply attending a meeting of a group or organization and showing by one's presence an interest in the group's activities.

Key Campus and Community Relationships

It is important for a student affairs staff to understand the special nature of its campus. Each campus has unique characteristics, traditions, and problems. The most successful student affairs staff members are very sensitive observers of their campuses, and what they are able to accomplish is often a result of their abilities to establish close ties to major groups and organizations. The following groups are found in all campus communities, and the student affairs staff should know them and learn to work with them well.

Faculty

The faculty represents the most important campus resource available to student affairs staff. Without the support, understanding, and participation of the faculty, no student affairs division can succeed for long. Within the faculty on every campus, there are talents that can be tapped for the benefit of students and their out-of-class education. All student affairs staff members — in admissions and orientation, residence life and student counseling, financial aid, career development, and student health — should be engaged actively in efforts to involve the faculty in their programs and policies. Establishing positive relationships with faculty entails getting to know individual faculty members and their specific interests, and then finding ways to invite their participation in programs. Some staff members, feeling that they have sufficient knowledge and independence to implement programs on their own, may be reluctant to approach the faculty. Yet failure to make this connection often results in the isolation of the student affairs staff from the faculty, a situation that eventually harms the division and does not serve students very well either. Younger staff members may not be as confident as those more experienced in initiating these contacts for program and policy development and may benefit from some encouragement in this regard.

The most successful student affairs staff understands that the faculty, even on small campuses, comprises many smaller groups, often related to academic disciplines but sometimes to other interests as well. Student affairs staff must know faculty members well enough to be able to match their talents with particular student needs. A student affairs staff should know, for example, what faculty member can be asked to help a Chinese student facing a family tragedy; which one should (and should not!) be invited to moderate a debate on gay and lesbian issues; which one should mediate a dispute between African-American and Hispanic students; which should be recommended to the president for membership on the trustee committee on student life; and which faculty members would be most helpful in reviewing the fraternity and sorority system. These are only a few examples of how a student affairs staff can work with faculty. In each of them, the success of the effort depends on a strong student affairs staff–faculty liaison. Student affairs needs faculty support in order to thrive, and its staff should initiate these contacts, which can improve the education and growth of students.

The President

It is important for all student affairs staff members to understand the president's goals, priorities, and style. Their job is to support their institution and the president's objectives. The chief student affairs officer should take the lead in establishing a positive connection to the president, but other student affairs staff should be active participants in this process as well. Student affairs policies and programs need the understanding and support of the president, and the best way to ensure this is to develop a close working relationship. Some presidents enjoy frequent personal involvement with students and campus programs, and student affairs staff members can benefit from encouraging this activity. Other presidents prefer to spend their time on external affairs or are not very comfortable being directly concerned with student life. It is important for all student affairs staff members to be aware of the special interests and skills of their presidents. If they have made the effort to get to know the president and to inform him or her about the most critical issues and problems affecting students, then it is likely they will earn their chief executive officer's support. Some student affairs staff members may disagree at times with their president's approach to or decision about a campus issue. If good relationships have been created, then such disagreements are less likely to cause difficulty. Presidents need the insights and information that a student affairs staff can provide; and if mutual respect has been established, frank discussions of issues can take place, and better decisions can be made.

Other Major Administrators

Student affairs staff members interact frequently with academic, business, and development officers on their campuses. The staffs of these offices have a major impact on policies, programs, and issues affecting student affairs. It is important that these individuals understand admissions, housing, placement, counseling, health, and other student-related issues. All student affairs staff members should share in informing and involving those in academic, business, and development offices about student life activities. If effective relationships can be fostered with these other major administrative areas, the success of student affairs programs will be enhanced. When problems occur, it may be essential for student affairs staff to solicit the support and cooperation of academic, business, and development personnel. In an atmosphere of trust, solutions to problems are more likely to be humane, timely, and successful.

Governing Board Members

The chief student affairs officer should keep the staff well informed about the activities, objectives, and preferences of the board. Some board members may not be very visible in campus programs and student life, whereas others may be frequent participants. At times, this situation can be awkward for the student affairs staff; for example, a board member may express a view contradicting what the president has stated. Those on the staff should understand that it is the president who speaks about the institution to the board. They should not attempt to do so or to initiate contacts with board members on their own. In the course of their work, however, it is very likely that they will get to know various members of the board, and in many cases, such interaction can be good for the institution. The staff should keep the chief student affairs officer informed of these contacts. If a president feels that people in student affairs are misrepresenting the institution to the board, a very serious situation has developed. Board members may be quite interested in issues such as student demonstrations, the disciplinary status of a student, the registration of a controversial student group, the admissions status of an applicant, or the invitation of a speaker to the campus. If the student affairs staff has done its homework and has taken the time to get to know individuals on the board, then their conversations on issues such as this can be more candid and helpful. In all of its dealings with board members, the staff should remember that it must defer to the president and keep its chief student affairs officer well informed.

Alumni

The student affairs staff can often improve the quality of student life by establishing good relationships with alumni. Staff members can speak about the kinds of experiences and opportunities for students that are meaningful to alumni. These contacts can often result in enhanced support and understanding of student affairs programs. With the assistance of the development staff, student affairs staff can establish good relationships with key alumni on specific issues. These relationships can be enhanced by inviting alumni to various campus events and by involving them in discussions of important policy and program issues. With the increasing complexity of student affairs divisions, it is very important that the efforts of the staff not contradict or duplicate each other. It is very likely that housing, admissions, financial aid, placement, recreation, and student health all have persuasive programs and proposals to present to alumni, so it is essential that the chief student affairs officer coordinate these efforts. The development staff is key to success for student affairs in this area, and those in student affairs, with the knowledge they have about former students, can often make very helpful suggestions to their colleagues in development.

Parents

On campuses with significant numbers of traditional-age students, establishing strong ties to parents can be very helpful to student affairs. Many institutions have well-developed parent programs, with a staff member assigned to this function. All in student affairs should have contacts with parents and be sensitive to their concerns and interests. Parents can be excellent partners with the institution in the education of students, and student affairs staff should be the initiators of programs to increase their involvement. The chief student affairs officer should make sure that the institution's contacts with parents produce a coordinated and coherent message—especially in large universities, where many departments and colleges may want to conduct their own separate parent programs. Special weekends, seminars, advisory groups, fund-raising efforts, publications, and other programs may be conducted by the student affairs staff, but the success of all these efforts depends on relationships with parents. These can begin, of course, with the introduction of the institution to prospective students and their parents and should continue with a variety of academic, student life, financial, and other activities through graduation. Each of the major functional areas of student affairs should have a special understanding of parents' needs and interests, and these should be developed into a coordinated program. In establishing connections with parents, student affairs staff should listen carefully to their concerns before initiating programs and policies. When parents feel a real sense of involvement in the activities of their children's university, they are more likely to be helpful participants.

Community Members

Student affairs staff members should be visible and active participants in their communities. They should know the elected officials, the city manager, the police, the business leaders, the clergy, and personnel from the various health-related agencies. Such relationships are essential if problems are to be solved or if campus and community services and support are to be coordinated. When a troublesome issue arises in an off-campus apartment complex, a student death occurs, or the student government petitions a city commission on a controversial issue, it is crucial for student affairs staff to have forged sturdy links with community officials in advance. The lead should come from the chief student affairs officer, but those working in admissions, housing, counseling, placement, and other areas also have much at stake. At many institutions, the campus-community relationship is very close, and regular meetings throughout the year may be called to ensure good coordination and communication. Student affairs staff members should be very active in initiating such contacts and should find ways to involve students themselves in the process. With the rapid turnover of students from year to year, this is an effort that requires constant attention. The staff may have a tendency to get involved with community leaders only in response to crises. In this case, so much potential support goes unexploited. Most colleges and universities do not have sufficient resources to meet all of the needs they have for students, and with community assistance, many improvements can be made. Student affairs staff, by establishing positive relationships with community leaders, can significantly enhance the quality of life for their students.

Students and Student Groups

The division's most important constituency, of course, is the students. Without close bonds with students, the division's programs and policies cannot be successful. The student affairs staff should work to establish good relationships with all students, not just those who are the most visible, accessible, or compliant. Among the various offices, many different insights about students may exist that can be shared with others. The financial aid staff understands student problems with housing, student life, and counseling. Those who work in recreational sports often have unusual insights about students and student groups. Faculty advisers to student organizations have the opportunity to discover student interests and talents that can improve the quality of student life. Those working in student religious centers can also provide very valuable information. Staff members will usually get a distorted notion of student life if they restrict their contacts to those who visit their offices during the day. Every college or university comprises many smaller student communities; to understand student life on any campus requires that the staff learn about their needs, concerns, and customs. Student affairs staff members should be the campus experts on student culture and should determine its effect on programs and policies. All campuses, large and small, are complex, and no one staff member can know or be effective with every student group. However, the staff as a whole should be able to develop good working relations with most groups. Being sensitive to the special traditions and thinking of smaller student communities will enable student affairs staff to earn their respect and support. Without these, little can be accomplished.

Relationships with students and student groups are not always positive, as they may be engaged in activities that violate institutional rules or standards. Moreover, the student affairs staff may intervene with certain student communities in efforts to change their behavior. Even in these situations, very little can be achieved if the student affairs staff has not earned the respect of the group beforehand. Student groups involved in negative behavior need to be approached with consideration and candor. If constructive change is to occur, the staff will need to work with individuals in the group over a period of time. Very little education takes place as a result of authoritative decisions imposed by the staff on student groups; after harsh disciplinary action is taken, the real education should begin by working with the group in efforts to rebuild its strengths. The same principle obviously pertains to individual students. Student affairs staff members build well-known reputations among students and student groups over a period of time. Most frequently, student perceptions of the staff are accurate, as they are based on actual experience. Good relationships with students are earned as a result of taking the time to reach out to them in all corners of the campus community, of listening carefully to their concerns, and of demonstrating through consistent actions a commitment to them.

Expected Outcomes

The following discussion outlines the potential outcomes that can be anticipated as a result of good campus and community relations.

Support for Programs and Policies

The student affairs staff achieves success in its work largely as a result of collaboration with others. The support of students, faculty, other administrators, parents, and community members is essential to create sound programs and policies. All of this depends on the ability of student affairs staff to establish good relationships with the campus and the community. The various activities initiated by the student affairs division cannot stand alone, isolated from the institution.

Opportunity for Joint Projects with Others

One of the most rewarding aspects of close campus and community relationships is that they open up all kinds of opportunities for cooperative projects and activities. Staff in all division offices can initiate such projects, whether in admissions and orientation, career planning and counseling, or housing and student health. The best and most creative staff members understand that they can do much more for students' education when they forge coalitions with others within and without the campus. As stated previously, collaborative programs with parents, faculty, alumni, and community organizations can greatly enhance the quality of life on the campus and can also significantly extend the impact of the student affairs program. Few student affairs staffs have sufficient financial resources to do all the things that they would like, and joint projects, especially with those outside the institution, often can expand opportunities for students.

Effective Problem Solving

All of the student affairs staff is involved in problem-solving activities, some with individual students, some with groups. Many of these involve complex personal matters, financial difficulties, political and ethnic disputes, or conduct problems. The skills that members of the student affairs staff demonstrate in handling these issues are crucial to their success and survival as professionals. Unfortunately, they can resolve very few of these problems by themselves. The best people in student affairs recognize that their effectiveness in these situations depends on their ties to faculty, students, other administrators, and community members. Solutions to most problems can be found when the most sensitive and knowledgeable people can be involved; staff members should know who these people are in their campus communities. Most important, they need to have already earned their confidence and support.

Improved Sense of Community

The student affairs staff has as a principal goal the enhancement of the quality of life on its campus and in its community. At the same time, the staff is only a small part of the total institution and unable to achieve a sense of community all alone. Thus, staff members must work with others and encourage values supportive of a caring and open campus. They can be very effective leaders in this activity by bringing people together to consider the essential character of their campus communities. However, they must realize that these efforts depend on the relationships they have been able to build over a period of time.

Better Education for Students

The student affairs staff exists for the education of students. Everything it does must be directed to the goal of improving student learning. The staff recognizes that students learn better when they are significantly involved in an activity and when they have opportunities to interact with others while engaged in real projects. Most of what student affairs staff members do in their work with students is based upon these assumptions. It clearly follows that it is essential for the staff to be able to link students with many others in the campus community for a variety of learning activities. If this link is to be accomplished, student affairs staff members must have established good relationships with the groups that can affect students. Much of what the student affairs staff does is to enable things to happen, and its ability to invent coalitions with a variety of groups will have a great deal to do with its success.

Thoughts for Consideration

The following thoughts are presented for the consideration of student affairs staff members as they work to establish good relationships on their campuses and in their communities.

Who Should Decide Division Priorities?

The staff in each of the division's offices may be eager to create close ties to various groups on and off the campus. There is more than enough work for everyone. However, it is important to convey a coordinated and consistent message from the student affairs division; and of course it is the responsibility of the chief student affairs officer to see that this happens. There are persons on every student affairs staff whose talents and interests are particularly suited to certain groups and issues. Efforts should be made to ensure that these pairings are not left entirely to chance. Not every staff member in the division needs to have a close working relationship with the city police, the community health providers, the faculty in the pharmacy school, or the alumni association staff. However, the chief student affairs officer should make sure that someone on the staff works very closely with each of these groups and that what they hear is consistent. The information gathered by individual staff members in their dealings with such groups must be shared with others in student affairs in regular conversations about the campus community and its many components. Only through this sharing can the best educational programs continue to grow and improve. The chief student affairs officer should create an atmosphere within the staff that encourages such contacts and stimulates such creativity.

How Can Staff Learn the Importance of Campus Relations?

Most individuals in student affairs probably do not need much encouragement to move out and meet new campus and community groups. They understand that developing such relationships is essential to the success of programs and policies they want to implement. There may be a tendency among some staff members, however, to think that they simply offer a "service" and that their only job consists of providing it to whatever students who happen to visit their office. These people may be reluctant to reach out to groups simply because they have not done it before or because they lack the confidence to try. More experienced staff members can be of real assistance. The way to get staff members to do something new is not to lecture them but to ask them to join in some activity. Once people learn for themselves how new relationships with campus and community groups can enhance their work with students, they usually do not need any more prodding. In may ways, student affairs administration is the art of the possible, and the most valuable asset staff members can possess is their own imagination and initiative.

Which Approach Works Best?

Is there a most effective way to establish good relations with the campus and in the community? The same approach may not work for each staff member, as some are more comfortable with informal contacts and others may prefer more structured and planned meetings. There does not seem to be any substitute for personal, face-to-face contacts with campus and community groups. On the basis of these contacts, the staff will learn that the same method will probably not work equally well with the Filipino Student Union, the Rugby Club, the Gay and Lesbian Association, the Coalition for Conservative Action, and a social fraternity. Some groups may be offended by direct contacts initiated by student affairs staff; thus, the preferred approach may be to arrange an invitation from within the organization. Others may have felt unwanted or unappreciated for some time and may welcome the attention and concern expressed by the student affairs staff. Sometimes the best way is to work through others who already have established contacts within the group. It is not uncommon for some student affairs staff members to fail in their efforts to establish good relations with campus and community groups because they have not taken the time to learn how to contact them appropriately. The process requires that those in student affairs be very careful listeners and observers and that they adapt their approach to fit the special nature of the group.

What If Others Resist Cooperation?

All student affairs staff members must recognize that not all of their efforts to establish good relations will be successful. Some student groups may actively resist almost any attempt at involvement, and some faculty members may be openly skeptical about what student affairs may have to contribute. Indeed, such resistance certainly contributes to the decisions of some student affairs staffs to conduct their programs in isolation, for there are fewer obstacles and difficulties! However, very little of consequence can be achieved in this manner, and eventually, isolation can result in obscurity. The best student affairs staff members are always seeking better ways to approach campus and community groups, especially those that present the biggest challenges. They may at times have to resort to authoritarian methods (such as disciplining a fraternity) in order to get these groups' attention. However, these staff members realize that if they are going to have any positive influence over time, they need to establish good relations. Persistence and consistent performance are excellent strategies to use in student affairs. Eventually, at least one member of the student affairs staff is usually able to build a trusting relationship with a group.

Who Is Accountable?

It is obvious that when student affairs staff members enter into cooperative arrangements with campus and community groups, things become more complicated. With more people from different interests and backgrounds sharing the work load, some campus administrators may become nervous about who is in charge and even about who may be responsible. This situation presents a dilemma at times for chief student affairs officers, who on the one hand encourage coalitions with student, faculty, and community groups and on the other are worried about how predictable the results might be and who might be held accountable for them. Establishing good relationships with various groups should lead to more creative and worthwhile programs and policies, but it also increases the risk of failure, as a good deal of the control may be lost. But there really is no workable alternative in student affairs, as the very nature of the profession is cooperation and collaboration. Of course, the chief student affairs officer is ultimately accountable for what happens in the division. However, each staff member should be actively involved in establishing good relationships with campus and community groups and should understand the responsibility that the institution and the division asume in any cooperative project or program.

Summary

Student affairs administration is not an end unto itself. Its success depends on the quality and diversity of the relationships that the staff can develop with campus and community groups.

Trustworthiness and honesty, proven competence, highly developed listening skills, a commitment to involve others effectively, respect for confidentiality, and skill in planning are all essential in developing strong relationships with campus constituency groups and individuals. The time and effort spent in this effort is important, for the result is inevitably improvement in the quality of programs, policies, and the educational experience of students. The chief student affairs officer must demonstrate commitment to building relationships, set priorities, purposely involve staff, and take responsibility to assure that attention is paid to this important aspect of student affairs administration. Staff members who understand the special nature of diverse constituent groups will be highly valuable to their institution.

21

Conflict Management Skills

Don G. Creamer

Managing conflict is a major function of student affairs administration. Some student affairs administrators may spend as much as 40 percent of their time managing conflicts among people, functional units, and constituencies of the organization (Creamer, personal interviews, 1991). Conflicts that require a student affairs administrator's involvement may be uncomplicated and have the potential for only minor repercussions, or they may be intricate and hold the seeds of serious consequences, including for the organization itself. In either case, the ability of student affairs administrators to manage conflict may be a crucial determinant of their success or failure as leaders (Sandeen, 1991).

Conflicts arise regularly in any organization where people work and live together (Walton, 1987) and may be destructive or constructive depending on the nature of the conflict and the way it is handled (Baron, 1990). Unresolved conflicts over resources, authority, and purpose, for example, may lead to territoriality, protectiveness, and narrow-mindedness. If properly addressed, these same conflicts may reveal needed changes in the organization and lead to qualitative modifications to the educational agenda, expanded vision, renewed energy, and increased cooperation among organizational members.

How conflict is managed reflects the basic values of the organization and its people (Likert and Likert, 1976). The organization's facility to deal compassionately with its own problems, a major indication of its vitality, reflects its culture and attitudes and beliefs. Where the principles of fairness and concern for the integrity and worth of each individual characterizes this culture, administrators will act responsively and skillfully to resolve existing strife while simultaneously strengthening the capacities of the organization to achieve its mission.

This chapter will portray the general nature of conflicts faced by student affairs administrators and their colleagues in the larger higher education community. The chapter also will describe appropriate perspectives for understanding and resolving disputes through the application of both conflict management and conflict resolution skills. Brief vignettes of specific conflicts will be offered to illustrate the application of many perspectives, approaches, and skills in conflict management.

Nature of Conflicts in Student Affairs

Conflicts arise in almost any human interaction. They originate in competition for resources or influence, incompatible goals, antagonistic actions, divergent ideas or interests, inconsistent demands, unfair distribution of work, unfulfilled expectations, inequitable application of policies or regulations, and personality clashes. Most conflicts can be classified according to issues of fact, methodology, goals, or values (Williams, 1985).

Higher education is a fertile environment for conflict. Its intellectual character makes it a magnet for opposing ideas, demographic and cultural diversity, and multiplicity of objectives. The purposes of higher education are complex and far-ranging, often requiring maximum individual autonomy by its members and at the same time a designed coherence or unified focus to achieve its goals. Faculty members often have loyalties that are divided between their disciplines, their independent research, their professional service, and their students. Such high levels of individual autonomy within a unified organization inherently breed conflict even though the institution may encourage specially tailored self-governance systems and decentralized authority for decision making.

Student affairs administrators are called upon to relieve conflicts among people across the entire spectrum of the organization, but especially to deal with discord that involves students in some way. Some common examples of conflicts that require student affairs administrators' intervention include disputes between students and faculty, those between students and other students, those between university officials and parents of students, those between university officials and student organizations, and those arising from the competing interests of student and academic affairs. Examples of actual conflicts will illustrate these typical situations.

Student-Faculty Conflict

> David is enrolled in political philosophy class. He admittedly
> holds ultraconservative political views and adamantly opposes
> most social programs of the government. He complains that his
> professor is extremely liberal about social programs and that
> this professor has consistently awarded him lower grades than
> deserved because his views contradict those of the professor.
> David asks the dean of students to intervene on his behalf.

David's contention that his professor unfairly evaluated his academic
performance represents a student-faculty conflict that goes to the heart of
the basic character of higher education. Do all members of the organization
share the values of unfettered thought in a pluralistic and scholarly community? Faculty members evaluate students' performance every day. On a
campus of average size, interactions between students and their professors
occur thousands of times each year and have the potential to cause numerous
complaints that require administrative intervention.

Student-Student Conflict

> Kelly, a computer science major, and Charlotte, a music major,
> are roommates. Both express resentment toward the other over
> incompatible study schedules associated with their academic
> majors and over the other's annoying habits. Kelly needs to study
> in groups with other computer science majors, whereas Charlotte
> requires time alone for practice. Both often interrupt the study
> and sleep schedule of the other. Furthermore, Kelly has a girl-
> friend from her hometown who likes to visit and to stay in the
> residence hall room. Kelly typically asks Charlotte if it is okay
> for her friend to stay over, and Charlotte generally says, "Sure
> it's okay." But she secretly harbors resentment for the intrusion.
> Charlotte complains to her parents and to others but not to Kelly.
> Both ask the director of residence life to be reassigned to another
> room.

This situation represents a classic student-student conflict. Roommate
disputes and other conflicts between students are the most common type
that demand attention by student affairs administrators (Hayes and Balogh,
1990). On the surface, this conflict may be relatively uncomplicated and
the solution obvious; yet meaningful issues for an educational institution
are embedded in the predicament. Is not diversity among students a fundamental condition for learning? If all students live and work only with others
like them and heterogeneity is removed, what are the educational conse-

quences for students' development? Here is a situation where a relationship is carried on without meaningful communication and represents a powerful "teaching moment" for student affairs administrators if the problem is handled properly.

University-Parent Conflict

Kimberly has attempted to take her life several times. The director of the counseling center, the director of the health services, and the dean of students have intervened. Kimberly's parents have been informed by these officials that immediate medical assistance and therapy are needed; yet the parents have resisted taking any action and have argued, "Kimberly wants to be in school." The university officials have considered forcing Kimberly to leave school and seek help but fear that to take such action may push her "over the edge."

This dispute between university officials and parents may literally conceal life-or-death consequences. What are the ethical implications of any decision that might be made by institutional officials? (See Chapter Twenty-Two in this volume.) Are there broader policy implications beyond this case? Many questions arise. University-parent disputes are fortunately not all life threatening or always complicated. Parents may simply have too little information about university services or may have heard only one side of a dispute involving their son or daughter.

University–Student Organization Conflict

The *Collegiate News* is the campus student newspaper and is the most prestigious of the student media organizations. It is housed free of charge in the student center, as are other student media groups, and is a profitable enterprise. Over time, the organization has purchased considerable equipment, some with its own funds and some with university funds offered by the administration out of a desire to support and promote the student press. Serious controversies have arisen between the university and the *Collegiate News* over its content, and the *News* has threatened to move off campus. The editors have been informed that the university owns the name of the publication and much of the equipment and that if the current editors and the other members of their organization move off campus, the university will reestablish the *News* on campus using other students. The editors dispute the university's claim to ownership and tacitly invite the university to sue them. The president of the university, alarmed over the public relations fallout from a situation pitting the university in court battle with one of its own student organizations, instructs the vice president of student affairs to intervene and find a solution.

This dispute places a powerful student organization in opposition to the university. It is a situation familiar to student affairs administrators on many campuses. Student editors and writers like to think of themselves as colleagues with members of the press in the larger society, and they want to exercise their freedom-of-the-press prerogatives. University officials also want a free press on campus, and they want students to have real-life experiences associated with the print media. But antagonism between a student-run press — not always demonstrating mature judgment or acceptance of the consequences of open expression — and university officials — concerned about many other issues than interpretations of the exercise of freedom of press rights — is rampant in American higher education.

Competing Interests of Student and Academic Affairs

The director of the university's honors program has proposed that Jackson Hall, the most homelike and sought-after residence hall on campus, be converted to the Morrill Center for Advanced Studies to house the faculty and administration associated with the honors program and seniors completing supervised honor projects. The center, named after the author of the Land-Grant Act of 1862, would signal respect for the land-grant tradition and underscore the university's commitment to academic excellence. The project is viewed by university academic leaders and by the president as a very attractive proposal that fits in with many other ongoing plans. The project is viewed by student affairs leaders as desirable for all the reasons cited by academic leaders but also as detrimental to efforts to enhance the overall quality of life for undergraduate students. Jackson Hall possesses a livable character not available in any other hall. It stands as a symbol for the priorities given to students in university decisions.

Student affairs administrators in this situation are torn between competing interests of equal importance. They know that their often-stated formal position, recognizing the "preeminance of the academic mission" (National Association of Student Personnel Administrators, 1989, p. 12), is on the line. Which is more important? The benefit to academic excellence or the priority given to student life? Should student affairs be forced to give up its best residence hall?

Seeking advantage, reciprocity, or fairness between student affairs interests and those of other administrators, faculty, governance systems, and external groups is a constant factor in student affairs administration. Other administrators may interpret policies from the perspective that student affairs concerns can cause conflict. Some faculty members who represent a value system unfriendly to student social and personal development may pit student affairs administrators against powerful political forces on campus. Governance systems in which student affairs interests are underrepresented may result in unfair competition for resources and authority over significant policies. And community interest groups with significant political clout sometimes force student affairs administrators to make compromises that represent serious threats to their values. Such wide-ranging conditions cast student affairs administrators into conflict management roles that are near constant and that have significant consequences for their institutions.

Perspectives for Constructive Conflict Management

Decisions about conflict management may be made from three interrelated viewpoints: student development, organizational development, and community development. Each represents a coherent set of values consistent with the core values and purposes of higher education. The student development perspective acknowledges the centrality of student learning and seeks to preserve the focus on learning in dispute resolution. The organizational development perspective recognizes the significance of institutional well-being as a prerequisite to carrying out all functions of higher education and attempts to maintain this condition in disputes. The community development point of view comprehends the connections between individuals, organizations, and society and encourages decisions that respect the moral commitments that bind these together.

Student Development Perspective

The student development approach recognizes that student learning and growth are the essence of education and that they should be preserved when disputes are handled. The central question here is, What resolution will ensure that students profit educationally from the outcome? A resolution that arises from this perspective may not guarantee student satisfaction or happiness, but it will maintain a healthy developmental environment, one enriched by challenge and support. The roommate friction described about Kelly and Charlotte offers a clear opportunity to apply the student development perspective in conflict resolution. The guiding principle in this case should be the following: How can this disagreement be settled so that both students involved directly, and possibly other students, learn or grow from the experience?

Organizational Development Perspective

The organizational development viewpoint links the achievement of all aims of education to organizational well-being. Educational purposes can best be accomplished and student development facilitated when the organization is fully capable of accomplishing its goals. The important question is, What resolution will make the institution better able to achieve its mission? A resolution that occurs using this perspective considers competing interests and strives for a resolution in which all organizational interests are served. The proposal to convert Jackson Hall from a standard residence hall to a center for advanced studies appears on the surface to pit traditional student affairs interests against basic academic affairs concerns; yet the application of the principle of shared advantage may yield benefits to the overall health of the organization that in turn may bestow gains on both student and academic affairs.

Community Development Perspective

The community development perspective recognizes that the foundation of higher education is built upon societal values that guide both organizational and participant goals. Thus, both student and organizational development interests are molded by the values or interests of society. The fundamental question is, What resolution will preserve the values of the largest community? A solution using this perspective would seek to preserve the human system as the highest virtue and to serve the interests of all people. The dissension between the university and Kimberly's parents described earlier ignores societal respect for life. The community development viewpoint applies universal principles that bind people together.

Each of these approaches to conflict management allows the student affairs administrator to seek moral resolutions consistent with the core values of higher education and the personal goals of individuals. The perspectives encompass ever-larger concerns, from ensuring student learning and development, to guaranteeing institutional well-being, to preserving societal values.

Approaches to Conflict Management

Student affairs administrators may approach conflicts within their institutions in two ways. First, they may strive to create and sustain a particular social system or organizational culture that reflects common values of the organization. This strategy, which results in the establishment of organizational predispositions to act when challenges to the system of the culture occur, may be called conflict management. Second, student affairs administrators may prepare to use a variety of professsional skills and competencies designed to reduce dissension within the organization. This tactic, which relies on human resources to restore organizational stability and direction, may be called conflict resolution.

Conflict Management

As conflicts between the organization's various units and between the people of the organization and its widely ranging constituents are inevitable, it is sensible to consciously install mechanisms that will permit the handling of potentially disruptive actions in a manner that results in positive, rather than negative, consequences. Most of the literature giving guidance for constructive action in conflict management comes from the field of organizational development (Boyer and Crockett, 1973; Likert and Likert, 1976; Schmuck and Runkel; 1985; Walton, 1987). A common theme of organizational development is that effective social systems are built upon democratic and humanistic values and are structured to empower the people of the organization to participate fully in all organizational actions.

Likert and Likert's (1976) argument will serve to illustrate the organizational development perspective. They suggest that "the management of conflict can be improved substantially by replacing the traditional structure and processes of organizations with those based on a more effective social system" (p. 71). Likert and Likert believe that a win-lose mentality in conflict management should be replaced by a win-win predisposition that strengthens capabilities of organizational members in communication, influence, responsibility, motivation, coordination, and decision making. A win-win predisposition creates a better social system and results in greater organizational performance, productivity, and satisfaction (Likert and Likert, 1976).

How can everyone "win" in a dispute? In reality, winning may not be possible for everyone involved, but the healthy organization, the one seeking a social system composed of democratic and humanistic values, will be working to achieve that end. The central task, says Baron (1990), is to manage the process to maximize the benefits and minimize the disruptive effects. The effective organization views conflict as revealing dysfunctional practices and as offering an opportunity for dialogue that may lead to remedies that further strengthen the organization's decision-making capacities (Walton, 1987). Conflict may also reveal new and important insights about the institutional character. This kind of organization does not fear conflict; it plans for it. Moreover, this organization does not seek to hide disagreement; it welcomes multiple views in its decision-making apparatus.

A key feature of the particular approach of Likert and Likert (1976) is the argument for using participative decision making, supportive relationships, and effective groups to develop a social system that undergirds strong conflict management capabilities. Each element of management then recognizes the interdependence of the people of the organization and of its goals (Tjosvold, 1990). *Participative decision making* means that members' views will be sought and valued when important decision are made. *Supportive relationships* means that people know that they will be called upon to support the efforts of others and that they in turn will be helped. *Effective groups* means that individuals understand that they are vital components of organizational teams with interconnected needs and rewards. When the principles of participative decision making, supportive relationships, and effective groups are widely known and practiced, members of the organization know that the vibrancy of the culture of which they are a part depends upon their individual and group contributions and that conflict must be resolved in a manner that does not destroy these sensitive interdependencies. Members in this type of organization also know that dialogue will precede and will be a part of solutions to all conflicts.

Thus, the manner in which an organization's people interact both routinely and in a crisis is a key variable in conflict management. The skillful conflict manager is a person who has prepared the organization for dealing with inevitable disputes by empowering each person to serve as an integral part of the organization in its everyday activities.

Conflict Resolution

In conflict resolution, student affairs administrators may approach a settlement through negotiation, mediation, or arbitration.

Negotiation may be viewed as joint decision making (Pruitt, 1981) that brings about agreement through conference, discussion, and compromise. Negotiation is the most common approach to conflict resolution. It often occurs as a routine duty for student affairs administrators as they carry on their daily activities. All student affairs professionals should be proficient in negotiation skills.

Negotiation may be indicated in the roommate conflict between Kelly and Charlotte, where an honest dialogue between the two is lacking. Negotiation also may be required in the case of Kimberly, even though the situation harbors a more immediate threat to the student's well-being. The negotiator's demonstration of communication skills in a relatively safe environment can have a healing effect.

Mediation refers to third-party intervention in a conflict (Burrell, 1990) that is "a voluntary, informal, confidential, and structural problem-solving and decision-making process that occurs within a cooperative environment" (Beeler, 1986).

Some suggest that the practice of mediation is growing (Hayes and Balogh, 1990; McCarthy, 1980) and is needed when a dispute is sufficiently serious or has proven unyielding to other methods of resolution. It may also be indicated in highly visible disputes. In a case where two highly acclaimed performing units, such as organized bands, expect to be scheduled at a prestigious event when only one can perform, a long-term compromise solution is necessary. A unilateral administrative decision in this case, no matter how wise, may not yield the best result. When two or more valued student affairs administrators have a history of implacable hostility toward one another, mediation by a third party, such as a trusted faculty member, may be indicated.

Arbitration employs the selection or appointment of a third party to determine final resolution of a dispute. Arbitration is "a quasi-judicial process in which the arbitrator listens to testimony and renders a decision based on this testimony" (McCarthy, 1980, p. 3). This approach to conflict resolution is rarely used by student affairs administrators and will not be discussed further in this chapter, though it may be employed in labor union contract disputes.

Skills in Conflict Management

Conflict management and conflict resolution skills are often indistinguishable from general abilities associated with good administration or management. It is likely that student affairs administrators who deal constructively with both the institution and its students are also sound managers of conflict. Thus, distinctions between skills associated with conflict management and those required for conflict resolution are difficult and could be challenged as imaginary or conjectural. One possible distinction is that actions taken for the benefit of the organization as a whole can be roughly associated with conflict management; those taken for the benefit of individuals can be linked to conflict resolution.

Conflict Management Skills

The ability to manage conflict stems from sensitivity to organizational culture, insight into internal and external forces inducing change, understanding of organizational behaviors, knowledge of organizational functioning, vision about the organization's future, the capability to plan for alternative futures, the talent to formulate unambiguous policies and procedures, the provision of leadership in implementing policies, a talent for personnel supervision and evaluation, and a respect for fairness. Conflict managers are shapers of organizational culture and most demonstrate keen insight into dynamics of institutional symbols, artifacts, values, and behaviors (Kuh and Whitt, 1988). They are magnets for collaborative actions of others and may, for example, create conflict resolution teams, composed of representatives of the organization trained to settle disputes. This tactic is recommended by Sandeen (1991).

Conflict Resolution Skills

Negotiation and mediation call for overlapping talents. The setting of the resolution activities is more likely to vary than the skills used. Mediation may occur more publicly than negotiation and may underscore the importance of patience, timing, self-confidence, and knowledge of the situation (Sandeen, 1991); it may also raise the stakes of the outcome.

Conflict resolution may require proficiency in making arrangements for meetings, establishing rules for decision making, collecting information, asking questions, listening, using interactive communication, reading cues, stating one's own views, making suggestions, summarizing views, setting agendas, diagnosing conflicts, and being fair (Beeler, 1986; Burrell, 1990; Hayes and Balogh, 1990; Walton, 1987). These are commonplace requirements for educators and administrators of educational institutions; their careful use is crucial for negotiation and conflict mediation, however.

A subtle issue in conflict resolution is the use of power. Most authorities agree that the exercise of some power is helpful, but its use is a sensitive issue. Power may come from at least two sources: (1) ascribed role or status in an organization and (2) knowledge of the issues and of the organizational culture. How much power is necessary or useful in negotiation or conflict mediation? Sometimes the nature of a conflict demands that it be handled by a certain institutional leader with specific responsibilities. A parent who is distressed by perceived mistreatment of a son or daughter may not be satisfied with a decision that comes from a midlevel manager. Sometimes unique or complex circumstances dictate the involvement of persons known to possess penetrating insights into a situation. The faculty may scorn a decision to add a freshman seminar to the curriculum if the decision is made unilaterally by student affairs personnel. Sometimes occasions call for a neutral party without specific administrative portfolio or unusual knowledge of the circumstances of the dispute. Instead, disputants may prefer a person with a reputation for fairness and objectivity to settle their differences.

Applications of Conflict Management Skills

The application of conflict management skills is appropriate to all disputes. Metaphorically, they act as a rudder to give direction to the course of the institution. The student affairs administrator is at the helm, steering the institution by preparing it for every contingency. The application of conflict resolution skills may vary according to the nature of the conflict and the approach taken. Their use acts as a tactical response to turbulence.

Sandeen reminds us, "The process used in settling disputes may be just as important as the eventual decision. Student affairs administrators often transmit stronger messages to students by the way they approach problems than they do by the actual policy outcomes" (1991, p. 124). This is sound advice and underscores the importance of choosing the proper approach when resolving conflicts—that is, recognize the prevailing values in a particular situation.

Examine the cases of David, Kelly and Charlotte, Kimberly, the *Collegiate News,* and the proposal to establish a center for advanced studies to consider the role of perspectives and specific application of talents and skills in handling these situations. At first glance, David's situation appears to identify a single impediment to his learning. The simple solution is to negotiate a reevaluation of his work in the class where the dispute arose, perhaps involving the instructor and the department head. Yet is David's grade all that is at stake in this situation? This situation calls for a broader perspective, one that considers the total organization and assesses whether its values are being eroded. Furthermore, intervention into this situation by a student affairs administrator might have politically explosive consequences. Issues of academic freedom and faculty-performance evaluation may loom just over the horizon and may call for intervention only by especially empowered individuals who, even then, may require extraordinary talents. David's situation demands action, but it involves institutional politics and sensitive issues that call for wisdom, vision, and patience. It also entails the use of some form of mediation to effect possible change in the attitude and behavior of the teacher. It is possible that a dispute about such fundamental academic issues could involve college- and university-level administrators, faculty governance systems, student honor court systems, and governing boards.

As stated previously, the dispute between Kelly and Charlotte offers a powerful teachable moment for the two students and—to the extent that the resolution may effect institutional policies—for all students. It calls for the application of the student development perspective that focuses on enhancing learning opportunities. The use of a negotiation approach seems warranted in this case, probably by the director of residential programs or someone acting for the director. The pressing issues in this dispute include a breakdown in communication between the two students and a seemingly incompatible schedule. The negotiator might show what good communication is and thereby teach the students to use the same skills in future interactions. Taking care to expose the students to all the administrative issues associated with such action, the negotiator also may involve the two students in a decision about whether they continue living together. Whether Kelly and Charlotte remain roommates may be a secondary issue. Whether they learn to encounter others constructively and to represent their own interests in productive dialogue is vital to the resolution.

Kimberly's case has such critical implications and represents such pervasive interests that only the community development perspective allows for consideration of all contingencies. Kimberly is desperate. Her cries for help have been ignored by her parents. University officials have undertaken all prudent actions. Yet the problem remains. What can be done to protect the fundamental value of this student's life? Many administrators may be involved in this case, including the director of residential programs, the dean of students, the director of counseling, the director of health services, the vice president for student affairs, and even the president. First, this is a situation that involves extensive knowledge of physical and mental health issues, institutional responsibilities, and the availability of community resources. It calls for interventions at many levels. Personal counseling and therapy are obviously indicated. Consultation among institutional "care teams" is needed as well as negotiation with the student and with the parents. Perhaps some form of mediation by an independent representative of the health agencies of the community would be helpful. Ultimately, an arbitration-like decision (perhaps by a medical-legal team) may be required, though the technical use of arbitration is not called for here. Each of these actions should be taken while exercising skills of communicating, information giving and collecting, diagnosing, and summarizing at their highest levels.

The conflict between the university and the *Collegiate News* represents an archetypal clash over interpretations of student rights and freedoms, ownership of property, and status and image. The concern of the university to provide an environment rich in opportunities for democratic living is pitted against the interest of the students to exercise constitutionally guaranteed freedoms in our society. This is a circumstance laden with threats to student development, organizational development, and community development perspectives. The dominant and most pressing threat, however, seems to be associated with organizational development. The situation calls for dialogue between student media organizations and university officials, clarification of rights and responsibilities, fact finding, articulation of opposing views, objective review of alternative solutions, and decision making. Intervention by the vice president for student affairs, the vice president for administration, the director of public relations, the institution's legal counsel, and possibly the president may be in order. It is a disagreement that suggests the use of negotiation first and, if necessary, mediation. Persons handling the resolution process should possess power associated with official status in the organization and with knowledge of the institutional culture, university policies, legal obligations and constraints, and educational philosophy. Compromise may be necessary; thus, patience with disputants and influence with university policy makers may be required.

The proposal to create a center for advanced studies for honors students and faculty reflects a real conflict of interests between student and academic affairs, but it also exhibits clear opportunities for all parties. It can be viewed from an organizational development perspective to hold advantages for all and involves the vice president for academic affairs, the vice president for student affairs, the director of advanced studies, and the director of residential programs. The essential tactic is to ensure that all members of the organization are given full information about the proposal. Through dialogue with representatives of student and academic affairs, all issues germane to both can be articulated. Although establishing the center will require substantial change, its presence in the academic community will produce real benefits for students, faculty, and other constituencies of the institution. It is a clear example of a win-win situation, and so long as the negotiators always keep that perspective in mind, everyone should gain.

Summary

Higher education is rife with conflicts, as well it should be, given its nature and purpose in American society. Managing these conflicts falls to some degree on student affairs administrators, who must help prepare the institution for disagreements among its members and act directly in the resolution of specific disputes. Appropriate approaches to conflict management and resolution are found in the overlapping conceptual perspectives of student development, organizational development, and community development. Conflict management skills are anchored in building an effective social system or culture for the institution. The foundation of conflict resolution skills lies in open dialogue, information sharing, and the exercise of fairness and good judgment.

References

Baron, R. A. Introduction. In M. A. Rahim (ed.), *Theory and Research in Conflict Management.* New York: Praeger, 1990.

Beeler, K. D. "Campus Mediation: A Promising Complement to Student Judicial Processes." *SACSA Journal,* 1986, *7* (1), 38–45.

Boyer, R. K., and Crockett, C. "Organizational Development in Higher Education: Introduction." *Journal of Higher Education,* 1973, *44* (5), 339–351.

Burrell, N.A. "To Probe or Not to Probe: Evaluating Mediators' Question-Asking Behaviors." In M. A. Rahim (ed.), *Theory and Research in Conflict Management.* New York: Praeger, 1990.

Hayes, J. A., and Balogh, C. P. "Mediation: An Emerging Form of Dispute Resolution on College Campuses." *NASPA Journal,* 1990, *27* (3), 236–240.

Kuh, G. D., and Whitt, E. J. *The Invisible Tapestry: Culture in American Colleges and Universities.* ASHE-ERIC Higher Education Report, no. 1. Washington, D.C.: Association for the Study of Higher Education, 1988.

Likert, R., and Likert, J. G. *New Ways of Managing Conflict.* New York: McGraw-Hill, 1976.

McCarthy, J. E. "Conflict and Mediation in the Academy." In J. E. McCarthy (ed.), *Resolving Conflict in Higher Education.* New Directions in Higher Education, no. 32. San Francisco: Jossey-Bass, 1980.

National Association of Student Personnel Administrators. "A Perspective on Student Affairs." In *Points of View.* Washington, D.C.: National Association of Student Personnel Administrators, 1989. (Originally published 1987.)

Pruitt, D. G. *Negotiation Behavior.* San Diego, Calif.: Academic Press, 1981.

Sandeen, A. *The Chief Student Affairs Officer: Leader, Manager, Mediator, Educator.* San Francisco: Jossey-Bass, 1991.

Schmuck, R. A., and Runkel, P. J. *The Handbook of Organization Development in Schools.* (3rd ed.) Prospect Heights, Ill.: Waveland, 1985.

Tjosvold, D. "The Goal Interdependence Approach to Communication in Conflict: An Organizational Study." In M. A. Rahim (ed.), *Theory and Research in Conflict Management.* New York: Praeger, 1990.

Walton, R. E. *Managing Conflict: Interpersonal Dialogue and Third-Party Roles.* Reading, Mass.: Addison-Wesley, 1987.

Williams, M. J., Jr. "The Management of Conflict." In R. J. Fecher (ed.), *Applying Corporate Management Strategies.* New Directions for Higher Education, no. 50. San Francisco: Jossey-Bass, 1985.

22

ತಿ

Maintaining High
Ethical Standards

Harry J. Canon

Jean Fortunato is director of student activities at Turner College. She and her assistant director, Jim Forbes, are working on plans for the annual student leadership retreat, a very successful event that Jean introduced to the Turner campus when she arrived three years ago. It appears that cuts in the student services budget may call for cancellation of the retreat, a $1,500 item.

Jim tells Jean that a service-club colleague, a vice president at one of the local banks, has said that it might have some money to invest in a student program in exchange for an opportunity to tell students about its automobile loan plan for graduating seniors. In fact, Jim is feeling pretty good about having set up a tentative deal with the banker, subject to Jean's approval, of course. Essentially, the bank will pay for a third of the cost of the retreat in exchange for a chance to make a twenty-five-minute presentation.

The real world of professional practice in student affairs contains a variety of circumstances that present ethical dilemmas. As Jean Fortunato and Jim Forbes are about to be reminded, these are an ongoing, and sometimes confounding, part of our professional existence.

In this chapter, we will explore clues to understanding that ethical problems exist, review principles that help focus on key issues in resolving ethical conflicts, discuss so-called practical and political implications of ethical decisions, identify and examine the critical roles played by the moral environment (the quality of the ethical community), and conclude with a review of emerging practices in academic communities that appear to pose new and infrequently considered dilemmas.

Ethical Sensitivity

If one had to identify the single most critical barrier to a sustained high quality of ethical practice in student affairs, it would probably be the difficulty of recognizing that an ethical problem has presented itself.

Jim Forbes might well take understandable pride in having arranged a deal with local business interests that promises to salvage a program that has benefited prospective student leaders and won praise for his agency in campus circles. All of this was accomplished in the entrepreneurial spirit consistent with initiatives in the academic community in the last decade or so. What remains to be assessed is the appropriateness of trading twenty-five minutes with a captive audience for the partial financing of the retreat, the permission of the participants, and the implied endorsement of the bank and its loan program. Indeed, it is as yet unclear whether Jean Fortunato will raise the issue with her subordinate or if it will even occur to her that accepting this particular solution to her problem may represent a moral compromise. Degrees of self-interest, even in the pursuit of laudable goals for others, could thus serve to blind Jean Fortunato and Jim Forbes to the existence of a potential ethical issue. Such lack of awareness in the face of other and seemingly more pressing professional challenges are not uncommon. It is an unfortunate but probably manageable part of our human and professional condition.

Rest (1984) acknowledges the importance of the first step in his identification of components essential to moral behavior. The first component, *moral awareness,* requires that the individual recognize "how . . . lines of action would affect the welfare of each party involved" (p. 19). For well over a decade and in a variety of forums, Brown (1985 and 1989; Brown and Canon, 1978) has reiterated his concern that student services professionals give greater priority to recognizing and addressing ethical issues. It is important to acknowledge the probability that failures in this direction are less likely to be the result of conscious wrongdoing on the part of practitioners than of mere oversight. How often have even the most ethically conscientious practitioners said to themselves, "I just never thought . . . ?"

It seems useful to start with the assumption that most people, especially our colleagues, want to do the right thing. That premise allows us and our colleagues to rethink hasty decisions. Assuming that others desire to do good also serves as an antidote to the appearance of self-righteousness. At times, some co-workers seem to be consistently unaware of the conflicts of interest in which they find themselves. As a mutual friend once said of such a person, "He needs a keeper." In truth, the individual in question seemed oblivious to certain kinds of ethical conflicts without a colleague willing to offer gentle guidance.

There are those who have been fortunate enough to have gained experience as professionals in settings where ethical discourse is a part of the ongoing professional exchange. Thanks to that circumstance, they have developed a set of clinical skills that serve as a kind of ethical radar. Regular exposure to a broad range of moral issues has fostered heightened sensitivity to the situational cues that serve as markers for ethical dilemmas. Those professionals who are in possession of such skills have a special obligation to place that awareness, that ability to recognize ethical concerns, at the service of their colleagues.

For still others, ethical discourse may have been confined to a particular graduate course or was limited to those situations specifically enumerated in a professional code of ethics. Raising a topic with ethical content then comes less easily, feels more intimidating, and if broached at all, may carry a note of apology or embarrassment. And because there has been little sustained experience in dealing with professional ethical concerns, the ability to identify them quickly and readily may be limited.

Probably for all of us, an acute awareness of our own human frailty serves as an impediment to expressing an ethical concern. Apprehensiveness about giving offense to a colleague or of appearing self-righteous need not be a significant barrier. If the issue is raised with appropriate tentativeness and in a mode that reflects clear concern for the parties involved (Canon, 1989, p. 77), the impediments just noted will seem much less overwhelming.

If ethical dilemmas are to be recognized, then, it is imperative that those who are most skilled in their identification speak out. The individual who takes such action implicitly gives permission to other colleagues to address the matter and, further, assists them to learn what constitutes a moral issue.

In our first case, it seems likely that Jean Fortunato, in her position as agency director and Jim Forbes's supervisor, is in the best position to raise the possibility of an ethical dilemma. Empowered individuals like Ms. Fortunato can assert potentially controversial positions with less personal and professional risk. *How* she broaches the matter to Jim will, of course, make a difference in how he responds to her query. Essentially, the professional who is able and willing to sustain a pattern of identifying and exploring moral concerns plays a key role in the formation of an ethical environment. Other dimensions that assist in the development of an ethical community will be discussed later in this chapter.

Application of Ethical Principles

Largely as a result of the work of Kitchener (1985), student services professionals have turned in increasing numbers to the use of certain principles in resolving moral dilemmas. Though there has certainly been no whole-sale abandonment of professional ethical codes, even the process of formulating these (American College Personnel Association, 1990) has been informed by selected ethical principles. Because they have been widely adopted and referred to by student services professionals, we will use the principles enunciated by Kitchener. It should also be noted that Kitchener has been careful to acknowledge that her contribution is rooted in the work of Beauchamp and Childress (1979). The review that follows is brief and is intended as a reminder; for an expanded discussion, see Kitchener (1985) and Kitchener and Harding (1990).

Five Ethical Principles

• Respect autonomy. It is assumed that individuals have the right to decide how they live their lives, as long as their actions do not interfere with the welfare of others. One has freedom of thought and choice.

• Do no harm. The obligation to avoid inflicting either physical or psychological harm on others and to avoid actions that put others at risk is a primary ethical principle in the helping professions.

• Help others. There is an obligation to enhance the welfare of others. Those in the helping professions assume that the welfare of the consumer comes first when other considerations are equal.

• Be just. To be just in dealing with others means to offer equal treatment to all, to afford each individual his or her due, to be fair. It presumes reciprocity and impartiality.

• Be trustworthy. One should keep promises, tell the truth, be loyal, and maintain respect and civility in human discourse. Only insofar as we deserve it can we expect to be seen as trustworthy.

In general, Kitchener observes that ethical principles commonly come into conflict with each other as they are applied to real-life situations. No principle is absolute. Occasions will occur when the violation of one or more principles is required to meet a higher standard of conduct. Nonetheless, Kitchener notes that violating any of the principles, whether because they are in conflict with each other or because a higher moral purpose might be served, places a strong burden on the individual to provide a rationale for rejecting the principle.

Let us see how the principles might be applied in one ethical dilemma.

Marty is nearing the end of the first semester of her internship in the office of the dean of students where she is being supervised by Dale, the college's conduct officer. After much soul-searching, Marty admits that she has strong feelings for Dale. Dale asks for some time to think about this development and comes back the next day to tell Marty that the feelings are reciprocated. Both Dale and Marty are shaken by this turn of events and wind up spending long hours discussing what to do. They are alternately exhilarated by the possibility of a shared future and distressed about a dual relationship that both find unthinkable.

They ultimately make an appointment with Dale's supervisor, the dean of students, to advise him of their emerging personal relationship and seek his assistance in finding a professionally acceptable solution. Almost before their description of their situation and expression of concern has been completed, the dean angrily charges Dale with unprofessional conduct, threatens to put a formal letter of reprimand in her folder, and tells Marty that her internship is terminated as of that moment.

The dilemma in which Marty, Dale, and the dean of students find themselves is complex, not unlike the circumstances that commonly accompany many ethical conundrums. The *autonomy* to which Marty and Dale might ordinarily be entitled as their relationship evolves is significantly constrained by the inequality in the professional dimension of their lives. As Marty's internship supervisor, Dale has the responsibility to evaluate and the presumed power to enforce outcomes of the evaluation process. That empowerment also calls on Dale to refrain from placing herself in situations that are potentially exploitative of Marty, and the exchange of affection under these circumstances has a clear potential for exploitation and *harm*. With that potential in mind, one might perhaps be inclined to forgive the dean of students for his hasty and possibly intemperate response to Dale and Marty's forthright plea for assistance.

Nonetheless, the dean has an opportunity to *benefit* his two charges by commending them for their open and thoughtful approach to their dilemma and thus reinforce professionally responsible behavior. With a little more attention to his responsibility to be *faithful* to Marty and Dale, we trust that he might take a deep breath, acknowledge his anger, and proceed to conduct a civil and respectful three-way discussion of the situation and possible solutions.

The reader will easily identify other ways that these principles might be applied, other issues that either sharpen or confuse the resolution process, and circumstances in which the principles come into conflict with each other. For example, allowing the dual relationship to continue raises the specter of other interns perceiving Marty as gaining privileged status; this issue has to be compared with the problem of Marty's having to move to another institution for the completion of the internship. The concern to "do no harm" to other interns must be balanced against that of impairing Marty's "autonomy" of choice. As so often in life, the Marty-Dale dilemma admits of no ready resolution, even after the ethical principles have been applied. What they do accomplish is a more orderly and informed exploration of the issues.

Perhaps ultimately what Kitchener's work has achieved is to provide student affairs professionals with a common language and set of precepts that can be effectively applied to moral problems. The utility of her model was clearly realized when the American College Personnel Association undertook a revision of its ethical code and explicitly employed her principles as the basis of the revised document (1990).

More recently, Upcraft and Poole (1991) have contributed some modest criticisms of Kitchener's approach, and their concerns deserve thoughtful reading. Essentially, Upcraft and Poole argue that the biomedical roots of the Beauchamp-Childress model (1979) on which Kitchener based a significant portion of her work is of somewhat limited utility when applied to student affairs functions outside of counseling. To illustrate the process for administrators who are not counselors, Upcraft and Poole offer a two-dimensional framework: the vertical axis reflects a management versus leadership role; the horizontal axis posits the needs of the individual versus those of the community. The framework is intended to inform the ethical decision-making process. The relative merits of the Upcraft-Poole matrix and the Kitchener model remain to be seen after more testing is done in case studies and real-life settings. In the meantime, we have the very refreshing and morally reassuring occasion for enhanced debate about ethical issues.

Practical and Political Implications of Ethical Decisions

"Let's get real." "There you go again." "We've got to be practical." Each of these administrative clichés has been pressed into service to disarm or discredit the professional who has raised an ethical concern. More recently, we've seen evidence in the professional literature that there may be a difference or conflict between "doing things right" (being politically astute) and "doing the right thing" (being ethical) (Upcraft and Poole, 1991). These semantic distinctions are clever, but I would again assert (Canon and Brown, 1985; Canon, 1989) that being ethical is a very practical course of action.

The imputation of a lack of political sophistication to the person showing a concern is commonly all that is required to render ineffective any further arguments in support of an ethical position. There are a variety of defenses against such labeling, and those will be discussed as we look at factors in an ethical community that offer sustained support. Several elementary precautions serve to reduce the effectiveness of stereotyping or labeling.

Reactions Appropriate to the Issue

Student affairs administrators need, where possible, to choose their issues wisely. Not every injustice, not every harmful policy, not every authoritarian position, is capable of redress by a single administrator. Responding to every occasion of ethical failure with the same level of intensity and expressed degree of concern falls into the trap of "There you go again." A prudent response gauged to the level of probable harm is the one most likely to be effective in the situation. After all, there is a very useful array of responses between "I'm feeling uncomfortable with that," and "I have no alternative but to resign." For some of us, the dramatic gesture is frequently tempting, but surviving, when possible, to fight another day will commonly result in greater change in the system.

Limitations to Control

Our working circumstances are further complicated by the fact that ethical agendas are frequently determined by events quite beyond our control. For example, the vice president, who is faced with the prospect of a student-sponsored erotic film festival, might wish to use the situation to focus community attention on the issue of the exploitation of women. An active student government and a collaborating student newspaper, by contrast, easily can shift the agenda to issues of student autonomy and possible censorship. The vice president may then have no choice of agendas and is thus constrained for the moment to deal with the ethical issues being advanced by the students.

Identification of Key Concerns

The choice of issues is more likely to be effective and focused when an individual student services administrator assesses the campus environment. On the basis of that assessment, he or she identifies a very few critical ethical concerns and makes those a part of an agenda that is held before the campus community over an extended period. With that kind of focus, the identified issues (racism, civility in interpersonal exchange, substance abuse) will be addressed in a consistent manner and are more likely to gain the community's attention than the transient crises that are always part of the campus scene.

Creation of an Ethical Environment

Brown's efforts to direct the attention of the profession to the creation of ethical campus environments were noted earlier. Briefly summarized, he asserts: "*The* [emphasis supplied] common mission of the student services profession is being the moral conscience of the campus" (1985, p. 68). In his view, because student services as a collective entity is involved with the whole student, it is best positioned to promote the development of students. Their moral growth is part of this charge and must be constantly considered. He notes that community norms are powerful determinants of the ethical standards to which students will eventually aspire (Brown, 1985).

Suppose for the moment that the staff-elected student affairs personnel committee had officially adopted the principles and standards of the American College Personnel Association (1990) and the standards of professional practice of the National Association of Student Personnel Administrators (1991) as official components of the division's personnel policy. Let us further suppose that the orientation packet mailed to each in-coming student affairs staff member included copies of each of the two associations' ethical statements. Finally, let us suppose that in addition to sessions describing job benefits, committee structures, personnel evaluation procedures, and the like, the new staff orientation program also included a two-hour workshop on making ethical decisions. Together, these actions could combine to establish a strong beginning for a communitywide focus on the moral quality of the campus environment.

The point of offering these ideas is to emphasize the importance of being *intentional* about the formation of ethical environments. Moral environments and communities do not come into being by chance; rather, they are created when members of that community, whether few or many, thoughtfully and persistently pursue a virtuous life. And that intentional pursuit often requires a willingness to deal with uncomfortable realities, to take unpopular stands, to give voice to concerns that colleagues are reluctant to express.

Lest words like *uncomfortable, unpopular,* and *reluctant* seem intimidating, it is important to note that the reference group's ease with these issues increases as it moves toward becoming an ethical community. One can expect more support and less dissent as discussions of ethical matters become more commonplace and as basic community values are made increasingly explicit. Indeed, those who venture to raise a concern are frequently pleasantly surprised by statements of support and commendation from co-workers.

Ultimately, the formation of an ethical community comes about as individuals with strong ethical commitments are able to seek each other out and very deliberately support each other in presenting their concerns to others. It is out of that sustained discourse about ethical matters that a critical mass of ethically concerned individuals is formed, and it is that critical mass that can carry the message to the larger community on a consistent basis.

Some Unaddressed Ethical Concerns

At the beginning of this decade, I took advantage of a professional forum to deliver a speech entitled "The Ethical Unmentionables: Seven Topics You Can't Discuss on a Convention Program" (Canon, 1990). Having survived that experience, I will, by way of illustration, offer several "unmentionables" here. They are *hazing in the African-American Greek community, corporate sponsorship of college programs and activities,* and *dual relationships.* Some readers will have their own cherished lists of unmentionables; these are simply ones that I find compelling and in need of thoughtful professional attention.

Hazing in the African-American Greek System

On many predominantly white campuses, the black Greek system serves as the primary source of social life for its members and the larger African-

American campus community. These organizations sponsor dances and other events that form the focus of weekend socializing.

Admission to full membership in the major fraternities and sororities is highly selective and involves a rigorous and demanding pledge program. Indeed, many members would assert that it is the demanding nature of the pledging experience that lays the foundation for ties that are sustained over the life spans of the members. Assistance in career advancement, support in moving into new social circles, and generosity in time of need are generally expected and provided without question.

The white campus community catches only a partial glimpse of what black Greek organizations require from pledges. For brief periods, small groups of costumed African-American men and women may move around the campus. Typically, fraternity pledges (said to be "on line" when moving about the campus in these small groups) will pause in their travels to engage in synchronized dance-style steps, a practice called stepping. Sorority pledges are more likely to restrict themselves to traveling about the campus in their small groups and in lock-step formation.

To many onlookers, these activities look suspiciously like public hazing. Yet if one were to suggest this reaction to a participating African-American pledge, he or she might evidence surprise and disbelief, for this display can be and often is an occasion for public recognition of enhanced status and an acknowledgment of the promise of acceptance into an elite community. Nonetheless (and as is sometimes the case in predominantly white Greek organizations), the pride of public recognition is paid for in the form of private ridicule and hazing. This issue was judged by black Greeks to be sufficiently acute to warrant the convening of a national symposium in early 1990. The matter is made more complex by the practice of branding that is carried out among the active members of a few African-American fraternities. The branding is asserted as a clearly voluntary sign of a deep commitment to the brotherhood.

After two decades of tangential encounters with all of these practices, I remain uncertain as to how they should be approached. What remains clear to me is my own reluctance, and the seeming general reluctance of Anglo student affairs administrators, to raise some fairly obvious questions. I seriously doubt that branding among white fraternity members or forced public appearances in costumes by their pledges would occur without comment. Our collective fear of being seen as racist or naive appears to prevent a process of inquiry about the welfare of these students or even the legitimate exploration about the effects on both the involved individuals and the larger community. This would thus seem to be a situation that calls for us to inform ourselves about the roles and traditions of African-American Greek organizations and, further, to assert concern for the welfare of student pledges in these organizations. To do less means only that we have again failed an obligation to a neglected student constituency.

Corporate Sponsorship of Campus Programs and Activities

In an era of declining fiscal resources, we have gotten in the habit of turning to the private sector to discover just which firm or enterprise might be interested in defraying the cost of a cherished program. The student services sector is not alone in this practice. Engineered genes, thirst quenchers for athletes, pharmaceutical concoctions, computer software, and sophisticated electronics, among other campus-created products, have paid off handsomely for their universities. By providing development funds in exchange for exclusive rights to the resulting products, the private funding sources and the institutions have occasionally done well for themselves, while concurrently providing stipends for graduate students and overhead funds to support faculty research. Access to sources of financial support during times of diminishing resources is clearly appealing, but consideration must be given to the long-term effects of such support on the direction of research and the consequences of agreeing to proprietary control of research findings by a private sector sponsor. A direct conflict with the academic tradition of the free exchange of ideas can result.

The student services profession is less likely to encounter many blandishments from the private sector, but it is hardly immune from them and their accompanying ethical dilemmas. The case study that opened this chapter illustrates just such a situation. The director of a student activities office needed to examine the various concerns that might accompany the private sponsorship of a university program in exchange for time to present a sales pitch to students. Other examples come readily to mind.

The brewing industry has been very astute in providing support for a variety of college and university activities and functions. Some are happy to furnish the numbered tags used by runners for a fund-raising five- or ten-kilometer run or the advertising for Greek Week, all in return for the right to print the name of their beer on the materials they supply. It is also instructive to watch one of the nationally televised football or basketball games of the week. The odds are excellent that the stadium or fieldhouse in which the events take place will contain billboard space that has been leased to a brewer.

Such relationships with an industry whose product has contributed substantially to vandalism and personal violence on our campuses would seem to warrant questioning. Left begging as well is the issue of leasing publicly owned space (in the case of public institutions) to private-sector entities. In addition, the question of whether there is any real difference between accepting advertisements for institutional publications and leasing empty wall spaces has not been addressed. The answers are not clear; the issues deserve more open discussion and review than they have been given thus far.

We might also consider some aspects of the relationships between vendors and our national professional organizations. It has not been uncommon for professional organizations to receive offers of event sponsorship (convention receptions, speaker fees, and the like) from for-profit vendors who may subsequently be bidders for residence hall food services, transportation contracts, and the like. The acceptance of such offers, always attractive to financially strapped volunteer organizations, leaves us with the potential for at least the appearance of conflict of interest. My past experience has been that when such issues are raised in organization councils, there is real reluctance to consider them. Not infrequently, a statement suggesting that these practices are common to other national higher education organizations is enough to lay the matter to rest. It is my sense that we have much to gain and little to lose by a more thoughtful review of what is involved. Our conclusion may well be that acceptance of some of these offers is ethically appropriate; after such discussion, we would at least have a defensible rationale for having agreed to them.

Dual Relationships

In spite of a literature that has clearly spelled out the problems generated by dual relationships (for example, Kitchener, 1988 and 1990), my own day-to-day experiences on the campus and the informal reports of colleagues from a variety of campuses suggest that the issue and its associated problems remain unresolved. There are several complicating factors. Those of us who teach at the graduate level will recognize the perplexing situations that arise when an instructor and a student, both clearly adults, begin a personal relationship. Lest we be too judgmental, a quick mental survey up and down the corridor would probably identify at least one faculty colleague who is in a long-term relationship with a former student. A second difficulty derives from the increasing number of dual-career couples who are appearing in faculty and staff roles on the same campus. These couples are often faced with a series of barriers to having the competencies and professional worth of each member honored, to being able to realize the professional potential of each of the partners. Additionally, a variety of pitfalls are inevitable for such partnerships. Should one accept promotion to a supervisory position in the other member's department or agency? Should either party function as a full member of personnel committees? Ultimately, how will either or both members be perceived by their co-workers when controversial issues arise and positions are taken on the issues.

In the main, student services professionals appear to be relatively sensitive to the serious ethical problems that are inherent in dual relationships. We are not without sin ourselves. But there is also clearly regular discussion of the issue within the profession, and some of that trickles down to home campuses. No one should have the least doubt about the impropriety of a sexual relationship between a faculty member and a student or between a supervisor and a subordinate staff member. Colleagues in other academic-professional staff areas are frequently less aware of the issue; in that circumstance, we do have a responsibility to serve as the conscience of the campus if only because we *are* aware.

Most campuses have personnel policies that outline the ways in which dual-career couples are constrained from involvement in personnel actions that affect either partner. We need to develop a supportive and caring climate in which both the formal and informal aspects of dual-career partnerships and the ways that these affect the working environment are openly discussed. Furthermore, we need to make the issue of sexual-affectional relationships between faculty members and their students a part of the agendas of our campus personnel committees. Without such efforts, our campuses will continue to ignore the exploitation of students.

Summary

Brown's call for an ethical community (1989) remains to be answered. There are responses at the level of our professional organizations that give cause for hope, particularly as codes and standards are developed and as ethical matters are increasingly debated on a national professional level. However, the single most critical event may be our willingness as individual professionals to speak out in the settings where we carry out our daily responsibilities. That is not an easy step to take, but the reward—in the form of the formation of an ethical environment for our students—could be profound.

References

American College Personnel Association. "Statement of Principles and Standards." *Journal of College Student Personnel,* 1990, *31,* 197–202.

Beauchamp, T. L., and Childress, J. F. *Principles of Biomedical Ethics.* Oxford, England: Oxford University Press, 1979.

Brown, R. D. "Creating an Ethical Community." In H. J. Canon and R. D. Brown (eds.), *Applied Ethics in Student Services.* New Directions for Student Services, no. 30. San Francisco: Jossey-Bass, 1985.

Brown, R. D. "A Visit with Don Quixote." Unpublished presidential address to the American College Personnel Association, Washington, D.C., 1989.

Brown, R. D., and Canon, H. J. "Intentional Moral Development as an Objective of Higher Education." *Journal of College Student Personnel,* 1978, *19,* 426–429.

Canon, H. J. "Guiding Standards and Principles." In U. Delworth, G. R. Hanson, and Associates, *Student Services: A Handbook for the Profession.* (2nd ed.) San Francisco: Jossey-Bass, 1989.

Canon, H. J. "The Ethical Unmentionables: Seven Topics You Can't Discuss on a Convention Program." Unpublished keynote address to the American College Personnel Association, St. Louis, Mo., 1990.

Canon, H. J., and Brown, R. D. "How to Think About Professional Ethics." In H. J. Canon and R. D. Brown (eds.), *Applied Ethics in Student Services.* New Directions for Student Services, no. 30. San Francisco: Jossey-Bass, 1985.

Kitchener, K. S. "Ethical Principles and Ethical Decisions in Student Affairs." In H. J. Canon and R. D. Brown (eds.), *Applied Ethics in Student Services.* New Directions for Student Services, no. 30. San Francisco: Jossey-Bass, 1985.

Kitchener, K. S. "Dual Role Relationships: What Makes Them So Problematic?" *Journal of Counseling and Development,* 1988, *67,* 217–221.

Kitchener, K. S., and Harding, S. S. "Dual Role Relationships." In B. Herlihy and L. Golden (eds.), *Ethical Standards Casebook.* Alexandria, Va.: American Association for Counseling and Development, 1990.

National Association of Student Personnel Administrators. "Standards of Professional Practice." *NASPA Member Handbook.* Washington, D.C.: National Association of Student Personnel Administrators, 1991.

Rest, J. R. "Research on Moral Development: Implications for Training Counseling Psychologists." *The Counseling Psychologist,* 1984, *12,* 19–29.

Upcraft, M. L., and Poole, T. G. "Ethical Issues and Administrative Politics." In P. L. Moore (ed.), *Managing the Political Dimension of Student Affairs.* New Directions for Student Services, no. 55. San Francisco: Jossey-Bass, 1991.

23

૭

Dealing with
Campus Crises

Marsha A. Duncan

It is almost impossible to work for any period of time in student affairs without facing a campus crisis: whether a student death (from murder, suicide, or an accident), student demonstrations, violent acts (assault or rape), or a natural disaster (hurricane, tornadoes, or earthquakes). Volumes have been written on the subject of crisis management, many of which provide clear information on the elements and development of formal organizational crisis management plans.

This chapter is not intended to provide guidance on the development of a formal institutional crisis management plan. The intent is, instead, to focus on those issues and circumstances that every student affairs administrator will face in the midst of a campus crisis, regardless of the existence of a crisis management plan or its content. And although some of the discussion centers on events surrounding a student's death, it is often applicable to any crisis, regardless of its origin. The chapter is written informally, and when the word *you* is used, it refers to the chief student affairs officer or the staff member in student affairs responsible for responding to the presenting crisis situation.

There are four broad categories that will be addressed: the hands-on management of the actual circumstances of the crisis, media management, attorney management, and personal management.

Confronting the Crisis

When that dreaded call comes, what do you do? How do you do it? How do you establish priorities? The answers to those questions will vary greatly, depending upon the nature of the crisis and the specific circumstances at the institution. However, there are a number of actions that are predictable and necessary if a crisis is to be managed well.

Inform the president. The president should be informed immediately and must be given *all* of the facts, as well as an understanding of the current circumstances (for example, have parents been informed?)

Encourage coordination. The president should be encouraged to identify a "point person" and to communicate that decision to the campus. The key players in any crisis usually include the chief of police, the chief student affairs officer, and the director of public information. It is, however, unlikely that those holding these positions report to the same person. Thus, someone must be assigned the responsibility for coordinating a response across administrative stems and ensuring that efforts are not duplicated or counterproductive.

Contact the top public relations official. The top person in the public relations–information office should be contacted and involved fully at the scene. This person's knowledge and understanding of the circumstances must be complete if he or she is to be effective.

Call the institution's attorney, if necessary. If the crisis involves a death or serious injury, contact the attorney for the institution immediately. There is, of course, no way to know whether or not a crisis will result in a lawsuit. However, the likelihood is often great, and the institution will be well served if you operate as if that will be an outcome.

Identify concerned parties. Early identification of the individuals and categories of people who have been or will be affected by the crisis is important if you are to make certain that information and support is provided quickly and appropriately. The list of individuals and groups that require a response includes not only the parents and friends of the victim, but the student body, the faculty and staff, the parents of your students, the alumni, the board of trustees, the media, the various law enforcement agencies, and the specific staff members who will be directly involved in the crisis and its aftermath.

Although the priorities will differ depending on the circumstances, you will need to provide timely and accurate information, respond to rumors (which will be rampant), and provide direct support for whatever specific requirements may arise. Written communications, if timely and specific to the audience, can be particularly useful. Every individual and group will need the facts. In addition, a letter to the faculty and staff might ask for their assistance in identifying and supporting students who require special attention. Another letter to the governing board might include a summary of how the campus is responding to the various aspects of the crisis. A third letter to the student body might supply information about temporary changes in policies and practices or encouragement to students to seek assistance if needed.

It is unlikely that a single written communication to each group will be sufficient. Circumstances change rapidly, and periodic updates will be both expected and necessary.

Use existing support systems. Existing support services should be mobilized to respond to the particular requirements of students and the close friends and family of the victim. The period immediately following the crisis will bring both predictable and unanticipated challenges. Residence hall, counseling center, and chaplain staff members are often the most significant and obvious resources; it is important to determine how those individuals can be used most effectively.

Although individual circumstances will differ, consider whether or not a professional counselor should be available "on site." To what extent do more seasoned staff members need to be directly involved in supporting both students and the less experienced staff? What are the wishes, needs, and demands of those most directly affected? Are you being responsive to these?

All student affairs divisions have support services in place and theoretically positioned to respond to the extent necessary. That is one of the dimensions of our services that we take most seriously. The successful delivery of support in times of crisis will depend, however, upon our care and flexibility.

Establish communication links. Depending upon the nature of the crisis, a temporary hot line may be appropriate. Such a hot line can be a valuable tool in disseminating accurate information, responding to rumors, and providing direct assistance. However, the individuals who staff the hot line must be carefully selected. They should be experienced individuals who have the capability to deal with both rational and irrational calls and who have the confidence and judgment to know when a situation must be handled immediately or can be referred. It is, of course, essential to keep those staff members answering inquiries fully informed and constantly updated about the facts and the university's response to the crisis.

Define the role of staff. The role that the staff plays in furnishing support for various police agencies, the district attorney's office, and the coroner's office (if appropriate) is critical. That role may take many forms depending on the specific requests or demands of those agencies, as well as the nature of the relationship that the university has with them. Regardless of what expectations those agencies have, the police, coroner, and district attorney are central players over which the university has no formal authority or control. Putting the staff at the disposal of agency representatives and responding efficiently and positively to their needs will increase the likelihood that the university will be better informed and involved in all aspects of an investigation.

The list of responses that are required at the time of a crisis is almost endless, and the circumstances will dictate priorities. However, the various and complex responses necessary must often be accomplished almost simultaneously and always at a time of enormous emotional stress. As a result, staff involvement in thinking about responses to crises before they happen will be time well spent.

Media Management

Interaction with the media takes many forms—from formal press conferences and interviews for the print or broadcast media to responses to individual inquiries and the preparation of a press release. At the time of a crisis, those interactions are often complicated by the fact that the institution is communicating "bad" news.

Most campuses have public relations–information offices with responsibilities for managing the institution's dealings with the media. Your public relations–information staff and the relationship that you have with them will become critical assets during crises. Interaction with the media is complex and risky. As a result, the student affairs staff should establish and develop a close working relationship with the public relations–information office and seek assistance in understanding the complexities of that world before a crisis happens. Then, when one does occur, the institution will be poised to maximize the opportunities and minimize the difficulties.

Depending on the magnitude of the crisis, the institution will be besieged with requests for information and interviews. Those requests may come from national and regional media, as well as the local press. And although the pressure that will be placed on the staff is often intense, a number of actions can reduce that pressure, as well as increase the likelihood that the relationships with the media will be positive.

Explain the context to your media representative. The fact that you may have your top public relations–information person on site and fully informed is not enough. That person also must understand the context of the crisis and the response of the campus. For example, if both the victim and the perpetrator are students, the friends of both will be dealing with the reality of what has happened. However, the friends of the perpetrator will also be confronting a different kind of loss and betrayal. Some students will be numbed by a crisis, others will take an activist role, and some may even seek revenge. It is those complex interactive dynamics that provide the context for effective support from the public relations–information office.

Listen to advice. It is important to remember that the public relations–information officer is the professional in the media world and knows and understands it better than you do. Once the facts and context are discussed fully, it is time to listen to that person's advice and trust his or her instincts. That certainly does not mean blind acceptance, but it does mean that the public relations–information officer is better trained and positioned than you are to make difficult decisions.

Use the resources. The public relations–information office should be responsible for calls and inquiries from the media. If that office is fully informed, many of the requests for information can be handled immediately. An additional tool that may prove helpful is a question-and-answer list that is jointly prepared by student affairs staff and the public relations–information personnel. Such a list will not only enable an immediate response to many more inquiries but its development will also create an occasion to think through the appropriate responses to complicated or sensitive questions.

Decide who will speak for the institution. The institution must decide who will be available for formal interviews and press conferences. Although the public relations staff can provide basic facts, the media will want an opportunity to hear from individuals who are directly engaged in managing the crisis. The president may or may not be the right person for this task, but he or she should be involved in deciding who is best able to handle that delicate role for the university.

Balance student privacy and press interests. Protecting students while simultaneously meeting the demands of the press will be a constant problem. Members of the media will not be pleased if you remove them and their cameras from a residence hall or prevent them from entering a building. Yet the primary responsibility of the student affairs staff is to provide support and care for students. The approach that is taken may depend upon whether or not the institution is public or private. It is therefore crucial to determine what press contact will be allowed by the institution and then to communicate those decisions to the students, the staff, the police, and the press.

Engage the student press. It will also be important to engage your student press fully. They are important players and will be covering the story long after the local, regional, and national media have left the campus. Give the editor of the student newspaper the facts, keep him or her current on developments, and ensure direct access to the significant persons managing the crisis.

Exercise candor. You can never control what the media prints or broadcasts, but you can manage how your institution is perceived by being cooperative, responsible, and truthful. There is no alternative to candor.

Handle privileged information with care. There may be circumstances or facts that cannot be communicated to the press. However, hiding behind the "no comment" response is not a good alternative. When handling a question from the press, it should either be answered directly, or you should indicate that you simply cannot respond at that time but will follow up as soon as possible.

Confront errors and misinformation prudently. No matter how clearly, openly, or thoroughly you communicate with the media, you should be prepared for the fact that there will be many times when you will be misquoted or quoted out of context. In addition, many of the "facts" that are reported will simply be wrong. Although it is a natural inclination to attempt to clarify or correct, that is often both impossible and imprudent. Seeking or even achieving a public correction, apology, or retraction may seem the right thing to do, but it can often result in unwanted extended coverage, with little to be gained.

Regardless of your skill or competence in dealing with the media, the student affairs staff will most certainly be expected to interact with the press. The time to develop those skills and to establish positive working relationships with the public relations–information office is before a crisis occurs. Working with the media is an excellent opportunity for a high-quality staff development program. Development of written protocols and procedures on events such as responding to a student death is also useful preparation for crisis management.

Attorney Management

Though there will be many major incidents and crises on campus that will not require the involvement of the legal world, it is clear that a general understanding of the law and litigation is increasingly necessary for those in student affairs administration. Yet attorney management involves an entirely different skill that is also important: how can student affairs staff members use their universities' attorneys most effectively? What are the realities of relationships with legal counsel?

Understand the nature of the relationship. It is important to understand the nature of the representation. Is the attorney employed by the university? Retained by the university for general purposes? Appointed by your insurance company? Representing you or the university? What are his or her specialties? Does that person have experience in or understand higher education and college campuses? For public institutions, the issue may be even more complicated. Depending on state status, the university may be represented by the office of the attorney general or the state's attorney in litigation matters. Knowledge of these factors is essential if the crisis is going to be managed effectively and the institution represented competently.

Be realistic. Unless your attorney works "in house," you should be aware that you and your campus crisis are not likely to be as high a priority for your attorney as for you; this situation also means that your attorney may not always be fully prepared. In addition, the process of preparing that person may be an extensive one if he or she has no previous experience with your institution and its values.

Understand the protections available to you. Before a suit is filed, you should understand the extent to which the university and you as an individual and an employee are protected. Institutions take many precautions to provide adequate protection. However, does your carrier for standard liability exclude coverage when personal damages are sought or when punitive damages are a part of the suit? Do your policies cover legal fees for your institution and for you?

You should know what is excluded and included in your coverage and — equally important — what circumstances can alter that coverage. As an example, your failure to immediately inform your insurance company of a suit could result in its failure to cover you. It is a complex world that can best be understood before a suit is filed.

Make no assumptions. Never assume that any attorney that is retained or employed knows anything at all about colleges and universities in general, your institution in particular, or student life on a college campus. Educating your attorney about the world of higher education may be the most important thing that you do.

Take notes. Careful notes are necessary; write down everything that you say and do and when you say and do it. You should also document what you have been told to do by attorneys; they do not always give good advice and that advice may sometimes be contradictory.

Get approval. Obtain attorney approval on everything you write that is in any way related to the circumstances of the lawsuit. Annual reports, correspondence, and policy statements may be the documents that you find yourself explaining in a deposition.

Train for a deposition. If you are going to be deposed, make certain that your attorney takes the time to train you for that experience in advance. There are a number of standard guidelines that seem obvious and are little more than common sense. However, understanding and thinking through the guidelines before a deposition will significantly improve the likelihood that you will do a good job.

Review and proof. Do not fail to review and proof everything that your attorneys write. Your role is not to approve the legal language; it is, however, your responsibility to see that the tone is consistent with the university's position and that the facts are correct. You should not hesitate to ask questions or disagree. Take your role as the client-consumer seriously.

Consider settlement carefully. The decision of whether to settle a lawsuit or to allow it to go to court is difficult, both institutionally and personally. The likelihood of winning or losing the suit will be only one of many factors. The decision will also depend on whether settlement is an option that all parties agree to pursue and whether you and the institution are willing to prolong the process and the expense (both human and financial) for months and often years.

Attorneys are not only a critical part of our lives in student affairs administration but they can be magnificent resources as well. However, monitoring and managing those relationships are responsibilities that are increasingly critical to our effectiveness.

Personal Management

Personal management could be the most important element of the crisis that you must contend with. If you cannot keep yourself under control and cannot function at the top of your form, chances are not very good that any other aspect of a crisis will be well managed.

It is always difficult to perform efficiently when you are tired and under stress. And in the midst of a crisis, you are not likely to be sleeping much, eating regularly, or finding any time for yourself. Those circumstances will make your body, your emotions, and your judgment vulnerable. Obviously and unfortunately, there is no one plan for personal management that works for everyone. There are, however, several suggestions that you can keep in mind.

Stay calm. Remember that your staff will need you and your support more than ever. No matter what the circumstances, it will be important to stay visibly calm and exude confidence (even if you have to fake it).

Identify a confidant. Find that single person in whom you can confide for support. That individual should be someone with whom you can safely share confidential information, a person who understands you well enough to help you manage your emotions, and someone with whom you can be emotional. It may be a colleague on your campus or a friend from far away that you can talk with freely and openly. An escape valve is essential, and finding and using it will enhance your ability to think clearly and respond with care.

Attend to your health. Take care of yourself. Eating and sleeping may seem like distractions, but they are critical to your effectiveness.

Clear the decks. Get everything you can that is unrelated to a major crisis off your desk and off your mind. You will find that colleagues are more than willing to help with ongoing functions and responsibilities that cannot be postponed. If you try to do everything you will most surely realize after the fact that deadlines have been missed and opportunities lost. Focusing your efforts on the management of the crisis, while delegating other current issues to staff, will not only result in a better managed crisis and operation but will also give the staff a wonderful opportunity to expand its understanding, to test new skills, and to contribute in new and significant ways.

Maintain a sense of humor. There will be nothing funny about the crisis that you are facing, but amusing things will happen. Let yourself enjoy those moments.

Only you can know what will serve you well, but maintaining strength and confidence in the midst of a crisis will be an essential survival and management skill.

Summary

The effective management of crisis is an essential skill for a student affairs administrator. In fact, a successfully managed crisis can result in positive visibility, increased confidence, and deepened appreciation for and understanding of the role of student affairs on a campus. By the same token, a poorly managed crisis can result in a very different outcome. Loss of respect, influence, and trust, individual reassignment, or even dismissal are also possible if the crisis is major and if it is badly handled.

More importantly, how student affairs professionals deal with crisis will have a lasting influence on the lives of the students who are touched. No greater opportunity exists for our profession to provide support and understanding than to individuals who are affected personally by a crisis. Many will come through that experience either strengthened or diminished. The role that student affairs plays in the management and response both to the crisis and its aftermath can make the crucial difference.

In many respects, the student affairs profession is uniquely positioned to manage these most difficult moments. We have support services in place; we work in communities with shared values; and our ongoing communication and relationships with students, faculty, and staff provide a positive context for dealing with crises well.

In other respects, we are not so well positioned or prepared. We may have a general understanding of the federal and state laws, as well as case law, that applies to higher education. However, our legal knowledge rarely extends to the world of litigation and the complexities of that process. The same gap often applies to the world of media relations. We all have a basic appreciation of the importance of public relations, and we often have regular interaction with the student press. But how many in our profession have the training to be successful in a press conference or to appreciate the subtle differences in dealing with the print versus the broadcast media or with national "entertainment" journalists versus the national or regional news?

The process of becoming more familiar with such areas as litigation and media relations increases the likelihood that we will be better equipped to handle a crisis when it comes; moreover, those issues provide wonderful opportunities for staff development and interaction within the student affairs division and across the campus.

The successful practitioner will recognize that crisis management can be as critical a task as any that we engage in and will take whatever steps are necessary to prepare for a sound performance in that role.

PART FOUR

❦

Acquiring
and Developing
Administrative Skills

We all have deficiencies in our academic training and preparation as we assume administrative positions in student affairs. The question becomes one of identifying what skills and competencies we must develop further, what knowledge we need to gain. Then we can design a plan to meet those requirements. Part Four discusses the means and methods to improve, update, or acquire the competencies necessary to be an effective administrator within student affairs.

Staff salaries are by far the largest item in our budgets and are our most important investment. It is essential that we assure that all professional and support staff members have the opportunity to refine their own skills to improve performance. Well-crafted staff development programs provide one method to achieve this goal, and in Chapter Twenty-Four, Frederick Preston discusses practical methods to assess staff needs for development and methods to institute a high-quality development program.

Professional associations create many opportunities for professionals to gain indispensable skills, competencies, and support. Elizabeth Nuss, in Chapter Twenty-Five, considers the role of professional associations in the ongoing development of staff. In addition, she provides suggestions for student affairs staff members to match their individual requirements with opportunities within such associations.

Some student affairs colleagues work in settings where it is not possible to engage in a full staff development program. In Chapter Twenty-Six, Susan Batchelor identifies how such individuals can engage in mentoring and self-directed learning to improve their professional capabilities. Her suggestions are equally applicable to staff members in other types of settings.

349

The decision of whether or not to engage in formal graduate education as a means for both advancement and growth is a difficult one for many student affairs professionals. In Chapter Twenty-Seven, Susan Komives explores the issues involved in choosing a graduate program, the possibilities associated with such a decision, and the alternatives available if a professional does not choose to pursue doctoral study.

Administrative internships provide a unique occasion for staff members to gain hands-on experience to increase their professional skills. Marlene Ross and Juan Mestas review the conditions and structures needed to develop a campus-based, system-based, or consortium-based administrative internship program in Chapter Twenty-Eight.

Each of these approaches can create opportunities for student affairs professionals to acquire the needed skills and competencies to be a successful administrator and manager. The commitment to improve professional skills and competencies rests, however, with each of us.

24

❧

Creating Effective
Staff Development
Programs

Frederick R. Preston

The quality and competence of a student affairs staff are primary components in creating and improving student development programming and service delivery. Although there has been continued advocacy of staff development in the literature (Stamatakos and Oliaro, 1972; Kanter, 1977; Komives, 1986; and Barr, 1990) and growing evidence of the need of student affairs professionals to engage in staff development (Roe, 1982), there remains considerable skepticism regarding the adequacy of such efforts within the higher education community (Baier, 1985). A continued climate of shrinking budgetary resources, coupled with higher public demand for accountability, has heightened the challenge to use creative and cost-effective programs to improve staff competency.

Two major determinants of staffing quality, selection and evaluation practices, are discussed elsewhere in this volume. This chapter focuses on the third strategy to foster potential: staff development. In this chapter, a rationale for investing in professional staff development programs is presented. Next, the goals for a high-quality program and the significant issues related to staff development are discussed. Third, the building blocks for a successful program are introduced. Fourth, a programming model is offered, and strategies for professional development activities are discussed. Finally, the need to evaluate efforts in this area carefully and adequately is emphasized.

The Rationale for Investing in Staff Development

Truitt and Gross (1966), who offer one of the early frameworks to justify in-service training, list six reasons for engaging in intentional staff development efforts. Their list includes the following: improving inadequate or unrelated preservice training, sustaining continued professional growth of staff, effecting productive changes in student service programs, providing continuity for a specialized and changing staff, assisting with the rising aspiration of staff members, and offering expanded opportunities for these individuals to contribute to the total student services program.

Others have presented reasons for in-service training that further emphasize the essential function of development programs in realizing the full potential of staff to meet the mission of student affairs (Shaffer, 1984; Stamatakos and Oliaro, 1972; Miller, 1975; and Merkle and Artman, 1983). Canon (1989) translates these rationales into three categories: (1) the need to remediate and rehabilitate professional staff with widely diverse types of preservice preparation, (2) the necessity of enhancing institutional accountability of staff roles to various constituent groups, and (3) the need for staff members to exercise professional responsibility for their continued growth and refinement of skills and professional attributes.

During the 1990s, significant emerging demographic and social patterns provided new impetus to the call for increased investment in the professional development of student affairs professionals. Many of these issues, including accelerated application of computer technology, increased student diversity, and intensification of student health issues, are discussed extensively in other chapters in this volume. Taken together, these factors place new demands and expectations on student affairs professionals and require new areas of staffing specialization and new skills. Given the historical curricular focus of student personnel graduate preparation programs (Stamatakos, 1981) and lack of change in program content over the years (Keim, 1987), responding to these new requirements falls to staff development programs. Shaffer (1984) reminds us that graduate programs serve only as the beginning phase of our professional education.

New trends suggest the evolution of at least two additional rationales for staff development programming: the need to facilitate team building across student affairs units and the importance of maximizing staff growth and proficiency in the area of cross-cultural literacy. Addressing contemporary student needs and issues requires coordinated and collaborative action by student affairs units. In addition, decreasing budgetary resources also challenge units to pool staffing resources to meet demands otherwise beyond the capability of any individual unit. Actively attending to teamwork and team building is essential to a high-quality staff development program.

Finally, as regards the growing diversity of the student population, overall enrollment of ethnic minority students increased 10 percent from 1988 to 1990, with increases of 12 percent for Asian Americans, 12 percent for Hispanics, 11 percent for Native Americans, and 8 percent for African-American students (Carter and Wilson, 1992). Also, recent substantial increases in the number of nonresident alien students have greatly expanded the presence of subethnic groups. Beyond the traditional homogeneous ethnic classifications, current college students are, for example, Haitian, Jamaican, Puerto Rican, Chicano, Cuban, Filipino, Korean, Chinese, Vietnamese, Cambodian, Indian, Pakistani, and Japanese. Each of these groups represents socioeconomic, religious, political, cultural, and emotional differences.

The expanding presence of ethnic minority students and foreign nationals creates a major challenge to student affairs to offer educational and developmental opportunities that engender appreciation and acceptance of cultural diversity. These new ethnic minorities possess a host of characteristics that will make it more difficult and complex for staff members to assist these students in satisfying their developmental needs. Success will depend heavily on the increased participation of student affairs professionals in related staff development programming.

Significant Issues Related to Staff Development

Any campus environment demonstrates a dynamic interplay of internal and external organizational factors. Within the student affairs division, a wide array of interdepartmental or unit functions operate to support the division's philosophy, goals, and management structure. Equally important is the relationship of the student affairs division with other organizations both within and without the institution. A thorough understanding of the political environment at all levels allows student affairs practitioners to manage their environment, instead of having their environment control them (Walker, 1979). It is this multidimensional system, which encompasses a complicated and often diverse set of values and priorities, that guides and influences the design and initiation of human resource development programs.

Staff development initiatives within the higher education community have usually been vulnerable to the bureaucratic ebb and flow of the organizational culture. In order to minimize this systemic weakness, careful evaluation and analysis of the following environmental factors should be considered: campus climate, financial support, job training relevancy, and affirmative action.

Campus Climate

A critical review of the institutional mission statement often reveals a philosophic basis that shapes the approach of the institution to staff development initiatives. The particular campus climate is often revealed by posing a series of probing questions. Does the institution subscribe to a central human resource development program? If so, what are the objectives and scope of this initiative? Is staff development viewed as a priority by senior campus administrators? Do existing personnel policies support or restrict staff development efforts? Is staff development perceived as a component of the strategic planning and goal-setting process? Answers to these questions should provide a fairly accurate picture of where staff development fits in the overall campus culture.

Financial Support

Staff development generally falls into one of two extreme positions on the financial continuum: either as a wise and long-term investment or as a token effort and sometimes burdensome expense. Institutions of higher education have rarely allocated substantial dollars to staff development. Miller (1975) reports the following funding strategies: 33 percent of the staff development funding at postsecondary institutions was spent for off-campus staff attendance at annual conventions and professional association meetings, 19 percent went to off-campus professional workshops, and 9 percent was allocated for specific on-campus, in-service education programs. (The remaining 39 percent went toward acquiring materials, and so forth.) Miller's study, which surveyed 560 American College Personnel Association members, also reports that fewer than one-fifth of the respondents reported any type of specific policy statement concerning staff development activities. The implications of this study deserve careful consideration.

In addition to the issue of allocation strategies, consistent availability of financial resources must be evaluated. Various forms of support can be tailored to a specific staff development program or activity. As campuses continue to struggle with shrinking resources, a renewed emphasis on long-term strategic planning, innovation, and creativity will become critical factors in maintaining vital programs. Student affairs divisions with large travel budgets in support of off-campus conference attendance are now being asked to design alternate methods to support staff development. Several different forms of resource support must be considered, including staff release time, paid study leaves, on-campus staff development programs, or more careful coordination of staff development expenditures. These can be effective approaches and are readily available in many campus settings.

Job-Training Relevancy

The issue of job-training relevancy is directly related to the goals and objectives of any staff development program. Many programs are designed to meet short-term objectives, developed in response to immediate service- and program-related requirements. The challenge is to look beyond current issues and design programs that transcend immediate job requirements. Constant changes in the institutional environment necessitate fluidity at all levels of the organization. Good staff development programs can help professionals deal with these issues.

Rapid changes in the environment also require task-related technical training. This type of short-term program has clearly defined and narrow objectives. The goal is often simple: teach the worker how to get the job done. To illustrate, in the case of a new computer system, all that is really necessary is familiarity with the system and effective entry and retrieval skills. Or is it? Student affairs practitioners are not used to a product-oriented system. Therefore, the training should not solely relate to specific tasks but rather to the broader mission and goals of the division and the college or university. In essence, student affairs staff development programs must practice what the field preaches: they must attend to the human development aspirations of participating staff members. In addition to the technological skill required for a new computer system, attention must be given to the misgivings of staff when new technology is introduced. Efforts must be made to aid staff in understanding how the new technology can assist them in more effectively serving their institution and their students. To do less would be shortsighted and would severely limit staff potential and organizational growth.

Affirmative Action

As the nation grows more heterogeneous, the mix of students will continue to grow more pluralistic. A major question thus becomes, How can we train a staff that is less diverse than the students they serve? Specialized multicultural training programs associated with enhancing the ability of staff to understand and respond to a wider range of student needs are essential in today's campus culture. These programs must examine and reexamine alternative approaches to help staff respond appropriately to new students.

Staff Development Building Blocks

To some degree, the current pop culture phrase "Just do it!" reflects a key premise regarding the initiation of a staff development program effort. Unlike many management functions, a lack of financial resources need not be debilitating in planning and executing specific training objectives for staff members. The most crucial element in implementing an intentional staff development effort is the desire of staff members, supervisors, or senior administrators to act. The impetus to engage in staff development can arise from the initiative of an individual staff member excited by reading an article in a professional journal or from a centrally coordinated, widely available series of programs utilizing in-house and outside presenters. Responsibility for staff development may rest with an individual, a department, or a division. Of course, all three approaches can provide opportunities for active professional enrichment related to a specific job function, departmental needs, or divisional objectives. However, it is generally accepted that divisionwide programs most effectively promote staff development (Merkle and Artman, 1983).

A sound strategy for launching a staff development program involves six steps: establishing the priority of staff development activities, assessing training needs, specifying training objectives, designing the program, implementing it, and evaluating it. Making staff development a priority is an often overlooked first step in the process. It is essential to establish the significance of this personnel management function at the departmental or divisional level. Expression of support from relevant senior administrators and the articulation of policies that encourage professional development generate credibility for these programs, enthusiasm, and investment by the staff. Policies allowing staff release time and broad-based staff participation improve chances for a successful program.

The assessment of training needs within the student affairs community is often afforded less attention than it deserves (Hall, 1982). Evaluation provides critical information necessary to both design and evaluate the training program. Goldstein, Braverman, and Goldstein (1991) advocate tri-level assessment to determine institutional needs, job-specific and task-related requirements, and employee-identified needs.

Training objectives flow from the needs assessment and should be specific. Without specific objectives, it is difficult later to measure meaningful achievement on the part of participating staff. (See Chapter Ten for additional information on setting training objectives.)

With needs identified and training objectives in place, a program can be designed and implemented that is relevant to the articulated mission and goals of the department, the division, and the institution.

A Model Program

Although isolated professional development activities can be beneficial, a model student affairs staff development program features comprehensive campus-based and off-campus opportunities that are responsive to identified staff needs. The following components should be a part of any model or program.

Orientation and In-Service Training

This component covers those activities that relate to assisting staff members in adjusting to new job assignments and in overcoming deficiencies in their job-related knowledge and skills. Attention to these basic requirements assures that staff members receive a general introduction to the institution and division policies, objectives, and available resources. It also ensures that staff members are exposed to thorough training in all aspects of their expected professional job performance.

Career Skills and Education

Activities that encourage staff members to enhance their professional development with particular emphasis on theory, exemplary practice, and the mission of student affairs are part of this component. Support for completion of degree requirements or reentry into graduate education is also involved.

Opportunities should be present to help individual staff members define issues related to their personal career paths and aspirations.

Organizational Climate

This component focuses on activities that promote sound administration and individual motivation for high-quality performance and accountability. Efforts related to improving staff morale and organizational design and change are also included.

Communications and Human Relations Training

Effective communication skills are a fundamental competency in student affairs. Part of every staff development program should focus on activities that support and improve communication skills and human interaction. Specific attention should be paid here to activities that upgrade staff cross-cultural literacy.

Staff Support

In addition to the content components just listed, a well-rounded development program also emphasizes involvement in the design and implementation of the program. A representative staff development committee can assist in achieving this goal. Examples of successful programs using a staff development committee model include those at Wichita State University, Texas A&M University, the University of Kansas, Drake University, and the State University of New York at Stony Brook. These programs have worked well because of the involvement of staff and ongoing and adequate senior-level administrative support and funding.

Strategies for Staff Development

A wide range of strategies can be utilized in planning and implementing a staff development program. Small campuses or institutions experiencing significant budget constraints can use many of the strategies discussed in this section with little financial outlay. The examples listed focus on cost-effective and easy-to-implement programs that also are equally useful in larger institutional settings.

Brown-Bag Discussion Groups

This type of informal noon program can be scheduled on a monthly basis, using rotating facilitators from within or outside the student affairs division.

A variety of formats is possible: focus groups addressing departmental or divisional issues, general staff forums for the exploration and analysis of current issues facing the campus community, or resource- and information-sharing related to professional practice. A thematic approach is taken on some campuses, where brown-bag luncheons are scheduled to assess topics such as integration of a customer service orientation in student affairs, demographic trends in higher education, or an introduction to the day-to-day operations of each department in the division. Whatever the approach, brown-bag lunch programs provide a resource-efficient and excellent method of staff interaction and learning.

Professional Staff Specialty Portfolios

Changes in the campus environment have motivated many staff members in student affairs to develop skills and competencies outside their required duties and responsibilities. Professional specialties like language fluency, research, program development, computer literacy, and others can be documented in the form of a specialty portfolio. The portfolio can then be added to the staff member's personnel file as a means of recognizing and substantiating the contributions gained from individual professional development efforts. In addition, valuable resource people can be identified whose skills can be used throughout the division of student affairs.

Temporary Staff Exchange Opportunities

A temporary shift in job assignment, either to a different student affairs department or to another university division, allows for concentrated practical learning experiences about different functional areas on campus. The exchange can be concentrated into full-day experiences over a short term, or partial-day periods can be developed over a longer period of time. An exchange opportunity strengthens understanding of interdepartmental operations and often bolsters communication and cooperation among units. Further, this type of opportunity broadens the experience base of developing professionals and may be helpful in determining long-term career goals and aspirations. Some campuses have formalized such exchanges in the form of administrative internships (as discussed by Ross and Mestas in Chapter Twenty-Eight).

Staff Development Newsletter

A staff development newsletter can be a simple yet excellent boost to staff development programs. The newsletter can furnish information on current programs and activities; recognize individual and departmental accomplishments; share the important life events of staff members (weddings, births) that enhance the sense of caring among staff; supply resource information on conferences, publications, and current research; and give staff members the chance to offer their ideas on current problems and issues. Production of a newsletter can also be tailored to meet available resources. In some instances, one staff member can produce a simple newsletter. A more comprehensive effort may require the involvement of the staff development committee. In any case, the newsletter should be published consistently, whether on a monthly or quarterly basis. Such newsletters aid in the perception of a strong organizational culture and increase a sense of individual belonging.

Teleconferencing

Teleconferences, now widely available from a range of excellent sources within the higher education community, provide exposure to national issues and expert commentary to a campus-based staff. Staff members who never leave the campus can benefit from this often intensive and thought-provoking interactive learning option. Through direct phone links with commentators and panelists, the staff can directly participate in the program. Teleconferencing can be expensive, and efforts should be made to approach other institutions to help with the cost. Sharing these experiences with staff members from other institutions often leads to useful, longer-term professional relationships.

Video Workshops

Requiring only a television monitor and a VCR, a video workshop can be an effective and cost-conscious program strategy. Creativity and a comprehensive video resource guide can assist in identifying a range of program ideas. For example, an affirmative action or cultural diversity program can utilize any number of popular videotapes depicting experiences from different cultural perspectives. Guided discussion after such presentations can enrich the understanding of all participants. In addition, there is also a wide range of videotapes on topics pertinent to the personal lives of staff members, such as nutrition, wellness, and first aid.

Social Events

Social events provide an opportunity for staff members and their families to get to know one another in a nonwork setting. For example, a summer-celebration picnic provides a festive occasion where staff members from all parts of the division can share in both recreational and social activities. Organized games such as volleyball add to the spirit of comradeship and fun. Other possible social events include departmental open houses, new-employee receptions, and holiday-season events. The importance of fun in a staff development program should not be overlooked, as this is one of the best ways to celebrate accomplishments collectively and possibly to make new friends.

Staff Awards Convocation

Annual recognition ceremonies do more than simply recognize individuals for their accomplishments and merit. Establishing high-achieving role models is often an effective and motivating learning experience for many staff members. Recognition of achievements within the division of student affairs can promote components of the total divisional program. Categories that might be used in defining such internal award criteria are student development promotion, systems innovations, extraordinary outreach efforts, research and assessment, and environmental enhancement. Such awards should not be limited to professional staff, for the support personnel contribute a great deal to divisional efforts. Acknowledging the outstanding effort of clerical or maintenance staffs makes a strong statement about institutional standards and expectations.

Citations or awards can also recognize excellence outside the division of student affairs. As campuses strive to develop more collaborative bonds of community, identifying faculty contributions to student development programs can reinforce a sense of value and prestige.

In addition to recognizing outstanding achievement, the convocation can also be used as a vehicle to promote learning, motivation, and self-renewal. Keynote addresses should be informative and inspirational and should reaffirm the value placed on individual accomplishments and divisional goals. The University of Massachusetts at Amherst has presented a staff development convocation for many years. Generally composed of a welcome address by senior administrators, a "state of the division" address, award presentations, entertainment, and a reception, this event brings the division together in a useful way.

A Staff Development Library

Accessible space can be used to house a collection of current research and student services literature. Not only will the collection serve as a valuable resource for staff members in their work, but it will also heighten staff awareness of the importance of staying current and maintaining scholarly connections with research and program development. In addition to housing books and periodicals, such a library could also be the repository for past staff development initiatives and video resources. Library management could be delegated to the staff development committee.

Intersession Staff Development Conference

An annual staff development conference provides staff members with the opportunity to create a program most suited to their particular needs for self-renewal and professional growth. This type of campus-based program is easiest to do over an intersession period, as everyone's time, energy, and resources are less taxed. Conference programs can focus on both personal enrichment or professional practice. This format also provides a vehicle for staff members to teach each other.

This can also be an occasion to use an outside speaker or consultant. One fine example of this type of initiative is the annual Student Affairs Conference at the University of Maryland at College Park. For the past eighteen years, this winter conference has concentrated on professional development issues and concerns and has also furnished an opportunity for social interaction. The model has been so successful that other professionals in the region annually join in the activity.

In those cases where both professional and support personnel are encouraged to attend, the program theme should be pertinent and geared to a common interest. A variety of topics should be offered on both general themes and specific skills to enhance performance and personal renewal. Typical examples might include time management, development of a multicultural perspective, basic first aid, and wellness. Both support and professional staff can participate in the sessions, and all will profit.

Who's Who in Committee Service

It is no secret that committee service is often the unappreciated source of substantial, innovative program development on college campuses. A divisional committee-service work-load profile, which includes student affairs divisional committees, university committees, and external service groups, can be devised and updated on an annual basis. A special report highlighting exceptional levels of individual committee service can then be distributed within the division. A listing in "Who's Who in Committee Service" can connote prestige, accomplishment, and recognition for outstanding and valued service. Aside from the recognition factor, this activity can help members of the division understand the committee structure and the ways that they can contribute to it. Further, by requiring the division to catalogue and analyze committee responsibilities, valuable data can be generated that often can be utilized in future planning efforts.

Evaluating the Program

The importance and usefulness of evaluating staff development programs cannot be overemphasized. Evaluation is a diagnostic tool that furnishes data to assist in planning and implementing future staff development programs. Further, the benefits of the program can be used to justify continued or increased support for staff develevelopment efforts. Through the use of specific and well-written program objectives, standards and measurement criteria can be applied to determine program success. Four levels of evaluation criteria are particularly suitable for assessing training and development offerings (Kirkpatrick, 1967).

Reaction Criteria

These measures focus on program delivery and on the reactions of participants to the program effort. Examples include participant response to items such as program content, materials, and facilities.

Learning Criteria

These measures assess how well participants have mastered the program's content. The emphasis is on what principles, facts, skills, techniques, or attitudes have been acquired.

Behavior Criteria

These criteria measure the extent to which changes in practice occur from the staff development experience. The measured behaviors must fit the training objectives and typically reflect feedback from supervisors, peers, and subordinates.

Results Criteria

These criteria involve objective assessment of both individual and organizational effectiveness: for example, increased quality or quantity of performance, reduced costs, less waste, reduction in staff turnover, or a reduction in absenteeism.

Summary

Although there is strong agreement on the part of student affairs professionals regarding the value of comprehensive staff development programs, implementation of such programs on a systematic basis in many institutions has not occurred. The progress of the student affairs profession is directly linked to the ability of staff members to accomplish student affairs' and the institution's missions and goals. Current and emerging issues, especially in the realm of cultural diversity within our student populations, require staff members to be exposed to new information in order to be effective. Shrinking financial resources and increased expectations for performance intensify the need to strengthen our commitment and resolve to implement and use staff development programs fully. Staff members in student affairs are, after all, our most important resource.

References

Baier, J. L. "Evaluation of Mini-University Staff Development Program at Texas Tech University." Unpublished research report, Texas Tech University, 1985.

Barr, M. J. "Growing Staff Diversity and Changing Career Paths." In M. J.

Barr, M. L. Upcraft, and Associates, *New Futures for Student Affairs: Building a Vision for Professional Leadership and Practice.* San Francisco: Jossey-Bass, 1990.

Canon, H. J. "Developing Staff Potential." In U. Delworth, G. R. Hanson, and Associates, *Student Services: A Handbook for the Profession.* San Francisco: Jossey-Bass, 1989.

Carter, D. J., and Wilson, R. *Tenth Annual Status Report on Minorities in Higher Education.* Washington, D.C.: American Council on Education, 1992.

Goldstein, I. L., Braverman, E. P., and Goldstein, H. W. "Needs Assessment." In K. N. Wexley (ed.), *Developing Human Resources.* Washington, D.C.: BNA Books, 1991.

Hall, C. L. "Needs Assessment: A Critical Component in Professional Development Planning and Programming." Unpublished manuscript, University of Southern Mississippi, Feb. 1982.

Kanter, R. M. *Men and Women of the Corporation.* New York: Basic Books, 1977.

Keim, M. "Data from the Directory of Graduate Preparation Programs in College Student Personnel (1973, 1977, 1980, 1987)." Paper presented at the annual Midwest meeting of faculty in student affairs, Michigan State University, Lansing, Oct. 1987.

Kirkpatrick, D. L. "Evaluation Training." In R. L. Craig and L. R. Bittel (eds.), *Training and Development Handbook.* New York: McGraw-Hill, 1967.

Komives, S. R. "Facing Crises: Counselors' Personal and Professional Responses." In M. Rose and S. Alexander (eds.), *Power Keys in America: Counseling Interventions.* Alexandria, Va.: American Association of Counseling and Development, 1986.

Merkle, H. B., and Artman, R. B. "Staff Development: A Systematic Process for Student Affairs Leaders." *NASPA Journal,* 1983, *21,* 55–63.

Miller, T. K. "Staff Development of College Student Personnel." *Journal of College Student Personnel,* 1975, *16* (4), 258–264.

Roe, B. B. "An Analysis of Career Enrichment Needs and Programs for Student Personnel." Paper presented at the annual convention of the American Personnel and Guidance Association, Detroit, Mich., Mar. 1982.

Shaffer, R. H. "Preparing for Student Personnel in the 1980's." In F. Kirby and D. Woodard (eds.), *Career Perspectives in Student Affairs.* NASPA Monograph Series, no. 1. Jan. 1984.

Stamatakos, L. C. "Student Affairs Progress Toward Professionalism: Recommendations for Action — Part 2." *Journal of College Student Personnel,* 1981, *22,* 197–207.

Stamatakos, L. C., and Oliaro, P. M. "In-Service Development: A Function of Student Personnel." *NASPA Journal,* 1972, *9,* 169–273.

Truitt, J. W., and Gross, R. A. "In-Service Education for College Student Personnel." *National Association of Student Personnel Administrators Bulletin,* no. 1. June 1966.

Walker, D. E. *The Effective Administrator: A Practical Approach to Problem Solving, Decision Making, and Campus Leadership.* San Francisco: Jossey-Bass, 1979.

25

୬

The Role of
Professional
Associations

Elizabeth M. Nuss

Professional associations have an important function in American higher education. The purpose of this chapter is to demonstrate to student affairs professionals how these organizations can help them enhance or develop their administrative and professional skills. The chapter provides a brief history of professional associations and describes what they are and do. It reviews the wide variety of forms of participation and the ways that involvement in a professional association may vary over the span of a career. Suggestions about how to become involved, tips for managing time commitments and personal resources, and issues related to affiliation in multiple associations are discussed.

The chapter gives examples of many professional associations but is *not* intended to be a definitive summary of the universe of professional associations. The sample listing is included for illustrative purposes only. Moreover, the chapter does not advocate membership in any particular organization. As should be evident from the following discussion, decisions about which professional associations to join and when to join them are based on the reader's current professional goals, talents, and institutional needs. Nevertheless, participation in these organizations is the hallmark of a professional. At a minimum, anyone intending a serious career in student affairs should be a member of at least one professional association.

Brief History of Professional Associations

Professional associations have many objectives. They seek to advance understanding, recognition, and knowledge in the field; to develop and promulgate standards for professional practice; to serve the public interest; and to provide professionals with a peer group that promotes a sense of identity. The oldest American professional society still in existence is the American Philosophical Society, founded by Benjamin Franklin in 1743. Of the nearly 21,000 national associations, there are approximately 1,217 educational associations (American Society of Association Executives, 1988). As societies grow and become technically and socially more complex and specialized, associations are created to represent those specialized interests (Bloland, 1985).

The founding of the major student affairs professional associations follows the history and development of higher education and the profession itself. Student affairs as a distinct entity emerged in the early 1900s as a result of alterations in the nature and purpose of public higher education and changes in the American professorate. Deans of men and deans of women were appointed to resolve student problems and to administer campus discipline systems (National Association of Student Personnel Administrators, 1987). In 1916, the first formal program of study in vocational guidance was offered at Teachers College, Columbia University (National Association of Student Personnel Administrators, 1987). The increased size and specialization of higher education fostered the establishment of appropriate professional associations to articulate the shared concerns of each institutional group (Bloland, 1985). The fact that many student services in the early 1900s were organized by gender also influenced the development of the professional associations.

The National Association of Deans of Women (NADW) was organized in 1916. Since its founding, the organization has focused its mission on serving the needs of women in education. In 1956, NADW became the National Association of Women Deans and Counselors (NAWDC). In 1972, a decision was made to change the group's name and purpose; the organization became NAWDAC—the National Association of Women Deans, Administrators, and Counselors (Sheeley, 1983). In 1991, the organization's name was changed to the National Association of Women in Education (NAWE) to reflect more accurately its contemporary scope and focus.

In January 1919, a meeting, referred to as the Conference of Deans and Advisers of Men, was held at the University of Wisconsin. That meeting is now recognized as the founding of the National Association of Deans and Advisers of Men (NADAM). After two earlier attempts (1948 and 1949) failed, the organization officially adopted NASPA (National Association of Student Personnel Administrators) as its name in 1951. This broadened the base of the association, and for the first time NASPA began to recruit members (Rhatigan, 1991).

The American College Personnel Association (ACPA) traces its founding to 1924, when it began as the National Association of Appointment

Secretaries (NAAS) (Sheeley, 1983; Bloland, 1972). The title of appointment secretary referred to persons who assisted in placing teachers and other college graduates. NAAS's first meeting in 1924 was held jointly with NADW. In 1929, NAAS's name was changed to National Association of Placement and Personnel Officers to reflect its broader professional role. In 1931, the name was again changed, to ACPA (Bloland, 1972). Bloland (1972) describes the historical cooperative relationships among these three major associations.

A sample listing (not by any means a complete one) of some other national higher education and student affairs associations and their founding dates is included in Table 25.1. The list provides a historical context for the development of the different associations and provides familiarity with the acronyms frequently used. For complete information, consult the *Encyclopedia of Associations* (Burek, 1992).

Table 25.1: A Sample Listing of Professional Associations by Year of Founding.

Association	*Year*
Association of American Universities (AAU)	1900
American Association of Collegiate Registrars and Admissions Officers (AACRAO)	1910
Association of College Unions—International (ACU-I)	1914
National Association for Women in Education (NAWE)	1916
American Council on Education (ACE)	1918
National Association of Student Personnel Administrators (NASPA)	1919
American Association of Community and Junior Colleges (AACJC)	1920
American College Health Association (ACHA)	1920
Association of Governing Boards of Universities and Colleges (ABG)	1921
American College Personnel Association (ACPA)	1924
National Association of College Admission Counselors (NACAC)	1937
National Orientation Directors Association (NODA)	1947
Association of International Educators (NAFSA)	1948
National Association of College and University Business Officers (NACUBO)	1950
American Association for Counseling and Development (AACD)	1952
Association of College and University Housing Officers—International (ACUHO-I)	1952
National Association of Personnel Workers (NAPW)	1954
American Association of State Colleges and Universities (AASCU)	1961
National Association of State Universities and Land Grant Colleges (NASULGC)	1962
National Association of Independent Colleges and Universities (NAICU)	1967
National Association for Campus Activities (NACA)	1968
National Association for Student Financial Aid Administrators (NASFAA)	1968
American Association of Higher Education (AAHE)	1969
Council for the Advancement and Support of Education (CASE)	1974
Association for Student Judicial Affairs (ASJA)	1987

Source: Adapted from Burek, 1992.

It should also be noted that over time many regional or state associations developed independently of the national organizations. Examples include the Western Deans and the Pennsylvania Association of Student Personnel Administrators.

Roles of Professional Associations

The mission of each organization describes the fundamental reasons for its existence, establishes the scope of its activities, and provides its overall direction. Like many other social institutions, these purposes evolve and change over time. It is also true that like a college or university, an association's mission may or may not be explicit or readily understood by its members or a wider professional audience. One of the marks of excellence in a voluntary association is the degree to which its mission is clearly articulated and serves as a guidepost for determining the appropriateness of the association's activities (Independent Sector, 1989). For example, the mission of NACUBO (National Association of College and University Business Officers) is "to promote sound management and financial administration of colleges and universities and to anticipate the issues affecting higher education" (Hines, 1982, p. 109). In 1991, NASPA reconsidered its mission statement as a part of the strategic planning process. The revised mission states, "The National Association of Student Personnel Administrators (NASPA) enriches the education experience of all students. It serves colleges and universities by providing leadership and professional growth opportunities for the chief student affairs officer and other professionals who consider higher education and student affairs issues from an institutional perspective" (p. 2). The financial and human resources of most associations are limited. As board members consider alternative programs and services, choices must be made among several desirable options. Determinations should be based on how centrally related the particular program or service is to the organization's mission.

Generally, associations are described by both their mission and scope. They may be local, regional, statewide, national, or international. They may be an organization composed of individual members, institutional members, or both. The specific types of services and programs offered may vary. As a general rule, most professional associations perform the following functions: conduct research; publish and disseminate research, information, and opinions; provide educational training and professional development programs; advocate on behalf of public policy or broad professional issues affecting members; assist members with career development issues; promulgate standards for professional preparation and practice; and create opportunities for professional peers to interact (American Society of Association Executives, 1988).

Professional associations are governed by their members and exist to serve their interests and needs. Most associations are legally incorporated nonprofit entities. The formal rules and structure for governance are various and are described in documents such as the articles of incorporation, constitutions, or bylaws. A governing board—composed of elected and/or appointed individuals—has the fiduciary responsibility to govern the association in compliance with the published bylaws.

A key characteristic of most student affairs professional associations is the degree to which their operations are managed by volunteers. Organizations such as NASPA, NAWE, ACUHO-I (Association of College and University Housing Officers-International), and others have small office staffs (fewer than ten full-time employees or the equivalent) that provide administrative services and assistance to the hundreds of volunteers responsible for program development and execution.

Professional associations are funded primarily by member dues; fees for programs, services, and publications; and corporate or foundation grants.

Like other organizations, associations are distinctive for many reasons, including those attributable to organizational culture. That culture is constantly evolving, incorporating changes in the beliefs, values, and attitudes of society as well as those of the members (Kuh, Schuh, Whitt, and Associates, 1991). The culture of the association determines in large measure how the governing board, staff, and volunteers behave, regardless of written policies (Independent Sector, 1989). Examples of organizational culture might include the dominant values espoused by the association, such as the degree to which volunteers have responsibility for program development, the emphasis placed on service to members, and the priority assigned multicultural participation and involvement.

Many associations collaborate on issues of common concern. For example, the American Council on Education (ACE) coordinates the Washington Higher Education Secretariat, composed of over thirty higher education associations based in Washington, D.C. NACUBO coordinates the Council of Higher Education Management Associations. Many of the organizations listed in Table 25.1 are members of one or both of these coordinating councils.

Reasons for Belonging to a Professional Association

Why do institutions and individuals belong to professional associations? There are a host of answers, but based on my conversations with colleagues, the majority of reasons fall into one of the following categories: opportunities for professional growth, a means to benefit from the services and programs provided, a chance to test professional competencies, a desire to join with others of similar interest to influence the future direction of the association or profession, and a professional sense of obligation to help advance the status of the profession and fund programs that assist it. Bloland (1985) argues that colleges and universities join the higher education associations based in Washington, D.C., because they need to have their case presented to Congress and the administration.

There are many different forms of participation and involvement, ranging from consumer to board member. These and the typical skills and time commitments required are summarized below.

Consumer

A consumer is an individual who is not a member but may (for example) periodically read the publications in the library; purchase a publication or audiotape; subscribe to a teleconference as a staff development tool; or attend a state, regional, or national conference.

Member

A member is a professional who has joined the association and receives copies of newsletters, journals, and other publications. The member follows the news of the association and responds to surveys on professional issues. These individuals have an opportunity to influence the direction and priorities of the association and are able to attend conferences or purchase resource materials and services at reduced costs. They may also volunteer and serve in a variety of leadership roles.

Contributor

A contributor may or may not be a member of the association. Working alone or in conjunction with colleagues, the contributor submits program proposals for workshops or conferences, makes presentations, prepares newsletter articles, or submits research results for publication. These tasks require good oral presentation and written communication skills and a solid conceptual understanding of research and the professional issues being addressed. The time commitment will depend on the scope and nature of the project.

Volunteer

A volunteer is a member who agrees to assist with an activity, project, or program. The assignment may be for as little time as one hour or an ongoing assignment that requires a considerable investment of time and expertise (such as service on a committee). A volunteer must have an ability to handle independent tasks as well as work as a team member. Examples of possible jobs include posting signs; planning programs; helping with registration, newsletter preparation, or surveys; conducting research; and recruiting members.

Coordinator

The coordinator is a member responsible for planning, coordinating, and directing the efforts of other volunteers and colleagues to deliver a program, event, or service. The assignment may be on a project, local, state, regional, or national level and usually requires involvement for six to eighteen months. The work typically involves coordination, administration, supervisory, interpersonal, and communication skills. Financial management skills may also be necessary. Because committee members may be located across the country, being a coordinator requires an ability to interact with and motivate others in person, on the telephone, and in written form. Possible assignments may include editing publications, chairing committees, planning educational programs, and coordinating commissions or networks.

Governance

A member can be elected or appointed to an advisory board or the governing board. This person is responsible for establishing major policies and long-range planning. It is work requiring understanding of budget and finance, a significant time commitment, and an appreciation of the important and emerging issues in the profession.

In summary, the major reasons why professionals join and become involved with associations are (1) to enhance their own professional development, (2) to make a contribution to the association, and (3) to help the profession. Individuals can assist their own professional development through all the forms of participation described above. However, making a contribution to the association and profession requires membership at a minimum and usually participation as either a contributor or a volunteer or in a governance capacity.

Involvement over the Career Life Cycle

It may be helpful to think about a career in student affairs as a life cycle. During the course of the cycle, we may be at various points or playing many different roles. Consider the student affairs professionals in a typical student affairs division. There are graduate assistants with varying amounts of previous professional experience, new professionals, persons who have made a career transfer from another field or discipline, midlevel professionals, senior student affairs officers, faculty members, and perhaps several retired staff members. In addition to their professional assignments, each of the individuals may have family responsibilities, may be involved in community or church activities, or may be working on an advanced degree. All of these factors influence the degree to which they are able to participate or interested in participating in professional associations and the types of involvement that they seek.

The examples listed below describe categories of participation and involvement for student affairs professionals.

Consumer and Member

Sally is a graduate assistant with limited time and financial resources. She is a resident director and a member of ACUHO-I. She subscribes to the NAWE journal *Initiatives* and reads other publications as required for her course work. Next year she plans to join ACPA so she can attend the annual conference and participate in career services.

Consumer, Member, Contributor, and Volunteer

Jim is a doctoral student who has three years' previous professional experience as a Greek adviser. Prior to returning to graduate school, he was a member of ACPA's Commission IV (student activities) and edited its newsletter. As a result, his writing and publication skills improved considerably. This year he joined NASPA and plans to attend the regional conference. He and his faculty adviser have submitted a program proposal and hope to present it at the regional conference.

Consumer, Member, Contributor, and Volunteer

George is the director of the counseling center. He is a member of AACD (American Association for Counseling and Development), ACPA, and APA (American Psychological Association). In the past fifteen years, he has served in numerous volunteer roles, has made frequent presentations at conferences, and has published his research regularly. Because of the demands of his current position and budget restrictions, he will not be able to attend any professional conferences this year. He has, however, agreed to serve as a reviewer of program proposals for the conference.

Member

Alice has recently been named director of the outdoor recreation program in the student center. Her previous professional experience was as a high school coach. She plans to maintain her membership in the National Intramural/Recreational Sports Association and has recently joined the Association of College Unions—International to learn more about the union field. Alice hopes to attend the summer institute sponsored by the association this year.

Member, Contributor, Volunteer, and Governance Participant

Sue has been a faculty member and a student affairs professional for twenty-five years. She has served as editor of the *NASPA Journal* for three years, was director of the research division, was director of the NASPA summer institute, and served as a member of the board of directors for both NASPA and NAWE. In 1985, she was elected president of ACPA, and she has recently agreed to be the program chair for the upcoming annual conference.

Consumer and Member

Bill is the dean of students and has been a student affairs professional for ten years. He has been a member of ACUHO-I, ACPA, and NASPA. He now has administrative responsibility for financial aid and the student health service. He has recently joined the National Association for Student Financial Aid Administrators and plans to accompany the health center director to the American College Health Association conference next year. Occasionally, he also attends the annual ACE meeting with the president of the college.

These are just a few examples of how participation and involvement in professional associations may vary over the course of a career. These examples are based on the patterns of contemporary professionals. Think about your own pattern of involvement and participation. How does it compare to these examples or to the experiences of your colleagues and other professionals whom you respect?

The Role of Associations in Professional Development

Professional associations provide programs and services designed to enhance their members' understanding of contemporary issues and to develop their professional skills. Though the benefits derived from participation often depend on the type of individual involvement, the potential positive outcomes are significant. The most often cited benefits are summarized below.

Colleagues

The reason members give most frequently for joining or belonging to an association is the opportunity it offers for professional networks. Individuals encounter colleagues and make friends with whom to exchange ideas, perspectives, and concerns beyond the scope of their current work. The professional is able to interact with individuals in similar types of institutions and to compare ideas on programs and services, as well as to gain a broader perspective on issues from professionals in other types of institutions and parts of the country. Someone who moves from a small liberal arts college in New England to a public four-year college in the Southwest may have an automatic network of colleagues as a result of involvement in professional associations.

For many members of underrepresented ethnic groups and women, participation in professional associations creates valuable contacts. In cases where few women or ethnic minorities are employed on a campus, the organization provides connections to valuable role models and colleagues with similar interests and concerns.

The social nature of professional associations is also a legitimate advantage of involvement. Friendships and personal relationships develop during graduate school, in employment settings, and as a result of professional work. As people move to different institutions and regions of the country, professional associations furnish opportunities for continued interactions and get-togethers. Individuals often develop strong friendships with those with whom they have served on committees or in other volunteer roles.

Opportunities for Understanding

The simple act of getting away from a single campus environment is important in gaining new perspectives. The chance to consider issues from the perspective of others is invaluable. For example, their current campus assignment may be in the area of health education, but individuals can learn more about residence life issues through participation in different professional associations. Staff members are also able to broaden their understanding of different types of institutions and the issues that they confront.

Ongoing Professional Development

Participation in professional associations creates access to the latest professional developments through publications and conferences. As a contributor or volunteer, an individual is able to expand and test a repertoire of skills and experiences beyond those required in a current assignment. It may be possible to perform duties and tasks not included in a full-time position. Many professionals gain the necessary experience and training for broader or more responsible career roles as a result of association involvement. Further, they also have a chance to establish a professional reputation beyond an individual campus as a result of their contributions.

Orientation to the Profession

New professionals and persons who transfer into student affairs from another career field receive an important orientation to the relevant issues and literature through participation in association-sponsored programs. Many chief student affairs officers are appointed to the leadership roles from faculty positions. The professional associations provide important opportunities to gain conceptual grounding as well as advice from more experienced colleagues.

Influence on the Direction of the Profession

Individuals do make a difference. The organizational culture, professional priorities, and the association's direction are all shaped by the concerns and perspectives of the members and those responsible for governance. By responding to research questionnaires, voting on membership issues, serving as a volunteer, and contributing to the professional literature, professionals help to document the current issues and influence the emerging ones.

Shaping of Professional Practice and Accreditation Standards

Professional associations establish professional standards that describe the characteristics of good practice for individuals and institutions. The general public's expectations and bench marks for sound professional and ethical practice are guided by the association's standards and directives. In many cases, accreditation and licensing standards are established, or at least influenced, by the professional associations.

This chapter has described the functioning of professional associations, the forms of participation and involvement, and the specific benefits to members' professional development and skills. Yet there are several other questions to consider. These include ways to get involved, decisions about time and resource management, and factors associated with joining more than one professional association.

Ways to Get Involved

If ten student affairs professionals were interviewed, the results might reveal fifteen different views on how to get involved, and they would all work for some people. No one correct way exists, and professionals should talk with respected colleagues and seek their advice. Listed here are some basic suggestions for getting started.

Assess Your Own Situation

What do you wish to accomplish? What contributions can a professional make? What talents do you have? In what areas do you wish to develop? Keeping your own personal and professional needs in focus is an important first step.

Investigate Alternatives

Once individual goals have been clarified and identified, investigate a variety of associations. The list contained in Table 25.1 is a good place to start. Consult with faculty members and colleagues. Be wary of persons who may try to persuade you that there is one best professional association. Review the association's publications, conference programs, and membership recruitment materials. Determine as much as you can about the association and its culture and assess their compatibility with your goals.

Join and Participate

As the previous examples illustrated, you are free to change your mind and belong to different associations at various points in your career. When possible, attend a state or regional conference so that you can get acquainted with people in an appropriate setting. Some straightforward advice for newcomers includes the following: attend with a colleague who may already be involved and ask that person to introduce you to the volunteers and leaders; attend sessions, especially those designed for newcomers, and ask questions; participate in group meals and sit with people you do not already know; take part in social events or small-group discussions; and wear your name tag.

Volunteer

Depending on individual needs and interests, a person may decide to become more involved. Do something: volunteer, submit a program proposal, newsletter article, or journal article.

Explore Other Alternatives

Always keep an open mind about other possibilities. As you mature professionally, shift your interests, or change positions or institutions, your professional goals and aspirations will invariably change. It may be a good time to seek out new challenges in your professional association or to find another one.

Ideally, there should be no limits to your ability to participate and become involved in professional associations. What are some of the realistic constraints?

Your first priority is to your institutional assignment. Most institutions are supportive of staff involvement, but you should not take things for granted. Consult with your supervisor before accepting a volunteer assignment. Be sure you have a clear understanding about the use of university time for association activities; release time to attend meetings; use of institutional resources for copying, mailing, and telephone calls; and so forth. Finally, clarify what types of support the association will provide for the volunteer experience.

Your ability to participate may also be limited by the needs and plans of other staff members. For a variety of sound administrative and financial reasons, not everyone on the staff can attend the same workshop or conference. Someone has to be on duty to handle the campus responsibilities. If the majority of the staff in a unit is active in one association, it may be a wise choice to pursue other opportunities. This approach provides the unit with access to the resources of more than one association and may allow greater possibilities for participation and involvement.

The Cost of Membership

In most cases, the individual and the institution combine to pay the cost of membership in professional associations. For example, you may be eligible for reduced membership dues because your college is an institutional member of NASPA. In other cases, the individual may pay the membership dues and the registration fees, but the institution allows release time for attendance and a van for transportation. As a professional, you are ultimately responsible for your own development. Institutional support is an important investment, but lack of campus funding is not a valid excuse for not joining a professional association. Obviously, finite time and financial resources will influence your decisions about whether or not to join more than one professional association.

Multiple Association Affiliations

It is not unusual for professionals to change their association memberships from year to year as their personal and professional circumstances change. It is also common for individuals to belong to more than one organization. The examples discussed earlier supplied several reasons, including a desire to learn more about issues in a new field, to collaborate with other colleagues, and to provide financial and moral support for the goals and purposes of several worthwhile organizations.

Good judgment is the determining factor in deciding whether or not to volunteer in more than one association simultaneously. There are limits on your time and energy. Avoid commitments that may cause you to give less than a very best effort to your assignments. The student affairs professional associations depend heavily on volunteers to plan and execute their programs, and your colleagues there will rely on you to complete your work. Failure to manage your time effectively can result in disappointments and frustrations for both you and your colleagues.

Much of your professional reputation depends on how well you handle your volunteer assignments. Reliability is an essential characteristic for volunteers. Equally valued will be the ability to delegate and share responsibilities, to assist or be a mentor to newcomers, to share recognition and credit appropriately with all involved, and to manage your commitments realistically. Of utmost importance are your professional standards and personal integrity.

As the examples illustrate, the degree of participation will vary at different points in your career. Your ability to make mature and responsible decisions about your professional involvement will influence the esteem in which your colleagues hold you.

Summary

Professional associations play an important role in continuing career development and represent a major strategy for professionals to consider when they think about ways in which they may acquire or improve their professional and administrative skills. Individuals and their institutions both derive advantages from participation in professional associations. The benefits include access to current information and research for ongoing professional development, a broader perspective and scope of understanding on contemporary issues, a network of colleagues and friends, an orientation to the profession for persons who transfer into student affairs from other disciplines, standards of professional practice and accreditation, and an opportunity to influence the future direction of the profession and the association.

Decisions to join and become involved should be based on your goals and talents, the flexibility and support of your institution, and the needs of the association. There is no one best association, and you should feel comfortable exploring alternatives at various points in your career.

Whether you are a new professional, someone who has made a recent career change, or a senior student affairs officer, associations should play a meaningful and significant part in your development. It is never too early or too late to consider and reconsider the variety of associations and the forms of participation and involvement available. It is my hope that you are inspired to take charge of your development and carefully analyze the possibilities that the professional associations may create.

References

American Society of Association Executives. *Principles of Association Management: A Professional's Handbook.* Washington, D.C.: American Society of Association Executives, 1988.

Bloland, H. G. *Associations in Action: The Washington, D.C. Higher Education Community.* ASHE-ERIC Higher Education Report, no. 2. Washington, D.C.: Association for the Study of Higher Education, 1985.

Bloland, P. A. "Ecumenicalism in College Student Personnel." *Journal of College Student Personnel,* 1972, *13,* 102–111.

Burek, D. M. *Encyclopedia of Associations.* Detroit, Mich.: Gale Research, 1992.

Hines, N. O. *Business Officers in Higher Education: A History of NACUBO.* Washington, D.C.: National Association of College and University Business Officers, 1982.

Independent Sector. "Executive Summary." In *Profiles of Excellence: Studies of the Effectiveness of Nonprofit Organizations.* Washington, D.C.: Independent Sector, 1989.

Kuh, G. D., Schuh, J. H., Whitt, E. J., and Associates. *Involving Colleges: Successful Approaches to Fostering Student Learning and Development Outside the Classroom.* San Francisco: Jossey-Bass, 1991.

National Association of Student Personnel Administrators. *A Perspective on Student Affairs.* Washington, D.C.: National Association of Student Personnel Administrators, 1987.

National Association of Student Personnel Administrators. *Mission Statement of Association.* (Rev. ed.) Washington, D.C.: National Association of Student Personnel Administrators, 1991.

Rhatigan, J. J. "NASPA History." In *NASPA Member Handbook.* Washington, D.C.: National Association of Student Personnel Administrators, 1991.

Sheeley, V. L. "NADW and NAAS: 60 Years of Organizational Relationships (NAWDAC–ACPA: 1923–1983)." In B. A. Belson and L. E. Fitzgerald (eds.), *Thus We Spoke: ACPA–NAWDAC 1958–1975.* Washington, D.C.: American College Personnel Association, 1983.

26

℘

Mentoring and Self-Directed Learning

Susan W. Batchelor

Did you think your formal education was concluded when you were awarded your last university degree? Even though we student affairs professionals understand better than most people the importance of continuous learning and cocurricular experiences for *students,* we often overlook the value of such activities for ourselves. In this changing global society, it is imperative to keep pace with changes, maintain cutting-edge knowledge, and stay mentally and physically healthy in the process. Sandeen directly addresses the need for professionals to be skilled leaders, managers, mediators, and educators to be effective in dealing with the evolving complexities of student affairs work (1991).

Theoretical perspectives are useful tools for increasing the student affairs professional's understanding of the cultural needs of students and staff. One suggested reading, *Evolving Theoretical Perspectives on Students* (Moore, 1990) is particularly helpful for professionals attempting to increase their understanding, skills, and competence. However, astute student affairs professionals must also expand their learning beyond student affairs.

This chapter will focus on lessons learned from other fields regarding mentoring and self-directed learning. Specific strategies will be explored that will assist professionals in developing and improving their administrative skills. Options and opportunities will be discussed and suggestions made to assist student affairs officers in creating a plan for continued professional development.

Lessons Learned from Other Fields

Significant literature exists on the benefits of mentoring relationships and self-directed learning in the fields of psychology and management.

Leadership

Business has long discussed and defined the terms *management* and *leadership*. Kouzes and Posner (1987) maintain that top executives and managers at all levels must accept the challenge of leadership. Their definition of management skills includes the ability to bring people together to accomplish extraordinary results. We can all learn leadership skills; they are not the province of a gifted few. Furthermore, leadership can perhaps best be learned by working with persons who possess and practice these skills.

Kouzes and Posner state, "Shared values foster strong feelings of personal effectiveness, promote high levels of company loyalty, facilitate consensus about key organization goals and stakeholders, encourage ethical behavior, promote strong norms about working hard and caring, and reduce levels of job stress and tension" (1987, p. 193). Further, Kouzes and Posner challenge leaders to reinforce intangible values through identification of key behaviors: how leaders spend time, the questions they ask, their reactions to critical incidents, and what leaders reward (1987, p. 201).

Warren Bennis, former president of the University of Cincinnati, concludes that there is a clear distinction between leaders and managers: "Leaders are people who do the right thing; managers are people who do things right" (1989, p. 18). He also indicates that American organizations are overmanaged and have too little leadership. Therefore, leadership enhancement must be just as much a part of the development effort as learning new technical skills; moreover, it should not be assumed that these necessary skills are learned in formal classroom settings, regardless of degree earned.

Identifying and discussing these key behaviors with a mentor accomplishes several goals. Leadership skills and the agreement on values necessary for sound management *at all levels* can be fostered and practiced with mentor assistance. Mentoring relationships are effective ways of establishing and transferring these shared values, also very much a hallmark of our work in student affairs.

Naisbitt (1982) indicates, "The failure of hierarchies to solve society's problems forced people to talk to one another — and that was the beginning of networks" (p. 191). These networks have become the foundations of problem solving and the exchange sources for developing mentor relationships and sharing leadership strategies.

Staying Balanced

Being mentally and physically healthy is what James Autry refers to as "staying balanced" (1991). He discusses the two extremes of professional behavior: the one person who cannot stay away from the office emotionally or physically, and the other who barely fulfills the time or job requirements. According to Autry, the balanced life lies somewhere in the middle, though where that is can fluctuate depending on career stage or work load. Therefore, we have to be persistent in rediscovering where the middle is to achieve a sense of personal balance. Failure to do so will result in the loss of resources, both professionally and personally.

Autry's method of finding the middle ground is more complex than it would at first seem. He advises one to consider everything to be equally important. That includes job, family, friends, exercise, church, volunteer work, sports, hobbies, carpools, and individual relaxation time. Acquiring the ability to balance is important for the successful student affairs administrator and is also an appropriate agenda for a mentoring relationship.

Mentoring

The advantage to every individual who actively engages in a mentoring relationship is that it is completely free and that the initiative for developing mentors and the plan for self-directed learning remain under that person's control. Consider the activity of mentoring an important professional growth opportunity, an investment in self.

Is mentoring a new concept or trend that will fade as we march toward the year 2000? It seems highly unlikely, as the tradition that exists today has its origins in Greek mythology. Odysseus asked his faithful friend, Mentor, to become the guardian of his beloved son, Telemachus. Mentor was the adviser, guide, and support for Telemachus during Odysseus' long absence. Hence, the term *mentor* has come to mean "trusted advisor and wise, faithful counselor" (*Random House College Dictionary,* 1988). Mentoring, as we examine it today, still includes the roles of adviser, supporter, and teacher. Implicitly, the relationship's foundation is built on trust, mutual agreement, respect, and confidentiality. Emotional and social interaction makes possible the transfer of attitudes, behaviors, and skills (Hill, 1989). Another outcome of mentoring relationships is improved and marketable administrative skills, and research strongly suggests that we need more mentoring as part of professional education (Kelly, 1984). Finally, Moore (1982) describes mentoring as a form of adult socialization for professional roles, especially leadership ones. The skills to be effective in all of these roles can be learned and practiced in mentoring relationships.

Professional development takes many forms where both formal and informal mentoring relationships can make a significant contribution. Selection of a mentor takes time, effort, and commitment. Mentor relationships should cross gender and ethnic lines and be a method of learning new information and gaining competencies.

It may not appear that there are logical connections between simultaneously occurring mentoring relationships, but they exist to meet specific objectives, complete a project, or provide counsel to work with specific concerns. For example, a professional, who was also a doctoral candidate, asked the director of an institute that she attended to help her with her dissertation by becoming an outside reader. The institute's director agreed, and an informal mentoring relationship was initiated. The connection occurred during a professional development institute; the project to be completed was the dissertation. It is always the responsibility of the person initiating the relationship to maintain contact as the two professionals may not be on the same campus or close geographically.

Mentoring relationships often develop into rich and helpful lifelong friendships. The positive outcomes and rewards are many. The significant key to successful mentoring relationships is to develop several ones at once, each with different expectations.

Informal Mentoring

Beginning with local campus contacts, determine who has a skill you would like to acquire. Take the initiative to approach that person to request their guidance. Even very busy administrators and faculty members are usually flattered by the compliment and will make time to meet your needs. Be direct and clear about what you want and what you hope to gain. Maintain regular contact and offer your reactions about the skills being learned and the status of the relationship. Finally, do not forget to express gratitude in both verbal and written form (with copies to your mentor's supervisor if appropriate) for time spent and lessons learned.

Never be discouraged if a professional indicates an inability to fulfill mentoring requests. Assume the timing of the request is a problem, and either make another attempt on a different occasion or move on to another professional.

As stated previously, several mentors can provide a variety of perspectives and offer different strengths. If improved writing skills or publication in professional journals is a goal, seek a mentor known for writing ability or someone who has published frequently. Ask for editorial feedback on work in progress, and learn the processes of and expectations for publishing. If understanding the politics of the institution is a goal (Barr and Keating, 1979), select a person held in high regard because of professional expertise, strong leadership, and communication style. Ask colleagues whom they consider to be effective politically. Job title is not necessarily relevant; rather, the high regard of diverse colleagues will validate the potential mentor. Again, take the initiative to contact this person in an appropriate fashion, explain your goal, and seek assistance. Obviously, confidentiality and trust are crucial in this particular relationship.

Another excellent opportunity for identifying potential mentors arises through volunteer work at professional association meetings. Development occurs during the planning, implementation, and evaluation of a conference and while working on the many tasks necessary to sustain this kind of organization. Many of the profession's finest leaders become readily available to, and share the credit for success with, persons willing to do the tedious chores, work the long hours, and contribute to the value of the program. These leaders have performed such tasks in the past on many occasions and view the volunteer's initiative as professional dedication. From volunteer work, you can establish a network of people to call on in your region and across the country (Chapter Twenty-Five).

Networking is not mentoring, of course; yet the connections created by a network can lead to a mentor. A new publication, *Connections: A Publication for New Professionals in Student Affairs* (Strange and Belch, 1990), lists different ways to become involved with networks within the National Association of Student Personnel Administrators (NASPA) and can be used as a guide to getting involved. Committee work is another way to meet someone with whom you would want to establish a mentoring relationship.

Formal Mentoring

Formal mentoring relationships can develop in a number of ways, including as the outcome of a performance review, through work with faculty advisers, or through a network.

Performance Reviews. A formal mentoring relationship might be the result of a performance review goal to improve skills. A formal internship program in the vice president's office, for example, can help achieve this objective and often leads to a continuing mentoring relationship. In this situation, a wide range of activities and agendas can be experienced from the viewpoint of the vice president over an extended period of time. Everyday management, decision-making, conflict resolution, and budget skills can be learned through the mentoring of an able and sharing vice president.

Faculty Advisers. Another formal mentoring relationship can develop through work toward an advanced educational degree. A professor or major faculty adviser is often someone who meets all the criteria of being a mentor. This relationship is usually long term and grows through structured contacts that include classroom and formal research activity. Again, it is the professional's responsibility to ensure that the formal relationship develops into a true mentor relationship by following the basic guidelines outlined earlier. For example, suggest to your major professor that you present a program together at a professional meeting. Follow through with the details of program requirements, and set out-of-class appointment times to work on the project.

Then utilize his or her expertise and experience to create an interesting and informative program. Outcomes of this initial investment might include skills that will enhance classroom learning, encounters with colleagues at the actual meeting, possible publication of the work, or additional presentations at future professional meetings.

Networks. A third strategy for developing formal mentoring relationships is to request that your supervisor nominate you for an institute or other concentrated professional experience. Several are offered by professional organizations: for instance, the Richard F. Stevens Institute for Vice Presidents and Deans; regional Mid-Management Institutes and New Professionals Institutes, sponsored by NASPA; and NASPA regional associations. The Interfraternity Institute, sponsored by Indiana University and the Fraternity Executives Association, which provides intense learning about the Greek community, and the Summer Institute for Women, sponsored by Bryn Mawr College and Higher Education Resource Services, Mid-Atlantic, are other examples of worthwhile investments of time, energy, and financial resources. Regardless of background, training, or graduate preparation, such professional opportunities meet common curricular requirements and establish networks for continued professional development (McDade, 1987; Hodgkinson, 1974).

Kerr (1984) and others have documented the need for administrators in senior positions to continue to grow as leaders in order to adapt to the changing environment. From these developmental experiences, the professional's store of knowledge is increased, and networks that foster mentoring relationships can be formed at all professional levels.

Investment in Self

Be prepared to invest personal funds to supplement the costs of attendance at institutes or professional meetings. Whereas business spends nearly $6 billion each year on professional development (Green, 1983), most educational institutions have restricted travel and professional development funds. To illustrate, a dean of education paid all of his expenses to attend a costly and highly respected summer institute. He was promoted within the institution shortly thereafter and was subsequently appointed provost at another university. Although this experience was not the only way that he improved himself, he credits it with establishing focus for his career goals and offering opportunities for developing several key mentoring relationships. Several new professionals at the NASPA Region III New Professional Institute also paid their own registration and travel costs. Their home institutions supported them by giving time away to attend. The written evaluations in each of these cases verified the high value that these professionals placed on their investments and on the networks and mentors that resulted from them.

Advantages of Mentoring

The advantages of informal relationships are that they can in a short period achieve a specific goal and that they afford the initiator a genuine sense of control. Formal relationships, by contrast, involve longer-term ties in order to accomplish ongoing goals and entail regular contact with the mentor, because of the usual proximity of the parties involved. The importance of both formal and informal mentoring relationships is that they provide diversity and breadth to professional growth. Numerous mentors provide many perspectives to complex issues and enhance understanding of current concerns through their knowledge and experiences.

Mentors Outside the Student Affairs Profession

There are also many opportunities to develop mentoring relationships outside the field of higher education. It would be an oversight not to use the same model when approaching and establishing relationships with business professionals, politicians, doctors, or other community leaders. The different perspectives and priorities provided by such professionals increase knowledge and broaden understanding of issues. Engaging in volunteer work in the community can extend opportunities for learning and development through mentoring. Whether it is the arts, social service agencies, or local schools, such community-based programs need and recruit volunteers with expertise and commitment. The professional can benefit from these activities by acquiring additional skills and connecting with potential mentors. From a practical level of involvement, greater visibility and responsibility can be gained through volunteer work. It is possible to become involved in agency governing boards, community task forces, and even election to public office.

Both the individual professional and the home institution derive advantages from these relationships and experiences. For example, many community professionals are willing to provide programs on your campus at little or no cost. Your own professional development can also be expanded through outside speakers and guest lecturers on your own campus. To illustrate, due to a special relationship between a student affairs professional and a nationally known speaker, an exceptional opportunity for help and advice was created for undergraduate students.

Equally important, diverse mentoring relationships enhance the personal development that everyone needs. Transferring skills and interests from the workplace to other arenas profits everyone. A student affairs vice president plays violin in the city's symphony. This activity not only gives her an outlet for her musical training and interest but also furnishes an entirely different opportunity for establishing mentoring relationships with others who have similar talents but varied professional backgrounds. Another professional was in charge of her community's efforts to establish citywide recycling with nationally recognized success; she is now involved with experts working on environmental issues. An experienced vice president was the mayor of his community for many years and worked regularly with local and state leaders. Success in both mentoring relationships and projects are outcomes of these efforts.

Never underestimate the power of your institutional position. Many professionals are invited to participate in community projects because of access to student volunteers and university resources. Use this advantageous position to become involved in the community, and develop mentoring relationships in the process.

Impact of Mentoring on Women and Minorities

According to researchers, women and minorities will be assisted by close relationships with mentors or sponsors who offer encouragement and support (Gappa and Uehling, 1979). Moore and Sagaria (1981) also suggest that mentoring creates opportunities that would not otherwise exist for women. They report that many senior women professionals acknowledge the invaluable contributions of their mentors. Other studies about the effect of mentoring on underrepresented individuals (Burke, 1984; Fagensen, 1989) who succeed in higher education and business are supportive of the concept that mentoring is helpful. Therefore, for women and minorities who aspire to becoming a dean or vice president or to assuming another administrative position, mentoring can be a very useful tool.

Because there are proportionally fewer women and minorities in upper-level positions who can serve as mentors, cross-gender and cross-cultural mentoring possibilities can be exploited instead. The "good old boy" (or "girl") networking and mentoring process must be replaced by genuine multidimensional relationships to prepare future leaders in the student affairs profession. As more women and minorities aspire to positions of responsibility in higher education, diverse strategies must be identified and fully taken advantage of. For example, the work of Gilligan (1982) describes certain characteristics as distinctly feminine. These kinds of cultural and gender differences can be used to solve complex problems. To attain positions in which major institutional policies and decisions are made, women and minorities must cultivate any opportunities to open doors.

Self-Directed Learning

Cervero (1988, p. 38) asks the question, "Which model of the learner is best?" He goes on to quote the psychologist Jerome Bruner, who states that no one model should be "enshrined" at the center of the practice of education, but that value judgments made by each of us as individuals and the choices that we make about what we want to achieve determine how professionals learn.

How we learn and what model is best are difficult questions to answer. Many educators believe professionals learn in many different ways and that forms of learning differ according to desired ends (Cervero, 1988). This philosophy suggests, or rather expects, that short-term and long-term goals should be identified *before* continued self-directed learning is attempted. Therefore, ask yourself some difficult questions. Do I want to increase my knowledge base merely for the sake of knowing? Do I want to commit myself to a formal educational setting (graduate school)? Do I want to improve my administrative and management skills in order to move up the ladder in my profession?

Once goals have been set, assume that learning will occur when committed participation in a self-directed plan occurs. The plan should be detailed, realistic, and appropriate to both your career stage and experiential level. For example, it would probably not be suitable for a first-year residence life staff member to intern in the dean's office, even if she desires to be a dean as the result of self-directed learning. This activity would be more productive for a midmanagement professional. A number of practical steps can be taken by professionals to assure a carefully planned program of self-directed learning.

Reading

It is productive and effective to begin professional learning by reading a variety of pertinent materials. *Points of View,* published by NASPA (1989), is essential in forming a framework on the profession of student affairs. *The Chronicle of Higher Education* should be read regularly to keep pace with current issues and trends in higher education. Professional journals such as those published by the American College Personnel Association (ACPA) and NASPA are excellent sources of theoretical knowledge and current practices. Several monthly newsletters associated with legal issues help to create perspective, and popular educational magazines such as *Change* supply timely and interesting background information. New books and monographs are also useful to the self-directed learner. Jossey-Bass publishes current offerings in all areas of education and is an excellent resource. An active learner should be a voracious reader of all types of literature, depending on individual interests as well as professional needs.

Staff Development Activities

Campus-based staff programs provide a readily available source of professional development. Attend programs even if they do not seem relevant to your current career expectations. Watch for special guests invited to the campus by various academic departments, and attend these programs. Volunteer to work with faculty members to help with their programming needs. Valuable mentoring relationships can be established within the institution and even with guests through this process. Again, their lack of financial cost and ease of accessibility should make these activities an integral part of well-rounded professional development.

Professional Associations

Hall (1976) defines the career stages that all professionals experience: early career, midcareer, and late career. He outlines specific characteristics and activities common to each stage and states that a function of professional associations is to meet the requirements of professionals during all three. Associations sponsor regional and national annual meetings, publish journals, conduct research, and provide the networking and mentoring opportunities previously discussed in this chapter. Therefore, involvement with at least one professional association is beneficial regardless of the career stage and should be a component of professional development.

Informal mentoring can occur if you attend a professional meeting and are impressed by a speaker. Take the initiative to meet this person. If possible, introduce yourself, invite the person for coffee, or speak briefly after the speech. Explain a related project; ask a question about a particular item in the speech; and if there is an opportunity, ask for additional information. Follow up with a letter and exchange any additional findings. In this way, a relationship is established (see Chapter Twenty-Five).

Classroom Education

Finally, consider enrolling in a continuing education course, a graduate-level administrative offering, or a departmental academic course. Also attend lectures and seminars offered at your university or college or in the community. These experiences will enrich professional continued learning.

Developing an Action Plan

Know what you want your end results to be, and then design your own plan. Following the premise of the learning theory previously discussed, learning will take place when goals are set and there is commitment to them. Developing goals and a plan for their implementation is an excellent agenda to bring to a mentor. Remember also that the desired objective is to stay balanced (Autry, 1991), and understand that workable strategies must include a time commitment. Be prepared to make adjustments, and anticipate the need to communicate goal changes to significant others in order for them to be supportive as well.

Read. Journals, periodicals, the Jossey-Bass New Directions for Student Services series, and major books about both student affairs *and* diverse areas of higher education are all appropriate.

Get involved. Become active in a professional association. Attend or present programs at conferences, and volunteer to help with association projects.

Follow through. Write to authors, and call when appropriate; take the initiative to get answers and develop professional relationships.

Engage in staff development. Attend staff development programs on your campus and video conferences. In addition, subscribe to newsletters and publications that appeal to your interests.

Engage in mentoring. Sustain mentoring relationships until goals are completed. Remember to share what you have learned, and thank your mentor for his or her contribution. Finally, establish formal mentoring relationships where possible, either through internship experiences, institute attendance, or pursuit of an advanced degree.

Summary

Integrating theories, fields, practices, and experiences enables the student affairs professional to improve professionally on a constant basis. Without oversimplifying complex issues and theories of self-development, two strategies have proven to be successful: mentoring and self-directed learning.

Review the suggestions made here and in other professional development literature, and incorporate them into professional life strategies that will improve administrative skills. Learning is continuous and takes place in many environments.

The game of baseball often offers excellent illustrations of important life lessons. The following is a short but telling parable about taking personal charge of professional development. I have found it especially helpful since first hearing it long ago.

In a game crucial to the success of the baseball season, the count was three and two on the batter. The next pitch was hurled from the pitching mound, and the umpire hesitated a split second before calling the pitch. The frustrated batter turned to the umpire and yelled, "Well, What was it?" The umpire confidently responded, "It's *nothing* until *I* call it!"

You call it. You define and control your destiny for professional development. Like baseball, this is best done by involving committed team players, having clear rules, and knowing the power of the umpire who hesitates only long enough to make a good decision and then acts confidently.

References

Autry, J. A. *Love & Profit: The Art of Caring Leadership.* New York: William Morrow, 1991.

Barr, M. J., and Keating, L. A. "No Program Is an Island." In M. J. Barr and L. A. Keating (eds.), *Establishing Effective Programs.* New Directions for Student Services, no. 7. San Francisco: Jossey-Bass, 1979.

Bennis, W. *Why Leaders Can't Lead: The Unconscious Conspiracy Continues.* San Francisco: Jossey-Bass, 1989.

Burke, R. J. "Mentors in Organizations." *Group and Organization Studies,* 1984, *9,* 353–372.

Cervero, R. M. *Effective Continuing Education for Professionals.* San Francisco: Jossey-Bass, 1988.

Fagensen, A. "The Mentor Advantage: Perceived Career/Job Experiences of Protégés Versus Non-Protégés." *Journal of Organizational Behavior,* 1989, *10,* 309–320.

Gappa, J. M., and Uehling, B. S. *Women in Academe: Steps to Greater Equality.* AAHE-ERIC Higher Education Research Report, no. 1. Washington, D.C.: American Association for Higher Education, 1979.

Gilligan, C. *In a Different Voice: Psychological Theory and Women's Development.* Cambridge, Mass.: Harvard University Press, 1982.

Green, M. F. "Review of Administrative Leadership: Effective and Responsible Decision Making in Higher Education." *Journal of Higher Education,* 1983, *54* (2), 209–12.

Hall, D. *Careers in Organizations.* Pacific Palisades, Calif.: Goodyear, 1976.

Hill, S. K. "Mentoring and Other Communication Support in the Academic Setting. *Group and Organization Studies,* 1989, *14,* 355–368.

Hodgkinson, H. L. "Adult Development: Implications for Faculty and Administrators." *Educational Record,* Fall 1974, *55* (4), 263–274.

Kelly, K. "Initiating a Relationship with a Mentor in Student Affairs." *NASPA Journal,* 1984, *21,* 49–54.

Kerr, C. *Strengthening Leadership in Colleges and Universities: A Report of the Commission on Strengthening Presidential Leadership.* Washington, D.C.: Association of Governing Boards of Universities and Colleges, 1984.

Kouzes, J. M., and Posner, B. Z. *The Leadership Challenge: How to Get Extraordinary Things Done in Organizations.* San Francisco: Jossey-Bass, 1987.

McDade, S. A. *Higher Education Leadership: Enhancing Skills Through Professional Development Programs.* ASHE-ERIC Higher Education Report, no. 5. Washington, D.C.: Association for the Study of Higher Education, 1987.

Moore, K. *What to Do Until the Mentor Arrives.* Washington, D.C.: National Association of Women Deans, Administrators, and Counselors, 1982.

Moore, K. M., and Sagaria, M. A. "Women Administrators and Mobility: The Second Struggle." *Journal of the National Association of Women Deans, Administrators, and Counselors,* 1981, *44* (2), 21–28.

Moore, L. V. (ed.). *Evolving Theoretical Perspectives on Students.* New Directions for Student Services, no. 51. San Francisco: Jossey-Bass, 1990.

Naisbitt, J. *Megatrends: Ten New Directions Transforming Our Lives.* New York: Warner Books, 1982.

National Association of Student Personnel Administrators. "A Perspective on Student Affairs, 1987." In *Points of View.* Washington, D.C.: National Association of Student Personnel Administrators, 1989.

Random House College Dictionary (rev. ed.). New York: Random House, 1988.

Sandeen, A. *The Chief Student Affairs Officer: Leader, Manager, Mediator, Educator.* San Francisco: Jossey-Bass, 1991.

Strange, C., and Belch, H. (eds.). *Connections: A Publication for New Professionals in Student Affairs.* Bowling Green, Ohio: Bowling Green State University, Department of College Student Personnel, 1990.

27

☙

Advancing
Professionally
Through
Graduate Education

Susan R. Komives

Time is going by. Your professional clock is signaling that it is time to decide. Do you need a doctorate or not? Will earning a credential be sufficient? Is a doctorate necessary to move into new professional roles, engage in meaningful research, or make possible a career shift into a faculty role? Are you considering graduate work because of a sense of "up or out" (Burns, 1982), a recognition of needing more competencies to handle your function more effectively, or an acknowledgment that you are burned out where you are and need to move onward and upward? Is the reason that you love to learn and want the stimulation of the classroom to push you to read whole books again, not just to collect them on your shelves? It may be time to decide. One issue in the application stage of professional development is the serious consideration of what additional education is needed to achieve professional goals (Miller and Carpenter, 1980).

Assuming that the reader has earned a master's degree or is engaging in master's-level study, this chapter focuses on the nature of doctoral preparation for student affairs administrative, teaching, and research positions. The chapter, an examination of specialization and growth within the study of student affairs and higher education, will emphasize perspectives on doctoral programs, both in higher education and student affairs administration.

Particular attention will be devoted to (1) curricular focus, (2) degree requirements, (3) faculty, (4) Ph.D. or Ed.D. degrees, (5) criteria and processes for admission, (6) financing of doctoral study, and (7) alternative preparation routes. The chapter concludes with observations on evaluating the appropriateness of a doctoral program, including self-assessment and program review. Future issues in doctoral preparation are briefly explored.

Doctorates for Career Success

Success in student affairs work should not be judged by upward mobility or degrees earned. A professional can stay renewed and effective with the help of good supervision, meaningful work, and the self-learning that can take place beyond a professional master's preparation. Few would argue, however, that there is a growing expectation of doctoral study for both advancement and credibility in student affairs. A current job could be retained without the doctoral degree, and promotions from within are one way that someone without a doctorate can advance; yet most opportunities for advancement or even lateral shifts are likely to be reduced when master's degree applicants are compared to similarly experienced peers who have doctorates. Many midmanagement and upper-management positions in most institutions simply will not be available without the doctoral credential. Conversely, prospective doctoral students without any prior experience in higher education may find the degree alone insufficient in seeking an administrative position in higher education.

The doctorate is much more than a union card, much more than a mere academic hurdle or a rite of passage to advance further in the academy. A good doctoral program should be a valuable experience establishing the developing professional as an expert about the student experience and student affairs administration. The doctorate should add a strong scholarly focus to an already established practitioner base, should empower educational leadership, should provide perspectives that enable the role of change agent, and should stimulate research inquiry.

The doctorate offers concentrated, formal opportunities for building additional competencies and skills whether one's career path is to be an expert in a functional area (for example, career development, residence life, or learning disabilities), to assume a faculty position teaching student development or student affairs administration, to take an institutional research role, or to move into upper management (such as becoming a vice president or dean). Indeed, seeking a doctorate for career advancement often requires shifting from functional-area specialty skills to advanced educational administration skills. Bloland (1979) states that the attitudes, competencies, and roles of vice presidents for student affairs must focus on being administrators and leaders and that new vice presidents actually have "changed career fields from student personnel to professional administration" (p. 58).

Paterson (1987) finds that 25 percent of chief student affairs officers hold doctorates in higher education or student personnel administration; of note is that only 63 percent of these vice presidents, deans, or vice chancellors have any type of doctorate at all. Other studies have found that 13 percent of all administrators with doctorates in four-year colleges and universities have theirs in higher education (Moore, 1981).

Doctorates in higher education are common in two-year colleges. One study of two-year colleges reports that 39.1 percent of chief student affairs officers and 41.2 percent of the presidents have a higher education doctorate (Moore, Martorana, and Twombly, 1985). In another study of 716 presidents, vice presidents for academic affairs, and vice presidents for student affairs in all types of institutions, Townsend and Wiese (1990) find uniformly positive impressions of a higher education degree in the community college sector. Approximately one-third of the presidents and vice presidents for student affairs in this study have doctorates in higher education. Whereas presidents and vice presidents of academic affairs at other types of institutions are unlikely to prefer the higher education doctorate for their role (viewing it as too practitioner-oriented), vice presidents for student affairs are more likely to value the degree. Nearly half (47 percent) of the respondents believe that the degree is more beneficial than one in an academic discipline for a vice president for student affairs position; 23 percent think it less desirable. Presidents are neutral in this opinion, and student affairs vice presidents are highly supportive. Sandeen (1982) reports that 83 percent of 219 chief student affairs officers in a national study view a professional degree in student personnel services as somewhat or very important for assuming entry-level staff and department-head positions, and 75 percent feel that it is very or somewhat important for the chief student affairs officer role.

The higher education doctorate is clearly valued in the community college setting and for student affairs and institutional management positions in other types of institutions. "It is possible that the degree is more useful for those seeking career advancement in lower-tier institutions than in those designated as Level I institutions, particularly for positions in academic administration. . . . Obtaining the doctorate . . . may now be the means for many prospective students to simply hold their current positions, rather than to advance" (Townsend and Mason, 1990, p. 79).

Specialization in Studying Higher Education and Student Affairs

The ever-growing list of new books in higher education signals the growth and specialization of scholarship in the fields of higher education and student affairs. These publications are an indication of the growing complexity of the American postsecondary system and the increased interest in studying higher education.

The first graduate course in higher education was offered at Clark University in 1893, and the first college student personnel (CSP) course was offered at Teachers College of Columbia University in 1916. The most recent transformation of student affairs graduate preparation came in the early to mid 1970s, with the expanding application of human development theory to students in higher education and the evolution of theory-to-practice models (Knefelkamp, Widick, and Parker, 1978; Miller and Prince, 1976).

Interest in the nature of graduate preparation in higher education and student affairs administration is strong and growing. In the early 1970s, the Association of Professors of Higher Education (APHE) became a division of the American Association of Higher Education (AAHE). APHE later changed its name to the Association for the Study of Higher Education, eventually establishing a separate identity apart from AAHE in 1985. Another sign of the interest in the study of higher education was the establishment of Division J in the American Educational Research Association in 1981 (Townsend, 1990).

Administrators, students, and faculty members concerned with graduate preparation in student affairs often belong to Commission XII of the American College Personnel Association (ACPA). This commission on graduate preparation has sponsored the *Directory of Graduate Preparation Programs in College Student Personnel* for nearly twenty years (Keim and Graham, 1990) and recently established a Syllabi Clearinghouse (Commission XII, 1990). In addition, approximately 10 percent of the membership of the Association for Counselor Education and Supervision is interested in student affairs preparation programs. In recent years, the National Association of Student Personnel Administrators (NASPA) and ACPA have jointly sponsored several activities to examine graduate preparation (Task Force on Professional Preparation and Practice, 1989; Moore and Young, 1987). Other associations, such as the National Association for Campus Activities, have proposed model curricula for their specialty (Allen, Julian, Stern, and Walborn, 1987).

As CSP is a field that begins professional study at the graduate level, entry-level preparation receives a great deal of attention in the student affairs literature. Many studies and opinions have been published on such topics as career options in student affairs (Komives, 1990; Rentz and Knock, 1990; Saddlemire, 1988), competencies for new professionals (Hyman, 1988; Ostroth, 1981), comprehensive developmental models (Beeler, 1991; Brown, 1985; Miller and Carpenter, 1980), and the curriculum and related experiences needed for effective practice (Delworth and Hanson, 1989; Knock, 1977; Saddlemire, 1988; Spooner, 1979; Task Force on Professional Preparation and Practice, 1989; Woodard and Komives, 1990).

Over one hundred institutions offer master's or doctoral study in student affairs (Keim and Graham, 1990). Until recently, however, far less attention has been paid to doctoral preparation (Beatty and Stamatakos, 1990; Coomes, Belch, and Saddlemire, 1991).

The Council for the Accreditation of Counseling and Related Educational Programs (CACREP), an independent accreditation agency affiliated with the American Association for Counseling and Development, is the only accreditation route for graduate programs in student affairs. Approximately two dozen CSP master's programs, most based within counseling departments, are accredited by CACREP. Most programs choose not to seek this accreditation. Voluntary master's preparation standards, created by the collaborative efforts of the Council for the Advancement of Standards (CAS), were published in 1986; however, no standards exist for doctoral preparation in student affairs or higher education (although study groups are currently considering the role of student affairs doctoral standards within CAS). Few if any references are made to accreditation in the broader field of study in higher education.

Within a college of education, prospective doctoral students might explore either a generalist degree in higher education (perhaps with an emphasis on student development or student affairs administration) or a specialized degree in student affairs administration (likely with emphasis in higher education administration or other developmental focus). There is more research on the higher education doctorate than the student affairs doctorate; information on both degrees is presented in this chapter. Other doctoral majors may be appropriate and are noted at the end.

Perspectives on Doctoral Programs in Higher Education or Student Affairs Administration

The taxonomy of three groups of higher education programs identified by Dressel and Mayhew (1974) remains useful in assessing today's higher education programs (Crosson and Nelson, 1984) and also appears to apply to student affairs graduate programs. The first group contains programs with a *national* perspective and reputation based on the research and professional activity of the faculty, their graduate placements, and their student applicants. Programs in the second group have a *local* or *regional* perspective with an emphasis on practitioner preparation and are frequently composed of part-time students or administrators from area institutions. The third group of programs is small, with little to no formal structure, and consists of several courses designed to serve a *local* need (often geared to community college personnel). Townsend (1990) suggests that very few programs admit to the latter orientation; most blend the national and local perspectives, with many aspiring to a national focus.

Many problems exist with ranking or listing exemplary national programs, and such reviews of a dozen nationally regarded higher education programs reveal few differences between them on such measures as faculty-to-student ratios, size, number of faculty, and courses offered. Indeed, Crosson and Nelson conclude that such programs are probably "distinguished by qualitative rather than quantitative factors, and that they have more visible, active and 'cosmopolitan' faculty and students" (1984, p. 21). Studies of program quality have generally asked professors of higher education to rank programs or have looked at such objective measures as faculty publications; few studies have looked at student-related outcome measures like the career paths of graduates, persistence in the field, satisfaction, or graduates' subsequent publications and research productivity.

Curricular Focus

Doctoral programs in higher education frequently provide specialization options. Two specialties exist in nearly 75 percent of the programs: student affairs administration or general administration and management. Two-thirds offer a specialization in academic administration or community college administration. Half make available an emphasis on curriculum and instruction or teaching or adult education; fewer than half, foundations or history or philosophy of higher education, institutional research, policy analysis, or financial administration or finance; and fewer than 25 percent, planning and comparative or international higher education (Crosson and Nelson, 1984).

Current estimates indicate a total of eighty-eight higher education doctoral programs in the United States, enrolling approximately seven thousand students (Crosson and Nelson, 1984; Townsend, 1990). Most programs enroll a majority of part-time students. Women and men are equally represented in higher education doctoral programs. Thirteen percent of all students are members of minority groups, and 8.5 percent are international students (Townsend, 1990). Two-thirds of those participating in student affairs doctoral programs are part-time students, of which approximately 79 percent are Caucasians and 21 percent are ethnic minorities (Coomes, Belch, and Saddlemire, 1991). Both higher education and student affairs doctoral programs report a trend toward an increasing proportion of women students, a finding that raises interesting questions about the feminization of the profession (McEwen, Engstrom, and Williams, 1990).

The department in which a program is based exerts a strong influence on program design. The *Directory of Graduate Preparation Programs in College Student Personnel* (Keim and Graham, 1990) notes forty-four student affairs doctoral programs; half are located in higher education or educational leadership programs, and the other half are in counselor education, counseling psychology, educational psychology, or other departments. Although 75 percent of all higher education administration doctoral programs claim a student affairs specialization (forty-seven programs), their resources should be examined carefully; the *Directory of Graduate Preparation Programs* lists only twenty-two doctoral programs in higher education with a student affairs specialization, and not all of those meet the minimal ACPA Commission XII criteria of at least one full-time faculty member, one practicum, and two student affairs content courses. Even allowing for some differences in the programs that were used in these two data sources, this is a troublesome discrepancy.

Both student affairs and higher education are "derivative field[s] of study" (Crosson and Nelson, 1984, p. 7). Course work ranges from applied management theory to sociology. Higher education administration programs and student affairs administrative doctoral programs may have only one thing in common: neither has paid serious attention to identifying a core of necessary knowledge. The need for progress in this area should consume more professional discussion in this decade (Cooper, 1986). "The question that remains unanswered is how doctoral programs continue to prepare professionals for more advanced levels of student affairs administration or prepare faculty for teaching and research in student affairs, without having mutually agreed upon guidelines and standards that relate to the field's needs and expectations" (Beatty and Stamatakos, 1990, p. 222).

Beatty and Stamatakos (1990) find agreement among student affairs practitioners and preparation faculty on the competencies needed for effective practice; the exception is that the faculty rank research and evaluation competencies as number one, whereas that skill was rated ninth for student affairs administrators.

Based on the general agreement of the practitioners and faculty members in their study, Beatty and Stamatakos (1990) identify six general competence areas that students should seek in a developmental framework for their doctoral preparation:

- Theoretical competence: an in-depth understanding of the historical, philosophical, and theoretical foundations on which student affairs administration is based
- Scholarly competence: the development and perpetuation of scholarship through inquiry, critical interpretation, investigation, research, and writing.
- Functional competence: the development, maintenance, or enhancement of those skills needed to perform both simple and complex functions in an effective manner
- Transferral competence: the ability to transfer theoretical and philosophical foundations of student affairs administration to practical situations
- Environmental competence: an understanding of and the ability to work with and to help shape the environment in which student affairs administration exists
- Human relations competence: the ability to understand, direct, communicate with, and interact with primary constituents, colleagues, and peers who are a part of the higher education environment

Those considering doctoral study might use this list as a self-assessment guide. If prospective students can demonstrate high-level competence in each area, then their academic study might extend beyond higher education or student affairs for further enrichment. If self-assessment reveals deficits in master's preparation or in experience, then a doctorate that would best round out those competencies is indicated.

Administrators believe the most useful experience in a higher education doctorate to be an internship, along with courses on finance and budgeting and organization and governance (Townsend and Wiese, 1990). The importance of field experience, including practicums and internships, is a consistent theme in master's degree programs related to student affairs (Council for the Advancement of Standards for Student Services/Development Programs, 1986; Richmond and Sherman, 1991).

Doctoral Degree Requirements

Doctoral degree requirements typically include course work, a residency requirement, and dissertation; in recent years, programs have added a course work core in higher education as well as statistics or research requirements (Crosson and Nelson, 1984). Student affairs doctoral programs require 3.7 research courses on average and an average of 18.1 courses beyond the master's degree (Keim, 1991b).

Most programs require comprehensive examinations to measure a necessary minimum subject competence usually including (1) the history of the field; (2) major professional issues therein; (3) the field's various dimensions, such as governance and organization, finance, and student development theory; (4) research skills sufficient to begin a dissertation; and (5) some applied, integrating, synthesizing experience like a case study, comprehensive question, or practical problem (Peters and Peterson, 1987). Programs may also require preliminary or qualifying examinations for a wide variety of purposes ranging from an opportunity to assess a student's writing and analytical skills to a major evaluation of the subject matter around which an individualized program of study is designed. Many programs also require some fieldwork experience, such as an internship.

The dissertation process is guided by a committee usually chaired by the student's adviser. The committee generally includes a methodologist, someone from outside the host department and often outside the college, and a faculty member from the program. The two major components of the process include the proposal and the oral defense. Students agree that acceptance of the proposal seems more crucial than the oral defense, which virtually everyone should pass (Peters and Peterson, 1987). Doctoral students nearing the end of their program are sorely tempted to accept a professional position before starting their dissertation, but they should be careful. Successfully completing a dissertation from long distance is understandably difficult, and students are advised to stay through the defense of their research if possible and at least conduct the proposal meeting before assuming new professional roles.

Faculty

Crosson and Nelson (1984) estimate that the number of full-time faculty in higher education doctoral programs increased 50 percent in the 1970s, with approximately 330 faculty members teaching higher education full time. Concurrently, part-time faculty members continue to play a strong role in all higher education programs; 58 percent of the part-time faculty hold appointments as administrators on their host campus. Although the size of the faculty varies greatly, most higher education programs are small, with a mean of 3.7 full-time faculty members along with 5.5 part-time affiliates (p. 12). Student enrollment has outpaced increases in full-time and part-time faculty. Over half of all higher education programs report more than twenty students per full-time faculty member (Crosson and Nelson, 1984).

Faculty numbers in student affairs doctoral programs are even smaller and are in many cases a subset of a larger group of faculty in the host department. In a study of both master's and doctoral program faculty, Keim (1991a) reports nearly 700 faculty members teaching in student affairs preparation programs; however, only 105 are full time (the remaining 595 being part time). Spread over nearly 177 programs, this averages out to fewer than one full-time faculty member per program). In a national study of the applications of CAS and CACREP standards to master's programs, Evans concludes, "Clearly the lack of staff is a major issue for programs trying to meet standards in terms of courses, supervision, and advising" (1988, p. 9). With the number of full-time faculty decreasing in existing student affairs programs, the field faces the problem of improving its professionalization, which requires greater demand on faculty resources.

There are few full-time faculty of color in either higher education or student affairs graduate programs. Moreover, women now compose over half of all higher education and student affairs doctoral student enrollments; yet women make up only 15 percent of all higher education faculty at all ranks, and many programs have no women faculty members. Faculty profiles of full-time and part-time student affairs faculty reflect similar proportions of men (approximately 72 percent) to women (approximately 28 percent) (Keim, 1991a).

Ph.D. Versus Ed.D.

Half of all higher education doctoral programs make available both the doctor of philosophy (Ph.D.) and doctor of education (Ed.D.) options; another 24 percent offer only the Ph.D. and 26 percent only the Ed.D. Where both options exist, it is frequently possible to switch programs if one degree becomes more relevant to the student's goals than the other. The Ph.D. is thought to reflect a greater research orientation, and the Ed.D. is often perceived as having a practitioner focus. In reality, reviews show little difference between Ph.D. and Ed.D. degree requirements even when a program offers both options (Crosson and Nelson, 1984). One difference is that research requirements in the Ed.D. program range from five to eleven hours, whereas the Ph.D. requires twelve to sixteen credits (Dill and Morrison, 1985). Prospective students often ask, "Which degree is better?" One could reply, "Which degree do you think I have? How about the degree of Professor Smith or well-known researcher Dr. Jones or outstanding Vice President Wilson or the president of one of our professional associations, Dr. Washington? It's probably not the degree but how good you are that counts!" Little difference exists in reality, leading some (Carpenter, 1990) to encourage academic departments to eliminate the valid but more confusing Ed.D. and offer only the Ph.D., which may be more readily understood.

Criteria and Processes for Admission

More than half of the higher education doctoral programs require similar credentials: letters of recommendation, a master's degree, English proficiency for international students, a satisfactory Graduate Record Exam score, and a stated minimum grade point average (GPA) for both baccalaureate and master's work (ranging between a 3.0 to 3.5). A few programs ask for such materials as a career goals statement, two to five years of professional experience, or an autobiographical statement (Crosson and Nelson, 1984). Student affairs programs use similar screening methods. Over 40 percent admit students on a rolling admissions deadline; 83 percent demand a GPA from 3.00 to 4.00 (Coomes, Belch, and Saddlemire, 1991). Over two-thirds of the student affairs doctoral programs require a personal interview and related work experience for admission (Keim, 1991b).

As many doctoral programs are offered by major research universities, the host graduate school will also have minimum academic standards for admission in good standing. Programs frequently recommend students who do not meet those minimums for provisional or probationary admission, so prospective students should not be deterred by published criteria. There is a movement to seek diverse indicators of academic promise that could influence graduate admissions beyond published cognitive indicators like GPA and test scores. Sedlacek's noncognitive factors to predict academic achievement (Tracey and Sedlacek, 1985) become very useful for effective consideration of racial and ethnic minorities. They are also useful for other students whose undergraduate leadership experiences and motivation signal a better prognosis of success than their test scores or undergraduate grades. Students who do not meet minimal academic standards should assertively build their case around these indicators and request an exception to stated minimums. They should use a persuasive cover letter, write a thorough personal statement if one is required, and include a résumé to build a strong set of credentials that exceed the stated requirements.

Financing Doctoral Study

Assistantships are valuable work experiences for master's students and offer an out-of-class setting to integrate the knowledge, attitudes, and skills needed in the student affairs field. By contrast, for doctoral students, assistantships generally serve as a source of financial support and usually provide less credibility and responsibility than full-time work experience prior to matriculation. Many doctoral programs offer limited assistantships because doctoral students tend to be part time and maintain full- or part-time work commitments. A survey of eleven major CSP preparation programs shows that only 36 percent of the doctoral students had assistantships, compared to 78 percent of the master's students. Doctoral assistantship stipends in 1990–91 ranged from $2,515 to $9,675 per year with a variety of fringe benefits, including tuition remission, office space, computer access, parking, professional travel, health benefits, and housing and meals for live-in positions (Olivetti, 1991).

Most assistantships are meaningful professional involvements with developmental supervision. Doctoral students should consider accepting assistantships that offer a research experience, particularly in offices that can make subjects or a data base available for dissertation research. Students seeking graduate assistantships should carefully assess the campus and office work climate. Graduate students' complaints about low wages, inadequate or nonexistent health insurance, increased work loads for teaching assistants, and the extended period required for doctoral study, as reported by the *Chronicle of Higher Education,* may be leading to a unionization movement among graduate students in some other disciplines (Blum, 1990). Certainly, even within student affairs, all professionals know that a supposedly twenty-hour assistantship as a head resident, student activities adviser, or student union programmer usually takes much more time. Considering that the relationships and reputation gained from assistantship employment will persist after graduate study, students should carefully assess the true work load, expectations, and office culture as students cannot afford not to do well in this related work experience.

Alternative Approaches

The approach to doctoral study in this chapter has valued an administrative degree in either higher education or student affairs earned in a traditional campus-based program. Other disciplines and modes of learning should also be explored to answer the diverse needs of professionals seeking doctorates.

Doctorate in Counseling, Counselor Education, or Counseling Psychology

Counseling degrees have become a specialty degree at the doctoral level for those preparing for professional roles in counseling centers, teaching, and human development in community colleges. They are also a legitimate route to becoming a director of agencies such as career development and counseling centers, services for students with disabilities, or learning assistance programs. Three-fourths of counseling doctoral graduates find positions in counseling, and 15 to 19 percent are employed in student personnel work, higher education administration, or higher education teaching (Zimpfer and De-Trude, 1990). For the administratively minded counselor, this degree may be a means to further administrative career advancement or teaching and may even be desirable in small college or community college settings. However, noticeably fewer doctoral counseling graduates are entering higher education work environments: 64.4 percent in 1970 compared to only 21.5 percent in 1985. There are more than one thousand doctoral counseling degrees conferred annually (Zimpfer and DeTrude, 1990), not including degrees in counseling psychology or clinical psychology.

Doctorate in Another Discipline

In this era of specialization, some argue for the competencies of a compatible behavioral science field (such as organizational behavior, social psychology, law, psychology, or sociology) as acceptable, if not desirable, for student affairs administrative roles (Canon, 1982). Using the base of a student affairs master's degree, this approach would clearly be a strong option and provide such additional benefits as adjunct teaching in almost any institution of employment and the unspoken credibility of a more clearly understood discipline. This author believes it essential that professional practitioners earn at least one graduate degree in student affairs or higher education. If another discipline is pursued as the only course of study for both the master's and doctorate, one would be advised to take student development or higher education administrative course work as a cognate area; do dissertation research on a related issue in higher education; use students, faculty, or administrators as the population of interest; and in essence develop a specialty in the higher education environment within the selected discipline. Some graduate preparation in and exposure to student affairs and higher education may be preferable to none, but they will be insufficient for professional practice. This course of action is not recommended.

External Degree Programs

Perhaps graduate education needs a paradigm shift. The known paradigm of a campus-based degree program is comfortable, has rigor, and is effective. If we truly believe in continuous lifelong learning, self-motivated learners, and new technologies that make teleconferencing and video and electronic communication a reality, then we might be more open to external degree programs.

One possibility would be a shift away from a "campus" perspective of traditional learning to explore the merit of such external degree programs as the Union Institute. Accredited by the same regional agencies that evaluate established colleges and universities, many of these programs help the advanced learner establish a doctoral committee of graduate faculty across the country that will guide learning, read papers, and direct research. Often combined with intensive weekend seminars, learning contracts, and regular progress checks, these programs claim that the quality of their doctoral dissertations compares positively with that of traditional programs. This approach may be successful for the most motivated self-directed learner and may be the only opportunity for advanced study for someone without ready access to a campus-based program. The external degree program does have significant disadvantages, including the lack of interaction with peer students and graduate faculty, but learning does occur. Additional competencies can be built through such a program, and the desired outcome — the doctoral degree — is obtained.

If there are clusters of colleges in a region of a state not served by a graduate preparation program, special offerings might be developed as a satellite program. This might create a source of new students for a nearby established program, support state outreach for public institutions, and bring degree advancement possibilities to professionals who might not otherwise be able to seek them.

Institutes, Workshops, Extended Study, and Professional Development

Continuous learning is essential for professional practice, whether or not an individual seeks a doctoral degree. Creamer and Shelton (1988) identify two perspectives on in-service education: institutional effectiveness and staff effectiveness. Assuredly, specific staff training in areas of institutional goals can and will advance the accomplishment of objectives. Likewise, staff training designed around staff needs and professional interests can advance individual skills (see Chapter Twenty-Four).

Adaptation of the model of requiring continuing education units (CEUs) for recertification in such fields as counseling and psychology should be on the national student affairs agenda. Such a credentialing system ensures professional renewal supported by professional associations (Paterson and Carpenter, 1989; Task Force on Professional Preparation and Practice, 1989). A professional could demonstrate a competence in such topics as conflict resolution, multicultural awareness, women's development, facilities development, or the like by earning a designated number of CEUs. Issues of a professional registry leading to systems of continuing education units and recertification are on the horizon (Task Force on Professional Preparation and Practice, 1989). Even without a formal registry, CEUs need to be embraced as evidence of important experiences beyond a formal degree program. Associations should establish the appropriate mechanisms, and professionals should request, perhaps demand, CEUs to encourage that process.

Professional associations sponsor numerous professional development activities. NASPA's Richard Stevens Chief Student Affairs Officers' Institute provides an annual opportunity for vice presidents and deans and those who seek those positions to meet in an intensive, week-long summer institute to explore major issues. The Harvard Institute for Educational Management is an intensive classroom-based program joining academic administrators, new presidents, and student affairs administrators in educational management strategies using the case-study method. The HERS program at Wellesley offers mentoring to women administrators, as does the program at Bryn Mawr. The ACE National Identification Project for Women develops and creates networks for women seeking administrative careers and advancement. Whether one has a doctorate or not, these special institutes refresh and refocus practitioners on central issues in student affairs and higher education administration.

Assessing a Doctoral Program — Is It Right for You?

Deciding to engage in doctoral study is a complex search for compatibility between the needs and characteristics of the student and the focus and environment of the graduate program. Finding an optimal match between personal needs and program characteristics is worth extensive study and research, for it may be the most important decision in the process.

Self-Assessment

The single most important variable in selecting a graduate program is *you*! Practitioners considering doctoral study should engage in probing self-assessment, including intermediate and long-term career goals, skill and competency strengths and needs, and ways to build on the focus of their master's degree. Perhaps more important is to evaluate family responsibilities and family support, necessary financial adjustments, stress and energy levels, and life events that might occur during the duration of graduate study (Belch and Ottinger, 1989).

A serious preliminary question is whether you will pursue a program part-time while employed (at least part time) or whether you will enter poverty again as a graduate student and enjoy full-time study. Townsend and Mason (1990) report that the time taken to earn a higher education doctorate has steadily grown, from 5.4 years in 1967 to 6.9 years in 1987. The average age at the time of awarding of the degree has similarly increased, from thirty-six to forty-three. Students in student affairs doctoral programs tend to be slightly younger (one-third are thirty-one to thirty-five years of age) (Coomes, Belch, and Saddlemire, 1991). If you plan to be a part-time student, explore your work culture. You should determine the support of members of your organization, particularly those who may feel that they might have to assume some of your responsibilities when you have to leave for class on such a regular basis. They may support your effort or may resent the increased work load.

If you are a part-time student, will you work on or off the host campus? Working on campus usually brings tuition-remission benefits, ease in getting to classes, and access to resources. And you do not have to find another parking place! However, on-campus work also brings the possibilities of complex relationships in which your supervisor may now also be a faculty member and an employee in your unit may be a doctoral student ahead of you in the program. These can be healthy experiences; or they can be stressful and uncomfortable, and you may feel that you are being evaluated on multiple fronts. Working at a nearby campus provides less role confusion—in fact, colleagues may not even know of your graduate study obligations; but it may not provide needed benefits and supports. You may wish to consult two extensive lists of self-assessment questions: those posed by Moore and Young (1987) and by Belch and Ottinger (1989).

Program Assessment

If you have identified what you want to study, have career and research goals, know if you can enroll in a national program or are adapting your life to accommodate a regional program, and have decided whether you will be part-time or full-time, you are ready to begin reviewing programs. You should consider many aspects of the programs of interest to you. The following list is not exhaustive but is representative of certain basic questions.

Faculty. Who are the current faculty members, and what are the faculty staffing projections for the four to six years required for you to get your degree? Are retirements or sabbaticals being planned? What are faculty research interests? What research methods are valued by faculty members—is their work predominantly qualitative, quantitative, or both?

Faculty-Student Interaction. What is the nature of student-faculty interaction? To what degree does the faculty act as mentor and sponsor and advise students (Merriam, Thomas, and Zeph, 1987; Rentz and Saddlemire, 1988)? Among full-time and affiliate faculty or campus practitioners, are there professionals that you could consider models for your gender, race, and interests if these are important to you?

Interest and Experience. How do your interests and experiences fit what you know about other students in the program who will now be your colleagues? What is the student culture? What are graduation rates from the program? What supports exist for job placement, and what positions do recent graduates hold?

Areas of Specialty. What are the areas of specialty in the program? Is there flexibility with department cognates, or is the one you want even available? Can you register in other departments' courses, or are they closed to non-majors? Do not assume you can take a wonderful psychology course or a doctoral-level course in managerial leadership in the business school; check it out.

Core Requirements. How does the focus of the host department influence core requirements like course work and comprehensive exam questions?

Teaching Modes. What are the predominant teaching modes in the department: seminar discussions, case studies, lecture classes? What is the nature of the learning activity: readings, research papers, group projects? Are the fieldwork experiences in settings that will stretch and challenge you? Do the modes used build on your preferred learning styles (Forney, 1989)? Is course content on the cutting edge or at least current?

Policies. What policies will influence your life — for example, required internships, residency requirements (used by over 80 percent of programs; see Coomes, Belch, and Saddlemire, 1991), procedures for interrupted study, language requirements, and policies about class absences due to work or travel?

Financial Support. Are there appropriate assistantships, fellowships, or other financial support if needed? Is there a tuition-remission limit on the number of credits per semester or number of semesters that are covered? What other benefits are included, such as health insurance? Are there special fellowships for students of color?

Ethics. What are the climate, culture, tone, and core values of the program? Are departmental relationships ethical and principled (Brown and Krager, 1985)? Is it a collaborative community with norms of supportive relationship, an impersonal atmosphere stressing individual accomplishment, or even a competitive environment providing a richer experience for the scholarly committed student? In which environment would you flourish? How realistic are your expectations?

Connections with Practice. Is there a healthy connection with the host campus student affairs program and nearby institutions? Are the practitioners and faculty tightly or loosely joined?

Future Content in Doctoral Preparation

Society has become a permanent "white water," with rapid change, ambiguity, and chaos becoming the norm instead of the exception (Vaill, 1989). These complexities are more than simply problems that must be solved (Barr and Golseth, 1990). We seek a community built on the talent and creativity that arises from our differences in an environment that values our shared visions and common dreams. Successful professionals, both those engaging in doctoral study as well as those in practice, will need to learn many new ways to function well in these rapidly changing times. Graduate programs should enrich their course work, experiential learning, research focus, and program culture to honor these changes and shift emphasis from the present, probably most comfortable for practitioners, to the ambiguities and unknowns of the future.

Graduate programs should strive to develop leadership perspectives, attitudes, values, and skills in doctoral students as an intentional outcome. Vaill (1989) admonishes leaders of the future not merely to work harder or longer, but to work collectively, reflectively, and spiritually smarter. Leaders (Lipman-Blumen, 1989) should connect individuals with each other in fashioning an inclusive community and link people with ideas about shared vision. New-age leaders must see connections, value collaboration, and empower all stakeholders to make a difference in campus change. It is encouraging that Rogers (1991) finds a commitment to this new collaborative paradigm of leadership among graduate preparation faculty and students.

Other chapters in this book have considered the benefit and challenge of diversity in college environments. Student affairs professionals have always shared a professional commitment to bring all students to the table, to value individual differences, and to ensure that all students' interests are taken seriously by the institution. Though not always implemented with consistency or insight, professionals for the future must possess "cultural competence" (Ebbers and Henry, 1990) and demonstrate an appreciation of multiculturalism in their attitudes and behaviors. This appreciation embraces all kinds of individuals, regardless of their gender, sexual orientation, race, ethnicity, disability, religion, or other characteristics. These individuals have talents and perspectives to bring to the larger purpose of being an inclusive learning community — not because it is "politically correct" but because it is "educationally correct." Indeed, it is an educational mandate. Further, graduate programs must search affirmatively for faculty members who can create more effective links to and models for diverse graduate students (Woodard and Komives, 1990).

The concept of campus community, which in the 1980s was so vigorously endorsed in the pages of the *Chronicle of Higher Education* and many national reform reports, needs nurturing champions: student affairs professionals. Yet few graduate programs teach an understanding of campus culture, elements of building a diverse community, or ways to become "involving colleges" (Kuh, Schuh, Whitt, and Associates, 1991) or developmentally powerful environments. The environmental assessment and redesign skills required to build real community should be a foundation of all student affairs graduate programs.

It would be folly to list the many additional competencies and skills necessary for effective student affairs administration in the future. Perhaps instead we should encourage prospective students, program faculty members, and practitioners to find regular mechanisms to bring important issues, as well as discussion of essential generalist skills, attitudes, and values, to the seminar table. This "liberal arts" approach to graduate study will serve us as well as it has served the liberal arts undergraduates, who traditionally know how to think, how to learn, and how to communicate within the higher education community.

Summary

Student affairs professionals desiring strong careers as administrators, researchers, graduate faculty members, and informed change agents must consider graduate study beyond their master's degree. Doctoral degrees are necessities in many positions and types of institutions. The reasons for pursuing a degree and decisions about when to start, what and where to study, and with whom are issues requiring personal reflection and self-assessment. Professional practice will advance when those who engage in it are prepared with advanced competencies, knowledge, skills, attitudes, and values and when institutions commit themselves to that kind of practice by hiring such professionals. "Chief student affairs officers who have their own graduate training in student personnel services in higher education attach considerably more importance to such graduate training in their hiring decisions than do their counterparts who have earned their graduate degrees in unrelated fields" (Sandeen, 1982, p. 53). Perhaps the decade's most profound challenge to employing institutions is to advance effective, professional practice by requiring professional graduate credentials of those seeking student affairs leadership roles—and stand for no less!

References

Allen, K. E., Julian, G., Stern, T., and Walborn, G. *Future Perfect: A Guide for Professional Development and Competence.* Columbia, S.C.: National Association of Campus Activities Educational Foundation, 1987.

Barr, M. J., and Golseth, A. E. "Managing Change in a Paradoxical Environment." In M. J. Barr, M. L. Upcraft, and Associates, *New Futures for Student Affairs: Building a Vision for Professional Leadership and Practice.* San Francisco: Jossey-Bass, 1990.

Beatty, D. L., and Stamatakos, L. C. "Faculty and Administrator Perceptions of Knowledge, Skills, and Competencies as Standards for Doctoral Preparation Programs in Student Affairs Administration." *Journal of College Student Development,* 1990, *31,* 221-229.

Beeler, K. D. "Graduate Student Adjustment to Academic Life: A Four-Stage Framework." *NASPA Journal,* 1991, *28* (2), 163-171.

Belch, H. A., and Ottinger, D. C. "To a Degree: Making a Decision About Doctoral Studies." *Connections,* 1989, *1* (1), 13-18.

Bloland, P. "Student Personnel Training for the Chief Student Affairs Officer: Essential or Unnecessary?" *NASPA Journal,* 1979, *17* (2), 57-62.

Blum, D. E. "Graduate Students on a Growing Number of Campuses Are Stepping Up Efforts to Organize Bargaining Units." *Chronicle of Higher Education,* Aug. 8, 1990, pp. A9-A10.

Brown, R. D. "Graduate Education for the Student Development Profession: A Content and Process Model." *NASPA Journal,* 1985, *22* (3), 38-43.

Brown, R. D., and Krager, L. "Ethical Issues in Graduate Education." *Journal of Higher Education,* 1985, *56* (4), 403-418.

Burns, M. A. "Who Leaves the Student Affairs Field." *NASPA Journal,* 1982, *20* (2), 9–12.

Canon, H. J. "Toward Professionalism in Student Affairs: Another Point of View." *Journal of College Student Personnel,* 1982, *23* (6), 468–473.

Carpenter, S. "Professional Development and Career Issues for Mid-Managers." In R. B. Young (ed.), *The Invisible Leaders: Student Affairs Mid-Managers.* Washington, D.C.: National Association of Student Personnel Administrators, 1990.

Commission XII, American College Personnel Association. *Catalog: Clearinghouse for Syllabi of Courses in College Student Personnel and Related Coursework.* Manhattan, Kans.: Kansas State University, 1990.

Coomes, M. D., Belch, H. A., and Saddlemire, G. L. "Doctoral Programs for Student Affairs Professionals: A Status Report." *Journal of College Student Development,* 1991, *32* (1), 62–68.

Cooper, J. A. "Higher Education as a Field of Study: Some Future Prospects." Paper presented at the annual meeting of the Association for the Study of Higher Education, Feb. 1986. (ED 268 905)

Council for the Advancement of Standards for Student Services/Development Programs. *Council for the Advancement of Standards: Standards and Guidelines for Student Services/Development Programs.* Washington, D.C.: Council for the Advancement of Standards for Student Services/Development Programs, 1986.

Creamer, D. G., and Shelton, M. "Staff Development: A Literature Review of Graduate Preparation and In-Service Education of Students." *Journal of College Student Development,* 1988, *29,* 407–414.

Crosson, P. M., and Nelson, G. M. "A Profile of Higher Education Doctoral Programs." Paper presented at the annual meeting of the Association for the Study of Higher Education, Mar. 1984. (ED 245 604)

Delworth, U., and Hanson, G. R. "Future Directions: A Vision of Student Services in the 1990s." In U. Delworth, G. R. Hanson, and Associates, *Student Services: A Handbook for the Profession.* (2nd ed.) San Francisco: Jossey-Bass, 1989.

Dill, D., and Morrison, J. L. "Ed.D. and Ph.D. Research Training in the Field of Higher Education: A Survey and Proposal." *Review of Higher Education,* 1985, *8,* 169–186.

Dressel, P. L., and Mayhew, L. B. *Higher Education as a Field of Study: The Emergence of a Profession.* San Francisco: Jossey-Bass, 1974.

Ebbers, L. H., and Henry, S. L. "Cultural Competence: A New Challenge to Student Affairs Professionals." *NASPA Journal,* 1990, *27* (4), 319–323.

Evans, N. J. "College Student Personnel Program Responses to Preparation Standards." Unpublished report to the American College Personnel Association, 1988.

Forney, D. S. "Relationship of Characteristics and Attitudes of Student Personnel Students and Learning Styles." Unpublished doctoral dissertation, Department of Counseling and Personnel Services, University of Maryland, College Park, 1989.

Hyman, R. E. "Graduate Preparation for Professional Practice: A Difference of Perceptions." *NASPA Journal,* 1988, *26* (2), 143–150.

Keim, M. C. "Preparation Program Faculty: A Research Description." NASPA Journal, 1991a, *29* (1), 49–54.

Keim, M. C. "Student Personnel Preparation Programs: A Longitudinal Study." *NASPA Journal,* 1991b, *28* (3), 231–242.

Keim, M., and Graham, J. W. (eds.). *Directory of Graduate Preparation Programs in College Student Personnel.* Washington, D.C.: American College Personnel Association, 1990.

Knefelkamp, L., Widick, C., and Parker, C. A. (eds.) *Applying New Developmental Findings.* New Directions for Student Services, no. 4. San Francisco: Jossey-Bass, 1978.

Knock, G. H. (ed.). *Perspectives on the Preparation of Student Affairs Professionals.* Alexandria, Va.: American Association for Counseling and Development, 1977.

Komives, S. R. "Careers in Postsecondary Settings." In N. Garfield and B. Collison (eds.), *Careers in Counseling and Human Development.* Alexandria, Va.: American Association for Counseling and Development, 1990.

Kuh, G. D., Schuh, J. H., Whitt, E. J., and Associates. *Involving Colleges: Successful Approaches to Fostering Student Learning and Development Outside the Classroom.* San Francisco: Jossey-Bass, 1991.

Lipman-Blumen, J. *Connective Leadership: Female Leadership Styles Meeting the Challenge.* Unpublished paper, Drucker Graduate Management Center, Claremont, California, 1989.

McEwen, M. K., Engstrom, C. M., and Williams, T. E. "Gender Diversity Within the Student Affairs Profession." *Journal of College Student Development,* 1990, *31* (1), 47–53.

Merriam, S., Thomas, T., and Zeph, C. "Mentoring in Higher Education: What We Know Now." *Review of Higher Education,* 1987, *11* (2), 199–210.

Miller, T. K., and Carpenter, D. S. "Professional Preparation for Today and Tomorrow." In D. G. Creamer (ed.), *Student Development in Higher Education.* Washington, D.C.: American College Personnel Association, 1980.

Miller, T. K., and Prince, J. S. *The Future of Student Affairs: A Guide to Student Development for Tomorrow's Higher Education.* San Francisco: Jossey-Bass, 1976.

Moore, K. M. *Leaders in Transition: A National Study of Higher Education Administrators.* University Park: Center for the Study of Higher Education, Pennsylvania State University, 1981.

Moore, K. M., Martorana, S. V., and Twombly, S. *Today's Academic Leaders: A National Study of Administrators in Community and Junior Colleges.* University Park: Center for the Study of Higher Education, Pennsylvania State University, 1985.

Moore, L. V., and Young, R. B. (eds.). *Expanding Opportunities for Professional Education.* New Directions for Student Services, no. 37. San Francisco: Jossey-Bass, 1987.

Olivetti, S. *Graduate Assistant Benefits Survey Summary.* Unpublished manuscript, University of South Carolina, 1991.

Ostroth, D. D. "Competencies for Entry-Level Professionals: What Do Employers Look for in Hiring New Staff?" *Journal of College Student Personnel,* 1981, *22,* 5–11.

Paterson, B. G. "An Examination of the Professional Status of Chief Student Affairs Officers." *College Student Affairs Journal,* 1987, *8* (1), 13–20.

Paterson, B. G., and Carpenter, D. S. "The Emerging Student Affairs Profession: What Still Needs to be Done." *NASPA Journal,* 1989, *27* (2), 123–127.

Peters, D. S., and Peterson, M. A. "Monitoring and Evaluating Doctoral Student Progress in Programs for the Study of Higher Education." Paper presented at the annual meeting of the Association for the Study of Higher Education, Feb. 1987. (ED 281 432)

Rentz, A. L., and Knock, G. H. *Student Affairs Careers: Enhancing the Collegiate Experience.* Washington, D.C.: American College Personnel Association, 1990.

Rentz, A. L., and Saddlemire, G. L. (eds.). *Student Affairs Functions in Higher Education.* Springfield, Ill.: Thomas, 1988.

Richmond, J., and Sherman, K. J. "Student-Development Preparation and Placement: A Longitudinal Study of Graduate Students' and New Professionals' Experiences." *Journal of College Student Development,* 1991, *32* (1), 8–16.

Rogers, J. L. "Leadership Education in College Student Personnel Preparation Programs: An Analysis of Faculty Perspectives." *NASPA Journal,* 1991, *29* (1), 37–48.

Saddlemire, G. "Designing a Curriculum for Student Services/Development Professionals." In R. B. Young and L. V. Moore (eds.), *The State of the Art of Professional Education and Practice.* Generativity Project, no. 1. Washington, D.C.: American College Personnel Association, 1988.

Sandeen, A. "Professional Preparation Programs in Student Personnel Services in Higher Education: A National Assessment by Chief Student Affairs Officers." *NASPA Journal,* 1982, *20* (2), 51–58.

Spooner, S. E. "Preparing the Student Development Specialist: The Process Outcome Model Applied." *Journal of College Student Personnel,* 1979, *20* (1), 45–53.

Task Force on Professional Preparation and Practice. *The Recruitment, Preparation, and Nurturing of the Student Affairs Profession.* Washington, D.C.: National Association of Student Personnel Administrators and the American College Personnel Association, 1989.

Townsend, B. K. "Doctoral Study in the Field of Higher Education." In J. C. Smart (ed.), *Higher Education: Handbook of Theory and Research.* Vol. 6. New York: Agathon, 1990.

Townsend, B. K., and Mason, S. O. "Career Paths of Graduates of Higher Education Doctoral Programs." *Review of Higher Education,* 1990, *14* (1), 63–81.

Townsend, B. K., and Wiese, M. "Administrative Perceptions of Doctorate in Higher Education." Unpublished manuscript, Loyola University of Chicago, 1990.

Tracey, T. J., and Sedlacek, W. E. "The Relationship of Noncognitive Variables to Academic Success: A Longitudinal Comparison by Race." *Journal of College Student Personnel,* 1985, *26,* 405–410.

Vaill, P. B. *Managing as a Performing Art: New Ideas for a World of Chaotic Change.* San Francisco: Jossey-Bass, 1989.

Woodard, D. B., Jr., and Komives, S. R. "Ensuring Staff Competence." In M. J. Barr, M. L. Upcraft, and Associates, *New Futures for Student Affairs: Building a Vision for Professional Leadership and Practice.* San Francisco: Jossey-Bass, 1990.

Zimpfer, D. G., and DeTrude, J. C. "Follow-Up of Doctoral Graduates in Counseling." *Journal of Counseling and Development,* 1990, *69,* 51–56.

28

ॐ

Administrative
Internship Programs

Juan E. Mestas
Marlene Ross

Other chapters in this volume have described the many challenges that student affairs professionals must meet in the changing environment of higher education. Professional staff must have skills and competencies to meet these new challenges, and the need for continued professional development is evident (McDade, 1989).

This chapter explores methods to increase staff skills and competencies through the use of an administrative internship program. The chapter begins with a discussion of how professional skills are learned. Next, suggestions of how to engage in planned professional development through an administrative internship program are offered. Finally, the types of administrative internships are discussed, and steps to implement an administrative internship program successfully are presented.

Traditionally, professional skills are acquired by a combination of three methods: formal training (for example, graduate school), on-the-job learning (apprenticeship or old-fashioned "sink or swim"), and enhancement activities (conferences, workshops, seminars, and retreats). Graduate programs in the field of student services are not always of high quality (see Chapter Twenty-Seven), and enhancement activities, though valuable, do not add up to a comprehensive education. Learning by trial and error and by observation is thus the most readily available method for current student affairs administrators to increase their skills. These ways of learning are also perilous and not always reliable.

Moreover, many student services administrators have received their training either in unrelated fields or in related but specialized fields, such as counseling and financial aid. Many student affairs administrators were not trained in their current field. In academia, lack of such training is not unusual. Few professors are taught how to teach, and few administrators of any kind are prepared for the jobs they actually do. In fact, some of the qualities and skills essential for success in a certain field (such as career counseling, for example) may be less fundamental to succeeding in a management position. The ability to empathize is central to the effectiveness of a counselor but only a desirable quality in a program director.

The nature of the "client" or "customer"—the student—has changed as well. The traditional student, who enrolled in college on a full-time basis immediately upon graduation from high school, is now in the minority. The majority consists of older students, part-time students, those with spouses and small children, and those with jobs. More women than men attend college. Individuals with physical or learning disabilities have gained access to learning services and facilities. And though some ethnic groups remain grossly underrepresented, the ethnic diversity of the campus is ever more evident (DeWitt, 1991; Kuh, 1990; Shaffer, 1984).

In summary, student services administration has become a complex, changing enterprise (Barr, Upcraft, and Associates, 1990; Delworth, Hanson, and Associates, 1989). The skills required to manage and lead its multiple operations should not be acquired through happenstance but through planned professional development. Such a systematic approach is in the best interest of both the profession and the professional. Even more importantly, it is in the best interest of institutions to support planned professional development (Woodard and Komives, 1990). In these times of economic stress, the first test of viability for any professional development initiative must be its appeal to institutional self-interest (Renick, Terrell, and Jones, 1989).

Planned Professional Development

Internship programs are a particularly effective form of planned professional development. A well-structured administrative internship program can combine the three basic methods of learning a profession identified earlier. The scope, size, format, and duration of internship programs can be adjusted to suit the specific conditions of each institution. They provide a flexible means of responding to the need for leadership and management abilities among senior and midlevel student services administrators. The growing complexity of these jobs requires that the individuals who hold them be trained with a purpose, rather than be brought in (or promoted) with hope and good intentions and then be expected to learn, almost exclusively, by developing survival skills.

A time may have existed when student services professionals had to bring only an alert mind, a good heart, and lots of energy to a position. Although these qualities are still desirable, they are no longer sufficient. Student services administrators, especially at the levels of greater managerial responsibility, are now expected to have experience and expertise in areas such as enrollment management, strategic planning, budgeting, labor relations, and interpretation of statutes (Carpenter, 1990; DeWitt, 1991; Garland, 1985; Renick, Terrell, and Jones, 1989; Trimble, Allen, and Vidoni, 1991; Benke and Disque, 1990).

Additionally, good student affairs administrators should have some familiarity with the operational units and functional areas that are a part of the administrative portfolio. And they must have the flexibility and know-how to address emerging issues, such as multiculturalism, date rape, AIDS prevention, drug abuse, and campus crime. Institutions may run out of money, but they retain their expectations.

An imaginative student services division can establish an excellent internship program at a fairly low cost and with minimal structural disruption. Through the establishment of such a program, a student affairs division can assist in developing flexible, up-to-date leadership at the top and in the middle levels of the organization. A core of administrators can be created who possess the essential skills, theoretical knowledge, and multiple exposures indispensable to the integration of a highly diversified enterprise (Bloland, 1979; Shaffer, 1984). The potential also exists for creation of a management team capable of responding to the changing needs of a diverse student body (McDade, 1989). Through carefuly planning, administrative internships can increase the representation of women and minorities in the upper echelons of management in the organization. Training individual staff members in several specific student services areas also increases the general competence of the divisional staff. Finally, administrative internships have the great potential for improving staff morale even when clearly discernible means of upward mobility are not available (Renick, Terrell, and Jones, 1989).

What Deegan, Steele, and Thielen say about the institution as a whole can be applied specifically to student services: "Today, college and university administration is too complex and the leadership needed too important not to develop planned work experiences that will enhance the leadership capabilities of individuals interested in administrative positions in higher education as a career" (1985, p. 61). Internship programs can be among the most valuable and readily available planned work experiences to address the management and leadership requirements of student services.

Types of Administrative Internships

There are many models of internship programs. The selection of the one best suited to a particular institution depends on factors such as institutional size and location, specific purpose of the internship, and the history and extent of professional development activities on the campus. The models described here were not conceived exclusively for student services but can be adapted to the needs of this division. It should be noted that there is a dearth of literature on these types of programs, especially as they apply to student services.

Internal Rotation Option

A model well suited to small or isolated colleges is internal rotation. Typically, the interns are selected from one office and assigned to another for a specified period of time — most often, a semester or two — to become participating observers and observing participants. Iowa State University (ISU) has implemented this model with remarkable success (Robinson and Delbridge-Parker, 1991).

In the ISU model, an intern is brought to the office of the chief student affairs administrator as an assistant for two years on a half-time basis (originally one year on a full-time basis). Only staff members (not deans or directors) who have been in the division for at least two years are eligible to participate in the program. The intern's job description is flexible and encompasses the areas of communication, administration, and program development. The staff member is guaranteed a position in his or her previous unit at the end of the internship. A pool of money from internal and external sources eases the financial burden on the intern's office of origin.

A ten-year follow-up study reveals that the feedback from interns and deans and directors at ISU has been overwhelmingly positive. Among the benefits of this experience cited by the interns are improved communication between student services units and the vice president's office, the acquisition of a global view of the division and the institution, enhanced professional development, and the learning of management skills. Deans and directors also mention positive results, such as professional growth of staff members, improved unit morale, and a better understanding of administrative processes by the returning interns. The student affairs division benefits through greater communication and "broadened perspectives" as well as more innovative ideas and greater use of skills (Robinson and Delbridge-Parker, 1991). The negative side effects, minor in comparison, include the break in work continuity and the net loss of staff time.

Rotation Outside Student Services

In a variation of this model, the intern is assigned to not one but several offices within the division, spending a month or two in each one. A more desirable option would extend the rotation to other units outside student services. For example, the intern could spend a month or two in the office of the academic vice president, in the public relations office, in the development office, and even in the president's office (Bloland, 1979; Robinson and

Delbridge-Parker, 1991). This approach would give interns a comprehensive view of the entire institution, thus enabling them to address the complexities and subtleties of higher education administration from multiple perspectives. Several studies have indicated the many positive outcomes of job rotation, including strengthened skills, higher morale, increased motivation and productivity, and greater job satisfaction (Deegan, Steele, and Thielen, 1985; McDade, 1989; Quartly, 1973; Robinson and Delbridge-Parker, 1991; Renick, Terrell, and Jones, 1989).

Consortium Option

Colleges and universities in the same geographical area can agree to sponsor one or more interns from each campus for placement either at their home institutions or at another one within the consortium. Interns could spend a year, a semester, or a month on a different campus, studying leadership styles, management methods, and organizational behaviors in an institutional culture unlike their own. Interns would see how things are done at different institutions and would return with new ideas and valuable insights.

The consortium option provides two other significant advantages: the possibility of reducing costs by spreading administrative expenses around; and the opportunity for interns to meet periodically, share experiences and reactions, support each other, learn from each other, and give each other helpful feedback. This idea of having periodic group meetings of interns has been used with great success in the American Council on Education (ACE) Fellows Program.

A natural tendency of educational institutions is to seek association with other institutions of the same "family": community colleges with community colleges, research universities with research universities, and so on. This same-family arrangement allows interns to gain insights that have practical applicability in their institutions but may be too restrictive in scope. We encourage the formation of consortia that include a broad range of universities and colleges — research, liberal arts, large public, small private, historically black, women's, two-year, land-grant — and perhaps private industry. This suggestion should not be taken lightly. For example, much can be learned from the corporate sector in the areas of management and quality control. Exposure to a variety of institutions is in itself a valuable learning experience that gives the interns not only a sense of the scope of higher education but an openness to change and a sensitivity to diversity that are much more difficult to acquire in any single environment.

Outside Agency Option

A variation of the consortium theme, increasing its scale and boundaries, would place the responsibility for managing the internship program on an outside agency. The ACE Fellows Program is one such model, probably the most successful of its kind. It is designed to identify and train future leaders in higher education administration. Its scope is national and covers most areas of institutional administration.

Approximately thirty ACE fellows are selected each year through a competitive process. They are nominated by their home institutions, which continue to pay their salaries and benefits, and participate in a year-long internship either at their home or host institutions under the president and other senior administrators. Typically, the ACE fellows learn about the operation of a college or university from several levels and perspectives, including those of its most senior officers and policy-making bodies.

The role of the mentors is central to the ACE fellowship experience (see Chapter Twenty-Six). Generally, these senior administrators take their mentoring responsibilities quite seriously, enjoying the opportunity to groom new leaders. Throughout the year, the ACE Fellows Program staff remains in contact with the mentors, who offer each other suggestions and feedback.

The internship experience is complemented by three week-long seminars sponsored by the ACE Fellows Program. These seminars consist of workshops, group discussions, case studies, simulation exercises, presentations, and informal dialogues with higher education leaders. Topics cover a wide range, including strategic planning, budgeting and financial management, academic administration, personal and interpersonal dimensions of higher education, contemporary issues and trends, and, of course, leadership. Through participation in these seminars and other regional meetings, as well as visits to a variety of colleges and universities, ACE fellows acquire a national perspective and a sense of the human and institutional diversity that characterize higher education in this country.

The ACE Fellows Program is administered from a central office in Washington, D.C., but functions with the support of participating institutions. The program staff remains available to the ACE fellows through the remainder of their careers, advising them and helping them along in their professional advancement. The ACE fellows themselves constitute a close, highly effective network of mutual support. All these factors combined have made this program one of the most comprehensive and successful leadership initiatives in higher education.

System Option

Many states have preestablished consortia of higher education institutions. These can be public university systems (such as the State University of New York) or private universities with multiple campuses (such as California's Claremont Colleges). It is only natural and quite advantageous for participating institutions to establish collaborative arrangements within their own multicampus structures. Where a systemwide approach to professional development is in place, an internship program can be incorporated with minimal mobilization of resources. When it is not in place, an internship program can become the incentive for launching a more ambitious professional development effort.

An instance of successful implementation of this model was the California State University (CSU) Administrative Fellows Program. Established in 1978, it extended career development opportunities to academic and administrative personnel, especially women, minorities, and individuals with disabilities, on the system's nineteen campuses. The program was discontinued briefly due to economic constraints; however, CSU has announced plans to revive the program with a new name and improved features. The Pilot Executive Leadership Development Program will add two significant elements: the program will be for two years, and there will be a guarantee of executive appointment within the system upon completion of the internship. Each CSU campus president will be allowed to nominate two candidates, and three participants will be selected from the nominees. In the first year, the restructured program will give preference to Latinos, and other underrepresented ethnic groups and women will be given priority in subsequent years.

Structurally, the CSU Administrative Fellows Program resembled its ACE counterpart, after which it was modeled. The participants were nominated by their institutions, were selected on the basis of qualifications and potential, and were sent to another campus to learn under senior administrators. The fellows participated in a series of seminars and workshops and met periodically to share their experiences. The home campuses continued to pay the fellows' salaries and benefits during the year of internship; the host institutions provided space and access to campus administrators.

The CSU program differed from ACE's in several aspects. It placed less emphasis on travel and campus visitations, was less concerned with national issues, and gave greater value to hands-on learning. Whereas ACE's primary purpose is to shape leaders, the CSU's main thrust was to develop administrators. In the ACE model, the president is typically one of the mentors; in the CSU's, the mentoring was often provided by a vice president, an assistant vice president, a dean, or a program director. In addition, the fact that the CSU Administrative Fellows Program was administered at each campus by the affirmative action office had a dual effect: it underscored the program's commitment to the advancement of underrepresented populations, but it also reduced its relative importance on the institutional agenda.

Designing, Developing, and Implementing an Administrative Internship Program

If campus-based, a student services administrative internship program should be part of institutional professional development for all personnel. Every college or university ought to invest in the future of its employees — for their benefit, of course, but also for the benefit of the students and of the institution itself. Although less desirable, an administrative internship program can also be created as a single-unit professional development effort. In that case, it could be conceived as a pilot project, whose success could inspire the creation of a more ambitious initiative within the institution.

The Importance of Leadership and Institutional Support

A crucial ingredient for the creation of a successful internship program is the backing of the campus's top leadership (Bryan and Mullendore, 1990). This support should be manifested through a clear and forceful statement of support issued by the president (or the chief student services officer), assurances of adequate resources and financial assistance, and long-term commitment. The presence of top-level support informs the college community that the internship program is important to the institution, that it has a high-priority ranking, and that the community's cooperation is sought and expected.

The Necessity of Widespread Commitment

The successful implementation of an administrative internship program requires widespread support throughout the campus community. This support cannot be assumed; it must be nurtured. If the institution has an established, recognized professional development initiative for all personnel, this readily available mechanism could be used to publicize the internship program. Otherwise, new mechanisms must be constructed to develop community support and program recognition.

Developing the Program and Defining Its Parameters

The first step in developing an administrative internship program is the establishment of a planning task force. The president can underscore the program's importance by issuing personal invitations to the members of the task force. Those invited to participate should include the chief student affairs officer, other student services staff members, faculty members, academic deans, and human resource personnel. It is very important that this task force have representation from several divisions of the institution and that it not be conceived as a private enterprise within student services. The agenda for the task force should be issues chosen (preferably) by the president or by the chief student affairs officer.

The fundamental purpose of the task force should be to define the parameters of the program. In so doing, it will design the program and will move it smoothly toward its implementation. In defining parameters, the philosophy of the program, its organization, the model to be implemented, and the timing all must be considered. At a minimum, the following questions should be answered. What are the philosophical foundations of the program? These should include the affirmation of ethical behavior, the appreciation of diversity, and the conception of the campus as an integrated entity. How will the program work? The actual organization of the program must be clearly stated, including time expectations for interns, requirements, and a calendar. What model will fit this institution best? When should the program begin? It is very important that a schedule be established, so the work will proceed in a timely manner and with a sense of urgency.

Selecting the Participants

Participant selection is a key element in assuring program success. Expected outcomes, the selection criteria, and the application and selection processes should all be carefully described. Answering the following questions will assist with that process. What will be the nomination or application process? Will the program be designed to increase employees' knowledge of the job that they do, to promote advancement, to develop leadership skills? What will be the eligibility requirements to participate in the program? What will be the criteria for selection? What information and documentation should be required in the application process? Who should serve on the selection committee?

Finding answers to these questions will take time and energy, but all are important. The approach used to identify candidates is critical and can occur through nomination, application, or a combination of methods. Whatever the chosen method, a competitive process is desirable.

Eligibility requirements must be clearly linked to the specific objectives of the internship program. For example, if the program is designed to develop top divisional management, a certain level of seniority and leadership experience may be critical. In almost all cases, the minimum length of employment at the institution or in the division must be specified. It is also legitimate to conceive an administrative internship program as a vehicle of upward mobility for traditionally overlooked populations such as women or minorities.

Criteria for selection must be precisely stated to avoid confusion, the appearance of arbitrariness, and unnecessary disappointment among non-selected candidates. The goals of the internship must be clear to both potential candidates and their supervisors. Finally, the selection committee should be broadly based to assure fairness and equity in the selection process.

Designing the Program

Careful design of the administrative internship program is essential. At least the following questions must be answered prior to program implementation.

Who should have the responsibility for running the program? The program director should be someone in a highly visible position and with easy access to either the president or the chief student affairs officer.

What types of experiences should the participants have during their internships? The program guidelines should recommend a combination of structured and unstructured experiences (Renick, Terrell, and Jones, 1989). The interns should be encouraged to observe process as well as product and to study decision making, leadership models, management practices, organizational methods, and interpersonal skills. While observing the work of offices and leaders, the interns should consider the following questions. Why did some people do something this way? What was the impact of their decision? How would they, the interns, have done it differently? What evidence is there that this decision or action was effective?

What will be the obligation of the current supervisors during the internship year? The interns should be released from their responsibilities but should be assured that they can return to their former positions.

What will be the obligations of the interns? Expecting them to write periodic reports will help them focus on the meaning of the experience and analyze and synthesize its contribution to their professional and personal growth. Such reports also provide the basis for meaningful dialogues with mentors.

What are the costs of the program, and whose budget should absorb what part of these costs? The expenses involved will vary according to the design of the program, but at a minimum, these should include each intern's salary and benefits. Ideally, a pool of money will be available to compensate offices that lose employees during the period of the internship. Some money should also be provided for the interns and their mentors to attend professional conferences and other pertinent activities.

How will the mentors be selected? Individuals who demonstrate their interest by volunteering are generally more effective teachers. Sometimes, however, administrators with the skills and knowledge to be good mentors are reluctant to take the initiative. The time and effort spent on developing their interest will prove worthwhile over time.

What written materials need to be developed? These should include guidelines for mentors and interns (Kelly, 1984; Schmidt and Wolfe, 1980), a core curriculum, background literature, time lines, and lists of expectations. A good manual can be a handy tool.

Evaluation

Determining if the administrative internship program is successful and meets the goals of the design is extremely important. Lack of evaluation can make the program vulnerable if resources become restricted or administrative leadership changes within the organization.

How will the success of the program be assessed? Appropriate data must be collected from the onset of the program. The expected outcomes must be specified, and a way of comparing them with actual outcomes should be developed. It is essential that a follow-up mechanism be established to receive feedback for interns, mentors, nominators, and supervisors and to evaluate the long-term impact of the program on the individual, the division, and the institution.

What is expected of the interns after the program is over? Will they be expected to return to their previous job for a specified period of time? If so, what is that period? How can the intern's newly acquired skills, talents, and knowledge be utilized by the home institution? The institution has invested in the development of this professional and should be eager to enjoy the fruits of that investment. If a position of greater responsibility is not available immediately, then other kinds of challenges must be created, such as participation in important committees or the assignment of significant projects.

What will be the mechanism for ensuring the continuity of the program? Once these questions have been answered and the parameters of the administrative internship program have been established, the rest is implementation.

Summary

A well-planned, comprehensive administrative internship program can be an asset to any institution or division of student affairs. An internship program can be a vehicle for assisting student affairs staff members in developing skills and competencies to meet new and changing responsibilities. Specificity regarding objectives, expected outcomes, and selection criteria is essential. Evaluation of the program is also critical so that adjustments can be made to meet changed needs and priorities. Administrative internship programs can be a cost-effective method to train potential institutional leaders and ultimately to improve services to students. Planning, accompanied by strong support, adequate resources, and a sense of commitment, is of vital importance.

References

Barr, M. J., Upcraft, M. L., and Associates. *New Futures for Student Affairs: Building a Vision for Professional Leadership and Practice.* San Francisco: Jossey-Bass, 1990.

Benke, M., and Disque, C. S. "Moving In, Out, Up, or Nowhere? the Mobility of Mid-Managers." In R. B. Young (ed.), *The Invisible Leaders: Student Affairs Mid-Managers.* Washington, D.C.: National Association of Student Personnel Administrators, 1990.

Bloland, P. A. "A Personal Point of View." *NASPA Journal,* 1979, *17* (2), 57–62.

Bryan, W. A., and Mullendore, R. H. "Professional Development Strategies." In R. B. Young (ed.), *The Invisible Leaders: Student Affairs Mid-Managers.* Washington, D.C.: National Association of Student Personnel Administrators, 1990.

Carpenter, D. S. "Developmental Concerns in Moving Toward Personal and Professional Competence." In D. D. Coleman and J. E. Johnson (eds.), *The New Professional: A Resource Guide for New Student Affairs Professionals and Their Supervisors.* Washington, D.C.: National Association of Student Personnel Administrators, 1990.

Deegan, W. L., Steele, B. H., and Thielen, T. B. *Translating Theory into Practice: Implications of Japanese Management Theory for Student Personnel Ad-*

ministrators. Washington, D.C.: National Association of Student Personnel Administrators, 1985.

Delworth, U., Hanson, G. R., and Associates. *Student Services: A Handbook for the Profession.* (2nd ed.) San Francisco: Jossey-Bass, 1989.

DeWitt, R. C. "Managing a Student Affairs Team: It's a New Ball Game." *NASPA Journal,* 1991, *28* (2), 185–188.

Garland, P. H. *Serving More Than Students: A Critical Need for College Student Personnel Services.* ASHE-ERIC Higher Education Report, no. 7. Washington, D.C.: Association for the Study of Higher Education, 1985.

Kelly, K. E. "Initiating a Relationship with a Mentor in Student Affairs: A Research Study." *NASPA Journal,* 1984, *21* (3), 49–54.

Kuh, G. D. "The Demographic Juggernaut." In M. J. Barr, M. L. Upcraft, and Associates, *New Futures for Student Affairs: Building a Vision for Professional Leadership and Practice.* San Francisco: Jossey-Bass, 1990.

McDade, S. A. "Leadership Development: A Key to the New Leadership Role of Student Affairs Professionals." *NASPA Journal,* 1989, *27* (1), 33–41.

Quartly, C. J. "Job Rotation Is More Than Musical Chairs." *Supervisory Management,* 1973, *18,* 21–27.

Renick, J. C., Terrell, M. C., and Jones, D. "Examining Leadership Opportunities: An Empirical Assessment." *NASPA Journal,* 1989, *27* (1), 42–50.

Robinson, D. C., and Delbridge-Parker, L. "A Model Job Rotation Plan: A 10-Year Follow-Up." *NASPA Journal,* 1991, *28* (2), 172–178.

Schmidt, J. A., and Wolfe, J. S. "The Mentor Partnership: Discovery of Professionalism." *NASPA Journal,* 1980, *17* (3), 45–51.

Shaffer, R. H. "Critical Dimensions of Student Affairs in the Decades Ahead." *Journal of College Student Personnel,* 1984, *25* (2), 112–114.

Trimble, R. W., Allen, D. R., and Vidoni, D. O. "Student Personnel Administration: Is It for You?" *NASPA Journal,* 1991, *28* (2), 156–162.

Woodard, D. B., Jr., and Komives, S. R. "Ensuring Staff Competence." In M. J. Barr, M. L. Upcraft, and Associates, *New Futures for Student Affairs: Building a Vision for Professional Leadership and Practice.* San Francisco: Jossey-Bass, 1990.

PART FIVE

❧

Administrative
Challenges
for the Future

We are currently in an age fraught with change, and it is likely that this cycle will continue and perhaps accelerate into the near future. This situation influences all areas in student affairs. Part Five is devoted to identifying the specific administrative challenges faced by student affairs in the future and provides suggestions about how we can prepare to meet them.

By now, we are all aware that our student bodies reflect the growing diversity in our larger society. We know that our college populations in the years ahead will be markedly different from the past in terms of their age, ethnicity, gender, and disabilities. The question of how we can effectively prepare for these differences remains, however. In Chapter Twenty-Nine, Blandina Ramirez focuses on the anticipated changes in the demographic characteristics of college students and the implications that those changes will have for our profesion.

The skilled practitioner in the future must be able to operate effectively in a nongrowth, reduced, or limited-growth fiscal environment. In Chapter Thirty, Ernest Ern provides a focus on the issues involved in managing a changed set of fiscal parameters and includes strategies that must be used if student affairs is to survive and flourish.

A critical need also exists to furnish both appropriate role models for students and opportunities for diversity in administrative and policy-making bodies. These needs are coupled with increasing pressure to provide better programs and services. In Chapter Thirty-One, approaches to meet these challenges, discussed by Michael Freeman, Elizabeth Nuss, and Margaret Barr, should prove helpful to administrators at all levels.

In Chapter Thirty-Two, Barbara Jacoby discusses assistance to the many kinds of students coming to college and university. Student affairs must find methods to supply services to students who are not enrolled full time, are older, are physically challenged, are commuters, study in off-site locations, study through the use of technology, and come from many ethnic backgrounds. This chapter offers a model to assess the response of the campus and design strategies to assist these new students.

Health care is a major issue in the United States, one that higher education must also be prepared to confront. Margaret Bridwell and Stanley Kinder in Chapter Thirty-Three explore questions involving health insurance and care for students and for their dependents. All will be major concerns in the decade ahead.

The relationship between public and private higher education and government is also evolving. Financial aid programs are being altered at the same time that federal and state government has begun to intrude in the management of higher education. It is essential to understand the consequences of the changes and to develop means of dealing with them. E. T. ("Joe") Buchanan identifies the problems and provides guidance on how to approach them in Chapter Thirty-Four.

Measuring effectiveness is often a difficult and illusive task for colleges and universities; yet accrediting agencies, governing bodies, and consumers are asking how well are we fulfilling our mission. William Bryan and Richard Mullendore discuss the role of professional standards in improving student affairs programs, activities, and services in Chapter Thirty-Five. Their examples and guidance will help us to assess how well we are doing our job.

Part Five and this volume conclude with Chapter Thirty-Six. No one book can provide all the information needed for the practitioner who seeks to be the best possible administrator and manager. However, this chapter by Margaret Barr summarizes the issues and provides guidance for continued professional development through reading and involvement.

29

❦

Adapting to
New Student Needs
and Characteristics

Blandina C. Ramirez

Several years ago, I witnessed a hit-and-run accident in which a young Mexican-American woman was run over by a speeding car as she walked from her residence hall to the campus library. After calling 911, we university officials proceeded to ascertain as much about the victim as we could. She was one of two sisters attending the university as the result of intensified efforts to recruit minority students. Her parents were non–English-speaking farmers living outside the city. After talking to the other sister, I concluded that the family was a very traditional one that had managed to educate their daughters by living simply on a farm, working hard, and adhering to strong religious values.

The president, the university's only high-ranking Spanish-speaking administrator, turned to me and asked if I would call the girl's family. For the twenty-two minutes it took the emergency medical services vehicle to arrive, I watched in anguish, attempting to frame what I would say to the parents according to what I would learn from the medics. As my usual response to any crisis involving bodily danger is to sink into a deep, frightened silence, I feared that I would not be able to say anything at all. I called up the image of my elementary school principal, Mrs. Cardwell. Speaking with great authority and greater sensitivity, she could always get exactly the reaction she desired from the parents of the Mexican-American students with whom I grew up. As the ambulance transported the young woman to a local hospital, I was grateful that I would not have to tell the parents that their daughter was in danger of dying.

Her mother answered the phone with a voice that conveyed greater strength and clarity of thought than I felt. I was very formal and used my doctoral title. I explained the situation and suggested that it would be important for her and her husband to come to the hospital. I asked if they had a car. When she said no, I offered to drive the thirty miles to get them. She explained that a neighbor could drive them more quickly. She told me that her husband was in the fields and that she needed to tell him what had happened. I requested her to leave the phone line open and said that I would wait to talk to him. He came on the line and in very formal Spanish thanked me for calling. He asked me to make sure that the doctors treated his daughter immediately upon arrival; he assured me that he would get the money to pay the hospital. I explained that the insurance that the university required would apply. He then said that he would call his son to transport them to the hospital and that his son knew English. After giving him directions to the hospital, using the landmarks that I thought he would easily recognize, I told him that I would stay by the phone until I knew that they had reached the hospital and that they should call me collect if they had any difficulties. Before too long, we got word that our student (their daughter) was going to be all right.

As I talk to student affairs professionals today, I am often reminded of the many skills and sensitivities required by that situation; the institution was called upon to respond to the needs of a student's family that was quite different from what we have considered typical in the past. Language, cultural nuances, and economic considerations came into play in creating a relationship of trust and respect between the institution and the family. More importantly, the institution had the opportunity to see beyond the stereotype of "disadvantaged minority student" and encounter familial strength and dignity that would make many affluent and more "typical" students appear truly disadvantaged. But the challenge facing higher education in general and the student services profession in particular is far more complex than increasing an institution's capacity to deal with any one cultural group.

Over the course of the next several decades, higher education will be transformed by the effects of two powerful trends in American society. The first is the continuing struggle in the institutions that shape that society to embrace populations that have experienced historical exclusion based on gender, race, culture, national origin, age, disability, and sexual orientation. Though the pace will vary for each group, the incompatibility of exclusion with the shared values, ideals, and needs of this country makes eventual inclusion inevitable. The second trend is the dramatic demographic shifts within the country; these include a rapid growth in the proportion of the population that lives into old age, a even greater increase in the number of children who grow up in poverty, an increase in students who are members of what we call the historical United States minority groups, and the immigration to the United States of new groups of people from highly populated areas of the world.

In short, America will become one of the most open, longest lived, and culturally and racially complex societies in the history of humankind. College and university campuses will face the turbulence and the promise of that diversity first and most intensely as traditional structural barriers to higher education are dismantled. Student affairs professionals will be required to respond to these changes at the human level and with increasing understanding, sensitivity, courage, creativity, and competence.

This chapter will discuss the need for a different paradigm in higher education and the evolving needs and characteristics that student affairs must confront. Finally, the implications of these changes will be discussed in detail. In a real sense, we have no models for creating campus communities in this new context, for the paradigm that defines equality and inclusion in this country, and perhaps around the world, has shifted markedly. That shift is a triumph for American values, not a repudiation.

Understanding the Paradigm Shift

History would indicate that issues of race, gender, and cultural equality and inclusion may well represent the most difficult challenges in human experience. Human beings of all cultures and all races tend to form a view of their world early in life, and some elements of that world view continue to influence their thinking and actions in spite of conscientious efforts to assimilate new information and experiences. The separateness of society in the United States is so powerful a reference that it continues to dominate and is reinforced by popular media, patterns and places of worship, and family and leisure activities. And that separateness is not limited to the many kinds of segregation experienced by Hispanics, African Americans, Asian Americans, and Native Americans.

Until very recently, for example, specialized institutional facilities for persons with one or more disabilities created a situation in which most Americans acquired neither the sensitivity, comfort, or competence needed for their interaction with persons with disabilities. Persons with disabilities were literally removed from the broader society's presence and consciousness.

Fortunately, that situation is changing. To illustrate, at the Dallas–Fort Worth airport recently, I waited at a gate while a team of basketball players in wheelchairs came off their flight. The manner in which the airline staff met the physical needs of these passengers was almost as inspirational as the strength, independence, and joy with which the basketball players assisted the airline staff in getting the job done. Then, as I stood there reflecting on this remarkable change in human behavior after centuries of devaluing and disregarding the disabled, a group of men and women traveling home after participating in the Senior Olympics came up behind me. Among them was a tall, strong woman — she could have been seventy or eighty — who wore several medals won in running events. She told me that she had always been "the best runner" until forced by her parents to stop when she reached her teens. She had resumed running three years before, when she joined a senior citizens group after her husband died. Now she was winning all the time. Although her manner was matter of fact, she spoke as if a great hunger had finally been satisfied.

Coming to understand this kind of change, both intellectually and through personal experience, is essential to student services professionals. It is certainly imperative in developing a conceptual framework for student affairs programs, minimizing dysfunctional responses to students, and building the institutional and individual strength for coping with both the turbulence and the promise of diversity. Most importantly, it is crucial to enabling student affairs professionals to make sense of their work and to derive from it the intellectual and personal satisfaction that is the hallmark of the profession.

The struggle for equality in American society is as old as the republic. From the moment that this nation based its right to exist on the premise that all men are created equal, it invited the agitation of thinking men and women who would resist laws and practices that belied that premise. Because we see ourselves as a nation ruled by law, rather than ruled by the personal whim or belief of those who have secured power, that struggle has affected government social policy, which eventually is translated into institutional policy.

Successive groups within society have confronted their discrimination and exclusion from its full benefits. Most have been able to overcome exclusion and discrimination within two generations by coming to understand and make use of the regular institutional processes. Incorporating each successive group has pretty much been a process of "seeing them like us, accepting them like us, and making them like us." But for women, racial and national origin minority groups, and the disabled — groups whose exclusion has been sanctioned in law, broadly institutionalized, and culturally and socially accepted — it has been necessary to change laws, reverse institutional practices and their persistent effects, and replace deeply held cultural biases, attitudes, and social behaviors.

Although the experience and development of both individuals and groups have differed in significant ways, the same remedies to discrimination and exclusion have been applied to all groups with minimal variation. As groups have succeeded in gaining political attention to their plight, they have become part of the "protected" classes and have been able to gain access to those remedies that would supposedly enable them to become one with the dominant group.

Like the traditional thinking in linear physics, both the history and the substance of social policy on equity have been additive, linear, and based on the existence of a mythical "typical" dominant standard and the relative deviation of each group from that standard. Like the 1950s fifth-grade science book picture of the solar system showing one sun and nine planets in a straight line, the old paradigm framed the equitable treatment of excluded groups solely in relation of their relative distance from the white, mostly male, "American" whole.

The old paradigm allowed those at the margin to approach the center only to the extent that they were willing or able to become like the group at the center. Responsibility for adaptation rested wholly on the formerly excluded and on those with the least resources to adapt. For European immigrants, this meant relinquishing languages, culture, and to a great extent identity, including the Anglicizing of family names. The old paradigm viewed equality as a finite resource and assumed that equity for one group necessarily resulted in loss for the others. Competition and domination were the primary forces upholding the old paradigm and were highly valued because they had always been the basis of success in the past.

It is new thinking that the universe itself is a nonlinear, chaotic balancing of overlapping energies in which, as Marilyn French says, "Nothing rules, yet there is peace as each segment follows its own course and exists in cooperative relation with everything else" (1985, p. 498). These attitudes provide the analogy for the paradigm and the challenge of serving students and creating campus communities in the midst of dynamic and accelerating diversity.

The paradigm shift, of course, requires a mind shift. Minorities in the United States are not only a majority in the world but may increasingly represent the majority population in certain parts of this country. We can no longer speak in a general way of minorities as a group or of any one minority group. We must instead seek to understand the immense diversity within as well as between groups. For example, though women wish to be accorded the same equality of being, they are (as they have always been) different in race, culture, sexual orientation, socioeconomic condition, age, and ability. The other characteristics of a disabled person outweigh any handicap. One ages but may not be "old" until the onset of a terminal illness.

Understanding Changing Student Needs and Characteristics

The extent and rate of change in the population of college and university campuses, though far from adequate, are still nothing short of revolutionary. It is important to understand the depth and extent of the change that has already occurred, even as we challenge ourselves to accelerate the pace of inclusion.

As Boyer tells us (Carnegie Foundation for the Advancement of Teaching, 1990), America's first colleges were guided by a vision of coherence. For the first two hundred years, college students were socially and economically very much alike. Campuses were populated by men, drawn primarily from the privileged class. Virtually no black students were enrolled in college until the appearance of the traditionally black institutions. When a few

Native Americans were provided higher education opportunities, these were also in segregated settings, and too often the consequences of isolation from home and culture were tragic. The number of Asian-American and Hispanic students in higher education was minuscule.

Although the benefits of the GI Bill following World War II increased the presence of working-class white and minority men in higher education, gender- and race-specific institutions provided the bulk of college opportunities to women and minorities. The postwar era did, however, begin to focus the value of a higher education for a more varied population. In 1950, 5 percent of women and 27 percent of men aged twenty-five to thirty-four had completed four or more years of college. By 1987, the comparable figures were 23 percent for women and 25 percent for men (Touchton and Davis, 1991).

At the same time, the traditions of higher education institutions, particularly those within the purview of student services professionals, continued to be firmly set in a distant era of homogeneity and privilege. It is a wonder that this institution designed by males for their male, privileged children functions as well as it does in the face of an exploding market with vastly different needs and characteristics.

Approximately 1.3 million (or 10.5 percent) of the 12.5 million students now enrolled in the nation's postsecondary institutions are students with at least one disability. They represent 10.8 percent of the undergraduate, 8.4 percent of the graduate, and 7.3 percent of the first-professional (medicine, business, and law) students (American Council on Education, 1991b). These percentages almost doubled in the period between 1978 and 1988. The disabilities most frequently reported by postsecondary students relate to vision, health, and hearing; however, improved early medical treatment, more equitable elementary and secondary educational opportunities, and increased legal protections will lead to greater participation of students with a broader spectrum of disabilities, including psychiatric and emotional disabilities (Unger, 1991).

The *Fact Book on Women in Higher Education* (Touchton and Davis, 1991) offers a fascinating account of the ways in which women's drive to empower their lives is affecting higher education institutions and will continue to alter the characteristics of student bodies. Since 1979, women have constituted a majority of students in higher education. In 1987, women were 53 percent of the 12.6 million students enrolled in higher education (6.7 million women; 5.9 million men). The substantial increase in part-time enrollment over the past two decades appears to be more significant for women, with almost one-half (47 percent) of women enrolled on a part-time basis, compared to 39 percent of men. Minority women have also experienced formidable increases in college attendance; in 1986, women constituted 60 percent of the African American students, 56 percent of the Native American students, 53 percent of Hispanic students, and 47 percent of Asian students.

Enrollment of women aged twenty-five and older has increased by more than one million in the past fifteen years. Today more than 40 percent of women college students (approximately 2.7 million) are age twenty-five or more. Men in this age group increased by .2 million, from 1.2 million in 1972 to 1.4 million in 1987. Between 1972 and 1987, the fastest-growing group of college students was made up of women over age thirty-five. Approximately 1.2 million women over age thirty-five are now in higher education — triple the number in 1972. Men over age thirty-five have doubled their presence in higher education since 1972, from slightly more than .3 million to .6 million (Touchton and Davis, 1991).

It is in the area of defining institutional responses to an aging society that we are least prepared. This is the first generation that will see massive numbers of individuals living into advanced age in relatively good health and having experienced the enriching value of education. The expectations of this population with regard to using continuing education for a variety of purposes are now barely beginning to surface. By the same token, we are only now starting to understand the physical, intellectual, and emotional passages encountered by these individuals and the ways in which we can more fully influence those passages. The exceptional older individual who completes a new venture in formal schooling later in life is becoming less exceptional all the time. Nonetheless, it is important that we understand that we can stereotype the older population, both negatively and positively, as easily as we stereotype minority groups, women, and the disabled. The fact is that in a society that continues to adulate youth, coping with the aging process is too often a confusing, lonely experience perhaps most popularly understood in relation to the "midlife crisis." As more than one wise women has said, "Growing old ain't for sissies."

The number of Native American, Hispanic, African-American, and Asian-American students on campuses is increasing rapidly (in spite of a percentage-rate decline in the college participation of Hispanics and African Americans). Native American, Hispanic, African-American, and Asian-American students will represent one-third of the school- and college-age population by the beginning of the next century. Still grossly underrepresented on predominantly white campuses, approximately 56 percent of Hispanic students, 46 percent of African-American students, 52 percent of Native American students, and 38 percent of American-Asian students in higher education attend two-year institutions, and fewer than one fifth transfer to four-year campuses. Approximately 20 percent of African-American students and 30 percent of Hispanics attend historically black institutions or Hispanic-serving institutions. In spite of these current patterns of institutional attendance, the rapid growth in the size of these populations will spur rapid increase in their presence on all college campuses (Carter and Wilson, 1992).

As we stated earlier, the most grievous and common mistake in assessing the needs and characteristics of members of minority groups is to generalize. This population will vary significantly in terms of socioeconomic circumstances, group identity, educational preparation, group and family experience with the educational system, articulation and influence of traditional culture, and family circumstances.

More than 40 percent of Native Americans, African Americans, Hispanics, some Asian-American groups, Native Hawaiians, and Alaskans come from homes where the income is below the poverty line. This is two and three times the rate for white non-Hispanic Americans, and that figure has increased in the last decade, not decreased. There is evidence that structural forces in the American economy are pushing greater numbers of the working middle class (and disproportionate numbers of middle-class minorities) into the low-income category (U.S. Census Bureau, 1992). The low rates of participation in higher education of these groups clearly show that most minority students who attend college will be among the first of their families to do so. Indeed, the data for Hispanics and Native Americans indicate that students from these groups are highly likely to be the first in their family to complete high school. Serving a population characterized by poverty or near poverty, little experience with higher education institutions, and often differing language capabilities, implies that all the assumptions about the students' ability to understand and comply with the fiscal, social, and academic demands of college must be reexamined. What are the information needs of students in these circumstances? What are the information needs of their families? How does one respond to those requirements in a manner that recognizes and builds on the strengths of these students, even as appropriate support systems are designed? Most importantly, how does the institution develop a capacity to recognize and appreciate those cultural and social elements within the family that can strengthen these students' college experience?

The experience of some historically black colleges and universities, some of the institutions now represented among the Hispanic Association of Colleges and Universities, the American-Indian Higher Education Consortium, as well as research analyzing the success of Asian-American groups, indicates that incorporating the students' culture in the creation of both the social and academic climates of institutions is an important element in their relative success. It is important, however, to understand that this approach does not merely entail the celebration of formal or superficial cultural manifestations; also required are deeper cultural forms of nurturing, relating, interacting, reflecting, and affirming, occurring in a manner that communicates to students an institution's expectation of and commitment to their success. Consistently and repeatedly, students sum up this experience (as well as successful experiences on predominantly white campuses) by explaining, "[Someone] believed I had it in me!"

Of course, a growing number (if not proportion) of minority group students come from homes where income levels and educational experiences are rising. These students may or may not know the language of their group, may have grown up in neighborhoods populated mostly by white non-Hispanic families, and may be supported by parents with high expectations of both their children and the institutions that serve them. These students, no less than their less privileged peers, face a unique developmental task for minorities in our society: to arrive at a sense of their own identity and to make choices about their identification with their own group and the larger society. What often makes the task more difficult for minority students of privilege is that college often represents their first day-to-day visceral encounter with the divisions in our society.

Understanding the Implications

For the student services professional, the implications of this exploding diversity in the student body are all-encompassing. There is a need to understand the many ways in which students are unique — and yet the same. The diversity that we confront grows exponentially as we learn to see each new element. It is as if we are looking at our campus communities through a kaleidoscope and every movement to improve the whole picture changes the design. But it is the student affairs professional who has the most accurate lens on the campus community and on the individual students within it. It is student affairs that has the responsibility to lead the campus community to an understanding of the implications of diversity. And it is our profession that must assess the institution's capacity to fulfill its mission and lead, cajole, and assist the institution in developing the ability to meet its emerging challenges. In short, the student affairs professional must be prepared to assume leadership at the institutional programmatic, and individual level.

Leadership

The exercise of leadership is a significant area of study; empirical research is now attempting to identify those elements of leadership that are art and those that are science (Gardner, 1990). It may be quite useful for the student affairs professional to engage in an examination of both writing and research and the training in the area of leadership. Ultimately, of course, those who would exert influence over others are alone with their own understanding of the skills, resources, and gifts available to them. Whether individuals rely on science or art, they are still required to know themselves; to have complete, specific, and accurate information; to develop consensus within diverse constituencies; to manage what is attempted well enough to enable it to succeed or fail on its own merits; and to have some way of testing whether they are doing the right thing well enough and whether it continues to be appropriate to the context that they originally wished to change.

Planning

Neither professionals nor the institution can fully and accurately envision the changes that will occur in the student body over the next several decades. The only thing we can be sure of is that change will occur and at an ever-accelerating pace. The American Council on Education (ACE) has developed an approach to comprehensive institutional planning that is contained in *Minorities on Campus: A Handbook for Enhancing Diversity* (Green, 1989). Although minorities are the focal point of this guide, the assessment, consensus-building, and implementation processes that are suggested can be adapted to include other groups. *Focus on Adults: A Self-Study Guide for Postsecondary Educational Institutions* (American Council on Education, 1991a) is helpful in developing programs and services for adult students. ACE's National Clearinghouse on Postsecondary Education for Individuals with Disabilities (telephone 800-544-3284) can be a source of assistance in understanding and responding to the needs of persons with disabilities (American Council on Education, 1991b), and perspectives on the needs of women are contained in *Educating the Majority: Women Challenge Tradition in Higher Education* (Pearson, Shavlick, and Touchton, 1989).

Information Gathering

The sources just listed can also be helpful to the student services professional as programmatic innovations are developed. Just as at the institutional level there is a need for accurate, timely, and relevant information, it is also necessary that such information be systematically examined at the program level. Quantitative and qualitative strategies must be created to gather information about the well-being of each identifiable group, as well as the perceptions, attitudes, and behaviors of all students. Too many of the problems faced by student affairs professionals with regard to diversity are a product of "squeaky wheel" program development and management. When only the squeaky wheel secures a response, being noisy is the most intelligent course of action.

Teamwork

Student affairs professionals, more than any other group in the institution, must develop a team that reflects the varied nature of the population. Not only does this variety improve the probability that the information used for program design and management will be more accurate and relevant, but that information will also have more meaning and importance for the team. Achieving a team commitment to the whole of the many different parts of a student body is vital, if not easy. The student services leader will need to be concerned about more than recruiting and hiring a diverse staff; staff training and development and the creation of consensus on shared goals are imperative.

Student affairs professionals working with a heterogeneous student population must arrive at a commonly held philosophy or guiding principles of student development programming. Basic understanding of what constitutes equitable treatment of all groups should be achieved. Student affairs staff members must appreciate that treating everyone equally does not always mean treating everyone the same. Differences exist and must be recognized. Guiding principles should be examined regularly and should evolve as greater understanding about diversity is gained.

Support

Programmatic development in an institution characterized by changing student populations ultimately comes down to choosing from an array of activities that will require fiscal and staff support. At the point of decision making at the budgetary level, the tension between supporting things as they have always been and changing them becomes most difficult. Again, it becomes necessary to rely on information to provide a rationale for the choices that will be made. What are the guiding principles for student affairs programming? What are the assumptions about students that shape the design of the student affairs program? How relevant and inclusive are current programmatic activities? What are needs that are not met by current programmatic activities? What are the views of students? How do the activities under consideration support the building of community on campus?

Summary

Examining the assumptions that we make about atypical students is essential to planning responsible student services activities. I remember the rage that I felt while visiting an institution that had become a predominantly minority institution after an early history as a somewhat elitist single-sex institution. When I asked why nearly all of the early cultural traditions of the institution had been abandoned, I was told that it was unlikely that low-income minority students would want to see a play or go to the symphony. What is even more tragic is that little cultural activity of any kind had replaced the traditional program. Two Christmas events at the institution proved that the institution's current students were eager to participate in these activities, both new and familiar. One was a songfest in the early English minstrel tradition; the second was a Mexican posada in which carolers recreated Mary and Joseph's search for lodging.

The most exciting challenges and implications for the student affairs professional, who faces ever-increasing diversity in the student body, are those that require the enhancement of individual understanding, perspective, skills, and gifts for living and serving in a varied society. Diversity requires that individuals take risks in challenging their view of their work, creating relationships with people whose differences may make them feel less competent than they would like, accepting the opinions and views of a broad range of individuals, and examining long-held values and beliefs. There is risk involved in attempting new ways of accomplishing objectives in the development of students, and there is risk in discarding the traditional. Only the certainty that things will never be the same again can sustain the quest for new answers.

References

American Council on Education, Center for Adult Learning and Educational Credentials. *Focus for Postsecondary Educational Institutions.* Washington, D.C.: American Council on Education, 1991a.

American Council on Education, National Clearinghouse on Postsecondary Education for Individuals with Disabilities. "Facts You Can Use." In *Focus on Adults: A Self-Study Guide for Postsecondary Educational Institutions.* Washington, D.C.: American Council on Education, 1991b.

Carnegie Foundation for the Advancement of Teaching. *Campus Life: In Search of Community.* Princeton, N.J.: Carnegie Foundation for the Advancement of Teaching, 1990.

Carter, D. J., and Wilson, R. *Tenth Annual Status Report on Minorities in Higher Education.* Washington, D.C.: American Council on Education, 1992.

French, M. *Beyond Power.* New York: Summit Books, 1985.

Gardner, J. *On Leadership.* New York: Free Press, 1990.

Green, M. F. (ed.) *Minorities on Campus: A Handbook for Enhancing Diversity.* Washington, D.C.: American Council on Education, 1989.

Pearson, C. S., Shavlick, D. L., and Touchton, J. G. (eds.) *Educating the Majority: Women Challenge Tradition in Higher Education.* New York: Macmillan, 1989.

Touchton, J. G., and Davis, L. *Fact Book on Women in Higher Education.* Washington, D.C.: American Council on Education, Macmillan, 1991.

Unger, K. "Servicing Students with Psychiatric Disabilities on Campus: Clarifying the DDS Counselor's Role." *Journal of Postsecondary Education and Disability,* Fall 1991, pp. 21–28.

U.S. Census Bureau. *Trends in Relative Income: 1964 to 1989.* Washington, D.C.: U.S. Census Bureau, 1992.

30

☙

Managing Resources
Strategically

Ernest H. Ern

The higher educational system in the United States, the largest, most complex, and most diverse in the world, faces its most stringent test during the concluding decade of the twentieth century. The combination of escalating college tuitions throughout the 1980s and the current and projected economic conditions of the 1990s portends an extended period of fiscal constraint, which could cause indelible changes in our system.

This chapter will discuss the problems of rising costs, the need for fiscal restraint and expenditure reduction, and the importance of strategic planning for institutions and student affairs units. Case examples at the University of Virginia and Stanford University highlight the need for an organized process and procedure. The discussion considers the hard decisions that must be made and includes suggestions for the management of necessary change.

The dramatic escalation of costs associated with collegiate attendance in recent years can be attributed to a multitude of factors that are compounded by our impressively varied assemblage of colleges and universities in both the public and the private sector. The elements that have caused these unprecedented changes are many: the need to compensate faculty better; an aging faculty that requires compensation at progressively higher levels; a

439

notable growth in administrative staffs; the necessity to expand and improve computer equipment to keep pace with technological changes; the mandate to address the increased expectations of both parents and students for service delivery, thus escalating educational and general expenditures; dramatic increases in financial aid budgets, combined with a decline in available federal support; substantial decreases in revenue for public institutions from state appropriations; and other factors related to the specific nature of an institution (see Chapter Four). In addressing the costs related to higher education, Bowen (1980) has formulated the "laws" of higher education costs; these state: "The dominant goals of institutions are educational excellence, prestige and influence; in questions of excellence, prestige, and influence, there is almost no limit to the amount of money an institution could spend for seemingly fruitful, educational ends; each institution raises all the money it can and each institution spends all that it raises." He concludes that the overall effect is one of constant, escalating expenditure.

In spite of sobering tuition costs, by the end of the decade of the 1980s, enrollments in colleges and universities reached an all-time high (National Center for Education Statistics, 1989). Families were willing to find ways to meet the ever-growing expense of college attendance due to the extraordinarily high value that contemporary American society places on this experience. However, the economic downturn of the 1990s not only has colleges and universities scampering to reduce costs, but also has caused families to assume a more rigid posture in challenging the unprecedented tuition increases that have occurred in both the public and independent sectors.

The 1990–91 academic year exposed widespread financial problems for the academy that were deemed to be acute, widespread, and persistent. El-Khawas reported in *Campus Trends, 1991* (1991) that issues of adequate financial support overshadowed by a wide margin all other matters facing administrators. Economic conditions forced nearly one-half of this country's colleges and universities to pare their operating budgets by midyear. This situation obtained in almost two-thirds of public four-year institutions, almost half of public two-year colleges, and slightly more than one-third of the independent institutions. This American Council on Education report makes clear that an extended period of fiscal retrenchment will be required for many institutions due to further deterioration in their financial circumstances in the years ahead. Some may say that doing more with less (both resources and personnel) will be the watchword of higher education throughout the 1990s; yet for an ever-increasing number of colleges and universities, the potential exists for doing less with less. It is instructive to note—in an environment where meticulous planning is a presumption—that most institutions lacked any contingency plan to address early budget cuts experienced in the first full year of the decade!

The realities of reduced resources have affected the complete spectrum of higher education institutions in this country, from Sweet Briar to Stanford, from Minnesota to Mississippi, from the largest to the smallest, and from the well endowed to the unendowed. The realization that what universities have become accustomed to doing is no longer possible has been difficult to accept.

Strategic Planning and Budgeting: The Inseparable Pair

Before addressing the inextricable linkage between budgeting and planning, it is appropriate to examine the role of student services and its relationship to academic affairs and to the stated mission of a college or university. Fiske (1985), as editor of the *Selective Guide to Colleges,* focuses on a unique system of rating colleges in three areas: academics, social life, and quality of student life. His work is an example of the importance placed on a balanced collegiate experience by prospective students and their parents. In such situations, time outside the formal academic setting is expected to be just as rich, worthwhile, and consciously structured to complement intellectual growth as what takes place inside the classroom. To be certain, education is not bound by walls or structures but consists of purposeful programmatic initiatives that occur both day and night and provide for a total experience.

Of course, individuals do not select colleges based on the quality of the steam generated from the heating plant or the friendliness and efficiency of the bursar's staff, no matter how important these services may be. And we would not contend that the student affairs profession is anything but a service adjunct to an institution's academic mission; however, the nature of our adjunct relationship *is* different. Assessment studies (Moomaw, 1990 and 1991) underscore that students, particularly during their first year, need to break away and manage independent lives. Students state their most important objectives in terms of personal growth rather than an academic discipline. Objectives such as independence, self-control, self-confidence, learning to learn, and learning to coexist with different kinds of people are paramount, according to these studies.

If what we do in student affairs is important and enriching for the development of the individual, then such undertaking must be a stated, recognized, and respected part of an institution's mission. Thus, our working principle must embrace at least the following: student affairs, through its professionals and support staffs, provides leadership in helping to develop a true community of learning by expanding the intellectual, social, and cultural horizons of the student body through a broad range of support services and programs outside the formal academic setting. In striving for diversity in the student body and in seeking the ablest and most promising students, a commitment exists to expand the educational opportunities for persons with special challenges, such as minority status, physical and mental impairment, ethnic heritage, or insufficient financial resources. Tasks are accomplished by setting goals and priorities; policy and program development, implementation, and evaluation; budgeting; and a variety of administrative procedures enhancing staff development and communications within and outside student affairs. Through various departments, we strive to contribute to students' academic progress, personal growth, and sense of well-being by helping them clarify and reach their educational objectives and develop their talents; by promoting integration of learning; by contributing to a college or university environment that promotes student development, good human relations, a sense of community, and individual responsibility; and by acting as role models, providing them leadership in a variety of settings.

Dawson (1991) offers the unsettling information that comprehensive strategic plans are anomalies on college and university campuses. Such plans evolve from institutional mission statements. It is truly puzzling that intensive self-examination is not under way on every campus to portray more accurately the purpose, values, and intended direction of the institution. The simplest and clearest statement on planning reminds us that the hardest thing in the world to do is to plan ahead; yet the dumbest thing is not do so. Most student affairs administrators take the annual budgeting process seriously, and we all should. That process permits modest planning from year to year within the parameters of available short-term resources and is absolutely necessary; but it is also short-sighted! Without benefit of an intermediate-to long-range planning activity by each unit, a chance to be accountable for what student affairs does and to clarify its importance to the institutional mission is lost. This activity must not be undertaken in isolation but should be an equal partnership with other institutional leaders to develop both the short- and the long-term vision of the institution we serve. It is vital that such planning occur not only during times that involve the happy prospect of numerical growth and increased revenues, but even more important, when economic reversals demand institutional realignment.

As a profession, we have been appropriately admonished by Williamson and Mamarchev (1990, p. 204) that there is "an inherent responsibility to accumulate the fiscal acumen that will enable us to maintain credibility in an educational enterprise increasingly limited by financial constraints. Those who do heed this challenge face the possibility of program and staff reductions. A grave danger then may be the absorption of student affairs into other components of the institution. While expertise in the financial arena is not the focal point of most student affairs operations, it can no longer be avoided if the student affairs mission is to continue safely into the 21st century."

Elements of a Strategic Plan

A comprehensive strategic plan is crafted to direct an institution to realize its aspirations more nearly and to provide an opportunity to evaluate what it is doing, why it does so, who does it, and how well and how efficiently it is being done. Further, a plan will help to determine if the institution is fulfilling its stated mission. Any plan, if effective, must possess methodology to measure outcomes. A basic strategic plan should consist of at least the following elements:

1. Clarity of purpose (mission)
2. Goal setting (to achieve the institutional purpose)
3. Prioritizing of the goals to be attained
4. Specific objectives (subgoals), both long and short term, stated in measurable outcomes
5. Review of both the required and available resources to accomplish these objectives
6. Action steps (strategies) based on both internal and external assumptions and the subsequent determination of the best alternatives
7. Assignment of responsibility and establishment of a timetable for implementation of the plan
8. Periodic evaluation of both programs and personnel (accomplishments and deficiencies)

Staff Evaluation

As student affairs professionals, we need to be mindful that ultimately our greatest impact is made by the persons who deliver the programs and services. Thus, there is a mandate for managers to assess periodically, in a way as complete as possible, the performance of each staff member. An effective job description must specify the elements that compose the major goals, projects, duties, and related assignments on which a staff colleague is to be evaluated. Further, specific elements of the job description need to be assigned relative importance. All aspects of a position must be discussed and clarified by the supervisor and the employee at the time of appointment. This approach assures that a staff person is totally familiar with the duties of the job and the criteria on which an annual evaluation will be based before the performance cycle begins.

This process can be enhanced further by requiring that each staff member submit an annual report covering the same cycle. Each report should consist of a personal assessment of one's accomplishments and shortcomings during the previous year, scholarship, and forms of service to the institution and to the greater community, with citations of professional activities and recognitions.

Together the performance appraisal and the annual report provide a sound basis for salary recommendations and other personnel decisions. As personnel costs count for at least 75 percent of our budgets, senior managers must ascertain whether each person provides a notable contribution to the operation or serves as a noncontributory resource drain. Sears Roebuck and Company got it right many years ago when it began marketing its various products under the classifications "good," "better," and "best." In student affairs, we hire good people; we hope that they will get better; and we expect, especially in today's marketplace, that they will become the very best at what they do.

A Case Example

The planning process at the University of Virginia has evolved in a meaningful way through a series of biennial evaluation and planning cycles (Ern, 1984, 1986, 1989, and 1991). This process was found to be an exceedingly useful one in coordinating planning with evaluation and resource allocation for the institution as a whole. The biennial evaluation and planning reports

- Project the major policy and program goals of the institution for the next ten years.
- Specify the program objectives and the strategies to be undertaken in order to realize them.
- Provide information on resources necessary to pursue the objectives and strategies.

Each unit, department, or school reporting to a vice president at the university is required to submit a prioritized listing of objectives and strategies for the next two academic sessions, which have direct bearing on the statement of purpose and institutional goals adopted by the university's Board of Visitors. Additionally, University of Virginia internal planning assumptions for an upcoming biennium are developed through consultation with administrators and faculty and are approved by the president and vice presidents before the initiation of a cycle. Typical planning assumptions might include the following elements:

- State tax appropriations will be flat during the planning period.
- Tuition increases will average under a given percent per year.
- Auxiliary enterprise revenues will remain self-sustaining within approved expenditures plans.
- Private support will become more critical during the biennium.
- Sponsored program revenue increases will be above the national average but below recent levels.
- The teaching of undergraduates will continue to be emphasized. The undergraduate curriculum will be studied for possible innovations and improvements. No new major instructional programs will be initiated during the biennium.
- Efforts will be made to improve academic advising.
- Undergraduate enrollments and first-professional enrollments (medicine, business, and law) will remain essentially stable; graduate enrollments will show moderate growth.
- The quality of the residential experience of undergraduate and graduate students will continue to receive greater attention; planning will take place for a total of four residential colleges by the year 2000.
- The work load and performance of instructional and administrative faculty and staff will be monitored more closely.
- Other appropriate planning assumptions for a designed time frame will be included.

Each department assesses the results of the earlier biennial period by examining previously cited objectives, the extent to which each was met, or the reasons why they were not achieved. The report's section on accomplishments and deficiencies has proven to be invaluable. Department heads also furnish more general descriptions of proposed future program changes and initiatives ranging from two to ten years beyond the current biennium. Each proposed program change must identify (if applicable) related staffing and fiscal consequences. Throughout the report, emphasis is on content rather than length, as brevity is not equated with lack of importance.

The most recent planning cycle (1990–1994) covered a period of fiscal constraint unknown since the Great Depression. Reports were required to contain incisive evaluations of the impact of budget reductions on programs and services that were imposed during the previous reporting cycle. Each report included an update of the plans for 1990–1992 based on the realignment of programs, services, personnel, and projected operations for 1992–1994. Given the economic forecast of perhaps another budget cut in the immediate future, contingency scenarios were also required. Managers identified activities that would be curtailed or personnel actions that would have to be initiated to achieve additional fiscal reductions. The contingency plan included versions ranging from 1 through 5 percent reduction of the base budget that might be imposed if the need arose. Each scenario addressed permanent personnel and operational reductions along with commensurate short- and long-term program implications. Each vice president refined the collective submissions of the divisional units by crafting coherent, consistent sections that followed established vice presidential budget targets and related institutional mission statements.

The level of confidence attained over the years through the experience of short- and intermediate-term strategic planning has empowered the development of a long-range vision and academic plan for the schools and programs at the University of Virginia. Known as the "plan for the year 2000," this effort entailed extensive public review and comment through a succession of departmental, schoolwide, and student forums. Specific universitywide themes regarding scholarship and academic innovation, information technology (including libraries), undergraduate education within a research environment, interdisciplinary academic programs, and the like were considered. Additionally, institutional support plans for enrollment, student assessment, residential life, land use, and computing were developed or updated. As colleges and universities prepare for the year 2000 and beyond, *detailed* planning and self-examination are crucial.

Making Hard Decisions: Retrenchment, Reallocation, Restructuring, and Repositioning

The ability and flexibility of colleges and universities to adhere seriously to the *R* words in the heading may very well predict their capacity to be fiscally solvent and competitive throughout the 1990s and beyond. Immediate or one-time financial adjustments will not begin to solve the basic problems currently facing the academy. Even assuming modest economic recovery by the mid 1990s, it is unlikely that the partners in the higher educational enterprise will ever again choose to return to the somewhat undisciplined spending patterns of the past. Higher education has the habit of using bottom-up budgeting procedures with inflational increases built into the unit-based budgets and with proposed enhancements treated as addenda (cost-plus pricing). We can no longer rely on escalating tuition charges or increases in state appropriations to cover such operational costs. Dramatic increases associated with educating citizens at public institutions, along with the drop in federal support for higher education, have placed states in the arduous position of keeping higher education affordable. Declining revenues; surging demands to fund highways, bridges, correctional institutions, and drug prevention and law enforcement programs; and the runaway costs of Medicaid and mental health facilities have forced states to expect residents to assume an ever-higher percentage of the cost of their education. Many have passed the full cost of education along to nonresidents. In the private sector, comprehensive fee charges have soared, and annual increases in costs often approaching twice the inflation rate have angered prospective consumers. For the independent institution, the prospect of pricing itself out of the competition has become a reality. Although differences exist in revenue sources between public and independent institutions, the expenditure side of the ledger looks the same.

Each institutional entity is accountable for what it does within the realm of designated responsibility and thus contributes to the collective good of the institution. Slippage in any one operational segment can be deleterious to an institution's ability to reach its stated goals. The partnership of professionals does not permit the luxury of any one unit's stating, "But the hole is not in my end of the canoe!"

Because of the service-oriented nature of our work, student affairs is especially vulnerable during times of budget stringency and resource constraints. As a profession, we have not been noted for our diligence in relating student affairs programming and services to the fulfillment of the academic mission of our institutions or for our assertiveness in educating the community about the importance of what we do; we certainly have been lax in making our case for a fair share of available resources. It only takes a cursory literature search to be reminded of the scarcity of instructive articles on matters such as the impact of enrollment and budget reductions on student personnel services (Nelson and Murphy, 1980), establishment of student affairs programmatic priorities for budgetary purposes (Moxley and Duke, 1986), and other planning and resource allocation concerns.

We have come with increasing frequency to call upon legal counsel for advice on what we can do without having a policy imposed upon us. Senior financial officers are also invaluable resources and allies who can help clarify the budgeting process. However, decisions regarding programmatic and fiscal allocations for student support services must ultimately rest with the chief student affairs officer (CSAO). The responsibilities of the CSAO are well known. Yet often overlooked is the fact that if something needs to be done, it *will* be done. If we do not do it, someone else will.

The ground swell of regulation and external micromanagement of institutions has resulted in substantial increases in administrative staffing. Demands for greater accountability and reporting to governmental and state agencies, public commissions, foundations, and boards of trustees have contributed significantly to explosive administrative costs. Grasmuck (1990) has reviewed a decade of Equal Employment Opportunity Commission data by comparing increases in administrative staff with faculty growth; he finds that staff increased faster than faculty by a ratio of ten to one. For at least the last quarter of a century, higher education has seen the demise of "Mr. Chips" on campus. Faculty are likely, especially in university settings, to identify with departments, specialties, or subspecialties rather than with the institution as a whole. Research, publication, professional service, and other nonadministrative pursuits essentially have removed faculty members from the responsibilities now undertaken by student personnel administrators. Administrative cost escalation is real, but many of the causes are apparent.

A most instructive example of institutional repositioning and retrenchment was undertaken by Stanford in the fall of 1989 (Gardner, Warner, and Biedenweig, 1990; Massy and Warner, 1991). In spite of a more than $2 billion endowment, Stanford University foresaw lean years ahead. The factors that prompted the move toward repositioning included operational deficits for the preceding three years with the prognosis of additional revenue shortfalls; concerns related to increases in the institution's indirect cost rate, which was limiting faculty research opportunities; mounting public resistance to Stanford's escalating tuition, compounded by an institutional reluctance to limit access to a Stanford education; and the devastation and capital problems created by the October 1989 earthquake. Action plans were created with the principal objective of bringing into existence lasting organizational changes built around the following four principles: to simplify processes, to simplify organizations and structures, to create more effective client-supplier interactions (regarding support services), and to change the management culture and decision-making processes to make these principles work.

This effort eventually led to a repositioning program with four basic objectives. The first was to hold student fee increases close to inflation and indirect cost rates below 78 percent. The second involved cutting the operating budget by $22 million through a 12 percent reduction in allocations for administrative and support areas. The third was to expand the effort for organizational reform by restructuring and reorganizing administrative and support offices instead of compressing the budget through across-the-board cuts. The final objective was to constrict the facilities construction program. Of paramount importance was the attainment of permanent budget reductions along with safeguards that would preclude reversion to prior spending patterns upon economic recovery. Faculty positions, student aid, and library acquisitions were protected from the budget reductions. In the student affairs area, the reduction was targeted at more than $2.6 million (14 percent of the division budget). Some student service management and support functions were merged, 5 positions in the student union and 19 in residence life were abolished, and the student infirmary was closed. To avoid duplication of services, a new vice presidency for student resources was created by eliminating two senior positions and by consolidating services previously spread over several departments.

In repositioning itself, Stanford University effected $22 million in planned reductions (including 450 positions) by eliminating management layers, consolidating functions, reducing services, and increasing risks. Through restructuring and reallocations, Stanford University arrived at an appropriate level of administrative and support activities. A review of academic productivity was scheduled to be the next area for consideration.

For other approaches to reduction, retrenchment, and reallocation, see Dawson (1991) and Gaither and DeWitt (1991).

Managing Change

In the economic climate of the 1990s, colleges and universities are in the throes of reassessing their roles and missions in the higher educational arena and seeking ways to maximize their efficiency and increase their allure to prospective students.

Cost containment traditionally has relied on hiring freezes, across-the-board cuts, low or no salary increases, elimination or substantial reduction in programs and services, abolishment of positions, or delays in maintenance and capital expenditures. *Simplification, consolidation, realignment,* and *reorganization* have become the catchwords of the moment in response to the need to balance efficiency and effectiveness. Concurrently, the basic requisites of control, authority, and high institutional profile must be maintained. Higher education is a labor-intensive enterprise, composed of an array of guilds whose members often are shielded from the impact of size reduction. It is a time, however, not only of great peril, but of great opportunity to enhance institutional vitality and to capitalize on institutional strengths while seeking fiscal solutions to problems. Self-examination is revealing, healthy, and wise.

Suggestions for Practice

The following "commandments" can assist chief student affairs officers in addressing the *R* words (*retrenchment, reallocation, restructuring,* and *repositioning*) and in attaining and maintaining efficient and functional programs and services:

- Remember that the forceful and instructive advocacy of the educational importance of student services to the institution rests primarily with the CSAO.
- Know your institution inside and out—its values, needs, and hidden pockets.
- Consider that budgets must evolve from goals and objectives and should reflect institutional and divisional priorities.
- Accept that nothing of substance happens until specific budget reduction targets are imposed from above.
- Ask yourself, "Who can do it any better?" If you do not, someone else will, and he or she will not do it as well.
- Remember that strategic planning is *just* as effective during periods of growth as it is in periods of decline; plan for both.
- Plan ahead and stick to your game plan. A recessional period forces us to employ a long-term view rather than short-term responses.
- Set deadlines, move rapidly to restructure, and be in command of the situation. Inconsistency sends mixed messages.
- Keep in mind that periods of recession destroy conventional planning and lead to ad hoc maneuvering in the absence of strategic planning.
- As painful as it may be, accept the fact that there will be certain things you cannot do any longer.
- Avoid one-time or short-term adjustments because such actions only delay the inevitable and certainly do not eliminate the basic problems.
- Get advice, listen, look, and then decide. There is lots of brain power around, both inside and outside the institution. Use it!
- *Shun* across-the-board cuts.
- Accept that shifting costs elsewhere does not equate to savings unless the shift is to sources outside of the institution.
- Be as open as humanly possible regarding what you are doing, why you are doing it, how you are planning to do it, and when it will happen. Communication is all-important.
- Train your mid- and lower-level managers how to manage change (to handle layoffs, survival guilt, and so forth).
- When developing a financial contingency plan, be certain to weigh the expected impact on your units before implementation.
- Keep a balance between line functions and staff functions (direct providers and those who support the effort).
- Find ways to recognize and express appreciation to your staff.
- Do not complain. The CSAO is the designated captain and cheerleader. Set the tone, keep a sense of perspective, avoid ambiguity and negativism, and try to maintain morale.
- Keep in mind that trying to do everything will result in mediocrity. Be selective.
- Get away from the "we-they" mentality. The fact is that there are two

enduring institutional cultures (academic and service), so do not fight the situation. Educate your colleagues on the faculty about what student affairs does and how it interrelates with their work.

- Your repositioning and restructuring should be permanent. When and if new money becomes available, it should be applied to new initiatives.
- On occasion, toot your own (student affairs) horn. Do not assume that others know what you are doing.
- Always hold some resources in reserve, thus maintaining some financial flexibility.
- Remember that initial budget cuts are easy; thereafter, they require creativity, knowledge, and commitment.

Needed Processes

The following processes are helpful in approaching the problems and the issues.

Empowerment of Unit Managers

Trust but verify (after the fact). Provide your deans and directors maximum freedom to make decisions while ensuring that they are accountable for their actions regarding fiscal expenditures. Encourage initiative and sound judgment. Let managers know how much they are valued, divisionally and institutionally.

Programmatic Prioritization

Initially identify which programs, if any, are to be protected because of institutional need (for example, student recruitment or underfunded but valued programs). This step requires categorizing programs as either nice or necessary. These are the hard calls to make, and they entail departmental, programmatic prioritization followed by an assessment by the CSAO of overall importance to the student affairs division. Most programs *are* important, but some are more crucial than others. Yes, there will be slippage in the quality of the student experience outside the classroom, but with proper planning it will be minimal to imperceptible. The easiest programs to protect are those that can be closely allied with the institutional mission. Evaluate what programs and services should be offered centrally by student affairs as opposed to those that should be supported by academic departments or schools (certain services for graduate students, for instance).

Jaguars Versus Jeeps

In times of fiscal stringency, services and programs must be scaled to basic institutional needs, consumer desires, and available resources. "Function lust" drives managers to create top-of-the-line offerings. Ask whether it is really necessary to be the best in the country in what student affairs does and offers. As CSAO, you must conduct a careful assessment of the design, performance, and practices of each unit to discern where budget savings may be effected.

Personnel

Although the case has been made that the strength of student affairs units lies with their personnel, remember that substantial cost containments can be achieved only by staff reductions. It may be instructive to review recently created positions to understand why they were established and to determine if any of those new functions should take precedence over preexisting position responsibilities. Savings can be achieved through holding turnover vacancies open for a period of time or by consciously hiring entry-level or junior staff to fill senior staff positions created through turnover. The use of interns and part-time staff avoids payment of major benefits. Consideration should be given to cost reductions effected through four-day work weeks during the summer months or nine-month appointments. Another consideration might involve an incentive-for-higher-pay plan. For example, a unit could be reduced from five to three employees who would be paid at a salary level equivalent to four staff members (work harder for more pay). Staff members with academic teaching responsibilities should have a proportionate amount of their salary assumed by academic departments. Likewise, the offerings of certain service providers may be good candidates for joint sponsorship with some university professional schools. Career planning and placement officers with specific career-field responsibilities, for example, can function well away from the central unit in satellite arrangements in schools of nursing, architecture, engineering, and so forth. In these situations, most operational costs, as well as a portion of the service provider's salary, may be assumed by the professional school. Finally, it is also appropriate to consider consolidating jobs within or even between departments where overlap of responsibility occurs.

The Return of Mr. Chips

You may conclude that it is time to reengage faculty members to a degree in some programs and services that were historically a component of their institutional responsibilities. As faculty size is less vulnerable to reduction, a strong case can be made for the reassignment of certain duties to members of the faculty as part of their institutional service commitment.

Operational Efficiencies

Determine the unavoidable costs of operation (such as telephone lines) and then proceed to make value judgments regarding discretionary expenditures (travel, equipment purchases, printing, long-distance calls, subscriptions, supplies, and the like) to achieve savings. Identify ways to reduce the scope of funded initiatives (consider scaling back summer session operations and using bulk mailings for new-student orientation materials). Use local talent for speakers and staff development presentations. (Not all of the experts are employed elsewhere!) Concentrate uninterrupted staff time by restricting formal office hours from 9 A.M. to 4 P.M. Combine duplicative services, eliminate layering in the decision-making process, reassign responsibilities, and simplify administrative procedures and processes. Ascertain the frequency of use of services and programs and by whom. Assess whether persons attend programs due to the quality of the offering or to the punch and cookies. Determine if cost savings can be made through contracting out (privatization of) certain services—dining, the bookstore, some specialized programming for the learning disabled, or programs related to sexual assault—to local agencies and hospitals. Any of these actions, of course, requires careful evaluation to ensure that the agency can do the job as well as the college service to which it is currently assigned. Refinance bond issues when appropriate. Compare the price of ongoing labor to that of replacement by one-time capital investments in automation. Determine if retired faculty in the community and student volunteers can be used on a mutually rewarding basis. Even in times of increased consumer expectations, the reality of retrenchment requires the deletion of certain programs and services.

"Full Serve" or "Self-Serve"

Identify new opportunities and programs that permit students to assume meaningful responsibility for their education through self-governance. Education by peers not only provides personal growth but teaches individuals how to learn and how to assume responsibility for their affairs. Examples of these opportunities might include involvement in programming, planning, and even budgeting for student union activities; use of undergraduate resident assistants in the residence halls; and use of peer advisers for new students. These are all realistic possibilities that would benefit the individual and the institution.

New Dollars

Every manager seeks ways to generate additional income above and beyond what is provided. There is a natural reluctance to consider fee-based services. Yet in a given collegiate setting, students may very well choose such an option if the high probability exists that their needs will be met better and less expensively than if services are procured outside the institution. Corporate support lends itself to some operations more than to others (for example, career services). Nonalumni parent programs have been established successfully at a host of institutions; of specific interest are those committed to enhancing the quality of undergraduate life for the student body. CSAOs should weigh the consequences of employing a development officer reporting directly to the dean or vice president.

Summary

No one has ever said that maintaining the rigor and handling the strong emotions associated with budgeting and planning would be easy; they certainly consume more time than is presently allocated. Student affairs professionals, particularly CSAOs, must take fiscal management seriously; to do less invites failure. Strategic planning, including both short- and long-term priorities, solutions, and options, is essential. Though creative approaches can be used to deal with reduced fiscal support, paying attention to detail and securing staff support are vital. Difficult decisions must be made, and data must be available to support those choices. Above all, dedication to the task of fiscal management presents an unparalleled opportunity for student affairs professionals to take a personal hand in helping to shape the future of their institutions.

References

Bowen, H. R. *The Costs of Higher Education: How Much Do Colleges and Universities Spend per Student and How Much Should They Spend?* San Francisco: Jossey-Bass, 1980.

Dawson, B. L. "The Incredible Shrinking Institution—A Five-Component Downsizing Model." *NACUBO Business Officer,* July 1991, pp. 26–30.

El-Khawas, E. *Campus Trends, 1991.* Higher Education Panel Report, no. 81. Washington, D.C.: American Council on Education, 1991.

Ern, E. H. "1982–1989 Biennial Evaluation Report and Plan for 1986–1990." Office of the Vice President for Student Affairs, University of Virginia, 1984.

Ern, E. H. "1984–1986 Biennial Evaluation Report and Planning for the Period 1986–1998." Office of the Vice President for Student Affairs, University of Virginia, 1986.

Ern, E. H. "1986–1988 Biennial Evaluation Report and Planning for the Period 1988–2000." Office of the Vice President for Student Affairs, University of Virginia, 1989.

Ern, E. H. "1988–1990 Biennial Evaluation Report and Planning for the Period 1990–2000." Office of the Vice President for Student Affairs, University of Virginia, 1991.

Fiske, E. B. (ed.). *Selective Guide to Colleges.* (3rd ed.) New York: Times Books, 1985.

Gaither, G., and DeWitt, R. "Making Tough Choices—Retrenchment and Reallocations During Hard Times." *NACUBO Business Officer,* July 1991, pp. 31–34.

Gardner, C., Warner, T., and Biedenweig, R. "Stanford and the Railroad—Something in Common After All These Years." *Change,* Nov.–Dec. 1990, pp. 23–27.

Grasmuck, K. "Big Increases in Academic-Support Staffs Prompt Growing Concerns on Campuses." *Chronicle of Higher Education,* Mar. 28, 1990, p. A1.

Massy, W. F., and Warner, T. R. "Causes and Cures of Cost Escalation in College and University Administrative and Support Services." Paper presented at the National Symposium on Strategic Higher Education Finance and Management Issues in the 1990s, Washington, D.C., Feb. 1991.

Moomaw, E. "Undergraduate Learning at the University of Virginia." Student Assessment Group, Office of the Provost, University of Virginia, Mar. 1990.

Moomaw, E. "Undergraduate Education at the University of Virginia—Second Year Report to the UVA Community." University Assessment Program, Office of the Provost, University of Virginia, Apr. 1991.

Moxley, L. S., and Duke, B. W. "Setting Priorities for Student Affairs Programs for Budgetary Purposes: A Case Study." *NASPA Journal,* 1986, *23,* 21–28.

National Center for Education Statistics. *Digest of Education Statistics.* Washington, D.C.: U.S. Government Printing Office, 1989.

Nelson, J., and Murphy, H. "The Projected Effects of Enrollment and Budget Reductions on Student Personnel Services." *NASPA Journal,* 1980, *17,* 2–10.

Williamson, M. L., and Mamarchev, H. L. "A Systems Approach to Financial Management for Student Affairs." *NASPA Journal,* 1990, *27,* 199–205.

31

౭

Meeting the Need
for Staff Diversity

Michael A. Freeman
Elizabeth M. Nuss
Margaret J. Barr

An African-American woman student was asked during a study of minority status on a campus why she had succeeded. She replied that a staff member in student affairs had recognized her potential, was willing to serve as a mentor, and cared about her success (Texas Christian University, 1991). Her statement is not unusual and could be repeated at countless institutions throughout the country. Student affairs staff members are professionally committed to making a difference in the lives of students. Whether students are old or young, African American, Caucasian, Asian American, or Hispanic, they must not feel marginal if they are to achieve educational and personal success (Schlossberg, Lynch, and Chickering, 1989).

The demographic characteristics of college students are changing and becoming more diverse (Kuh, 1990). However, higher education's ability to ensure that minority groups are fully represented has been deservedly criticized (Washington and Harvey, 1989). Some question higher education's level of commitment and argue that momentum has been lost (Business–Higher Education Forum, 1990). *One Third of A Nation* (American Council on Education and the Education Commission of the States, 1988) concludes, "America is moving backward—not forward—in its efforts to achieve the full participation of minority citizens in the life and prosperity of the nation" (p. 5).

The American Council on Education (Green, 1989) has called upon higher education to renew its commitment, intensify its efforts, and lead the way for other institutions in society. ACE has identified three principles that should guide the effort: (1) the need for leadership in establishing a vision and building a sense of community; (2) an integrated approach to change that goes beyond simply adding a staff member or a program; and (3) an examination of our assumptions, structures, and priorities to build campuses that are truly pluralistic.

Diversity is one of the greatest challenges facing higher education today, and student affairs has a critical role to play. Levine (1991) laments that the diversity portfolio has been largely delegated to student affairs officers because it warrants the attention of everyone in the institution. Many reject or fear the concept because they lack a proper understanding (Levine, 1991). Wu (1991) states, "The trouble with universities' interest in diversity is, they embrace it as a panacea for racial tension" (p. B2). At the same time, campus administrators understand that concerns in this area will not disappear.

Questions about how to deal with the issue are evident on almost all college and university campuses. Under different labels since the 1960s, campus officials have encouraged cross-cultural relations, pluralism, racial awareness and understanding, and multiculturalism as methods for increasing understanding and acceptance of minorities at traditionally white campuses. The challenge for student affairs is how to respond to the changing and varied needs of college students now and in the future.

In this chapter, the necessity for diverse role models for students within a student affairs staff will be explored, as well as the importance of including a range of viewpoints in policy development and implementation. The demographic characteristics of current professionals in higher education and student affairs will then be described, emphasizing those enrolled in graduate preparation programs. Finally, suggestions will be provided to assist student affairs administrators in accomplishing staff diversity as part of our quest to serve both our students and our institutions responsibly.

The Importance of Staff Diversity

Arturo Madrid describes the sense of being seen as different and the feelings of isolation that result: "Being *the other* means feeling different; is awareness of being distinct; is consciousness of being dissimilar. It means being outside the game, outside the circle, outside the set. It means being on the margins, on the periphery. Otherness means feeling excluded, closed out, precluded, even disdained and scorned. It produces a sense of isolation, of apartness, of disconnectedness, of alienation" (1988, p. 56). Many of us—male or female, old or young, African American or Asian American—have at times in our lives felt that we were "the other." Whether that feeling has come from being the only male in a class of women, the only minority member on a residence hall staff, or the only older student participating in a community service project, we have felt that we were different. And we have searched for ways to connect and become connected in a meaningful way. For college students, however, those feelings of isolation can be disastrous in terms of personal development, academic achievement, retention, and graduation. One of our fundamental assumptions as a profession is that "feelings affect thinking and learning" (National Association of Student Personnel Administrators, [1987] 1989), but all too often we have not devised means to help students deal with these feelings in productive ways.

Language, institutional traditions, policies, and practices all influence the sense of community or inclusiveness on a campus (Kuh, Schuh, Whitt, and Associates, 1991). Obviously, a first step is to increase staff members' awareness of these issues and to help them gain understanding of what it means to be "different" within the campus collegiate environment. Staff development programs can assist with this process (see Chapter Twenty-Four), but a student affairs division committed to diversity must go beyond mere understanding. Fundamental assumptions about enrolled students must be challenged and data provided to help current staff members "internalize" what it means to be different on a specific campus (Smith, 1989). Further, skills and competencies among staff must be improved in the areas of cross-cultural communication, work with adult students, and work with students who face physical challenges.

In addition, policies and practices should be reviewed to ensure that they are fair and are understood by all persons who join the learning community. As Minow (1990) states, "All of this means looking at the issues . . . from the vantage points of people who were not in mind when our institutions were designed" (p. 25). An institution's commitment to diversity comes to life when members of previously underrepresented groups are influential in shaping the policies, practices, and traditions of the college or university. The first step in achieving this goal is to ensure that the composition of the faculty, staff, and student bodies is representative of the larger society.

The need for role models is evident on our campuses: "For many students, minority people in positions of leadership and influence are rare. More important, however, is the integration of values from other cultures into the institutional structure that minority administrators bring with them. A minority student who, for example, needs specific intervention because of cultural obligations that conflict with a college responsibility may find him or herself better understood by an administrator who understands and can communicate to others the values of his or her culture" (Astone and Nuñez-Wormack, 1990, p. 68). These administrators can also help influence other staff and shape the campus climate and the curriculum to respond to the requirements of many different populations.

Minority students are not alone in their need for positive and affirming role models. Women, for example, now constitute a majority on college campuses (Pearson, Shavlick, and Touchton, 1989). Ponterotto (1990) indicates that "despite their protection under civil rights laws, elderly people still face discrimination in society and on college campuses. As 1992 approaches and forced retirement is legally abolished, the elderly population on campus will grow and the chances for intensified 'ageism' will increase. Student affairs administrators are professionally and ethically responsible for their own and their staff's affirmative action–based knowledge with respect to this group" (p. 9). Only 15 percent of disabled high school graduates enroll in two-year or four-year college programs (Evangelauf, 1989). "Students and staff with physical disabilities do have special needs, and yet their academic and professional potential is as high as other students. Administrators must work toward making campuses more hospitable and welcoming to these individuals" (Ponterotto, 1990, p. 9).

A diverse staff also benefits whatever the "majority" group is on a campus. As a profession, we are failing *all* our students if we do not prepare them for postgraduate opportunities where their supervisors, students, and co-workers may be very different from them. Exposure to a variety of role models within a student affairs organization can assist students in understanding, accepting, and becoming comfortable with difference in very concrete ways. All students will appreciate a demonstrated strong commitment to diversity and pluralism.

Characteristics of Student Affairs Staff Members

To estimate the representation of women and minorities in student affairs requires extrapolation using several data sources. National data collection efforts record data for administrators but do not segregate them by administrative specialty. The recent ACE report *Minorities in Higher Education* (Carter and Wilson, 1992) provides a good overview.

Since the 1960s, minorities have attained only modest increases in higher education employment. African Americans and Hispanics have made the most progress in increasing their respective share of administrative positions. Minority women have made larger gains at this level than minority men (Carter and Wilson, 1992). Many of these individuals have been hired to staff or direct minority or special support service units. Minority administrators are also more likely to serve in staff positions (as assistants, for example) rather than in senior-level positions such as vice president or president.

As of 1989, the Equal Opportunity Employment Commission reported that 39 percent of full-time administrators were women and 13 percent were minorities. Nearly 9 percent of the full-time administrators were African Americans, and 2.3 percent were Hispanic. The number of Asian-American and Native-American full-time administrators was less than 2 percent and 1 percent respectively (Carter and Wilson, 1992).

The demographic data on members of professional associations are another source of information. As of June 1991, 44 percent of the members of the National Association of Student Personnel Administrators (NASPA) were women, but only 27 percent were chief student affairs officers (National

Association of Student Personnel Administrators, 1991). Eleven percent of NASPA members were minorities. The largest of these groups (7.2 percent) were African Americans. Among chief student affairs officers, 8.5 percent were minorities, and 6 percent were African Americans (National Association of Student Personnel Administrators, 1991).

A recent dissertation study by Talbot (1992) examined diversity in ten of the largest student affairs master's degree programs. Almost 45 percent of the thirty-eight full-time faculty members in these programs were women, and 5 percent were minorities. Only eight of the participating programs had compiled relevant data on their students. Of the 320 students enrolled in these programs, 17.5 percent were minorities, and 80 percent were women. Of the minority students, over one-half were African Americans, 27 percent Hispanic, Latino, or Chicano, 11 percent Asian Americans, and 4 percent Native Americans. A little more than 7 percent of the graduate students reported that they were gay, lesbian, or bisexual.

The data provide insights into the diversity of higher education administration, student affairs, and the graduate preparation pipeline. They indicate some progress but clearly demonstrate that higher education must make continued and persistent efforts to create faculties and staffs that will be representative of the students enrolled on the campus.

Strategies for Increasing Staff Diversity

The need for increased diversity on student affairs staffs is evident, but the means to achieve those goals remain illusive for many. Developing a comprehensive, multifaceted approach is the most effective way to achieve representative staffing. For example, there are ways to increase the number of minority undergraduates who consider careers in student affairs. Staff development and educational training for current staff must be furnished. Opportunities must be developed for minority or other underrepresented staff to provide leadership and direction for revision of campus policies, procedures, and traditions. The contributions of minority and other underrepresented staff members must be recognized and celebrated. And talented individuals throughout the country must be identified and recruited. The following strategies offer examples to institutions and student affairs divisions and institutions interested in creating an approach to staff diversity. Many of these are related. After consultation and discussion, campus leaders should decide which ones are most appropriate for their campus.

Adopt Real Affirmative Action Programs

Too often affirmative action plans are established and then ignored. A commitment to affirmative action requires more than just paper goals; campus administrators must set expectations and priorities and discuss the philosophical issues surrounding affirmative action. The decision to select new staff members should result from an examination of campus needs. Who should be hired? What goals should an office have regarding affirmative action? A viable affirmative action philosophy and plan will guide hiring decisions and answer difficult questions (see Chapter Ten for further information).

Carefully Examine Job Qualifications

Legally, hiring unqualified candidates is *not* an acceptable affirmative action mechanism (Bullington and Ponterotto, 1990). Student affairs administrators, however, need to examine job qualifications carefully (Green, 1989). Ponterotto asks: "Does excellence in the field include being able to relate to, mentor, and be a role model for minority students, or would this just be a nice extra for a candidate?" (1990, p. 71). The same question could be asked regarding age, gender, or disability. If we wish a staff member to develop social relationships with certain groups of students, then that expectation should be reflected in the qualifications necessary for the position. This approach does *not* exclude individuals who are not of that particular group from applying for the position and receiving full consideration, but it *does* make explicit that they must possess specific skills and abilities.

Extend the Recruitment Network

Development of an affirmative action pool requires effort in the search process. It is not enough merely to list the vacant position in standard places with the hope that a range of qualified candidates will apply. Special efforts must be made through personal contacts, letters, and advertisements in specialty journals.

Address Bias in the Selection Process

Conscious and unconscious issues related to prejudice in the selection of candidates may erect unnecessary barriers to finding qualified minority candidates. Selection committee members are urged to examine objective and subjective criteria related to the search for qualified candidates (Wilson, 1989). Examples of possible sources of prejudice include answers to the following questions: Do members of the committee place greater emphasis on a reference that comes from people they know? Is it important for the candidate to belong to specific associations or to have been present at particular conferences? Does the candidate publish in journals that the committee members are familiar with and respect? Does the candidate have broad interests (beyond minority issues)? Is the candidate a graduate of a "highly regarded" preparation program? Answers to these and other questions seriously influence the objectivity and outcome of a search process. As a result of subjective biases, Wilson (1989) finds that "some committees throw up their hands and say, we'd love to hire a minority but we just can't find one who meets our standards" (p. 8).

Make the Hard Decisions

An administrator committed to affirmative action is often placed in a position of making a hard decision regarding an applicant pool. If it does not reflect affirmative action goals, careful consideration must be given to extending the search in some manner. Prior to the time that screening and selection committees recommend candidates for consideration for campus interviews, the responsible administrator must make every effort to assure that the candidate pool reflects the goal of diversity. Sometimes the administrator must even decide not to fill a position, even though everyone else disagrees.

Look for Candidates at All Times

Often we wait until we have a specific position in mind before we begin to identify candidates who may meet its requirements. One highly useful technique is to be constantly on the look out for potential staff members through daily contacts or professional associations. Actively identify individuals who may have the characteristics that may be needed to achieve diversity goals and get to know them. Professional association meetings provide many opportunities to create relationships with potential employees. If a position becomes available, a personal contact will increase the possibility that an individual will respond to a letter or an advertisement.

Develop Current Personnel

Members of underrepresented groups are often employed in support functions within a division of student affairs. Campus leaders should identify those with the potential to assume increasingly responsible professional positions. Every attempt should be made to enable these individuals to develop the necessary credentials for new positions. This effort may require that the supervisor develop flexible work schedules so that formal degree training might be pursued. Or it may mean encouraging professionals to participate in professional associations for development and exposure to issues beyond their current job assignment (see Chapter Twenty-Five). It may require sponsoring the individual's participation in management and leadership institutes, such as Harvard University's Institute for Educational Management, NASPA's Richard F. Stevens Institute, or another comparable program.

Another approach is systematically to offer staff members committee assignments or special projects that allow them to demonstrate their potential for broader administrative and leadership roles on the campus. In some cases, release time from the current assignment should be provided so the individual has sufficient time and energy to devote to the special assignment.

All that may be necessary is to help a person in a support position to change aspirations while concurrently supplying training in an administrative capacity. Of course, those roles do not have to be limited to student affairs. Diversity is needed throughout the campus community. Encouraging staff members at all levels to pursue other options affirms faith in their abilities and the contributions that they can make.

Provide a Postgraduate Entry-Level Position

Some institutions have developed a postgraduate option for exceptional undergraduate students to be employed in an entry-level position on the campus. The range of qualified potential candidates for such a position is enormous, and an experience can be created in which a member of an underrepresented group can learn and do at the same time. This is one area where athletics has led the way in higher education by offering graduate assistantships or assistant coaching positions to talented undergraduate athletes. If this option is employed, however, specific attention must be paid to the in-service training of such individuals. It is also useful to develop a careful approach to career advising for such staff members as they begin to explore permanent career options. Admissions offices all over the country have hired recent graduates to act as recruiters in the field. There is no reason why such methods cannot be applied to some of the generalist areas in student affairs.

Provide Summer Internships

Summer internships are a variation on the approach just described but require less financial investment on the part of the institution. A specifically designed summer internship program either in a generalist area or in a specialty such as campus recreation can provide unique opportunities for minority, older, or disabled students to assess whether employment in higher education is a viable career alternative.

Develop Part-Time Affiliate Positions

Often institutions of higher education cannot compete financially with business and industry. Qualified individuals understandably take positions outside of higher education because of financial concerns related to their own particular life circumstances. There may be, however, a means to use some of these professionals to add a dimension to our work with students on the campus. For example, a minority professional working in human resources in a local company might very well be interested in assisting at a career planning and placement center one evening a week or might be available for conducting trial interviews. Such appointments, which may come with or without compensation, can create greater staff diversity.

Consider the Potential of Alumni

Alumni from underrepresented groups who were active and involved undergraduates may be excellent candidates for staff positions. They are an often-overlooked pool of professional employees who may be interested in changing careers or returning to the academy. The worst outcome from such efforts is that an individual will know that someone in the institution is interested in his or her professional progress and career. The best outcome is that there will be an expanded pool of candidates for positions that may come open.

Develop a Strong Paraprofessional Program

A strong paraprofessional program that is installed throughout a division of student affairs can attract a number of individuals to the field. Involvement at the undergraduate level can help potential staff members understand the complexity of student affairs and the opportunities available. When coupled with a strong affirmative action program extending beyond the professional staff to all levels in the division, the possibilities for recruiting diverse potential employees to student affairs positions within an institution increase dramatically.

Often paraprofessional programs are focused on traditional-age students. Intentional efforts should be made to expand the concept of paraprofessionalism to include students of widely ranging ages. This approach has been used successfully for both older students and disabled students in the Office of the Dean of Students at the University of Texas at Austin (as one example).

Redefine the Work Environment

Student affairs offices have often followed traditional patterns in creating work spaces and environments. However, the literature suggests that cooperative opportunities for communication are critical to enhancing the understanding of cultural differences and developing appreciation for others (Manning and Coleman-Boatwright, 1991). Campus administrators working separately in secluded individual spaces have fewer chances to collaborate and exchange ideas.

Time should thus be taken to assess the work environment in student affairs functional areas. Walk-in or open-door hours will increase staff availability and lower structural barriers to student-staff interactions. Images and symbols of diverse groups can be included on the walls of the office; staff members should also read and display magazines from varied sources in the office. The ultimate goal is the development of a safe place where staff members can candidly discuss issues of diversity (Weiner, 1990).

Orient New Staff

An effective orientation of new staff members will reinforce the expectations and values of diversity and multiculturalism within the institution, division, and functional area. Green (1989) urges that senior-level administrators establish clear expectations about these issues with new staff. A comprehensive orientation also should include information about the surrounding community, especially if ethnic neighborhoods are in close proximity. Upcraft (1988) suggests that a senior staff member be assigned as a mentor to the new staff person. The mentor will need to have a thorough understanding of the campus community mores and the values important to different cultural groups. By combining cultural and institutional information in the mentoring activity, the new staff member will grow to understand the institution's serious commitment to diversity. Finally, new staff members can spend orientation time in offices that primarily serve underrepresented groups. Much valuable information and insight can be gained by exposure to the minority affairs office; the women's studies office; disabled student services; or gay, lesbian, and bisexual programs.

Integrate Appreciation and Celebration with Opportunities for Learning

On many campuses, student affairs has been thrust into the role of leadership on issues of diversity (Levine, 1991). Student affairs staff members spend a considerable amount of time planning diversity celebrations and appreciation events for students throughout the academic year. Although these programs for students are important, staff members also need opportunities to increase their knowledge and understanding of the relevant issues. These should include historical and cultural information about the various groups.

In situations where staffs are not representative of the campus community, individual staff members can be specifically encouraged to learn about underrepresented groups. Staff comfort levels with the issues involved (positive or negative) will affect co-workers, students, and the campus climate. To address these concerns higher education currently depends primarily on finding minority group members or women to represent and address the needs of their particular populations. Minority group role models are important; however, all staff members can demonstrate a desirable level of understanding and comfort with differences.

Transform Training Programs and Course Material

Credit or noncredit training courses for peer counselors, student leaders, residence hall staff, and those in career development are taught by student affairs staffs on many campuses. Residence life programs on some campuses also offer courses to help prepare resident assistants for the requirements of varied student populations. However, the course content may not reflect the diversity that student staff members should embrace.

Many voices should be included in courses required for student staff members or those enrolled in courses taught by student affairs staff members. In addition, opportunities must be created in the classroom to inform students about the thinking of a range of scholars from underrepresented populations. During the 1950s, references were made to blacks such as Booker

T. Washington and W.E.B. Dubois; today, Martin Luther King, Jr., Malcolm X, and a few others are invoked. Student affairs administrators and faculty should be encouraged to discover and incorporate less-known African-American, Hispanic, and Native American, as well as gay, lesbian, and bisexual, references into lectures and course reading materials.

Within the last decade, many excellent resource materials about these many groups have been written and would be useful in courses or training programs. Consider some of the following ones: *Kemet Afrocentricity, and Knowledge* (Asante, 1991), *Black Indians* (Katz, 1991), *The Joy Luck Club* (Tan, 1989), *Bury My Heart at Wounded Knee* (Brown, 1970), and *A People's History of the United States* (Zinn, 1980). These works and others can help instructors and students examine relevant social topics from the perspectives of different cultures.

When examining the most appropriate strategies for a campus, it is important to keep in mind that the goal is to develop, in conjunction with representatives of previously underrepresented groups, a comprehensive approach with many parts. Any of the suggestions listed previously will also need to be adapted to meet the requirements of the mission and climate of a specific campus.

Summary

There is no question that diversity is an issue that must be confronted and effectively managed by student affairs administrators. Two primary challenges must be met: creating opportunities for the staff in student affairs to reflect the variety of emerging student populations *and* creating a climate where many kinds of individuals feel valued and welcomed in the campus community. Each involves special problems that can be overcome with careful planning, commitment, and a long-term plan for change. Recruiting and encouraging underrepresented populations to enter the field of student affairs — and then retaining them — requires new modes of thinking. But if student affairs organizations are to be successful in the future, these new approaches must be undertaken. Making the commitment to an environment where many points of view and different cultural perspectives are honored and appreciated also requires time and energy. The results, we believe, will be well worth the effort.

The suggestions in this chapter provide alternatives to consider, debate, and modify within the context of a specific institutional setting. All will not be appropriate at every college and university, but careful assessment of what might work will go a long way to meet the challenges of diversity.

References

American Council on Education and Education Commission of the States. *One Third of a Nation: A Report of the Commission on Minority Participation in Education and American Life.* Washington, D.C.: American Council on Education and Education Commission of the States, 1988.

Asante, M. K. *Kemet Afrocentricity, and Knowledge*. Trenton, N.J.: Holt, 1991.

Astone, B., and Nuñez-Wormack, E. *Pursuing Diversity: Recruiting College Minority Students*. ASHE-ERIC Higher Education Report, no. 7. Washington, D.C.: Association for the Study of Higher Education, 1990.

Brown, D. *Bury My Heart at Wounded Knee*. Trenton, N.J.: Holt, 1970.

Bullington, R., and Ponterotto, J. G. "Affirmative Action: Definitions and Philosophy." In J. G. Ponterotto, D. E. Lewis, and R. Bullington (eds.), *Affirmative Action on Campus*. New Directions for Student Services, no. 52. San Francisco: Jossey-Bass, 1990.

Business–Higher Education Forum. *Three Realities: Minority Life in the United States*. Washington, D.C.: American Council on Education, 1990.

Carter, D. J., and Wilson, R. *Tenth Annual Status Report on Minorities in Higher Education*. Washington, D.C.: American Council on Education, 1992.

Green, M. F. (ed.) *Minorities on Campus: A Handbook for Enhancing Diversity*. Washington, D.C.: American Council on Education, 1989.

Evangelauf, J. "Small Percentage of Disabled Youths Enroll in College, Study Finds." *Chronicle of Higher Education*. Apr. 19, 1989, p. A32.

Katz, W. L. *Black Indians*. New York: Atheneum, 1991.

Kuh, G. D. "The Demographic Juggernaut." In M. J. Barr, M. L. Upcraft, and Associates, *New Futures for Student Affairs: Building a Vision for Professional Leadership and Practice*. San Francisco: Jossey-Bass, 1990.

Kuh, G. D., Schuh, J. H., Whitt, E. J., and Associates. *Involving Colleges: Successful Approaches to Fostering Student Learning and Development Outside the Classroom*. San Francisco: Jossey-Bass, 1991.

Levine, A. "The Meaning of Diversity." *Change,* 1991, *23* (5), 4–5.

Madrid, A. "Missing People and Others." *Change,* 1988, *20* (3), 54–59.

Manning, K., and Coleman-Boatwright, P. "Student Affairs Initiatives Toward a Multicultural University." *Journal of College Student Development,* 1991, *32,* 367–374.

Minow, M. "On Neutrality, Equality, and Tolerance." *Change,* 1990, *22* (1), 17–25.

National Association of Student Personnel Administrators. "A Perspective on Student Affairs, 1987." In *Points of View*. Washington, D.C.: National Association of Student Personnel Administrators, 1989. (Originally published 1987.)

National Association of Student Personnel Administrators. *Annual Report*. Washington, D.C.: National Association of Student Personnel Administrators, 1991.

Pearson, C. S., Shavlick, D. L., and Touchton, J. G. (eds.) *Educating the Majority: Women Challenge Tradition in Higher Education*. New York: Macmillan, 1989.

Ponterotto, J. G. "Racial/Ethnic Minority and Women Administrators and Faculty in Higher Education: A Status Report." In J. G. Ponterotto, D. E. Lewis, and R. Bullington (eds.), *Affirmative Action on Campus*. New Directions for Student Services, no. 52. San Francisco: Jossey-Bass, 1990.

Schlossberg, N. K., Lynch, A. Q., and Chickering, A. W. *Improving Higher Education Environments for Adults: Responsive Programs and Services from Entry to Departure.* San Francisco: Jossey-Bass, 1989.

Smith, D. G. *The Challenge of Diversity.* ASHE-ERIC Higher Education Report, no. 5. Washington, D.C.: Association for the Study of Higher Education, 1989.

Talbot, D. M. "A Multimethod Study of the Diversity Emphasis in Master's Degree Programs in College Student Affairs." Unpublished data, 1992.

Tan, A. *The Joy Luck Club.* New York: Ivy Books, 1989.

Texas Christian University. *A Report of the Chancellor's Task Force on Minority Affairs.* Texas Christian University internal report, 1991.

Upcraft, M. L. "Managing Staff." In M. L. Upcraft and M. J. Barr, *Managing Student Affairs Effectively.* New Directions for Student Services, no. 41. San Francisco: Jossey-Bass, 1988.

Washington, V., and Harvey, W. *Affirmative Rhetoric, Negative Action.* ASHE-ERIC Higher Education Report, no. 2. Washington, D.C.: Association for the Study of Higher Education, 1989.

Weiner, D. D. "Accrediting Bodies Must Require a Commitment to Diversity When Measuring a College's Quality." *Chronicle of Higher Education,* Oct. 10, 1990, pp. B2-3.

Wilson, R. *Effective Strategies and Programs to Increase Minority Faculty.* A paper prepared for the Office of Minority Equity, Michigan State University, 1989.

Wu, F. "The Trouble with University Interest in Diversity Is, They've Embraced It as a Panacea for Racial Tension." *Chronicle of Higher Education,* Mar. 12, 1991, p. B2.

Zinn, H. *A People's History of the United States.* New York: HarperCollins, 1980.

32

⁂

Service Delivery
for a Changing
Student Constituency

Barbara Jacoby

Many aspects of higher education are changing as we move towards the end of the twentieth century. The very foundation and fabric of the curriculum are evolving. The complex web of relationships between higher education and the federal government, state and local governments, and the private sector is becoming more challenging to negotiate. Even as the financing of colleges and universities is being questioned, institutions are called upon to be more accountable to their multiple constituencies. And the demographics of college students in the United States have changed and are continuing to change dramatically. Students at all institutions of higher education are increasingly diverse with regard to age, race, ethnicity, gender, disabilities, attendance patterns, and living arrangements.

Despite these changes, many institutions of higher education have continued to operate as though a college education means 120 credit hours of course work completed between the ages of eighteen and twenty-two. The majority of today's faculty members and administrators earned their undergraduate and graduate degrees at traditional residential institutions and often expect the colleges and universities where they are now to be like the ones that they attended (Lindquist, 1981; Lynton and Ellman, 1987). Many student affairs practitioners have had similar collegiate experiences and were professionally trained in programs that emphasize, perhaps inadvertently, traditional college students. Student personnel graduate programs tend to be located at institutions where policies, services, and programs focus on traditional-age, full-time students who live on campus (Jacoby, 1989). Several theories of student development, which form the foundation for research and which are studied in student personnel preparation programs, are based on the experiences of white, middle-class males who attended mainly private four-year residential institutions (Barr and others, 1988; Stodt, 1982). In practice, as Schlossberg, Lynch, and Chickering observe, "Staffing patterns, scheduling arrangements, annual cycles of activity, and areas of expertise for student personnel professionals continued to be established for traditional-age, full-time, mostly on-campus students" (1989, p. 228).

Student affairs professionals must learn about the diversity of today's college students and must develop an understanding of how the traditional nature of higher education institutions continues to exert tremendous influence on their experiences. This chapter offers a framework for conceptualizing how colleges and universities need to change in order to provide a high-quality educational experience for all students. A model that enables student affairs professionals to develop a comprehensive approach to meeting the needs of many different kinds of students, together with examples, is then presented.

The Need for Institutionwide, Systemic Change

Throughout its history, higher education has placed the burden of adaptation on students. Often, despite the growing presence of greater numbers of students who are "different" from the norm, the environmental accommodation has been minimal and peripheral. In order to provide truly equal opportunities for success for a diverse student body, the institution must adjust policies, practices, and programs to meet current student needs rather than expecting the students to adjust to the institution.

Ackell's (1986) model, which describes the process of institutional adaptation to the presence of adult students, is useful in understanding the broad scope of the changes necessary in most institutions. The model may be used by an institution to assess the nature of its environment for all groups within the student population. Ackell views the process of institutional adaptation and change as three stages ranging from a relatively primitive organizational stage, through a more specialized type of adaptation, to a final stage where an institution has fully adapted to all its students and where all students are treated with equity.

Stage 1: The Laissez-Faire Stage

The first stage for most institutions consists of simply removing obvious barriers or artificial constraints and permitting students to do the best they can for themselves within a system that works neither for nor against them. Although in this stage no organized administrative intervention is made on their behalf, students are allowed to be as entrepreneurial and aggressive as they like in dealing with the institution. The general assumption on the part of the administration is that variables such as age, race, and disability are not relevant to students' role at the institution. In other words, the institution is as it is and students who choose to attend must accept it as such. No active recruitment of diverse student groups is carried out.

The mission statement and publications of institutions at stage one reflect usually only the institution's majority or traditional students. Policies and practices regarding admissions, financial aid, and the curriculum favor the institution's traditional students as well, and institutional planning fails to take into account the growing diversity of the student body. No special support services are offered to nontraditional students, and no efforts are made to encourage them to participate in the life of the campus community. It is unknown whether such student subpopulations are consistently less satisfied with their college experience than others or whether some groups leave the institution at a higher rate.

Stage 2: The Separatist Stage

Most institutions that enroll an increasingly heterogeneous student body will eventually move into the "separatist" stage. At this point, certain groups (for example, adults at a predominantly traditional-age institution, commuters on a primarily residential campus, or minority students at a historically white university) are essentially separate from the majority. Some recognition exists that certain students are different from the majority, usually accompanied by the assumption that different means "lesser." Recruitment and admissions practices and publications acknowledge these groups of students but address them as distinct, "special" populations. Programs and services continue to be geared for majority students, but some separate and different programs and services are offered (for example, orientation and mentoring). Minimal attempts are made to meet special needs (referrals to child care providers or interpreters for deaf students) without changing basic institutional priorities. It can be argued that institutions in this stage subject certain student groups to a subtle form of economic exploitation in that the institution expects them to function with substantially less support from general fund dollars than is appropriated for services and programs for the institution's traditional or majority students. Students referred to as special populations feel that they are marginal rather than integral members of the campus community, are consistently less satisfied with their experience, and leave the institution at a higher rate.

Stage 3: The Equity Stage

Equity entails an "active use of the principles of justice and fairness to correct inequities in a system that *de facto* discriminates against one group in favor of another" (Ackell, 1986, p. 3). An institution has begun to evolve towards the equity stage when it takes significant steps to treat all students fairly and to provide the same quality of experience for all. It is unlikely that any college or university has fully reached this stage, but some institutions have moved sufficiently in that direction that some of its characteristics can be observed.

The mission statement, publications, and institutional leadership highlight the varied nature of the student body. Recruitment, admissions, and financial aid practices are appropriate for all students. In addition to specialized services for particular groups of students, programs and services are designed to benefit the entire student body. The members of the campus community understand and appreciate the diversity of the student population, and knowledge of the educational goals and needs of all students is incorporated into curriculum development and class scheduling. All students feel included as members of the campus community and are so recognized. There are few differences among student groups regarding their rate of persistence to graduation or their degree of satisfaction with the institution.

The process of development to the equity stage is complex, difficult, and slow. As part of this process, student affairs agencies must change their traditional methods of delivery of services and programs. In fact, professionals in our field must be aware of who our students are and how their diversity is increasing. It is appropriate for student affairs to take the lead within the institution in adapting to meet students' many requirements. To be effective, however, changes in service delivery require a comprehensive approach. The next section provides a practical model to help in moving our institutions from the laissez-faire stage to become institutions of true equity.

The SPAR Model: A Comprehensive Approach to Meeting Students' Diverse Needs

Throughout its history, our profession has existed to help students. In the late 1960s and early 1970s, the numbers of women, adults, commuters, minorities, and students with disabilities increased, and many colleges and universities created new student affairs offices or departments to serve special populations. Often, these offices received federal or other funding that recognized the growing presence of new student groups on campuses throughout the nation. Typically underfunded, situated at lower levels of the administrative hierarchy, and staffed by individuals with relatively little experience, these offices were charged with the responsibility of providing services, programs, and support.

Having created special services, many institutions felt they could continue to go about their business as usual and assumed that their special students were being taken care of. However, operating under unrealistic expectations, many such services failed to make a substantive difference in the success and satisfaction of the students that they attempted to serve. Increasing numbers of diverse students, together with shrinking institutional budgets and the loss of grant funding, have led to the demise of special services at many institutions. On other campuses, although population-specific offices continue to function at widely varying levels of effectiveness, they have generally failed to bring about the institutionwide change that is required to enhance the educational experience of diverse students significantly.

As stated previously, student affairs staffs must take a comprehensive approach to their diverse student bodies. A model developed by Jacoby and Girrell (1981) serves as a framework for the development of such an approach. Because it is organized around basic functions rather than administrative units, the model works equally well in institutions where population-specific offices exist as in those where they do not. The model assumes that student affairs professionals—no matter what position they hold in the organizational structure—will work for, with, and on behalf of all groups of students. The responsibility of student affairs professionals to advance comprehensive institutional change regarding diversity is an integral part of the model.

Four essential areas form the core of a comprehensive approach to enhancing the educational experience of a diverse student body: services, programs, advocacy, and research. This comprehensive approach is referred to as the SPAR model.

Services

Functions or services performed for students should be both general to the entire student body and specifically designed for particular student groups. Each student affairs unit should examine itself from two perspectives: (1) making all services more appropriate and accessible for all students and (2) providing specific services to identified groups of students.

In ascertaining whether services are suitable and readily available, the answers to the following questions should be sought:

- Are services and facilities open at hours convenient to the schedules of all students (early morning, lunchtime, evenings, weekends)?
- Are advisers, counselors, and other staff on flextime schedules so that they are available whenever students are on campus?
- If the institution has off-campus centers, are student services available there?
- Are all facilities and services fully accessible to students with mobility, visual, hearing, and speech impairments?
- Are current technologies used to enable students to transact business (for instance, registration or bill payment) and obtain campus information via telephone or computer?
- Is information disseminated in a wide variety of ways, both on and off campus (handbooks, calendars, bulletin boards, direct mail to students' homes, campus and local newspapers, radio stations, cable television)?

In addition to assuring general access to its services, each student affairs functional area should act to meet the specific needs of each group within the student population. For example, institutional financial aid should be available to part-time evening students as well as to full-time day students. The career center should be prepared to assist those making career changes as well as those seeking a first professional job. Learning-assistance centers should offer services to assist international students having difficulty with the English language or in adapting to American pedagogical methods. Health services should be able to respond to the particular health needs of women, older adults, and minorities. Likewise, counselors should be trained to deal with issues facing adults (such as marital problems or threats to self-esteem as a result of returning to college), traditional-age commuter students (conflicts with parents or feeling "left out" of the mainstream of college life), and racial and ethnic minorities (acculturation or racial identity). Counseling services should be available in different formats to accommodate various interpersonal-style preferences.

Some population-specific services may be offered by offices established to serve particular groups of students. Frequently, an office is designated to provide the services of, or referrals to, interpreters, personal care attendants, and assistance to blind or partially sighted students. International education specialists may be appropriately charged with furnishing immigration assistance. Minority student services may supply specialized tutoring or support services, whereas commuter services may provide housing and transportation information and referrals.

Programs

The emphasis in programming is on meaningful interactions; that process has two directions. Because activities and programs are carried on *with* rather than *for* students, they are usually more staff-intensive than services.

As is the case with services, student affairs professionals should encourage the participation of all students in a broad range of programs and should provide some geared to the needs and interests of each student group.

Programming efforts should be evaluated by answering the following questions:

- Are programs and activities scheduled at a variety of times to accommodate students' varied schedules (early morning, lunchtime, late afternoon, evenings, weekends, between classes)?
- Does information about upcoming programs sufficiently explain the offerings and intended audience so that all students are able to understand what the programs are about and who is encouraged to attend?
- Is program information disseminated in a wide range of formats and sufficiently in advance so that students who must rearrange their family, work, and transportation schedules can attend?

- Are all types of students encouraged to participate in campus governance and student government? To apply for leadership positions?
- Do large-scale campus programs (such as homecoming) explicitly provide opportunities for all students to participate?

Units responsible for general campus programming, as well as population-specific departments, should design and implement programs for each subgroup within the student body. For example, orientation programs should encompass all students and should make all of them feel equally welcome to the campus community. Orientation should include general sessions plus components that focus on the unique transition needs of each student group (for example, overcoming "math anxiety" for students returning to college after a long break in their education and a special campus tour for mobility-impaired students). Spouses and children of adult students should be included in orientation programs, and sessions should be held for commuting students' parents to prepare them for the life-style adjustments that they will face having a college student in the home. Various options for orientation programs should be available (weekday, evening, and weekend formats; individualized programs; videocassettes for home use).

Recreational sports programs, including high- and low-impact aerobic sports, martial arts, dance, and intramural sports, should be appropriate for all students. Individualized fitness programs may appeal to adult students, for example, whereas team sports may be preferred by traditional-age students. Activities staffs and student program boards should provide a range of educational, cultural, and social programs. Besides the rock groups and comedians that majority, traditional-age students may enjoy, a wide variety of other entertainment options (such as dinner theater) should be sponsored. On-campus activities that bring together members of racial and ethnic minorities in ways that are comfortable for each group can increase harmony within the institutional environment and help create a sense of community.

Counseling services, career centers, health services, and financial aid offices should offer information sessions, support groups, and workshops for specific groups, such as reentry women, Native Americans, or gay, lesbian, and bisexual students, as appropriate. Whether adults or of traditional age, students who live with their families appreciate opportunities to involve them in campus life. Events held specifically for this purpose include family picnics, activities for couples, and parents' weekends. Some institutions offer weekend programs (movies, arts and crafts) for children of students simultaneously with programs for adult students (lectures, study groups).

Programming efforts should also be developed for faculty, staff, and all students to encourage their appreciation of diversity and multiculturalism. If colleges and universities are to become multicultural and multigenerational environments, all members of the campus community must learn about diversity and about the values associated with it. Thus, programs to assist Hispanic students to adjust to the institution should be accompanied by those to introduce other students, faculty, and staff to various aspects of Hispanic cultures. Events such as ethnic days or international fairs can achieve the dual purposes of bringing groups of students together in a context of cultural identity and mutual support and of exposing the larger community to the richness of many perspectives.

Advocacy

As the Ackell model makes clear, simply adding services and programs for various groups is not sufficient to provide a high-quality experience for all students at an institution. Advocacy means working on behalf of students to assure that their needs are recognized and integrated into all levels of planning, policy development, and practice.

It is appropriate and important for student affairs professionals to assume the role of advocate on behalf of students. This role involves three fundamental tasks (Likins, 1986): (1) to become informed about the characteristics and requirements of the various groups of students at the institution, (2) to raise the awareness of all members of the campus community about the diversity and needs of students, and (3) to encourage institutional change to enhance the educational experience of the entire student population.

The following questions can form a sound basis for advocacy efforts by a student affairs staff.

- Does the composition of the faculty and staff reflect the diversity of the student body in key ways (race, gender, cultural background, national origin)?
- Do selection criteria for faculty and staff specify knowledge of and experience in dealing with a varied student population?
- Are employee development programs that focus on the wide range of student characteristics and their implications offered to all levels of faculty and staff?
- Do faculty members understand learning-style differences and structure their courses based on that understanding?
- Do faculty members integrate out-of-class experiences (work, family, cultural) into the curriculum?
- Is there a program that identifies students having academic difficulty and offers them assistance?
- Do all students benefit equally from fee-supported services and programs?
- Have shifts in the composition of the student body been accompanied by appropriate changes in funding priorities?
- Do students in some groups drop out of the institution at a higher rate than others? What is the institution doing about it?
- Are the needs of all students considered in planning for the construction and renovation of buildings, roads, and parking facilities?

Advocacy efforts can be simple or complex, short- or long-range, informal or formal, unofficial or official, indirect or direct. The best advocates use several approaches, are creative in developing strategies, and are persistent. The many avenues for advocacy include volunteering to serve on committees that search for candidates to fill vacant positions, plan programs, or set policies; inviting a colleague to lunch to discuss an idea for how his or her area could better serve a group of students; convening a task force to study and recommend action on some issue; informing student groups of appropriate advocacy targets and assisting them to organize constructive efforts; suggesting the creation of advisory boards to the president and other officials to inform them about issues regarding certain student groups (for example, women, students with disabilities, or minority students); submitting a proposal recommending modifications in services, programs, or policies; offering to conduct a workshop for faculty, staff, or student leaders about the diversity of the student body; and becoming involved in institutional development to encourage the solicitation of funds targeted for students with special needs.

Advocates ask questions, encourage colleagues to focus on student needs, and work to bring about institutional change. The chances for success are significantly increased if advocates are knowledgeable about the institution's history and values and work within these contexts. It is equally critical to assess where one is likely to find support (or resistance) to advocacy efforts. Cultivating the acquaintance and respect of decision makers who may be either potential supporters or critics is essential to establish personal credibility. Timing is another key factor; knowing what other issues confront decision makers can indicate whether they are likely to be receptive to advocacy efforts or whether it is better to wait for another time.

Research

For student affairs units, research regarding characteristics and needs is the foundation upon which services, programs, and advocacy efforts are developed. Closely related to research is evaluation of services and programs. It is a fundamental responsibility of higher education institutions to conduct research and evaluation to determine to what extent students' educational goals are being met. As Astin writes, "A high-quality institution is one that knows about its students . . . [and] has a method for gathering and disseminating this information, enabling it to make appropriate adjustments in programs or policies when the student data indicate that change or improvement is needed. In other words, quality is equated here not with physical facilities or faculty credentials but rather with a continuing process of critical self-examination that focuses on the institution's contribution to the student's intellectual and personal development" (cited in Keller, 1983, p. 132).

National studies are useful for institutional research, but it is not good practice to transfer findings to a particular institution or from one institution to another. What may be an accurate and useful statement about women or

Asian students on one campus, for example, may be inaccurate or misleading on another. Only specific assessment can reveal how well each component of the institution responds to the needs of each group in the student body.

Like advocacy, research ranges from simple and informal to complex and formal. There are many research methodologies that can be employed by student affairs professionals.

• Data already existing at an institution can be compiled and examined. The admissions office, the registrar, the counseling center, and the institutional research office routinely collect data on students. Many institutions also receive individual reports from such sources as the College Board and the Cooperative Institutional Research Program.

• Unobtrusive measures of student behavior entail observation of student activities (for example, counting those attending programs or using a lounge area) or of the environment (carpet wear, bulletin boards).

• Valuable information can be gathered by the simple addition of one or more key variables (age, place of residence, employment status) to institutional data already collected upon admission or at course registration.

• Surveys—conducted in person, by telephone, or by mail—can yield a wealth of descriptive information as well as data regarding students' needs, experiences, and satisfaction with various aspects of the institution.

• Student interviews or focus groups (structured small-group discussions led by a facilitator) provide rich qualitative information that can supplement quantitative data collected by surveys.

• In-depth study of students' experiences or development generally requires longitudinal research, in which the same group of subjects is followed over time (for example, from matriculation to graduation). Such studies often combine quantitative and qualitative measures.

The work of research and evaluation can at first seem overwhelming. However, according to the SPAR model, if each student affairs unit conducts research related to its functions, the task becomes far less burdensome. In addition, data collected by those individuals who provide services and programs for students are more likely to be used in planning and evaluation. For example, counselors can keep records of the kinds of issues presented by certain groups of students (women, minorities, commuters). Programmers can assess whether international or commuter students participate in proportion to their presence in the student body. Student union staffs can determine which areas of the building are most heavily used by particular groups of students so that bulletin boards, information racks, and banners announcing events can be displayed there.

Another effective way to use the SPAR model in conducting research is for several student affairs units or staff members to join together to gather information about a specific group during a set time period using several of the research methodologies just described. A joint report of the findings of such a coordinated effort could provide powerful data to serve as the basis of advocacy efforts as well as to encourage additions or improvements to services and programs.

Table 32.1. An Example of How the SPAR Model Can Be Applied to Adult Students.

	Services	Programs	Advocacy	Research
Activities	Make child care available during programs	Provide leadership development programs for working adults		Collect statistics on adult-student preferences for activities
Career planning		Sponsor programs for adults seeking career changes or advancement	Work to eliminate "ageism" by area employers	
Counseling	Train counselors to deal with adult issues	Create support groups for adult students on relevant topics (elder care, marital problems)	Inform faculty and staff on adult-student issues	
Health	Sponsor clinics on age-related problems (backache, menopause)	Give workshops on relevant topics (fitness, diet for adults)		Assess adult students' needs for health services
Housing	Ensure that buildings or units are designed for older students or families		Work with area apartment complexes to offer reduced rents to students	
Learning assistance	Provide math and writing tutoring for adults by peers	Sponsor programs on returning to college after a long break	Promote faculty awareness of adult learning preferences	
Orientation		Provide programs in multiple formats and at various times	Encourage academic and other departments to offer programs to welcome students	Investigate different transition needs of older versus traditional-age students
Union	Create lounge for adult-student interaction			Measure use of union services by adults

Table 32.1 indicates how the SPAR model can be applied to one student group. It does not list all applications or student affairs areas. The four functions—services, programs, advocacy, and research—appear across the top of the table, and representative areas of student affairs work are on the left. Each box provides an example of a function that can be performed for (in this instance, adult) students.

Table 32.2 is an example of how professionals in our field, in no matter what area of work, can apply the SPAR model to various student groups. This example is useful for smaller colleges and universities and for institutions where student affairs professionals play generalist roles.

Summary

As the students pursuing higher education become more diverse, institutions must change to meet their needs and education goals. In this era of accountability, the burden of adaptation must shift from the students themselves to institutions. Those that fail to change appropriately will find their enrollments, their financial solvency, and their very existence threatened.

Because each institution consists of a unique combination of students, faculty, administrators, mission, history, curriculum, facilities, and setting, there is no universal plan or blueprint that can be used to move institutions toward Ackell's equity stage of development. Student affairs professionals must be the leaders at their institutions in seeking to appreciate the range of objectives and needs that students bring to the campus. Knowledge of the characteristics of the diverse student groups at each institution and the nature of the institutional environment is the essential basis for developing appropriate services and programs. In addition, professionals in our field must use their understanding of students to work as advocates for systemic institutional change.

Table 32.2. An Example of How Student Affairs Professionals
Can Apply Each Function of the SPAR Model to Various Student Groups.

Adults	Ascertain that services and facilities are available when adult students are on campus (lunchtime, evenings, weekends)
Commuters	Provide information about services and programs that reaches commuter students (direct mail to students' homes, local radio stations and newspapers)
Internationals	Provide a handbook of campus and area services and resources especially needed by students adjusting to U.S. culture.
Minorities	Offer menu choices, books, grooming items, and other products and services preferred by different groups of minority students
Students with disabilities	Make all services fully accessible to students with mobility, visual, hearing, and speech impairments.

References

Ackell, E. F. "Adapting the University to Adult Students: A Developmental Perspective." In W. H. Warren (ed.), *Improving Institutional Services to Adult Learners.* Washington, D.C.: American Council on Education, 1986.

Barr, M. J., and others. "Toward an Expansion of Theory and Application in Human Development." *A Proposal to the Executive Council of the American College Personnel Association from the Senior Scholars of ACPA,* Feb. 1988.

Jacoby, B. *The Student as Commuter: Developing a Comprehensive Institutional Response.* ASHE-ERIC Higher Education Report, no. 7. Washington, D.C.: Association for the Study of Higher Education, 1989.

Jacoby, B., and Girrell, K. W. "A Model for Improving Services and Programs for Commuter Students." NASPA Journal, 1981, *18,* 38–41.

Keller, G. *Academic Strategy: The Management Revolution in American Higher Education.* Baltimore, Md.: Johns Hopkins Press, 1983.

Likins, J. M. "Developing the Commuter Perspective: The Art of Advocacy." *NASPA Journal,* 1986, *24,* 11–16.

Lindquist, J. "Professional Development." In A. W. Chickering and Associates, *The Modern American College: Responding to the New Realities of Diverse Students and a Changing Society.* San Francisco: Jossey-Bass, 1981.

Lynton, E. A., and Ellman, S. E. *New Priorities for the University: Meeting Society's Needs for Applied Knowledge and Competent Individuals.* San Francisco: Jossey-Bass, 1987.

Schlossberg, N. K., Lynch, A. Q., and Chickering, A. W. *Improving Higher Education Environments for Adults: Responsive Programs and Services from Entry to Departure.* San Francisco: Jossey-Bass, 1989.

Stodt, M. M. "Psychological Characteristics of 1980's College Students: Continuity, Changes, and Challenges." *NASPA Journal,* 1982, *19,* 3–8.

33

∽

Confronting
Health Issues

Margaret W. Bridwell
Stanley P. Kinder

In the late nineteenth and early twentieth centuries, college and university health centers were designed as infirmaries offering a limited range of care. Such health care units were intended primarily to give students suffering from acute minor illnesses and infectious diseases a supportive environment in which to rest and recuperate. Infirmaries also helped to prevent the spread of these minor infectious diseases by isolating the sick students from the rest of the student population. The role of the early college health centers was limited to treating the sick and injured and protecting the campus's community health.

The mission for health centers remained relatively unchanged until the late 1960s and early 1970s, when the social and cultural revolution sweeping our nation altered forever the way colleges and universities dealt with students. The sexual liberation movement, the popularization of drug and alcohol use on campuses, and an aggressive new student activism brought change to the student health agenda. These new issues demanded new approaches: drug and alcohol treatment and education programs; specialized services, such as women's clinics offering gynecologic and contraceptive services; and many others. And during this period, students became much more vocal in expressing their discontent with campus agencies or services that were not meeting their needs. All of these forces served as catalysts leading to the health centers that we see on today's campuses.

Although the size, programmatic scope, and staffing levels in college health centers are as variable as the institutions at which they are located, there is a set of common characteristics that define the best of today's programs. As stated by the American College Health Association (ACHA) in its document *College Health 2000: A Perspective Statement in Higher Education,* "Today, the following vital characteristics define the college health model: preventive and educational health programs, quality care, cost effectiveness, and active involvement with the higher education community" (1990, p. 1). A college health center must actively embrace this model to be successful in fulfilling its responsibilities to the students and institution that it serves.

This chapter focuses on the administrative issues that must be addressed regarding student health services, including the appropriateness of providing student health care, the financing of campus health services, the need for student health insurance, and issues of confidentiality and ethics. Further, the chapter considers the medical issues on college campuses, the need to build campus partnerships, and the role of accreditation for health services.

Administrative Issues for the Student Affairs Administrator

Senior student affairs officers are often faced with difficult issues concerning the administration of student health programs. These problems range from pragmatic problems—how best to finance health programs on the campus and how to ensure that students have access to affordable health insurance—to the ethical issues related to student confidentiality. College health centers often confront conflicting interests. To illustrate, what is the appropriate balance between the privacy interests of an individual student and concern for the broader interests of the campus community? Should a residence hall staff member be informed of a particular student's health problem if there is potential risk to others? Finally, should a discipline officer be made aware of a health problem prior to adjudicating a case? Balancing these conflicting interests can be a formidable challenge for health center directors and chief student affairs officers.

The Issue of Providing On-Campus Student Health Services

Perhaps the first question that the chief student affairs officer must answer in regard to student health programs is whether or not the institution should be in the business of providing health care. There are few places in this country where a readily available range of treatment choices are not available in the private practice community. Should colleges also offer health services on campus? This question is legitimate, particularly in a climate of shrinking resources for higher education. It is reasonable to conclude that a sore throat or sprained ankle can be treated just as well in a private physician's office as in campus health service. And with the cost of the care being borne exclusively by the student, there is no cost to the institution. Yet however potentially persuasive on the surface, this limited perspective of clinical care and cost concerns begs broader and much more meaningful questions for the institution. Boyer says it well:

> Students spend most of the undergraduate years outside the classroom, and what they do during this time profoundly shapes the form and quality of their experience. . . . The college that deserves support is one that sees academic and nonacademic functions as related. Because college is intended to prepare students for life, the lessons of the classroom should first be applied in the college community itself. . . . There are health matters to be considered, too: Are students at the college educated about the importance of nutrition and exercise and encouraged to participate in a program of regular physical activity? Does the college cafeteria provide a healthful diet? Do college administrators back local and state laws regarding the use of drugs and alcoholic beverages? Does the college sponsor programs to help deal with these problems? In short, does the college have standards not just in academic matters but in nonacademic matters, too — expectations that help define the college as a community [1987, pp. 292–293].

It is within the broader institutional context that the question of providing student health services must be answered. Campus-based health services, if structured to meet the requirements of the campus community, will offer the necessary clinical care coupled with strong programs of prevention and wellness that address the problems of drug and alcohol use, sexually transmitted diseases and unwanted pregnancy, nutrition, stress, and other major problems of the college student. These programs can favorably influence retention rates and generally help to create a supportive and caring campus environment.

Financing of Campus Health Services

In an era of shrinking resources, senior student affairs administrators will increasingly confront challenges regarding the financing of student health programs. As tuition grows and other costs of attending college continue to escalate, there will be greater pressure to hold expenses down. Under these conditions, backing for the health center may erode. However, a combination of fee-based support, combined with reasonable fees for services, may provide needed financial flexibility in the future. Such an approach is based on the assumption that all enrolled students share a common responsibility in ensuring a certain baseline of campus health services and that they should consequently pay a mandatory fee.

Under this assumption, the health center operates on the same premise as most health maintenance organizations (HMOs). Students who actually use the service would pay an incremental fee, thus taking on a proportionally larger share of the health center's budget. Many health centers charge for ancillary services such as laboratory tests, pharmacy, and X ray (when these services are available). Others have implemented a small per-visit charge to students using the service. It is in the area of these self-generated fees that health centers have their greatest flexibility. With ceilings being placed on mandatory fees and reductions in general funding for health services, locally generated income is an area where revenue can be increased. Health centers that are entrepreneurial in thinking about funding strategies are much more likely to weather periods of fiscal difficulty on campus than those that are not.

Student Health Insurance

One element of the continuing national debate on the seemingly endless escalation of health care costs is related to health insurance. Health insurance is an issue that most senior student affairs administrators cannot avoid. With many, if not most, colleges and universities sponsoring a student health insurance program, decisions must be made regarding scope of coverage, benefit limits, policy provisions relating to issues such as pregnancy and abortion, and mandatory versus voluntary insurance. Many of the answers to these questions can only be determined in the context of local circumstances. For example, scope of coverage may be influenced by the level of service available at the campus health center, a variable that may increase or decrease the need for external insurance coverage. These are matters of significance to students and to the institution and should be carefully considered by the senior student affairs administrator or the health center director. It is generally not appropriate for this issue to be decided exclusively by someone in the institution's business office or purchasing department.

Debate has occurred in recent years about the relative benefits of mandatory and voluntary student health insurance policies. The principal difference is that for most mandatory programs a student must show evidence of current health insurance coverage or purchase the university-sponsored policy, whereas voluntary programs have no set requirement. The value of mandatory student insurance programs rests on two points: with increased enrollment (as a consequence of the plan's mandatory feature), the policy can be priced more competitively; the institution can also be reasonably assured that a student's academic work will not be interrupted due to unpaid medical bills. With the cost of a single, short-term hospital stay potentially running into thousands of dollars, the latter is no small concern. The advantage of voluntary approaches is that they allow students to make independent decisions as to whether or not they want insurance and do not force them to purchase potentially unnecessary coverage that they may not be able to afford. Strong arguments have been advanced supporting both positions. Each chief student affairs officer and other administrators must evaluate the characteristics of the student population, the real and perceived need for a mandatory student insurance program, availability of care in the community for uninsured students, and existing state and municipal programs that could serve students. Statistics suggest that 4.6 million adolescents lack insurance coverage of any kind nationally and further that the rapid escalation of insurance costs is threatening the coverage of the dependent children of the working insured (U.S. Congress, Office of Technology Assessment, 1987).

Most health care professionals, both clinicians and administrators, would support any program that broadens access to adequate health insurance, for they have seen firsthand the difficulties created by its absence. There are two factors that will have profound influence on this debate in the future. First, mandatory insurance programs are currently being tested in the courts. In several instances, students who had been forced to buy a policy have brought suit, alleging that the practice is not legal. Second, there seems to be growing political support for some type of national health insurance legislation. Although the details are as yet unpredictable, the final outcome may well determine how colleges and universities proceed on this issue. For additional assistance on student health insurance, ACHA has published a set of guidelines for schools to use as they evaluate their insurance programs. These can be obtained by writing to ACHA at 780 Elkridge Landing Road, Linthicum, Maryland, 21090.

Confidentiality and Ethics

The issue of confidentiality is at the heart of the relationship between college health centers and the students that they serve. The nature of the problems for which many students are treated — alcohol and other drug abuse, sexually transmitted diseases, unwanted pregnancy, mental health issues, and countless other sensitive concerns — necessitates that a strong sense of trust exist between student and health center. In an institutional environment where many students consider the organized college or university bureaucracy to be adversarial, it is essential that student health centers be perceived as advocates for the interests and welfare of students. Absent this type of relationship, students requiring care may opt not to go to the campus health service, a practice that can lead to complication or exacerbation of their problem if no alternative treatment is obtained. Further, if they sense a lack of confidentiality, students may not be honest about the real nature of their problem when talking with clinicians. The failure to be candid may compromise the treatment plan.

It does not require an active imagination to envision these kinds of circumstances. A young woman suspects that she is pregnant but forgoes clinical testing even as the pregnancy advances to the point of limited options.

Fearing exposure and social stigma, a student with a sexually transmitted disease avoids treatment while continuing to be sexually active. A student apprehensive about parents finding out about a problem of alcohol abuse does not seek help although the pattern of abuse becomes more advanced.

Effective response to students in stressful and health-threatening circumstances includes the absolute requirement for confidential treatment of student records by campus health practitioners. At the same time, student affairs professionals must wrestle with ethical aspects of this issue in instances where the institution might be well served by access to confidential information contained in a student's medical record. An excellent hypothetical example of this dilemma might involve a student in a residence hall who is suspected by fellow students on the floor and by the resident assistant of being HIV positive. The resident life director contacts the health center and demands to know the truth but is rebuffed on grounds of confidentiality. She contacts the vice president for student affairs and demands to know the answer. How does the vice president respond? Obviously, there is no real reason to reveal the student's HIV status because there is no risk to anyone in the hall, even if the individual is seropositive (unless this student engages in intimate sexual relations with others). However, the emotion and paranoia surrounding this issue sometimes make rational conclusions difficult. In the belief that the interests of other residents should be protected, there can be strong pressure to release the information.

Ethically, what is appropriate, even if one assumes that a real risk to others exists? How does one strike an appropriate balance between the community's and an individual student's interests? Given that strong arguments supporting each position can be made, historical precedent and generally accepted practice must be relied on to guide our decision making. Historically, any information pertaining to a particular patient has been considered absolutely confidential unless one of the following conditions applies.

1. There is imminent danger to the patient or others. *Imminent* has generally been defined as implying that there is an immediate risk, absent intervention of some kind.

2. Public health officials consider the medical circumstances as requiring a structured follow-up. Illnesses in this category include meningitis, certain sexually transmitted diseases (AIDS is not yet among these), tuberculosis, and others. These are commonly known, and there are often federal, state, or local regulations concerning them.

3. On campus, the patient is so medically compromised as to be unable to function independently in the academic or residence hall environment. This case differs from the first one listed here in that the situation would generally be a function of a physical illness, as opposed to a willful act such as suicide or assault. An example would be a bulimic-anorexic student who denies the illness but is so physically debilitated that continued class attendance is a significant health risk.

It is important to understand that in each of these instances the determination to be made is essentially a medical one. These are not judgments to be arrived at by an administrator, but rather by a competent health care professional. Outside of college health, this individual is usually a physician but on many campuses may be a nurse or other midlevel provider. Once the medical judgment is made by the campus health service, the senior student affairs administrator may then need to take administrative action. Action that could result from a medical concern might be suspension or forced withdrawal from classes or a residence hall.

How do these criteria apply to our earlier hypothetical example? As stated previously, there is no medical evidence supporting a conclusion of imminent danger to other students in the residence hall. HIV infection has not been treated as a public health risk that should be followed in the same manner as other infectious diseases. There is no compromise in the student's ability to function on campus as a result of medical status. One can only conclude that there is no basis to disclose any medical information on the student in question.

Testing individual situations against the three criteria just identified is a sound approach to navigating the difficult waters of medical confidentiality. Although obtaining medical information on a particular student may sometimes understandably be a great temptation for student affairs administrators, confidentiality must be maintained. All concerned must understand the inestimable damage done to the campus health service's credibility each time the implicit contract of trust between student and health service is broken.

Medical Issues on Today's Campus: Bugs or Behavior?

If student affairs administrators are to make informed decisions regarding the appropriate mix of programs and services in their campus health centers, they must first understand the nature of health problems most often experienced by students. They must start by understanding that the most significant health risks to college students are usually related to their behavior and risk taking. Keeling states, "The future consequences of their current behavior pose the greatest health challenges facing college and university students today in the United States. Foremost among the problems challenging young people, as well as their parents, and colleges and universities, are the epidemics of HIV and other sexually transmitted diseases; substance abuse; sexual assault; and unwanted pregnancy — all problems related to behavior and relationships" (1991, pp. B1–B2).

Other problems that may manifest themselves much later in life but have their origins in behavioral patterns established during the young-adult years include cardiac disease, hypertension, obesity, and the physical and social problems secondary to alcohol use. This is not to say that students do not present campus health centers with serious illnesses or injuries that are not related to behaviors — they do. These medical problems, even those considered more serious, tend to be episodic, to be acute only in the short term, and to respond well to treatment interventions. Measured in terms of lifelong impact, the consequences of the behavioral issues are much more profound and persistent.

The U.S. Public Health Service is developing national health objectives for the year 2000. This plan will be an extension of earlier efforts establishing specific national goals for health promotion and disease prevention and will set the agenda for the next decade. The 1990 goals for the adolescent and young-adult population (ages fifteen to twenty-four) include 20 percent fewer deaths, with special focus on alcohol and drug issues and motor vehicle injuries.

In the process of building its agenda for the college student population, ACHA held open hearings at its annual meeting in May 1987. Oral and written testimony on the key health issues confronting students on our college campuses for the next decade and beyond was gathered from a wide range of individuals: practicing professionals in the field of college health, professionals in related student affairs disciplines, and students. Five issues were established as being of primary concern.

1. Over 90 percent of the experts identified sexual health concerns as a threat to the emotional and physical health of young adults.
2. Substance abuse, including that of alcohol, other drugs, and tobacco, was considered the second leading health risk for students on the college campus.
3. Mental health concerns related to stress, anxiety, achievement pressure, fear of failure, low self-esteem, and lack of social support were identified as the third most significant problem for students.
4. Another major issue was food and its relationship to nutrition, weight management, and chronic disease prevention.
5. The more efficient and effective use of resources to provide comprehensive, low-cost health services for students and their families was the final concern (Guyton and others, 1989).

These findings further demonstrate the relationship between students' behaviors and the most commonly occurring health problems on the college campus. The evidence supporting the need for student health programming that addresses these behaviorally driven problems is incontrovertible.

Programming for Prevention and Wellness

College students are naturally at risk for many of the problems just described. Making fully independent decisions for the first time and being exposed to a wide variety of influences, many students do not possess the maturity of life experience to make good choices. During these transitional college years, many students experiment and take risks in the course of finding their limits.

Very often, the results of this struggle to establish an independent identity and set of values are behavioral patterns and habits that will persist for a lifetime. The challenge to staff members providing student services, especially those in campus health services, is to design interventions that give students the ability to make better, more informed decisions.

As a result of the research of student health professionals and others interested in the field, it has become increasingly clear that students very often possess the knowledge to make sound decisions. As Keeling states, "The simple truth is that young people do not *do* what they *know*" (1991, p. B2). Helping students translate knowledge into action is fundamental to successful health education programs. Programs must be designed and delivered that fight the tendency of students to believe that they are immortal or invulnerable to the problems that affect "other" people. Further, students need practical help in developing the skills necessary to negotiate or communicate well in difficult social and interpersonal circumstances. For example, it is hard to discuss protection with a first-time sexual partner or to refuse alcohol in a party situation where everyone else is drinking. Anecdotal evidence collected in survey research studies suggests that students find it very difficult to talk about these issues. A student's ability to exercise the best judgment in these kinds of situations may well hinge on his or her assertiveness or strength of self-identity. Understanding how and why students make the choices that they do is the best hope we have of developing programs that will influence their decision making.

Educational programs that give students a strong role or sense of ownership are among those that are best received. Programs using strong, well-trained, and motivated student peers have dealt effectively with issues like alcohol and other drug abuse, sexually communicated diseases and contraception, AIDS, and depression awareness. Student educators, who face the same issues, are generally much more credible than staff members would be lecturing on the same subjects. Peer programs are also an excellent means of extending the effort of a campus health service staff, particularly in situations where the number of employees is limited. One of the best features of these programs is that the only resources necessary to get them started are a staff trainer or supervisor and a group of interested students. Peer programs embody the concept of empowering students to solve their own problems — the ultimate aim of all wellness education and prevention programs.

Smaller health services often show their commitment to health education by informing their patients. Without the luxury of a full-time health education staff, small health centers must rely on their clinical staff, most often nurse practitioners and nurses, to fill this role. Sensitive to the issues and problems that students experience, these clinicians use the opportunity created by the student's need for health care (sometimes referred to as a teachable moment) to educate about prevention and wellness. Health education takes many forms on college campuses. Small initiatives with limited funding and staff can have just as good results as larger programs.

Partnerships for Success

To be successful, campus health services must be active players in the larger community; they must reach out to form the necessary partnerships to achieve the best outcome for their student and institutional constituencies. It is important that the health service is viewed as an involved, proactive, and credible member of the campus community. The year 2000 health objectives testimony discusses the kind of partnerships that are important: "Expert testimonies described the need for institution-wide responses to problems of substance abuse, sexual health, mental health, and stress. They suggested a model of a unified, multidimensional, community-based approach to prevention, education, diagnosis, and treatment with increased funding for physical and mental health services. . . . Respondents said health services should be strongly linked with academic programs, as well as with athletic departments, food services, residence halls, and social organizations" (Guyton and others, 1989, p. 12).

Specific examples of how these partnerships might work include credit internships for students working in the health center, integration of prevention-oriented information into the academic curriculum, and the building of a strong liaison and support system for paraprofessional staff in the residence halls. The synergy that results from these informal networks of individuals and organizations not only helps to solve a problem but also serves to create and enhance a sense of community.

It is extremely important that other caregivers on the campus work closely with the health center. These include the staff of the counseling center (if a separate center exists), the chaplains, and those working at minority student centers. All too often, relationships between health services and counseling centers have been strained. Tension has existed regarding overlap of services and mission, allocation of resources, and long-standing conflicts about therapy between psychiatry and the fields of clinical and counseling psychology. It may not be possible to eliminate these tensions entirely, but the senior student affairs administrator has an obligation to minimize them and to ensure that students' interests remain the focus of all student service agencies. Being clear about mission, responsibilities, and objectives can be very helpful. The leadership of the campus health service—more specifically, its mental health staff—should seek opportunities to work in collegial fashion with those at the counseling center. Coming together to improve the health and welfare of students puts into practice the values that are of greatest concern to health and counseling centers alike.

College and university health services should also look beyond the borders of the campus in building relationships that will benefit students. At a minimum, they should have some knowledge upon which to base referrals when off-campus care is required. Appropriateness of fees, insurance practices, professional reputation, and willingness to see students are just a few of the criteria that should be used to screen physicians. Moreover, if the health service refers patients or campus emergency transports them to a particular hospital or emergency room, the health service should be building a strong working relationship with that hospital. Managed care and HMOs are increasingly populating the health care landscape. To the degree that these kinds of organizations are important in the college or university community, the health service should have some contact and ongoing communication with them.

The world in which students live is increasingly complex and fast paced and the problems that they experience do not lend themselves to simple, one-dimensional solutions. Multidisciplinary, community-based responses are needed. Senior student affairs administrators should challenge the leadership in their student health services to engage the campus and community in addressing the health issues confronting our universities.

Commitment to Quality: The Role of Accreditation

Accreditation is a term familiar to colleges and universities. On a regular basis, academic programs are forced to undergo the careful scrutiny of a wide variety of accreditation processes. The process is essentially the same in the health care arena. There are two nationally recognized accrediting bodies, Accreditation Association for Ambulatory Health Care and the Joint Commission for the Accreditation of Healthcare Organizations. These two bodies publish a set of specific and objective standards under which ambulatory health care organizations are expected to operate. The standards consider virtually every major aspect of a health service's operations: quality of care, patients' rights, administration and governance, medical records, and many others. Given that student health practice has traditionally been held in low regard by other sectors of medicine, accreditation can become an unequivocal means of stating and verifying program quality. Independent assessment using a set of external standards is truly one of the best means of ensuring a defined level of quality, for internal as well as external audiences.

An additional resource to use in creating and measuring program duality is *Recommended Standards for a College Health Program,* published by the American College Health Association (1991).

Summary

The following quotation captures much of what has been communicated in this chapter.

> College health services have a unique position within institutions of higher learning. Society has become increasingly aware of the impact of physical and mental health on social and public health issues. College health services can play a major role in encouraging college students to attend to these critical issues.

New partnerships are being forged with institutional groups, so that both clinical and educational concerns are being integrated into campus and community practices. While the American College Health Association Standards outline recommended standards of practice and operation, it is important to identify and address certain special characteristics of college health that place it in a position of influence among a population receptive to education and self-exploration. Although institutions differ in size and scope of services, there are universal concepts that impact upon the provision of health promotion, health protection, disease prevention, and clinical care to college students. Current sociological trends, public health issues, and changes in preventive medicine have broad institutional implications. College health services are now recognized as valuable resources to help meet those new challenges [American College Health Association, 1991].

College health practice is an exciting arena in which to operate. Many of the most profound social, public health, and public policy issues surface in the day-to-day business of college health services. Student affairs administrators, in partnership with their campus health services, are afforded a rare opportunity to contribute to a better and healthier campus community.

References

American College Health Association. *College Health 2000: A Perspective Statement in Higher Education*. Linthicum, Md.: American College Health Association, 1990.

American College Health Association, Committee on Standards for College Health. *Recommended Standards for a College Health Program*. Linthicum, Md.: American College Health Association, 1991.

Boyer, E. L. *College: The Undergraduate Experience in America*. New York: HarperCollins, 1987.

Guyton, R., and others. "College Students and the National Health Objectives for the Year 2000: A Summary Report." *Journal of American College Health,* 1989, *38* (1), 9–14.

Keeling, R. P. "Student Health in the 1990's." *Chronicle of Higher Education, 1991,* 38 (7), B1–B2.

U.S. Congress, Office of Technology Assessment. *Adolescent Health: Summary and Policy Options*. Vol. 1. Washington, D.C.: U.S. Congress, 1987.

34

The Changing Role
of Government
in Higher Education

E. T. "Joe" Buchanan

This chapter examines the impact of statutory and regulatory action by federal, state, and local governments on student affairs administration in higher education. An underlying theme of the chapter is that governmental bodies continue to display a willingness to regulate and micromanage higher education, often by placing unfunded mandates on institutions. The chapter will discuss the involvement of governmental entities in higher education with specific emphasis on religion, race and admissions, disability, sex discrimination, environmental quality, employment, and privacy. In addition, issues surrounding televised football, the sale of goods and services, and campus crime will be examined. Finally, concerns related to state government and higher education will be discussed.

Although the U.S. Constitution does not refer to higher education explicitly, it is often referred to in state constitutions. In a few states, public higher education is constitutionally autonomous, but public and to an extent private higher education is increasingly regulated by both state and federal agencies.

Federal statutes have had a profound influence on colleges and universities. For example, the G.I. Bill of 1944 brought new and different students to American campuses. Returning veterans were older, often married, academically dedicated, *and* supported by the federal government. Colleges and universities had to respond to these new students; the results included construction of married-student housing, new-student support services, and a reexamination of institutional policies.

The G.I. Bill was the precursor to the Federal National Defense Education Act (1958). This program was the initial phase of the development of a federal student financial aid program and provided low-interest student loans. Since that time, federal programs related to financial aid have expanded and have become a major influence on both institutional and student welfare. Examples include Pell Grants, college work-study programs, the Supplementary Educational Opportunities Grant Program, the Guaranteed Student Loan Program, and Auxiliary Loans to Assist Students.

During the 1950s and 1960s, a series of court cases opened higher education institutions and the public schools to the enrollment of students regardless of race, but most institutions entered the 1970s little changed by federal and state law or regulations. Land-grant institutions continued to teach engineering or agriculture to a predominantly male student body with a mostly male faculty. Women were largely absent from the schools of business, law, and medicine. Few minorities were enrolled in institutions, as both de jure and de facto segregation existed. Disabled students were found at only a few institutions. Date rape was an unheard-of concept. Students were routinely dismissed from colleges on marginal hearsay evidence, without notice or hearing. And campus security was often the province of a handful of retired men whose usual role was that of night watchman. All of this was to change dramatically over the next two decades, largely as a result of increased federal and state regulatory activity, That activity is the focus of this chapter.

These issues never appear to be completely settled, for the law itself is always changing and evolving. However, those discussed in this chapter are likely to remain on the future agenda of higher education.

Religion

A concern that continues to be significant to colleges and universities (and their student affairs staffs) is the use of facilities by religious groups. There is no federal statute governing that use, but the case of *Widmar* v. *Vincent* (1981) provided the framework for congressional policy. The principles of *Widmar* were codified by Congress in the Equal Access Act (1984), which applies to K–12 schools. In *Widmar,* the fundamental policy basis of the Equal Access Act was enunciated. The decision in *Widmar* held that once a public college or university authorizes meetings by student groups in public facilities, student religious groups may not be barred from their use on the basis of the religious content of their activities.

The Equal Access Act, which was held constitutional in *Board of Edu-*

cation of Westside Community v. *Mergens,* (1990) requires K–12 schools that receive federal support to allow student religious groups to meet on campus during noninstructional hours if other noncurriculum-related student groups are permitted to use these facilities during such times.

It should be noted that religious activity deemed unduly intrusive may still be regulated. The Fourth Circuit held in *Chapman* v. *Thomas* (1984) that a public university in North Carolina could prohibit a student from going door to door in the residence halls to advertise religious Bible study, while at the same time authorizing candidates for student government offices to campaign door to door. Also, a recent K–12 case held that when a public school was not open to noncurriculum-related student groups, the school had no duty to permit noncurricular student religious groups to meet before school (*Garnett* v. *Renton School District No. 403,* 1989). In another case, a prefootball-game prayer in a Georgia public school setting was held to violate the establishment clause of the First Amendment (*Jager* v. *Douglas Co. School Dist.,* 1989). Free distribution of Bibles on a sidewalk abutting a public school was held to be constitutional, provided other groups who wished to distribute material were similarly treated (*Bacon* v. *Bradley-Bourbonnais High School District No. 307,* 1989). Finally, the courts held that public school libraries could include Bibles in their collection if other religious materials were also included (*Roberts* v. *Madigan,* 1989).

Federal and local government involvement in the affairs of a private religious institution is illustrated by *Gay Rights Coalition of Georgetown University* v. *Georgetown University* (1987). In the same year that the U.S. Supreme Court decided *Widmar,* the District of Columbia City Council adopted the Human Rights Act (1981). The Gay Rights Coalition applied for use of Georgetown University space and sought recognition on campus on the basis of that act. Georgetown University refused to recognize the organization or to provide meeting space for the Gay Rights Coalition on the basis of the First Amendment "free exercise" of religion clause. Georgetown claimed that church doctrine did not permit recognition of homosexual groups. The District of Columbia Federal District Court required Georgetown to provide the Gay Rights Coalition equal access to facilities and services but held that the university need not recognize or endorse the Gay Rights Coalition. The U.S. Congress thereafter adopted the Nation's Capital Religious Liberty and Academic Freedom Act (1988), which made it lawful for religiously oriented colleges and universities in the District of Columbia to discriminate against persons promoting a homosexual life-style or homosexual acts. Apparently departing from traditional views of the supremacy of the federal government and from the axiom that federal law preempts any contradictory statute adopted by state or local government, the District of Columbia Council attacked Congress's act as a violation of free-speech rights of the members of the District of Columbia Council. Both the federal district court and the court of appeals sustained the plaintiffs, holding in part that "voting . . . is the individual and collective expression of opinion" (*Clark* v. *United*

States, 1989, at 406). Georgetown University was compelled to honor the District of Columbia Human Rights Act.

One final issue concerns the extent to which federal, state, or local funds may be provided to religiously oriented institutions of higher education. An extensive technical discussion of these matters is provided in the *Journal of College and University Law* (McClamrock, 1991), and the reader is referred to that source. The author concludes that student-based financial aid may be provided to both "controlled" and "affiliated" institutions to assist students, but student aid to "controlled" institutions should generally be provided for a secular purpose.

Admission and Race

Brown v. *Board of Education* (1954) declared public school segregation illegal. A series of cases often involving law school admission (*Missouri ex rel Gaines* v. *Canada,* 1938, and *Sweatt* v. *Painter,* 1950) had already applied the principle that would be articulated in Brown to postsecondary education. The law school cases laid the ground for a series of litigations that began as *Adams* v. *Richardson* (1973) and continued with various Department of Education secretaries named as defendants until it became *Adams* v. *Bell* (Kaplin, 1985). *Adams* v. *Bell* (1983), involving desegregation of public colleges and universities in ten southern states, has been the most massive assault on de jure segregation in the history of higher education. Under *Adams,* the U.S. Department of Education was compelled to require those ten southern states with a history of de jure segregation to submit and enforce compliance plans designed to meet the *Adams* criteria, including enhancement of historically black institutions, greater participation by African-American students in Euro-American institutions, and elimination of duplicate programs. The court of appeals for the District of Columbia dismissed the *Adams* case in 1991. An appeal may be pending.

One of the remedies authorized by *Adams* was race-conscious scholarships. This issue became a controversial subject of debate in the early 1990s. The U.S. Department of Education initially announced that such scholarships were constitutionally suspect but eventually withdrew that opinion. Ward (1991) provides a helpful review of this important issue. It should be noted, however, that when the question was litigated (*Poderesky* v. *Board of Regents,* 1991), the federal district court upheld the University of Maryland's award of race-conscious scholarships initially developed under the *Adams* criteria.

Disability

The Federal Rehabilitation Act of 1973, the Americans with Disabilities Act of 1990, state statutes such as the Virginians with Disabilities Act (1991), and a range of county and city ordinances provide the regulatory framework for working with students with disabilities. Further, extensive work on behalf of disabled K–12 students pursuant to the federal All Handicapped Children Act (1988) has increased both the demand for services from institutions of higher education and the likelihood of litigation in the future.

Laura Rothstein (1991) summarizes the status of many of the Section 504 issues. Section 504 protection has been extended by state courts, federal district courts, and federal courts of appeal to a variety of handicapping conditions. She cites the following examples: AIDS victims (California), persons sensitive to tobacco smoke (Washington), transvestites (District of Columbia), those suffering from heart disease (Pennsylvania), alcoholics (Wisconsin), learning-disabled students (Massachusetts), kleptomaniacs (Maryland), epileptics (California), compulsive gamblers (Pennsylvania), and drug addicts (California). It is important to note, however, that only two of these cases involve colleges and universities. The only substantive U.S. Supreme Court decision (*Southeastern Community College* v. *Davis,* 1979) found that a hearing-impaired nursing student was not "otherwise qualified" due to safety concerns about her clinical performance. She was therefore not entitled to Section 504 protection.

Similarly, the U.S. Supreme Court refused to hear *Doherty* v. *Southern College of Optometry* (1989); in effect, this action sustained the Sixth Circuit Court opinion that a student with retinitis pigmentosa whose vision was not correctable to 20/20 need not be admitted to an optometry program. In *Samuelson* v. *Texas Women's University* (1989), a student with deformed fingers was not required to be admitted to a physical therapy program because he could not perform clinical procedures. Section 504 protection has also been denied to individuals who were left-handed, who feared heights, who had varicose veins, who experienced occasional stress disorder or depression, who had crossed eyes, who suffered from posttraumatic stress disorder, or who were chronically late.

Matters currently in litigation include many policy issues affecting colleges and universities. These include whether a university can charge for auxiliary services to disabled persons based on that person's ability to pay and whether a faculty member can refuse to grant an accommodation (such as additional test time) for a learning-disabled student. Facility questions are also under court challenge, including the construction of residence halls without an elevator, the level of support required for a deaf law student, and the issue of whether a medical school can give examinations to learning-disabled students only in a multiple-choice format.

Both state statutes and the Americans with Disabilities Act may significantly increase the remedies available to a disabled person. For example, under the Virginia statute, a disabled person has a statutory right to sue for damages, a remedy not available under Section 504 until 1990. It is also important for student affairs professionals to analyze the Americans with Disabilities Act, particularly in such areas as campus transportation systems, remedies available to plaintiffs, and the right to sue. The status of these issues is unclear as of this writing.

Gender

With the adoption of Title IX of the Higher Education Amendments of 1972 and its implementing regulations, the U.S. Congress has had a significant influence on institutions of higher education and the student affairs profession. Title IX, which prohibits discrimination on the basis of gender in public colleges and universities, covers such issues as admissions, access to services and programs, and athletics. Although Title IX specifically exempts the admissions practices of institutions that were single sex on the effective date of the statute, it ushered in an era in which many institutions voluntarily abandoned their single-sex status. The educational impact of admission of both sexes continues to be studied, particularly for women's colleges, and the issue of single-sex education in the public sector is still being litigated. An appeal has been taken regarding a district court decision that recently sustained the males-only admissions policy of the Virginia Military Institute.

Sexual assault currently is also the subject of keen congressional interest. The Student Right-to-Know and Campus Security Act (1990) was in significant part a response to concerns about sexual assault. In the 1991 congressional session, Senator Biden and Representative Boxer introduced companion legislation in the house and senate that treats campus rape as sexual discrimination (S 15 and HR 1502). In May 1991, the Campus Sexual Assault Victims Bill of Rights Act (HR 2363) was introduced by Representative Ramstead. This bill would have required colleges and universities to implement a sexual assault bill of rights. The Ramstead bill did not survive, and it appears, as of this writing, that Congress will adopt the California approach requiring each institution to adopt its own set of policies and procedures to support rape victims.

Also under consideration is whether Title IX should be amended to define rape as discrimination based on sex. No reported court case has extended Title IX protection to campus-based rape of students. Terry Nicole Steinberg, a lawyer and advocate for such legislation, urges amendment of the Title IX regulations to include providing mandatory orientation of new students regarding rape awareness, written documents for each student defining rape and outlining procedures to deal with it, twenty-four-hour access to medical and counseling support, an administrative review board to adjudicate cases, and designation of a victim assistance advocate assigned by the institution (1991). Steinberg also recommends that students who are raped be authorized by federal statute to sue their institution in federal court if the elements of the proposed Title IX amendment just listed are not met. Steinberg's proposal differs from the Violence Against Women Act of 1991, which authorizes suits only against the rapist, not the institution.

It should be noted that there is currently a conflict between the federal circuit courts of appeal on the issue of the award of compensatory damages to plaintiffs in Title IX claims. The Seventh and Eleventh Circuits have denied compensatory relief, whereas the Third Circuit in *Pfeiffer*

v. *Marion Center Area School District* (1990) authorized compensatory damages in a Title IX claim. In the case, Pfeiffer was not invited to join the National Honor Society because her premarital pregnancy was not consistent with the "good conduct" standard of the group. This matter has now been sent back to the lower court for further trial.

State governments are also introducing legislation on sexual assault. For example, under recently adopted legislation in California, both public and private institutions are required to provide supportive services to rape victims.

A closely related issue is that of sexual harassment. Sexual harassment is defined in regulations issued by the Equal Employment Opportunity Commission (1980). Two forms of sexual harassment have been defined by the courts. The first is quid pro quo: harassment that requires sex in return for job advancement, a pay increase, or similar rewards. The second is "hostile-environment" harassment, in which the behavior creates a hostile or abusive working environment. Sexual harassment, as currently defined by federal law, primarily involves the employment context, but it should be noted that a private institution was subject to a Title IX claim when a professor made a grade for a student contingent on a sexual relationship (*Alexander* v. *Yale University*, 1980).

The leading case in employment-related academic sexual harassment may be *Lipsett* v. *University of Puerto Rico* (1988). Lipsett was a surgical resident who left involuntarily after three years of a five-year residency. She alleged that she was driven out of her surgical residency by acts that included a list of sexually charged nicknames for female residents posted on bulletin boards, a sexually explicit drawing of Lipsett's body that was posted on a bulletin board, repeated sexual propositions by other residents, and repeated comments by other residents about her body. When she complained, no action was taken, and eventually she was dismissed for alleged behavioral problems. The First Circuit held that an employed student who is sexually harassed or assaulted by a professor or fellow student can file a Title IX claim of hostile-environment sexual harassment. The employee student may prevail if an institutional official knew or should have known of the harassment.

Consensual amorous relationships between faculty and students also provide unusual problems. A consensual relationship may deteriorate, and sexual harassment charges may be filed. Some institutions, including the University of Iowa, have developed sexual harassment policies that forbid such relationships. As part of their sexual harassment policy, other institutions strongly urge faculty not to get involved in such relationships. For a full discussion of the issues surrounding consensual relationships, the reader is referred to Keller (1988).

In addition, for sexual harassment that does not occur in the context of employment and that involves a student, other remedies are afforded. Institutional processes and state and local human rights commissions currently provide multiple avenues for resolution. In addition, hazing has been banned in most states, and sexual harassment may constitute hazing under many of the state statutes. Either a criminal prosecution or a civil tort suit may provide viable options for a victim.

Employment Issues

Executive Order 11246 (1981) requires federal contractors to practice non-discrimination and to take affirmative action in employment. The order is enforced by the Office of Federal Contract Compliance in the Department of Labor, and that office can require audits of institutions to assure compliance with employment law.

In 1972, the Equal Employment Opportunity Act was passed. The act expanded Title VII of the Civil Rights Act of 1964 to cover educational institutions. As a result, the Equal Employment Opportunity Commission (EEOC) now has a two-decade history of involvement in higher education. Perhaps the influence of the EEOC on higher education is most apparent in *University of Pennsylvania* v. *EEOC* (1990). At issue was the refusal by the university to comply with an EEOC subpoena of presumably confidential faculty-written evaluations of a candidate who was seeking tenure. The candidate, an Asian female, asserted that the refusal of tenure constituted sexual harassment and discrimination based on sex, race, and national origin. The U.S. Supreme Court held that the presumably confidential evaluations were subject to subpoenas by the EEOC and returned the case to the lower court for adjudication. Prior to this case, the EEOC had broad investigative authority with regard to institutional hiring and promotion practices. This case, however, brings that investigative authority into the very heart of the tenure-granting process, one of the most significant procedures in higher education.

Privacy

As recently as 1965, there was no legal battle for students to assert any privacy rights. Many students were at that time minors, and their academic records and residence hall rooms enjoyed no federal privacy protection. The first suggestion that students enjoyed some limited privacy rights came in cases involving searches of residence halls. Fourth Amendment protection from residence hall room search and seizure is not yet assured in all jurisdictions, but the Fifth Circuit has sustained this position (*Piazzola* v. *Watkins,* 1971). However, the U.S. Supreme Court in *State of Washington* v. *Chrisman* (1982) sustained a "plain-view" warrantless seizure of drug contraband in a college residence hall room.

Comprehensive privacy protection for student academic records was afforded by several federal statutes enacted in the early 1970s. The Federal Privacy Act of 1974 limited the administrative use of a student's social security number for institutional class rolls, grading reports, and other institutional purposes. The Family Educational Rights and Privacy (FERPA) Act (1974) and its implementing regulations established student control over unauthorized release of academic records. And the Federal Computer Fraud and Abuse Act (1986) made unauthorized access of computer data bases, including institutional student data bases, a federal criminal offense. Many states also have similar statutes to protect privacy.

Are campus crime police incident reports subject to federal privacy laws? This issue has been litigated in Missouri (*Bauer* v. *Kincaid,* 1991), where the court held that FERPA did not cover campus police incident reports provided to other offices of the institution and that such reports could be released to the press without student authorization. The *Bauer* case illustrates the long reach of both state and federal law into the operations of colleges and universities. In many states, laws require arrest records to be open to the public and to the press. Under FERPA, as recently interpreted by the Department of Education, student arrest records, once turned over to other college offices, become educational records. Such arrest records are then releasable only under a subpoena or pursuant to student permission. In states with such open-records laws, institutions are on the horns of a dilemma. Does not disclosing arrest data violate state law, or does disclosing such data violate federal law? In a press release, Department of Education secretary Lamar Alexander (May 1991) announced that he expected institutions to release campus crime records where state open-records laws require that action and that an amendment to FERPA to require such would be proposed by the Department of Education.

Campus Crime

The issue of campus crime—both its extent and nature—has been the subject of legislation at the state and the federal level. By 1991, twelve states had adopted a campus crime bill. The federal interest in campus crime began during the Nixon administration, and federal grants to institutions were provided to improve the quality of campus justice. Grants were intended to strengthen the professionalism of campus police departments, which were faced with the challenge of student dissent.

During the Reagan administration, the nation began a "war on drugs," and federal law and regulation (Drug-Free Schools and Communities Act, 1989) required colleges to develop and disseminate to students institutional policy on substance abuse. This was preceded by the 1988 Drug Free Workplace Act, which required similar policies and information for faculty and staff. Several states have also adopted state drug-free workplace acts that may broaden the federal definition.

The year 1990 also saw the adoption of the Hate Crimes Statistics Act. This act requires the U.S. Attorney General to establish guidelines and to collect (as part of the Uniform Crime Reporting Program administered by the Federal Bureau of Investigation), additional data about certain types of crimes. These include those that manifest evidence of prejudice based on race, religion, sexual orientation, or ethnicity. Of special interest are crimes of murder, manslaughter, forcible rape, assault, intimidation, arson, destruction, damage or vandalism to property, burglary, larceny and motor vehicle theft. Review of the illustrative examples of hate crimes in the *Hate Crime Reporting Guidelines* (U.S. Department of Justice, 1990) suggests that it may not be easy to characterize a given act as "hate based." In the guidelines, the theft of a purse from a Jewish woman, with the thief shouting anti-Semitic comments, is not considered hate based. Nonetheless, if institutions provide information to the Uniform Crime Reporting System, they will be expected to report hate crimes starting in 1990.

The most comprehensive congressional action on campus crime is the Student Right-to-Know and Campus Security Act of 1990. This act requires colleges to collect data on certain crimes; to advise students, faculty, and staff in writing of such crimes; and to furnish information on police and other crime prevention services on an annual basis. Crime data for a prior three-year period is to be included in the information, and applicants to institutions must also receive such reports. Final regulations for this bill are scheduled to be published in 1992; compliance will begin in the fall of 1992.

Environmental Quality

The late 1990s witnessed a major increase in environmental awareness and an extension of environmental statutes to colleges and universities, which had traditionally been unregulated in this area. Institutions were included in statutes covering such areas as disposal of hazardous waste, water quality, medical and infectious waste management, asbestos, radioactive waste, underground petroleum storage tanks, clean air, safe drinking water, and employee and community public awareness efforts regarding hazardous waste.

The greatest initial impact on universities has been the necessity to remove asbestos. Many institutions have completed or have in process costly asbestos abatement projects in residence halls, classrooms, and auxiliary services. Institutional claims against asbestos manufacturers and suppliers are in litigation. Technical guidance for asbestos abatement can be found in *Guidance for Controlling Asbestos-Containing Materials in Buildings* (U.S. Environmental Protection Agency, 1985).

Health centers have also been made to comply with medical waste disposal requirements. Additional requirements to document medical waste disposal were also established; technical guidance can be found in the *Guide for Infectious Waste Management* (U.S. Environmental Protection Agency, 1986).

Televised Football

The most unusual example of the influence of a federal bureaucracy on colleges and universities is the effort of the Federal Trade Commission (FTC) to assert jurisdiction over the televising of College Football Association (CFA) games. The FTC is statutorily authorized to enforce antitrust statutes against the for-profit sector. The CFA membership includes sixty-six superpower football teams in both public and private nonprofit institutions of higher education.

After an investigation, the FTC charged the CFA and a television holding company (which owns ABC and ESPN) with antitrust constraint of trade in the marketing of college football. The FTC objected to the CFA contracting for all its member institutions. The CFA and some of the member institutions challenged the FTC's assertion of jurisdiction on the fundamental ground that the CFA and its member institutions are not for-profit. The FTC staff took the position, supported by the Knight Commission Report on Intercollegiate Athletics, that the CFA member football programs are in fact for-profit.

In August 1991, an FTC administrative judge held for the CFA and the member institutions. However, an appeal has been taken by the FTC. Two factors argue against the success of the appeal. First, the Internal Revenue Service has ruled that revenue from athletics is generally not taxable. Second, the U.S. Congress has rejected the FTC's efforts to broaden its jurisdiction to nonprofit organizations.

Should the FTC jurisdiction over the televising of CFA football programs be sustained on appeal, the impact on the higher education community will be substantial. Colleges and universities have been considered nonprofit for many years. To define higher education or some of its components as for-profit ventures would influence policy far beyond football. Among many others, questions would arise over the legitimacy and the tax status of joint technology ventures, real estate development, research, and medical centers.

The effort by the FTC to assert jurisdiction over college football during a time when it stood by passively and watched leveraged buyouts and the resulting closing of facilities and loss of jobs leaves one puzzled about the mission of the FTC. This example, perhaps more clearly than any other in this chapter, shows how pernicious and how cynically applied some aspects of federal influence have become on higher education.

In a related example, in August 1991, Representative McMillen introduced legislation granting the National Collegiate Athletic Association (NCAA) a limited antitrust exemption in return for some "reforms." Under the proposed Collegiate Athletic Reform Act, individual colleges would be prohibited from contracting for televising of games, and the NCAA would be the sole contracting agent. Television revenues would be shared among NCAA members.

Tuition Price Fixing: Sherman Anti-Trust Act

As the preceding section suggests, colleges and universities have historically been little concerned with issues related to antitrust laws. Televising of college athletics, the FTC investigation of CFA football, and the *NCAA* v. *Board of Regents* (1984) case are notable exceptions.

In 1989, however, the Justice Department began a tuition price-fixing investigation of twenty-three highly selective institutions in the Northeast and added an additional group of institutions later on. The Justice Department asserted that these institutions' practice of sharing financial aid award information, tuition and fee increases, and faculty and staff salary raises prior to implementation was a violation of the antitrust act. The institutions asserted that the sharing of information was intended to equalize the opportunity for students to attend any institution regardless of parental resources. The matter was eventually settled, in part by a consent decree in which the institutions agreed to cease sharing this information.

The message in this case is clear. Barring some congressional action, the Department of Justice, like the Federal Trade Commission, will seek to apply the Sherman Anti-Trust Act to nonprofit entities. Nonprofit status by itself will not be sufficient to avoid the effect of the Sherman Act when the Justice Department raises the issue. A full discussion of these issues is provided in "Private Colleges and Tuition Price Fixing: An Anti-Trust Primer" (Richmond, 1991).

Sale of Goods and Services

An issue publicly debated in the 1980s concerned nonprofits' competing with the private sector in offering for sale goods or services. This competition is most visible in the sale by nonprofit colleges and universities of computers and computer supplies, time, and records; textbooks; and travel services. Also at issue was the rental of residence hall space during summers to non-student groups. At least two cases were litigated. *Sunshine Books* v. *Temple University* (1982) had to do with retail sale of textbooks by a university bookstore. *Cowboy Books, Ltd.,* v. *Board of Regents* (1989) involved the extension of credit to students by the university bookstore, a practice that the plaintiffs declared was anticompetitive.

There has been a long history of nonprofit colleges and universities providing housing, food, and medical services in direct competition with the private sector, and the U.S. military establishment's base stores directly compete with the private sector. Nevertheless, nearly forty states have considered bills or executive orders requiring public colleges not to compete with the private sector in the provision of goods and services (*Business Officer,* July 1991). These bills, which require that auxiliary enterprises be contracted out to private, tax-paying vendors, suggest that an institution must rent out student union space to a group outside the institution at a rate equivalent to that charged by a commercial hotel in the community for meeting space.

Debate on this subject will be accelerated by difficult economic conditions. One national lobbying group, which tried to get federal legislation on this subject, is now proceeding state by state and is promoting a "model" bill in the state legislatures; this would prohibit any nonprofit college or university from selling any product or service that could be provided by a for-profit, tax-paying business unless an exclusion is specifically authorized by law. The model bill could open the door for legislative interference into traditional internal institutional services such as concerts, dances, janitorial services, maintenance, psychological counseling, catering, health centers, recreational facilities, and security.

Two states, Ohio and Louisiana, have recently considered legislation based on the model bill. The Ohio bill would create the Private Enterprise Review Commission, which would be empowered to review the commercial activities of state agencies and to prohibit any activities that it finds inappropriate. The Louisiana bill is similar and includes the authority of the review commission to seek injunctive relief and to authorize private companies to sue for damages or injunction (*Business Officer*, Sept. 1991).

Higher Education and State Government

During the last two decades, two major changes have occurred in the relationship of higher education to state government. First, state legislatures are increasingly adopting legislation affecting institutions. Second, higher education state bureaucracies and national professional associations serving them have been created. For example, the city of Denver now hosts both the Education Commission for the States and the Office of State and Higher Education Executives. These associations reflect the general trend toward the establishment of a state-level higher education bureaucracy standing atop a college- or university-system bureaucracy. The state bureaucracy typically exercises a number of powers, including data collection, academic program review and control, student assessment, and budget control.

Traditionally, the relationship of the states and higher education in the public sector fell into one of two categories. In the first, a handful of states have provided constitutional autonomy for the state university. In the second category, public higher education is considered a public agency, fully accountable to the governor and the legislature and treated the same as any other stage agency. A third option that has emerged over the years is called by some a quasi-independent partnership. In this option, a state provides enabling legislation, financial support at some level, a bureaucracy that links state government to the institutions, a requirement to adhere to some fundamental state policies, and a separate lay board to establish policy for a system or an institution of higher education.

State higher education commissions or boards are, however, exercising a much more significant role in the governance of public institutions in recent years. In the next decade, it seems likely that the role of the state higher education bureaucracy may further strengthen. Factors such as the economy, a change in national defense posture, and work-force demographics — combined with more intense competition for state resources — all increase this likelihood. Under such conditions, the higher education bureaucracy will more and more often act as an arbitrator for both public and private higher education (Hines, 1988).

Summary

This chapter has briefly discussed some of the issues where federal or state legislation or judicial decisions have had a significant impact on the higher education enterprise. The list is not exhaustive but is representative of the influence of government on colleges and universities. A major theme of the chapter is that the influence of both federal and state government on higher education in general, and on student affairs in particular, has grown significantly since 1970 and appears likely to continue to increase in the next decade. Economic conditions, tax-law reform, junk bond financing of corporate takeovers, and major shifts in national defense procurement and deployment priorities may heighten governmental deficits and intensify competition for scarce resources between all levels of education and other state and social entities. The extent to which institutions obtain resources and the content and character of their academic programs, student services, campus environment, and research and service efforts will be increasingly affected by federal and state policy.

It is indeed paradoxical that in the 1970s and 1980s — when many service industries in this country, including airlines and savings and loans were deregulated — higher education has come under increasing control. Perhaps the positive side of that regulation is that colleges and universities, unlike the savings and loan industry, are still alive. In addition, in comparison to other types of regulated industries, institutions of higher education appear to reflect more closely the intent of the framers of the Declaration of Independence and their belief that "all men [and women] are created equal." Despite the all-too-obvious flaws and failures, governmental regulation has brought higher education to women, minorities, and the disabled. It has encouraged the creation of learning environments that are more likely to be fundamentally fair communities of scholars and students, places where judgments are based on facts. Further, through such regulation, the possibility exists for communities less affected by crime and environmental error. The expense and burden of governmental regulation are, however, not insignificant, and the continued adoption of statutes and regulations by federal and state government with no appropriation to cover attendant institutional costs remains a matter of considerable concern.

References

Alexander, L. Press release. May 1991.

Business Officer. Sept. 1991, pp. 46–49.

Business Officer, July 1991, pp. 7–8.

Equal Employment Opportunity Commission. *Guidelines on Sexual Harassment.* Washington, D.C.: Equal Employment Opportunity Commission, 1980.

Hines, E. R. *Higher Education and State Government: Renewed Partnership: Cooperation or Competition.* ASHE-ERIC Higher Education Report, no. 5. 1988.

Kaplin, W. A. *The Law of Higher Education: A Comprehensive Guide to Legal Implications of Administrative Decision Making.* (2nd ed.) San Francisco: Jossey-Bass, 1985.

Keller, E. "Consensual Amorous Relationships Between Faculty and Students: The Constitutional Right to Privacy." *Journal of College and University Law,* Summer 1988, *15* (1), 21–42.

McClamrock, D. "The First Amendment and Public Funding of Religious-Controlled or Affiliated Higher Education." *Journal of College and University Law,* Winter 1991, *17,* 381–428.

Richmond, D. R. "Private Colleges and Tuition Price Fixing: An Anti-Trust Primer." *Journal of College and University Law,* Winter 1991, *17,* 271–306.

Rothstein, L. "Students, Faculty, and Staff with Disabilities: Current Issues for Colleges and Universities." *Journal of College and University Law,* Summer 1991, *18,* 471–482.

Steinberg, T. N. "Rape on College Campuses: Reform Through Title IX." *Journal of College and University Law,* Summer 1991, *18,* 39–71.

U.S. Department of Justice. *Hate Crime Reporting Guidelines.* Washington, D.C.: U.S. Department of Justice, 1990.

U.S. Environmental Protection Agency. *Guidance for Controlling Asbestos-Containing Materials in Buildings.* Washington, D.C.: Environmental Protection Agency, 1985.

U.S. Environmental Protection Agency. *Guide for Infectious Waste Management.* Washington, D.C.: Environmental Protection Agency, 1986.

Ward, J. A. "Race-Exclusive Scholarships: Do They Violate the Constitution and Title VI of the Civil Rights Act of 1964?" *Journal of College and University Law,* Summer 1991, *18,* 73–103.

Cases

Adams v. *Bell,* 711 F.2d 161 (D.C. Cir. 1983) en banc.

Adams v. *Richardson,* 356 F.Supp. 92 (D.D.C. 1973), affirmed 480 F.2d 1159 (D.C. Cir.) 1973.

Alexander v. *Yale University,* 459 F.Supp. 1 (D. Conn. 1977), affirmed, 631 F.2d 178 (2d Cir. 1980).

Bacon v. *Bradley-Bourbonnais High School District No. 307,* 707 F.Supp. 1005 (C.D. Ill. 1989).

Bauer v. *Kincaid,* 759 F.Supp. 575 (W.D. Mo. S.D. 1991).

Board of Education of Westside Community v. *Mergens,* 110 S.Ct. 2536 (1990).

Brown v. *Board of Education,* 347 U.S. 483 (1954).

Chapman v. *Thomas,* 743 F.2d 102 (4th Cir. 1984).

Clark v. *United States,* 886 F.2d 404 (D.C. Cir. 1989).

Cowboy Books, Ltd., v. *Board of Regents,* 782 F.Supp. 1518 (W.D. Okla. 1989).

Doherty v. *Southern College of Optometry,* 862 F.2d 570 (6th Cir. 1988) cert. den. (1989).

Garnett v. *Renton School District No. 403,* 874 F.2d 608 (9th Cir. 1989) cert. granted and judgment vacated, 110 S. Ct. 2608 (1990).

Gay Rights Coalition of Georgetown University v. *Georgetown University*, 536 A.2d 1 (D.C. 1987).

Jager v. *Douglas Co. School Dist.*, 862 F.2d 824 (11th Cir. 1988), cert. den. 109 S. Ct. 2431 (1989).

Lipsett v. *University of Puerto Rico*, 864 F.2d 881 (1st Cir. 1988).

Missouri ex rel Gaines v. *Canada*, 306 U.S. 337 (59 S.Ct. 232 1938).

NCAA v. *Board of Regents*, 468 U.S. 85 (1984).

Pfeiffer v. *Marion Center Area School District*, 917 F.2d 779 (3rd Cir. 1990).

Piazzola v. *Watkins*, 442 F.2d 284 (5th Cir. 1971).

Poderesky v. *Board of Regents*, (U.S.D.C. Md. 1991).

Roberts v. *Madigan*, 702 F.Supp. 1505. 1505 (D. Colo. 1989).

Samuelson v. *Texas Women's University* (unreported S.D. Tex. 1989).

Southeastern Community College v. *Davis*, 442 U.S. 397 (1979).

State of Washington v. *Chrisman*, 102 S.CT. 812 (1982).

Sunshine Books v. *Temple University*, 697 F.2d 90 (3rd Cir. 1982).

Sweatt v. *Painter*, 339 U.S. 629 (1950).

University of Pennsylvania v. *EEOC*, 1105 S.Ct. 577 (1990).

Widmar v. *Vincent*, 102 S.Ct. 269 (1981).

35

Applying Professional Standards in Student Affairs Programs

William A. Bryan
Richard H. Mullendore

Professional standards for student affairs have been developing for more than twenty-five years. During this time, there has been an ever-increasing thrust toward professionalism in student affairs practice. The field of student affairs has also become widely recognized as an essential partner in the higher education enterprise. The field has grown in stature, and its professionals have gained greater competency and credibility on the modern-day college campus. This chapter focuses on the use of professional standards as a means to assess the overall effectiveness of student affairs programs. Readers will be provided with an overview of standards and their uses. It is hoped that they will also be motivated to implement standards on their campuses if they have not already done so.

Development and Impact of Professional Standards

Since the early 1960s, student affairs staffs, through their national associations, have articulated standards for the profession.

Professional Standards — A Perspective

As Mable (1991, p. 5) states, "During the past decade, student affairs professionals have become increasingly aware of the need for a well defined set of standards for student services and development programs." Leadership has been provided by numerous professional associations, which have undertaken efforts to establish standards and guidelines in specific, as well as general, student affairs service areas (Bryan, Winston, and Miller, 1991). Major initiatives undertaken by professional associations include the following:

• 1964 — The American College Health Association published standards and practices for college health programs.

• 1964 — The Council of Student Personnel Associations in Higher Education (COSPA) "submitted to the profession at large for its consideration the document 'A Proposal for Professional Preparation in College Student Personnel Work'" (Miller, 1991, p. 46). (A final statement was published after the dissolution of COSPA.)

• 1970 — A task force composed of counseling center directors wrote guidelines for university and college counseling centers.

• 1973 — The Association for Counselor Education and Supervision sponsored a set of professional standards to be used for accrediting counseling and personnel services programs.

• 1979 — The National Association of College and University Food Services called for standards to assess levels of operational performance.

• 1979 — The American Council on Education (ACE) prepared six guidelines for colleges and universities related to student affairs: "(1) Policy Guidelines for Refund of Student Charges, (2) Joint Statement on Principles for Good Practice in College Admissions and Recruitment, (3) Collegiate Athletics Policy Statements, (4) Joint Statement on Transfer and Award of Academic Credits, (5) Joint Statement on Standards of Satisfactory Academic Progress to Maintain Financial Aid Eligibility, [and] (6) Academic Integrity and Athletic Eligibility" (Mable, 1991, p. 6).

• 1979 — The American College Personnel Association Executive Council adopted "Standards for the Preparation of Counselors and College Student Affairs Specialists at Master's Degree Level" as official preparation standards (Miller, 1991, p. 47).

• 1981 — The National Intramural-Recreational Sports Association adopted collegiate recreational sports standards.

• 1981 — The National Association for Foreign Student Affairs approved self-regulation principles for international education exchange.

• 1984 — The National Association of State Universities and Land Grant Colleges published the *Statement of Principles on Student Outcomes Assessment.*

• 1984 — The American Council on Education published a series of resource documents: *Achieving Reasonable Campus Security* (1984a), *Student Athletic Drug Testing Programs* (1984c), and *Alcohol and Other Substance Abuse: Resources for Institutional Action* (1984b).

- 1985 — The Association of College and University Housing Officers — International established standards pertaining to "staff and graduate educational programs, accreditation self-studies, collegiate community information projects, and assistance to outside agencies concerned with student housing" (Mable, 1991, pp. 7–8).
- 1985 — The Council for the Accreditation of Counseling and Related Education Programs published the revised *Accreditation Procedures Manual and Application for Counseling and Related Educational Programs*.
- 1986 — The Council for the Advancement of Standards for Student Services/Development Programs (CAS) published a set of general standards and sixteen statements of standards and guidelines for functional areas in student affairs.

The guidelines and standards statements listed here have provided a major impetus for our developing profession. The primary focus for this chapter will be the use of the CAS standards, due to their comprehensiveness and their application to many functional areas.

CAS Standards Background Information

The American College Testing Program, on behalf of CAS, made these standards available to the higher education community in 1986. They represented over six years of collaborative work by student affairs leaders in twenty-two professional associations. Mable (1991, p. 11) describes the process leading to the development of the CAS standards and guidelines:

> In June 1979 a meeting of student affairs professional association representatives was held to consider the desirability and feasibility of establishing professional standards and accreditation programs in student affairs. This meeting was indeed a milestone as it evidenced the need for an interassociation approach to addressing standards in student services and development programs, as well as an interest in accreditation initiatives. Subsequently, an invitational conference was held in October 1979 to bring together representatives from as many interested student services associations as possible. Their goal was to examine accreditation as a quality-assurance function for the student affairs profession, both for academic professional preparation programs and functional areas for the practice of student services.

The conference led to the initiative to create standards for the profession. Jim Vickrey, president of the University of Montevallo, states in the foreword to the guidelines (1986, p. vii), "CAS has moved ahead commendably . . . to set forth standards and guidelines for professional practice. In doing so, CAS not only has established the student affairs profession as a leader in the self regulation movement, but also has encouraged other higher education associations to go and do likewise."

CAS initially published sixteen functional-area standards and guidelines for student affairs programs. More recently, standards for three additional functional areas have been added: women, student programs, and services; admission programs and services; and alcohol and other drug programs. As a result of the publication and distribution of CAS's work to every institution of U.S. higher education, student affairs professionals are now more aware of the need for and the valuable assistance provided by well-defined standards and guidelines for student affairs functional areas.

The CAS publications are historic documents for our field. Never before have so many student affairs professional associations worked together for the common good in student services and development programs. As can be seen with the continued work of CAS, development of standards is a process that will evolve as necessary for professionals to continue providing high-quality services to students. As Bryan and Mullendore remark (1991, p. 29), "From the upper ranks of the chief executive officer and the chief student affairs officer on down the administrative hierarchy, a challenge is presented to those who work in the student affairs profession on a daily basis: effectively apply and operationalize these standards in the collegiate setting."

Impact of Professional Standards on Student Affairs

The development of professional standards in the past twenty-five years has assisted student affairs staffs in meeting the goal of increased professionalism. This increased emphasis on professionalism, according to Winston and Moore (1991, p. 63), "has necessitated the formulation of a new mission that goes beyond the mere provision of support services for the academic development of college students and the maintenance of discipline."

Student affairs standards provide focus, direction, and a greatly needed new perspective to student affairs practice. They "proffer a guiding vision of substance and integrity and stable and permanent criteria against which to measure out of class education, involvement, and learning pertaining to student development" (Mable, 1991, p. 16). Our practice is now more substantial as we support and enhance the total education of the student; it calls for a monitoring of services and programs to determine their true value.

Additionally, professional standards can have significant impact on student affairs in the following areas:

1. Program development: standards and guidelines can provide an excellent blueprint for program establishment and enhancement as divisions of student affairs seek to determine ways to respond to the unique needs of students.

2. Staff development: using professional standards sets the stage for self-assessment and evaluation and the comprehensive study of one or more different program areas; this can lead to positive development experiences when staff members are involved in the assessment of their areas of responsibility as well as those beyond their purview.

3. Comparisons across institutions: using professional standards and guidelines provides the opportunity for staff members to compare their programs with those at similar institutions due to consistency of language and format.

4. Development and enhancement of program credibility: professional standards can be helpful in reducing the credibility gap between the student affairs staff and other constituencies when the process of their development involves varied university personnel and when many different occasions and settings are used to deliver information.

5. Institutional acceptance of programs and departments: professional standards assist student affairs divisions to define clear missions and objectives; articulate the value of services and student development programs to many different university constituencies; and involve students, faculty, and staff in identifying the needs for programs and services.

6. Education of the campus community and external constituencies (discussed later in this chapter): professional standards and their implementation make it possible for faculty, staff, and students to participate collaboratively in assessment and evaluation of functional areas; they create an occasion for these constituencies to understand the value of division-initiated proposals and recommendations.

7. Improved political maneuverability: as in the academic, business, and athletic arena, student affairs professional standards can provide minimal national statements that are easily understood and accepted as a rationale for needed institutional and political change.

8. Budgetary assistance: professional standards, as a minimum statement of expectations, can be helpful in making a case for additional program financial support that can be developed over a period of time.

9. Accreditation self-study (discussed later in this chapter): the development of program statements for functional areas following the outline of CAS standards can be extremely helpful in completing divisional self-studies.

10. Program evaluation and assessment (discussed later in this chapter): professional standards provide a comprehensive and consistent framework for program evaluation and assessment activities (Bryan and Mullendore, 1991, pp. 31–32).

As we will see, professional standards can have influence in even more areas. Yet they cannot make a difference if they remain a set of documents on an office shelf. Standards must be fully operationalized in each functional area, and they must be used frequently to maintain their value and import. The next section provides guidance on ways to use the standards on an ongoing basis.

Use of Professional Standards

With the development of professional standards, student affairs staff have excellent tools to create, expand, explain, and defend important campus services and student development programs. The challenge for the student affairs professional continues to be the development and implementation of ways to use these standards in a coherent manner.

Use of Professional Standards for Planning

As Tincher (1983, p. 436) suggests, planning involves "a conscious choice of ideas, goals, objectives, program structure, and action patterns designed to coordinate efforts of people for some period of time toward chosen broad goals." Professional standards provide statements of consensus by professional leaders in higher education regarding minimum essential elements expected of any institution conducting student services–development programs in higher education. CAS standards and guidelines, for example, give direct guidance to campus student affairs efforts to devise programs that meet student needs and make it possible to evaluate student affairs functional areas against minimum requirements.

Bryan and Mullendore state (1991, p. 38), "By integrating CAS standards into a student affairs planning process, each functional area can determine future (or annual) objectives that relate to each component within the functional area standard." Divisions of student affairs can maintain viability as well as visibility through the use of professional standards if they are integrated into their annual planning materials and if they are shared beyond department and division lines. As a division of student affairs is initially developing statements of functional-area standards, it is important to involve faculty and staff in the self-evaluation to ensure objectivity and credibility. Bringing faculty into the process is especially helpful in other ways, too. Faculty members can learn how various student affairs departments operate and what types and levels of services are provided. As a result, they often become advocates for student affairs programs. Once the standards are in place, those on the staff should continue to communicate with and involve others in planning and in annual review of compliance with standards. This process can assist the division in moving beyond minimal compliance, justify additional budget requests, and provide impetus for change. For a discussion of applying CAS standards and guidelines to a division's program planning materials, refer to Bryan and Mullendore (1991).

Use of Professional Standards for Assessment and Evaluation

Professional standards establish a bench mark that a division of student affairs can use to assess strengths and deficiencies as it seeks to improve programs. CAS has published self-assessment guides that provide an opportunity for an in-depth assessment of a program and its compliance with the CAS standards. Another approach is the development of program statements (Bryan and Mullendore, 1991) for functional areas and of recommendations where there is noncompliance with CAS standards and guidelines. These program statements can be developed by an advisory group or ad hoc committee through a self-study process. Group participation is quite helpful to a program director who is seeking independent, objective assessment of a functional area. Using either approach (self-assessment guides or program statements) can assist in the initial and ongoing evaluation of a program. If student affairs professionals are good stewards and use professional standards appropriately, they can enhance the learning and development of students and can also be accountable to their various constituencies on campus.

As Winston and Moore (1991, p. 77) suggest, the use of standards is "a double edged sword. The standards clearly require that student affairs divisions carefully evaluate the effectiveness of the services and programs offered and investigate the effect or outcome associated with them. If a student affairs division fails to institute effective, comprehensive outcomes assessment programs, it conspicuously falls short of the minimum CAS standards and probably forfeits the protection that standards potentially afford." Standards are virtually useless unless there is consistent movement toward compliance through an ongoing outcomes evaluation program within each functional area.

Use of Professional Standards for Division and Program Productivity

Consistent use of professional standards in a division of student affairs should enhance program productivity. A division that develops a planning and evaluation process and integrates professional standards into its work can significantly increase productivity by focusing on appropriate goals and establishing suitable priorities.

The value of CAS standards and guidelines has been affirmed by many professionals. Terrence Hogan (letter to the authors, Nov. 15, 1991), director of student activities, Ohio University, states, "The standards have provided us with a sense of collective professional opinion of our colleagues as to what our mission, goals, and objectives should be. They have served as a common point of reference for us as we work toward defining our future." Paula Rooney (letter to the authors, Nov. 11, 1991), vice president for student affairs, Babson College, views the standards as a mechanism for evaluation; she says, "I feel it was a useful tool in finding our weak areas, which could then be incorporated into the following year's plan. It was also valuable as a gauge of how well we were doing, which was helpful in being able to clearly articulate the services we provide."

Martha Brown, associate dean of students, Creighton University, also sees the standards as useful in planning and assessment. In addition, she indicates, "They have also been instrumental in demonstrating to other administrative and academic areas on campus that student services departments have a common base across institutions" (letter to the authors, Nov. 18, 1991). Angela Terry, assistant vice president and director of planning and assessment, University of Connecticut, says, "CAS standards proved invaluable to department heads in the identification of functional areas in need of further development. Furthermore, these standards were a useful tool for reasoned decision making relative to resource and goal-objective priorities" (letter to the authors, Nov. 1, 1991).

Dana Burnett, vice president for student services and dean of students, Old Dominion University, believes that the standards have filled a void and states, "I only hope that they will be utilized more broadly in the future by groups, such as accrediting bodies and state governing boards in the resource allocation process" (letter to the authors, Nov. 5, 1991).

Use of Professional Standards for Regional Accreditation Self-Studies

"Accreditation is a system for recognizing educational institutions and professional programs affiliated with those institutions for a level of performance, integrity, and quality which entitles them to the confidence of the educational community and the public they serve" (Council on Postsecondary Accreditation, 1988, p. 3).

As stated previously, CAS standards and guidelines can be used as a self-study tool in reviewing basic components: mission, program, organization and administration, human resources, funding, facilities, campus and community relations, ethics, or evaluation in student affairs functional areas. Whether an institution uses CAS self-assessment guides or follows a procedure of developing program statements with recommendations, either approach will be extremely helpful in preparing for regional accreditation review.

Regardless of purpose, this can be an annual process. Statements for all functional areas can be prepared for a division and made available to any management group within the university. They can assist a division in its annual process of determining new objectives, solutions to problems, and future innovations that will enhance the work of a particular functional area.

Case Examples of Professional Standards Use

Since the appearance of the CAS standards, their use has been encouraged and discussed at professional meetings. Although "the utilization of student services standards is in its infancy" (Marron, 1991, p. 95), divisions of student affairs at institutions of higher education are increasingly using CAS standards and guidelines for a variety of purposes, some of which are described here.

Using CAS Standards for Accreditation Self-Study

The division of student affairs at the University of North Carolina at Wilmington (UNCW) began using CAS standards when they were available in draft form in 1985. Before the publication of the final document in 1986, the division developed an approach for operationalizing standards and guidelines designed to provide campuswide education regarding the division's mission and purpose, increase division-department credibility, and assist some program areas in responding to budget needs. Bryan and Mullendore (1991) describe the process followed at UNCW as the "program statement approach"; it produced a comprehensive program overview and a thorough examination of CAS standards and guidelines as a total package for application to a division's work. Individual functional-area standards were reviewed and revised where necessary on an annual basis as part of the divisional planning process. All functional-area program statements incorporated the basic components listed previously.

As UNCW approached the accreditation process conducted by the Southern Association of Colleges and Schools (SACS) during 1990–1991, the division thoroughly reviewed all program statements and added an additional section with specific recommendations for moving programs into compliance with CAS standards and guidelines. In responding to requests for information from the institutional subcommittee dealing with student development services, the division extracted content from existing CAS program statements for functional areas. These program statements were developed from an intensive self-study process that had occurred four years before the institutional reaccreditation self-study began. (Each functional area updates these program statements annually.) The content from the program statements, with minimal additional information, created a basis for the institutional subcommittee to conduct its study and to complete the section on student development services responding to the requirements of SACS. According to the members of the campus subcommittee dealing with education and support services and the Self-Study Steering Committee, the material provided by the division greatly assisted the development of this section of the self-study report. As opposed to that occurring on a ten-year basis, self-study using CAS standards and guidelines takes place on an annual basis within the division of student affairs at the University of North Carolina at Wilmington.

Using CAS Standards for Salary Justification

In the fall of 1990, a memo was distributed from the North Dakota Office of Central Personnel in Bismarck, North Dakota, to every state agency indicating that most personnel classification categories had been appraised and were to be adjusted as of January 1, 1991 (Gordon H. Henry, letter to the authors, Jan. 3, 1992). Attached to the memo was a document showing the various state job classifications separated into three categories: (1) position classifications that were currently graded below where they should be and therefore needing to be increased in pay grades; (2) position classifications to be maintained at the current pay grades; (3) position classifications above appropriate pay grades and therefore needing to be downgraded. Most of the position classification categories for student affairs positions were in the number-three category. These positions were to be reclassified to lower pay grades unless information came forward that could influence the state Central Personnel Office to reconsider. Gordon Henry, vice president for student affairs at the University of North Dakota, Dick Jenkins, vice president for student affairs at Minot State University, and Jennifer Gladden, dean of student services at Bismarck State College, used CAS standards and guidelines to educate the state Central Personnel Office regarding job responsibilities and position requirements for all student affairs positions. CAS standards, along with updated position descriptions from throughout the state, were so convincing that the Central Personnel Office developed a new set of specifications. As a result, the average pay grades were determined to be two to six pay grades *below* where they should have been. Therefore, instead of taking severe downgrading of their pay grades, most student affairs staff in North Dakota received significant equity raises.

Reflecting on this incident, Gordon Henry (letter to the authors, Jan. 3, 1992) states, "Overall, the CAS standards provided the foundation and the support to assist in helping people to understand the profession. I'm not sure that we would have been able to pull this off if it had not been for the CAS standards."

Uses Identified by Survey

In the fall of 1991, the authors conducted a review of the 1990–91 National Orientation Directors Association Data Bank and identified institutions stating that they currently used CAS standards. Typically, a survey was sent to the chief student affairs officer and the orientation director on each campus. One hundred and thirty-nine individuals were surveyed on seventy-four university campuses. Seven schools indicated they were not currently using these standards. Thirty-eight usable surveys (27 percent) were returned out of a total of 139. Institutions asked to identify the ways in which they had used CAS standards responded as follows:

Orientation. The standards were employed to evaluate and improve orientation programs amid a changing student population; assess them in terms of compliance with the CAS standards and guidelines; design a program for new, transfer, and special-population students; train orientation team members regarding the purpose of their work and the needs of new students; evaluate the position of coordinator of orientation, the team, and the program's goals; set goals for the university's new-student orientation program; and develop a mission statement for student-parent orientation and a checklist in developing a comprehensive program.

Self-Study. As we saw earlier, CAS standards made an invaluable contribution to UNCW's self-study. They have also been used to guide a North Central Association self-study; produce an accreditation report; assist (in preparation for a SACS accreditation visit) in redefining goals, objectives, and assessment processes in the division; conduct a unit-by-unit review within a division in preparing for a site visit by the commissioner on higher education of the Middle States Association of Schools and Colleges; provide for evaluation, planning, and review and help in planning all student affairs functional areas (as part of the planning document). They have assisted in creating universitywide strategic planning, in focusing required components of research and evaluation activity for department heads, in furnishing the primary criteria for faculty committees assigned to evaluate and offer recommendations about specific student services programs, and in meeting strategic planning efforts for the entire division of student affairs. They have been the basis of an evaluation process involving departments in a student affairs division (CAS self-assessment guides) and have offered a means to evaluate deficiencies and determine whether or not particular areas were in compliance. The standards have acted as an instrument for self-assessment, a guide to assess the structure and purpose of new programs, an evaluation instrument for gathering data to build programs and services, a self-evaluation instrument for all departments, a guide in supplementing institutional effectiveness standards and assuring student development needs were addressed (with a focus on effectiveness and emphasis toward excellence), and a baseline for long-range planning.

Other Uses

CAS standards can be helpful for many other tasks. They can be used to develop a framework to evaluate the counseling and development center; to define departmental mission, goal, and objective statements; or to assist in a formal review of the university judicial system. As we have seen, the most common use of CAS standards and guidelines is for evaluation, planning, and review within a division of student affairs or within individual functional areas.

Summary

With the continuing development of professional standards, student affairs appears to be an emerging profession, one that is continuing its growth to maturity. The use of professional standards in student affairs is greatly dependent on the chief student affairs officer's awareness of their value. Professional standards provide a valuable educational tool for student affairs professionals to educate various constituencies regarding the mission of a division of student affairs. If operationalized, they can assist in program development, accreditation self-study, and enhancement of program and division credibility. They can also greatly aid a division in dealing with the political climate on a college campus. Standards create an opportunity for the staff to view strengths and weaknesses and thereby provide justification for program expansion and funding needs. By involving the faculty in the review process, they also assist academic colleagues in better understanding programs and services in student affairs and subsequently their contributions to the mission of the university. As Marron states (1991, p. 96), professional standards "provide an excellent tool for achieving the kind of successful practice to which all student affairs programs and personnel should aspire."

References

American Council on Education. *Achieving Reasonable Campus Security.* Washington, D.C.: American Council on Education, 1984a.

American Council on Education. *Alcohol and Other Substance Abuse: Resources for Institutional Action.* Washington, D.C.: American Council on Education, 1984b.

American Council on Education. *Student Athletic Drug Testing Programs.* Washington, D.C.: American Council on Education, 1984c.

Bryan, W. A., and Mullendore, R. H. "Operationalizing CAS Standards for Program Evaluation and Planning." In W. A. Bryan, R. B. Winston, Jr., and T. K. Miller (eds.), *Using Professional Standards in Student Affairs.* New Directions for Student Services, no. 53. San Francisco: Jossey-Bass, 1991.

Bryan, W. A., Winston, R. B., Jr., and Miller, T. K. (eds.). *Using Professional Standards in Student Affairs.* New Directions for Student Services, no. 53. San Francisco: Jossey-Bass, 1991.

Council for the Accreditation of Counseling and Related Education Programs. *Accreditation Procedures Manual and Application for Counseling-Related Programs.* Washington, D.C.: Council for the Accreditation of Counseling and Related Education Programs, 1985.

Council for the Advancement of Standards for Student Services/Development Programs. *Council for the Advancement of Standards: Standards and Guidelines for Student Services/Development Programs.* Washington, D.C.: Council for the Advancement of Standards for Student Services/Development Programs, 1986.

Council on Postsecondary Accreditation. *The COPA Handbook.* Washington, D.C.: Council on Postsecondary Accreditation, 1988.

Mable, P. "Professional Standards: An Introduction and Historical Perspective." In W. A. Bryan, R. B. Winston, Jr., and T. K. Miller (eds.), *Using Professional Standards in Student Affairs.* New Directions for Student Services, no. 53. San Francisco: Jossey-Bass, 1991.

Marron, J. M. "Example Applications of CAS Standards and Guidelines." In W. A. Bryan, R. B. Winston, Jr., and T. K. Miller (eds.), *Using Professional Standards in Student Affairs.* New Directions for Student Services, no. 53. San Francisco: Jossey-Bass, 1991.

Miller, T. K. "Using Standards in Professional Preparations." In W. A. Bryan, R. B. Winston, Jr., and T. K. Miller (eds.), *Using Professional Standards in Student Affairs*. New Directions for Student Services, no. 53. San Francisco: Jossey-Bass, 1991.

National Association of State Universities and Land Grant Colleges. *Statement of Principles on Outcomes Assessment*. Washington, D.C.: National Association of State Universities and Land-Grant Colleges, 1984.

Tincher, W. A. "Time Management and Planning for Student Affairs Professionals." In T. K. Miller, R. B. Winston, Jr., and W. R. Mendenhall (eds.), *Administration and Leadership in Student Affairs: Actualizing Student Development in Higher Education*. Muncie, Ind.: Accelerated Development, 1983.

Winston, R. B., Jr., and Moore, W. S. "Standards and Outcomes Assessment: Strategies and Tools." In W. A. Bryan, R. B. Winston, Jr., and T. K. Miller (eds.), *Using Professional Standards in Student Affairs*. New Directions for Student Services, no. 53. San Francisco: Jossey-Bass, 1991.

36

ᔍ

Becoming Successful
Student Affairs
Administrators

Margaret J. Barr

The agenda for student affairs and higher education is constantly evolving, and no one volume can describe all the issues and problems that are a part of each professional setting. This book is designed to cover the major issues involved in effective practice in student affairs. Without doubt, new concerns will arise in the decades ahead.

In this chapter, major themes regarding the conditions necessary for success as a student affairs administrator will be presented as well as advice on enjoying the profession of student affairs. The chapter closes with a list of readings recommended by the authors of this volume.

Each student affairs professional must make a commitment to ongoing development in order to meet the challenges of the future. We must keep current with issues, problems, and trends so that we can anticipate what is going to happen in our field of work. In addition, those in student affairs must undertake a program of lifelong learning through formal education, professional development programs, and personal investment of time and energy. Many options and opportunities have been discussed throughout this volume, but the commitment to improve skills and competencies has to rest with each individual. A broad range of resources are available— student affairs literature and professional associations, business and industry, government, other academic disciplines, and the popular press — but each professional must be willing to take advantage of them.

There is no question that higher education will be different in the future. New students, new agendas, changed fiscal support, changed expectations, and more complex problems will face each and every professional in student affairs. As we have seen, governmental influence within the academy is increasing from the legislative, executive, and judicial branches. At the same time, fiscal support for higher education is declining. Questions of liability and accountability are having more and more impact. Management responsibilities are becoming more complicated, and requirements for performance in administering budgets, facilities, and programs are stringent. Ethical questions are part of the daily lives of our students and each of us.

The following list highlights specific themes from this volume for student affairs professionals who wish to increase their administrative effectiveness.

Invest time, energy, and resources in staff. Never has the need for qualified staff in student affairs been more evident. Staff members in student affairs must be supported in their efforts, challenged to meet emerging priorities, exposed to theoretical constructs, assisted in translating theory to practice, and trained to accomplish necessary tasks. Failure to provide staff development programs, strong supervision, a good design for staff selection, training programs, and attention to the individual will mean mediocrity in the service that we offer our students and our institutions. In addition, we must devise means and methods to attract and retain qualified professionals in student affairs through graduate education and other means.

Make a commitment to diversity. The commitment to diversity must be real. Each of us is required to learn more about those who are different, to translate that learning into our daily lives, and to help our current students and our institutions prepare for the future challenges of diversity. Any tendency toward stereotyping and bigoted behavior must be confronted, both within ourselves and others, and it will not be easy. Support for diversity, which is demonstrated in large and small ways, is vital if we are going to serve today's and tomorrow's students.

Understand the implications of changing demographics. The demographic trends that will influence higher education in the coming years are clear. The goal is to adapt facilities, programs, and services to meet the needs of the new students entering higher education. Much of what we currently do must be evaluated to determine if our institutions are really responding to "new" students. Accommodations must be made that relate to ethnicity, age, part-time status, gender, sexual orientation, and disability. This approach does not mean that standards should be lowered or altered; rather, it reflects our responsibility to provide equal access for new learners to our programs, services, and facilities.

Increase your management skills. No longer can student affairs professionals assume (if they ever did) that management is someone else's responsibility.

fiscal constraints, huge facilities, a litigious society, and complex and diverse staffs require each of us to increase our management skills in order to be able to continue to provide high-quality services and programs. Technological advances must be carefully evaluated and integrated into management tasks to increase efficiency. In an era of more restricted fiscal support, lack of sound management judgment will result in lost effectiveness for student affairs.

Increase skills in managing conflict and crises. The choices faced in the future by higher education will create a competition for both resources and support. Demonstrated skills in conflict resolution and crisis management are essential. In an environment filled with ambiguity, ethical conduct is essential, and adherence to professional and ethical standards must be above question. Our work in student affairs will be directly related to our collective abilities to resolve difficult situations and demonstrate our commitment to the worth and dignity of every individual.

Gain understanding of your institution. It is crucial that each professional in student affairs know the institutional mission, the governance structure, and the key relationships on campus. Student affairs never stands alone and must be an integral part of the decision-making, policy development, and ongoing work of the institution. In order to function in that way, each professional must appreciate the unique characteristics of the institution and translate that understanding into appropriate management structures, staff supervision, and program development.

Understand that assessment and evaluation are essential. As we face our shared future, we must be able to articulate clearly what we do and why it takes so many of us to do it. Careful evaluation of programs, in concert with a commitment to modify or abandon ones that no longer meet student or institutional goals, is essential. Additive budgeting will not be the norm in the future, and it is only through reallocation of resources that we will be able to respond to emerging situations. A prerequisite to all evaluation is good program planning and the ability to set goals that are measurable or observable. We must be able to answer the key question of what will *not* be accomplished if a particular program or activity supported by student affairs is unavailable.

Assessment requires each student affairs professional to think beyond the immediate and to look at the long-range influence that student affairs interventions have on the growth and development of students. New skills and competencies will be necessary; no longer will our many publics be satisfied with vague answers about outcomes. Additional research on students and student subpopulations is also important. We can design programs successfully only if we understand the environment that our students negotiate on a daily basis and their needs, wants, and skills. Such research and assessment activities are no longer a luxury but are a necessity in a new age of accountability and increased expectations.

Understand the legal environment and governmental influence on student affairs. Ignorance of legal issues is not bliss. Each student affairs professional should remain current with the ever-changing legal, statutory, and regulatory factors influencing student affairs and higher education. Statutory requirements create new burdens that are unmitigated by additional funding; this circumstance, combined with concern about liability, means that careful planning and legal advice are essential.

Develop relationships across and beyond the campus. Strong and supportive relationships sustain all of us. They can also offer opportunities for collaboration and joint problem solving. If higher education is going to achieve the goal of creating communities of learning, it is my firm belief that student affairs professionals must take the lead. Strong and cooperative relationships with faculty and other administrative staff are necessary to the objectives of student affairs and higher education. In addition, key off-campus constituency groups must be identified, and communication must be established in positive and productive ways. Failure to establish these ties could cause problems that could have been avoided. Finally, both intrinsic and extrinsic rewards result from community involvement. That kind of involvement and volunteer experiences can help us to learn and develop as well as to form new personal and institutional connections.

Become involved professionally. Each of us needs challenge and stimulation in our work. Of course, many of us feel that we get enough challenge and more than enough stimulation in our daily work, but that is a faulty premise and will doom our efforts. Professional involvement assists us to be aware of current issues, helps us gain new skills, and creates a network of resources to call upon when needed. Participation can be at the local, state, regional, or national level. It can be in a specialty association in student affairs, in an academic discipline group, or in one of the generalist organizations serving student affairs. Whatever the choice, involvement is critical to professional staffs as we face the challenges of tomorrow. If we choose to remain isolated, relying on what we know and closing ourselves to new possibilities we may not be prepared for the future.

Read the literature. It is important to read not only the literature in student affairs and higher education but also news magazines, books about major issues, and business publications. We naturally cannot read everything, but a cooperative arrangement with colleagues can evolve where each pledges to keep others informed of new developments in a particular journal, magazine, or area of interest.

Enjoyment of Work

The following advice is from one professional to another. It focuses on the enjoyment of work, but it is my firm belief that these suggestions will also contribute to more effective administrative practice.

Enjoy the students. Students are essentially the reason why we got into this business in the first place. In the daily challenges of discipline problems, crisis situations, and chronic health and psychological problems involving students, we forget that most of them are doing just fine. In addition, when we spend hours with those in student government, fraternity and sorority leaders, and the "stars" of the campus, it is easy to forget the average student who is the mainstay of each of our campuses. It would behoove all of us to take time to enjoy the wonder of learning that many students experience and to appreciate their enthusiasm. I must often remind myself that I could fall into the trap of spending 80 percent of my time with 20 percent of the students. My goal is always to change that investment strategy in a significant way.

Become involved in the institution. Higher education is a stimulating environment in which to work. For the most part, we are surrounded by bright people who often do exceptional things. We must take advantage of those opportunities whenever our demanding schedules permit. We should hear lectures, attend plays, go to student concerts, take new faculty members to lunch, or play basketball at noon with a group of faculty and staff colleagues. Each of our institutions is rich in occasions for fun, excitement, enjoyment, and learning. If we fail to take advantage of our unique environment, we are the losers.

Maintain perspective. A sense of perspective and a sense of humor may be our most important qualities. All problems cannot and probably should not be solved at once, all plans will not go exactly as we would like them to, and all of us make errors. Keeping a proper perspective and a sense of humor can help each of us in maintaining balance and in finding joy in our chosen profession.

Take time to smell the roses. Each of us has favorite aspects of our lives: our family, our friends, our neighborhoods, favorite restaurants, walks in the park, travel, or sports. So often we student affairs professionals forget that we also have needs that must be attended to. If we fail to take care of ourselves, we will be unable to take care of others.

These suggestions are certainly not all that must be accomplished, but they are a way to start thinking about what might be useful in our professional practice. I strongly believe that this is a wonderful time to be a student affairs professional, even with all the challenges and problems that we face. My hope is that this volume will be of help to readers as they face those challenges on their own campus.

References

The authors in this volume were asked to recommend some additional readings that they felt would be particularly helpful to practitioners. The list that follows includes their suggestions but should not be seen as complete. It is merely a starting point.

Althen, G. (ed.). *Learning Across Cultures.* Washington, D.C.: National Association for Foreign Students, 1981.

Appleton, J. R., Briggs, C. M., and Rhatigan, J. J. *Pieces of Eight*. Portland, Oreg.: National Association of Student Personnel Administrators, Institute of Research and Development, 1978.

Association for the Study of Higher Education. *Directory of ASHE Membership and Higher Education Program Faculty*. Washington, D.C.: Association for the Study of Higher Education, 1987.

Astin, A. W. *Assessment for Excellence: The Philosophy and Practice of Assessment and Evaluation in Higher Education*. New York: American Council on Education, Macmillan, 1991.

Barr, M. J., Upcraft, M. L., and Associates. *New Futures for Student Affairs: Building a Vision for Professional Leadership and Practice*. San Francisco: Jossey-Bass, 1990.

Bennis, W. *Why Leaders Can't Lead: The Unconscious Conspiracy Continues*. San Francisco: Jossey-Bass, 1989.

Birnbaum, R. *How Colleges Work: The Cybernetics of Academic Organization and Leadership*. San Francisco: Jossey-Bass, 1988.

Boyer, E. L. *College: The Undergraduate Experience in America*. New York: HarperCollins, 1987.

Brown, R. D. *Performance Appraisal as a Tool for Staff Development*. New Directions for Student Services, no. 43. San Francisco: Jossey-Bass, 1988.

Carnegie Foundation for the Advancement of Teaching. *Campus Life: In Search of Community*. Lawrenceville, N.J.: Carnegie Foundation for the Advancement of Teaching, 1990.

Cohen, A. M., and Brawer, F. B. *The American Community College*. (2nd ed.) San Francisco: Jossey-Bass, 1989.

Council for the Advancement of Standards for Student Services/Development Programs. *Council for the Advancement of Standards: Standards and Guidelines for Student Services/Development Programs*. Washington, D.C.: Council for the Advancement of Standards for Student Services/Development Programs, 1986.

Cross, K. P. *Adults as Learners: Increasing Participation and Facilitating Learning*. San Francisco: Jossey-Bass, 1981.

Deegan, W. L. *Managing Student Affairs Programs: Methods, Models and Muddles*. Palm Springs, Calif.: ETC Publications, 1981.

Delworth, U., Hanson, G. R., and Associates. *Student Services: A Handbook for the Profession*. (2nd ed.) San Francisco: Jossey-Bass, 1989.

Erwin, T. D. *Assessing Student Learning and Development: A Guide to the Principles, Goals, and Methods of Determining College Outcomes*. San Francisco: Jossey-Bass, 1991.

Evans, N. J. (ed.). *Facilitating the Development of Women*. New Directions for Student Services, no. 29. San Francisco: Jossey-Bass, 1985.

Flawn, P. T. *A Primer for University Presidents: Managing the Modern University*. Austin: University of Texas Press, 1990.

Fleming, J. *Blacks in Colleges: A Comparative Study of Students' Success in Black and in White Institutions*. San Francisco: Jossey-Bass, 1984.

Guba, E., and Lincoln, Y. *Fourth Generation Evaluation.* Newbury Park, Calif.: Sage Publications, 1989.

Hall, R. M., and Sandler, B. R. *Out of the Classroom: A Chilly Climate for Women.* Washington, D.C.: Association of American Colleges, 1984.

Hanson, G. R. *The Assessment of Student Development and Outcomes: A Review and Critique of Assessment Instruments.* Trenton: College Outcomes Evaluation Program, New Jersey Department of Higher Education, 1989.

Jacoby, B. *The Student as Commuter: Developing a Comprehensive Institutional Response.* ASHE-ERIC Higher Education Report, no. 7. Washington, D.C.: American Association for Higher Education, 1989.

Jenkins, H. M., and Associates. *Educating Students from Other Nations.* Washington, D.C.: National Association of Foreign Student Advisors, 1981.

Kaplin, W. A. *The Law of Higher Education: A Comprehensive Guide to Legal Implications of Administrative Decision Making.* (2nd ed.) San Francisco: Jossey-Bass, 1985.

Keim, M., and Graham, J. W. (eds.). *Directory of Graduate Preparation Programs in College Student Personnel, 1990.* Washington, D.C.: American College Personnel Association, 1990.

Kuh, G., and McAleenan, A. (eds.). *Private Dreams, Shared Visions: Student Affairs Work in Small Colleges.* Washington, D.C.: National Association of Student Personnel Administrators, 1986.

Kuh, G. D., Schuh, J. H., Whitt, E. J., and Associates. *Involving Colleges: Successful Approaches to Fostering Student Learning and Development Outside the Classroom.* San Francisco: Jossey-Bass, 1991.

Kuh, G. D., and Whitt, E. J. *The Invisible Tapestry: Culture in American Colleges and Universities.* ASHE-ERIC Higher Education Research Report, no. 1. Washington, D.C.: Association for the Study of Higher Education, 1988.

Levine, A., and Associates. *Shaping Higher Education's Future: Demographic Realities and Opportunities, 1990–2000.* San Francisco: Jossey-Bass, 1989.

Lynton, E. A., and Elman, S. E. *New Priorities for the University: Meeting Society's Needs for Applied Knowledge and Competent Individuals.* San Francisco: Jossey-Bass, 1987.

May, W. (ed.). *Ethics and Higher Education.* New York: American Council on Education, Macmillan, 1990.

Miller, T., Winston, R., and Associates. *Administration and Leadership in Student Affairs.* (2nd ed.) Muncie, Ind.: Accelerated Development, 1991.

Moore, L. V. (ed.). *Evolving Theoretical Perspectives on Students.* New Directions for Student Services, no. 51. San Francisco: Jossey-Bass, 1990.

Moore, P. L. (ed.). *Managing the Political Dimension of Student Affairs.* New Directions for Student Services, no. 55. San Francisco: Jossey-Bass, 1991.

National Association of Student Personnel Administrators. *Points of View.* Washington, D.C.: National Association of Student Personnel Administrators, 1989.

Pascarella, E. T., and Terenzini, P. T. *How College Affects Students: Findings and Insights from Twenty Years of Research.* San Francisco: Jossey-Bass, 1991.

Pfeffer, J. *Power in Organizations.* Marshfield, Mass.: Pitman, 1981.

Rentz, A. L., and Saddlemire, G. L. *Student Affairs Functions in Higher Education.* Springfield, Ill.: Thomas, 1988.

Richardson, R., and Bender, L. *Fostering Minority Access and Achievement in Higher Education: The Role of Urban Community Colleges and Universities.* San Francisco: Jossey-Bass, 1982.

Sandeen, A. *The Chief Student Affairs Officer: Leader, Manager, Mediator, Educator.* San Francisco: Jossey-Bass, 1991.

Schein, E. H. *Organizational Culture and Leadership: A Dynamic View.* San Francisco: Jossey-Bass, 1985.

Schlossberg, N. K., Lynch, A. Q., and Chickering, A. W. *Improving Higher Education Environments for Adults: Responsive Programs and Services from Entry to Departure.* San Francisco: Jossey-Bass, 1989.

Schuh, J. (ed.). *Financial Management for Student Affairs Administrators.* American College Personnel Association Media Publication, no. 48. Washington, D.C.: American College Personnel Association, 1990.

Smart, J. V. (ed.). *Higher Education: Handbook of Theory and Research.* Vol. 6. New York: Agathon, 1990.

Task Force on Professional Preparation and Practice. *The Recruitment, Preparation and Nurturing of the Student Affairs Profession.* Washington, D.C.: National Association of Student Personnel Administrators, American College Personnel Association, 1989.

Tierney, W. G. (ed.). *Assessing Academic Climates and Cultures.* New Directions for Institutional Research, no. 68. San Francisco: Jossey-Bass, 1990.

Walker, D. E. *The Effective Administrator: A Practical Approach to Problem Solving, Decision Making, and Campus Leadership.* San Francisco: Jossey-Bass, 1979.

Wright, D. J. (ed.). *Responding to the Needs of Today's Minority Students.* New Directions for Student Services, no. 38. San Francisco: Jossey-Bass, 1987.

Young, R. (ed.). *The Invisible Leaders: Student Affairs Mid-Managers.* Washington, D.C.: National Association of Student Personnel Administrators, 1990.

Young, R., and Moore, L. (ed.). *The State of the Art of Professional Education and Practice.* Washington, D.C.: American College Personnel Association, 1988.

Name Index

Subject Index

A

Academic advising, technology for, 186–187

Academic affairs, students in conflict with, 317–318, 319, 325

Access, for students with disabilities, 54

Accountability: and assessment, 231–233; and campus relations, 312; for middle manager, 128

Accreditation: and doctoral programs, 393–394, 401; and health services, 491; and professional associations, 373–374; restructuring, 232; standards used in self-studies for, 513, 516–517, 518–519

Accreditation Association for Ambulatory Health Care, 491

Action Trac, for advising, 187

Ad hoc and advisory committees, role of, 22–23

Adams v. *Bell*, 496, 507

Adams v. *Richardson,* 496, 507

Administration: aspects of, 1–92; and constituent groups, 69–82; enjoying, 525–526; and fiscal pressures, 49–68; future challenges for, 425–529; and governance, 16–29; of health services, 482–487; and institutional context, 30–48; internship programs for, 412–423; and mission, 3–15; overview of, 1–2; and presidents, 83–92; relations with, 305

Admission: to doctoral programs, 399; legal issues of, 283, 293–294, 496; president's view of, 85–86; technology for, 186

Advocacy, for changing constituencies, 475–476

Affinity of services model, for organizational structure, 117–118

Affirmative action: legal issues of, 500; and staff development, 355; for staff diversity, 459–460; in staff selection, 138, 139–140, 144

African-American students: and demographic trends, 51, 52, 353; fraternity and sorority hazing by, 334–335

Age Discrimination Act of 1975, 286

Age Discrimination in Employment Act of 1967, 286

Alabama, University of, in court case, 283, 298

Alaska, University of, mission of, 9

Alcoholic beverages: legal issues of, 279; sponsorship by brewers of, 336

Alexander v. *Yale University,* 284, 295, 499, 507

All Handicapped Children Act of 1988, 497

Allegheny College, mission of, 7–8

Alumni: relations with, 306; staff from, 462–463

American Association for Counseling and Development, 78, 366, 371, 394